Since its birth two thousand years ago, Christianity has been in large measure a religion of diasporic communities. Just as the early disciples found a receptive audience among the God-fearers of the Roman Mediterranean and the Jews of Persian Mesopotamia, today the gospel message has borne an abundant harvest among the Chinese scattered across Southeast Asia – in the Philippines, Indonesia, Malaysia – and elsewhere. Though the field of diasporic studies has burgeoned in recent decades, the study of diaspora religion, and especially of religious change among men and women uprooted from their ancestral homelands, is still in its infancy. Jean Uayan's pioneering book on the early days of Protestantism among Chinese Filipinos shows what diligent research and the careful weighing of evidence can accomplish. Her work sheds light on the spread of Reformation Christianity among Chinese Buddhists in the Catholic Philippines, deepening our understanding of the emergence of what Philip Jenkins has dubbed "the next Christendom." It has my highest recommendation.

George W. Harper, PhD
Program Director, Theological Studies and Church History,
Asia Graduate School of Theology, Quezon City, Philippines

Dr Jean Uayan's *A Study of the Emergence and Early Development of Selected Protestant Chinese Churches in the Philippines* is another important addition to historiography of religion of the Chinese-Filipino community in the Philippines. There has been erstwhile little known information and data on the emergence and evolution of Protestant Chinese churches in the Philippines, which is a vital institution in the Tsinoy community then and now. How the six churches emerged in the predominantly Catholic Philippines, how the membership and leadership were formed and how they related to the Christian missions of early years, and how the churches resolved issues and challenges, enlighten the readers and fill a serious gap in the body of literature on the study of the Chinese Filipinos.

Teresita Ang See
Founding President, Kaisa Para Sa Kaunlaran Inc.
Executive Trustee, Kaisa Heritage Foundation
Former President, International Society for the Study of Chinese Overseas
Former President, Philippine Association for Chinese Studies

This book is a comprehensive account of the emergence and early development of Chinese churches in the Philippines. The focus is on the individual stories of the churches but the stories are examined within their historical, social, and religious setting. Thus, it includes the history of the Chinese in the Philippines and the histories of the cities where the churches are situated. It also describes the history of early Christianity in the Philippines and China. Dr Jean Uayan is to be commended for her hard work and careful research.

In a recent gathering of theological educators in Asia, a church history professor lamented, "There is a dearth of materials on Asian Church History, we need local textbooks, please write about the history of Christianity in your country." This book meets such a need!

Theresa Roco Lua, PhD
General Secretary, Asia Theological Association

This is a great and significant work on the history of Chinese churches in the Philippines. The author has critically researched, studied and evaluated primary resources and come up with this history. Aside from helping the existing Chinese churches in the Philippines to go back to see God's graciousness in establishing his church, the book can be a tool for critical researchers, church historians, and church pastors to study and plan on how to establish new churches in Asia and beyond. Reading this book gives us missional principles on church growth, the proper relationship between mission and local churches.

Joseph Shao, PhD
General Secretary, Asia Theological Association (2007–2016)
President, Biblical Seminary of the Philippines
Board member, Chinese Congress on World Evangelism International

Historians have previously shown some interest in Protestant church history in the Philippines, but recently the topic has become more developed. Jean Uayan's study is one of very few in this area; this is specifically so of Chinese churches.

This book tells of the birth of Protestantism in China before it proceeds to the emergence of Chinese churches in the Philippines. It contains countless illuminating stories, facts and illustrations of the various denominations such as Baptist, Episcopal and Presbyterian; individual lives, efforts and contributions are described in detail. Numerous pages of early photographs and lists, as well as the author's final reflections, round out the narrative. This is a well-documented work.

Anne C. Kwantes, PhD
Retired missionary of Christian Reformed World Missions
Former professor of Church and Mission History in Asia,
Asian Theological Seminary, Quezon City, Philippines

A Study on the Emergence and Early Development of Selected Protestant Chinese Churches in the Philippines

Jean Uy Uayan

🌐 **Langham**
ACADEMIC

Published 2017 by Langham Academic (Previously Langham Monographs)
An imprint of Langham Publishing
www.langhampublishing.org

Langham Publishing and its imprints are a ministry of Langham Partnership

Langham Partnership
PO Box 296, Carlisle, Cumbria CA3 9WZ, UK
www.langham.org

Isbns:
978-1-78368-281-2 Print
978-1-78368-282-9 Epub
978-1-78368-284-3 PDF

British Library Cataloguing in Publication Data
A catalogue record for this book is available from the British Library

ISBN: 978-1-78368-281-2

Cover & Book Design: projectluz.com

Dedication

Every accomplishment is beautiful when done according to God's time and to God's will. I could have accomplished my doctoral studies much earlier, at the prime of youth, but God saw fit to let it happen at a later time. This is the decade when the study of the history of Asian Christianity has come of age and become a central focus of scholarly studies produced by the global academic community. This is also the time when the histories of a good number of Philippine Chinese churches have reached the centennial or half-centennial mark.

I am whole-heartedly grateful to our Heavenly Father, Lord and Savior Jesus Christ, and the Holy Spirit for being the Author and Finisher of this dissertation. It was he who sent me on this journey and traveled with me all the way until the finish line was reached. When exhaustion overwhelmed me, he was there for me to lean on. When doubts started to creep in, his steadfast love was a protective hedge encircling me. To him who is my Lord and Savior and the God of history, I dedicate this work first and foremost.

I also dedicate this work to two groups of people. The first group is my family and friends. Although my father and mother (Marcos Uayan/Xiao TianRui 蕭天瑞 and Uy Sun Ti/Huang ShunZhi 黃舜治) are now experiencing and sharing my joy in their heavenly abode, their loving nurture and all-encompassing support while they were still on earth continue to sustain my life and uphold me in my academic pursuits. This attainment is but a fruit of their lifelong investment in my life. Another person who stood by my parents' side and has continued to shower me with loving concern is my aunt, Mameng Uy, a.k.a. Uy Ma Bin/Huang MaMin 黃媽敏. A retired schoolteacher, she instilled in me a disciplined lifestyle and thirst for academic excellence. I owe a debt of gratitude to this family that only God can adequately repay.

I will always be grateful to God for my friends Jane Chuaunsu/Cai ZhenRu 蔡真如 and Jenny Bee Tin Ting/Ding MeiZhen 丁美珍. Jane has been with me through thick and thin in this academic endeavor. She has been extra supportive and caring, challenging me to pursue excellence for the glory of the Lord. She also rendered tireless assistance in proofreading and typing archival materials throughout the stages of research and dissertation writing. Jenny is a childhood friend who has shown confidence in me and extended her close friendship to me throughout the years, despite the distance that divides us. Both of them and other friends have sustained me with their unceasing prayers.

The other group to whom I want to dedicate this work are two missionaries whose exemplary lives as teachers – one in history and the other in education – continue to inspire me in my own life as a teacher. Dr Carol B. Herrmann (1936–2012) was a missionary-friend and former director of the AGST EdD program (first and second cycles). Our friendship began in the late 1970s when she taught Christian education subjects and served as acting Academic Dean at the Biblical Seminary of the Philippines. She became a "Barnabas" to me till the end of her life. She never failed to encourage and show her confidence in me whenever we met in fellowship. Another dear missionary-friend is Dr Anne C. Kwantes who is truly a model for teaching history and an author that makes history come alive to both listeners and readers. As a friend, she prayed for and nudged me on, especially when it would have been easier to give up on this project. As a mentor, she went through my dissertation with meticulous attention and gave valuable insights and suggestions.

Lastly, I dedicate this work to the Biblical Seminary of the Philippines and all the people who are part of this institution. I was first trained as the Lord's servant in Biblical Seminary of the Philippines (BSOP), and I have continued to serve our God in this place for nearly four decades. I am proud to be a product of this seminary and to be a part of its great ministry of equipping God's workers with God's word for God's work.

SOLI DEO GLORIA!

Contents

Abstract

Whereas most of the recorded history of the Philippine Protestant Chinese churches point to Protestant Chinese as their founders, a minority recognizes that missionaries from the Christian and Missionary Alliance, Episcopalian, Presbyterian and Southern Baptist mission organizations assisted in the establishment of such Chinese churches, without giving extensive details of their ministry. This dissertation shows that there were Protestant Chinese in the Philippines during the time of the Spanish regime, but no church was formed until the coming of the Protestant missionaries during the American occupation (1898–1946). This study of six representative Protestant Chinese churches in the Philippines shows that missionaries from these mission organizations pioneered the work that resulted in the emergence of four of the churches. Only one church can be considered as a result of the labor of a group of Protestant Chinese resulting from the influence of the church in China. Using annual reports, minutes and publications of these mission agencies and the correspondence and writings of individual missionaries, with supplements from church records, published anniversary materials and oral interviews, the emergence and early development of these six churches are carefully described.

The individual histories of the "Chinese Presbyterian Church in Iloilo" (1900), St. Stephen's Chinese Mission (1903), Cebu Gospel Church (1916), Chinese United Evangelical Church (1929), Davao Evangelical Church (1951), and Dagupan Chinese Baptist Church (1952) are examined within the frameworks of the mission history of the four mission organizations in the Philippines and in China, the history of Protestantism in South Fujian, the history of the Chinese in the Philippines, the history of the United Church of Christ in the Philippines, and the local histories of the cities where the six churches emerged.

The earliest Protestant Chinese church to be established in the Philippines is not what is known today as St. Stephen's Parish, as generally acknowledged by the Philippine Chinese community. It is rather the congregation that this study has named the "Chinese Presbyterian Church in Iloilo." No record of this church can be found in the historical publications of the Philippine Protestant Chinese community. The book shows that this church and four others were mission-established, a pattern manifestly prominent during the first half of the twentieth century. This study discerned common patterns as well as unique distinctions regarding the historical emergence of these six churches. The common patterns of emergence are: the majority of missionaries did not originally intend to work among the Chinese as primary targets of mission, hence, they did not purposely learn the *Hokkien* dialect despite the fact that it was predominantly used by the Chinese who were from South Fujian, China. Point of contact was made through visitation and other meetings; invitations to attend such meetings were extended and accepted. As a result, a core group gathered and formed the church, subsequently supplying the leadership for all six churches. Chinese church members and leaders were very zealous in drawing non-believers into the church and in working closely with the missionaries in many functions of the church. Missionaries involved with these Chinese churches and the earliest pastors from China who came in later periods, normally stayed in the field for one or two decades, thus providing continuity in pastoral ministration and spiritual nurture. During the emerging years, however, these churches lacked Chinese pastors who were linguistically and culturally capable of ministering to the church members. In fact, this deficiency, on top of a weakened missionary oversight, had devastating effects on one of the churches. These churches had to rely on the Church of Christ in China to supply pastoral training and staffing for four decades until this avenue was permanently closed in 1949.

One distinction that surfaced from this study is that only the Chinese United Evangelical Church was truly native as it was founded by a group of Protestant Chinese. It was self-governing, self-supporting and self-propagating, receiving missionary assistance only in the form of preaching and pastoral advice for a brief period during its emerging years. In contrast, Cebu Gospel Church maintained its mission ties and association with the

United Church of Christ in the Philippines for fifty years, but functioned as an independent church during the last half of this period. Only the Southern Baptist mission had the foresight to establish its own training school for Chinese pastors soon after missionaries began working among the Philippine Chinese, but this endeavor did not last long. Another significant point is that four out of the six churches became independent in less than ten years, unlike mission-established churches in China during the nineteenth century. This study, however, brings out the need for more investigations regarding the Philippine Chinese church in areas of inter-faith and inter-cultural, ecclesiastical, missiological and theological concerns.

Acknowledgments

I thank my adviser Dr Floyd Cunningham and my mentor Dr Anne C. Kwantes for their careful supervision and sustained concern throughout the whole process of research and writing this dissertation. I also thank my readers Dr David Cheung and Dr George Capaque for taking time and for their effort in examining my manuscript. My gratitude goes to Dr Theresa Roco Lua for her professional administration and personal assistance as Dean of the Asia Graduate School of Theology.

I thank Dr Winston Crawley, Dr Daniel Frederick Doeppers, Professor Go Bon Juan, Professor Teresita Ang See, and Dr Edgar Wickberg for their insightful and critical evaluation of different sections of this work. I also thank close friends and sincere brothers and sisters in Christ who extended assistance in defraying expenditures incurred during the course of research.

Researching for materials for this dissertation was greatly facilitated by kind-hearted librarians from local and foreign institutions that I visited. Fellow librarians of the Brent Library of St. Andrew's Theological Seminary, the Rizal Library of Ateneo De Manila University, the Henry Luce III Library of Central Philippine University, the Chin Bin See Library of Kaisa Para Sa Kaunlaran Heritage Center, the libraries of Alliance Graduate Seminary, Asia Pacific Nazarene Theological Seminary, Asia Pacific Theological Seminary, Asian Theological Seminary, De La Salle University, Lopez Memorial Museum Library, Philippine Baptist Theological Seminary, Philippine National Library, Philippine Union Theological Seminary, University of the Philippines, University of San Carlos, and University of Santo Tomas, were more than hospitable and helpful in allowing me to access their general and special collections, some of them granting permission to take digital photographs of rare materials that could not be photocopied. I owe my deepest gratitude to the following archivists for going out of their way to assist me in locating and sending documents: Joan Duffy and Martha Smalley of the Day Missions Library and Divinity School Library of Yale University; Geoffrey Reynolds of the Joint Archives of Holland, Hope College; Patty McGarvey of Christian and Missionary Alliance National Archives; Steve Lucht of the Archives of the Episcopal Church; and Robert D. Shuster of the Billy Graham Archives. I also thank my former students Ding ShiEn and Mina Anne Tian for procuring library and documentary materials in China and in Hong Kong respectively. Lastly, I owe a debt of gratitude to my own library staff: Raquel D. Cruz, Adiel Danganan, Jessica Malubay, Rebecca Danganan and Norabel Villanueva.

It is my deepest hope that this research work may prove beneficial and useful, not only to fellow historians, but also to the Chinese churches in the Philippines and to the whole kingdom of God both in this age and in the succeeding generations.

List of Tables

Abbreviations

Churches and Organizations

ABB	American Baptist Board (formerly ABMU)
ABCFM	American Board of Commissioners for Foreign Missions
ABEO	Association of Baptists for Evangelism in the Orient
ABHMS	American Baptist Home Mission Society
ABMU	American Baptist Missionary Union
ABWE	Association of Baptists for World Evangelism
BCBC	Baguio Chinese Baptist Church
BFM-PCUSA	Board of Foreign Missions of the Presbyterian Church in the United States of America
BFMRCA	Board of Foreign Missions of the Reformed Church in Americ (formery RPDC)
BFMRPDC	Board of Foreign Missions of the Reformed Protestant Dutch Church
BIOP	Bible Institute of the Philippines
BSOP	Biblical Seminary of the Philippines
CCC	Church of Christ in China
CCS	Cebu Christian School
CGC	Cebu Gospel Church
CMAFMB	Christian and Missionary Alliance Foreign Mission Board

CPCM	Commission on Philippine-Chinese Mission
CUEC	Chinese United Evangelical Church
DCBC	Dagupan Chinese Baptist Church
DCGC	Davao Chinese Gospel Church
DEC	Davao Evangelical Church
ECP	Evangelical Church of the Philippines
EPM	English Presbyterian Mission
EUPI	Evangelical Union in the Philippine Islands; short form, Evangelical Union
FEM	Federation of the Evangelical Missions
ICCC	Iloilo Chinese Christian Church
ICGAC	Iloilo Christian Gospel Assembly Center, Inc.
IEMELIF	*Iglesia Evangelica Metodista en las Islas Filipinas* (Evangelical Methodist Church in the Philippine Islands)
LMS	London Missionary Society
MEC	Methodist Episcopal Church
MSMEC	Missionary Society of the Methodist Episcopal Church
NCCC	National Christian Council of China
NCCP	National Christian Council of the Philippines; National Council of Churches in the Philippines
PBTS	Philippine Baptist Theological Seminary (formerly PBTSBS)
PBTSBS	Philippine Baptist Theological Seminary and Bible School
PCGS	Philippine Christian Gospel School
PEC	Philippine Episcopal Church
PFCC	Philippine Federation of Christian Churches
PFEC	Philippine Federation of Evangelical Churches

PIC	Philippine Independent Church or *Iglesia Filipina Independiente* (also known as *Aglipayan Church*)
PPCC	Philippine Protestant Chinese churches (collectively used)
PRC	People's Republic of China
PrECBFDM	Protestant Episcopal Church Board of Foreign and Domestic Mission
RCA	Reformed Church in America (formerly RPDC)
RPDC	Reformed Protestant Dutch Church (1819–1867, now RCA)
SBC	Southern Baptist Convention
SBCFMB	Southern Baptist Convention Foreign Mission Board
SPCM	St. Peter's Chinese Mission
SPP	St. Peter's Parish
SSCM	St. Stephen's Chinese Mission
SSP	St. Stephen's Parish
UBC	United Brethren Church
UECM	United Evangelical Church of Manila (formerly CUEC)
UECN	United Evangelical Church of Naga
UCCP	United Church of Christ in the Philippines (formerly UECPI)
UECP	United Evangelical Church of the Philippines (formerly UECM)
UECPI	United Evangelical Church of the Philippine Islands (formerly ECP)
UNIDA	*Iglesia Evangelica Unida de Cristo* (United Evangelical Church of Christ)
UPCUSA	United Presbyterian Church in the USA
UTS	Union Theological Seminary
YMCA	Young Men's Christian Association

Notations

a.k.a.	Also known as
b.	Year or date of birth
d.	Year or date of death
ff.	Following
n.	Note/footnote
r.	Year of retirement as missionary
RG	Record Group
vda.	*viuda*, widow

Works or Sources Cited Repeatedly

BRPI	Blair and Robertson, *Philippine Islands*
CGCGJS	*Cebu Gospel Church Golden Jubilee Souvenir 1916–1966*
HDPO	*Historical Documentary of Protestantism in the Orient. 40ᵗʰ Anniversary of the United Evangelical Church of Manila*
JAC	*Journal of the Annual Convocation of the Missionary District of the Philippine Islands*
JGC	*The Journal of the Bishops Clergy and Laity Assembled in General Convention*
PNA	Philippine National Archives

Explanatory Notes

This dissertation has been written for the benefit of English and Chinese readers in the Philippines and worldwide, hence, all Chinese titles, authors' names, names of publishers and other proper names have been retained in their original form. Such names have been transliterated into either *Hanyu pinyin* or *Hokkien* romanization or both.

Hanyu (Chinese language) *pinyin* (literally, "spell" – "sound") 漢語拼音, commonly called *pinyin* 拼音, is the most common variant of the Standard Mandarin romanization system in use. It is also known as the scheme of the Chinese phonetic alphabet or *Hanyu Pinyin Fangan* 漢語拼音方案. *Hanyu pinyin* was approved in 1958 and adopted in 1979 by the government of the People's Republic of China (PRC). It superseded older romanization systems such as Wade-Giles (1859; modified 1892, used extensively by missionaries) and Chinese Postal Map Romanization, and replaced Zhuyin 注音 as the method of Chinese phonetic instruction in PRC. *Hanyu Pinyin* should not be pronounced according to English conventions. See Yin BinYong 尹斌庸 and Mary Felley, *Chinese Romanization, Pronunciation and Orthography* (*Hanyu pinyin he zhengcifa* 漢語拼音和正詞法) (Beijing: Sinolingua, 1990). For a conversion table on the *Hanyu pinyin* and the Wade-Giles system, see Conrad Schirokauer, *A Brief History of Chinese and Japanese Civilization* (New York: Harcourt Brace Jovanovich, 1978), ix–xi (also readily available from the World Wide Web).

In the case of *Hokkien* romanization, the main reference work used is Rev William Campbell's *A Dictionary of the Amoy Vernacular Spoken throughout the Prefectures of Chin-Chiu, Chiang-Chiu and Formosa* (Taiwan) (Xiamenyin Xinzidian) 廈門音新字典, 19th edition (Tainan: Ren Guang Chubanshe 人光出版社, 1997). Originally published in 1913, it has been re-issued over the decades until the present. For simplicity and because the Chinese characters are given in full, no accent marks will be used in this work. It is the writer's opinion that romanization is still important, especially for place and personal names, because they are what Chinese Filipinos are familiar with, and because the *Hokkien* dialect is still widely used today. For place names, the *Hanyu pinyin* is followed as much as possible, without using hyphens, for example, Anhai (instead of Oa^n Hai) or Tongan (instead of Tang Oa^n).

Furthermore, several comments should be made concerning the style used in this work, particularly in relation to:

1) Chinese Proper Names
For names of people related to local histories of the six churches, the *Hokkien* version is given before the *Hanyu pinyin* version, followed by the Chinese characters, then by the legal anglicized or Filipinized name, if available, in parenthesis. Once the full information is given, only the *Hokkien* version is given in succeeding mention of the names. An example would be: Kho Ju Soat/Xu YuXie 許逾雪 (a.k.a. Elizabeth Co). In this example of the *Hanyu pinyin* system, the first character (Xu) is the family name, followed by the personal name (YuXie) in mono-syllabic or multi-syllabic (with no space in-between). The second character (Xie) is capitalized in order to facilitate distinction from the first character and pronunciation purposes. Names that are pre-set or with no record written in Chinese, and for which the *Hanyu pinyin* form cannot apply, are retained in their original forms (e.g. Wung Kuanty).

The transliterated *Hokkien* surnames of persons referred to in this study normally appear in the beginning of the whole name, for example, Keng Lin Kiat, Kho Ju Soat, Kho Seng Iam. However there are exceptions such as Ben Ga Pay/Bai MingYa 白萌芽 and Rector J. B. Wei Hsi Jin/Wei XiRen 魏希仁, where Pay and Wei are the surnames.

For names of authors, editors, or publication committees in general, no *Hokkien* equivalent is given. If the Chinese characters are known, the *Hanyu pinyin* may be included. This will not apply to works published in English by Chinese authors, for example, Wong Kwok-chu and Wang GungWu. Some books are bilingual and give the author's name in English and in Chinese (for example, Teresita Ang See). For such works the *Hanyu pinyin* will be given. The same author may publish his or her work purely in English, hence, no *Hanyu pinyin* will be given.

2) Place Names
In discussing South Fujian place names, the *Hokkien* pronunciation will be given first, followed by the *Hanyu pinyin* and the Chinese characters, for example, E-Mng/Xiamen 廈門. Archaic names such as "Amoy," although employed by missionaries in China, will be avoided unless it is part of a proper name, for example, "Amoy Classis." The province is called Fujian 福建, unless used in connection with the ecclesiastical unit, for example, *Hokkien* Ban Lam Tai Hoe 福建閩南大會. For the benefit of *Hokkien* readers, some of the colloquial versions and *Hokkien* place names in South Fujian can be found in Appendix D, E, and G.

3) Names of Churches
With reference to the churches being studied, period names have been used all throughout except for Cebu Gospel Church, due to the variety and inconsistent usage of its early English names as found in the Presbyterian mission records.

4) Bibliography
The bibliography collected in this study has been categorized into the following sections: English, French and Spanish, and Chinese sources. The English source has been further sub-divided into the Archival Materials, Official Documents and Anniversary Publications, Interviews and Other Materials, Books, Articles and Addresses, Dissertations and Theses, while the Chinese source, into the Anniversary Publications, Books and Articles and Addresses. With regard to the style of writing these bibliographic sources, it should be noted that:
   a.   Titles of Chinese works are written before the English titles, preceded by the *Hanyu pinyin* equivalent, and followed by the given translation (either in sentence or heading style) or my own translation (written in sentence style). Translations are placed in ( ) or [ ], the latter being used when a parenthesis is part of the original title. When English titles are written before the Chinese titles, this indicates that the book is either written in English with

the Chinese title supplied, or the text is bilingual. If the source is
published bilingually or if the translation is already supplied, the
translation is in heading style according to the given form. Some
bilingual sources give the English title before the Chinese title;
while others do the reverse. In case of the former, the Chinese
title would no longer be rendered in the *Hanyu pinyin* form. For
example, Chen YanDe 陳衍德. *Xiandaizhong de Chuantong –
Feilübin Huaren Shehui Yanjiu* 現代中的傳統 – 菲律濱華人
社會研究 (Tradition in Modern Times: A Study on Philippine
Chinese Society). Xiamen, Fujian: Xiamen Daxue Chubanshe 廈
門大學出版社 (Xiamen University Press), 1998.

b. Even when English equivalents of the publisher are given, the
Chinese name is still included. When only Chinese data is
available, the place of publication is rendered in *Hanyu pinyin*
form preceding the publisher's name in Chinese.

c. When page numbers are followed by the note "(in Chinese
style)," this means that the pages should be viewed starting
from the right to the left, contrary to the paging style of English
books. The page numbers, however, are still written in the logical
order.

d. Annotations are given to some books giving information relevant
to its publication or content. Annotations following the names of
persons interviewed give information that is extremely relevant to
the six churches being studied.

e. Official records of the same title periodically published by the
same organization are arranged chronologically according to
dates of publication. This applies to journals of regular meetings,
annual reports, minutes, and year books (for examples, see pp.
406–420).

CHAPTER 1

Introduction

A. Global Perspective

We live in an age in which the gospel of Christ is established on all continents and in virtually every nation. The history of the church can now be written from a global perspective, not just from a Western viewpoint. This was the essence of Wilbert R. Shenk's introduction to an essay which he presented at the consultation on World Christianity and the Teaching of History, held at Yale Divinity School in June 1995. At this consultation Shenk discussed his agenda of moving "Toward a Global Church History."[1] He rightly critiqued the writing of history from a Western perspective for assuming the history of the churches of Asia, Africa, and Latin America as a subcategory of Western mission history. He urged that we must "recognize that the global extension of the church represents a different kind of history from what church historians in the West usually write and teach." He suggested that people move "beyond the conventional framework," and declared: "What is needed today are historical studies that trace the founding of the church in those places where it was not present before, paying particular attention to the nature of the initial insertion and the issues it raised."[2]

Shenk then presented many examples showing how such a global interpretation of history has already taken place. He mentioned the works of

---

1. Wilbert R. Shenk, "Toward a Global Church History," *International Bulletin of Missionary Research*, 20, no. 2 (Apr 1996), 50–57.

2. Ibid., 50.

Western scholars John King Fairbank, Andrew Porter, Maurice Leenhardt, Roland Oliver, as well as some non-Western, mostly African scholars, but not excluding those from Latin America and Asia. As an outgrowth of these pioneers' efforts, the Church History Association of India and the Roman Catholic Bishops' Council of Latin America have undertaken major projects of writing the history of Christianity in their respective localities. Both projects are voluminous and both are being written by non-Western historians.

Based on Paul Cohen's investigation of how the history of China has been written for the past 150 years, Shenk presented his own model for writing from such a global approach at the end of his essay.[3] Just as Cohen recommended a "China-centered approach," Shenk gave four recommendations. First of all, the internal criteria of a country, rather than the external (Western) criteria, should be the basis for determining what was significant in the past. Shenk advised that we must reject Western Christendom as the starting point for church history in a country such as China. Second, Cohen maintained that China's history must be approached horizontally in terms of such units as regions, provinces, prefectures, cities, and the like. For Shenk, this means that church historians must recognize the parity between the local and the global – "each local, regional, or national unit of the church must recognize that it is incomplete in and of itself." Third, Cohen's proposal identified discrete levels of Chinese society and encouraged the writing of a history accessible to the wider populace. Shenk, in turn, suggested that one must write history using media on various levels, so that the final product serves not only the specialists but also the whole people. Lastly, Cohen's approach embraced "theories, methodologies and techniques" developed in other disciplines (such as the social sciences). Shenk suggested using the tools of narrative and social history as building blocks.[4]

---

3. Ibid., 56. He was citing and adapting from Paul A. Cohen's book, *Discovering History in China: American Historical Writing on the Recent Chinese Past* (New York: Columbia University Press, 1984), 186–187.

4. Shenk, "Toward a Global Church History," 50.

B. Background of the Problem: Local Challenges

The Philippines is not lacking in initiative and results when it comes to writing its own history, both secular and ecclesiastical. The history of the Roman Catholic Church in the Philippines has been well researched.[5] Commendable efforts have been made to understand the history of Protestant Filipino churches, with more studies having been published during the past decades.[6] With regard to the Chinese-Filipino community, the Asian Center of the University of the Philippines and the China Studies Program of De La Salle University and the Ateneo de Manila University, as well as the Kaisa Para Sa Kaunlaran 菲律濱華裔青年聯合會, have collected or massively produced books, monographs, and dissertations over the past decades that address multiple issues arising from and concerning this community.[7] Several of Shenk's proposals have already been applied

5. John N. Schumacher, SJ, has a detailed list in his book, *Readings in Philippine Church History*, 2nd ed. (Quezon City: Loyola School of Theology/Ateneo de Manila University, 1987), 385–401 and 411–415. See also Miguel A. Bernad, SJ, *The Christianization of the Philippines: Problems and Perspectives* (Manila: Filipiniana Book Guild, 1972).

6. For example, Gerald Harry Anderson, ed., *Studies in Philippine Church History* (New York: Ithaca, 1969); Peter Gordon Gowing, *Islands under the Cross* (Manila: National Council of Churches in the Philippines, 1967); Arthur Leonard Tuggy, *The Philippine Church: Growth in a Changing Society* (Grand Rapids, MI: Eerdmans, 1971); and the recent work of Anne Catherine Laninga Kwantes, ed., *Chapters in Philippine Church History* (Manila: OMF Literature, 2001).

7. The Kaisa Para Sa Kaunlaran (Unity for Progress)/Feilübin Huayi Qingnian Lianhehui 菲律濱華裔青年聯合會 was launched on 29 Aug 1987. It is a non-governmental organization aimed at promoting the integration of Chinese Filipinos into the mainstream of Philippine society. See Chinben See/Shi ZhenMin 施振民 and Teresita Ang See/Shi Hong YuHua 施洪玉華, *Chinese in the Philippines: A Bibliography* (Manila: De La Salle University China Studies Program, 1990). This is the third edition of the late Professor Chinben See's work, painstakingly compiled from collections of books located in the US Library of Congress, Harvard University, Ann Arbor Michigan Microfilm collections, University of the Philippines, Ateneo de Manila University, De La Salle University and other libraries. Works of major significance include: George Henry Weightman, *The Chinese Community in the Philippines* (MA thesis, University of the Philippines, 1956); Edgar Wickberg, *The Chinese in Philippine Life, 1850–1898* (New Haven, CT: Yale University Press, 1965); Jacques Amyot, *The Manila Chinese: Familism in the Philippine Environment*, Institute of Philippine Culture Monographs, no. 2 (Quezon City: Ateneo de Manila University, Institute of Philippine Culture, 1973); and Teresita Ang See, *The Chinese in the Philippines: Problems and Perspectives Volumes 1 and 2* (Manila: Kaisa Para Sa Kaunlaran, 1997). Unfortunately, Chinben See's bibliography has not been updated although countless works on the Philippine Chinese have been published since 1990.

and this continues to be done, as manifested by volumes of work on secular as well as religious history.[8]

However, concerning the Protestant Chinese in the Philippines, there is a paucity of historical writing, especially by non-Western scholars. The oldest existing (albeit not the first) Protestant Chinese church in the Philippines celebrated its 100th anniversary in 2003. St. Stephen's Chinese Mission, now known as St. Stephen's Parish, was founded in 1903. Other churches emerged over the following decades, and to date there are ninety-three Protestant Chinese churches (formally organized Christian communities), excluding the Little Flock group, in the Philippines. From that beginning until now little has been done to study the history of the Protestant Chinese churches on a comprehensive scale.

C. Statement of the Problem

The central problem addressed in this study is, how did the Protestant Chinese churches emerge in the Philippines? Was there a single pattern in their emergence or not? What were the features of the early development of these churches? In order to address this problem, I studied the history of six representative churches and their respective patterns of emergence and early development. By emergence I mean the period when groundwork was laid by a group of persons, whether missionaries or Protestant Chinese pastors or believers, until the time when an organized church was formed. The study covered churches that emerged at different times during the years 1900 to 1952. The ecclesiastical heritage of these churches include the Christian and Missionary Alliance, Baptist, Episcopal, and Presbyterian (Presbyterian Church in the United States of America) denominations. Hence the study of the emergence of these Protestant Chinese churches cannot be detached from the history of mission work done by these four Protestant denominations. The early history primarily covered the period right after the formal organization of the church and into the first few decades, when Sunday School, prayer or other meetings, Chinese leadership

---

8. See sections on "History and Culture Change" and "Religion" of Shiro Saito, *Philippine Ethnography: A Critically Annotated and Selected Bibliography* (Honolulu, HI: University Press of Hawaii, 1972), for a partial list of works.

and pastoral work force, and/or financial capability to construct church buildings began to develop.

Sub-problems that guided the study include: (1) Were the Chinese churches planted solely by Western missionaries or by immigrant Chinese? (2) Where and how were these early churches established? What was the earliest leadership structure? (3) Was the first generation of pastors and leaders mostly Westerners or Chinese? (4) Where did the original members come from? (5) What was the social, economic, and religious background of these members? (6) Were there other features in the patterns of emergence distinguishable within the histories of these churches? (7) How soon did these churches devolve or become self-supporting, self-governing and self-propagating?[9]

These questions will be the sub-foci of this study. The main focus, however, will be on the circumstances surrounding the emergence of the six representative Protestant Chinese churches. These churches, listed chronologically according to their original names and respective dates of first meeting or founding, are as follows: (1) The "Chinese Presbyterian Church in Iloilo" (henceforth, CPCI) – first meeting 8 April 1900; (2) St. Stephen's Chinese Mission (SSCM) – first meeting 4 October 1903; (3) Cebu Gospel Church (CGC) – first meeting 1916; (4) Chinese United Evangelical Church (CUEC) – founded 14 July 1929; (5) Davao Chinese Gospel Church (DCGC) – formally organized June 1951; and, (6) Dagupan Chinese Baptist Church (DCBC) – formally organized 19 February 1952.

The main consideration for choosing CPCI, SSCM, CGC, and CUEC as representatives of the Philippine Protestant Chinese churches (PPCC) during the pre-WWII period was the early dates of their founding and the certainty that different Western denominations were involved in their emergence. Three other churches were formed during the same period

9. According to David Cheung, in his study of the first native Protestant churches in South Fujian, "devolution consists of the transition from missionary to native leadership within an organised [sic] Christian community involving the attainment of structural independence and sovereign self-determination on the part of the Chinese party." See David Cheung, "Ecclesiastical Devolution and Union in China: The Emergence of the First Native Protestant Church in South Fujian, 1842–1863" (PhD diss., University of London, 2002), 12–13.

– St. Peter's Chinese Mission (SPCM, 1932), what is today called United Evangelical Church of Naga (UECN, 1936) and the Christian Union (1929). Because SPCM was formed by the Episcopalian missionaries as a Cantonese congregation in contrast to the *Hokkien* membership of SSCM, while UECN was a daughter church of CUEC, they belong to a category unrelated to the focus of this book, and it is adequate to study the churches with the earliest dates of emergence. As for the Christian Union, which has now divided into the Christian Gospel Center/Jidutu Juhuisuo 基督徒聚會所 and the Church Assembly Hall/Jiaohui Juhuisuo 教會聚會所, a search for historical writings and mission records met with no success, since these groups take the stand of not writing their own history and do not welcome non-members who desire to investigate their past for academic purposes.

Both DCBC and DCGC, founded soon after WWII, were among the earliest to be formed during the transition period when the American occupation of the Philippines had ended and China had been overrun by the Communists. Religious conditions in China, the socio-political context of the Chinese community in the Philippines, and the mission environment in both countries were undergoing changes that brought beneficial effects, leading to the emergence of DCGC and DCBC in the early 1950s. However, instead of studying the Baguio Chinese Baptist Church (BCBC) which emerged two years earlier than DCBC, I chose to study DCBC because it was the first among all the Southern Baptist Convention (SBC)-established churches to acquire a Chinese pastor and this pastor was directly involved in assisting the missionaries form DCBC, whereas SBC missionaries were pastors of BCBC from 1951–1964.[10]

Geographical location was another determining factor. These six churches were chosen because they cover a wide sweep of the Philippine archipelago (see App. A): DCBC is in Region 1; SSCM and CUEC are in the National Capital Region; CGC and CPCI are in Region 7; and lastly, DCGC is in Region 11.

---

10. The missionary-pastors were Dr Winston Crawley (1950–1951), Rev James Foster and Dr Frank Lide (alternating during 1951 to 1964). See pages 241–264 and "Baptist Work in the Philippines," in Baguio Chinese Baptist Church/Biyao Huaren Jinxinhui 碧瑤華人浸信會, *Blueprints BCBC 1950–2000* (Baguio City: Baguio Chinese Baptist Church, 2000), n.p. (hencefort, *Blueprints BCBC*).

D. Purpose of the Study

The purpose of this study is to investigate the circumstances that gave rise to the emergence of the Protestant Chinese churches by focusing on six representative churches, and by discerning common and distinctive patterns in their emergence. Part of this investigation includes finding out who were involved in forming the churches and where and when the events happened. The period of emergence overlaps into the stage of early development, wherein the membership composition, organizational formation, and leadership structure of these churches are examined. In cases where the churches were established by mission organizations, the investigation may extend further from the early stage until the time when full independence from these organizations in terms of pastoral leadership, financial stability, and evangelistic outreach was attained. It is anticipated that in the course of gaining a proper understanding of the emergence and early history of these six churches, along with the study of how each evolved and developed, new discoveries regarding the past can be made and recommendations for further studies can be proposed. This study aims to contribute toward filling the lacuna of research done on the roots and heritage of the PPCC, and to be of benefit to the Chinese Christian community worldwide.

E. Methodological Framework

The method used in this investigation was the qualitative style of research wherein data and facts found in documentary material and oral evidence were gathered and historical narratives were constructed for six Protestant Chinese churches.[11]

I am aware that modern-day Christian historians feel the tension between history as a subdivision of theology and history as an empirical science. According to Mark A. Noll, there are three positions that historians may hold: the premodern or ideological, the modern or scientific and the postmodern or deconstructive views. However, Noll points out that

---

11. Cesar M. Mercado, *A New Approach to Social Research/Thesis Writing* (Quezon City: Development Consultants for Asia Africa Pacific, 2004), 9; Mark A. Noll, "The Potential of Missiology for the Crises of History," in *History and the Christian Historian*, ed. Ronald A. Wells (Grand Rapids, MI: Eerdmans, 1998), 106–123.

all three positions have their respective flaws. Premodern history, which is also called providential or ideological history, presumes to know where and how God acted historically and thinks of history as vindicating the right and true. However, this view often leads to non-reflective partisanship and parochialism. Historical modernism, on the other hand, tends to assume that knowledge of the past is merely discovery of pristine fact and recording of what actually happened.[12] This viewpoint can dangerously lead to the conclusion that justly arranged facts can interpret themselves.[13] In Shirley Mullen's analysis, the postmodernist view has raised crucial questions about the meaningfulness of the historian's self-understanding, has portrayed the ideal of objectivity as unattainable, and has posited that all narratives are creating their own realities and cultures, not reflecting what was in the past, because language is assumed to be creative and manipulative.[14]

In light of these views, I have therefore attempted to do the following: First, avoid the pitfall of presuming to know what God did or did not do for the Philippine Chinese churches and approach the study purely as a historian, but without taking the position that all the facts and data that I gather can lead to a definite interpretation on their own. While aiming to strike a balance between theology and history, I believe that objectivity can be attained even as I become part of the interpretation process. This means rejecting any pre-conception about how events transpired before research begins. For instance, one cannot presume that the PPCC were established solely by the Protestant Chinese. Many of the commemorative publications produced by the PPCC presume that their churches were either established by Protestant Chinese or that these believers were the key persons in their emergence. Even if some churches acknowledged as fact that missionaries were instrumental in their formation, hardly any detail is given regarding their roles and involvement. Equal attention must be given to the contributions made by non-Chinese as well as Chinese figures involved in forming the PPCC. Furthermore, as Mark Noll states,

---

12. For a sample of this view, see George Burton Adams, "History and the Philosophy of History," *American Historical Review* 14 (1909): 223, 226.

13. See Noll, "Potential of Missiology," 116.

14. Shirley A. Mullen, "Between 'Romance' and 'True History': Historical Narrative and Truth Telling in a Postmodern Age," in *History and the Christian Historian*, ed. Ronald A. Wells (Grand Rapids, MI: Eerdmans, 1998), 23–40.

"Missiology is now of heightened importance for church history because the next great challenge for writing the history of Christianity is to attempt a genuinely global history."[15] The historical context of the history of the PPCC must extend beyond this nation in order to be global, hence, the investigation must be examined within the larger frameworks of the mission history of four mission organizations in the Philippines and in China, the history of Protestantism in South Fujian, the history of the Chinese in the Philippines, the history of the United Church of Christ in the Philippines (UCCP), and the local histories of the cities where the six churches emerged.

Second, while heeding the warning that the "agents of history – those who act and witness actions, those who make and transmit records, those who attempt to reconstruct past actions on the basis of those records – people with worldviews, biases, blindspots, and convictions," I have tried to be empirical in gathering and analyzing data concerning the six churches.[16] Pieces of evidence scattered here and there in mainland Chinese, Philippine Chinese and Western sources were meticulously scrutinized with regard to accuracy and veracity. Seemingly unrelated events were logically and chronologically integrated without bringing deductive explanations into the process. Finally, a significant narrative of the past was reconstructed as objectively as possible, giving due consideration to how the Chinese and the Westerners perceived what they recorded.[17]

Since history is a story of *human* experiences, it manifests both the positive (good) and negative (fallen) nature of mankind. The universal church that Christ built is not perfect, neither are the six Protestant Chinese churches under study. The fact that one of these churches came into existence through internal and interpersonal conflict was not covered up; neither were the flawed character of some of the missionaries, pastors and early leaders.

In recent years, the value of oral history has been increasingly acknowledged by the Western academic world. In its contemporary meaning,

---

15. Noll, "The Potential of Missiology," 107.

16. Ibid., 121.

17. See Ronald H. Nash, *Christian Faith and Historical Understanding* (Grand Rapids, MI: Zondervan/Probe Ministries International, 1984), 12–16.

oral history means a collection of reminiscences of persons with intimate knowledge of, or who are in positions of authority on, certain topics.[18] Understandably, some historians do not recommend this method, but for a nation such as the Philippines, where documentary records cannot survive the ravages of time, climate and human destruction or neglect, oral history cannot be dispensed with as a supplementary source of information.[19] In Philippine historiography, Marcelino Foronda acknowledges that this methodology is a relatively new tool, but by and large, Filipinos (including Chinese Filipinos) are "a *talking* rather than a *writing* people."[20] The interview process was employed in this study to add confirmation to the historical data gathered from church and mission records. It was also useful toward furnishing minor details that were missing from these records. Descendants of pastors and leaders who were involved with or were instrumental in founding the six churches provided fuller biographical accounts of their forebears, thus enhancing the personal background materials that were relevant to the histories of these churches. However, interviews are never free from inaccuracies, subjective interpretations, memory gaps, and even errors, therefore, only one-third out of a total of thirty-five interviews were used in this study because they were credible, corroborative and more relevant to the scope of this study (see App. B).

F. Scope and Delimitations

In studying the general history of the PPCC, the delimitation of this investigation was not set in terms of a certain chronological period. Rather, the study was limited to the emerging stage of the six Protestant Chinese

---

18. American historian Allan Nevins founded an oral history program at Columbia University in 1948. The Oral History movement has since then gained momentum with the formation of the Oral History Association (1967) and the projects it undertakes. See David K. Dunaway, "Introduction: The Interdisciplinarity of Oral History"; 7–22; Louis Starr, "Oral History," 39–61; and Gary Y. Okihiro, "Oral History and the Writing of Ethnic History," 199–214, all found in David K. Dunaway and William K. Baum, eds. *Oral History: An Interdisciplinary Anthology*, 2nd ed. (Walnut Creek, CA: AltaMira/Sage, 1996).

19. This is the reason why De La Salle University launched the Chinese in the Philippines Oral History Project in 1979. A catalogue of this project is compiled in Marcelino A. Foronda, *Kasaysayan: Studies on Local and Oral History* (Manila: De La Salle University Press, 1991), 59–74, 139–167.

20. See discussion in Foronda, *Kasaysayan*, 25–39.

churches that took place at different points of time from 1900 until 1952. The devolution of the churches, being a sub-problem, was not examined extensively in the three areas of self-support, self-rule, and self-propagation. Five of these churches have reached or passed fifty years of history. This means that churches established from the 1960s onward were not included in the study.

Another delimitation was budget and work-related time constraints that did not allow me to travel and visit archives in Hong Kong and Fujian, China, which may have more materials relevant to Sino-Philippine historical relationship, the history of the Church of Christ in China, the history of overseas Chinese, or records containing observations made by churches or missionaries in China concerning the PPCC.

The scope of the study focused only on the historical emergence and early development of the PPCC. It did not include the historical study of Protestant migration from South Fujian to the Philippines. Neither was a comparison made between the emergence and early development of Protestant Filipino and Chinese churches which were connected to the same mission organizations.

G. Definition of Terms

Different terms have been used in this study to refer to the Chinese in the Philippines. There are varying degrees of meaning in these terms, hence further elucidation is necessary:[21]

Alien Chinese and *Xin Qiao* 新僑 are the Chinese who have not acquired Filipino citizenship. The first term can refer to Chinese from Southeast Asia or the People's Republic of China, who came to the Philippines in the past decades, while the second term refers especially to those who have recently entered the country primarily for business interests, most likely to initiate a new wave of migration whose outcome awaits further study.

21. Many of these terms and definitions follow the data given in "Factsheet 1 by the Kaisa Para Sa Kaunlaran/Feilübin Huayi Qingnian Lianhehui 菲律濱華裔青年聯合會," accessed 3 Nov 2006, http://www.philonline.com.ph/~kaisa/kaisa_fact.html. Kaisa coined and popularized the term "tsinoy" to differentiate the Chinese Filipino from alien Chinese and the *xin qiao*.

Chinese Filipino 菲華 refers to the young, mostly Philippine-born ethnic Chinese who identify themselves as Filipinos first, but still maintain their Chinese cultural identity and retain some Chinese customs and traditions – enough to consider themselves and be considered by their neighbors as Chinese. The Tagalog equivalent for this term is *tsinong* (Chinese) *pinoy* (Filipino), and in modern use this is shortened to *tsinoy*. In this term "Filipino" is the noun suggesting the person's fundamental identity, while "Chinese" is the modifying adjective that indicates the Chinese heritage.

Philippine Chinese. In this study this term refers generally to the community of Chinese living in the Philippines, without distinguishing them as temporary or permanent residents, having acquired Filipino citizenship or not, or having pure or mixed blood lineage. But it does refer to certain cultural identifications: (1) Chinese ancestry; (2) knowledge of a Chinese dialect (aural, oral, or both); and (3) an acquaintance (however unconscious) with distinctive Chinese core values such as filial piety and familism.[22]

Banlam (Hokkien)/Minnan (Hanyu pinyin) 閩南. This term, that literally means "south of the River Min," is used to refer to the region in South Fujian (excluding the towns and cities on the border of Fujian and Guangdong, which are not relevant to this work). This is the region where the three Protestant missions belonging to the Reformed Church in America (RCA), English Presbyterian Mission (EPM), and London Missionary Society (LMS) began mission work in the nineteenth century. The term *Banlam* will be consistently used in the text except where *Minnan* is part of a nomenclature.

Hokkien is the Minnan transliteration of Fujian 福建. Technically, *Hokkien* can encompass all the dialects spoken in the northern and southern parts of the province, but the Minnan language or dialect *Banlam-oe/Minnanyu* 閩南語 from South Fujian is popularly known as *Hokkien*, Hokkienese, or

---

22. See Gerald A. McBeath, *Political Integration of the Philippine Chinese*, Research Monograph No. 8 (Berkeley, CA: Research Monograph Series, Center for South and Southeast Asia Studies, University of California, 1973), 1–3; for filial piety, see Wanda Liam Giok Po, "A Philosophical Analysis of Filial Piety: An Integrated Approach" (EdD diss., Asia Graduate School of Theology, 1997); for familism, see Amyot, *The Manila Chinese: Familism in the Philippine Environment*.

Fukienese in Southeast Asia. In this study I have chosen to use *Hokkien* consistently to refer to the people who came to the Philippines from Minnan and to the dialect spoken by up to 98.5 percent of these immigrants. There are many variants of *Banlam-oe*, but in the Philippines, the Xiamen 廈門 話區 and the Quanzhou 泉州話區 variants are the most commonly used.

Protestant Chinese refers to the Chinese in the Philippines who have embraced the Protestant faith and practice. The term has been used consistently in this work in lieu of the words "Chinese Christian" in recognition of the fact that the more generic term can also refer to the Roman Catholics.

H. Organization

The study is organized into four chapters. After the Introduction, the second chapter reviews the resources that have direct or indirect relevance to this study. The third chapter presents and evaluates the research findings with the first section dealing with the historical, social and religious background of the Philippine Chinese. Subsets in this section include: a brief survey of the relationship between China and the Philippines; the historical trends of immigration and population growth of the *Hokkien* Chinese in the Philippines from the Spanish era to the American occupation; the social and religious history of the Chinese in Manila; and a historical sketch of Protestantism in China in general and South Fujian in particular.

The second section of chapter 3 begins with the history of Protestant mission attempts among the Chinese in Manila from 1900–1903, followed by the individual histories of the emergence and early development of the sixth Protestant Chinese churches. Each sub-set in this section follows a pattern of examination involving the following steps: (1) first the history of each of the Chinese community (Iloilo, Cebu, Dagupan and Davao) is analyzed, except for Manila, which is discussed in a prior section. (2) After this and starting with the history of the endeavors of various Protestant mission groups working among the non-Chinese in these cities, the focus is narrowed down to their work among the Chinese. (3) Finally, the minute details of the emergence of the Protestant Chinese congregations in these cities, the contributions of Western missionaries and Chinese preachers, the leadership and organizational structures of the established churches are examined and the story of each church is discussed within the set parameters of this study.

The fourth and last chapter brings together all the significant findings of the previous chapter and analyzes the emergence and early history of the six Chinese churches, in one case covering until the stage when full devolution had occurred. Common patterns of emergence and early development are first discerned, followed by highlighted distinct or unique features of some of the churches. These patterns and features are then considered with regard to certain issues and situations observed within the six Chinese churches in the present context, such as devolution, relationship to mission bodies and missionaries, pastoral training, church membership and leadership. This study will not only produce a clearly detailed and documented history of how these six churches emerged and developed, it will also provide a paradigm for studying the history of other Protestant Chinese churches in the Philippines.

CHAPTER 2

Review of Literature and Related Studies

Research on the emergence of the Philippine Protestant Chinese churches (henceforth, PPCC) entails a study of literature on four aspects: (1) the historical, social and religious background of the Chinese in the Philippines during the Spanish colonial period; (2) the history of Protestantism in China and in South Fujian from 1807 to the Republican period of China's history; (3) the history of Protestantism in the Philippines during the American occupation (1898 to the 1930s), and especially, how Protestant missionaries and Chinese believers or pastors established churches in Manila, Iloilo, Cebu, Davao and Dagupan, and (4) more specifically, how six of the Chinese churches in these cities were formed.

A. Historical, Social and Religious Background

The first area of study concerns the history of the immigration of the Chinese from South Fujian to the Philippines and their social and religious conditions under Spanish and American rules, with particular attention given to the social phenomenon of Chinese immigrant-sojourners turning into long-term residents of the Philippines. Spain's political and religious policies toward the Chinese undulated from welcoming them as commercial and industrial assets to reluctant tolerance to outright expulsion and massacres from the sixteenth to the nineteenth centuries. These trends and events are richly documented in the definitive 55-volume work

The Philippine Islands, 1493–1898 edited by Emma H. Blair and James A. Robertson.[1]

Many Chinese scholars have produced excellent studies on the relationship between China and the Philippines, on the migration patterns of *Hokkien* Chinese, and on the history of their sojourn in Manila and other urban centers in the Islands. Chen TaiMin 陳台民 (1927–1983), a Filipino-Chinese graduate of Adamson University, wrote two volumes on *Zhongfei Guanxi yu Feilübin Huaqiao* 中菲關係與菲律賓華僑 (Sino-Philippine relations and oversea Chinese in the Philippines, my translation) using *BRPI* and other primary sources. This work, published in 1961, is especially commendable for its use and quotations of Chinese primary sources dating as far back as the Jin dynasty 晉朝 (AD 265–420), but unfortunately, Chen's study was limited to the Spanish colonial period.

Covering the Spanish era are the works of Alfonso Felix, Jr, entitled, *The Chinese in the Philippines: 1570–1770*, vol. 1, and *The Chinese in the Philippines: 1770–1898*, vol. 2. Particularly relevant are the essays in the first volume, dealing with the Chinese colony in Manila (ch. 3) and the situation inside the *Parian* (chs. 4 and 12). Another study covering the Spanish period, the American occupation, and the 1950s is the book *Ten Centuries of Philippine-Chinese Relations (Historical, Political, Social, Economic)* by Eufronio Alip. This book deals more with the economic and cultural contributions of the Chinese in Philippine society, but has relevant chapters on Christian faith among the Chinese and their educational system. Similar books focusing on the historical role of the Chinese in Philippine economy include the dissertation by George Henry Weightman entitled "The Philippine Chinese: A Cultural History of a Marginal Trading Community" and Wong Kwok-chu's *The Chinese in the Philippine Economy 1898–1941*.

---

1. See Wu Ching-Hong 吳景宏, "References to the Chinese in the Philippines during the Spanish Period Found in the Philippine Islands by Blair and Robertson," *The Bulletin of the Institute of Southeast Asia* 1 (Singapore: Nanyang University, 1959): F1–90, and *The Philippine Islands, 1493–1898* (electronic resource), eds. and trans. Emma Helen Blair and James Alexander Robertson. CD–ROM design and programming, Antonio E. A. Defensor (Cleveland, OH: Arthur H. Clark, 1903–1909; Quezon City: Bank of the Philippine Islands, 2000). Henceforth cited as BRPI. Most important are volumes 7, 9, 13, 14, 15, 16, 18, 20, 22–27, 29–31, 34–39, 41–43, 48–49, and 51.

Two dissertations – "The Chinese in the Philippines during the American Administration" by Tomás S. Fonacier and "The Chinese in the Philippines during the American Regime: 1898–1946" by Khin Khin Myint Jensen – focus on the economic and political situation and their effects on Chinese residents in the Philippines, but only the issue regarding American administrative policy toward Chinese immigration is relevant to this study.

By far, the authoritative book by the leading scholar on overseas Chinese, Edgar Wickberg, entitled *The Chinese in Philippine Life 1850–1898*, is the most relevant to this study. Many of his works have been translated into Chinese by the Kaisa Para Sa Kaunlaran, an organization serving the academic needs of the Chinese-Filipino community through its publications, the most up-to-date being *Tsinoy: The Story of the Chinese in Philippine Life*.

Other specialized books that focused on the Chinese in Manila (*The Manila Chinese* by Jacques Amyot and *The Chinese in Manila* by Eufronio Alip), in Cebu (*A Social History of the Economy of the Chinese in Cebu* by Go Bon Juan) and in Iloilo (*Chinese Merchant Families in Iloilo: Commerce and Kin in a Central Philippine City* by John Thomas Omohundro) provided background material for the individual mission histories in these cities. Daniel Doeppers' demographic and sociological works also contributed further to understanding the concentrations and social conditions of the Chinese in the above-mentioned cities. Works by Doeppers that were useful to this study include: "Ethnicity and Class in the Structure of Philippine Cities" (PhD diss., Syracuse University, 1971); *Population and History: The Demographic Origins of the Modern Philippines* (1998); and his 1986 article in the *Journal of Historical Geography* entitled, "Destination, Selection and Turnover Among Chinese Migrants to Philippine Cities in the Nineteenth Century."

When the Americans occupied the Philippines in 1898, the situation of the Chinese did not escape their notice. Books published from 1903 to 1908 contain references to the Chinese, either as targets for evangelism or with regard to two most pressing issues, immigration and the use and sale of opium. These books with their respective authors and dates of publications are:

- *The Philippine Islands and Their People* by Dean Conant Worcester (1898);

- *Report of a Visitation of the Philippine Islands* (1902) and *The New Era in the Philippines* (1903) by Arthur Judson Brown;
- *The Philippines and the Far East* (1904) by Homer Clyde Stuntz;
- *The Philippines Circa 1900: Book One. Philippine Life in Town and Country* (1905) by James Alfred Le Roy;
- *The Philippines under Spanish and American Rules* (1906) by C. H. Forbes-Lindsay;
- *The Philippines* (1906) by John Foreman.

These books give Western perspectives on the cultural, economic, political, religious and sociological circumstances of the Philippines and the Filipinos, many of them including descriptions about the Chinese and the roles they play in relation to the various aspects of Philippine life. Among these works, the two by Brown were the most valuable since both detailed information about the Chinese as an ethnic group and their early participation in worship services conducted by Protestant missionaries. This leads to the next category of related literature – resources on how Protestantism developed in China, and how independent (devolved) churches emerged in South Fujian.

B. History of Protestantism in China

The history of the Protestant Chinese churches in the Philippines cannot be fully understood without knowledge of the historical development of Christianity in China, but what is surveyed in this book covers the mid-1800s to the 1950s. The Philippine Chinese churches were intimately related to the Protestant churches in China, particularly those in South Fujian because many of the founders and members of the former came from China. Books on the history of Protestant missions are more than abundant, written by Chinese as well as Western historians. Among Western sources, Kenneth Scott Latourette's *A History of Christian Missions in China* remains the definitive reference work although it only covers events until 1929. In 1987, a Chinese scholar, Christopher Tang/Tang Qing 湯清, finally came out with a scholarly volume the English translation of which is *The First Hundred Years of Protestant Mission in China*. It is a rich source of information describing how major provinces in China were evangelized by different mission agencies, missionaries and Chinese evangelists or pastors, but as the title indicates, this volume only deals with events prior to 1907. It also provides substantial details on the nature of the mission work carried out by these workers.

Two Chinese scholars have produced works on the critical decade wherein the church in China struggled with anti-Christian sentiments and theological issues. One of these is Wing-hung Lam's book entitled *Chinese Theology in Construction*, published in 1983. It deals with the response of the church in China to Communism and Nationalism and the rise of indigenous churches with their particular views of the church and Christian theology. The other work is Jonathan T'ien-en Chao's dissertation entitled, "The Chinese Indigenous Church Movement, 1919–1927: A Protestant Response to the Anti-Christian Movements in Modern China" (PhD diss., University of Pennsylvania, 1986). This work details the growth of the Church of Christ in China/Zhonghua Jidu Jiaohui 中華基督教會 (CCC), focusing on how the Church dealt with factions espousing anti-Christian ideas during the prescribed timeframe. Chao also wrote an article, published earlier in 1981, dealing with the Banlam Church as a model for self-support, entitled *Minnan Ziyang Jiaohui de Dianfan* 閩南自養教會的典範 (The Model of the self-supporting Minnan Church). Both of these works were useful toward understanding the context of the emergence of the CCC.

With regard to Protestant missions in South Fujian, especially Xiamen, Fuzhou and their vicinities, two relevant micro-studies are *The Reformed Church in China 1842–1951* (1992) by Gerald Francis De Jong and *Working His Purpose Out: The History of the English Presbyterian Mission 1847–1947* (1947) by Edward Band. The latter begins with the introduction of Christianity in China and the birth of the Protestant English Presbyterian Mission. The author then relates the Presbyterian experiences in Xiamen 廈門, Shantou 汕頭 (written as Amoy and Swatow, respectively, in early missionary writings), and Taiwan 台灣 (formerly known as Formosa).

Several Chinese Christians have written their own stories about the Minnan Church, but I could only avail of these Chinese sources through the work of a Hong Kong scholar, Kinia C. Ng/Huang CaiLian 黃彩蓮, written in Chinese but with the English title translated as *Research on*

Hong Kong Min-nam [*sic*] Church (2005). Some of the resources she used were the writings of Chen QiuQing 陳秋卿, published between 1914–1925 in the *China Christian Church Year Book*, which I have translated as "The Progress of the Union of the Presbyterian and London Missions in Minnan," "The Process of the Union of the Minnan Church," "The Minnan Church of Christ in China," and "The Minnan Gulangyu Church of Christ in China." Another article by Xu ShengYan 許聲炎, published in 1933 in the same source, is translated as "An Overview of the Minnan Church of Christ in China Pursuing Self-Support and Self-Governance."[2]

Recent trends in the West and in Asia have focused on specific mission fields such as Xiamen and Fuzhou. For Fuzhou, the work of Ryan Dunch, *Fuzhou Protestants and the Making of a Modern China 1857–1927* (2001) is seminal. However, Fuzhou is beyond the South Fujian region and this study is not focusing on Christian involvement in the socio-political situations in China and in Fujian, hence, Dunch's work is not too useful to this study. In commemoration of the 200th anniversary of Robert Morrison's ministry in China, the Cosmic Light Holistic Care Organization in Taiwan has published a 70-volume anthology on various aspects of Christian mission in China. One of the books in this collection is entitled *Kaiduan yu Fazhan – Huanan Jindai Jidujiaoshi Lunji* 開端與發展 – 華南近代基督教史論集 (Beginning and Progress: Collected Works on the Modern History of Christianity in South China), written by Wu YiXiong 吳義雄. A few chapters in this work dealing with Christianity in Quanzhou were relevant to this study.

Two of the oldest churches in Xiamen have written their own brief histories commemorating their 150th founding anniversary: *Xiamenshi Jidujiao Xinjietang Jiantang 150 Zhounian (1848–1998) Jinian Tekan* 廈門市基督教新街堂建堂*150*週年 〔*1848–1998*〕紀念特刊 (The 150th Founding Anniversary of the Xinjie Christian Chapel of Xiamen City) and *Xiamenshi Jidujiao Zhushutanghui Jiantang Lihui 150 Zhounian (1850–2000) Jinianche* 廈門市基督教竹樹堂會建堂立會*150*週年 〔*1850–2000*〕紀念冊 (The 150th Founding Anniversary of the Zhushu Christian Chapel of Xiamen City). The former church is better known as

---

2. See Bibliography for the complete titles in Chinese and in *Hanyu pinyin* form.

the Sinkoe/First Amoy Chapel, while the latter, as the Tekchhiu/Second Amoy Chapel in history books and mission reports of the mid-nineteenth century. Along with other mission churches, these two churches were studied with regard to the issue of devolution and union by David Cheung, a Chinese Filipino (and my former student) who received his PhD in History from the University of London. His published study, entitled *Christianity in Modern China: The Making of the First Native Protestant Church* (2004),[3] shows that the Reformed Church in America and the English Presbyterian Mission had a blueprint for church formation that was consciously pro-devolution. His dissertation thesis is that "the Talmage ideal [of a devolved church] constituted the long-term theoretical motivation of Banlam [=Minnan] devolution (1856–63)."[4] The Banlam devolution and organic union of churches in this region exhibit both design and circumstance. Despite being advanced for its time, "the Banlam accomplishment had many limitations and fell short of twentieth-century ideals" (p. 18). Cheung's analysis of the devolutionary process in mission churches established in and near Xiamen provides a paradigm for examining how rapidly the PPCC developed into self-supporting, self-governing and self-propagating churches (except for Cebu Gospel Church).

C. History of Protestantism in the Philippines

The history of Protestantism in the Philippines relevant to this study required an examination of the records of American Protestant missions such as the Christian and Missionary Alliance, Episcopalian, Methodist, Presbyterian, and the Southern Baptist Convention, in two categories. First, their ministry among the Filipinos and then their work within the Chinese community. Kenton J. Clymer carefully studied the entry and work of the Presbyterian missionaries in his book, *Protestant Missionaries in the Philippines, 1898–1916: An Inquiry into the American Colonial Mentality* (1986). However, more relevant to this study is the dissertation of Anne

---

3. David Cheung (Chen Yiqiang), *Christianity in Modern China: The Making of the First Native Protestant Church*, Studies in Christian Mission, ed. Marc R. Spindler (Leiden: Brill, 2004), 28.

4. Cheung, "Ecclesiastical Devolution and Union in China," 18.

Catherine Laninga Kwantes: "Presbyterian Missionaries in the Philippines: A Historical Analysis of their Contributions to Social Change (1899–1910)" (PhD diss., University of the Philippines, 1988). Although this work mainly studies the lives and ministries of three pioneer Presbyterian missionaries who worked in the Philippines from 1898 to 1910, its findings are relevant to the formation of Protestant Chinese churches because James Burton Rodgers, Joseph Andrew Hall, and David Sutherland Hibbard had contact with the Chinese in Manila, Iloilo, and Cebu. In one way or another, Presbyterian missionaries were key figures in the formation and development of Chinese congregations, especially in Manila (1900–1903), Iloilo (1900–1925) and Cebu (1916–1966).

Since the late 1990s, Filipino historians have been producing critical analyses of the history of Protestantism in the Philippines in relation to American colonialism. Two very influential works are: Mariano Casuga Apilado's *Revolutionary Spirituality: A Study of the Protestant Role in the American Colonial Rule of the Philippines, 1898–1928* (1999) and Oscar S. Suarez' *Protestantism and Authoritarian Politics: The Politics of Repression and the Future of Ecumenical Witness in the Philippines* (1999). Both works advocate that today's Filipino church should engage in transformative theology and practice revolutionary spirituality in reaction to a tradition of political acquiescence inherited from American colonial rule. They see Protestant missionaries as willing participants not only in Christian expansionism but also in American political "imperialism." Concurring with Filipino historians such as Renato Constantino, they attribute the "erosion of [Filipino] revolutionary consciousness at the turn of the [twentieth] century" to these missionaries who discouraged or even repressed the nationalism of Protestant Filipinos.[5] From my study of the interaction of Protestant missionaries with the Chinese churches in the Philippines, there was hardly any mention of the political consciousness of the Chinese community

---

5. Suarez quotes extensively from Renato Constantino, *Neocolonial Identity and Counter-Consciousness: Essays on Cultural Decolonization* (London: Merlin Press, 1978). I personally feel that historians should not use current ideological paradigms to judge *en bloc* the actions and political motivations of early twentieth-century missionaries. Pacifism may have been the best recourse in pursuing the main goal of doing mission work in the Philippines.

during the American occupation, but frequent discussion on socio-religious issues such as the opium scourge or Roman Catholicism.

One aspect of the mission history of the Philippines that cannot be neglected is the development of the United Church of Christ in the Philippines, for it is vital to the history of Cebu Gospel Church. The Filipino church historian, T. Valentino Sitoy, Jr, has written an exhaustive history of the UCCP from 1898 to the year 1958 entitled *Several Springs, One Stream: The United Church of Christ in the Philippines*, composed of volume 1: *Heritage and Origins (1898–1948)*, and volume 2: *The Formative Decade (1948–1958)*. Many sections of these volumes provide background information not only with regard to the organization of UCCP, but also with reference to Presbyterian mission work in Manila and the provinces. Sitoy even included a short section on the relationship between four Chinese churches and the UCCP in his second volume. Two of these, the UECP and CGC, are being studied in this book.

An unpublished thesis relevant to the study of the Cebu Gospel Church (CGC) is "The Protestant Churches and Their Contribution to the Socio-Economic and Cultural Development of Cebu City, 1916–1988" (MA thesis, University of San Carlos, 1995) by Himlal Pradhan, a Nepalese pastor of a Protestant Chinese church in Cebu City. He studied the development and growth of Protestantism among the Chinese in Cebu in terms of its early experience and its individual contributions to the socio-economic and cultural development of Cebu City, making use of interviews with CGC members on the history of their church and their life testimonies. Since this was his focus, there was not much historical detail on the early formation and the leadership structure of CGC. He basically relied on the work of Bill T. C. Yang, whose work will now be discussed and evaluated.

D. Emergence of the Philippine Protestant Chinese Churches

To date, only two sets of materials have been produced on the history of the PPCC. The first set, which is more academic, is composed of two doctoral dissertations: that of Bill T. C. Yang/Yang DongChuan 楊東川 (a.k.a. William Young) entitled, "The Chinese Protestant Churches in the

Philippines" (University of Santo Tomas, 1980) and that of Joseph Young/ Yang QiYao 楊其燿 (1928–1979), entitled, "A Survey of the Overseas Chinese in the Philippines with a Suggested Program of Evangelism for the Chinese United Evangelical Church" (Columbia Bible College, 1958). The second set is more popular and is a collection of the historical writings and ministry reports of five of the Protestant Chinese churches being studied.

Bill T. C. Yang's work is divided into six chapters, four of which are of central significance: "Christian Missionary Movement in the Philippines," "History of Christian Missions in China: A Record of Evaluation," "The Chinese-Filipino: An Overview," and "The Emerging Chinese Churches in the Philippines." The first three chapters provide a general survey of the seedbed from which the Protestant Chinese churches emerged. The fourth chapter directly touches on the beginnings of these churches, but in the middle of narrating the emergence of the SSCM/SSP and the CUEC and the daughter churches of the latter, Yang digressed to a history and critique of the Little Flock or Local Church movement initiated by Watchman Nee/Ni TuoSheng 倪柝聲 (1903–1972).[6] Yang briefly mentioned the Christian Gospel Center and the Church Assembly Hall, which are "local churches" in the Philippines recognizing Watchman Nee and Witness Lee/ Li ChangShou 李常受 (1905–1997) as their respective leaders.[7] Following this digression, Yang goes back to discuss other post-WWII churches. As one of the pioneers in writing the history of the Protestant Chinese churches in the Philippines, Yang contributed in bringing together the historical

---

6. These two terms are used by outside observers. The followers of Nee and Lee prefer the terms "Meeting Halls" or juhuisuo 聚會所, distinguished by adding the name of the cities where each individual congregation is located. For a brief history, see Shangkuan, Shih Chang 上官世璋, "Benhui Sishi Zhounian Qingdianjian Manila Huaqiao Jidu Jiaohui Jianshi 本會四十周年慶典前馬尼拉市華僑基督教會簡史 (Pre-fortieth Anniversary Celebration: Short History of Overseas Chinese Christian Churches in Manila)," in *Historical Documentary of Protestantism in the Orient: 40th Anniversary of the United Evangelical Church of Manila (Feilübin Zhonghua Jidu Jiaohui Sishi Zhounian Lishi Wenxian Fu Yazhou Duoguo Jidu Jiaohui Lishi 1929–1969)* 菲律賓中華基督教會四十週年歷史文獻附亞洲多國基督教會歷史 *1929–1969*, 141–146 [pages in Chinese style] (Manila: United Evangelical Church of Manila, 1969) and Bill T. C. Yang/Yang DongChuan 楊東川 (a.k.a. William Young), "The Chinese Protestant Churches in the Philippines" (PhD diss., University of Santo Tomas, 1980), 157–166.

7. See further pp. 107–108, 200–201.

strands of the Roman Catholic, Protestant Filipino and Protestant Chinese segments of the Christian church in the Philippines.

However, my observations regarding Yang's work are: (1) Yang's dissertation does not really have a thesis, only a purpose, which is to trace the early development of the Protestant Chinese churches in order to propose a strategy for evangelism. (2) The work is already twenty-six years old. Much of the statistical data needs to be updated. (3) As this review of literature has shown, more studies on the history of Christianity in the Philippines, of evangelical Protestantism, of the Chinese in the Philippines and of the mission work in South Fujian, have been made within the past two decades. (4) Individual Protestant Chinese churches have produced their own historical writings during the same period. (5) As a historical work, Yang's work suffers from the tendency of shifting from a discussion on a certain period of history and suddenly moving to the present-day context. The deficiency of a consistent historical and chronological flow creates a skewed perspective of the main objective of his work. (6) Yang was writing his dissertation for his PhD degree requirement at the University of Santo Tomas, a Roman Catholic university. After reading his work carefully, I feel that he has not been totally free from the tendency to portray the Roman Catholics and the Spanish religious history in too positive terms and the Western Protestant missionaries and their work sometimes rather too negatively. (7) There are too many sections – such as general discussions on missions and church growth principles, and political criticisms of the Communist regime – that are not relevant to the main focus of the work. (8) Of the two hundred eighteen pages written on the history of the PPCC, only sixty pages are devoted to this main theme. Of the sixty pages, nine pages give a directory of each church, the current (1980s) pastor, address, year founded and average Sunday attendance. Ten pages refer to the current situation of the PPCC; while yet another eighteen are on the current (1980s) situation of Chinese churches in China and the world, along with an evaluation of how evangelism was being done. There are actually just twenty-three pages in which the history of how the Chinese churches were established in the Philippines is discussed. (9) Yang never made use of oral history although he did conduct interviews.

The work of Joseph Young is more organized and logically presented. He starts with a description of the land, the overseas Chinese, and the Chinese contribution to the racial composition of the Philippines, to its economy and culture. He then proceeds to discuss family system, language, religions and customs, occupation and social scale and organizations, educational system, characteristics, and political situation of the Chinese in the Philippines during the sixties. In the third chapter, Young surveys the planting of the PPCC beginning with a very brief overview of how Christianity entered and prospered in China. He then goes on to discuss the historical development of six Protestant Chinese churches briefly in seven pages, along with two others – Cebu Gospel Church and Davao Evangelical Church – being mentioned by name but without further explication. Like William Yang's work, this book does not have a thesis and the problem is the great need of evangelizing the Philippine Chinese. Since his purpose was to examine viable methods of evangelism and develop a suggested program for reaching this group of people, the historical survey is much too brief to be of use to my research.

The second set of materials includes: the 60th, 70th, 90th and 100th anniversary publications of St. Stephen's Parish (former SSCM); the founding, 40th, 50th and 70th anniversary publications of United Evangelical Church of the Philippines (former CUEC); the 50th, 80th and 90th anniversary publications of Cebu Gospel Church; the 20th, 40th, and 50th anniversary publications of Davao Evangelical Church (former DCGC); and finally, the 50th anniversary publication of Dagupan Chinese Baptist Church. These publications sought to document the formation and early development of the six churches as witnessed by the founders and/or early leaders, and transmitted to the present members. Some of these works were carefully researched, but others simply relied on the memories of early or second-generation leaders. Lack of professional skill in writing history tended to allow human errors and reductionist tendency to lessen the credibility of such publications. One vital aspect often missing in these works is the use of Protestant mission records to construct local church histories. Had both church and mission perspectives been given in these publications, there would have been more opportunity to achieve balance in the historical narrations, as well as the possibility for readers to crosscheck both sources.

I recognize that I have few predecessors in this area of research. Still, by persistent searching in libraries here and abroad (mainly in the United States), I found rare primary materials such as a photocopy of the founding issue of CUEC, the original of which cannot even be located in UECP today. I have also discovered Presbyterian mission records concerning a Chinese church in Iloilo, the existence of which has remained hidden for the past hundred years, except for a brief and vague reference in the 40th anniversary publication of UECP. Using both local church records and mission reports, it is expected that the credibility of this study has been adequately ensured.

CHAPTER 3

Presentation and Evaluation of Findings

A. The Historical, Social, and Religious Setting

The influx and social circumstances of the Chinese in the Philippines underwent many changes during the pre-hispanic and the Spanish regime. To appreciate and understand the significance of the entrance of Protestantism and its influence upon the Chinese in the Islands during the late nineteenth century, it is necessary to review briefly the historical relationship between China and the Philippines, examining the social phenomenon of the migration of Chinese from South Fujian to the Islands and specifically focusing on the Chinese in Manila. This section also includes a discussion on the attempt of Protestant missions to establish a foothold in the predominantly Roman Catholic nation. From there, the focus will shift to China and the work of Protestant missions during the nineteenth century, particularly in the province of Fujian. The stage will then be set to discuss the emergence and early development of six PPCC in the second section.

1. China and the Philippines

The history of the relationship between the Philippines and China during the pre-hispanic period will begin this section, followed by a discussion of the social situation of the Chinese in the Philippines under the Spanish regime.

a) Pre-Hispanic Period

Chinese presence in and trading relationship with the Philippines is far
older than the Spanish era (1521–1898) and may even date as far back as
the Zhou dynasty 周朝 (1122–225 BC).[1] This is based more on archaeo-
logical evidence than on written records.[2] There are, however, many written
sources from the Tang 唐朝 (AD 618–917), Song 宋朝 (AD 960–1279),
and Yuan 元朝 (AD 1277–1367) dynasties that evidence China's knowledge of various societies in the Nanyang 南洋 (referring to the regions
to the south of China). The Sung Dynasty Annals 宋史 (vol. 186), for
instance, recorded Arab traders bringing goods to Guangzhou 廣州 in AD
982, from "Ma-I 摩逸國," the name by which the Philippines was known
to China.[3] It was at this time that the merchant class, with its ability to
gain wealth, was beginning to assume a vital status in the empire. Maritime
trade in the southeastern coastal provinces of China became more important after the tenth century. The earliest account of Filipino traders, on the
other hand, is that in AD 982 merchants from Manila visited Guangdong

---

1. See Wu Ching-hong, "A Study of References to the Philippines in Chinese Sources
from Earliest Times to the Ming Dynasty," *Philippine Social Science and Humanities Review*
24 (1959): 1–181, and also by the same author, "Supplements to a Study of References to
the Philippines in Chinese Sources from Earliest Times to the Ming Dynasty (?–1644),"
University of Manila Journal of East Asiatic Studies 7 (1958): 307–393. A recent source
examining the earliest Sino-Philippine contacts is Li TianXi 李天錫. *Quanzhou Huaqiao
Huaren Yanjiu* 泉州華僑華人研究 (A study of overseas Chinese from Quanzhou) (Beijing
北京: Zhongyang Wenxian Chubanshe 中央文獻出版社, 2006). For an exhaustive
reference list (published up to the 1990s) regarding the history of the Chinese in the
Philippines, see Chinben See 施振民 and Teresita Ang See 施洪玉華. *Chinese in the
Philippines: A Bibliography* (Manila: De La Salle University Press, China Studies Program,
1990), 16–39.

2. Cf. Go Bon Juan 吳文煥, ed. *Huafei Ziku Shi Yijia: Feiren Yu Huananren Yuanyuan
Zhiliao Huibian* 華菲自古是一家：菲人與華南人淵源資料匯編 (One Family Since
Ancient Times) (Manila: Kaisa Para Sa Kaunlaran, Feilübin Huayi Qingnian Lianhehui 菲
律賓華裔青年聯合會, 2002).

3. The text reads, "There is also the country of Ma-i, which in the seventh year of
the Taiping Xing-guo period [982] brought valuable merchandise to the Guangzhou [
廣州] coast," or, in Chinese: 『又有摩逸國，太平興國七年〔九八二〕載寶貨，至
廣州海岸。』 Ma-I has previously been identified with Mindoro because of the Mait
people there and there are sources identifying Ma-I as Manila. See Chen TaiMin 陳台民,
Zhongfei Guanxi yu Feilübin Huaqiao 中菲關係與菲律賓華僑 (Sino-Philippine Relations
and the Philippine Chinese) (Hong Kong: Chao Yang Chubanshe 朝陽出版社, 1985),
14–19. Henceforth cited as *Sino-Philippine Relations*. Recently Go Bon Juan has proposed
that Ma-I is Ba-I, now known as Laguna de Bay (pronounced as Bai). For his argument
regarding the location of Ma-I, see Go Bon Juan, "Ma'I in Chinese Records – Mindoro
or Bai? An Examination of a Historical Puzzle," *Philippine Studies* 53, 1 (2005): 119–138.

廣東 for trade.[4] In AD 1003, the first Filipino diplomatic mission in China was established when King Qiling of Butuan 蒲端國主其陵 paid tribute to the Emperor of China.[5] During the twelfth and thirteenth centuries, a definite record of this trade relationship was described by Zhao RuGua 趙汝適 (variant name Chau Ju-Kua), who was appointed as superintendent and commissioner of customs in Quanzhou 泉州. He obtained his information by interviewing Chinese junk sailors and merchants who returned from the Philippines, and compiled these and other materials in the *Zhu Fan Zhi* 諸蕃志.[6] This is where the early names of the islands – Ma-I (Ma Yi Guo 摩逸國), San-su (San Yu 三嶼 or three islands) and P'i-sho-ye (Bei Wei Shi Ye 北未獅耶), probably a miscalling of Visaya or Bisaya – are found along with historical narratives of the trading activities.[7]

During the Ming dynasty 明朝 (AD 1368–1644), maritime trade within the interiors and beyond the boundaries of China, specifically the Philippines, greatly flourished.[8] This is evidenced by the Ming artifacts found all the way from Luzon (or Lü Song 呂宋, the name by which the

---

4. Liu Chi-tien, "Centuries of Sino-Philippine Relations," eds. Philip H. and Liu Chi-tien, *Sino-Philippine Research Journal* 1 (Sep 1940): 22–23. Between AD 976–983, China established trade relations with eight nations through the port at Guangdong.

5. See Chinese texts in Go Bon Juan 吳文煥 and Teresita Ang See 施洪玉華, eds. *Heritage: A Pictorial History of the Chinese in the Philippines (Wenhua Chuantong – Feihua Lishi Tupian)* 文化傳統—菲華歷史圖片 (Manila: Kaisa Para Sa Kaunlaran, Feilübin Huayi Qingnian Lianhehui 菲律賓華裔青年聯合會 and Professor Chinben See Memorial Trust Fund/Jinian Shi Chenmin Jiaoshou Jiangxuejin Jijinhui 紀念施振民教授獎學金基金會, 1987), 10–14.

6. Chau Ju-Kua/Zhao RuGua 趙汝適. *His Work on the Chinese and Arab Trade in the Twelfth and Thirteenth Centuries, Entitled Chu-fan-chi* 諸蕃志, trans. and annotated by Friedrich Hirth and W. W. Rockhill (St. Petersburg: Imperial Academy of Sciences, 1911). Originally published as *Chu-fan-chi* (諸蕃志) in 1225, *Chu-fan-chi* is now written as *Zhu Fan Zhi*, literally, "All barbarians of Southseas-record," and also translated as "Reports on the South Seas barbarians," or "An Account of Various Barbarians." The annotation by Hirth and Rockhill has been translated into Chinese, with Chinese text and additional corrections and comments, by Han ZhenHua 韓振華, *Zhufanzhi Zhubu* 諸蕃志注補 (Supplement to *Zhufanzhi*) (Hong Kong: Center of Asian Studies, The University of Hong Kong, 2000), henceforth cited as *Supplement to Zhufanzhi*.

7. Hirth and Rockhill identify Ma-it as Manila, the three islands as Calamians, Palawan and Busuanga, and P'i-sho-ye as Visaya. Cf. Han ZhenHua, *Supplement to Zhufanzhi*, 273–280. See also Liu Chi-tien, "Centuries of Sino-Philippine Relations," 24–27 and Chen TaiMin, *Sino-Philippine Relations*, 40. For Chinese texts mentioning Philippine locations in the Sung and Ming Dynasty Annals, see Go and Ang, eds. *Heritage*, 10–14.

8. See Wang GungWu, *The Nanhai Trade: Early Chinese Trade in the South China Sea* (Singapore: Eastern Universities Press, 2003).

islands were known to China during this period) south to the Visayan islands.[9] At least ten *rajahs* (princely rulers) and *sultans* (Muslim monarchs)
from the Philippines sent tribute missions to China from the eleventh to
the fifteenth centuries AD, with the last one reaching China in 1421, a
century before the coming of Ferdinand Magellan to the Philippines.[10] The
Ming Dynasty Annals 明史 even mentioned several tribute embassies from
Luzon, Pangasinan (called "Pin-ka-shi-lan," Ping Jia Shi Lan 馮嘉施蘭)
and Sulu (Su Lu 蘇祿).[11] The Chinese traders became cultural brokers who
introduced a wealth of knowledge and technology to the local people with
whom they conducted business.

Among the most active traders were the people from South Fujian
(Minnan), better known as the *Hokkiens*. During the short-lived independent kingdoms established in Guangdong and Fujian provinces in the
tenth century, these regions were frequented by foreign traders, giving rise
to a maritime commerce that flourished for centuries. At first, Quanzhou
was the major center for this trade during the thirteenth and fourteenth
centuries.[12]

It was during the Ming dynasty, specifically during the reign of Emperor
Yong Le 永樂 (1403–1424), decades before the Europeans ever set out
to sea, that China undertook an extensive exploration of the Pacific and
Indian Oceans. However, it was also during this dynasty that the policy
changed and the government imposed restrictions on foreign trade banning
overseas travel for all Chinese doing private trade. Trade was bureaucratized

9. *Tsinoy: The Story of the Chinese in Philippine Life,* eds. Teresita Ang See, Go Bon
Juan, Doreen Go Yu, Yvonne Chua (Manila: Kaisa Para Sa Kaunlaran, 2005), 18–29.

10. Liu Chi-tien, "Centuries of Sino-Philippine Relations," 28.

11. For a brief history of the Philippines paying tribute to China and a list of *Hokkien*
names for places in the Philippines that were known to China, see Wang Teh-Ming,
Sino-Filipino Historico-Cultural Relations (Quezon City: University of the Philippines,
1967), 295–310.

12. Quanzhou was the "Zeitun" described by Marco Polo in 1275 as "one of the two
greatest havens in the world for commerce." Marco Polo, *The Travels of Marco Polo: The
Complete Yule-Cordier Edition, including the unabridged third edition (1903) of Henry Yule's
annotated translation, as revised by Henri Cordier; together with Cordier's later volume of notes
and addenda (1920),* vol. 2 (New York: Dover Publications, 1993), 235. The other important
ports that later overshadowed Quanzhou were Fuzhou and Yuegang 月港 in Zhangzhou.
See Lau Yee-cheung and Lee Kam-keung, "An Economic and Political History," in *Fujian:
A Coastal Province in Transition and Transformation,* eds., Yue-man Yeung and David K. Y.
Chu, 25–55 (Hong Kong: Chinese University Press, 2000), 26–28.

and centralized in Guangzhou, using inland routes to distribute goods to the north. As a result, the ports in Fujian were bypassed. Quanzhou never regained its former greatness as a port. Despite the isolationist policy of the Ming dynasty, *Hokkien* sailors and traders maintained commercial links with the small port communities of Chinese traders in East and Southeast Asia.[13] Except for the community in Manila, these port communities were small. What made Manila different was the initial Spanish policy of welcoming and nurturing trade with China.

b) Spanish Regime

When the Philippine Islands were colonized by Spain, beginning in 1565, the Spaniards were not allowed to embark on trading expeditions to China because of the *Patronato Real* (royal patronage), a system whereby the Roman Catholic Church granted certain rights to the patrons and demarcated Spanish and Portuguese territorial jurisdictions.[14] In China, foreigners remained barred from the coastal ports until 1685 when the government allowed them to enter Guangdong under highly restrictive rules. Spain, however, was given special port rights in Xiamen 廈門 during the sixteenth century onward.[15] Taking advantage of this special treatment and skirting the stipulations of the *Patronato* system, Spain gained a foothold in China. The reason for this special privilege was the defeat by the Spaniards of Lin Feng or Limahong 林鳳/林阿鳳 in 1574, since Lin Feng

13. Some of the notable communities were in Faifo, Malacca, Patani, Hirado, Nagasaki, Manila, Bantam and Batavia. See Wang Gung Wu, *China and the Chinese Overseas*, Ethnic Studies Series (Singapore: Times Media Private Limited, Eastern Universities Press by Marshall Cavendish, 1991), 87–97.

14. According to Hernando M. Coronel, "The Spanish *Patronato* and Portuguese *Padroado* were generally described as the sets of rights, privileges, exemptions, duties and responsibilities granted by the papacy to the Crown of Spain and the Crown of Portugal as patrons of Roman Catholic missions in the rediscovered territories." This arrangement was based on the bull *Universalis ecclesiae* issued by Pope Julius II (1443–1513) on 8 Jul 1508. See his book, *The Early Filipino Priests: Boatmen for Christ* (Manila: Reyes Publishing, 1998), 15–16.

15. Although the Portuguese had cunningly secured a foothold and established on-shore trading depots in Macau in 1553, China did not officially open its doors to foreign trade until 1685, during the Qing dynasty 清朝 (1644–1911/12), when custom houses were set up in Guangdong 廣東, Zhangzhou 漳州, Ningbo 寧波, and Yuntaishan 雲泰山 (in Jiangsu 江蘇). The Guangdong port became prosperous when the British, followed by other Western nations, started to build factories there. See Immanuel C. Y. Hsü, *The Rise of Modern China*, 3rd ed. (New York: Oxford University Press, 1983), 92–97.

was considered a pirate by the Fujian authorities.[16] According to Chen TaiMin, the defeat of Lin Feng resulted in improved relations between the two countries but also brought negative repercussion since Spain's view of the Chinese residing in the Philippines turned from cordiality to distrust. Trading relations also flourished despite the existing ban and restrictions. In fact, the port of Xiamen was closed from 1730 to 1842 to all foreigners except the Spaniards.[17] The Spaniards were able to enjoy relative ease in defending and developing their colony, for the local Muslims had been cut off from their allies in Asia and Arabia by the Portuguese, and the Japanese and Chinese were not interested in the Islands, politically.[18] According to Benito Legarda, the silk for silver trade between China and the Philippines was carried out by "sampans," more properly called Chinese junks, from the ports in Fujian, such as Xiamen and Quanzhou.[19] According to Lau Yee-cheung and Lee Kam-keung, the expansion of foreign trade in Fujian produced economic growth in Fujian as well as in the southeast coastal areas. The increase of Minnan merchants and emigrants led to social and cultural changes in southern Fujian.[20]

With the eventual decline of the ports in Quanzhou and Zhangzhou during the seventeenth century, Xiamen became the center of coastal trade with Taiwan and Southeast Asia. During the eighteenth and nineteenth

----

16. Lin Feng was a native of Raoping, Chaozhou, 潮洲饒平, which is in Fujian. He should not be identified with Lin DaoGan 林道乾 who was also a pirate. The latter is from Huilai, Chaozhou 潮洲惠來. Chen TaiMin holds the view that Lin Feng did not only attack Manila for plunder, but was intending to settle in the Philippines since he was a hunted fugitive in his own country. This supposition is based on the number of ships and persons that came with him: 15,000 women and artisans, 2,000 sailors, and 2,000 soldiers in 62 ships. *BRPI* 4:24–44. For details on this incident and its political impact, see Chen TaiMin, *Sino-Philippine Relations*, 87–136; and *BRPI*, 6:92–125 and Wang GungWu, *China and the Chinese Overseas*, 99.

17. Henry Thurburn Montague Bell and Henry George Wandesforde Woodhead, eds., *The China Year Book, 1912* (Nendeln, Liechtenstein: Kraus–Thomson Organization Limited; Rep. Germany: Lessingdruckerei Wiesbaden, 1969), 73.

18. Wang GungWu, *China and the Chinese Overseas*, 96.

19. The better term to use is Chinese junks, which were usually three-masted and between 200 to 800 tons in size (see App. H). Sampans 舢舨 were wooden boats ranging from 12 to 15 feet long, suitable for inland or coastal travel but not for ocean voyages.

20. Lau and Lee mentioned extravagance and materialism among the people, sprouting of the ideas of freedom and equality, and academic success in Quanzhou and Zhangzhou, as seen from the rise in the number of advance scholars or *jinshi* 進士. See Lau and Lee, "An Economic and Political History," 29.

centuries, the Chinese who came to the Philippines were no longer just merchants or laborers, for some of them gradually became sojourners in the Islands.

2. Chinese Migration to the Philippines

As the preceding section has shown, the Chinese have been visiting and trading in the Philippine Islands for numerous centuries. They continued to enter the Islands even when it was under Spanish control. To understand the situation of these Chinese when the Americans occupied the Islands, one must first comprehend the complexities involved in the phenomenon of migration from China during the Spanish era.

a) Phenomenon of Migration

Migration to the Philippines is but part of the extensive phenomenon of Chinese migration that transpired from the seventeenth century until the Republican period of China's history. This phenomenon was analyzed by Wang GungWu in his study entitled, "Patterns of Chinese Migration in Historical Perspective," in *China and the Chinese Overseas* (1991).[21] He identified four patterns of Chinese migration in the last two centuries (since about 1800). The traders or *huashang* 華商 were merchants, miners, skilled workers or artisans who personally, or who sent their colleagues, agents, or family members, to work abroad and set up bases as ports, mines or trading centers. After a generation or two, these traders would settle down and bring up their emigrant families.

The coolies or *huagong* 華工 were normally men of peasant origin, land-less laborers and the urban poor. Being associated with plantation econo-mies in foreign lands it was therefore transitional, since many of the con-tract laborers returned to China after their contracts ended.

The sojourners or *huaqiao* 華僑 are the most relevant to this study; however, this term is controversial. Wang explained that the term can refer to all overseas Chinese in general, but it took on political, legal or ideo-logical content during the nineteenth century. It came to be applied to the *huashang* and *huagong* plus the teachers, journalists and other profes-sionals who went out to promote greater awareness of Chinese culture and

---

21. See Wang GungWu, *China and the Chinese Overseas*, 3–23.

national needs. Because of these three dimensions that developed during the Republican and Communist eras, the *huaqiao* came to be known as Chinese residing outside China but were still considered part of and legally protected by the Chinese nation. In the twentieth century, the term came to be ideologically associated with both the Nationalist Party (Guomindang 國民黨) and the Communist Party of China. Unlike the other two patterns, this pattern focused on education in the Chinese language and the fostering of nationalism. It was dominant until the 1950s.

The re-migrant or *huayi* 華裔 pattern is a new phenomenon describing the re-migrants of Chinese descent, largely foreign-born but including those born in China who have acquired foreign citizenship. This pattern, however, is beyond the scope of the historical context of this study.[22] Since the *huagong* were so transient due to the nature of their work, the *huashang* and the *huaqiao* were most likely the two types of Chinese emigrants that would later become Protestants and make up the membership of the Chinese churches in the Philippines. Furthermore, as the succeeding paragraphs will show, most of these immigrants originated from the Tongan, Xiamen and Jinjiang (South Fujian). But first the reasons for migrating need to be examined.

b) Reasons for Migration

In 1934 the Chinese sociologist Ta Chen surveyed 905 families in South China and listed the causes of migration as: (1) economic pressure (unemployment or underemployment), (2) previous connection with the Nanyang, (3) losses from natural calamities, (4) plans to expand specific enterprises, (5) being expelled for bad conduct, (6) local disturbances, and (7) family quarrel. However, the chief motivation for migration, which remains true until the present, was economic, or financial gain. Those who went abroad during the nineteenth and twentieth centuries were from the middle and lower classes, and of the latter, fully two-thirds were coolies. One of the biggest inducements for them to go abroad was the higher wages that they could earn. In 1912 Philip Wilson Pitcher, missionary of

---

22. In relation to the present age, Wang GungWu comments that the *huagong* pattern is gone and unlikely to revive; the *huaqiao* pattern survives but is now peripheral; the *huayi* pattern is new and its future uncertain; only the *huashang* pattern remains and is the foundation for Chinese migration from ancient times to the present.

the Reformed Church in America from 1885–1915, stated that in China a coolie might earn 5 or 6 Chinese *yuans* per month, but in the Straits and in Manila he could easily double this amount.[23] Ta Chen's observation that emigrants from Zhangzhou and Quanzhou mainly preferred to go to the Philippines complements Doepper's findings which will be discussed later.

c) Waves of Migration

Throughout the Spanish colonial period, from around 1561 to 1899, the relationship between Chinese immigrants and the Spanish government vacillated between periods of influx, uprisings, restrictions in travel or residence, massacres, and re-admission of immigrants (see App. C). By 1588 the Chinese in the Philippines had increased to 10,000, causing the Spanish authorities to become apprehensive.[24] Significantly, less than twenty years later in 1603, the figures jumped to 30,000. One of the worst massacres of Chinese occurred during this year, but this did not hinder the migration of Chinese into the Philippines. This phenomenon reached its highest mark in 1886 when 100,000 Chinese reportedly lived in the Islands.

d) Origins and Concentration of Immigrants

Since ancient days, Guangdong, Shantou, and Xiamen were the three places where the greatest stream of migration from China flowed. William Alexander Parsons Martin (1827–1916), the Presbyterian missionary who served in China from 1850 to 1916, briefly described these places in his book published in 1907.[25] The Chinese from Guangzhou and other provinces were consistently a minority group in the Philippines. The majority of immigrants came from South Fujian. In the 1890s, for example, more than 90 percent of the Chinese in the Philippines were from the *Hokkien*-speaking areas of Xiamen and Quanzhou (see App. D).

---

23. In 1934, one yuan 元 was equivalent to USD $0.34. See Ta Chen, *Emigrant Communities in South China: A Study of Overseas Migration and Its Influence on Standards of Living and Social Change*, ed. Bruno Lasker (New York: Secretariat, Institute of Pacific Relations, 1940), 259–261; Philip Wilson Pitcher, *In and About Amoy: Some Historical and Other Facts Connected with One of the First Open Ports in China*, 2nd ed. (Shanghai and Foochow: Methodist Publishing House in China, 1912), 159–169.

24. *BRPI* 3:167–168.

25. See details in William Alexander Parsons Martin, *The Awakening of China* (London: Hodder & Stoughton, 1907), 7–16.

Hence, migration from Fujian, particularly from Xiamen and Quanzhou, will be the center of focus. Concerning the nature of this migration, Doeppers explains:

> Migrations usually involved a feedback process of some historical continuity and the movement of *Hokkien* Chinese to the Philippines conforms to this expectation. . . . During this same period, the overseas trade activity of the *Hokkien* region, which had been handled by five ports, ended up highly concentrated in Amoy [Xiamen] in a pattern of major port emergence and minor port decline that was widely replicated along the inhabited coasts of the world. The flow of immigrants to the Philippines in the 1890s from Chin-chiang [Jinjiang 晉江] and Lung-chi [Longxi 龍溪], which contained the ports of Ch'uan-chou [Quanzhou 泉州] and Chang-chou [Zhangzhou 漳州], respectively, and from Tung-an [Tongan 同安] and Hai-teng [Haicheng 海澄], which each contained minor ports of the same names, represents a continuation of emigration patterns established before the rechanneling of foreign trade and travel through the deep water port of Amoy [Xiamen].[26]

Doeppers studied the places of origin of the Chinese population of Manila around 1822 and 1894, and compared this with the Chinese in other provincial centers during the 1890s. His findings indicate that Chinese immigrants in Manila originated mainly from Quanzhou, Longxi, and Tongan (see App. E).[27]

Additional information given in Doepper's research locates the Chinese in Philippine cities and towns according to their predominant *xian* 縣 (county) or place of origin, among them Manila, Dagupan, Iloilo, and Cebu (see App. F). Doeppers' findings show that the Chinese in these four

---

26. Daniel Frederick Doeppers, "Destination, Selection and Turnover among Chinese Migrants to Philippine Cities in the Nineteenth Century," *Journal of Historical Geography* 12, no. 4 (1986): 387.

27. For the names and locations of the places listed in this table, compare with App. G.

cities were mainly from the Jinjiang and Tongan-Xiamen localities of South Fujian (see political divisions in App. G).[28]

By law, immigrants to the Philippines had to land first in Manila. However, during the mid-nineteenth century, restrictions that had closely limited the number of Chinese and forced them to live in the vicinity of Manila were removed.[29] Doeppers' study significantly points out that in Manila, Dagupan and Iloilo the predominant place of origin is Jinjiang, while for Cebu, it is the Tongan-Xiamen region (App. F).

e) Patterns of Migration

Pitcher gave the following information regarding Xiamen as a central source of emigration (App. H). Based on the latest statistics, he reported that around ten million Chinese were scattered all over the world, and among them, 80,000 were in the Philippines.[30] It was estimated that among these emigrants, an average of about 65,000 annually left Xiamen while 50,000 returned. They went out to make their fortunes or, in many instances, their homes in foreign lands. Pitcher provided a chart showing the emigration statistics of departure and return within a period of six years, 1904–1909 (see App. I). It shows a distinctly different pattern for departure to and return from Manila in comparison to Formosa (Taiwan), Hong Kong, the Straits, and other coastal ports. This may indicate that more emigrants who went to Manila stayed and did not return immediately within four years. It might even indicate that such emigrants settled in the Philippines, but more *Hokkiens* migrated to the Straits, primarily Singapore and Malaysia, than to other Asian countries, including the Philippines.[31] If Protestant

---

28. As in the preceding table, the terms that were altered from Wade-Giles romanization to *Hanyu pinyin* include: hsien = *xian*, Chin-chiang = Jinjiang, Tung-an/Amoy = Tongan/Xiamen, Nan-an = Nanan, Lung-chi = Longxi. See Doeppers, "Destination, Selection and Turnover," 389.

29. Daniel Frederick Doeppers, "Ethnicity and Class in the Structure of Philippine Cities" (PhD diss., Syracuse University, 1971), 72–73; Rosario Mendoza Cortes, *Pangasinan, 1572–1800* (Quezon City: New Day, 1974), 100, 104. See 101–103 for a chart of the number of Chinese in Dumaguete, Dagupan and Davao for the years 1903, 1918, 1960 and 1968, in order to get a perspective of how the Chinese population grew in these provincial urban areas.

30. Pitcher does not provide the year for this "latest" statistics, but his book was first published in 1909 and what is available to me is the 1912 edition.

31. The Strait Settlements were a collection of territories of the British East India Company in Southeast Asia. It consisted of Penang, Malacca, Singapore, the Dinding

Chinese were part of these waves of emigrants, and even during the 1890s, the Straits would have been a more attractive destination since Singapore and Malaysia were colonized by relatively Protestant-friendly governments unlike the staunchly Roman Catholic Spanish regime in the Philippines.

3. Growth of the Chinese Population in the Philippines

Wong Kwok-chu compiled the following data regarding the number of Chinese in the Philippines during the American occupation, comparing these numbers to the whole Philippine population. He wanted to show that the Chinese population was relatively small compared to the total Philippine population, unlike in other Asian countries, but for this study the significance of table 1 is the number of Chinese from 1899 to 1918 (shaded cells). The figures for these years held steady, unlike in succeeding years (1921–1939).

The fact that during the first decade of American rule the population of the Chinese remained at about forty thousand was the result of the enforcement of the Chinese Exclusion Act issued by General Elwell Otis on 26 September 1898.[32] This Act refused all Chinese persons permission to land in the Islands; only former residents who left the Islands between 31 December 1895 and September 1898, and those Chinese belonging to the exempt classes, were allowed to land.[33] The exempt classes included skilled

---

territories, and Province Wellesley and scattered islands in the region. These places were also used as mission headquarters by the British and Americans at the beginning of Protestant entry into China.

32. See the text of the orders of General Elwell Stephen Otis (1838–1909) in *Annual Report of the Military Governor in the Philippine Islands, 1899–1903*, 6 vols. (Manila: n.p., 1899–1903) 1: 55–56. Otis was enforcing this Act as an extension of the United States federal law, which was passed on 6 May 1882, prohibiting Chinese coolies from entering its territory. The law was renewed by President Theodore Roosevelt on 29 Apr 1902 and formally approved in the Philippines on 3 Mar 1903. "In 1905, Chinese worldwide united to protest against the Exclusion Act by boycotting American products, dealing huge financial losses to American businesses," according to Clark L. Alejandrino. See further details and analysis of the effects of this Act in his book, *A History of the 1902 Chinese Exclusion Act: American Colonial Transmission and Deterioration of Filipino-Chinese Relations* (Manila: Kaisa Para Sa Kaunlaran, 2003), 1–50. The Act was finally repealed by the Magnuson Act, or Chinese Exclusion Repeal Act of 1943. "Repeal Act," *Digital History*, accessed 27 Oct 2006, http://www.digitalhistory.uh.edu/asian_voices/ voices_display.cfm?id=46.

33. *Census of the Philippine Islands* 1903, 2: 491.

or unskilled Chinese laborers who were former residents, Chinese officials, teachers, students, merchants, tourists and pastors.[34]

Table 1: Number of Chinese in the Philippines 1899–1939

YEAR	NUMBER OF CHINESE (1)	TOTAL PHILIPPINE POPULATION (2)	(1) (2) %
1899 (June)	40,000	data not available	data not available
1903 (2 March)	41,035	7,635,426	0.54%
1904 (29 April)	49,659	data not available	data not available
1918 (31 December)	43,802	10,314,310	0.42%
1921	55,212	10,956,000	0.50%
1933	71,638	data not available	data not available
1935	110,500	13,099,405	0.84%
1939 (1 January)	117,487	16,000,303	0.73%
1939	130,000	data not available	data not available

Source: Wong Kwok-chu, *The Chinese in the Philippine Economy 1898–1941* (Quezon City: Ateneo de Manila University Press, 1999), 5. Reprinted by permission of The Ateneo de Manila University Press.

Note: The last column gives the percentage of the Chinese (column 2) in relation to the whole population of the Philippines (column 3).

34. Annual Report of Major General Arthur MacArthur, US Army, Commanding, Division of the Philippines. Military Governor in the Philippine Islands, *Reports of the Military Governor*, Vol. 2 (Manila: n.p., 1901); Graciano Cabusora Abulog, "The Chinese Immigration Question in the Philippines" (MA thesis, University of California, 1940), 23.

No longer confined to Manila, Chinese enclaves in the provinces began to grow rapidly. During the first decade of American rule (1899–1909), the number of Chinese in the provinces more than doubled (see App. J). A more detailed survey exhibits data from various censuses taken in 1903, 1918 and 1939, showing the steady increase of the Chinese population in Manila and the provinces. Prominent increases were in Cebu and Davao, where we find 5.26 times and 189.21 times increase respectively when compared to 1903 (see App. K). The Chinese were now able to travel and live in many ports and cities, from as far north as the Ilocos province to as far south as Zamboanga. Manila, however, had always been and continued to be the prime destination for *Hokkien* traders during the first few decades of American rule. The history of the Chinese in Manila and other places pertinent to this study will now be highlighted.

4. History of the Chinese in Manila

An investigation of the history of the Chinese churches in the Philippines entails a preview of the historical background of the Chinese as immigrants, from their early settlement, places of residence, living situation under the Spanish rule, the effect of Roman Catholicism throughout the Spanish colonial period, and the observations of Protestant missionaries regarding the Chinese as potential mission targets. This section will focus on the Chinese in Manila. The Chinese in Iloilo, Cebu, Dagupan, and Davao are discussed within the context of the mission history of these cities in succeeding sections of this chapter.

a) Early Settlements

Manila was the main entrepot for extensive commercial activity; the city soon became the trading center of the archipelago. Chinese junks annually made voyages to the Philippines, but it seems that only a few of the Chinese traders settled in the country. When the Spaniards finally colonized the Philippine Islands in 1571, they found a settlement of one hundred fifty Chinese and twenty Japanese in Manila living peacefully with the natives.[35] This number rapidly increased to ten thousand by 1588.[36] The

---

35. "Relation of the Conquest of the Island of Luzon, Manila, Apr 20, 1572," in *BRPI*, 3:168. See also Jacques Amyot, SJ, *Manila Chinese*, 45.

36. *BRPI*, 3:167–168.

Spaniards called the Chinese traders "Sangleyes," according to the account of Domingo Fernandez Navarrete recorded around 1650. He explained that when asked who they were and what they came for, the Chinese replied: "Xang Lei" – that is, we come to trade. The Spaniards, who did not understand their language, conceived it to be the name of their country. Putting two words together into one, they called them Sangleyes, a name by which they continued to distinguish the Chinese.[37] The Chinese sources, on the other hand, referred to these settlers in Luzon as *yadong* 壓冬, but this term has since become obsolete.[38] However, recent studies have proven that the proper basis for this term is *chang lai* 常來 or in the *Hokkien* dialect, *siong lay* (literally, "visiting or to come frequently") and not based on the terms *shang ren* 商人 (traders) or *shang lü* 商旅 (doing business), as previously accepted.[39] It is argued that since the early traders were mostly from Fujian and spoke the *Hokkien* dialect, the term *siong lay* is closer in sound to "sangley" than the term *shang lü* in the Mandarin language, a language they were unlikely to have been using since they were predominantly *Hokkien*-speaking traders.

---

37. Domingo Fernandez Navarrete, *Tratados historicos, politicos, ethicos, y religiosos de la monarchia de China* (An account of the empire of China, also many remarkable messages and things worth observing in other coasts in several voyages) (Madrid: *Imprenta Real*, 1676), quoted in *Census of the Philippine Islands Taken Under the Direction of the Philippine Commission in the Year 1903, Vol. 1: Geography, History, and Population* (Washington, DC: United States Bureau of the Census, 1905), 484.

38. This term is found in the *Dong Xi Yang Kao* 東西洋考 (Studies on the ocean east and west), written by Zhang Xie 張燮 (1574–1640) in 1618. Zhang Xie 張燮, *Dongxi Yangkao* 東西洋考 (Studies on the ocean east and west) (N.p.: n.p., 1618; reprint, Beijing: Zhonghua Shuju 中華書局, 1981), 174; in Chen TaiMin 陳台民, *Sino-Philippine Relations*, 139–140. See n. 43.

39. In a collection of 75 drawings of early Filipinos done in 1590, called the Boxer Codex, there is a picture of a male and female Chinese in traditional garb with the words "常來" (*chang lai*) in the upper right corner. See *Tsinoy: The Story of the Chinese in Philippine Life*, 47, for a full-spread reproduction of this drawing. This collection belonged to Charles Ralph Boxer, but he donated it to the Lilli Library of Indiana University, where it is referred to as the Sino–Spanish Codex. See Charles Ralph Boxer, *South China in the Sixteenth Century: Being the Narratives of Galeote Pereira, Fr. Gaspar Da Cruz, O.P., and Fr. Martin De Rada, O.E.S.A.* (London: Hakluyt Society, 1953), 260. Fifteen of these pictures can be found in the 10–volume *Kasaysayan: The Story of the Filipino People*. In particular, see Jose S. Arcilla, SJ, Vol. 3: *The Spanish Conquest*, ed. Gina Apostol (Hong Kong: Asia Publishing Company; New York: Reader's Digest, 1998), 34, 39, 40, 55, and Go Bon Juan, "Gems of History: Earliest Chinese Drawings," *Tulay Fortnightly* (23 May 2006): 5–6.

b) Alcaiceria *and* Parian

Originally, the Chinese were free to live among the Filipinos and Spaniards
and most of them lived in the Binondo and Tondo area. Because of the
need to protect the goods brought by the Chinese traders, the Spanish
government provided a building in 1580 called the *alcaiceria* (silk market)
on *Calle San Fernando* in Binondo (see App. L).[40] Alarmed by the rapidly
increasing number of Chinese immigrants and fearful of further uprisings after the attack of Lin Feng in 1574,[41] the Spanish governor Gonzalo
Ronquillo de Peñalosa built the *Parian* (marketplace) in 1582 in an area
close to Intramuros or the Walled City, within range of its cannons (see
App. L).[42] This became a place where the Spaniards restricted the Chinese
in Manila to reside and do business. Records in China referred to this place
as the *jiannei* 澗內 (literally, lying between two rivers, which may have reference to the geographical location of the original *Parian*), or *shichang* 市
場 (market), or *tangrenjie zhi qianshen* 唐人街之前身 (the predecessor of

---

40. The word is of Arabic derivative and refers to a combined customhouse, wholesale
mart, and merchants' quarters. John Foreman gave a brief description of the construction
and administration of the *alcaiceria*. In later years, it became a ruin where government
built stores which were in use until 1863. John Foreman, *The Philippine Islands: A Political,
Geographical, Ethnographical, Social and Commercial History of the Philippine Archipelago
Embracing the Whole Period of Spanish Rule with an Account of the Succeeding American
Insular Government*. 3rd ed. Filipiniana Book Guild, 2nd series, Vol. 2 (New York: Charles
Scribner's Sons, 1906; reprint, Manila: Filipiniana Book Guild, 1980), 110. Wickberg,
however, gives a late date (late 1750s) for its construction. Wickberg, *Chinese in Philippine
Life*, 23, 81.

41. Lin Feng killed several Spaniards, including camp-master Martin de Goiti, then
burned much of Intramuros. He was aided by some Filipinos and for this action two native
chieftains paid with their lives. The Spanish authors called him Limahon, based on the
Hokkien pronunciation, Lim-hong or Lim-a-hong. See detailed narration in Fray Gaspar
de San Agustin, *Conquista de las islas Filipinas* (Madrid: Iimprenta de Manuel Ruiz de
Murga, 1698); Antonio de Morga, *Events in the Philippine Islands*, trans. J. S. Cummins.
(Cambridge: Cambridge University Press for the Hakluyt Society, 1972). Originally
published as *Sucesos De Las Islas Filipinas* (Mexico: Shop of Geronymo Balli, 1609).

42. Foreman notes that the word "*Parian*" is a Mexican word for marketplace.
Foreman, *Philippine Islands*, 110. But there are sources that claim its origin is Chinese,
while Alberto Santamaria, OP, claims that it is a Tagalog word signifying "go there" from *pa*
= command prefix and *dian/diyan* = there. See discussion in Alberto Santamaria, OP, "The
Chinese *Parian* (El Parian de los Sangleyes)," in *The Chinese in the Philippines: 1570–1770*,
ed. Alfonso Felix, Jr (Manila: Solidaridad Publishing, 1966), 1:67–72. Interestingly, the
phonetics of one of the Chinese terms is Ba Lian 八連 | 八連埠 | 八連基 (meaning "eight
sides") where "b" is pronounced as the English "p." In the *Hokkien* dialect, the pronunciation
is pat-lian (meaning eight joined segments), which may be a transliteration of the term, or
may be referring to the octagonal shape of the *Parian*.

Chinatown).[43] The equivalent in Tagalog is *palengke* (market). The *Parian* should not be confused with the *alcaiceria*, but because of the common nature of the trade going on inside these two places, the terms acquired the tendency of being interchangeably used.[44] The Chinese population in Manila grew rapidly: from 10,000 in 1588, to 24,000 in 1596, and finally to 30,000 in 1603 (App. C).[45] However, this number was soon depleted by the massacres of the same year and in succeeding periods.

Despite taking control measures, oftentimes extreme and cruel, the Spanish government recognized that the Chinese were indispensable to the growth of the economy and infrastructure of their colony. For "the Chinaman is the most available, the most desirable, and the most useful immigrant obtainable for the Philippines. Being docile, amenable to law, industrious, frugal, he accepts any proffered task which assures him of regular wages; or will till the soil if a market for its products is available."[46] "The Chinese residents in Manila became the bakers, cooks, barbers, tailors, carpenters, gardeners, printers, smithers, jewelers, bazaar owners, and

---

43. 『華人既多詣呂宋, 往往久住不歸, 名為壓冬. 聚居澗內為生活, 漸至數萬, . . . 』 ["Many of the Chinese are in Luzon where they settle and don't return, they are called *yadong*. They live inside the *jiannei* to make their living, and their numbers gradually rose to several tens of thousands . . ." – my translation] Zhang Xie, *Dongxi Yangkao*, 174; in Chen TaiMin 陳台民, *Sino-Philippine Relations*, 139–140. For a detailed history of the *Parian* see Sonia L. Pinto, "The *Parian*, 1581–1762" (MA thesis, Ateneo de Manila University, 1964), Susan L. Pe, "The Dominican Ministry Among the Chinese in the *Parian*, Baybay and Binondo: 1587–1637" (MA Thesis, Ateneo de Manila University, 1983), Eufronio M. Alip, *The Chinese in Manila* (Manila: National Historical Commission, 1974), 16–18, and Amyot, *Chinese Community of Manila*, 11–12.

44. For authors who used the two terms separately and for those who used it interchangeably, see Santamaria, "Chinese *Parian*," 71–72. As an example, Teresita Ang See wrote: ". . . the first *Parian* was built in 1581, when the Chinese were given a place to use as their silk market." Teresita Ang See 施洪玉華, "The Chinese and the *Parian*," in Jose S. Arcilla, *Kasaysayan*, 136. In contrast, see Wickberg, *Chinese in Philippine Life*, 23, 28, 81, 84, 115. Using the term interchangeably may have arisen due to the fact that the eighth *Parian* was later built on the site of the *Alcaiceria* of San Fernando. Cf. Sonia Pinto, "*Parian*," 10 and *Tsinoy: Story of the Chinese in Philippine Life*, 144. Other sources consider 1581 as the year of construction. Santamaria argues that it was being built during the closing months of 1581 until the opening months of 1582. Santamaria, "Chinese *Parian*," 84.

45. See Shubert S. C. Liao, ed. "How the Chinese Lived in the Philippines from 1570 to 1898," in *Chinese Participation in Philippine Culture and Economy*, ed. Shubert S. C. Liao (Manila: by the editor, 1964), 19–33.

46. Quoted without indicating source in Juan Mencarini, "The Philippine Chinese Labour Question" *Journal of the China Branch of the Royal Asiatic Society for the Year 190—1901*. Vol. 33 (reprint, Nendeln, Liechtenstein: Kraus Reprint, 1967), 163.

restauranteurs [*sic*]," according to Eufronio Alip.[47] Later they became big importers and exporters, financiers, and bankers.

In Manila, the Chinese lived and engaged in business in two areas from the Spanish era until the American occupation. The districts of Binondo, Santa Cruz, and Tondo were adjacent to each other. The *Alcaiceria de San Fernando*, the *Parian*, the San Gabriel Hospital, Binondo Church and the Walled City or Intramuros were relatively close in position within these districts (see App. L).[48] Binondo and Santa Cruz eventually became the bastions of the Chinese and Chinese *mestizo* (children of mixed parentage).

c) *Binondo and Santa Cruz*

According to a report dating from 1838, the chief commercial and residential centers in Manila were "Binondo, *Calle San Fernando* [which is in the San Nicolas district], and Santa Cruz" (see App. L and M).[49] This remained true until the days of American rule, for in 1930 it was reported that "Binondo and San Nicolas remain the dominant Chinese districts."[50] Binondo and Santa Cruz, which were part of the province of Tondo during the early nineteenth century, were not only commercial centers, but were also the mission parishes of the Dominicans and Jesuits, respectively.[51]

---

47. Eufronio M. Alip, *Chinese in Manila*, 11.

48. However, it should be noted that in this map, the *Parian* is not the first one built in 1582. The original *Parian* was then located outside Fort Santiago, which is within the present-day Intramuros, for the Walled City had kept expanding as the centuries passed. Go Bon Juan points out that it was the fifth and seventh *Parians* which were within cannon range. Go Bon Juan, telephone interview by Jean Uayan, Manila, 19 Dec 2006.

49. Rafael Díaz Arenas, *Memoria sobre el comercio y navegacion de las islas Filipinas* (Report on the Commerce and Shipping of the Philippine Islands), trans. Encarnacion Alzona (Cadiz: *Imprenta de Domingo Féros*, 1838; reprint, Manila: National Historical Institute, 1979), 74–75. Around 1790 the Chinese were allowed to move into Tondo and Cavite, many going to Binondo and Santa Cruz, and the segregation of Chinese Christians and Chinese non-Christians ceased. By 1828, 90 percent of all Chinese lived in Tondo, with Binondo as its chief urban center. See Wickberg, *Chinese in Philippine Life 1850–1898*, 23, n. 55.

50. American Chamber of Commerce Journal 10, no. 1 (Jan 1930): 10.

51. In the beginning of Spanish colonization, Manila was designated a province. It covered almost all of Luzon, including the modern territorial subdivisions of Pampanga, Bulacan, Rizal, Laguna, Batangas, Quezon, Mindoro, Masbate and Marinduque. These later became provinces, leaving only Manila province with a territory roughly equal to the present City of Manila proper (except Intramuros, the capital site), and the northwestern two-thirds of Rizal province. Early in the province's history, the provincial name was changed from Manila to "Tondo" province, by which it was known for most of the Spanish era. Around

Binondo was founded in 1594, during a time when the king of Spain had decreed the expulsion of all Chinese. Governor Luis Perez Dasmariñas gave a tract of land across the river from Intramuros to a group of prominent Chinese merchants and artisans.[52] Although the original purpose was to insure the availability of goods and services for Manila, it became a bastion where non-Catholic Chinese and Chinese *mestizo* were missionized and baptized, thus creating a Catholic community.[53] On the other hand, the Jesuits had established a similar mission settlement in Santa Cruz between 1619 and 1634 during which time the Santa Cruz Church was constructed.[54] Both of these communities were segregated from the non-Catholic Chinese of the *Parian* until the policy ended in 1790. Furthermore, the hispanized Chinese *mestizos* became predominantly Catholic, and identified themselves with the Philippines and with Spain, not with China.

The alien Chinese likewise became Roman Catholics in large numbers, especially during times of impending expulsions. Medical care of Chinese patients in the Dominican-operated *Hospital de Sangleys de San Gabriel*, for example, resulted in 30,000 conversions to Roman Catholicism over the years of its existence until it closed in 1766.[55] But by the nineteenth century, the Spanish administration increasingly gave up its long-held efforts of converting and assimilating the Chinese. Wickberg attributes this

---

1859, Tondo Province was renamed Manila Province. During American rule, the Philippine Commission dissolved the former province of Manila, and merged its pueblos with those of the District of Morong, forming the new province of Rizal. In 1911, the province of Tondo was dissolved, and its towns given to the provinces of Rizal and Bulacan. Today it is just a district of the city of Manila. Zoilo M. Galang, ed. *Filipiniana*. Vol. 1: *Land and People* (Manila: Philippine Education, 1937), 93.

52. For Chinese Catholics and *mestizos*, see Wickberg, *Chinese in Philippine Life 1850–1898*, 17–20, 23–25, 134–145.

53. In 1810 there were around 120,000 *mestizos* in a total population of around 2,500,000. Tomas de Comyn, *Estado de las Islas Felipinas en 1810* (State of the Philippines in 1810: Being an Historical, Statistical and Descriptive Account of the Interesting Portion of the Indian Archipelago), trans. William Walton, Filipiniana Book Guild, 15 (Madrid: *Imprenta de Repulles*, 1820; reprint, Manila: Filipiniana Book Guild, 1969), 186. The *mestizos* became concentrated in the most westernized, most economically advanced parts of the Philippines, especially in Central Luzon (Tondo, Bulacan, Pampanga). Although fewer in number elsewhere, they were also significant in Cebu, Iloilo, Samar, and Capiz.

54. For a complete and illustrated history of this Church, see Anna Maria L. Harper, *Santa Cruz Church: A Living Heritage* (Manila: Sta. Cruz Parish Pastoral Council, 2004). Today only the tower, which dates back to the eighteenth century, remains.

55. Wickberg, *Chinese in Philippine Life*, 189. See App. L.

loss of initiative to the developments after the *Parian* was destroyed and the Chinese began to populate Binondo and Santa Cruz. When many Chinese sided with the British during the uprising of 1762, the Spaniards lost confidence in their acceptance of Catholicism as an insurance of loyalty. Evidences of declining interest in converting the Chinese included: (1) Revoking special privileges given to Chinese Catholics. (2) No longer requiring Chinese engaged in agricultural colonization to convert. (3) No longer classifying the Chinese as "Catholics/non-Catholics" but as "residents/transients." (4) No longer requiring Catholic Chinese hacienda laborers to attend Mass and those who were not Catholics were no longer catechized or baptized. (5) The old policy of granting land to Catholic Chinese disappeared. (6) Taxation was now based on income, not on religious status. (7) The practice of cutting off the queue as a pre-requisite to conversion and of forbidding the Chinese from dressing like the Filipinos or *mestizos* passed out of use.[56]

On the part of the Chinese, Roman Catholicism also lost its importance and pragmatic relevance when the restrictions listed above were lifted and special privileges were revoked. As news about political events in China reached the Philippine Chinese, it also became increasingly clear that Spain lagged behind other nations militarily and technologically. Such developments among the Chinese and Chinese *mestizos* began to create a social, religious, and economic reality that made these two ethnic groups receptive to a new economic and political force – American democracy and free enterprise – as well as an alternate belief system, Protestantism. The former is beyond the scope of this study, but the latter is a subject of concern, as it relates directly to the Chinese communities in Cebu, Dagupan, Davao, Iloilo and Manila. Writing at the beginning of the twentieth century, Arthur Judson Brown (1856–1963) reported on the situation of the Roman Catholic Church in the Philippines as follows:

> The ecclesiastical registry for 1898 claims 6,559,998 souls, or
> the entire population of the Islands except the Mohammedan
> Moros and the scattered wild tribes of the mountain fastness.
> The Islands are divided into 851 parishes, of which 746 are

---

56. Wickberg, *Chinese in Philippine Life*, 189–194.

"regular" and 105 "mission." In addition, there are 116 missions, so that the total number of subdivisions is 967.[57]

When the Protestant missionaries attempted to enter the Islands, they were met with fierce opposition from priests and devout Roman Catholics, but there were areas such as Tondo and Cavite where resistance was less strong.

d) The Past and the Present

There are two streets that are highly significant with regard to the religious history of the Chinese in Manila. One of these is *Calle Reina Regente* in Binondo and the other is *Calle San Fernando* in San Nicolas.[58] Joseph Young claimed that "the first Chinese-speaking church was established in San Nicolas District, Manila City."[59] This concurs with Hobart Studley's writing in 1924.[60] The significance of these two streets lies in the fact that both are the "birth places" of two Protestant Chinese churches in Manila. Unlike the Filipino and Western Protestants of the early twentieth century, the initial meetings of the earliest Chinese churches in Manila – SSCM, CUEC and SPCM – took place in the Binondo and San Nicolas districts. This is further evidence that these two districts were no longer Roman Catholic strongholds at the turn of the twentieth century.

During the American era, SSCM first conducted services on *Calle San Fernando* in San Nicolas in 1903 (see App. M). From 1912 to 1944 the believers met in a large building located on *Calle Reine Regente* (App. M). Today this has become the site of its Cantonese-speaking sister church, the St. Peter's Parish (former SPCM), while the *Hokkien*-speaking congregation has moved to Masangkay Street (former *Calle Magdalena*) in Trozo, which presently is part of the Santa Cruz district. The CUEC, on the other hand, first met in 1929 in the mezzanine floor of an improvised "*accesoria*"

---

57. Brown, *The New Era in the Philippines* (New York: Revell, 1903), 125.

58. Note that on the map in App. M, Reina is written as "Reyna" and the street is located to the east of the Meisic Police Station. Today, the Meisic Mall is located on Reina Regente Street. According to Santamaria, Meisic is a contraction of the term "Mainsik," meaning, a place that has Chinese residents. Santamaria, "Chinese *Parian*," 72.

59. Young, "Survey of the Overseas Chinese," 31.

60. Hobart Earl Studley, "A Chinese Experiment in Christian Union: The Fruits of Twenty Years' Effort Are Worthy of the Effort Made," *The Spirit of Missions* 89 (Sep 1924): 577.

or accessory building, also located on *Calle Reina Regente* (see App. FF, Fig. 2).[61] It is presently located on Benavidez Street, which during colonial times was part of Binondo. However, both Benavidez and Masangkay streets are now part of the Santa Cruz district, unlike Reina Regente Street which remains part of Binondo (App. N).[62] *Calle San Fernando* and *Calle Reina Regente* were located in former strongholds of the Roman Catholic Chinese community, but these two streets became the seedbed where three of the earliest Protestant Chinese churches in Manila (SSCM, CUEC and SPCM) emerged. Such a great significance cannot and should not be overlooked.

e) Synopsis

Thus far, this introductory portion of the research has put in perspective the historical, social and religious background of the Chinese in the Philippines. When the American military forces occupied the Philippines in 1898, there was a significant number of Chinese in Manila and in the provinces. Most of these immigrants had come from South Fujian. Whether for convenience or out of sincere conversion, many of these immigrants had become Roman Catholics. There was as yet, however, no Protestant church in the Philippines. During this period, Christians in the USA were engaged in a debate which asked the question: "Can the World Be Evangelized in the Present Century (by the year 1900)?" The chief advocate of the view that it could be done was the Presbyterian pastor, Arthur Tappan Pierson (1837–1911). The historical development of this debate has been summarized by Todd Johnson in his article, "The Crisis of Mission." In it Johnson surmised that Pierson's enthusiasm was fired by the Shanghai conference of May 1877, a conference attended by one hundred twenty missionaries representing most Protestant denominations then working in China. One

---

61. *Historical Documentary of Protestantism in the Orient. 40th Anniversary of the United Evangelical Church of Manila (Feilübin Zhonghua Jidujiaohui Sishi Zhounian Lishi Wenxian Fu Yazhou Duoguo Jidujiaohui Lishi)* 菲律賓中華基督教會四十週年歷史文獻附亞洲多國基督教會歷史 1929–1969 (Manila: United Evangelical Church of Manila, 1969), 11. Henceforth, this source will be cited as *HDPO*.

62. The current address of SSP is 1267 G. Masangkay Street, Sta. Cruz, Manila, while that of UECP is 1170 Benavidez Street, Sta. Cruz, Manila. The address of St. Peter's Parish is 1018 Reina Regente Street, Binondo, Manila. Santa Cruz was downgraded from a *pueblo* (town) into a mere district of Manila in 1901 with the enactment by the Philippine Commission of the Charter for the City of Manila. See Harper, *Santa Cruz Church*, 78.

of the issues discussed was the evangelization of China.[63] Congruent to this optimistic mission perspective, American politicians spoke of the "manifest destiny" of America during the second half of the nineteenth century, and part of this destiny was her mission to spread the Christian gospel to all the people on earth. Even though the aspiration to evangelize the world by 1900 had begun to fade by 1894, with Pierson giving up on the year 1900 but still believing it could be achieved in a short time, many missionaries went to the Philippines carrying the same spirit of fulfilling this "manifest destiny" and looked at the inhabitants of their new possession as the "white man's burden," as Anne Catherine Kwantes stated in her dissertation. She noted that some "Filipinos and Americans ascribed American intention to annex the Philippines to a combination of this concept, motives of greed and political opportunism."[64] The Chinese living in the Islands were indeed a large and attractive target for evangelism, though not as large a target as the Filipinos. The earliest Protestant missionaries who arrived in the country immediately took note of this ethnic community.[65] In 1902, after recommending many measures on doing mission among the Chinese, Arthur Judson Brown commented that although mission work among the Chinese was important, it was "subsidiary as compared with the Filipino work."[66] Was this merely the view of the Presbyterian Mission? Were the Chinese, as Filipinos and Americans were, part of the mission focus of the other denominational mission groups? What patterns were manifested when Chinese churches began to emerge in Manila, Iloilo, and Cebu during the American occupation? Before these questions can be investigated, there is one more historical background that needs to be examined, and this is the extensive context of Christianity in China – how the Christian

---

63. Todd Johnson, "The Crisis of Mission: The Historical Development of the Idea of the Evangelization of the World by the Year 1900," *Mission Frontier Supplement* 10, no. 8 (Aug 1988): 2–32, accessed 11 Oct 2006, http://www.missionfrontiers.org/1988/08/a8812.htm. See also, Dana L. Robert, "The Crisis of Missions": Premillennial Mission Theory and the Origins of Independent Evangelical Missions," in *Earthen Vessels: American Evangelicals and Foreign Missions, 1880–1980*, eds. Joel A. Carpenter and Wilbert R. Shenk (Grand Rapids, MI: Eerdmans, 1990), 33–39.

64. Kwantes, Presbyterian Missionaries in the Philippines, 38–40, App. A.

65. Brown, *The New Era in the Philippines*, 79–83; Charles Henry Brent, "Religious Conditions in the Philippines," *Missionary Review of the World* 28 (Jan 1905): 51–52.

66. Brown, *Report of a Visitation*, 59.

faith was planted in China, how the Protestant churches grew and became independent in Fujian, and how this development affected the emergence of PPCC.

5. The China Connection

Before discussing the emergence of the six Chinese churches in the Philippines, this section will describe Protestant mission work in China and in Fujian covering three historical periods: (1) The first period when Protestant mission work in China began when Robert Morrison entered China in 1807; (2) the second period when David Abeel and other RCA, EPM, and LMS missionaries gained a foothold in Xiamen from 1842 onward; and lastly, (3) the Republican period (1911–1949) when the Church of Christ in China became an independent entity.[67] In the latter part of the second period Protestant Chinese churches (CPCI, SSCM and CGC) began to emerge in the Philippines. The birth of CUEC took place during the Republican period. Its original Chinese name – "Church of Christ in China Sojourning in the Philippines" or Lüfei Zhonghua Jidujiaohui 旅菲中華基督教會 – reflects its ties with the Church of Christ in China/ Zhonghua Jidujiaohui 中華基督教會.

When Hobart Earl Studley/Shi HeLi 施和力牧師 (1871–1961), the first missionary-pastor who served at SSCM from 1903–1931, wrote concerning his twenty year ministry in Manila, he gave credit to three persons as having laid the foundations in him when he had to build his work "from the ground up."[68] Two of these were "Dr Boone" and "Dr Abeel" (see App. O). The first name referred to Bishop William Jones Boone, Sr (1811–1864), the American Episcopal missionary who went to Xiamen in 1842 but stayed only until 1845.[69] The second name referred

---

67. For a vital study on the church-state relationship during the Republican period, see Zha ShiJie 查時傑, *Minguo Jidujiaoshi Lunwenji* 民國基督教史論文集 (Anthology on the history of Christianity in the Republic of China) (Taipei: Christian Cosmic Light Communication Center, 1993). Henceforth cited as *Anthology on the History of Christianity*.

68. Studley, "Chinese Experiment," 576.

69. Due to the death of Boone's wife (Sarah Amelia De Saussure) and on account of ill health, Boone's ministry in Xiamen was too short to have any impact. The Episcopal Church abandoned the field in South Fujian. Boone moved to Shanghai in 1845, serving there until his death in 1864 and leaving a lasting legacy. He was involved in the early development of almost all Protestant Episcopal Church mission endeavors in China. He translated the Book of Common Prayer and the Bible into the Wu dialect as well as into

to Rev Dr David Abeel III (1804–1846), founder of the Amoy mission of the Reformed Protestant Dutch Church (RPDC).[70] This was the mission with which Studley was originally connected in China before he went to the Philippines in 1903. This significantly highlights the fact that one of the earliest Protestant missionaries in the Philippines had served in South Fujian and considered his forerunners, Dr Abeel and Dr Boone, as the ones who laid the inner foundation for his own ministry in the Islands. Because of this mission link, it is necessary to survey the history of Protestantism in China and in South Fujian.

a) Christianity in China (7th–18th Centuries)

(1) Early Attempts of Evangelization

Recorded history of Christianity entering China began in AD 635 when the arrival and succeeding events of Aluoben 阿羅本, a Nestorian bishop from Syria, were engraved on the Nestorian stele.[71] Aluoben reached the capital, Changan 長安, and for a short period during the Tang dynasty (AD 618–907), Christianity flourished in China, but lost its foothold after two centuries. Roman Catholic missionaries managed to regain this foothold during the Mongol or Yuan dynasty (1271–1368), but Pope Gregory X (term of office 1271–1276) failed to take advantage of the invitation of Kublai Khan 忽必烈 (1215–1294; reigned 1260–1294) to

---

the classical Chinese style. *The China Mission Handbook. First Issue* (Shanghai: American Presbyterian Mission Press, 1896; rep. Taipei: Ch'eng Wen Publishing, 1973), 180; "Boone, William Jones, Sr" *Biographical Dictionary of Christian Missions*. For a full biography, see Muriel Boone, *The Seed of the Church in China* (Philadelphia, PA: United Church Press, 1973). Cf. *The Spirit of Missions* 63 (1898): 26.

70. The RPDC was renamed the Reformed Church in America (RCA) in 1867.

71. Missionary writings mostly use the name Alopen whereas "Aluoben" is the *Hanyu Pinyin* of the Chinese name. *The China Year Book, 1912*, 401. For resources on Nestorianism and the Nestorian stele, discovered in Xianfu 西安府 in 1625, see Nicolas Standaert, ed. *Handbook of Christianity in China*, Vol. One: *635–1800*, Handbook of Oriental Studies Section 4, eds. Erik Zürcher, S. F. Teiser, M. Kern, vol. 15/1 (Leiden: Brill, 2001), 1–42. An extensive discussion of Nestorian mission history is found in Rufus Anderson, *History of the Missions of the American Board of Commissioners for Foreign Missions to the Oriental Churches*, Republication of the *Gospel in Bible Lands*, vol. 1 and 2 (Boston, MA: Congregational, 1872).

send a hundred teachers of science and religion to instruct the Chinese in the learning and faith of Europe.[72] The pope was more preoccupied with the Crusades in Palestine, reunion with the Greek Orthodox Church and clerical reform. It was not until the sixteenth century that Christian missionaries once again tried to penetrate China. Portuguese missionaries based in Macau and Spanish missionaries from the Philippines attempted to convert China, although China technically belonged to the Portuguese *padroado*.[73] The Middle Kingdom, however, with its Confucian-based and Buddhist-infused culture, was like an impregnable fort. The Portuguese, however, were allowed to establish their trading post on Langbogao island in 1556, but this was later moved to Macau.[74] Surmounting great obstacles, the Roman Catholic Church was able to develop a community in China nearly 200,000 strong under the care of around seventy missionaries at the close of the eighteenth century.[75]

(2) Protestant Missions Before 1842

Although Roman Catholic missionaries provided Christian literature and sinologic materials quite extensively, the whole Bible was never translated. It was Robert Morrison (1782–1834), a Scottish Presbyterian born in

---

72. Samuel Hugh Moffett, *A History of Christianity in Asia*. Vol. 1: *Beginnings to 1500*, Rev. ed., (Maryknoll, NY: Orbis, 1998), 445–446.

73. See p. 33, n. 14. For a fuller treatment on the Philippines as a land-bridge to China, see Jean Uayan, "The Manila Connection: The Philippines as a Land-bridge for Roman Catholic Mission to China during the 16th and 17th Centuries" (lecture, Asia Graduate School of Theology, Taytay, Philippines, 26 Feb 2004).

74. Macau is called 澳門 in Chinese and *Provoaçâo do Nome de Deos na China* in Portuguese. Samuel Hugh Moffett, *A History of Christianity in Asia* Vol. 2: *1500–1900* (Maryknoll, NY: Orbis, 2005), 105.

75. Robert E. Entenmann, "Catholics and Society in Eighteenth-Century Sichuan," in *Christianity in China*, ed. Daniel H. Bays (Stanford, CA: Stanford University Press, 1996), 8. Standaert, *Handbook*, 307–308 gives a list of Roman Catholic missionaries from 1590–1815. The number of foreign missionaries for 1800 is 76, while the number of Chinese priests is 50. This number of 76 missionaries seems quite high, as Latourette, citing Marchini's map of Catholic mission found in the *Chinese Repository*, Vol. 1 (1833), 443, lists only 31 European missionaries and 80 Chinese priests in 1810. See page 180 and n. 142 of his book. The statistical value of Roman Catholic mission endeavors remains as rough estimates and many figures have been given throughout the first half of the 19th century. See Kenneth Scott Latourette, *A History of Christian Missions in China* (New York: MacMillan, 1929), 129, 174, 182–183. Cf. Joseph Schmidlin, *Catholic Mission History* (Techny, IL: Mission Press, 1933), 610, in Moffett, *History of Christianity in Asia*, vol 2: 190, n. 32.

Northumberland, England, who accomplished this task in 1819.[76] Sent by the interdenominational London Missionary Society, he arrived in Guangdong (then called Canton) on 7 September 1807. This event marked the beginning of Protestant mission in China. Missionary activity was forbidden throughout the empire at this time.[77] The penalty for spreading the gospel was strangulation; yet, Morrison and later missionaries persevered in learning the language, as well as doing one-on-one evangelism and preaching during Sundays. In 1842, eight years after Morrison's death, there was a partial lifting of the prohibitions, but before this happened, foreign missionaries suffered greatly in China.[78]

Early in his ministry, Morrison was joined in 1813 by a Scotsman named William Milne (1785–1822).[79] The literary accomplishments of both men laid the foundation that would facilitate mission work for later generations. During the last decade of Morrison's ministry, several developments helped lay a strong foundation for the next century of mission work in China. First, on his way to China, Morrison was invited to be the corresponding secretary of the American Board of Commissioners for Foreign Missions (ABCFM). He was also able to use ABCFM's magazine, the *Missionary Herald*, as a platform for missions in China. The ABCFM responded to this mission call by sending four missionaries: Elijah Coleman Bridgman (1801–1861) and David Abeel III (1804–1846) in 1830, Samuel Wells Williams (1812–1884) in 1833, and Dr Peter Parker (1804–1888) in 1834.[80] These four pioneers – Bridgman and Parker in Guangdong, Abeel in Xiamen, and Williams in Macau – made great strides in evangelizing China throughout

---

76. Murray A. Rubinstein, *The Origins of the Anglo-American Missionary Enterprise in China, 1807–1840*, ATLA Monograph Series No. 33, ed. Kenneth E. Rowe (Lanham, MD: Scarecrow Press, 1996), provides detailed information about the family background, education, training and missionary life and work of Morrison. The definitive biography, however, is written by Eliza Morrison, entitled *Memoirs of the Life and Labors of Robert Morrison* (London: Longmans, Orme, Green & Longmans, 1839).

77. For the persecutions of 1784, 1805 and 1811, see Latourette, *History of Christian Missions in China*, 171–180.

78. Moffett, *History of Christianity in Asia, vol 2*: 290–291.

79. See P. Richard Bohr, "The Legacy of William Milne," *International Bulletin of Missionary Research* 25, 1 (Oct 2001): 173–178.

80. The Chinese names of these four, respectively, are: Bei ZhiWen 裨治文 [Bridgman], Ya BeiLi 雅裨理 [Abeel], Wei ShanWei 衛三畏 [Williams] and Bo Jia 伯駕 [Parker].

their lifetime when China was still averse to Christianity. They carried out preparatory work such as composing dictionaries, grammars, vocabularies and translations, publishing Bibles, religious tracts, prayer books, rendering medical and educational services, and conducting evangelistic meetings in chapels and on a person-to-person basis, despite being restricted within the Macau and Guangdong areas.[81] The first thrust of mission into China was a British endeavor (1807–1830), but American missionaries soon followed British missionaries during the second stage of Protestant mission in China (1830–1842) [see App. P].

(3) Protestant Missions After 1842

The Treaty of Nanjing 南京條約, signed on 29 August 1842, stipulated that China would cede Hong Kong and neighboring islands to Great Britain and open the ports of Guangdong 廣東, Xiamen 廈門, Fuzhou 福州, Ningbo 寧波 and Shanghai 上海 to foreign trade. In addition to 21 million ounces in silver paid as indemnity, fixed tariffs, extraterritoriality for British citizens on China soil, and gaining the "most favored nation" status, British missionaries were able to work with greater freedom and gradually went beyond the boundaries of these ports. Later treaties, such as the Treaty of Tianjin 天津條約 (1858) and the Conventions of Beijing 北京條約 (1860), secured protection and special status for both foreign missionaries and their converts, and even permitted the former to reside and build churches in the heartland of China. The conventions, due to a translation error in the Chinese text, permitted missionaries to "rent and purchase land in all the provinces and to erect buildings thereon at pleasure."[82] This study will only focus on events that transpired in South Fujian, in particular, Xiamen and several other neighboring districts within this region.

b) Protestantism in South Fujian (1842–1898)

Guangdong was the first entry point of Protestant mission in the nineteenth century, but it took almost thirty years before reinforcements arrived

---

81. See "Sketch Reports," in *China Mission Handbook* (1896), 4–7.

82. Jonathan T'ien-en Chao, "The Chinese Indigenous Church Movement, 1919–1927: A Protestant Response to the Anti-Christian Movements in Modern China" (PhD diss., University of Pennsylvania, 1986), 35. See also Latourette, *History of Christian Missions in China*, 276–278.

to assist Morrison. But after 1842, in less than thirty years, there were approximately thirty mission agencies throughout China.[83] A quick view of Appendix P manifests the great difference in mission activity and influx *before* and *after* 1842 (as divided by the shaded row of 1842).

After 1842, Fujian province was a choice location for evangelistic work (App. Q). Fujian, meaning "Fortune Established" in Chinese, is one of the five smallest provinces in China. Ports in Fuzhou 福州, Quanzhou 泉洲, Xiamen 廈門 and Zhangzhou 漳州 made the province a strategic trading and commercial center. After the eighteenth century, Xiamen rose as the center of coastal trade with Taiwan and Southeast Asia.[84] Many overseas Chinese hailed from Fujian and continued to form a strong link to the province, even until today. After Xiamen and Fuzhou became treaty ports in 1842, they became beachheads of Western civilization and Christian mission. Appendix R summarizes the initial phase of the work of Protestant mission agencies in Fujian province.

In 1847, three missions were set up in Fuzhou city, namely, the ABCFM, the Methodist Episcopal Mission (MEM) and the Church Missionary Society (CMS).[85] The mission gateway to Fujian, however, was the port of Xiamen. The gospel seed in China was planted there on 24 February 1842, even before the signing of the Treaty of Nanjing. At that time, Xiamen was lying in the department of Zhangzhou and the district of Tongan 同安. When it was officially opened to foreign trade in November 1843, the trading area was in Shisan Lutou 十三路頭, or "Thirteen Street Entrances." In 1860 foreigners began moving from this location to Gulangyu 鼓浪嶼, or

---

83. See G. Thompson Brown, *Earthen Vessels and Transcendent Power: American Presbyterians in China, 1837–1952* (Maryknoll, NY: Orbis, 1997), 26. For detailed records of these mission agencies and their ministries in different parts of China, see Christopher Tang/Tang Qing 湯清. *Zhongguo Jidujiao Bainianshi* 中國基督教百年史 (The first hundred years of Protestant mission in China), ed. John Fan 范約翰 (Hong Kong: Tao Sheng Publishing, 1987), 169–398 (henceforth cited as *First Hundred Years*).

84. Lau and Lee, "Economic and Political History," 29.

85. For details on the work of these three mission in Fuzhou, see Tang, *First Hundred Years*, 187–188 and 193 (ABCFM), 424–427, 436–437 (MEM), and 227–229 (CMS). See also Alexander Wylie, *Memorials of Protestant Missionaries to the Chinese: Giving a List of their Publications, and Obituary Notices of the Deceased. With Copius Indexes* (Shanghai: American Presbyterian Mission, 1867. Reprint, Taipei: Ch'eng Wen Publishing, 1967), 80, 166, 199.

"Drum Wave Island."[86] Gulangyu became an international settlement in 1903 (see App. S).

c) Protestantism in Xiamen and Its Vicinity

Although the beginning of the mission enterprise in Xiamen is usually dated as 1842, the planting of the gospel seed in China actually began as early as 1830. The first American Protestant missionaries to enter China were Elijah Coleman Bridgman (1801–1861, term of service 1829–1861), and David Abeel III (term of service in Xiamen 1842–1845). They arrived in Guangdong on 25 February 1830.[87]

Abeel graduated from New Brunswick Theological Seminary in 1826. After a brief pastoral duty at the Reformed church in Athens, New York, he accepted the call from the American Seamen's Friend Society to serve as chaplain to sailors in Guangdong and during Sabbath evening services, preached at the Thirteen Factory District 十三行 outside the city walls.[88] Abeel strongly believed in foreign missions and in the need for sending single female missionaries, unheard of during his days. On his return to America in 1836 his enthusiastic exhortation stimulated his church (RPDC) to begin mission work in Asia.

The RPDC had been a member of the ABCFM since 1826 but was unable to play a significant role due to financial and other problems. In 1832 the RPDC General Synod formed its own Board of Foreign Missions (BFMRPDC) but still related cordially with the ABCFM, needing its expert advice and support.[89] Abeel thus joined the ABCFM on 20 December 1830 and after leaving Guangdong due to ill health in 1831, this mission board instructed him to explore Southeast Asian cities for possible sites for

---

86. Lau and Lee, "Economic and Political History," 33; Pitcher, *In and About Amoy*, 251.

87. For a descriptive report of Abeel's work from 1829–1833, see David, *Journal Abeel of a Residence in China and the Neighboring Countries from 1829 to 1833* (New York: Leavitt, Lord & Co., 1834). For Bridgman's ministry, see Latourette, *History of Christian Missions in China*, 217–218 and Wylie, *Memorials of Protestant Missionaries to the Chinese*, 69.

88. This was the residential and business district purposely constructed for foreign merchants outside the walled city of Guangdong. See Rubinstein, *Anglo-American Missionary Enterprise*, 1–43.

89. Abeel, *Journal*, 3. The ABCFM Amoy Mission was transferred to the Board of Foreign Mission of the RCA in 1857.

establishing mission stations.[90] He toured Thailand, Malaysia, Singapore and Java, then on his way back to America, he visited France, England and Switzerland to promote two causes: missions and the plight of women in China as well as sending female missionaries to meet these needs.[91] From 1833–1834, he went around churches and seminaries, awakening his countrymen and women in particular to do mission in the Middle East and in China. As a result, the BFMRPDC established a mission in Borneo and many missionaries from this station later moved into Xiamen. In 1839 he attempted to return to China but was hindered by the Opium War that erupted in June 1840.[92] He instead took another tour of Southeast Asia in 1841, finally re-entering Macau on 21 December 1841.[93]

In February 1842, Boone and Abeel sailed from Macau to Xiamen. They were received by the commandant at Gulangyu and settled in a Chinese house. Due to their language proficiency, they soon became invaluable as interpreters for the Amoy people who were less averse to Christianity than the Cantonese due to their desire for trade expansion.[94] The short ministry of these two men who most inspired Studley was described by Boone, who said:

> Many came to our house daily to enquire about the new religion we came to teach and to ask for books, and in this

---

90. David Cheung explains that the term "Amoy Mission" could refer to the missionary administrative category which started in Amoy town but eventually spread beyond it. He prefers to use the term *Banlam* 閩南 to refer to the geographical area of about 18,000 square miles for the space of mission work but reserves "Amoy Mission" for the operational unit of the RCA and EPM in the said region. See Cheung, *Christianity in Modern China*, 11–12.

91. Abeel inspired the formation of the Society for Promoting Female Education in the East in London in 1834. He graphically described the plight of Chinese women in his *Journal*, 126–133.

92. For a concise history of the Opium War, see Hsü, *Rise of Modern China*, 168–195.

93. Gerald Francis De Jong, *Reformed Church in China 1842–1951*, The Historical Series of the Reformed Church in America, no. 22 (Grand Rapids, MI: Eerdmans, 1992), 14–15.

94. Both had ministered to overseas Chinese who spoke the *Hokkien* dialect. See Cheung, *Christianity in Modern China*, 96, and Kinia C. Ng 黃彩蓮, *Xianggang Minnan Jiaohui Yanjiu* 香港閩南教會研究 (Research on Hong Kong Min-Nam Church). Fangyan Jiaohui Yanjiu Xilie Zhiyi 方言教會研究系列之一 Chinese Study Series 6 (Hong Kong: Alliance Biblical Seminary, 2005), 26. Ng quotes a Chinese translation of Alvin John Poppen's (卜沃文) book, *Ya Bi Li De Shengping* 雅裨理的生平 (The Life of David Abeel), trans. Li HuaDe 李華德譯 (Hong Kong: Jidujiao Fuqiao Chubanshe 基督教輔僑出版社, 1963), 112.

way many heard of the only name under heaven by which
we can be saved. Should this place, in the providence of God,
be thrown open to missionary effort by the English taking
possession of the Island of Amoy [this was written before
the treaty was negotiated], or by the arrangements by which
peace is concluded, there will not be a more desirable place in
the Empire.[95]

Boone did not stay long in Xiamen due to the death of his wife, but
moved to Shanghai.[96] Abeel first confined his ministry to Gulangyu, using
one of his rooms as a dispensary for Dr William H. Cumming who arrived
in June 1842 to treat patients. Six months later the number of Sunday
listeners reached fifty.[97] They were soon joined by Dr James C. Hepburn
of the American Presbyterian Church.[98] The work of this mission was very
soon turned over to the RCA after John Lloyd died in 1848. In 1843,
Walter Lowrie and Abeel boldly visited Zhangzhou and nearly created an
international incident because the city was not within the bounds of the
Treaty of Nanjing. In spite of this, they were given a tour of the city in
sedan chairs provided by local officials. The three began making occasional
visits to Xiamen City, located on the western end of Xiamen island, until
regular ministry was begun in January 1844. Abeel had never been strong
physically, and his health deteriorated, forcing him to leave in late 1844.
Hepburn departed in 1845 and Cumming left in 1847. Two couples – the
Dotys 羅啻 and the Pohlmans 波羅滿 – arrived on 22 June 1844 a few
months before Abeel's departure.[99]

---

95. Boone, *Seed of the Church*, 85.

96. For Boone's contribution to mission, see MeiMei Rose Lin 林美玫, "Zhongguo
Kaimen: Wen Huilian Zhujiao yu Shijiu Shiji Zhongye Meiguo Shenggonghui Zaihua
Caichuan Shiye De Kaichuang 中國開門: 文惠廉主教與十九世紀中葉美國聖公會
在華差傳事業的開創 (China's Door Opens: Bishop Boone and 19th Century Mission
Enterprise of the American Episcopal Church in China)," in *Zuixun Caichuan Zuji—
Meiguo Shenggonghui Zaihua Caichuan Tanxi* 追尋差傳足跡—美國聖公會在華差傳探
析 *(1835–1920)* (In Search of Missionary Footsteps: The Study of Protestant Episcopal
Mission and Its Development in China from 1835 to 1920) (Taipei: Cosmic Light Holistic
Care Organization, 2006), 85–140.

97. Cheung, *Christianity in Modern China*, 20, n. 56.

98. See Robert, "Crisis of Missions," 27–29.

99. Elihu Doty (1809–1865) and his wife Clarissa Dolly Ackley (1806–1845),
together with William John Pohlman (1812–1849) and his wife Theodosia R. Scudder

Other mission agencies entered Xiamen within the same decade – the most important were the LMS and the EPM. LMS missionaries William Young and John Stronach came in July 1844.[100] James Hume Young, MD, an EP missionary, arrived in May 1850. However, the first missionary sent out by the EPM was the itinerant missionary William Chalmers Burns/ Bin WeiLian 賓維廉 (1815–1868; term of service 1847–1868) [App. T]. Born at Dundee, Scotland, Burns entered China in 1847 and worked in the South Fujian region for six years (1851–1855, 1858–1859). He moved to Beijing in 1863 and died at Niuzhuang 牛莊.[101] He was a forerunner of other Irish and Scottish Presbyterians, among whom was Carstairs Douglas 杜嘉德 (1830–1877; term of service 1855–1877) [App. T]. He devoted his life to extending and developing a self-supporting, self-propagating Chinese church, to training church workers and to producing the Chinese-English dictionary of the *Hokkien* dialect (1873).

(1) First Fruits

The first fruits of the RPDC missionaries, reputedly led to Christ by Abeel's preaching, were Ong Hok Kui/Wang FuGui 王福貴 (d. 10 August 1850, aged 75) and Lau Un Sia/Liu YinShe 劉殷舍 (d. 1 November 1858, aged over 80).[102] They were baptized on 5 April 1846, becoming the first baptized converts in Fujian. Since foreigners were not allowed to purchase and own property, Ong Hok Kui bought a small piece of land with four ramshackle houses in 1847 for $550, and turned this over to the Reformed

---

(d. 30 Sep 1844), had been ministering to the Chinese in Borneo since 1838. It was Abeel who urged them to transfer to Xiamen. Wylie, *Memorials of Protestant Missionaries to the Chinese*, 97–98, 111–112; De Jong, *Reformed Church in China*, 17. The discrepancy between these two sources regarding the name of Doty's first wife and the year of service in Borneo should be noted. Wylie's source is more accurate than De Jong's and is confirmed in Jean R. Walton, "Elihu Doty's Garden – New Brunswick, Borneo and China," *Journal of the New Jersey Postal History Society* 3, no. 4 (Nov 2004): 127–142, accessed 5 Oct 2007, http://www.bernehistory.org/local/ ELIH_DOTY_NJPH_article.pdf.

100. De Jong, *Reformed Church in China*, 16, 23.

101. For a short biography, see James Alexander Stewart, *William Chalmers Burns: A Man with a Passion for Souls* (Philadelphia, PA: Revival Literature, 1964); Latourette, *History of Christian Missions in China*, 258; Cheung, *Christianity in Modern China*, 24–31.

102. Cheung, ""Ecclesiastical Devolution and Union in China," 37, n. 162; Wilson, *In and About Amoy*, 232; 27, n. 12. Ng's source is a Chinese article: Wu BingYao 吳炳耀, "Bainianlai De Minnan Jidujiaohui 百年來的閩南基督教會 (Minnan Christian Church after a Hundred Years)," 廈門文史資料, 第13輯 *Literary and Historical Sources from Xiamen* 13 (1998): 78.

mission by a perpetual lease. This was located on Sinkoea/Xinjiezi 新街
仔 "Little New Street," and one of the houses was fitted for a chapel.[103]
The Sinkoe chapel 新街堂會, began in late 1847, was inaugurated on 11
February 1849 (App. U).[104] This was the very first Protestant church building in Fujian as well as in the whole of China. The second church was
erected in Tekchhiukha/Zhushujiao 竹樹腳 "Bamboo Tree Foot" in 1859,
where John Van Nest Talmage 打馬字約翰 (1819–1892) was ministering,
and was called Tekchhiu chapel 竹樹堂會 (App. U). The first and crowd-
drawing pastor of this church was Iap Han Chiong/Ye HanZhang 葉漢
章 (1832–1914) [App. T].[105] Originally an elder of Sinkoe chapel, he was
ordained on 29 March 1863 and served at Tekchhiu chapel until 1864.[106]
Ordained at the same time with Iap Han Chiong was Lo Tau or Lo Ka Gu/
Luo JiaYu 羅嘉漁 (1826–1870).[107] He was an elder at the Tekchhiu chapel
but was assigned to Sinkoe chapel, and later became pastor at Peh Tsui Iaⁿ/
Baishuiying 白水營 and Chioh Be/Shima 石碼.[108] Other stations of the
Reformed mission included: Tang Oaⁿ/Tongan 同安 (1871), An Khoe/

---

103. De Jong, *Reformed Church in China*, 25, quoting "Semi-Annual Report,"
Christian Intelligencer (27 Apr 1848): 166.

104. Lin WenRen 林溫人, "Zhushu Tanghui Jianshiy 竹樹堂會簡史 (Short history
of Tekchhiu Chapel)," in *Minnan Zhonghua Jidujiaohui Jianshi* 閩南中華基督教會簡
史 (Short history of Minnan Christian Church of China, vol. 4, *Xiamenqu Jiuguizheng
Gonghui Getanghui Jianshi* 廈門區舊歸正公會各堂會簡史 (Short history of Reformed
chapels in the Xiamen district), ed., Xu ShengYan 許聲炎 (N.p.: Zhonghua Jidujiaohui
Chubanshe 中華基督教會出版社, 1934), 4–5. Henceforth, this source shall be cited as
Short History of Minnan CCC. This joyous occasion was at the same time a memorial service
for Pohlman who had perished at sea on his way back to Xiamen from Hong Kong. De
Jong, *Reformed Church in China*, 26.

105. Iap was born in Xiamen, Fujian. He hid in a church because a gang was
threatening him, and thereafter became a believer. See Ng, *Research on Hong Kong Min-
Nam Church*, 28, n. 20.

106. Two Chinese sources erroneously give the date of ordination as 11 Feb 1862.
See Ng, *Research on Hong Kong Min-Nam Church*, 28 and Jiang JiaRong/Keung Ka Wing
姜嘉榮, "Jindai Zhongguo Zili yu Heyi Yundong Zhishiyuan: Minnan Jiaohui 近代中
國自立與合一運動始源: 閩南教會 (The origins of the independent and ecumenical
movement in China: the church in Southern Fujian)," *Jindai Zhongguo Jidujiaoshi Yanjiu
Jikan* 近代中國基督教史研究集刊 *Journal of the History of Christianity in Modern China*
5 (2002/2003): 7.

107. Lo was from JinMen HuangXiang 金門黃鄉; he was baptized at an early age.
See Ng, *Research on Hong Kong Min-Nam Church*, 28, n.19.

108. De Jong, *Reformed Church in China*, 69–70; Ng, *Hong Kong Min-Nam Church*,
28, n. 19 and 20. The missionary terms Pechuia and Chiohbe will be used throughout
this work.

Anxi 安溪, Chiang Chiu/Zhangzhou 漳州 (1871), Koan Khoe/Guanxi 琯溪 (1880), Piⁿ Ho/Pinghe 平和 (1883).[109]

Aside from Xiamen, the fields where the English Presbyterian missionaries worked were at Pechuia and Chiohbe.[110] The Pechuia station was turned over to the RPDC in 1854. Cheung "argues" that the RPDC was ahead of the EPM by a decade in terms of having church formation as an objective. The EPM missionaries were held back by health and/or language hindrances whereas the RPDC leadership was maintained in terms of both efforts and results. By 1857 the RPDC, EPM, and LMS had a combined church membership of 415 in Xiamen and other outstations. By 1902 there were thirty-eight churches and 3,361 members in these churches.[111]

The missionaries were assisted by ardent converts in spreading the gospel to Lam Khoe/Nanxi 南溪, Tsoan Chiu/Quanzhou (1863), Chin Kang/Jinjiang 晉江, Lam Oaⁿ/Nan-an 南安 (1867), Ha An Khoe/Xia Anxi 下安溪, Chiang Pho/Zhangpu 漳浦 (1889) and Eng Chhun/Yongchun 永春 (1893). The London Missionary Society also established stations at Hui Oaⁿ/Huian 惠安, Be Kang/Magang 馬港 and Koan Khau/Guankou 灌口 (1862) in the Tongan region, Hai Tin/Haicheng 海澄 in Zhangzhou, and in Pak Khoe/Beixi 北溪 and Teng Chiu/Dingzhou 丁洲.[112]

(2) Church Growth

All three missions experienced steady growth from the start of their work in China until the early decades of the twentieth century (App. V). The EPM reported that from 1,500 adults and baptized children in 1888, the number increased to 4,082 in 1911. The number of congregations grew from forty-seven to ninety-seven, the pastors from six to twenty-five, and the preachers from thirty-three to fifty-five.[113] The focus must now turn

---

109. Years in parenthesis indicate dates of founding or organization. For detailed histories of these and other churches in Fujian, see the multi–volume work edited by Xu ShengYan, *Short history of Minnan CCC*.

110. See details in Band, *Working His Purpose Out*, 17–21.

111. Cheung, *Christianity in Modern China*, 13–60, 255; Ng, *Research on Hong Kong Min-Nam Church*, 30–33.

112. See further, C. Silvester Horne, *The Story of the LMS 1795–1895* (London: London Missionary Society, 1894), 328–333.

113. Band, *Working His Purpose Out*, 287.

to three outstations that are significantly related to overseas Chinese in the Philippines.

(3) Three Stations

(a) Tongan-Xiamen

Three of these stations in or near Xiamen deserve more comments since they were the places of origin of majority of the Protestant Chinese in the Philippines. These are Tongan-Xiamen, Oa[n] Hai/Anhai 安海, and Quanzhou. Many of the early members of CPCI and CGC came from such towns as Hosan/Heshan 禾山 and Su Beng/Siming 思明 in Xiamen (see App. B). Tongan was situated about 32 kilometers to the north of Xiamen and was at that time the capital of the township where Xiamen was located. Talmage visited this place in 1866 and Pohlman reported in 1847 that, "Large and attentive assemblies listened to our exhortations."[114] Tongan as a mission station was officially established in 1871; by 1900 the communicant membership reached 199. One of the fruits of the missionaries' labor was Sio Tsu Bi/Shao ZiMei 邵子美, the father of Sio Kheng Chiong/Shao QingZhang or Wesley Kho Shao 邵慶彰. Although the date of the visit of RPDC missionaries is not given exactly in his autobiography, Wesley Shao wrote that it was during the late nineteenth century.[115] Kho Seng Iam, however, states that it was Talmage who first visited Tongan in 1866.[116] The Shao clan lived at Ka[n] Na Nia/Ganlan Ling 橄欖嶺, located about five kilometers from Tongan. Out of the whole clan only two men were converted, one of whom quickly recanted due to pressure from

---

114. Lin ChaoCe 林朝策, "Semi-Annual Report, 1847," *Christian Intelligencer* (20 Apr 1848): 162; quoted in De Jong, *Reformed Church in China*, 50. See also pp. 48, 92–93.

115. Shao even purposely went to the RCA headquarters in New York to inquire regarding the names of the missionaries who visited Tongan, but could not find their names in the record books. Wesley Shao/Shao QingZhang 邵慶彰, audio-taped interview by the writer, 16 Dec 2003, Sta. Cruz, Manila, Philippines, audio-taped transcript, Philippine Chinese Church Archives, Biblical Seminary of the Philippines, Valenzuela City, Philippines.

116. Lin ChaoCe 林朝策, "Tongan Tanghui Shilue 同安堂會史略 (Short History of Tongan Chapel)," in *Short History of Minnan CCC*, vol. 4, 7. According to mission records, the first converts were baptized in 1870 by Pastor Iap. *The Fortieth Annual Report of the Board of Foreign Missions of the Reformed Church in America . . . for the Year Ending April 30, 1872* (New York: Board of Publications of the Reformed Church in America, 1872), 11, accessed 24 Sep 2015, http://digitalcommons.hope.edu/cgi/viewcontent.cgi?article =1014&context=world_annual_report.

his town mates. They believed that becoming a Christian was tantamount to betraying their ancestors and would result in their bloodline being cut off. Shao ZiMei, however, remained firm in his faith and even became a preacher of God's word. Not only did his bloodline continue – he had five sons and four daughters – but his family even produced many Christian school principals and pastors. All of Wesley Shao's five children and their spouses have become pastors, missionaries or seminary professors and are serving in America, Australia and the Philippines.[117] This then is a clear and direct legacy of the work of the RPDC missionaries in Tongan traversing from the nineteenth to the twenty-first centuries and crossing from China to the Philippines.

(b) Anhai

The second place is Anhai, situated on the coast halfway between Xiamen and Quanzhou. Carstairs Douglas visited Anhai several times in the course of his evangelistic tours. He saw the need for occupying this town first before entering Quanzhou. His first visit was in July 1857 when he met an encouraging reception. Although the place was in a pirate-infested zone, he paid four more visits in the early summer of 1859 and left two Chinese evangelists there.[118] This time there was opposition as well as interest, which culminated in a sudden attack one night in May 1860. Douglas was beaten by a mob using the backs of heavy knives and he would have suffered more had not a Chinese Christian named Song-peh helped him

---

117. Wesley Shao/Shao QingZhang 邵慶彰, *Ta Chuangshi Ta Chengzhong – Shao Qingzhang Mushi De Shengming Pianzhang* 祂創始祂成終—邵慶彰牧師的生命篇章 (God, the author and perfecter – the life of Rev Wesley Shao) (Taipei: Cosmic Light Holistic Care Organization, 2006), 11–17.

118. These two evangelists are identified as Cai ZeJu 蔡擇聚 and Fu Kuan 傅寬 in Zhang ZhongXin 張鍾鑫, "Bentuhua Yu Xinyi Congjian – Jindai Quanzhou Jidujiao De Bentuhua Licheng 本土化與信譽重建—近代泉州基督教的本土化歷程 (Reconstructing localization and prestige: the journey of localizing Christianity in modern Quanzhou)," in Lin JinShui 林金水. *Fujian Jidujiaoshi Chutan* 福建基督教使初探 (Initial studies on Christianity in Fujian), Malisun Ruhua Xuanjiao Erbainian Jinian Wenji – Lunwen 馬禮遜入華宣教200年紀念文集—論文 (Collected essays in commemoration of the 200th year of Morrison's entry into China) 12 (Taipei: Caituan Faren Jidujiao Yuzhou Quanren Guanhuai Jigou/Shijie Huaren Fuyin Shigong Lianluo Zhongxin 財團法人基督教宇宙光全人關懷機構; 世界華人福音事工聯絡中心 Cosmic Light Holistic Care Organization/Chinese Coordination Center for World Evangelism, 2006), 181.

return to the "gospel boat" so that he was able to get to Xiamen.[119] After a few months, Douglas returned and found that the situation had improved. On 1 September of that year, four Anhai Christians were baptized on board the "gospel boat."[120] From 1865 onwards, the gospel spread to the vicinity of Anhai in such places as Siong Si/Xiangzhi 祥芝 (1865), Koa^n Kio/Guanqiao 官橋 (1867), Toa Ih^n/Daying 大盈 (1880), Chioh Chi^n/Shijing 石井 (1882), Chhim O/Shenhu 深滬 (1883), Eng Leng/Yongning 永寧 (1884), Kim Chi^n/Jinjing 金井 (1888), and Chioh Sai/Shishi 石獅 (1889).[121] Anhai also became the gateway to Quanzhou, producing many pastors, one of the most well known being Rev Kho Seng Iam, and a large number of lay preachers. His story and that of two members of the Anhai Church who later migrated to the Philippines are found in the section on the history of the Chinese United Evangelical Church.

(c) Quanzhou

In June 1859 Douglas knelt on a hill in Anhai overlooking Quanzhou and prayed for the people in the bustling city. From December 1859 until his death in 1877 Douglas devoted himself to the city that had three or four hundred thousand inhabitants at the time. The second time he entered Quanzhou in December 1860, he was accompanied by Hur Libertas Mackenzie 金輔爾, Song-peh and two Chinese evangelists.[122] They preached to Confucianists, Muslims and Buddhists – the three major religious groups in the city. In 1867 the first group of believers was baptized and the church was established with fourteen communicants.

---

119. The name Song-peh is most likely referring to Zheng Shuang 鄭爽 with peh 伯 as a title of respect equivalent to "senior uncle," but using only the single character name Shuang 爽, pronounced as Song in the *Hokkien* dialect. See Zhang ZhongXin, "Reconstructing," 183–184.

120. Band, *Working His Purpose Out*, 53–54. The four Chinese were: Zheng Shuang 鄭爽, Zheng Tan 鄭坦, Wu Jiang 吳江, and Chen Wei 陳尾. Xu ShengYan 許聲炎, "Anhai Tanghui Shilue 〈安海堂會史略〉 (Short history of Anhai Chapel)," in *Short History of Minnan CCC*, vol. 3, *Beifang Jiaohui Shilue* 北方教會史略 (Short history of northern churches), 2.

121. Zhang ZhongXin, "Reconstructing," 183. Refer to 181–207 for the relationship of Jinjing to the Chinese United Evangelical Church.

122. Aside from Zheng Shuang, the Chinese who accompanied Douglas on this trip are identified as Cai ZeJu 蔡擇聚, Chen Qiang 陳强, Fu Kuan 傅寬 and Chen ZiLu 陳子路 in *Short History of Minnan CCC*, vol. 3, 9–10.

Although the work was disturbed by the Taiping Rebellion (1851–1864) and the literati (literally, "read book men") who used all means to discourage it, the ministry continued.[123] In fact, William Sutherland Swanson 宣為霖 (1861–1919; term of service 1860–1893) reported in 1868 that there was a constant stream of inquirers of the faith from morning till evening. By 1875 there were forty adult members, and elders and deacons were elected, making the church in Quanzhou a separate congregation no longer under the supervision of Anhai chapel. This was the beginning of the Lam Koe Ki Tok Kao Hoe/NanJie Jidujiaohui 南街基督教會 (South Street Church). In 1895 the Se Koe Ki Tok Kao Hoe/XiJie Jidujiaohui 西街基督教會 (West Street Church) was opened.[124] Many members of CGC and CUEC refer to these two oldest Protestant churches in Quanzhou, as well as churches from the nearby towns of Jinjiang (Ge Khau/Yakou 衙口, Tsuiⁿ Kang/Qiangang 前港, Tan Te/Chendai 陳埭), as their home churches (see App. B).

---

123. This rebellion created ill–will toward the Christians because non–Christians identified the movement with Christianity. Hong Xiuquan 洪秀全 (1812/14–1864) had been influenced by reading 勸世良言 (*Good Words for Exhorting the Age*), written by Liang Fa but given mystic overtones by Hong, and had studied with Issachar Roberts. The major work is Franz H. Michael, with Chung-li Chan, *The Taiping Rebellion: History and Documents*. 3 vols. (Seattle and London: University of Washington Press, 1966–1971). See also Jonathan Spence, *God's Chinese Son: The Taiping Heavenly Kingdom of Hong Xiuquan* (London: Harper Collins, 1996), and Thomas H. Reilly, *The Taiping Heavenly Kingdom: Rebellion and the Blasphemy of Empire* (Seattle, WA: University of Washington Press, 2004). For Chinese sources, see Tang, *First Hundred Years*, 148–158 and Liang YuanSheng 梁元生, "Panluanzhe: Jidujiao yu Taiping Tianguo 半亂者：基督教與太平天國 (The Rebel: Christianity and the Taiping Heavenly Kingdom)," in *Jidujiao yu Zhongguo* 基督教與中國 (Christianity and China).Malisun Ruhua Xuanjiao Erbainian Jinian Wenji – Lunwen 馬禮遜順入華宣教200年紀念文集—論文 (Collected essays in commemoration of the 200th year of Morrison's entry into China) (Taipei: 基督教宇宙光全人關懷機構 Cosmic Light Holistic Care Organization, 2006), 87–106.

124. Band, *Working His Purpose Out*, 55–56, 222–223. Aside from the Tsoan Chiu Tong Hoe/Quanzhou Chapel 泉州堂會, which was later renamed as Tsoan Lam Tong Hoe/Quannan Chapel 泉南堂會, the other churches included Tsoan Se Tong Hoe/Quanxi Chapel 泉西堂會 and Hong Lai Tong Hoe/Honglai Chapel 洪瀨堂會. Each of these churches supervised smaller congregations according to the districts they were located in. See *Short History of Minnan CCC*, vol. 3, 8–20, 40–41, 74–77.

(4) Ecclesiastical Union—The Banlam Model

(a) Mission and Church as Partners

The work in South Fujian became one of the best examples of mission partnership in the nineteenth century. Inter-mission cooperation between the RCA and the EPM had already begun around the mid-1800s. Using Xiamen (and later, Gulangyu) and Jiulong River 九龍江 as the home base and reference points, a "comity of missions" was arranged whereby the region was divided into three approximately equal parts. The RPDC worked toward the west of the province plus a small area to the north; the EPM, toward the south and part of the east, and the LMS toward the north and the remainder of the east.[125]

This partnership eventually led to the ecclesiastical union of the churches that were set up by two of the three missions. On 2 April 1862, the first meeting of the Amoy Classis (Presbytery) was held at Chiohbe, attended by five RPDC, two EPM missionaries and fourteen Chinese elders from five organized churches.[126] Since the English Presbyterians had their own assembly of elders (Tiuⁿ Lo Hoe/Zhanglaohui 長老會) it was decided to adopt the name "Great Assembly of Elders" (Toa Tiuⁿ Lo Hoe/Da Zhanglaohui 大長老會), or, for short, Tai Hoe/Da Hui 大會.[127] Another name for this assembly was Quanzhang Dahui 泉漳大會, literally, the Great Assembly of Quan [zhou] and Zhang [zhou].[128] With the ordination

---

125. De Jong, *Reformed Church in China*, 63.

126. The name "Amoy Classis" is not changed to Xiamen Classis, as in some sources, since it is considered as a proper name in a specific time frame. Cf. Brown, *Earthen Vessels*, 123. Kho Seng Iam was a delegate to this meeting, which he termed Zhang Quan Zhanglao Dahui 漳泉長老大會 (Great Assembly of Zhang[zhou] Quan [zhou]). Cf. n. 129. See Xu ShengYan 許聲炎, "Shima Tanghui Shilue 石碼堂會史略 (Short history of Shima Chapel)," in *Short History of Minnan CCC*, vol. 5, *Guizheng Zhanglaohui Shilue* 歸正長老會史略 (Short History of the Reformed Presbyterian Church), 3.

127. Cheung, *Christianity in Modern China*, 253. The five congregations were Sinkoe, Tekchhiukha, Chiohbe, Pechuia, and Be Piⁿ/Maping 馬平 (established 1857). The five RCA missionaries were Doty, Talmage, Alvin Ostrom 胡理敏 (1831–1898; term of service 1858–1864), Daniel Rapalje 來坦履 (1837–1901; term of service 1858–1901), and Leonard William Kip 汲澧瀾 (1826–1901; term of service 1861–1901). The two EP missionaries were Carstairs Douglas and William Sutherland Swanson.

128. Ng and Keung give the Chinese name Quan Zhang Da Hui 「泉漳大會」 and list the fourteen chapels that were members of this classis in 1875 as: Sinkoe (Xinjie) chapel 新街堂, Tekchhiuka (Zhujiao) chapel 竹樹堂, Emngkang (Xiagang) chapel 廈港堂, Pechuia (Baishuiying) chapel 白水營堂, Chiohbe (Shima) chapel 石碼堂, Bepiⁿ

of the first pastors (Iap and Lo) the missionaries relinquished their pastoral duties, as seen from the 1864 annual report of the RPDC, where the responsibilities of these two pastors were described:

> They have full charge of the Churches, whose Pastors they are. They preside at the Consistory meetings of their respective Churches, and along with the Elders decide who are to be received and who are not. The Consistories thus constituted, exercise discipline also, sometimes after consulting with the Missionaries, and sometimes without such consultation. These Native Pastors administer the Sacraments, using translations of our Church Forms. They also perform the marriage ceremony. Their people pay them $12 per month as salary, and furnish houses for them and their families to live in.[129]

Thus the local churches started to devolve, or become self-governed and self-supportive. As the Chinese Christians began to take initiative in doing evangelism and mission work, self-propagation was likewise achieved.

David Cheung gave the following reasons which, he considers, made devolution essential at this point in history: quantitative and qualitative growth of the churches, the performance of the native Christians in relation to gospel propagation, the demonstrated ability, personal growth, and adherence to strict admissions policy by the pastors, and the attainment of gradual and then full financial independence by 1862. Besides these reasons, there was also the need for a higher church court to settle disciplinary cases and the desire for ordaining native pastors in order to achieve the full organization of the church and free the missionaries for mission work.[130]

(Maping) chapel 馬坪堂, Longbun (Longwen) chapel 龍文堂, Khengbe (Kengwei) chapel 坑尾堂, Okang (Hujiang) chapel 湖江堂, Wahai (Anhai) chapel 安海堂, Chiangchiu (Zhangzhou) chapel 漳州堂, Tangwah (Tongan) chapel 同安堂, Kiolai (Qiaonei) chapel 橋內堂, and Tsoanchiu (Quanzhou) chapel 泉州堂 [their way of *Hokkien* transliteration has been retained]. Ng, *Research on Hong Kong Min-Nam Church*, 32; Jiang JiaRong, "The origins of the independent and ecumenical movement in China," 8.

129. *Thirty-second Annual Report of the Board of Foreign Missions of the Reformed Church in America . . . for the Year Ending April 30th, 1864* (New York: Board of Publication of the Reformed Protestant Dutch Church, 1864), 14, accessed 24 Sep 2015, http://digitalcommons.hope.edu/cgi/viewcontent.cgi?article=1006&context=world_annual_report.

130. See discussion in Cheung, *Christianity in Modern China*, 254–268.

With the formation of the Tai Hoe, the missionaries, Chinese pastors and evangelists, and congregations of the various churches now looked upon themselves as one single Christian church and met occasionally to discuss their common problems.[131]

(b) RPDC-EPM Union

The chief motivation for ecclesiastical union was the peculiar relationship between the RPDC and EPM during the 1850–1862 period. Using Cheung's work as main reference, the process of this union is summarized as follows.[132] The two missions had the same vision for their outstations and Talmage and Douglas were like-minded in their ideals for devolution. Talmage's concept of the three-self ideal was expressed by William Swanson in 1894, after the former had died, in this way: "The ideal of the church in China which [Talmage] had set before him[self], the goal he desired to reach, was a native, self-governing, self-supporting, and self-propagating church."[133] He further said that: "[Douglas] saw clearly that what he had to do was so to work as, by God's blessing, to be instrumental in setting up a native Church so organized as to be self-supporting and self-propagating."[134]

Moreover, the two missions were denominationally compatible with regard to doctrine and church polity. They shared the same creeds, confessions and catechisms: two creeds (the Nicene Creed and the Apostles' Creed); three confessions (Scots – 1560, Second Helvetic – 1566, Westminster – 1646); and three catechisms (Heidelberg – 1563, Westminster Larger and

---

131. De Jong, *Reformed Church in China*, 62–77. For a profile of Chinese evangelists during this period, see Jessie G. Lutz, "A Profile of Chinese Protestant Evangelists in the Mid-nineteenth Century," in *Authentic Chinese Christianity: Preludes to its Development (Nineteenth and Twentieth Centuries)*, ed. Ku Wei-ying and Koen De Ridder (Leuven: Leuven University Press/Ferdinand Verbiest Foundation, 2001), 67–85.

132. Cheung, *Christianity in Modern China*, 253–308.

133. William Sutherland Swanson, "In Memoriam: Dr. Talmage – the Man and the Missionary," in John Gerardus Fagg, *Forty Years in South China* (New York: ADF Randolph & Co., [1894], reprint, Whitefish, MT: Kessinger, 2004), 114 (page citation is from the reprint edition).

134. William Sutherland Swanson, "His Missionary Career," in John Monteath Douglas, *Memorials of Rev Carstairs Douglas, M.A., LL.D., Missionary of the Presbyterian Church of England at Amoy, China* (London: Waterlow & Sons, [1878]), 63; quoted in Cheung, *Christianity in Modern China*, 54.

Shorter Catechisms – 1649).[135] It wasn't this compatibility that alienated the LMS, but the reason for LMS not joining the 1862 union was church polity. Comparatively in North Fujian, inter-mission relationship was not always pleasant, especially after the CMS withdrew from the comity of missions.[136] A third factor facilitating union was similarity in their methodology: intensive oral instruction given by the missionaries and a strict policy of admission and quality control of church membership. There was harmony among the missionaries as well, especially among the three who stayed longest (Doty, Talmage and Douglas). In particular, Swanson could say of Talmage and Douglas: "to them more than to any others do we owe almost all that is distinctive there [in Xiamen] in union and in methods of work."[137]

(c) Synod of South Fujian

In 1892, two presbyteries (called classes in the RCA) – the Northern Presbytery 泉屬大會 and the Southern Presbytery 漳屬大會 – were formed due to increased membership. In 1893 the Synod of South Fujian (Ban Lam Tion Lo Tai Hoe/Minnan Zhanglao Dahui 閩南長老大會) was officially established and it consisted of the three-tiered system of church 堂會, presbytery 區會, and synod 大會. Devolution was further enhanced when Iap Han Chiong was elected as the senior moderator of the Synod during its meeting in Gulangyu in 1894. In 1901, representatives of all the Presbyterian churches in China met in Shanghai and formed the Zhonghua Jidujiaohui Lianhehui 中華基督教會聯合會 (literally, The United Assembly of Christian Churches in China). This union body became the Zhongguo Zhanglaohui Quanguo Zonghui 中國長老會全國總會, or the National Assembly of Presbyterian Churches in China in 1918.[138] The Banlam churches in this assembly were mostly self-propagating and

---

135. Today, the *Book of Confessions* further includes the *Confession of 1967* (USA), the *Theological Declaration of Barmen* (1934), and *A Brief Statement of Faith* (1983). See Jack Rogers, *Presbyterian Creeds: A Guide to the Book of Confessions* (Louisville, KY: Westminster John Knox, 1985, 1991).

136. Ellsworth C. Carlson, *The Foochow Missionaries 1847–1880* (Cambridge, MA: East Asian Research Center, Harvard University Press, 1974), 96ff; cited in Cheung, *Christianity in Modern China*, 290.

137. Swanson, "In Memoriam: Dr. Talmage," 115–116.

138. See Ng, *Research on Hong Kong Min-Nam Church*, 31–35 and n. 48.

self-governing but not yet self-supporting, since majority of them could not yet fully pay the salaries of their pastors.[139]

On 6 January 1920, the Banlam region established the Zhonghua Jidujiaohui Minnan Heyihui 中華基督教會閩南合一會 (United Chinese Christian Churches of South Fukien), later known as Minnan Zhonghua Jidujiaohui 閩南中華基督教會 (South Fukien Church of Christ). Chen QiuQing 陳秋卿 reported on the process of forming this union in his article, "Minnan Jiaohui Heyi De Jingguo 〈閩南教會合一的經過〉 (The process of uniting the Banlam churches)," and gave the objective as follows: "To unite the Banlam churches in order to pursue self-support, self-government, and self-propagation, and to proclaim the whole truth of the Christian faith in order to save the whole world."[140] The method of governing these churches was through conferences, presbyteries and synods. This spirit of union and devolution was what Rev Kho Seng Iam was referring to when he declared the need for establishing the CUEC in Manila in 1924.[141]

d) Protestantism in China (Republican Period, 1911–1949)

(1) The Rise of Independent Churches

While Protestant Chinese churches were emerging in Iloilo, Manila and Cebu, churches all over China were moving toward independence, cooperation and union on a nationwide scale. G. Thompson Brown analyzed three patterns in the Presbyterian effort to organize the churches in China. The first pattern propagated the distinctive Presbyterian manner

---

139. By 1900, there were eleven Reformed churches and a total membership of 1,133 in South Fujian, distributed as follows (with dates of organization): First Amoy/Xinjie Chapel 新街堂 (1856) –98; Second Amoy/Zhushu Chapel 竹樹堂 (1860) –165; Chiohbe Chapel 石碼堂 (1854) –88; Okang/Hujiang Chapel 湖江堂 (1868) –109; Hongsan Chapel 洪山堂 (1870) –88; Tongan/Anhai Chapel 安海堂 (1871) –199; Zhangzhou Chapel 漳州堂 (1871) –114; Sio Khoe/Xiaoxi [written as Sio Khe] Chapel 小溪 (1881) –176; Thian-san/Tianshan Chapel 天山堂 (1891) –117; Lamseng/Nansheng [written as Lam-sin] Chapel 南勝堂 (1892) –72; and Poaⁿ–a/Banzi [written as Poa–a] Chapel 坂仔 (1894) –107. See De Jong, *Reformed Church in China*, 92. The Chinese names are listed, slightly different in number, in *Short History of Minnan CCC*, vol. 4, 1.

140. Chen QiuQing 陳秋卿, "Minnan Jiaohui Heyi De Jingguo 閩南教會合一的經過 (The process of uniting the Banlam churches)," *Zhonghua Jidujiaohui Nianjian* 中華基督教會年鑑 *Chinese Christian Church Yearbook* 6 (1921): 186; quoted in Ng, *Research on Hong Kong Min-Nam Church*, 36.

141. See history of CUEC on 171–200 and App. EE.

of organizing the churches, forming the Synod of China (長老會中國大會) under the PCUSA General Assembly in 1870. In 1898 the PCUSA General Assembly divided the Synod into the Synod of North China and the Synod of Central and Southern China, reflecting the linguistic differences and the logistical difficulty of gathering for synod meetings. The second pattern developed with the entry of the Southern Presbyterians, whose policy was *not* to have any appendages of their church in foreign lands. Two reasons were given: (1) They did not want to be members of a "mixed presbytery" (Chinese and Caucasian), fearing that eventually, the Chinese would outnumber the missionaries and the latter would be subject to the discipline of "immature" Christians of another race; (2) If the foreigners and natives were united in a presbytery and this attaches to the General Assembly, it was feared that this might prevent the union of the native Christians. Without a presbytery, the Southern Presbyterians held annual conferences for workers. These two patterns both had flaws, according to Brown. The first one accented the foreign nature of the enterprise and prevented union with other mission boards. The second pattern, on the other hand, was too racist and delayed the transfer of authority to Chinese pastors and elders.[142]

The third pattern, which can be termed the "Banlam Model," proved to be the best model and pointed the way to the future. Subsequent unions created both in China and in later generations followed or were influenced by this model. In this model, the missionaries retained their relationship to their home church but sat as "provisional" voting members of the Amoy Classis. This body had the right to withdraw recognition of any missionary involved in misconduct as well as the right to vote and hold office. Missionaries and native Christians administered their own funds independently, and only Chinese pastors of self-supporting churches were eligible for ordination. The entry of different groups into practically all major cities and villages and the common endeavors (education, evangelism, literature, medical and relief work) of these mission groups made cooperation both a possibility as well as a necessity in order to avoid wasteful duplication of effort and to facilitate such vital projects as Bible translation and relief

---

142. See Brown, *Earthen Vessels*, 118–126.

distribution. But the coalescence of widely different denominations did not begin to take place until after the Centenary Conference of Protestant Missionaries 百年傳教大會, held at Shanghai in 1907, commemorating the hundredth year of Protestant mission. Despite the fact that there were only two Chinese representatives in the Conference and all the addresses and minutes were done in English, the Conference was able to draw 445 missionaries from over fifty mission societies. Plans were set, but not immediately actualized, for the formation of a "Christian Federation of China." In 1910, the World Missionary Conference was held at Edinburgh, Scotland, and one of its outgrowths was the formation of the China Continuation Committee 中華基督教繼行委辦會 in 1913.[143] That was also the year in which the China Council of the Presbyterian Church, USA 美北長老會中國理事會, was organized.[144] By 1920, the number of ordained Chinese had for the first time exceeded that of ordained foreigners (1,305 vs. 1,268).[145]

Parallel to this development within the mission field, the spirit of nationalism among both Christian and non-Christian Chinese was greatly invigorated when the Republic of China was established in 1911.[146] Before this event took place, churches in China were already rapidly moving toward independence and many eventually severed their ties with foreign denominations and missions.[147] Three models began to emerge: (1) The Banlam Model, wherein Presbyterian churches in South Fujian, encouraged by missionaries themselves, developed independence and self-support

---

143. De Jong, *Reformed Church in China*, 184–185; Latourette, *History of Christian Missions in China*, 662–672. This Conference gave priority to uniting missions of similar ecclesiastical makeup, expanding educational and medical facilities, improving standards of training of missionaries, placing greater responsibility upon the Chinese, and pushing evangelism where little was being done.

144. For details on the union movement of Presbyterians in China, see Wu YiXiong 吳義雄. *Kaiduan yu Fazhan – Huanan Jindai Jidujiaoshi Lunji* 開端與發展—華南近代基督教史論集 (Beginning and progress: collected works on the modern history of Christianity in South China) (Taipei: Cosmic Light Holistic Care Organization, 2006), 133–172.

145. Latourette, *History of Christian Missions in China*, 801.

146. For the whole history of the Republic of China, see *The Cambridge History of China* Vol. 12: *Republican China 1912–1949, Part 1* and Vol. 13: *Republican China 1912–1949, Part 2*, ed. John K. Fairbank (Cambridge: Cambridge University Press, 1983).

147. See Latourette, *History of Christian Missions in China*, 674, n. 375, for publications advocating such a movement.

within a denominational framework and in cooperation with foreign missions. (2) The Central China Model – In 1902 the Shanghai Presbyterian pastor Yu GuoZhen 俞國楨 or Zong Zhou 宗周 and his colleagues formed the Chinese Christian Union 基督徒聯會 to promote propagation of the gospel by the Chinese. From the organization of the Independent Church of Shanghai in 1906 until 1931, over 600 Chinese independent churches sought to become completely separated from missions. A federation of churches called the Chinese Independent Churches of Jesus 中國耶穌教自立會 was established. (3) The Northern China Model – Around Shandong, Beijing and Tianjin, another federation of Chinese churches, called the Christian Church of China/Church of Christ in China 中華基督教會, was formed. This group, with Cheng JingYi 誠靜怡 (1881-1939) as one of the leaders, advocated that churches established by Chinese Christians should be independent and united, yet friendly relations with missionaries were maintained.[148]

Jonathan Chao significantly pointed out that the stages of development of the Protestant Chinese churches differed from that of the missionary sequence of establishing churches. The pattern for the latter was self-support, self-government, self-propagation. Missionaries began their work with the purchase of buildings as bases for educational and medical work as means to evangelism, using funds that came from their mission boards or churches from where they originated. Self-support became the goal as congregations began to form. Self-government was attained only when a congregation was able to call and then pay the salary of its own Chinese pastor. After these two stages were attained, the work of self-propagation was carried on by the Chinese pastor and the church members, frequently with the assistance of the missionaries. In contrast, the pattern for the Protestant Chinese churches was self-propagation by the leaders and church members, then self-government, then self-support and calling of a pastor. After this, the congregation would develop financial growth for erecting a church building and start other institutional work. This was the pattern followed

---

148. Daniel H. Bays, "The Growth of Independent Christianity in China, 1900–1937," in *Christianity in China: From the Eighteenth Century to the Present*, ed. Daniel H. Bays (Stanford, CA: Stanford University Press, 1996), 307–316; Zha ShiJie, *Anthology on the History of Christianity*, 33–35; Jonathan Chao, "Chinese Indigenous Church Movement," 65–89, n. 21, 22.

by CGC, CUEC and DCGC. Chao further analyzed that this movement introduced three new concepts influencing the approach to establishing new churches in the next decades: *identity*, which motivated the Protestant Chinese to assume responsibility for church development; *independence from foreigners*, financial and administrative wise; and *separation* as a necessary step toward creating autonomous Chinese churches.[149]

(2) Move toward Ecumenism

After the China Continuation Conference of 1913, and under the leadership of John Raleigh Mott (1865–1955), chairman of the International Missionary Council and general secretary of the World's Student Christian Federation, five regional meetings were set up in the same year by the China Continuation Committee. The drafted findings included: (1) a call for a survey to show the state of occupation by Protestant mission and a suggested comity procedure for entering new territories inside China; (2) a declaration that much of the evangelism effort could now be assumed by the Chinese churches; (3) the formation of the "Christian Church of China," or Zhonghua Jidujiaohui 中華基督教會 as a manifestation of the unity that was already existing among all Christians in China; and (4) an emphasis upon the training of Chinese leaders. Other measures discussed were aimed at expanding the existing missionary endeavors. Two men were selected as full-time secretaries: Edwin C. Lobenstine (term of service 1898–1937) of the American Presbyterian Mission (North) and Cheng JingYi, pastor of the independent, formerly LMS-connected *Beijing Zhonghua Jidujiaohui* 北京中華基督教會 (literally, the Chinese Christian Church of Beijing).

In 1919 an organization evolved when representatives from the RCA, EPM, LMS, ABCFM, United Brethren, and other Presbyterian missions jointly drafted a preliminary plan for establishing a broad church union.[150] Cheng JingYi served as presider during the National Christian Conference (replacing the China Continuation Conference); as the first General Secretary of the National Christian Council of China (NCCC), which

---

149. Jonathan Chao, "Chinese Indigenous Church Movement," 86–90.

150. See Latourette, *History of Christian Missions in China*, 803–804 for a survey of how these missions and denominational churches were experiencing the same process of devolution and indigenization.

replaced the China Continuation Committee;[151] and as the first secretary of the Church of Christ in China General Assembly.

(3) Decline and Recovery

It was during this period of the emerging church of China, that anti-foreign and anti-religious sentiments began to foment in Beijing, finally reaching boiling point during the May Fourth Movement 五四運動 (1919–1923). This movement was sparked by intellectuals and students in Beijing who protested on 4 May 1919 over what they considered unjust treatment of China at the Versailles Peace Conference in Paris. This incident and its aftermath served to catalyze the intellectual revolution in China, leading an increasing number of Chinese intellectuals to adhere to Marxist socialism under the New Cultural Movement.[152] Historian Peter Wang made this remark regarding the effect of these two movements on Christianity:

> These latter movements stimulated Chinese intellectuals to look upon questions of national affairs and social realities from the viewpoint of democracy and science. Under these influences, intellectuals began to criticize the warlords for obstructing the development of democracy and the foreign powers for imperialist transgressions in China and for providing assistance to the warlords. As a result, anti-imperialist and antiwarlord [sic] sentiment was widespread in Chinese society. At the same time, the spirit of scientism, accompanied by the growing popularity of pragmatism among intellectual circles, promoted the iconoclastic rejection of superstition and religious beliefs. Under these circumstances, Christianity, with all its Western cultural baggage, had not yet been criticized seriously, but it was soon to encounter organized anti-Christian sentiment.[153]

---

151. Brown, *Earthen Vessels*, 214.

152. For the roots and intellectual development of Communism in China, see Charlotte Furth, "Intellectual Change: From the Reform Movement to the May Fourth Movement, 1895–1920," in *The Cambridge History of China* 12 322–405.

153. Peter Chen-Main Wang, "Contextualizing Protestant Publishing in China: The Wenshe, 1924–1928," in *Christianity in China: From the Eighteenth Century to the Present,* ed. Daniel H. Bays (Stanford, CA: Stanford University Press, 1996), 293.

As a result of the growing anti-foreign, anti-religious spirit in China, which later became explicitly anti-Christian, Chinese churches and foreign missions suffered setback and decline. The situation was intensified by the Shanghai incident of 30 May 1925. The killing of eleven Chinese students by British police led to class boycotts and protests in twenty-eight other cities. The effect of these combined incidents was most felt in mission schools: enrolment dropped, discipline became difficult, student-initiated strikes forced suspension of classes, and finally, the government decreed that religious schools now had to register and be regulated by the education bureau.[154] Fortunately, the schools weathered the storm and recovery began to take place in 1932. However, it became clear that the Chinese churches had to make their own stand with regard to national events and their future as a religious community. They had to defend their faith and to justify their existence. To be fully identified with and under the domination of foreign missionaries – in churches and Christian organizations – no longer seemed a viable option. The consensus gradually developed that the Chinese church had to become an indigenous church, which Jonathan Chao described as "independent, non-denominational, suited to the ethnic characteristics of the Chinese people, and integrated with Chinese culture and ways of life."[155] However, unlike the Chinese churches in Taiwan, Hong Kong, and to some extent, the Philippines, the total devolution of the Chinese churches in China was complicated by patriotic movements, the Marxist ideology and liberal theology that affected the ideals of integrating the Christian faith with Chinese culture and society.[156]

(4) The Church of Christ in China

It was in this context that the transition from mission to church transpired. After the NCCC convened more meetings, the first General Assembly of the Church of Christ in China, was held from 1–11 October 1927, attended by the representatives of fourteen denominations, fifty-six presbyteries, and

---

154. It was stipulated that religious schools could not make religion a required subject or compel students to attend religious activities. Brown, *Earthen Vessels*, 259–266.

155. Jonathan Chao, "Chinese Indigenous Church Movement," 271.

156. Latourette, *History of Christian Missions in China*, 805, 809–810.

twelve synods.[157] When the union was formed, it was composed of 12,000 churches and 113,000 communicants from thirteen of China's eighteen provinces,which actually represented only one-third of the total number of Protestant Chinese.[158] Three-fourths of the delegates at this assembly were Chinese, including the moderator (Cheng JingYi) and vice-moderator (Xu ShengYan).[159] A constitution and a statement of faith were adopted and various committees were set up. Their theology was simple, according to Cary-Elwes: faith in Jesus Christ as Redeemer and Lord (with no mention of the Godhead of Christ) and in the Bible as the supreme authority "in matters of faith and duty," and acceptance of the Apostles' Creed as the expression of their faith.[160] The formation of this union was caused by the political instability of the Republican government, the exodus of many foreign missionaries in 1926–1927, and the need for uniting and contextualizing the Chinese churches in order to face the socio-cultural realities.[161] During this assembly, as in previous NCCC conferences, tribute was paid to churches and missions in South Fujian for having set the pattern for the China-wide union movement.

Despite the emergence of the CCC and the ideals it pursued, the indigenous movement of the 1920s did not transform the CCC into a truly Chinese church. After anti-Christian pressures were lifted at the end of this decade, the old pattern of dependency on missions and denominations resurged, but the function of missionaries was changing.[162] In South Fujian, by the 1930s, more and more churches had either reached complete

---

157. The Anglicans, Methodists, Lutherans, Southern Baptists and the China Inland Mission did not join the CCC.

158. Brown, *Earthen Vessels*, 213; Latourette, *History of Christian Missions in China*, 800.

159. Asher Raymond Kepler (1879–1942) of the PCUSA was elected as General Secretary, but later became the associate of Cheng when the latter was elected to the position. Kepler, however, was the organizing force behind the union. See Brown, *Earthen Vessels*, 212.

160. De Jong, *Reformed Church in China*, 185–186; Columba Cary-Elwes, *China and the Cross: Studies in Missionary History* (London: Longmans, Green & Co., 1957), 255.

161. See Kenneth Scott Latourette, *The Chinese: Their History and Culture*, 3rd ed. (New York: Macmillan, 1949), 454–484 for an assessment of the economic, intellectual and religious changes taking place in China during the turbulent period from 1894–1944.

162. Latourette, *History of Christian Missions in China*, 821–822.

independence or were on the way to devolution. The whole of China was becoming more nationalistic in the political as well as the religious realms.

B. The Six Philippine Protestant Chinese Churches

After giving the backdrop of the history of the Philippine Chinese and an overview of Protestantism in China and in South Fujian, the histories of six Protestant Chinese churches in the Philippines will be discussed according to the founding dates of each church. The historical presentation will be preceded by focusing on the initial attempts of doing ministry among the Philippine Chinese, based on evidence gathered from mission reports, missionary correspondence and interviews that I conducted.

In the August 1898 issue of *The Gospel in All Lands*, a missionary journal published by the Missionary Society of the Methodist Episcopal Church, it was reported regarding the Philippines that,

> A few years ago the London Missionary Society sent three missionaries there, but soon after they had landed and commenced preaching the Gospel to the natives they were put into prison. They appealed to the British consul, and the consul to the government on their behalf; but as the laws of the country would not allow of any strange religion being preached within its boundaries the three missionaries were obliged to return home. [taken from] *The Christian*.[163]

The incident most likely took place before 1898, when the journal was printed, and before the Spanish-American War which lasted from May to August of the same year. It highlights the reality of Spanish intolerance despite religious toleration being established in Spain in 1876. It is also significant that this failed attempt was made by a British mission organization. The British had made an earlier attempt, but for economic and military rather than religious reasons, of occupying Manila in 1763–1764.[164]

When Presbyterian missionaries began working among the Chinese in Iloilo in 1900, they found two Protestant Chinese from Xiamen who

---

163. "The Gospel in All Lands." Illustrated (Aug 1898), 383.

164. See Horacio de la Costa, SJ, ed. *Readings in Philippine History: Selected Historical Texts Presented with a Commentary* (Manila: Bookmark, 1965), 98–105.

had previously been connected with the LMS.[165] Nine other Protestant Chinese, also from Xiamen who had been living in Iloilo from nine to sixteen years, were gathered for worship by the missionaries. Taking the year of publication of Arthur Judson Brown's *Report of a Visitation of the Philippine Islands* (1901–1902) as a marker, this would mean that these eleven believers had lived in Iloilo from 1885 to 1892. In China, this was a time of rapid growth of the Protestant churches, from 21,560 members in 1883 to 55,093 in 1893 (App. V). One can only speculate at this point whether the LMS missionaries made the attempt because they knew there were Protestant Chinese in Iloilo or whether these believers had anything to do with their daring entry into the Philippines. The fact remains that there were Protestant Chinese in Iloilo during a time when it was practically impossible for Protestant missionaries to work in the Spanish Catholic nation.

Another prelude to the formal entry of Protestant mission into the Philippines is related to David Abeel III. As the Philippines was one of the preferred destinations for trade and migration, especially for the *Hokkiens*, it could have been a logical development for the gospel seed to be transplanted in the Islands at the time or soon after the Protestant churches started to emerge in South Fujian during the nineteenth century, just as this was happening in Indonesia, Singapore, and Malaysia.

Abeel did indeed cast his eyes on the Philippine Islands even before China's doors were finally opened to Protestant Christianity in 1842. The first RCA missionary to minister in Xiamen had already sounded a call for doing mission in the Philippines eight years before setting foot in that city. He reported concerning the Philippines in his 1834 book, entitled, *Journal of a Residence in China and the Neighboring Countries*. Although he did not personally visit the Islands, he utilized extracts from another book whose author, C. W. King, had resided for a time in Manila. King's untitled work was published in India and reviewed in the *Chinese Repository*.[166] Full

---

165. Arthur Judson Brown, *Report of a Visitation of the Philippine Islands* (New York: Board of Foreign Missions of the Presbyterian Church in the USA, 1902), 58; John Marvin Dean, *The Cross of Christ in Bolo–land* (Chicago, IL: Revell, 1902), 77.

166. Although Abeel neither cited the title of this manuscript nor the specific issue of *The Chinese Repository*, the writer, through the special assistance of the Yale Library staff, located the review but it was without the name of C. W. King as author. The title of the small volume, published in 1828, is *Remarks on the Philippines, and on Their Capital Manila*.

of positive outlook regarding the land and its wealth, Abeel's description of the people, especially the natives and *mestizos* and even of the Chinese residents, was, however, less than positive, and even prejudiced. From the religious aspect he stated that the Church of Rome had "proselyted" the whole population and the natives had become "bigoted Catholics." The nearly one thousand priests held "the minds of the miserable natives in complete subjection." Importation of Bibles was strictly forbidden. Abeel ended his report with these words: "The city of Manilla [*sic*] . . . would be a most advantageous post for missions. Let every Christian pray that the power of the Beast may be destroyed, and the scepter of Jesus be extended over these perishing souls."[167]

Although his observation of the people reflects insufficient information and most likely some prejudice on the part of his source, Abeel's report manifests the fact that the Philippines was not a potential mission field during the mid-nineteenth century because of the overpowering hold and influence of Spanish Catholicism in that country. It would take another sixty-four years before this hindrance was removed during the American occupation, and for Abeel's prayer to be answered.

1. Protestant Missionary Attempt among the Philippine Chinese

The conversion of the Chinese immigrants and the eventual emergence of the Protestant Chinese churches is part of a larger Protestant missionary enterprise that includes the founding of the Presbyterian mission in Manila, its initial concern for the Chinese and the participation of the Protestant Chinese in worship services conducted by this mission.

a) The Founding of the Presbyterian Mission

When the Presbyterian missionaries entered Manila in 1899, they started their ministry in Binondo.[168] Meetings were held on *Calle San Fernando*

See "Miscellanies," *The Chinese Repository*, vol. 2 *from May, 1833, to April, 1934*, 2nd ed. (Canton: Printed for the Proprietors, 1834), 350–355.

    167. Abeel, *Journal*, 353–360.

    168. James Burton Rodgers, *Forty Years in the Philippines: A History of the Philippine Mission of the Presbyterian Church in the United States of America 1899–1939* (New York: Board of Foreign Missions of the Presbyterian Church in the USA, 1940), 32–43.

and *Calle Sacristia*, and soon spread to Intramuros (*Calle Beaterio*), Ermita/ Malate (*Calle Nueva*), Paco and Tondo. The fear that Filipinos would be embittered by war and refuse to hear the gospel message had actually been in vain. Instead, the Presbyterian missionaries found the people quite ready to consider and listen to the gospel. But among all these meeting places, it was in Tondo, where the Binondo services were transferred in 1903, Ermita/Malate and Cavite where the Presbyterian work took deeper roots.[169] According to Rocky Divinagracia, chairman of the Tondo Evangelical Church (former Tondo Presbyterian Church), this was due to the fact that Tondo and Cavite were the hotbeds of rebellion in 1896.[170] James Rodgers stated regarding the leaders of the Tondo Presbyterian Church: "It can be said with 90 percent of truth that of the first officers of the Tondo church, the deacons had been to jail once, the elders twice, and the secretary of the session Sr [Don Agustin] de la Rosa, three times."[171] The Roman Catholic Church and the Spanish government were both hated by many people, including the Chinese and Chinese *mestizos*, in Tondo and Cavite. Hence, resistance to the "new" religion and hostility toward Protestant missionaries was least felt in these two places. In fact, when the Presbyterian mission in the Philippines was formally constituted in December 1899, it was reported that James Burton Rodgers (1865–1944) and David Sutherland Hibbard (1868–1966) were "received more cordially than they had expected both by US authorities and by the people."[172] Plans to erect a church in

---

169. T. Valentino Sitoy Jr, *Several Springs, One Stream: The United Church of Christ in the Philippines*. Volume I: *Heritage and Origins (1898–1948)* (Quezon City: United Church of Christ in the Philippines, 1992), 84–87. The Presbyterians started working in Cavite in 1901, after the Methodists turned over their field to the former according to the comity arrangement of the Evangelical Union of the Philippine Islands. Rodgers, *Forty Years*, 44–45.

170. Rocky Divinagracia, telephone interview by Jean Uayan, 27 Jun 2005, Manila, Philippines. Transcript. Philippine Chinese Church Archives, Biblical Seminary of the Philippines, Valenzuela City, Philippines.

171. Rodgers, *Forty Years*, 6–7, 34. Rodgers further stated that Don Agustin, member of the Federalist Party aiming for Philippine statehood within the American federal government and also of the Aguinaldo Cabinet, was a friend of General Emilio Aguinaldo y Famy (1869–1964) until their relationship soured due to a dispute on how to use the funds paid by the Spanish government to the revolutionary leaders.

172. *The Sixty-third Annual Report of the Board of Foreign Missions of the Presbyterian Church in the United States of America, presented to the General Assembly, May, 1900* (New York: Presbyterian Building, 1900), 209.

Manila were taken up during a meeting on 20 November 1899.[173] By 1900 there were already many Protestant services in and near Manila. For example, the first meeting of the Philippine Mission of the Methodist Episcopal Church was held on 5 March 1899 at the *Teatro Filipino* on *Calle Echague* in Quiapo. The Methodist chaplain George C. Stull conducted services assisted by lay preacher Arthur W. Prautch.[174] The Presbyterian congregation, on the other hand, worshiped in a YMCA tent in Tondo under the leadership of James Burton Rodgers and Leonard Palmeter Davidson (d. 1901).

b) Initial Concern for the Chinese

As Presbyterian missionaries started working among the Filipinos and American soldiers, they showed concern for the large number (50,000–60,000) of Chinese as well.[175] In a letter to Rev Dr Frank Field Ellinwood (1826–1908), then senior secretary of the Presbyterian Foreign Board, William H. Lingle wrote that the Chinese consul informed him that there were 50,000 Chinese men in the Philippines. The number of women and children was not known.[176] This concern took even more concrete form in 1900.

In the *Sixty-fourth Annual Report* (1901) of the Board of Foreign Missions of the Presbyterian Church in the United States of America (BFM-PCUSA) it was stated that,

> It is felt that at Manila, as at the other Stations, a work is demanded in the interest of the Chinese who are settled there in large numbers, and who seem to be accessible and more or less responsive to religious effort. This work has been started by employing Chinese evangelists. Weekly services are held and a number of Chinese are always in attendance. The Mission

---

173. *Sixty-third Annual Report*, 212.

174. Sitoy, *Several Springs* 1: 43. See details in Ruben F. Trinidad, *A Monument to Religious Nationalism: History and Polity of the IEMELIF Church* (Quezon City: Evangelical Methodist Church in the Philippines, 1999), 43–44.

175. Brown, *Report of a Visitation*, 57–58.

176. William H. Lingle, Manila, Philippine Islands and the United States of America, to Rev Frank Field Ellinwood, New York, Jan 17, 1899. Yale Divinity School Library Special Collection, Sp. Col. MS 11 287. Yale Divinity Library, Yale University, New Haven, CT. Ellinwood is also known as Francis F. in other sources. Both names will appear in this work as the sources indicate accordingly.

is hoping to secure a native evangelist from Amoy who can speak in the dialect of his countrymen resident in Manila.[177]

Not only did this report reveal the situation of the Chinese – that they were in large number and mainly spoke *Hokkien* – it also gave another confirmation that even before mission work began, there were already Protestant Chinese, called "evangelists" in the report, in Manila around 1900.[178] Another piece of information is the attendance of "a number of Chinese" in the weekly services conducted by the Presbyterian missionaries.

c) Gathering the Protestant Chinese

Arthur Brown's report, published in 1902, is crucial to the study of the first attempt at reaching the Philippine Chinese. He provided more information as to how many Chinese were attending these services when he wrote:

> Our missionaries in the Philippines early saw this inviting opportunity and began service for the Chinese in connection with their other work. Although hampered by the fact that the medium of communication [Spanish] was a language foreign alike to preacher and hearer, the effort speedily thrived. A few Christian Chinese who had been converted in China were discovered, and these, like the devout Jews whom Paul found in the cities of the Roman Empire, were the nucleus around whom the new movement gathered. In Manila, two of these were able to preach, and while supporting themselves in their shops during the week, reasoned out of the Scriptures with considerable power on the Sabbath. Mr Gelwicks, being

---

177. *The Sixty-fourth Annual Report of the Board of Foreign Missions of the Presbyterian Church in the United States of America, presented to the General Assembly, May, 1901* (New York: Presbyterian Building, 1901), 260.

178. As difficult as it is to determine the exact number of Roman Catholic Chinese in the Philippines at the turn of the nineteenth century, Homer Stuntz reported in 1904 that there were 25,000 Chinese Catholics in Manila. It is even harder to know how many Protestant Chinese there were. Homer C. Stuntz, *The Philippines and the Far East* (Cincinnati, OH: Jennings & Pye; New York: Eaton & Maine, 1904), 275. Jacques Amyot, SJ wrote that "Statistics are not too meaningful because of the state of the records and the relatively large number of purely nominal [Roman Catholic] Christians, but it is certain that churchgoing Christians constitute a small minority in the total Chinese community. Some Chinese were Christian, either Catholic or Protestant, when they came to this country." Amyot, *Manila Chinese*. 275.

under appointment for China, naturally interested himself in this service, which has a congregation of from forty to fifty.[179]

The missionary that Brown was referring to was George L. Gelwicks who served in Hunan, China, from 1901–1922.[180] Gelwicks and his wife worked among the Americans in Manila, but because of their experience in China it is quite likely that they also assisted their colleagues with the work among the Chinese during their short seven-month stay before moving on to China.[181] At this early stage, the lack of skilled workers for the Chinese was already keenly felt, as Brown continued to report:

> A native pastor is now urgently needed. The missionaries can-
> not spare from their other work the time necessary to properly
> develop this attractive field among the sixty thousand Chinese
> in the city. Nor can this comparatively intelligent congrega-
> tion be permanently built up by the necessarily *unstudied talks*
> [emphasis mine] of Chinese who must devote their energies
> to a trade or a shop.[182]

The primary focus of the missionaries (the "other work") was evidently among Filipinos and Americans, hence it was desired that "native" pastors from China be called. It was also evident that the efforts of the two Chinese Christians who were preaching were not adequate because the men were not properly trained. Despite the critical observation that their messages were "unstudied," Brown did add that one of these preachers had praise-worthy qualities: he was "an intelligent, consecrated man" who led an ex-emplary life. He spoke with fluency and force, and he had the advantage of "a good knowledge of English." What's more, he was unpaid and his service required sacrificing a good earning job as a cabinetmaker.[183]

Despite the large number (40–50) of Chinese reportedly attending the services, no source has been found, as yet, indicating how many of these Chinese worshipers were new converts to Protestantism, since it would

---

179. Brown, *Report of a Visitation*, 57.
180. *Sixty-fourth Annual Report*, 209.
181. Rodgers, *Forty Years*, 39.
182. Brown, *Report of a Visitation*, 57–58.
183. See Brown, *Report of a Visitation*, n. 72, 58.

seem from Presbyterian and other mission records that these worshipers were already Christians and members of Presbyterian, Methodist Episcopal, or other denominational churches in China.

d) Short-lived Ministry

The question that arises is this: did the Chinese worshipers remain in the Tondo Presbyterian Church or did they join the St. Stephen's Chinese Mission when it was formed in 1903? There seems to be a hint that the latter was the case in Rodgers' book, *Forty Years in the Philippines*. His information confirms that Chinese Christians attending the Presbyterian and Methodist services before 1903 were Christians who had already been members of denominational churches while still living in South Fujian. Furthermore, he wrote that,

> both the Presbyterian and Methodist Missions had gathered groups of Chinese Christians from their churches in Fukien [Fujian] Province. In fact, practically all these Christian Chinese had been members of these two churches in their own country. It was found, however, that neither Mission had the personnel, either foreign or Chinese, to carry on this work. They therefore turned the work over to the Episcopal Mission which had a missionary who knew the Amoy dialect.[184]

From what Rodgers wrote concerning the short-lived Presbyterian and Methodist work among the Chinese, it would seem that the Chinese worshiping among the Filipinos in both of these Mission churches were channeled to SSCM. This would have been the most logical move to resolve their lack of mission workers for the Chinese, and at the same time benefit the Episcopalians who did not desire to overlap the work of other missions in Manila. Hobart Studley confirmed as much when he reported to Bishop Henry Brent saying, "We have now on our communicant list nearly all of those who were formerly members of Protestant churches in China and are now resident in Manila."[185] Another late source states that the SSCM congregation "included converts of the Anglican, Roman, Presbyterian,

---

184. Rodgers, *Forty Years*, 155.

185. Donald MacGillivray, ed., *The China Mission Year Book Being "The Christian Movement in China"* (Shanghai: Christian Literature Society for China, 1910), 423.

Congregationalist, Methodist, and English Wesleyan Churches."[186] In another report, Studley wrote: "Among the worshipers on that first Sunday was the entire congregation of a Filipino Presbyterian Church."[187] This can only have reference to the Tondo Presbyterian Church.

e) Place of Worship

As to the location where the earliest Protestant Chinese worshiped in Manila, the history of the Tondo Presbyterian Church, organized in 1902 and now called the Tondo Evangelical Church, may provide a clue. In 1903 this congregation, under the care of Paul Frederick Jansen and Elizabeth White Jansen, erected a wooden sanctuary on the corner of *Calle Santo Cristo* and *Paseo Azcarraga* (now Recto Street), on the north side of the San Nicolas district, which was then part of Tondo province (small circle in App. M).[188] Rocky Divinagracia, current elder of Tondo Evangelical Church, further confirmed that some aged members of his church can recall that there were Chinese who joined the Filipino service at 8:00 on Sunday mornings, followed by the English service at 10:30–12:00 noon.[189] This site could very well be the place where the earliest Protestant Chinese worshiped.

However, Brown mentions another site that may predate the Tondo meeting place. In his *Report*, he noted, "We can continue to give the congregation the free use of our *Trozo chapel* [emphasis mine] on Sunday afternoons."[190] In a later source (1903), Brown stated that the Presbyterians had four congregations in Manila: "the Trozo, the Tondo, the Chinese and the Americans."[191] According to Sitoy, the Trozo Presbyterian Church was

---

186. Vincent Herbert Gowen, *Philippine Kaleidoscope: An Illustrated Story of the Church's Mission* (New York: The National Council, Protestant Episcopal Church, [193?]), 22.

187. Studley, "Chinese Experiment," 576.

188. For more details on Elizabeth White's ministry see pp. 213–216. Due to termites and typhoon ravages, this church lot was sold and a new concrete church was built on the corner of *Calle Folgueras* and *Calle Padre Rada* in 1933. Rodgers, *Forty Years*, 36–37.

189. Rocky Divinagracia, telephone interview.

190. Brown, *Report of a Visitation*, 58.

191. Brown, *New Era in the Philippines*, 200. The 1903 date of publication does not necessarily indicate that these four congregations did not exist earlier. This is already the third edition of Brown's book; hence, we may accept that these four congregations may date back to 1900–1901. Note also the use of the word "congregation" to refer to the Presbyterian churches in Trozo and Tondo.

already in existence in 1900 and was located on *Calle Magdalena*, Trozo, Binondo (see App. M). He wrote, "Sometime before April 1900, the congregation was organized as the 'Trozo Presbyterian Church' – the first Presbyterian Church in the Philippines, starting with 15 members but increasing to 31 within a few months."[192] The work in Binondo, where Trozo was located, branched out to Tondo in 1901. The Trozo Presbyterian Church thus *preceded* the Tondo Presbyterian Church. However, in 1903 the Trozo services were transferred to Tondo where the church building was erected. From these reports, it can be logically constructed that the 40–50 Chinese were using the Trozo chapel from 1900–1903, conducting services in their own dialect, that they then worshiped at the newly built Tondo Presbyterian Church from some time in 1903 until they ultimately joined the SSCM in the last quarter of 1903. Hence, the earliest, pre-SSCM sites where Protestant Chinese gathered as worshipers were in Trozo and Tondo.

f) Time of Worship

Sitoy further noted that on Sundays, there were two regular meetings at the Trozo Presbyterian Church: one in Spanish in the morning and the Tagalog service in the afternoon. Brown's report revealed that the Chinese were using the Trozo chapel on Sunday afternoons, but since he also reported that the Chinese evangelists were conducting the services in their own dialect, it would seem that the Protestant Chinese were not attending the Tagalog service conducted by the missionaries and Filipino evangelists, but were merely using the building at another hour on Sunday afternoons. This arrangement probably ceased when the meetings were concentrated in the Tondo Presbyterian Church, during which time the Chinese began to attend the Tagalog services. Thus it comes as no surprise that the whole congregation would transfer and join the inaugural meeting of SSCM, because the services were being conducted in their mother tongue (*Hokkien*) by Hobart Studley, the Reformed turned Episcopalian missionary from Xiamen. To the Presbyterians and Methodists, the formation of this new congregation was not seen as competition but rather, in the spirit of evangelical union that was prominent during that period, as an opportunity for

---

192. Sitoy, *Several Springs* 1: 86.

Protestant Chinese to receive adequate and proper spiritual nurture, for which they had neither the personnel nor professional skill to offer.

2. The "Chinese Presbyterian Church in Iloilo"

While these events were taking place in Manila, the Presbyterians were also starting mission work in Iloilo. Was the "Chinese Presbyterian Church in Iloilo" (CPCI) the first Chinese church in the Philippines? Did it cease to exist after a few decades? This name does not appear either in the records of the Philippine Mission of the PCUSA or in other sources, but in 1930, the name "Chinese Presbyterian Church–Manila" does appear in the *Minutes of the Executive Committee*.[193] Note that at this stage CUEC had just began as a congregation, but the term "church" is applied to the group. Taking this record as a cue, I have coined the name "Chinese Presbyterian Church in Iloilo" for the Chinese congregation established by the Presbyterians in Iloilo. I choose the word "church," but consider this term and "congregation" as interchangeably used, based on Presbyterian mission usage.[194] In Cebu, for example, the Matilda Bradford Memorial Church is often referred to as the "Visayan congregation," distinct from the "Chinese congregation" (see pp. 152–153, 156–157). Another name, which I consider as referring to another congregation, is the "Iloilo Chinese Church of Christ Chapel." This is a translation of the Chinese name 『怡郎中華基督教會禮拜堂』 given by Shih Chang Shangkuan in reference to the church that existed *after* 1934. At this point, there is no source indicating that it is the same congregation as the CPCI.[195]

Based on the records and historical books of the Philippine Protestant Chinese churches, St. Stephen's Parish has always been considered the first Protestant Chinese church established in the Philippines. The only record regarding the Chinese church in Iloilo was a passing statement made by

---

193. See Minutes of the Executive Committee of the Philippine Mission of the Presbyterian Church in the United States of America, Baguio, P.I., May 3–6, 1930, 33.

194. See Archival Materials section of Bibliography for a list of Presbyterian mission records.

195. Shih Chang Shangkuan 上官世璋, "Xinyang Chunzheng Baochi Wei Difang Benshe Jiaohui – Feilübin Nandao Huaqiao Jidu Jiaohui Shilue 信仰純正保持為地方本色教會—菲律賓南島華僑基督教會史略 (Pure faith preserved in contextualized local churches: History of overseas Chinese Christianity in the Southern Philippines)," in *HDPO*, 151 (pages printed Chinese style).

Shi Chang Shangkuan 上官世璋 in the fortieth anniversary publication of the United Evangelical Church of the Philippines (UECP), a publication that sought to cover the history of Protestantism in the Philippine Chinese community as well as in Asia.[196] My translation of his statement is: "There is an oral report that as early as 1911 church services were held among the Chinese in Iloilo. These were held in the mission hospital, led by Dr Hall [Ho i seng/Hao yisheng 浩醫生], but they were meeting on and off. There is no written historical record, this is based only on the oral report of Elder Ng Guan Ko/Huang YuanGe 黃元戈."[197] Shangkuan's statement, however, is both inaccurate ("meeting on and off") and incorrect ("no record"). It is imperative that the record be brought to light and allowed to speak for itself. The story of this unique church has been reconstructed from Presbyterian missionary correspondence and minutes and supplemented by personal interviews of the descendants of Protestant Chinese who lived in Iloilo before WWII. However, to understand the beginning and eventual outcome of this church, it is necessary to start from the history of the city and from the work of the Presbyterian missionaries among the Chinese people of Iloilo.

a) History of Iloilo

Iloilo province is located on the island of Panay in the central region of the Philippines known as the Visayas. It is situated about three hundred miles southeast of Manila.[198] Foreign traders visited Iloilo even before the Malayan settlers came. The Chinese have been trading with Filipinos in the Iloilo area since perhaps the Song dynasty (AD 960–1279). They entrusted their goods to Filipinos without any receipts and when they came back six to eight months later, there was no difficulty collecting payment from them.[199]

---

196. Shih Chang or S. C. Shangkuan 上官世璋 (1915–1996) was an elder of CUEC/ UECP. His publications concerning this church's fortieth and fiftieth anniversaries, in 1969 and 1979 respectively, are vital contributions to UECP, to the Chinese Filipino Christian community, as well as to the Asian church as a whole.

197. Shangkuan wrote in Chinese: "據説早於一九一一年, 怡朗華僑既有舉行禮拜, 假差會醫院, 由浩醫生主持, 惟聚會時斷時續。 此事無歷史記錄, 惟得自一位信徒黃元戈長老所口述者。" Shangkuan, "Pure Faith," in *HDPO*, 151.

198. *The Iloilo Enterprise* 1, no. 6 (8 Oct 1908): 37.

199. See Chau Ju-Kua, *Zhu Fan Zhi*, 160.

During Spanish times, there was a *pariancillo* in Molo where Chinese merchants sold goods brought over from China.[200] The Spanish government opened the port of Iloilo to foreign trade in 1855.[201] Its physical features made it a very strategic commercial port and a center of trade in the West Visayas (App. W).[202] By 1893, Iloilo had become a regular province and its capital a city. Iloilo became the Philippines' premier province and the city was the second largest, next to Manila.[203]

During the Spanish regime, the number and freedom of the Chinese in Iloilo, and elsewhere, were limited by legal and other factors.[204] Yet Berthold Laufer (1874–1934), a German American anthropologist and orientalist, could boldly claim, "The entire Spanish colony subsisted until the nineteenth century exclusively on the Chinese trade."[205] During the mid-1800s, the Chinese shifted from being artisans and importers of Chinese goods to coast-wide traders, middlemen, and wholesalers. In 1850 the Spaniards reversed their policy and allowed unrestricted immigration and unbounded settlement of Chinese in the Philippines. By the late 1890s Chinese firms had expanded their trading contacts to include countries other than China, functioning as Western firms did.[206] Increased frequency of transportation

---

200. John T. Omohundro, *Chinese Merchant Families in Iloilo: Commerce and Kin in a Central Philippine City* (Quezon City: Ateneo de Manila University Press; Athens, OH: Ohio University Press, 1981), 15.

201. Foreman, *Philippine Islands*, 261.

202. Galang, *Land and People*, 31, 35, 80.

203. The City of Iloilo was created by Commonwealth Act No. 57, known as the Charter of the City of Iloilo, approved on 20 Oct 1936, amended by Commonwealth Act No. 158, approved on 9 Nov 1936. Zoilo M. Galang, ed., *Filipiniana* Vol. I: *Land and People* (Manila: Philippine Education Co., 1937), 80.

204. Between 1750 and 1850, the expulsion laws (1755), heavy taxes and hostility from both Filipinos and Spaniards, made living and doing business for the Chinese difficult for the Chinese. Wickberg, *Chinese in Philippine Life*, 20–41. Cf. Bowring, *Visit*, 208–210, 255; Antonio Tan 陳守國, *Feilübin Wubainian de Fanhua Qishi* 菲律賓五百年的反華歧視 (Five hundred years of anti–Chinese prejudice), trans. Joaquin Sy 施華謹 (Manila: Kaisa Para Sa Kaunlaran, Feilübin Huayi Qingnian Lianhehui 菲律濱華裔青年聯合會, 1989), 3–17.

205. Berthold Laufer, *Relations of the Chinese to the Philippines*, Smithsonian Miscellaneous Collections Vol. 50 (Washington, DC: Smithsonian, 1907; reprint, Manila: Philippine Historical Ass., 1967), 11.

206. Francisco Yap Tico, for example, combined his commission agency in Iloilo with his hemp- and sugar-exporting firm, with branches in Manila and Cebu; other Chinese firms worked along the same lines as Western firms. See Wickberg, *Chinese in Philippine*

facilitated immigration from Xiamen and Macau and the number of immigrants to the Philippines began to swell.[207] In Iloilo, however, the number of Chinese remained below 2,000, as indicated in the Census for 1903 and 1908. Of this number, 90 percent were from Fujian province, and of these, 50 percent were from the district (*xian* 縣) of Jinjiang.[208]

The Filipino revolutionary government replaced Spanish rule on 24 December 1898, but Filipino resistance to American forces ended only on 2 February 1901, and the American civil government was set up in Iloilo on 11 April 1901.[209] The Americans quickly built an economic base in the province and the Chinese traders were the backbone of this enterprise, despite the fact that, by September 1898, the American administrators instituted the Chinese Exclusion Acts that were in force in the United States.[210] After WWI, some Chinese began to bring their wives along, thus increasing the population. The prominent families in Iloilo's Chinese community were highly cultured and wealthy, coming mostly from the urban areas of Xiamen.[211] They were educated, gentlemanly and polite, as pioneer missionary Joseph Andrew Hall observed. They readily bestowed favors and were liberal with their money. When the missionaries built their small *nipa* [a kind of palm branch] hospital at a cost of about $300, Brown reported that the Chinese merchants and clerks subscribed $145 [almost 50%] of the cost while the rest was raised among the other foreigners.[212] The story of the work of these Protestant missionaries will now be discussed.

Life, 87–88, and Raul Rodrigo, *Phoenix: The Saga of the Lopez Family* Vol. 1: *1800–1972* (Manila: Eugenio López Foundation, 2000), 14–17.

207. Cf. Wickberg, *Chinese in Philippine Life*, 61.

208. See Omohundro, *Chinese Merchant*, 17; Wickberg, *Chinese in Philippine Life*, 172.

209. Felix B. Regalado and Quintin B. Franco, *History of Panay*, ed. Eliza U. Griño (Jaro, Iloilo City: Central Philippine University Press, 1973), 185, 187–189.

210. See pages 40–42 and Abulog, "Chinese Immigration Question in the Philippines," 22; Alejandrino, *History of the 1902 Chinese Exclusion Act*, 12–17. By late 1898, the 1,600 virtually all male Chinese in the province were distributed in Molo, Jaro, La Paz and Iloilo City as well as outlying areas in the province.

211. Omohundro, *Chinese Merchant*, 19–20.

212. Brown was then Secretary of the Foreign Board of PCUSA; he visited the islands for about a month in September 1901. See Rodgers, *Forty Years*, 38–39 and Brown, *New Era*, 80–81.

b) *The Chinese Presbyterian Congregation*

Soldiers and Presbyterian missionaries were the first Americans to enter Iloilo during the turbulent years of 1898–1900.[213] As early as May 1898, the Presbyterians' original plan was to begin work in Manila and Iloilo simultaneously. They believed that just as Manila was the key to Luzon, Iloilo was the key to the Visayas.[214] One of the secretaries of the Young Men's Christian Association (YMCA), Rev John Marvin Dean, witnessed the coming of the first Presbyterian missionaries to Iloilo.[215] Dr David Sutherland Hibbard (term of service 1899–1938) arrived in the Philippines on May 1899; his wife, Laura Catherine Crooks, arrived in June 1899. Joseph Andrew Hall (1867–1960; served from 1900–1937) and his wife, Jean Hotson Russell, arrived in Manila in January 1900 (App. X, Fig. 1). All four missionaries arrived in Iloilo on 13 February 1900,[216] having been delayed by outbreaks of cholera and smallpox in Panay and fighting between American and Filipino forces.[217] John Dean narrates, "I had been in Iloilo but a few brief weeks when my heart was gladdened by the arrival of the first missionaries to the Visayas, the Hibbards and the Halls. As David Hibbard had acquired some knowledge of Spanish they were soon able to open up a service for the natives."[218]

The first Sunday Service for English-speaking people in Iloilo was held on 8 April 1900 and attended by Chinese, Malay, Spanish, Mestizo, English and American. On the following Easter Sunday (15 April), the first service for Filipinos was attended by about seventy people. Their work was greatly helped by the assistance of Adriano Osorio y Reyes, a young

---

213. Lewis E. Gleeck, Jr, "Iloilo: Missionaries, Merchants and the Colonial Establishment I–IV," in *Iloilo in American Times: Excerpts from Bulletin of the American Historical Collection*, 23 (Manila: American Historical Collection Foundation, 1995), 7.

214. Brown, *Report of a Visitation*, 23, and T. Valentino Sitoy, Jr, *A History of Christianity in the Philippines* Vol. 1, *The Initial Encounter* (Quezon City: New Day, 1985), 99.

215. John Bancroft Devins, *An Observer in the Philippines or Life in Our New Possessions* (Boston, MA: American Tract Society, 1905), 330.

216. See *The Sixty-third Annual Report*, 209. For a detailed study on the life and contributions of these four missionaries, see Kwantes, "Presbyterian Missionaries in the Philippines,"143–261.

217. Sitoy, *Initial Encounter*, 99.

218. Dean, *Cross of Christ*, 76–77.

Protestant Visayan converted in Spain.[219] The Presbyterian Church of Iloilo was organized in September 1900. After only six months, the church had ten members.[220] Emily Bronson Conger observed and described the new mission thus, "A Protestant mission was established at Jaro, in a bamboo chapel, pure bamboo throughout, roof, walls, windows, seats, floor. The seats, however, were seldom used, for the natives prefer to squat on the floor. The congregation consisted of men, women, and children, many of whom came on foot for a distance of twenty or some miles, the older people scantily clad, and the children entirely naked."[221] The beginning, then, was truly difficult.

Not only did the Presbyterian missionaries minister to the Westerners and Filipinos, they also worked among the Chinese, as Dean further described:

> There were in Iloilo not a few Chinese merchants whose shops lined the long stretch of *Calle Real* and in addition to the weekly services for Filipinos they were also led to take up work for their profit. This was aside from the main purpose of the mission and was due to the providential presence in Iloilo of a second bright young convert, a Chinaman formerly of the London Mission in Amoy, who only needed slight encouragement to undertake a weekly Bible class among his countrymen.[222]

The encounter with the Chinese, not long after Hall and Hibbard arrived, was quite dramatic. Arthur Brown wrote that the missionaries discovered "two Christian Chinese from Amoy."[223] These Protestant Chinese approached Dr Hall, asking that worship services be held, offering to

---

219. Dean, *Cross of Christ*, 76–77; Joseph Andrew Hall, "Conference on the Philippines," in *Men and Modern Missionary Enterprise: History, Call, Addresses, Deliverances, Conferences and Deliberations of the First Inter–Synodical Foreign Missionary Convention for Men, Held at Omaha; Nebraska, February 19–21, 1907*, ed., Charles Edwin Bradt (Chicago, IL: Winona, 1907), 146. Cf. Rodgers, *Forty Years*, 65–66.

220. Sitoy, *Initial Encounter*, 100.

221. Emily Bronson Conger, *An Ohio Woman in the Philippines Giving Personal Experiences and Descriptions Including Incidents of Honolulu, Ports in Japan and China* (Akron, OH: Richard H. Leighton, 1904), 149.

222. Dean, *Cross of Christ*, 77.

223. Rodgers, *Forty Years*, 66. This may be the same Protestants referred to by Dean.

interpret and also to explain the teachings themselves. In April 1900, as Hall and Hibbard were passing a Chinese shop, one of these Christians ran out and implored Dr Hall to come in and see a man who was very sick. Entering, the missionaries found a raving maniac being held down on a bed by several excited Chinese. The man's condition was very bad, and the Chinese wanted to send him back to China to die in his homeland, but Dr Hall said he would not survive the voyage. The doctor persuaded the Chinese to keep him by promising to do all he could to save his life. The issue was long and doubtful, but under the missionary's skillful care, the patient slowly improved to the point that he was again earning his living. The wonder, delight and gratitude of the Chinese knew no bounds. Dr Hall took advantage of the influence he thus acquired to speak to them of Christ. Soon he began to hold services in that very shop. The work prospered from the beginning, with the result that on 6 October, at the request of Dr Hall, Brown had the great privilege of baptizing ten adult Chinese men. They had faithfully attended the preaching service for a year and a half, and for six weeks they had been specially instructed by Dr Hall in an evening class at his home. With another who was baptized in China, the number of Protestant Chinese believers in Iloilo rose to eleven.

Following this incident, Andrew Hall wrote to Dr Francis F. Ellinwood, then secretary of the Presbyterian Mission for the work in the Philippines and through whose initiative this mission entered the Islands soon after the American occupation.[224] Hall reported:

> I was called in a short time ago to treat a Chinaman who had become temporarily insane and was quite maniacal when I saw him first. In a week he was better and we sent him home to Amoy at the request of his wife. Later I treated several other Chinaman and thought this an opportune time to commence work among this class. A week ago last Sabbath we held our first meeting with five present. . . . We convinced a number of these people last Saturday with the result that thirty were out last Sabbath at 8 o'clock in the morning as that is the hour we

---

224. Today, the Ellinwood Malate Church is named after him. Richard P. Poethig, *60 Years Mission in Manila* (Manila: Ellinwood Malate Church, 1967), [7].

are holding the Chinese service. As there are over one thousand Chinaman in Iloilo, Molo and in Jaro together, this will be an important branch of our work.[225]

The Philippine Mission, meeting in Manila from 18–19 December 1900, upon the proposal of Andrew Hall, resolved that:

(1) This class of men [Chinese] be kept before our minds and that we try to reach them with the gospel in some form in all places possible. (2) That we aim at putting the Bible and other Christian literature into the hands of as many of this people as possible. (3) That since the missionaries in this field cannot undertake to train preachers or evangelists among these people, we take steps to cooperate with the Amoy missionaries with a view to supplying helpers for this work as time may develope [sic].[226]

The following year, the Presbyterian Mission took a step toward enacting this resolution through a preaching tour of Dr and Mrs Arthur Brown. Leander C. Hills[227] confirmed that they went to Iloilo from Dumaguete and were there from 3–8 October 1901. He testifies that "In all he spoke to about 60 Americans, 40 Chinese and 500 Natives. In the Sunday he was here we had . . . for the reception of ten Chinese converts who have been under Dr Hall's instructions for nearly a year, some of them longer. Dr Brown baptized them. *This was really the beginning of our Chinese congregation* [emphasis mine]."[228]

From the records cited above, it becomes clear that at the start the work among the Chinese had the following distinctions: (1) This ministry was

225. Joseph Andrew Hall, Iloilo, P[hilippine] I[slands], to Dr Ellinwood, New York City, 1 May 1900. Yale Divinity School Library Special Collection, text–fiche, 1–2, Sp. Col. Film, MS 11 Reel 287. Yale University, New Haven, Connecticut.

226. *Minutes of Annual Meeting Philippine Mission Held in Manila December 18ᵗʰ to the 19ᵗʰ, 1900.* Yale Divinity School Library Special Collection, text–fiche, 4, Sp. Col. Film, MS 11 Reel 289. Yale University, New Haven, Connecticut.

227. Both Rodgers, Sitoy and other sources used the name Leon C. Hills, but a much earlier source officially used the name Leander C. Hills, although in subsequent minutes the name Leon is also used. *Sixty-third Annual Report*, 209.

228. Leander (a.k.a. Leon) C. Hills (1874–1950), Iloilo, to Dr Ellinwood, New York City, 29 Oct 1901. Yale Divinity School Library Special Collection, text–fiche, 1–2, Sp. Col. Film, MS 11 Reel 288. Yale University, New Haven, Connecticut.

"aside from the main purpose of the mission," (i.e. not planned but a happenstance). (2) It began at about the same time the missionaries ministered to Filipinos and Americans in Iloilo in April 1900. (3) There were several Protestants from Xiamen living in Iloilo who assisted in reaching Chinese non-believers and building up the new converts. One of them, however, soon moved to another place, while the remaining one preached every Sunday and helped as interpreter because his English was quite good.[229] This seems to be the one referred to as "formerly of the London Mission in Amoy" by John Dean. (4) The medical skill and kindness of the missionaries were the points of contact attracting the Chinese to the gospel of Christ. (5) These converts were carefully instructed in the Christian truth before they were baptized.

(1) Growth of the Chinese Congregation

Missionary correspondence and the annual reports of the Presbyterian Mission, as well as a substantially long report found in *The China Mission Year Book* of 1915 attest to the growth of the Chinese congregation.[230] These records differ from what Valentino Sitoy wrote, "When the Presbyterians opened their Iloilo mission station that same year [1900], Dr David S. Hibbard shortly thereafter won to conversion one or two of the Iloilo Chinese merchants. But for the lack of missionaries able to speak Amoy [*Hokkien*] or Cantonese, these tentative efforts had to be abandoned."[231] Sitoy's statement gives the impression that there never was a congregation when in fact there was; it even lasted almost thirty years. The records also differ from the comment by William Yang that the work in Iloilo started in 1911 and there is no "official record of permanent organization."[232] Yang is using Shangkuan's work as the basis of his claim, but both the year and the non-permanent organization are inaccurately presented. On the contrary, the Presbyterians persisted in this work until the late 1920s. The historical

229. *The Sixty-fourth Annual Report*, 262.

230. MacGillivray, ed., *The China Mission Year Book Being "The Christian Movement in China" 1915*, 579.

231. Cf. T. Valentino Sitoy, Jr, *Several Springs, One Stream: The United Church of Christ in the Philippines*, Volume 2: *The Formative Decade (1948–1958)* (Quezon City: United Church of Christ in the Philippines, 1997), 941.

232. Yang, "Chinese Protestant Churches in the Philippines," 170–171.

development, covering the period from around 1901 to 1925, can be reconstructed from the minutes of the Presbyterian Mission in the Philippines and the annual reports that were submitted to the New York headquarters.

Around 1901, after visiting the Islands, Arthur Brown reported to the BFM-PCUSA regarding the Chinese work being done in both the Manila and Visayan stations. Brown contended that the Chinese should not be ignored by the mission; that there is no need for a full-time missionary to oversee the work. The missionary need not learn the Chinese language because the Chinese could understand either Spanish [the medium used by pioneering Protestant missionaries], Tagalog, or Visayan, but Brown acknowledged that the work was hampered because Spanish was, after all, foreign to both speakers and their hearers. Furthermore, in his opinion, the Chinese, being well-to-do, would soon become self-supporting and the missionaries could seek the help of mission boards in China to send visiting preachers. A native pastor was urgently needed, and the members could be induced to pay for his salary. The mission would continue to allow the Chinese congregation free use of their church for their meetings. Brown concluded his assessment by stating: "The work, while important, will always be under native helpers and subsidiary as compared with the Filipino work."[233]

The Philippine Mission, meeting from 8–15 December 1902, reported that the Chinese believers were taking turns as preachers during the Sunday services while the missionary, using Visayan, conducted a weekly Bible class attended by an average of seven, four of whom joined the church during the year. In August the Chinese themselves set aside $40 per month for a year to support a preacher "who could give all his time to teaching others and so double our membership in a year as well as train some of them to continue the work." But in reality no such preacher was available, for in China, every available man was needed.[234]

In a letter to Francis Ellinwood dated 15 June 1903, Andrew Hall reported that the work was progressing nicely, but attendance was not regular.

---

233. Brown, *Report of a Visitation*, 57–59.

234. *Minutes of the Third Annual Meeting of the Philippine Mission, Iloilo, P[hilippine] I[slands], December 8–15, 1902.* Yale Divinity School Library Special Collection, text–fiche, Sp. Col. Film, Ms 11 Reel 289. Yale University, New Haven, Connecticut.

He wrote that "All but four of our Chinese members are in China or else-where and our audience was reduced to six and seven for a few Sundays but is now up to twenty the past two weeks again and we hope to increase it still more."[235]

Finally, in 1908, an evangelist named Tan Su Wong took charge of the Chinese congregation. Meetings were held every Sunday afternoon, attended by about twenty-five Chinese, and a well-attended prayer meeting was held every Thursday evening. Wong was very active in pastoral visitation; he also conducted a school for Chinese children. Twelve adults were added to this congregation during the year. However, a portion of the thirty-five members were always absent from Iloilo.[236]

The 1909 report was less than positive as well. Many members were absent for a great part of the year, and such mobility starts to give a hint as to why CPCI eventually declined. Mr Wong, the evangelist, was attending college in Xiamen and it was hoped that he could be sent back for a third year and ordination, in order that he may become its resident pastor. Though few in number, CPCI members had maintained their allegiance to the church, and had even given liberally of their means to support its work.[237]

Beginning in 1910, the reports became more infrequent and less de-tailed. There is evidence that the Baptist and Presbyterian missionaries were cooperating in the ministry among the Americans in Panay, but there is no hint whether this cooperation also included CPCI. This cooperation, as will be seen subsequently, would lead to an exchange of mission territory that would in turn affect the future of the Presbyterian ministry among the Chinese. It was also reported that Mr Wong continued to preach to the Chinese and was teaching English to help support himself.[238]

---

235. Joseph Andrew Hall, Iloilo, to Dr Ellinwood, New York City, 15 Jun 1903. Yale Divinity School Library Special Collection, text–fiche, 2, Sp. Col. Film, Ms 11 Reel 288. Yale University, New Haven, Connecticut.

236. *The Seventy-first Annual Report of the Board of Foreign Missions of the Presbyterian Church in the United States of America Presented to the General Assembly, May, 1908* (New York: Presbyterian Building, 1908), 381.

237. *The Seventy-second Annual Report of the Board of Foreign Missions of the Presbyterian Church in the United States of America Presented to the General Assembly, May, 1909* (New York: Presbyterian Building, 1909), 374.

238. *The Seventy-third Annual Report of the Board of Foreign Missions of the Presbyterian Church in the United States of America Presented to the General Assembly, May, 1910* (New

In the report of 1911, there was only a passing remark that CPCI was one of the ten congregations organized in the Iloilo station.[239] In 1915, Andrew Hall published a report in *The China Mission Year Book*. After a decade of mission work, the missionaries had baptized fifty-five Chinese believers, but most of these had either moved elsewhere or returned to China or died. The report gave more details regarding the background and performance of the evangelist Tan Su Wong. In 1905, he had given up a good position with one of the leading firms in Iloilo, and had gone back and forth to Xiamen for his college education, his expenses being underwritten by the Chinese congregation. However, as this was the time when a revolution was taking place in China and overseas Chinese were sending funds to help the revolutionists, the congregation was facing financial difficulties. The missionaries, however, hesitated to ordain the evangelist because since his return from Xiamen he had not been performing well in his work and they could not find out why. The congregation was not increasing in number, and they would not ordain elders or officers as recommended by the missionaries.[240]

By 1917, the growth seems to have tapered off and that year's report stated as much: "The *Chinese congregation* has not grown in numbers during the year, but the services have been kept up regularly and have been fairly well attended by the members and a few who are not members."[241] The next year, not only was there a problem of declining membership, the pastor in charge was resigning, leaving the congregation without a leader. Attendance had decreased to around ten to twenty.[242]

In the next decade, the situation remained the same, with a new Chinese worker and a missionary in the field. The Rev Herman Ray Berger (term

York: Presbyterian Building, 1910), 353.

239. *The Seventy-fourth Annual Report of the Board of Foreign Missions of the Presbyterian Church in the United States of America Presented to the General Assembly, May, 1911* (New York: Presbyterian Building, 1911), 338.

240. MacGillivray, ed., *China Mission Year Book 1915*, 579–580.

241. *The Eightieth Annual Report of the Board of Foreign Missions of the Presbyterian Church in the United States of America Presented to the General Assembly, May, 1917* (New York: Presbyterian Building, 1917), 319.

242. *The Eighty-first Annual Report of the Board of Foreign Missions of the Presbyterian Church in the United States of America Presented to the General Assembly, May, 1918* (New York: Presbyterian Building, 1918), 299.

of service 1915–1924), reporting that Mr Wung Kuanty alternated with him in preaching, stated that, "Two young men were baptized this year, with promise of several others before long. Two others are beginning to help in the services."[243] James Rodgers added that "Yung Kuanty" was a teacher in the Chinese Commercial School. However, Dr Hall, who was on furlough, was the pastor of the Chinese congregation, and he would again take charge on his return to Iloilo.[244]

Note that the surname of the Chinese worker was spelled differently by Berger and by Rodgers. This might be a typographical error or a variation in the phonetical notation of the same Chinese character. Unfortunately, without other sources of information in Chinese, there is no way of finding out which spelling is the right one. In another source, *The Philippine Presbyterian*, mention is made of the same pastor Yung and his assistant, a Ms Si, daughter of a pastor in China and a very active worker. She played the piano and even sometimes preached a sermon.[245]

(2) Decline and Disbandment

The major event in Panay, occurring in 1925, was the turnover of the Presbyterian territory in Iloilo Province to the American Baptists. Early in 1901 a division of territory in this region had been agreed upon, wherein the Baptists would work in the northern half of Iloilo province, Capiz and Concepcion provinces, and the Presbyterians would work in Iloilo City, the southern half of the province and Antique.[246] A year later, there was a modification whereby a demarcation line was drawn running from Iloilo to the northwestern tip of the island. The Presbyterians worked west of this line while the Baptists worked to the east. Throughout the years there was mutual cooperation and respect, although there was considerable tension over such issues as mode of baptism. By virtue of the Presbyterian-Baptist

---

243. *The Eighty-fourth Annual Report of the Board of Foreign Missions of the Presbyterian Church in the United States of America Presented to the General Assembly, May, 1921* (New York: Presbyterian Building, 1921), 353.

244. Rodgers, *Twenty Years of Presbyterian Work*, 55.

245. "Evangelistic Work: A Chinese Woman Preaches," *The Philippine Presbyterian* 13, no. 1 (Jan 1922): 9.

246. Milton Walter Meyer, "The Course of Early Baptist Mission in the Philippines (2)," in *The American Era in the Philippines. Bulletin of the American Historical Collection* 15, no. 3 (Jul–Sep 1987): 41.

Comity Agreement of 1925, the Presbyterians and the Baptists exchanged mission territories, the latter surrendering Samar and the former giving up the province of Antique and the southern part of Iloilo.[247] A spirit of cooperation still prevailed during this time.

Before the turnover much time was spent in considering the withdrawal of the Presbyterian staff from the Iloilo station, as manifested in the 1925 *Minutes of the Executive Committee of the Presbyterian Mission*. As recommended by the Philippine Mission and approved by both the Presbyterian and Baptist Boards, the resolution for Presbyterians to withdraw from Panay was passed on 1 April 1925. However, the report states, "the step is taken because we are fully convinced that our acceptance in exchange for the Panay field of the large unevangelized, but more conveniently situated island of Samar means much for the larger interests of the Kingdom in the Philippines."[248]

CPCI is nowhere mentioned in this document. What happened to this congregation? I surmise that it eventually declined and ceased to exist. The question is why? Omohundro's analysis of the socio-economic condition in Iloilo during the thirties might provide a clue to the first reason:

> Dissipation, growth of family without commensurate economic success, troubles in China, and the world depressions of the 1930s, all served to break up these *Hokkien* families, destroy or disperse their wealth, and remove them from the Iloilo limelight. Many mestizo branches of these *Hokkien* families merged into Filipino society. Some members moved to more enticing economic climates elsewhere in the Philippines, especially the sugar-rich areas or cities like Bacolod and Cebu. Some returned to China.[249]

After the economic depression hit Iloilo in October 1929, a perfectly timed strike led by the principal union leader Jose Nava in May 1930 put the

---

247. Henry Weston Munger, *Christ and the Filipino Soul* (Iloilo: Mrs Laura Lee Munger and Mrs Laura Lee Marques, 1967), 67.

248. *Minutes of the Executive Committee of the Presbyterian Mission in the Philippine Islands, Iloilo, March Sixteenth through the Twentieth Nineteen Twenty-Five*, 25–26.

249. Omohundro, *Chinese Merchant*, 21.

waterfront out of business.[250] These social and economic upheavals may have caused Protestant Chinese from CPCI to transfer to other places in order to find work or better business opportunities.

The turnover of Presbyterian mission territory to the American Baptist Mission in 1925 might be another factor. Sitoy writes that after this event, "there was an alienation between the Presbyterian Board and the Panay Presbyterian churches. When the Philippine Synod joined in the union of 1929, the latter constituted themselves into an Independent Presbyterian Church, thus proclaiming a *de facto* schism."[251] This tension and rift within Presbyterian ranks lasted until 1935 when the Panay Presbyterians finally joined the United Evangelical Church in 1935. As far as I can gather, there seems to be no record whether CPCI remained with the Philippine Synod or allied themselves with the Independent Presbyterian Church in Panay, but it can be easily surmised that the situation may have left the Chinese congregation with a much-weakened missionary oversight, at a time when there was also no Chinese pastor. This may have hastened the decline in membership and caused CPCI to disband around 1928.

c) Other Chinese Churches in Iloilo

With regard to the question of whether the Baptists ever took charge of the Chinese congregation after the turnover, the only record I found is a short entry in *The Message*, a publication of the Baptist mission, cited by Elaine Kennedy.[252] This source gives a hint regarding the year that CPCI disbanded. It shows that Baptist missionary Ellen Martien organized English Bible classes for the Chinese in Iloilo from 1933–1936. In June 1934, Simon Meek/Miao ShaoXun 繆紹訓先生, a Chinese evangelist from the Christian Gospel Center (Little Flock) in Manila, conducted evangelistic meetings among the Chinese of Iloilo resulting in the "*re-opening of a Chinese church that had been abandoned six years before*" [i.e. in 1928,

---

250. Lewis E. Gleeck, Jr "Iloilo: Missionaries, Merchants and the Colonial Establishment (I)," in *Iloilo in American Times*. Bulletin of the American Historical Collection 23 (Manila: American Historical Collection Foundation, 1995), 77.

251. See Sitoy, *Initial Encounter*, 381–386, for a complete discussion of the succeeding developments within the two missions.

252. *The Message* (Oct 1934 and Jun 1936), 3–4; quoted in Elaine J. Kennedy, *Baptist Centennial History of the Philippines (1900–1999)* (Makati City: Church Strengthening Ministry, 1999), 133.

emphasis mine]. A Filipino Baptist pastor named Mr Galila [first name unknown] preached at the Wednesday afternoon evangelistic services. Soon after the Iloilo Chinese Christian Church 怡郎中華基督教會禮拜堂 (ICCC) was established, and Rev Lim Siong Hong/Lin XiangFeng 林翔鳳牧師 (1905–1990), also known as by his legal name Joseph Lim Tiao Hong, came from China to pastor the church (App. X, Fig. 3). Rev Lim was a convert of Leland Wang Dai 王戴, and a graduate of the Wuchow Alliance Bible Seminary 梧洲宣道神學院 in Guangxi, China 中國廣西.[253] Miss Martien described him as thoroughly fundamental with Baptist convictions. The Baptist record thus reveals that the Chinese church established by the Presbyterians was eventually abandoned and closed.

The establishment of the ICCC was recorded in the 1969 publication of Shih Chang Shangkuan. He wrote that in 1934, some Christians residing in Iloilo took turns holding services in their homes. They were Mr and Mrs Ong Siong Kim/Wang ShangQin 王尚琴夫婦 (App. X, Fig. 3), Mr and Mrs Kua Eng Chiong/Ke RongZhang 柯榮章夫婦, and Mr Yu Un Tian/Yang EnDian 楊恩典 (a.k.a. Yu Ka Bo/Yang JiaMo 嘉謨). Shangkuan provided the same information regarding the visit of Simon Meek's visit, but added that it was Meek who recommended Lim Siong Hong to be the pastor. The worship services after Lim arrived were held in Liang Fu Baptist Church 良福浸信會. I surmise that this is a transliteration of the name of a Baptist church, most likely Filipino, in Iloilo City. When interviewed, Rev Ong Kim Ja vda. de Chua/Cai Wang JinXia 蔡王錦霞牧師 (b. 1927), the daughter of Ong Siong Kim, mentioned that as a child she attended services at the Doane Hall Baptist Church with her mother, before their

---

253. The name of the CMA seminary written in Kennedy's book is Christian Alliance Bible Institute of Wuchow, South China. In Chinese the name is *Jiandao Shengjing Shuyuan* 建道聖經書院, which was the name used in 1899 when Robert Hall Glover established the Bible school. Because of the Boxer Rebellion (1900), the school was moved to Macau, then it was reopened in 1902 in Wuzhou 梧洲. The name of the school was changed to Alliance Bible Seminary/*Jiandao Shenxueyuan* 建道神學院 in 1936. In 1950 the seminary, after many relocations, was permanently situated in Hong Kong. See Leung Ka-lun 梁家麟, *Huaren Xuandaohui Bainianshi* 華人宣導會百年史 (A centenary history of the Chinese C&MA) (Hong Kong: Alliance Bible Seminary Christianity and Chinese Culture Research Centre, 1998), 35–36; Philip Loh 羅腓力, *Xuanjiao Yu Zhongguo – Xuandaohui Zhaoqi Zaihua Xuanjiao Shilue* 宣道與中國 —宣道會早期在華宣教史略 (Send the Doves to the Dragon: Footprints of Christian Alliance Missionaries in the Early 20th Century China) (Hong Kong, China Alliance Press, 1997), 129–132.

family set up the Iloilo Chinese Christian Church, but she has no recollection of any Presbyterian Chinese church.[254]

Shangkuan further wrote that in 1939, a piece of land was donated by Ong Siong Kim and a church building was constructed. The inauguration was held in March 1940, but WWII broke out in December the next year. Japanese troops entered Iloilo on 16 April 1942 and the new building went up in flames. After WWII the Christians regathered and renamed their church as Iloilo Christian Assembly 怡郎基督徒聚會所. When the membership was around 170–180, the officer-in-charge was Chuang Tek Tiam/Chuang DeTian 莊德添, one of the Chuang brothers from Dumaguete City.[255]

However, my view differs from the information found in both *The Message* and in Shangkuan's account. Based on what I have learned through mission records and the eyewitness accounts of the descendants of the founding members of the ICCC, this church should not be identified with the one established by the Presbyterians (CPCI). The three second-generation witnesses who were interviewed were: Ong Kim Ja, Kua Bee Tin/Ke MeiZhen 柯美珍 and Kua Ka Tin/Ke JiaZhen 柯佳珍 (the daughters of Mr Kua Eng Chiong), and Lim King Hua vda. de Ong/Wang Lin JingHua 王林璟華 (b. 1928, the daughter of Rev Lim Siong Hong). None of them were aware of the work of the Presbyterians among the Chinese of Iloilo City or of CPCI. They all claim that there was no Chinese church before their parents organized the ICCC. The Kua sisters affirmed that meetings were held in their home and the Christians mentioned by Shangkuan took turns leading.[256] Ong Kim Ja confirmed that her father donated the land and a church was built, and all recall that the pastor during and after the war was Lim Siong Hong.

Ong Kim Ja provides additional information regarding the second Chinese church in Iloilo. She claims that the Christian Gospel Center was not present in Iloilo before the war; it was only after liberation that they

---

254. Ong Kim Ja vda. de Chua/Cai Wang JinXia 蔡王錦霞, telephone interview by Jean Uayan, Quezon City, 9 Nov 2004 and 7 Apr 2005. Audio-taped transcript, Philippine Chinese Church Archive, Biblical Seminary of the Philippines, Valenzuela City, Philippines.

255. Shangkuan, "Pure Faith," in *HDPO*, 151.

256. Kua Bee Tin/Ke MeiZhen 柯美珍 and Kua Ka Tin/Ke JiaZhen 柯佳珍, telephone interview by Jean Uayan, Manila, 6 Oct 2005. Audio-tape transcript, Philippine Chinese Church Archive, Biblical Seminary of the Philippines, Valenzuela City, Philippines.

approached her mother about the vacant lot. Her mother agreed to sell it to them. This may not be entirely accurate since the Baptist source cited above does indicate that Simon Meek of the Christian Gospel Center conducted meetings in Iloilo around 1934. Soon after, people from CUEC, which had come into existence in Manila in 1929, approached her mother for the same purpose. Another difference was the year when the church edifice was built. She says construction did not start immediately in 1934/1935, but only in 1940 and the inauguration was at the beginning of 1941. By this time Rev Lim Siong Hong was already pastor of ICCC. The name of the church would lend support to Ong Kim Ja's assertion that the Christian Gospel Center did not establish this church in Iloilo before the war. They would never have used the word "Church" in their nomenclature since they despised the denominational connotation of the term and preferred to be known as "local assemblies." It was the view of Watchman Nee that denominations divide Christians, that believers of Christ should be members of Christ's body, not of a certain church. This group also holds that in every locality, there should only be one church.[257] All of their assemblies use either the name "Christian Gospel Center" or the "Church Assembly Hall" and add their geographical locations for specific identification.

According to Lim King Hua, the Chinese, including the church members, scattered when the Japanese attacked Iloilo, many hiding in the mountains. A Japanese pastor who went around asking about the pastor of the Chinese church, found Rev Lim and assured him no harm would come to his members if they continued their service, so they met at Rev Lim's home. This was around 1944. Since the church membership was small and conditions difficult during wartime, he was not being supported financially. He therefore went into business, his wife selling *toge* (bean sprouts) in order to augment their meager income.[258] Ong Kim Ja said that after

257. See Watchman Nee, *The Normal Christian Church Life* (Anaheim, CA: Living Stream Ministry, 1980), 110–111; for Nee's ecclesiology, cf. chapters 8 and 12 of this work. Witness Lee, *The History of the Church and the Local Churches* (Anaheim, CA: Living Stream Ministry, 1991), 73. The complete texts of both works are available online at http://www.ministrybooks.org/books.

258. Lim King Hua vda. de Ong/Wang Lin JingHua 王林璟華, personal interview by Jean Uayan, Malabon City, 9 Jul 2005. Transcript. Philippine Chinese Church Archives, Biblical Seminary of the Philippines, Valenzuela City, Philippines.

the war, this church also disbanded because the members were scattered. The Iloilo Christian Gospel Assembly Center, Inc. (ICGAC), was set up in 1953. Significantly, the name includes terminology from both groups belonging to the "assembly" movement led by Watchman Nee and Witness Lee. In the 1980s the UECP and the Bacolod Trinity Church 描戈律基督教三一堂 formally established the Iloilo Trinity Christian Church 怡郎基督教三一堂. Today, these two are the only Chinese churches existing in Iloilo City. At present, the four-story building owned by the ICGAC occupies the lot where the burned-down ICCC used to be located.[259]

This study has established that the Presbyterian missionaries did start work among the Chinese the moment they arrived in 1900 and throughout the succeeding two decades, albeit they considered such ministry subsidiary in status to the Filipino ministry. The church actually existed and was even known in China, for the report in *The China Mission Year Book* affirmed its existence in 1915. It states, "There are only two congregations of Chinese in the Philippine Islands – one connected with the Cathedral of the Episcopal Church in Manila, and one with the Presbyterian Mission in Iloilo."[260] Although we may never know for certain its official name, and even if it did cease to exist in the 1920s, CPCI should rightfully be considered the *first* Chinese church in the Philippines. This church, according to Andrew Hall, tried to be self-supporting in the sense that the members paid for a major portion of the salary of their pastor or Christian worker. Yet there were times when the congregation dwindled and such support became insufficient. However, throughout its existence, the Presbyterian Mission closely monitored its needs for native preachers and pastors. The church never reached a point of total devolution because of this deficiency in terms of native leadership. Furthermore, it ceased to exist due to deteriorating economy that subsequently caused migration among the Chinese of Iloilo, and also because of the exchange of mission territories between Presbyterians and Baptists in the mid-1920s.

The next section will focus on the mission of the Episcopalians among the Chinese in Manila five years after the Americans occupied the Philippines.

---

259. Ong Kim Ja vda. de Chua, interview.
260. MacGillivray, ed., *China Mission Year Book 1915*, 577.

Today, St. Stephen's Parish (SSP) can and should be considered the *oldest existing* Philippine Protestant Chinese church, but not the first to be established in the Philippines. In reality, it is actually the *fourth* Chinese congregation to emerge in the Philippines, following two unnamed congregations in Manila, one belonging to the Presbyterian mission and the other to the Methodist mission, and the third one in Iloilo (CPCI). As already noted, the Presbyterian work among the Chinese in Manila began in 1900, hence, the Manila and the Iloilo congregations can be said to have emerged in the same year, but mission records do not indicate the exact date for the emergence of the former. With regard to the Methodist Chinese congregation, it is a known fact that the first Methodist meeting in Manila took place on 5 March 1899, and that the Chinese work was turned over to the Episcopalians in 1907. There is, however, a remote possibility that the Methodist Chinese group also began in 1900. The following history of the establishment of SSP, or what was then called "St. Stephen's Chinese Mission (SSCM)," will shed more light on this matter.

3. St. Stephen's Chinese Mission

The oldest existing Chinese church in the Philippines is St. Stephen's Parish/ Feilübin Huaqiao Shenggonghui Sheng Sitifen Tang 菲律賓華僑聖公會聖司提芬堂, formerly called the Cathedral Mission of St. Stephen (Chinese),[261] or St. Stephen's Mission for Chinese,[262] and, in some sources, St. Stephen's Chinese Mission (SSCM), or, even shorter, St. Stephen's Church/Sheng Sitifen Tang 聖司提反堂.[263] St. Stephen's Chinese Mission is the name used in all the reports of the Missionary District of the Philippine Islands,

261. *Diamond Jubilee: Sixtieth Anniversary Souvenir of the St. Stephen's Parish (Feilübin Huaqiao Shenggonghui Liushi Zhounian Jinian Tekan)* 菲律賓華僑聖公會六十周年紀念特刊 (Manila: St. Stephen's Parish, [1963]), 1 (henceforth cited as *St. Stephen's Diamond Jubilee*); and Gowen, Philippine Kaleidoscope, 22.

262. Studley, "Chinese Experiment," 576 and *The Twentieth Annual Report of the Missionary District of the Philippine Islands for the Year Ending December 31, 1927* (Manila: n.p., 1928), 41.

263. This name is found in the *St. Stephen's Church Episcopal Golden Jubilee Souvenir 1903–1953 (Huaqiao Shenggonghui Wushi Zhounian Jinian Tekan)* 華僑聖公會五十周年紀念刊 (Manila: St. Stephen's Parish, [1953]), 3 (henceforth cited as *St. Stephen's Golden Jubilee*). It should not be confused with the American congregation that had the same name until it was called Cathedral of St. Mary and St. John. On the other hand the name "St. Stephen's Chinese Mission" is used in Charles Henry Brent, "Sixteen Years in the Philippines," *The Spirit of Missions* 82 (Mar 1918): 177.

110
A Study on the Emergence and Early Development of
Selected Protestant Chinese Churches in the Philippines

hence, I have consistently used SSCM throughout this work. The date for the establishment of SSCM is officially recognized as 8 November 1903, when, according to SSP anniversary publications, the first Episcopalian service conducted in the *Hokkien* dialect was held in rented quarters on *Calle San Fernando*.[264] However, the pre-history of SSCM can be traced back to 5 October 1898, with the following events leading up to its emergence: (1) the deliberation of the Protestant Episcopal Church in the United States of America (henceforth PEC) to set up the Missionary District of the Philippines; (2) the coming of Episcopalian chaplains during the Spanish-American War and the work of the Brotherhood of St. Andrew; (3) the attempts and setback of these chaplains as they ministered among the Chinese; (4) the Methodist and Presbyterian work among the Chinese in Manila; (5) the consecration of Charles Henry Brent/Bou LanDe 勃藍 [or 蘭] 德主教 (1862–1929, term of service 1901–1917) as Protestant Episcopal Bishop of the Missionary District of the Philippine Islands; and finally, (6) the appointment of Rev Hobart Studley (App. Y, Fig. 1) as pastor of SSCM.

a) Deliberation and Indecision

Felipe Agoncillo sent a letter on 5 October 1898 to the Protestant Episcopal Church (PEC) and it was presented for discussion during its Triennial General Convention. Agoncillo asked on behalf of the Philippines that the Americans pray for friendship and union between the two countries to become permanent, and that an "evangelical fraternity" be impressed by the PEC prelates. As a result of this meeting, it was considered that the accession of territory meant increased missionary responsibility, but no action was taken with regard to establishing a missionary foothold in the country.[265]

Mark Douglas Norbeck writes that this was the first time the PEC debated whether or not to send missionaries to the Philippines. Despite the political uncertainty at the time, there were many, including Bishop Daniel S. Tuttle of Missouri, who urged immediate and bold action in the

---

264. Kate Chollipas Botengan, *Transformed by the Word; Transforming the World: One Hundred Years of Episcopal Church in the Philippines* (Quezon City: Episcopal Church in the Philippines (ECP), 2001), 11; St. Stephen's Golden Jubilee.

265. *The Journal of the Proceedings of the Bishops Clergy and Laity of the Protestant Episcopal Church in the United States of America Assembled in a General Convention Held in the City of Washington from October 5 to October 25 Inclusive in the Year of Our Lord 1898 with Appendices* (Boston, MA: Alfred Mudge & Son, 1899), 217–218, 458.

Islands. Yet there were also those who were uneasy about the PEC rushing into the Philippines. One of those who expressed doubt was the Bishop of New York, Henry C. Potter (who would later recommend Brent as bishop). Writing in *The Churchman* in 1900, he expressed concern whether it was worthwhile to send missionaries to the Philippines since the Filipinos were "largely a Christian people." It would seem to be an intrusion to send teachers and teachings which the Roman Catholic Church had taught them to regard as belonging to the devil. It might inflame prejudice on the part of the Filipinos and "awaken violent religious controversy."[266] Thus the decision was tabled until the next Convention in 1901.[267] The PEC was therefore dependent upon military chaplains and short-term measures to keep the Philippines open for future mission work, while at the same time frustrations grew over the meager effort being done in the Islands.

b) Chaplains and the Brotherhood of St. Andrew

Chaplains who represented both the United States Army and the PEC arrived in 1898. Charles Campbell Pierce held the first public Anglican service in late August 1898 in the residence of English businessman Frederick Wilson.[268] This congregation became known as the Anglo-American Church.[269] He also started to minister to the Filipino residents of Manila, on top of his mortuary duties and oversight of the Anglo-American Church. He became popular among the Filipinos because of his generous heart and sweet character. At first hesitant to proselytize among the Roman Catholic Filipinos, he acceded to the Filipinos' plea for a Spanish language service. Finally, on Christmas morning, 25 December 1898, Pierce inaugurated the

266. Henry C. Potter, "Bishop Potter: On the Church Question in the Philippines," *The Churchman* (24 Mar 1900): 354, quoted in Mark Douglas Norbeck, "The Protestant Episcopal Church in the City of Manila, Philippine Islands from 1898–1918: An Institutional History" (MA thesis, University of Texas at El Paso, 1992), 193–194.

267. Mark Douglas Norbeck, "False Start: The First Three Years of Episcopal Missionary Endeavor in the Philippine Islands, 1898–1901," *Anglican and Episcopal History* 62, no. 2 (Jun 1993): 226–227.

268. Norbeck, "False Start," 215–216.

269. Another source gives the date 4 Sep 1898 and the location as #4 General Solano, San Miguel, Manila. Kate Chollipas Botengan, "The Horizon of the Past," in *Pearl for the Episcopal Diocese of Central Philippines "Recapturing the Zeal for Mission* (Quezon City: Episcopal Diocese of Central Philippines, 2002), 1; Conrad Myrick, "The Episcopal Church in the Philippines," in Joseph Graessle Moore, *A Study of the Episcopal Church in the Missionary District of the Philippines* (Quezon City: n. p., 1962), 1.

first Filipino PEC in a schoolhouse in Malate.[270] It was his custom to hold two services each day: one in the morning for Americans and Englishmen, and another in the evening for Filipinos.[271]

The Protestant Episcopal Bishop of Shanghai, the Rt Rev Frederick Rogers Graves (1858–1940), was given temporary jurisdiction over the work in the Philippines in September 1899.[272] A missionary to China since 1881, Graves visited the Philippines in 1899 to confirm five persons and receive seven Filipinos into the communion.[273] However, Pierce wrote that the outbreak of hostility between Filipinos and Americans scattered the communicants, the Filipino congregation numbering one hundred fifty by this time, and "the failure of the Church at home" prevented the normal development of this church. In 1900, the bishop himself requested that he be relieved of this distant responsibility, and that a bishop be elected to have exclusive jurisdiction in the Philippines.[274]

c) Attempts and Setback in Chinese Work

(1) The Ministries of Pierce, Marvine and Clapp

Pierce also ministered to the Chinese, baptizing twelve of them in Manila during his term of service. However, he credits his colleague, Walter Marvine, as being the first to baptize three "Chinamen."[275] Hence, the earliest records on Chinese work by the PEC sets the number of baptized

---

270. Charles Campbell Pierce, "Philippine Beginnings and Philippine Possibilities," *The Spirit of Missions* 65 (1900): 378.

271. *The Outlook* 63, no. 11 (11 Nov 1899), 611–612, accessed 31 Dec 2015, https:// www.unz.org/Pub/Outlook–1899nov11–00611.

272. See Botengan, "The Rt Rev Frederick Rogers Graves, DD," in *Transformed by the Word*, 113 and *The Journal of the Bishops Clergy and Laity Assembled in General Convention in the City of San Francisco on the First Wednesday in October A.D. 1901 with Appendices* (Boston, MA: Alfred Mudge & Son, 1902), 12–14. Cf. *The Living Church Annual and Whittaker's Churchman's Almanac: A Church Cyclopedia and Almanac 1910* (Milwaukee, WI: Young Churchman Co., 1910), 333.

273. Pierce, "Philippine Beginnings," 379; Botengan, "Horizon," 1. The PEC had two missionary districts in China, one in Shanghai 上海 and the other in Hankou 漢口. Graves served as "bishop-in-charge" of the Philippines from 1899–1902, then again from 1918–1920.

274. *Handbooks on the Missions of the Episcopal Church, Number 3: Philippine Islands* (New York: National Council of the Protestant Episcopal Church Department of Missions, 1923), 13 (henceforth cited as *Handbooks*). This is a series of work, hence, the plural title.

275. Pierce, "Philippine Beginnings," 380–381.

Protestant Chinese at fifteen. Concerning this ministry among the Chinese, Pierce wrote that a large number of Chinese and Filipinos attended the meetings that were conducted in Spanish. Some of the most influential Chinese in the city expressed great interest in the establishment of an Episcopal church in the Philippines and even asked for the privilege of aiding it financially. Furthermore, Pierce envisioned that this ministry would impact mission in China as the Chinese who embraced the Protestant faith in the Philippines would be burdened for the conversion of their kinsmen in their homeland.[276]

Norbeck adds that it was the three Chinese men who approached Chaplain Marvine for baptism. However, Marvine's ministry with the Chinese was short-lived, for he left the Philippines in 1900 with his regiment to help suppress the Boxer Rebellion in China. Norbeck further comments that, "like Pierce's work with the Filipinos, Marvine's effort with the Chinese withered and died until the Board of Managers found someone to pick it up."[277]

The next missionary to come into contact with the Chinese was Rev Walter C. Clapp. He had been sent by the Board of Missions to investigate prospective sites for mission work, which he did from 19 November to 20 December 1901.[278] This venture was part of the actions taken by the PEC during its Triennial General Convention held in San Francisco a month before Clapp's journey, on 5 October 1901, when the Philippines was finally made into a missionary district. On 14 October, Charles Brent, rector of St. Stephen's Church, Boston, was elected bishop of this district.[279] Pierce, who had returned to the States for health reasons, was elected bishop of the Missionary District of North Dakota.[280]

Part of the observation and report made by Clapp concerned "the Chinese opportunity." He narrated that a Roman Catholic Filipino brought two or three Chinese men for instruction preparatory to baptism. One of

---

276. Pierce, "Philippine Beginnings," 381.

277. Norbeck, "Protestant Episcopal," 248–249.

278. Walter C. Clapp, "Some Notes of Matters Philippine," *The Spirit of Missions* 68 (May 1903): 329.

279. *JCG* (1902), 219, 256, 262, 276, 339.

280. See also Norbeck, "False Start," 222–234, for a more complete picture of Pierce's work in the Philippines.

the candidates was a small boy who attended the Chinese public school, where he learned enough English to enable him to use a simple English catechism. The other knew some Spanish, so Clapp prepared a Spanish catechism for him. He further stated that "There are some 60,000 Chinese in Manila, and many scattered through the provinces. All my observation leads me to think that they constitute an especially inviting field, and a legitimate one, for our efforts at evangelization. The prospect that after a little [sic] a specially trained worker may be assigned to this work is certainly very welcome."[281]

Note the similarity between the experiences of Marvine and Clapp: the Chinese approached them for baptism. The missionary who formally initiated Chinese mission in Manila, Bishop Brent, revealed in a comment made in 1905 the reason why the Chinese were so interested in being baptized. He wrote that "the Christianity of the Manila Chinese in the past has been largely a matter of social or commercial convenience. There is a good deal of intermarriage with Filipinos . . . It has been impossible for a Chinese to get married hitherto unless baptized."[282] Other benefits of being baptized included: reduced taxes, land grants, freedom to reside anywhere, and acquiring of Spanish godparents who could be depended upon as bondsmen, creditors, patrons, and protectors in legal matters. During the early years of American occupation, the Chinese apparently thought that this practice was still in force. Thus when Hobart Studley began his ministry, several people came to him the day before their weddings and offered the priest generous fees if he would administer the rite. Homer Stuntz stated that a fee of from $5 to $100 was required by the friars for baptism. Studley refused and was indignant that they believed Christianity could be bought for a fee.[283] He was further incensed when he found out that many of these men already had wives back in China and intended to maintain two families simultaneously.

---

281. Clapp, "Some Notes on Matters Philippine," 329–330.

282. Brent, "Religious Conditions in the Philippines," 51–52.

283. Rafael Comenge y Dalmau, *Cuestiones Filipinas 1ª Parte Los Chinos (Estudio Social y Politico)* [Philippine questions: Part 1, the Chinese (social and political studies)] (Manila: Tipo–litografia de Chofre y Comp., 1894), 195–197. See also Wickberg, *Chinese in Philippine Life*, 16; Stuntz, *Philippines and the Far East*, 275.

(2) False Starts and Early Developments

As explained above, the first three years (1899–1901) of Episcopal work in the Philippines can be considered a "false start," because what could have begun in 1898 or 1899 had to wait until late 1901 when the Philippines officially became a missionary district and concerted efforts began. Norbeck finds that the PEC and the executors of its mission board were not able to deal quickly with the backlog of demands from the old as well as the new mission fields during the period from 1897 to 1899. During this period the Episcopalians were generally apathetic about foreign missions, as reflected by their dismal financing of mission work. Its diocesan system hampered the rapid establishment of a new field because a missionary district had to be created first, before any major expenditures could be made toward its propagation. This often had to wait for three years because the General Assembly met only triennially.[284]

Thus, despite the early contacts made by Chaplains Marvine, Pierce, and Clapp, no Episcopalian congregation was established within the Chinese community in Manila before Brent arrived in Manila on 24 August 1902. Kate Botengan's claim that "work among the Chinese started with the baptism of three Amoy Chinese by Army Chaplain Marvine at the beginning of 1900 and an additional twelve at the end of the year" gives the false impression of a sustained ministry.[285] This could not have been possible without permanent missionaries and funds from the mission board from 1900–1901. It would be more accurate to say that the work formally began with the coming of Rev Walter Clapp, although it was likewise in an interim stage. My view also varies with what Kate Botengan wrote in the centennial publications of the Episcopal District of the Philippines. She claims that SSCM,

> at the start was composed mostly of Caucasians with a sprinkling of Chinese in the congregation. It was decided to continue St. Stephen's as a mission station of the Cathedral of St. Mary and St. John to the Chinese community. On 4 April 1904, a congregational meeting was held and the decision was

---

284. Norbeck, "False Start," 223–226.
285. *Handbooks*, 13. Cf. Botengan, *Transformed by the Word*, 3.

made to become a self-supporting parish with the Rev Mercer
G. Johnston as the first rector.[286]

In an earlier publication, she expressed a similar view that "the original
St. Stephen's was the Anglo-American congregation in Manila in 1902,
served by Fr Clapp, as priest and Fr [H. Russell] Talbot as his assistant."[287]
Botengan claims that it continued to be the ministry of the PEC to the
Chinese community after the Caucasian members were absorbed by the
Cathedral of St. Mary and St. John. The Rev Mercer Green Johnston was
assigned as the first rector, and the congregation decided to become a Parish
on 4 April 1904. Botengan therefore presents the view that there was only
one Episcopalian congregation, which she termed the St. Stephen's Chinese
Mission, composed of both Chinese and non-Chinese.

Other early sources, however, differ from Botengan's records. In 1962
Conrad Myrick, then professor of history at St. Andrew's Seminary, wrote
that the Anglo-American Church was composed of the American and
British residents of Manila. Originally, this congregation was called the
Anglo-Saxon Church, then the Anglo-American Church in 1898 during the time of Pierce. From 1899–1902 it was known as Holy Trinity
Church, but when Rev Russell Talbot replaced Walter Clapp as rector in
1902, he renamed it St. Stephen's Church.[288] Again, in 1905, it was named
the Pro-Cathedral of St. Mary and St. John,[289] and finally, as the Cathedral
of St. Mary and St. John 聖瑪利亞和聖約翰座堂 during its dedication
on 3 February 1907, an event attended by seven hundred Americans,
Englishmen, Chinese and Filipinos. Meanwhile, in 1905 the city government decided to cut a street through the center of the church property in

---

286. Botengan, *Transformed by the Word*, 11.

287. Botengan, "Horizon," 7.

288. See *Report of the Bishop of the Missionary District of the Philippine Islands, 1911–
12. The Church in the Philippines: A Review of Events Since 1898, with Bishop Brent's First
Annual Report*, 2nd ed., photocopy (New York: Protestant Episcopal Church of the USA,
1904), n.p.

289. "Pro-Cathedral" is a church named by a diocesan bishop to serve as a cathedral
but which remains under the governance of the vestry and dean. It is used as a cathedral for
diocesan purposes, but it is not the official cathedral of the diocese. This status ends when
the bishop no longer holds the diocesan jurisdiction, but may be extended by the next
bishop. "Pro-Catheral," *An Episcopal Dictionary of the Church*, ed. Don S. Armentrout and
Robert Boak Slocum (New York: Church Publishing, 2000), 417.

Ermita. Therefore Bishop Brent negotiated the sale of this property. The city also agreed to move the first wooden church building from *Calle Nueva* (now A. Mabini Street in Ermita) next to the Settlement House in Trozo, Binondo, where it was renamed St. Luke's Mission Chapel for Filipinos and placed under the charge of Rev George C. Bartter.[290]

A concrete structure replaced this chapel in 1915. Able to withstand destruction during WWII, it served for a time after the War as the Pro-Cathedral when the Cathedral on *Calle Isaac Peral* (now United Nations Avenue) and *Calle Florida* was burned in 1945. In 1959, it became the permanent church building of the St. Stephen's Chinese Parish (Myrick's term), which did not evolve from the St. Stephen's Church but was a mission station of the Cathedral. An even earlier source, *Handbooks on the Missions of the Episcopal Church* (1923), confirmed and stated, "The work was started in 1902, as a mission of the cathedral, under the name St. Stephen's Mission."[291]

The Chinese congregation, according to Studley who wrote in 1924, first met on *Calle San Fernando*. They then moved to #132 *Calle Nueva* in 1904 (a Chinese source gives #64 遠勝寶號樓上).[292] By 1912, the Mission had built its own church and school building on *Calle Reina Regente* and occupied this until the great fire of 1945 (App. Y, Figs. 2, 3). After WWII, they were allotted certain hours of service in the Pro-Cathedral, while the building on *Reina Regente* was repaired and given to St. Peter's Chinese Mission/ Sheng Bide Tang 聖彼得堂 (now St. Peter's Parish), the Cantonese congregation that was officially formed in 1932.[293]

Lastly, Myrick stated that "St. Stephen's Mission became the second parish in the District on 23 February 1941, when senior warden H[uy] G[uan] Ty [Zheng HuiYuan 鄭輝元主理] presented its keys to the

290. Norbeck, "Protestant Episcopal," 210–212.

291. Myrick, "Episcopal Church," 1–4; *Handbooks*, 25.

292. *St. Stephen's Diamond Jubilee*, 11. I have, however, not found any source explaining this discrepancy.

293. Myrick, "Episcopal Church," 4 and *Report of the Bishop of the Missionary District of the Philippine Islands, 1913* (Manila: by the Secretary, 1914), Box 1, RG76–13, 2. St. Andrew's Seminary Archives, Quezon City, Philippines. Cf. Botengan, *Transformed by the Word*, 11.

Rev H[si] J[in] Wei [Wei XiRen 魏希仁牧師], its first rector."[294] In the
Episcopalian system, it takes three stages to reach the status of becoming
a parish, which means "a self-supporting congregation under a rector, as
opposed to a mission or other congregation under a vicar."[295] First, a congregation is set up as a mission (not fully self-supporting and without a
full-time priest). Then, while still not fully self-supporting, it becomes an
aided parish. Finally, upon gaining financial independence, it gains the status of a parish.[296] Thus, SSCM could not have become a parish as early as
1904. Before the Episcopalians began this work, however, the Presbyterians
and Methodists were already doing work among the Chinese of Manila.
The work of the Presbyterian mission has already been discussed earlier; the
work of the Methodists will now be examined.

(3) Methodist Work in Manila

When Bishop Brent arrived in the Philippines in 1902, he is said to have
consulted "the leaders of other missions which had definite work among
the Chinese before deciding to begin work among them."[297] These "other missions" refer to the Presbyterians and Methodists who had already
been doing ministry in the Philippines since 1898 and 1900 respectively.
There are very few written records regarding Methodist ministry among
the Chinese. What is more richly documented is their work among the
Filipinos, which was began by Arthur W. Prautch and his wife in May
1898, and the subsequent organization of the Methodist church by Bishop
James Miles Thoburn (1836–1922) who visited Manila on 2–14 March

294. J. B. [Hsi Jin] Wei/Wei XiRen 魏希仁, "A Brief Note on St. Stephen's Parish," in
*Fifty Years of Protestantism in the Philippines: The Manila Time (Morning Daily) and the Daily
Mirror* (Manila: Manila Times Publishing, 1949), 67 and Myrick, "Episcopal Church," 4.
Cf. Botengan, *Transformed by the Word*, 11. Wei (1893–1987) served from 1938–1963.
Shih Chang Shangkuan 上官世璋, "Benhui Sishi Zhounian Qingdianjian Manila Huaqiao
Jidu Jiaohui Jianshi 本會四十周年慶典前馬尼拉市華僑基督教會簡史 (Pre-fortieth
anniversary celebration: short history of overseas Chinese Christian churches in Manila),"
in *HDPO*, (Manila: United Evangelical Church of Manila, 1969), 142–143 (pages in
Chinese style).

295. "Parish," *Episcopal Dictionary of the Church*, 384.

296. Patrick Tanhuanco, telephone interview by Jean Uayan, Manila, 7 Nov 2005.

297. Studley, "Chinese Experiment," 576.

1899.[298] Chaplain George Stull held the first Protestant service in the Philippines in an old Spanish dungeon facing Manila Bay on 28 August 1898. Services for Filipinos began in June 1899. Services for Americans took place earlier. Subsequent services during Thoburn's time were held at *Teatro Filipino* on *Calle Echague*.[299] On 18 November 1899, the General Missionary Committee of the Methodist Missionary Society officially classified the work in the Philippines as a foreign mission and recognized it as the Philippine Islands District in the Malaysia Mission Conference, and the work was known as "The Philippine Islands Mission of the Methodist Episcopal Church."[300] This placed it under the jurisdiction of Bishop Thoburn. The statistical report (1904–1907) in Appendix Z indicates the steady growth of the Methodist church in the Philippines.

The Methodist Chinese work may have begun as early as 1900, for in his report to the General Conference for that year, Bishop Thoburn states: "We have also a small but hopeful band of Chinese Christians, and in the early future hope to have a vigorous Chinese work among the large Chinese populations of Manila."[301] Homer Stuntz provided a glimpse to the characteristics of these Chinese Christians being nurtured by the Methodists when he described: "Those whom we have baptized, after careful sifting of motives and pledging to prayer and public worship, show an almost pathetic eagerness for religious instruction, and read any book we put in their way, buy any books we recommend, and attend upon Divine worship with a regularity most gratifying."[302]

In September 1907 the Methodist mission decided to hand their Chinese work over to SSCM. The reason for this decision, according to

298. See Camilo Osias and Avelina Lorenzana, *Evangelical Christianity in the Philippine* (Dayton, OH: United Brethren Publishing, 1931), 85; Ruben F. Trinidad, *A Monument to Religious Nationalism: History and Polity of the IEMELIF Church* (Quezon City: Evangelical Methodist Church in the Philippines, 1999), 63, and Jose Gamboa, Jr, Gamaliel T. de Armas, Jr, Roela Victoria Rivera, Sharon Paz C. Hechanova, *Methodism in the Philippines: A Century of Faith and Vision* (Manila: Philippine Central Conference, United Methodist Church, 2003), 18–21.

299. Richard L. Deats, *The Story of Methodism in the Philippines* (Manila: National Council of Churches in the Philippines, for Union Theological Seminary, 1964), 3–4.

300. Deats, *Story of Methodism*, 7.

301. Stuntz, *Philippines and the Far East*, 433.

302. Ibid., 276.

Norbeck, was the repeated but futile attempt to find a qualified American missionary to oversee the work. Deciding to close their small church but desiring to make sure that their members were cared for, the Methodists turned to the Episcopal Church and asked Brent and Studley to assume this task.[303] Their local Chinese preacher became Studley's assistant and one of the teachers in the night school that the Episcopalians had established in 1905. More will be said concerning Ben Ga Pay/Bai MengYa 白萌芽牧師 (served from 1907; d. 1923)[304] in another part of this chapter (App.Y, Fig. 4). This turnover is confirmed by the mission report for 1908, which, unlike previous years, no longer has any entry for the Chinese work in Manila.[305]

The Presbyterians, who ministered in the Trozo district, also "handed their Chinese work over to Bishop Henry Brent, of the Episcopal Mission."[306] It is interesting to note that the hope of the Presbyterian mission for a Christian worker who could speak *Hokkien* was realized in the person of Hobart Studley, a former American Reformed missionary working in Xiamen. He, however, joined the Episcopalian mission, and, under the helm of Bishop Brent, the Episcopalians continued the work among the Chinese in Manila.

d) Contribution of Brent and Studley

(1) Charles Henry Brent

Attention must now turn to Bishop Brent, the person who formally initiated the Chinese ministry in the Philippines for the PEC. He served at St. Augustine's in Boston's West End and later became assistant minister at

---

303. See Hobart Earl Studley, "Report of the Cathedral Mission of S. Stephen," *The Journal of the Ninth Annual Convocation of the Missionary District of the Philippine Islands* (3 Aug 1912): 33–35, accessed 31 Dec 2015, https://imageserver.library.yale.edu/digcoll:239983/500.pdf. This source is henceforth cited as *JAC 1912*.

304. *St. Stephen's Golden Jubilee*, 7; John C. H. Pan/Pan ZhenHan 潘振漢, ed., *The 70ᵗʰ Anniversary of the St. Stephen's Parish* (Feilübin Huaqiao Shenggonghui Qishi Zhounian Jiniance) 菲律賓華僑聖公會七十週年紀念冊 (Manila: St. Stephen's Parish Philippine Episcopal Church, [1973]), 8 (henceforth cited as *St. Stephen's 70ᵗʰ Anniversary*).

305. *Annual report of the Board of Foreign Missions of the Methodist Episcopal Church for the year 1908* (New York: Board of Foreign Missions of the Methodist Episcopal Church, 1909). See also Rodgers, *Forty Years*, 155.

306. Sitoy, *Several Springs* 2:941, Rodgers, *Twenty Years*, 4–5.

St. Stephen's Church in Boston until his consecration as bishop in 1901.[307] Brent never married. His fiancée, Mary, was strongly against his coming to the Islands, hence he remained single until the end.

Upon arriving in Manila, Brent worked in four directions: the American and English ministry in St. Stephen's Church[308] in Ermita with Rev Mercer Green Johnston as rector; the Settlement House[309] with kindergarten and neighborhood work among Filipinos but without holding religious services, located at *Calle Magdalena* in the slum district of Trozo, Tondo; the medical work in St. Luke's dispensary[310] that was opened in two rooms of the Settlement House on 1 February 1903; and the Chinese ministry in Binondo and in Trozo.[311]

Bishop Brent's concern for the Chinese work must be considered in light of his philosophy of mission, that is: education, medical services and evangelism.[312] The thrust of his mission strategy reflected a shift in focus that differed from that of Pierce whose ministry was more of a straight forward evangelism. Bishop Brent manifested the general policies of the PEC to concentrate on a few key areas and on people groups that Roman Catholics had not been able to convert – the Muslims, the tribal people (Igorots in

---

307. The best biographical work on Brent is Zabriskie's, but a short biography can be found in "The Rt Rev Charles Henry Brent, First Bishop of the Philippines, 19 December 1901 to 20 October 1917," in Botengan, *Transformed by the Word*, 111–112. After his consecration as Bishop, he devoted the months from December 1901 to May 1902 to secure funds for the ministry, raising about US $150,000.

308. Once every Sunday the service was in Spanish for the benefit of the Filipinos. Myrick, "Episcopal Church," 2.

309. Margaret P. Waterman and Harriet B. Osgood helped establish the Settlement House for the purpose of introducing Filipinos to the American style of living. *The Episcopal Church in the Philippines Celebrating One Hundred Years of Ministry*, accessed 14 Jun 2005, http://episcopalphilippines.net/History1.htm. It formally opened on 13 Dec 1902 and later became an orphanage for girls of American fathers and Filipina mothers in 1906. Myrick, "Episcopal Church," 3. The location is significant, for this is where St. Stephen's Parish is presently located.

310. An army nurse named Clara Thatcher headed its operation. In 1907 it became a hospital, the precursor of today's St. Luke's Hospital located in Quezon City and Taguig City.

311. Stuntz, *Philippines and the Far East*, 466–467. See also *The Journal of the General Convention of the Protestant Episcopal Church in the United States of America Held in the City of Boston from October 5th to October 25th, Inclusive in the Year of Our Lord 1904 with Appendices* (New York: Winthrop Press, 1905), 436, henceforth cited as *JCG 1904*.

312. Botengan, "Horizon," 2.

the Mountain Province), and the Chinese. Initially, Brent sincerely believed that most Filipinos were already Christians and his high church sensibilities would not allow him to raise "altar against altar." He declared:

> I could not from conviction undertake or promote that attack on the Roman Catholic Church which, directly or indirectly, seems to be necessary for success. The raising of altar against altar is a process of which I am temperamentally incapable. My theory has been that constructive presentation of the truth as God has made it known to us would win those who ought to be won. Even those doctrines in another communion which I cannot accept, I am unable to condemn.[313]

Hence, when the Evangelical Union (formed in 1901) offered membership to the PEC, Brent declined and stayed aloof from the Union. The Union also agreed to leave the Muslims, Chinese and tribal people under the exclusive care of the PEC, without, however, any agreement on Bishop Brent's part to regard such limitation as binding or permanent. Two years later Bishop Brent reevaluated his policy regarding the Roman Catholics and urged his missionaries to give basic religious instruction to constituents of the PEC.[314] Ironically, while declining to be part of the union movement that united other Protestant mission bodies in the Philippines, he became involved with and was eventually propelled into leadership position in the growing worldwide ecumenical movement.[315]

(2) Hobart Earl Studley

Bishop Brent initially focused on the *Hokkien*-speaking Chinese in Binondo and Trozo. These Chinese originated from South Fujian which was not a

---

313. Brent, "Sixteen Years in the Philippines," 167; Constance White Wentzel, *A Half Century in the Philippines* (New York: National Council, 1952), 14.

314. Charles Henry Brent, Manila, to Margaret P. Waterman (Fall 1904), Mercer G. Johnston Papers, Box 38, Library of Congress Manuscript Division, Washington, DC, quoted in Norbeck, "False Start," 235.

315. Norbeck, "False Start," 236. Before his death on 27 Mar 1929, Brent was active in organizing the World Conference on Faith and Order held at Lausanne, and in bringing about a sense of fellowship among the attending members of the various denominations. Arthur Stanwood Pier, *American Apostles to the Philippines*. Biography Index Reprint Series (Freeport, NY: Books for Libraries Press, 1950, reprint, 1971), 151; Zabriskie, *Bishop Brent*, 143–159.

center for Episcopalian work, hence Bishop Brent needed an experienced missionary who could speak the dialect. He wrote to Bishop Graves in Shanghai asking if he could spare someone from his mission to work in Manila. Bishop Graves did not have anyone to spare, but he had just written back to Hobart Studley, turning down his request for joining the Episcopalian as a staff in Xiamen, because they did not anticipate any work there in the future.[316] An American Reformed minister and a graduate of the New Brunswick Theological Seminary, Studley had worked in Xiamen for seven years (1896–1903). His wife Edith was an Episcopalian but served with the Reformed mission.[317] There was an issue behind Studley's desire to change mission fields. Upon investigation Bishop Brent found that it was due to some women who tried to overturn Studley's management of affairs, but the bishop was convinced of his good character. Hence he was very favorable toward his appointment to the Philippines. Studley and his family arrived in Manila on 13 September 1903 and resided temporarily with Bishop Brent. He was confirmed the following Sunday and made a candidate for the Episcopal priesthood and ordained as deacon on 12 June 1904.[318] His reordination as priest took place on 24 September 1905.

e) The Emergence of St. Stephen's Chinese Mission

(1) Early History

The beginning of SSCM in 1903 was described in 1924 by Studley in the following way:

> After about three weeks spent in making the acquaintance of as many of the Chinese Christians as possible, especially those who were Protestant but not enrolled in any local congregation, services were begun in an upstairs rented room on *Calle San Fernando*, the First Sunday in October [4], 1903.

316. Norbeck, "Protestant Episcopal," 249–250.

317. Edith J. Holbrow Studley (b. 17 Jun 1872; d. 8 Nov 1929) served in Xiamen from 1898–1903. De Jong, *Reformed Church in China*, 347. Rong En 榮恩, "Short History of the Philippine Episcopal Church," in *St. Stephen's 70ᵗʰ Anniversary*, 12; William Robertson Angus, Jr, "The United Church and the Existing Chinese Churches," TMs (photocopy), 24, H00=1381 Box 1, Angus Papers, Joint Archives of Holland, Hope College, Hope, Michigan.

318. *JCG 1904*, 506.

Seventeen Chinese were present at that first meeting and among them were members of the Anglican, Presbyterian, Congregationalist, Methodist and English Wesleyan Communions.[319]

The date given by Hobart Studley should be noted in particular. Every other source, from the two anniversary publications of the Episcopal Diocese of Central Philippines to the fiftieth, sixtieth, seventieth, ninetieth and centennial publications of SSCM/SSP, gives 8 November 1903 as the date of the "first-ever Amoy [*Hokkien*] dialect worship service" to be held in the Philippines.

This record appears to be different from mission records and Studley's article in two aspects. First of all, the date given by Studley makes more sense and should be taken as more reliable, since he distinctly says that it was after three weeks of visitation that the first service was held. Mission records indicate that Studley arrived in the Philippines on 13 September 1903. If the service was held on 4 October 1903, that would be "about three weeks." If it were held on 8 November 1903, then there would be a discrepancy with his memory of spending three weeks in visitation before the first service started. An explanation, albeit without documentary support, is offered that the October service may have been just a morning service, not a formal Holy Communion service where an ordained priest (Studley had not yet been ordained at the time) would have to be present. The 8 November service may have been the formal one and this has been celebrated as the anniversary of the founding of SSP ever since.[320] Another source, however, records that the 20th anniversary of the Parish was celebrated in October.[321] Despite this discrepancy, I would consider the date when Studley first conducted a Protestant service for the Chinese in Manila as factual and as the founding date of SSCM.

Second, this service in *Hokkien* should not be considered the "first" as the Presbyterians and Methodists had already been holding services in the

---

319. Studley, "Chinese Experiment," 576.

320. Patrick Tanhuanco, telephone interview.

321. "Philippine Islands – 1923, Supplement No. 1 to the Philippine Handbook" in *Handbooks on the Missions of the Episcopal Church,* No. 3: *Philippine Islands* (New York: National Council of the Protestant Episcopal Church Department of Missions, 1923), n.p.

vernacular for the Chinese in Iloilo and Manila (from 1900–1903), respectively. Since most of the Chinese in these two places were from Xiamen and the "native" evangelists that the two missions employed were also Protestants from Xiamen, then it would be logical to assume that they used the *Hokkien* dialect in their services. Hence Botengan's statement may have been made due to the lack of knowledge of the existence of the Chinese congregations established by these two missions before the year 1903.

Studley further reported that most of the participants were people baptized in China under the Roman Catholic Church, the PEC and several other Protestant churches. This fact caused Vincent Gowen to remark: "From its first service, held upstairs in a rented room in October 1903, and attracting a congregation which included converts of the Anglican, Roman, Presbyterian, Congregationalist, Methodist, and English Wesleyan Churches, the Cathedral Mission of St. Stephen has been – as Mr Studley termed it – 'a Chinese experiment in Christian union.'"[322] This "union" is affirmed by publications such as the sixtieth and seventieth anniversary publications of SSP, and the pearl and centennial anniversary publications of the Episcopal Diocese of Central Philippines. However, the number given in these two sources, of persons attending the October service, is again different from Studley's report. All of the more recent sources record that only ten were in attendance whereas Studley stated that there were seventeen. Obviously, Studley should be considered the more reliable source since he was an eyewitness of the event.

Another piece of information that Studley gives is the presence of the Chinese constituents of the Tondo Evangelical Church (former Tondo Presbyterian Church) at the same service. He wrote:

> Among the worshipers on that first Sunday was the entire congregation of a Filipino Presbyterian Church. They insisted on coming, against my protest, because they desired the leadership which the Presbyterian mission was not at that time prepared to give them but which they believed Bishop Brent's work had. Every one of those men, except for one who soon retired to China and one who became a Roman Catholic for

---

322. Gowen, *Philippine Kaleidoscope*, 22.

his wife's sake, became a communicant of St. Stephen's, being confirmed by Bishop Brent.[323]

Regarding the formation of this congregation, Norbeck's study gives more analysis as to the reason behind their transfer. He wrote that "Studley's initiative and demeanor impressed several Chinese during the first three weeks of his ministry in Manila." He further cited Bishop Brent's belief that "Studley's success came because 'He . . . so identified himself with the Chinese that he is Chinese in manner.'"[324] Frank Laubach also noted that Studley could speak Chinese "better than the Chinese themselves."[325] In other words, his command of the Chinese language and custom made a good impression and attracted the Chinese to the new congregation.

Norbeck gave the second reason for the membership transfer in reaction to what Arthur Brown wrote in 1903. Brown had written that "Separate missionaries will probably not be required, nor will it be necessary to learn the Chinese language." He also believed that the work could be carried out by Chinese Christians who came from China, for they had found two of these in Manila and they "were able to preach, and while supporting themselves in their shops during the week, reasoned out of the Scriptures with considerable power on Sunday."[326] Norbeck, however, maintains that the Chinese congregation was "not as enthusiastic," as Brown surmised, regarding missionaries who could not speak Chinese or believers taking the role of part-time preachers. He reasons that the Chinese converts were not as well-to-do as Brown had assumed during his brief tour of Manila, and that they wanted a full-time leader. They turned to Bishop Brent and Studley whom they believed would give them the attention and guidance that the Presbyterians were unwilling to provide.[327]

---

323. Studley, "Chinese Experiement," 576.

324. Charles Henry Brent, Manila, to John W. Wood, 27 Dec 1909, 3. St. Andrew's Seminary Archives, Quezon City, Philippines.

325. Frank C. Laubach, *The People of the Philippines: Their Religious Progress and Preparation for Spiritual Leadership in the Far East* (New York: George H. Doran Co., 1925), 365. Laubach may have been voicing the opinion of others since he himself did not speak *Hokkien*.

326. Brown, *New Era*, 88–89.

327. Norbeck, "Protestant Episcopal," 252–254.

The year 1904 brought many changes to the Chinese Mission. In March the mission relocated itself to a more suitable building at #132 *Calle Nueva* in the Binondo district. The new facilities consisted of two rooms, a small one used as a chapel and a larger hall for other church functions.[328] The Chinese Mission was officially recognized as a mission station of the Cathedral on 24 September 1905, when it was named the St. Stephen's Cathedral Mission for Chinese by Bishop Brent.[329] Hobart Studley, having been examined four days earlier, was also reordained by Bishop Brent during this auspicious occasion. In the afternoon of that same day, the bishop confirmed the first fruits of the Chinese mission by performing the apostolic rite for three men, as part of the Episcopalian order of Confirmation.[330] According to Norbeck, when the Chinese congregation became an official auxiliary of the Cathedral of St. Mary and St. John, there was lack of publicity and funds for the Chinese Mission because throughout most of Bishop Brent's episcopate the cathedral and American community were always the primary concern of the Episcopalians. The Chinese work was seen as a mere extension of their primary work. Norbeck's point, it should be noted, was made in reference to the financial status of the Chinese Mission, for he went on to state that the situation "forced the Chinese to rely upon their own resources and stewardship to build and sustain their mission which made St. Stephen's all the stronger."[331] Before the end of 1905, SSCM had achieved self-supporting status and even paid the salary and rent of Hobart and Edith Studley.

(2) Growth Factors

The new congregation grew rapidly under Studley's leadership. Factors for this growth include: (1) the establishment of a night school and, much

---

328. Hobart Earl Studley, Manila, to [first name not recorded] Kimber, 23 Mar 1904, RG76–73; in Norbeck, "Protestant Episcopal," 256–257.

329. Charles Henry Brent, "Various Notes on Philippine Matters," *The Spirit of Missions* 71 (May 1906): 374; *JCG 1904*, 506. This name is found in Bishop Brent's *Report of the Bishop of the Missionary District of the Philippine Islands, 1911–12* Box 1, St. Andrew's Seminary Archives, Quezon City, Philippines.

330. This is a rite where baptized believers are confirmed by laying on of hands and the ceremony may include the recitation of the Apostle's Creed. For the order of administration, see *The Order of Confirmation*, accessed 12 Nov 2006, http://prayerbook.ca/bcp/ confirmation.html.

331. Norbeck, "Protestant Episcopal," 257–258.

later, of the girls' school; (2) membership increase, financial stability and the contribution of Ben Ga Pay after the turnover of the Methodist Chinese congregation; and (3) Bishop Brent's and Hobart Studley's involvement in fighting the opium scourge.

(a) Educational Factor

In 1905, a night school for boys was established and this ministry was maintained until 1909. It immediately attracted forty-seven boys in the first few months of operation (App. Y, Fig. 5). One of the teachers who contributed to the success of St. Stephen's Night School was Soat-hoag Yin.[332] He was brought up in the Presbyterian Church of South Formosa, educated at the Methodist School in Fuzhou and had taught in a prestigious school in Xiamen. He came to the Philippines in 1902 as a partner in the firm of S. C. Choy and Co., worked as a custom broker and also taught in the night school for the United States government. He began attending SSCM and was in Studley's second confirmation class. When the night school opened, Yin decided to teach there, but before starting, he went back to Fuzhou and married a well-educated Christian. They returned on 18 July 1906. While her husband helped the school, Mrs Yin volunteered as organist at SSCM. Brent even encouraged Yin to prepare for ordination but he felt it was not his calling. For some unknown reason, the couple left SSCM in 1908.[333]

SSCM established a day school, and both schools started to charge fees in January 1906.[334] This greatly affected attendance in the day school and it became unsustainable. Another factor leading to the failure of this school was the competition from the Anglo-Chinese School 中西學校. Considered the first Chinese school in the Philippines, it was opened by

---

332. Hobart Studley, "Report to the Cathedral Mission St. Stephen's for Chinese for the Year Ending December 1905," *JAC* (1905): 30. Unfortunately, I have not found any source giving the Chinese name of this teacher.

333. Charles Henry Brent, Manila to Dr John W. Wood, New York, 20 May 1907, RG76–13. St. Andrew's Seminary Archives, Quezon City, Philippines; Hobart Earl Studley to Kimber, 29 Jun 1907, RG76–13; in Norbeck, "Protestant Episcopal Church," 259–260.

334. Bi Chin Y. Uy/Huang Yao MeiZhen 黃姚美真, "Chinese Education in Philippine Society: An Analysis of Its Structure and Implications," (EdD diss., Philippine Women's University, 1969), 2–5 and *Anglo Chinese School Golden Jubilee Book: 1899–1949* (Manila, 1949).

the Chinese community on 15 April 1899, in response to the dilemma created by the Chinese Expulsion Acts that made sending the children of immigrant Chinese to study in China a great problem. The school started offering night classes in 1911. Despite the competition, the principal of the Anglo-Chinese School, a Chinese Presbyterian minister named Rev Yang NaiFu 楊迺甫牧師 invited Studley to help teach in the English department.[335] This paved the way for friendly relationship not only between the two leaders but also between the two schools. Certain members of the church became board members of the Anglo-Chinese School, while students from this school provided a constant stream of new members for SSCM.

In 1917, realizing that the other free night schools were doing well, the Chinese Mission committee decided to concentrate on a school for Chinese girls and established such a school in July under the leadership of Mrs Edith Studley. Vincent Gowen praised her by saying: ". . . she was one of those rare characters who can make personal goodness objective and who can transfigure mere efficiency into an active and visible presentation of love."[336] The Protestant Episcopal Mission appointed Miss Georgie M. Brown/Bu Lang 布郎女士 (term of service, 1920–1925) as principal (App. Y, Fig. 6). Hobart Studley wrote that "with the exception of Miss Brown's salary and other allowances, and one or two hundred *pesos* in specials from America, the school has received absolutely no help from America and none from the missionary district other than the loyal support of St. Stephen's Church and many Chinese friends not connected with the Mission."[337]

(b) Various Factors

When the Methodists turned their Chinese congregation over to the Episcopalians, the latter decided to move SSCM from *Calle Nueva* to the Methodist quarter that was located on the third story of a business edifice on a hot narrow street. This provided a bigger space that gave separate rooms

---

335. Rev Yang was formerly a minister of the Pechuia Church 白水營堂, a fruit of the missionaries of the RPDC and EPM. He was also involved in education in Gulangyu and Xiamen. He came to the Philippines upon the invitation of the school and became a member of SSCM. See *St. Stephen's Golden Jubilee*, 29.

336. Gowen, *Philippine Kaleidoscope*, 25.

337. Botengan, "Horizon," 22; Studley, "Chinese Experiment," 578–579.

for the church, the parsonage and the school. Hobart Studley also added new worship services to the weekly schedule – the regular Sunday evening services that the Methodist constituents were used to, and Thursday evening catechism classes.

Another major influence was the ministry of Rev Mr Ben Ga Pay.[338] He came to the Philippines in 1900 and taught at the Anglo-Chinese School before the Methodists invited him to serve as their interpreter and evangelist. He was ordained as deacon on 16 February 1913 by Hobart Studley, thus becoming the first resident Chinese to enter into sacred service. Pay did exceptional work as Studley's assistant, so that the latter credited him with whatever success the Mission had. He continued the Sunday evening evangelistic meetings, and Studley reported in 1908 that: "Much to our satisfaction we found attendance on the services to be much better than formerly, in fact, the congregations were much larger than the combined congregation had been before, and a new spirit of greater earnestness was shown in many ways."[339] In 1916, Pay studied at St. John's University in Shanghai, then returned to Manila where he rendered faithful and dedicated service until he suddenly died on 25 September 1923.[340]

Not only did attendance increase, the offerings also went up, causing the Chinese Mission to voluntarily relinquish the annual grant from the American mission board and become self-sufficient. As early as 1906, in a letter written to Dr John W. Wood, Bishop Brent reported:

> Mr Studley asks for no money for buildings or running expenses beyond rent for the time being, as he thinks that in the course of time his people will contribute funds for the erection of a church and for running expenses. . . . This includes expenditure for Chinese literature. We have two printing presses

---

338. This is how Bishop Mosher referred to him in his letter. See Rt Rev Governeur Frank Mosher, Manila, to Dr John W. Wood, New York, 30 Aug 1920, 1. St. Andrew's Seminary Archives, Quezon City, Philippines. Under the Episcopalian system, deacons can be addressed as "Reverend." In *St. Stephen's Golden Jubilee*, the same title (牧師) appears in Chinese.

339. Hobart Earl Studley, "Report of the Cathedral Mission of St. Stephen, Manila," *JAC* (2 Aug 1911): 21; *JAC* (5 Jun 1908): 14–15.

340. *Handbooks*, 25.

now, and I hope before another budget is sent in we shall be able to handle a good deal of our printing on our own presses.[341]

Of this financial strength Vincent Gowen goes to the extent to remark that, in his estimation, "Not even in China has St. Stephen's record been approached."[342] Not only was the mission financially stable, it also had an able treasurer in the person of George C. Bartter, an Englishman. Bishop Brent reported that he came to the Islands as a colporteur of the British and Foreign Bible Society in 1900, could speak Spanish, Bicol and Visayan, and was admitted as a candidate for Holy Orders in March 1906. He also gained proficiency in Tagalog and translated portions of the Prayer Book and Communion Service into this language.

The mission began raising funds in September of 1909 for a more permanent church structure. In 1911, utilizing the amount of 5,650 pesos from the members and $500 from America, the church purchased an 839-square meter lot along *Calle Reina Regente* and built a two-story building (App. Y, Fig. 2). The contractor – Mr Cai ShaoQing 蔡少菁 – was a Chinese communicant who did not accept any remuneration for his work. Worship services were conducted on the ground floor and the living quarters of the pastor and three big classrooms were on the second floor. The inauguration of the new building, the first of its kind among the Philippine Protestant Chinese churches, was held on 31 March 1912 (Palm Sunday). A school building was later constructed beside the church (App. Y, Fig. 3).

(c) The Opium Scourge

One of the islands' most pressing social problems at this time was opium addiction, especially prominent in the Chinese community. The Spaniards dealt with the problem by farming out concessions, allowing a person or company to receive a government approved monopoly on the drug in return for a share of the revenue.[343] The United States immediately ended this

---

341. Charles Henry Brent, Manila, to Dr John W. Wood, New York, 15 Feb 1906, 2, 8. St. Andrew's Seminary Archives, Quezon City, Philippines.

342. Gowen, *Philippine Kaleidoscope*, 23.

343. Regarding concessions for farming opium, see Wong Kwok-chu, *The Chinese in the Philippine Economy 1898–1941*, 24–25, 30–31, Wickberg, *Chinese in Philippine Life*, 114–118, Fonacier, "The Chinese in the Philippines During the American Administration," ch. 5, Jensen, "Chinese in the Philippines during the American Regime: 1898–1946," 175–

concession after occupying the Philippines. Congress and the Philippine Commission imposed a harsh tax on the sale of the product and opium dens were prohibited. However, this only made the situation worse, and addiction rapidly spread throughout the populace. The Philippine Commission drafted a bill that reinstated a modified version of farming out the drug, but allowed only Chinese addicts to purchase the drug.

A huge public outcry arose, with Bishop Brent and Homer Stuntz spearheading the opposition to this bill. They felt that addiction, whether among Chinese or Filipino, was a moral evil that should never be tolerated. With few exceptions, the Chinese community agreed with this view and submitted a petition against the bill. An Opium Committee was formed with Brent as a member in order to find an alternative solution. It recommended a policy, following Japan's lead, of the government monopoly on the substance. Opium importation was gradually phased out over a four-year period until it was prohibited except for medicinal purposes. Free medical treatment was given to confirmed addicts but they were deprived of the right to vote or hold public office. Schools launched anti-drug campaigns. Government monopoly on the substance was implemented and eventually helped to bolster a growing movement in China and elsewhere to end the opium trade.

It also led to the debate on the legality of the opium trade in Great Britain. Bishop Brent wrote to President Theodore Roosevelt proposing an international conference to eradicate the opium trade. With additional lobbying of the religious leaders and missionaries in China, the first International Opium Conference was eventually held in January 1909. President Roosevelt appointed Brent and two other delegates to represent the United States, with Brent being elected president of the conference. His subsequent involvement in this movement at the international level and Hobart Studley's local anti-opium crusade combined to gain the respect of the Chinese community for the PEC Mission.

Studley also scoured the law courts, hospitals, prisons and several Chinese homes, urging addicts to quit and offering them free help at St.

---

181 and Zabriskie, *Bishop Brent*, 97–98. The information regarding the roles played by Brent and Studley in helping to eradicate the opium scourge in the Philippines is based mostly on Norbeck, "Protestant Episcopal," 266–275.

Luke's Hospital and Dispensary. In 1913, for example, he took more than eighty addicts to the hospitals (St. Luke's and San Lazaro) for treatment. Many addicts went to SSCM to seek help and were successfully treated at St. Luke's, and from this dispensary it was but a short step into the church. As Studley testified, "they come from the dispensary to the Church, cured, glorifying God and His servant, the Christian physician [Dr Saleeby]."[344]

f) Developments after Brent's Departure

(1) Decade of Growth (1917–1928)

Bishop Brent retired in 1917 and was succeeded by the Rt Rev Governeur Frank Mosher (1871–1941, term of service 1920–1940) on 25 February 1920. During the interim period, Bishop Graves of Shanghai served as the "bishop-in-charge" of the Missionary District of the Philippine Islands. In 1922, when separate services in *Hokkien* and Cantonese were conducted, a Cantonese-speaking congregation was begun. Ten years later this group officially formed a separate church called the St. Peter's Chinese Mission. Bishop Mosher attended the General Assembly held in China in April 1924 and was introduced to Mr Yip Yat Tsing/Ye RiQing 葉日青, who accepted his invitation and arrived in Manila on 27 March 1925. When Hobart Studley ended twenty-eight years of service in 1931 and left SSCM, he went to serve at this church for two years before retiring in the United States in 1933.

SSCM continued to progress, as can be seen by the data collected from reports for the years 1923, 1926, and 1927, with the last column listing the data for 1929 for purposes of comparison (see App. AA). The table in Appendix AA shows a larger number of communicants in 1923, compared with 1926 and 1927. However, in 1929, only six adults were baptized, the number of communicants remained almost the same as in 1927 and the

---

344. Hobart Earl Studley, "Report of the Cathedral Mission of St. Stephen," *JAC* (4 Aug 1913): 22; Studley to Llyod, 13 Jan 1907, RG76–73, cited in Norbeck, "Protestant Episcopal Church," 274–275, n. 68 and 69. See also Ricardo M. Zarco, "The Philippine Chinese and Opium Addiction," in *The Chinese in the Philippines 1770–1898*, ed. Alfonso Felix, Jr, vol. 2 (Manila: Solidaridad, 1969), 96–109. Bertil Arne Renbord, *International Drug Control: A Study of International Administration* (Washington, DC: League of Nations, [1944]), *Traffic in Opium and Other Dangerous Drugs: Report by the Government of the United States of America* (Washington DC: US Government Printing Office, 1931).

total number of baptized persons dropped from 682 to 500. Furthermore, it is unusual that no entries were recorded for the day school and Sunday School, along with its teachers and pupils. This is a departure from the traditional manner of reporting statistics that Studley had always done in the past. From events that transpired in 1929, it is possible to conjecture that SSCM not only lost many members, but many of those who left the church were teachers either of the day school or of the Sunday School, thus leading to these blank entries.

(2) Discord and Division

Before this happened, however, a series of events in 1928 led to the "secession" (Studley's term) that happened in 1929, casting a dark shadow upon SSCM. In April 1928, the Studleys went on furlough and SSCM was left without any Chinese-speaking clergyman. Those appointed to take charge kept changing due to interruptions such as furloughs and vacations, thus creating a situation of discontinuity in pastoral oversight. The perception of inadequate staffing was already being felt as early as 1920, more acutely in 1923 when Pay died, and this is evident from the *Twenty-First Annual Report*:

> The Rev E. L. Souder visited the Mission several times to hold celebrations of the Holy Communion, and the Rev V[incent]. H. Gowen was appointed Priest-in-Charge in July, but his departure on furlough interrupted this arrangement after only a few weeks' service. The Rev R. F. Wilner arrived in August, and has since given what assistance he can as a deacon without knowledge of the Chinese language. Since August, the Rev B. H. Harvey, Canon Missioner, has taken all celebrations of the Holy Communion, except during this vacation in November, when we had the ministrations of Chaplain Thomas E. Swan, USA, Fort Mills, Corregidor. In the absence of any Chinese-speaking clergyman all the preaching and the conduct of non-sacramental services has fallen to our faithful catechists, Mr

Sia Tsu Keng [Xie ZiGeng 謝子耕] for the Fukienese group, and Mr Yip Yat Tsing for the Cantonese.[345]

In a letter to Dr John Wood, Bishop Mosher referred to this as a "precarious condition" because the work at SSCM was hanging entirely upon one man, referring to Studley. When Studley goes on furlough, Mosher said, Rev Mr Ben Ga Pay has "neither the strength of character, the learning, nor the initiative necessary to the [sic] head of such a work."[346] The difficult situation was further aggravated by the fact that the Chinese Christians originated from Xiamen and not from their mission fields in other parts of China, so that the Bishops there could not send either American missionaries or Chinese clergymen that they had trained. Hence he was requesting for two clergymen to come from America to minister among the Chinese. Both would need language training first, one in Xiamen and the other in Canton. He was already envisioning the start of a Cantonese congregation two years before one was officially formed. He even wanted to reach the Chinese in other parts of the Islands. In another letter dated 30 November 1926, that is, six years later, Bishop Mosher lamented that nothing had been done with his request.[347] The furlough of the Studleys in 1928 placed SSCM in an acutely vulnerable position.

When the Studleys returned on 30 September 1929, five months after their furlough had already expired, two secessions shattered the unity of the church. The immediate result was the formation of the Christian Union, which in turn split into two new congregations. The first group was called the Chinese United Evangelical Church/Lüfei Zhonghua Jidu Jiaohui 旅菲中華基督教會 (literally, Church of Christ in China Sojourning in the Philippines), known today as the United Evangelical Church of the Philippines (UECP)/Feilübin Zhonghua Jidu Jiaohui 菲律賓中華基督教會. The second group initially called itself the "Prayer Room/Qidao Shi 祈禱室" or "Gospel Hall/Fuyin Tang 福音堂." This church further split on 22 August 1961 into what is known today as the Christian Gospel Center

---

345. *The Twenty-first Annual Report of the Missionary District of the Philippine Islands for the Year Ending December 31, 1928* (Manila: by The Secretary, 1929): 26.

346. Mosher to Wood, 30 Aug 1920, 1.

347. Rt Rev Governeur Frank Mosher, Manila, to Dr John W. Wood, New York, 30 Nov 1926, 1. St. Andrew's Seminary Archives, Quezon City, Philippines.

基督徒聚會所 and Church Assembly Hall 教會聚會所.[348] The full history of CUEC will be discussed in another section. From the perspective of SSCM, however, the sad events were described by Studley in the following way:

> This is the most difficult report that we have ever had to write in our thirty-three years of missionary service, for it covers a period of successive misfortunes to St. Stephen's Mission brought about by the return of the Priest-in-Charge to Manila. First came a secession of a considerable proportion of our following, including most of our unbaptized adherents, who were dissatisfied with the way in which we handled the situation which we found here on arrival. Nearly all who had been attending the Fukien Sunday evening service ceased to attend the services of the Church, and it has proved impossible to maintain that service. This, following a previous secession earlier in the year, due principally to the absence of the Priest-in-Charge when his furlough had already expired, was a very severe blow. The result of these two schisms is seen in the most unsatisfactory statistical report that we have rendered since the establishment of the Mission.[349]

As a result, in an appended chart on statistics for 1929 it was listed that 118 were "lost without transfer."[350] Total membership at 682 dropped to 500, which, when compared with the 1927 statistics, shows a decrease of 182. Hobart Studley suggested that the reason the group left was due to their delayed return. But there were certainly other factors causing the separation.

One factor is connected to Pastor Sia Tsu Keng who left Xiamen and became a full-time worker of SSCM in 1925. In 1928 a Men's Fellowship

---

348. John C. H. Pan/Pan ZhenHan 潘振漢, "Yijiulingshannian Souci Juhui – Feilübin Jidu Jiaohui Fayuan Shihua 一九〇三年首次聚會—菲律賓基督教會發源史話 (First Meeting in 1903: Historical Beginnings of the Chinese Filipino Protestant Churches)," in *HDPO*, 139 (pages in Chinese style) and Shangkuan, "Chinese Christianity in Manila," 143–144 (pages in Chinese style).

349. *The Twenty-second Annual Report of the Missionary District of the Philippine Islands for the Year Ending December 31, 1929* (Manila: by the Secretary, 1930), 50.

350. Ibid.

was organized and started to publish its quarterly bulletin. In January of 1929, conflict arose between the pastor and a church member, Keng Jin Kiat/Gong RenJie 龔人傑 [1901–1974; the legal name Keng Lin Kiat will be used hereafter], over the distribution of this bulletin. Keng Lin Kiat left the church. In March there was a strike among teachers of the St. Stephen's Chinese Girls' School/Shenggonghui Nüzi Xuexiao 聖公會女子學校. Some of the teachers who criticized the chaplain were dismissed and also left SSCM. In October, another conflict arose between Pastor Sia and Rev Henry Mattocks (served from 1929–1939), who had arrived in September. Pastor Sia and Rev Studley also had a difficult working relationship, supposedly due to the former's inability to adjust to the Episcopalian system. He resigned in 1929 and ended up forming the Christian Union.[351]

Another tragedy experienced by Hobart Studley was the death of his wife on 8 November 1929.[352] Before this happened, a letter dated 2 November 1929 from Dr John Wood to the Bishop Governeur Frank Mosher, gives an intimate glimpse of the personality and situation of Hobart Studley. Dr Wood wrote that Studley lamented the fact that he had had no sympathetic and friendly letter from Bishop Mosher about how things were going in Manila. He "felt very much cut off," even to the point of "saying that he would not go back." The incident that caused Studley to feel hurt was the lack of consultation regarding purchase of a new property for constructing a church building that SSCM was planning to undertake. Dr Wood felt that Bishop Mosher had acted on his best judgment, and "perhaps at a time when it was not practicable to consult with Dr Studley." However, he advised Mosher:

---

351. See more discussion in the section on CUEC. Cf. *St. Stephen's Golden Jubilee*, 10; *St. Stephen's Diamond Jubilee*, 11–12; *St. Stephen's 70ᵗʰ Anniversary*, 12; "St. Stephen's Parish 1903–1983," in *St. Stephen's Parish 90ᵗʰ Jubilee Souvenir1903–1993* (Gaoju Yesu Wanren Guizhu Huaqiao Shenggonghui Shengsitifentang Jiushi Zhounian Jiniankan) 高舉耶穌 萬人歸主華僑聖公會聖司提芬堂九十週年十週年刊, ed. Patrick Tanhuanco (Manila: St. Stephen's Parish Philippine Episcopal Church, [1993]), 8; Shangkuan, "Chinese Christianity in Manila," 143. The breaking up of St. Stephen's Chinese Mission is nowhere mentioned in the Pearl or Centennial souvenirs published by the Episcopal Diocese of Central Philippines.

352. This happens to be the day that the church presently celebrates as its founding anniversary. As noted in Studley's letter to Kimber, dated 23 Mar 1904, the anniversary up to 1923 was still celebrated in October, and Vincent Gowen's book, *Philippine Kaleidoscope*, published during the 1930s, stated as much.

> You may be sure that I recognized that there are some at least
> of the difficult elements in Studley's make-up. . . . He may at
> times, as you suggest, seem inclined to criticize unfairly, but
> the situation is not going to be helped by returned criticism.
> A nature like his will only have its best qualities brought out
> I think by patience and by kindness. If you want to help a
> member of your staff to realize what is best, I hope you will
> exercise a great deal of patience. . . . I hope that you will do
> your best to bring out the best good and undoubted devotion
> that are stored up in him, and that you will work with him to
> help him realize his hopes for St. Stephen's Mission.[353]

These words of Dr Wood reflect a tension between Mosher and Studley
over the issue of purchasing a new property for the church, which, in turn,
may have affected the relationship between Studley and SSCM. Without
a doubt Hobart Earl Studley can be considered the founder and the shep-
herd who served the longest at SSCM. He devotedly gave more than thirty
years of his life to minister to the Chinese in Manila. It is unfortunate that
his tenure ended with the pain of losing both his wife and one-fifth of
his congregation.

g) Summary

This section has looked into the history of the fourth Protestant Chinese
church to be established in the Philippines. SSCM was a product of
Episcopalian and to a certain extent, Methodist and Presbyterian mission
work. It started auspiciously, growing steadily for two decades after its
emergence in 1903. It pioneered in setting up a night school for boys, and
subsequently, the first Protestant school for girls in the Chinese community.

For almost three decades, SSCM was the only Chinese church in Manila.
However, a very significant difficulty experienced by the Episcopalian work
among the Chinese was the lack of trained clergymen who could assist
Rev Studley throughout this period. There was only one Chinese deacon
for the first two decades – Rev Mr Ben Ga Pay – and he never reached the
stage of being ordained as a priest. The situation became even more critical

---

353. Dr John W. Wood, New York, to Rt Rev Gouverneur Frank Mosher, Manila, 2
Nov 1929.

between 1923, when Mr Pay died, and 1933, when Mr Go Beng Un/Wu MingEn 吳銘恩 joined the workforce. There was practically no one helping Studley during this period. Thus, in terms of pastoral leadership and despite earlier financial strength, the church only reached full independent status in 1941. Before this year, in 1926, when a plan to purchase another lot for the church was proposed, it was initially estimated that the New York head office of the Episcopal Church of the United States of America would cover $20,000 and the Chinese themselves would raise $5,000. This plan never materialized but Studley was not pleased with the way the plan was arranged.[354]

Furthermore, the furlough of the Studleys in 1928 left SSCM in critical condition, making it vulnerable to internal disunity and pastoral conflict. In 1929, SSCM became the first Chinese church to experience internal division, when a large number of constituents left, resulting in the formation of two new Chinese congregations.

The stage must now shift to the Visayas, to the history of the fifth Chinese congregation to emerge in the Philippines, namely, the Cebu Gospel Church (CGC), another church established by the Presbyterian missionaries (App. CC). Part of the history of this church, especially with regard to its devolution, is related to the history of the union body called the United Church of Christ in the Philippines (UCCP), of which the Presbyterian mission and their churches were members. A brief summary of the development of this organization is found in Appendix BB. In the course of presenting the history of CGC, attention must be directed occasionally toward this summary for a better comprehension and correlation of events.

4. Cebu Gospel Church

The Cebu Gospel Church/Shuwu Jidu Jiaohui 宿務基督教會 was formed in 1916 by a handful of Protestant Chinese in Cebu City through the ministry of Rev Dr George Williamson Dunlap and other missionaries

---

354. The plan to purchase a lot on *Calle Azcarraga* was proposed by Studley and was explored in 1926, but it was never realized as negotiations fell through. See Dr John W. Wood, New York, to Rt Rev Governeur Frank Mosher, Manila, 27 Feb 1926, and Rt Rev Governeur Frank Mosher, Manila, to Dr John W. Wood, New York, 23 Mar 1926.

of the Presbyterian Mission (App. DD, Fig. 1).[355] Rev Jorge Patalinghug, the Filipino pastor of the Matilda Bradford Memorial Church (hereafter shortened to Bradford Church), a Filipino church also established by the Presbyterian missionaries, assisted the work among the Chinese of Cebu City (App. DD, Fig. 1).[356] Joseph Que/Guo YuXian 郭毓賢, who was an elder in CGC and during his lifetime, a faithful chronicler of church events, considers Patalinghug the first pastor of the Chinese congregation as well as of the Filipino congregation.[357] A native of Mactan Island, Patalinghug was one of the earliest believers in Cebu. Rev Paul Frederick Jansen (App. DD, Fig. 1) helped send him to Silliman Institute in Dumaguete City where he studied from 1905 to 1910. He then went on to study at the Union Bible Theological Seminary in Manila from 1912–1914. He was ordained an elder in 1914 and as pastor on 17 September 1916. Installed as pastor of the Visayan congregation of Bradford Church in 1918, Patalinghug served there until 1938. That the Presbyterian Mission was able to form an American, a Visayan, and later a Chinese congregation in the Islands testifies to their diligence, for Cebu was not a promising mission field. Presbyterian missionaries had been working in Cebu and its vicinity since the year 1902.[358]

---

355. The City of Cebu was created by Commonwealth Act No. 184, known as the Charter of the City of Cebu and approved 20 Oct 1936. It was inaugurated on 24 Feb 1937. Zoilo M. Galang, ed., *Filipiniana*, 1: 67. The Church celebrates its date of founding as Mar 1916.

356. Originally called the Matilda Bradford Memorial Church, this church was built from funds donated by Mrs Dwight Day, wife of the treasurer of the Board of Foreign Mission, and named after the mother of Mrs Day. It was constructed in 1912 and dedicated on 26 October 1913. Today it is known as the Bradford United Church of Christ in the Philippines and is located at 85 Osmeña Boulevard (formerly called Jones Avenue). See Pascual Emelio S. Pascual, "Presbyterian Protestantism in Cebu: A Historical Study, 1902–1938" (Master's thesis, University of San Carlos, 1988), 62.

357. That Rev Jorge Patalinghug was the first pastor of the Chinese congregation is publicly stated in a late source. See Joseph Que/Guo YuXian 郭毓賢, "Benhui Xintang Libai Anli Zhanglao Ji Muzheng Jiuzhi Shengdian 本會新堂開堂禮拜按立長老暨牧正就職盛典 (New Sanctuary Dedication Service, Elders' Ordination and Installation of the Minister)," *Wuguang* 務光 *Gospel Quarterly* 10, no. 1 (Mar 1966): 9.

358. This information regarding Patalinghug appeared in the October 1922 special issue of *The Philippine Presbyterian* featuring Cebu. See *The Philippine Presbyterian* 13, no. 4 (Oct 1922): 14; Pascual, "Presbyterian Protestantism," 76.

a) Presbyterian Work in Cebu

The island of Cebu had been targeted as a mission field as early as 1899, when Dr David Sutherland Hibbard made a tour of the area.[359] In a letter to Rev Francis F. Ellinwood, Dr Hibbard wrote that with five large stone churches and convents and a press constantly printing Catholic literature written in Visayan and Spanish, Cebu was one of the strongholds of Roman Catholicism. However, Dr Hibbard found the natives friendly and eager to learn English, and they were not against the Protestants. Hence any opposition that the missionaries might meet would not be from the curious natives but "will be with the approval and through the agents of Rome, i.e. the priests and friars in the islands."[360] The Roman Catholic believers and priests used all means to disrupt and hinder the work of the missionaries. It was also very common to have stones thrown at the congregation during meetings, although no one was seriously injured.[361]

(1) Ministry of the Jansens

On 13 September 1902 the Jansens – Paul Frederick (term of service 1901–1935) and Elizabeth "Bessie" White (formerly with the CMA, term of service 1900–1935) – were sent from Manila to serve in Cebu. They first

359. Dr Hibbard made the tour in October, not long after he arrived in the Philippines in May 1899. Brown, *New Era*, 181; James Burton Rodgers, *Twenty Years of Presbyterian Work in the Philippines Supplement to the Philippine Presbyterian, Being a Summary of Preceding Years and the History of the Year Nineteen-nineteen [sic] as Shown by Station Reports* (Manila: n.p., 1920), 5.

360. David Sutherland Hibbard, Manila, to Dr Francis F. Ellinwood, New York City, 28 Nov 1899, 1–2. Archives of the Presbyterian Church in the USA Board of Foreign Missions, 1833–1964, MS 11, Reel 287. Special collection, Day Missions Library, Yale Divinity School, Connecticut. Dr Ellinwood was then secretary of the Presbyterian Mission for the work in the Philippines and he served at the Presbyterian Board of Foreign Missions from 1871–1907.

361. Francis J. Purcell, Presbyterian Mission, Cebu, to Dr Arthur J. Brown, New York City, 9 Sep 1903, 1–3. MS 11, Reel 287. Special collection, Day Missions Library, Yale Divinity School, Connecticut; *Seventy-fourth Annual Report, May, 1911*, 340. For the miraculous events and details of Jansen's ministry in Cebu (1902–1917), Batangas (1917–1921) and Palawan (1921– c.1953), see Rodgers, *Forty Years*, 89–92. See also Sitoy, *Several Springs* 1: 108–110; *The Sixty-seventh Annual Report of the Board of Foreign Missions of the Presbyterian Church in the United States of America, presented to the General Assembly, May, 1904* (New York: Presbyterian Building, 1904), 278. For other evangelists and more details on their background, see Kwantes, "Presbyterian Missionaries in the Philippines," 130–131.

served as affiliate missionaries, then as full members in November 1903.[362]
The Cebu Mission Station began under the sponsorship of the East Liberty
Church of Pittsburgh.[363] The next year, Hibbard wrote to Ellinwood and
mentioned that "the Jansens in Cebu are having a tough struggle. The first
six were baptized a short time ago but the opposition is terrific. Have them
remembered especially in your prayers."[364] Evangelists Alonzo and Angel
C. Sotto (1885–1978) were among the six baptized in the second group
of converts. The Jansens conducted the first Protestant service in Spanish
at the basement of their residence in October 1902, attended by only five
local residents. Three months later, attendance in the three weekly services
varied from thirty to forty people.

(2) Missionary Reinforcement

The Jansens laid the foundation of Presbyterian mission work in Cebu for
the next fifteen years until they went on to another mission field in 1917.
The minutes of the Presbyterian Mission described this couple as having
"eminent efficiency," "spiritual character," "alert mind [s]," and as being
"valued worker[s]" and "good organizer[s]."[365] They were soon joined by
Rev Alexander A. Pieters and his wife Elizabeth Campbell Pieters (term of
service 1902–1903); Dr Rev James Alexander Graham and his wife Lillian
Holmes Graham (term of service 1905–1909); Rev Dr George Williamson
Dunlap/Lan Na mushi 蘭納牧師 (App. DD, Fig. 1) and his wife Devee
Taylor Dunlap (term of service 1907 until retirement in 1935). From
1905–1908, mission work in Cebu experienced rapid growth, with eighteen congregations and 359 baptized in 1905.[366] This growth paralleled the
overall advance of Presbyterian mission work in the archipelago, for, by
1907, four presbyteries had been organized in Manila, Iloilo, Cebu, and

362. Rodgers, *Forty Years*, 90. For White's early connection to CMA, see pp.
213–214.

363. Pascual, "Presbyterian Protestantism," 39.

364. James Burton Rodgers, Presbyterian Mission, Manila, to Dr Francis F. Ellinwood,
New York City, 5 Mar 1903, 5. MS 11, Reel 287. Yale Divinity Library, Yale University,
New Haven, Connecticut. A brief profile and background of the Jansens' ministry in
Manila can be found on page 88.

365. *Minutes of the Third Annual Meeting of the Philippine Mission, Iloilo P.I. January
18th–28th, 1902*, insert.

366. Sitoy, *Several Springs* 1: 156.

Dumaguete. After these four presbyteries were organized, the Philippine Presbyterian Synod was created in the same year.[367]

However, a constant shuffling of personnel between the Cebu Station and other Visayan stations made conditions unstable. For example, Mr and Mrs Pieters replaced the Hibbards in Dumaguete in 1903, while Graham was transferred to Bohol in 1909. This left the Jansens working in Cebu without moving from one station to another. That the work could expand was largely due to the work of the converts themselves. They either brought others into the fellowship or became evangelists who laid the groundwork for the coming of more missionaries. By 1911, the Cebu Mission Station had 2,700 members and nine "self-supporting" churches, with fifty young men studying at the Silliman Institute (now University), founded by Presbyterian missionaries in 1901.[368]

By 1913, the Cebu Station had already acquired its own property at a site that was then outside the city. Charles Gunn reported that a desirable piece of property was purchased, and five buildings were erected within the year – two missionary residences, two dormitories (Sneed and Emerson) and a church (Matilda Bradford Memorial Church).[369] Undoubtedly, the building of the two dormitories helped to increase the number of converts (including Chinese students) and members in the church.

(3) A Pre-1916 Chinese Church?

By 1913 Charles Gunn reported that the nationwide Presbyterian mission had,

> over 13,500 baptized church members; one self-supporting Chinese congregation and sixty-five Filipino congregations contributing in part to their own support; 155 Sunday Schools; about 150 public school students living each year in dormitories run under Christian influence; two dozen graduates of

367. See Rodgers, *Twenty Years*, 30–41, 51–56, 57–64, 76–99. Sitoy, *Several Springs* 1: 186.

368. Sitoy, *Several Springs* 1: 162; *Seventy–fifth Presbyterian Board Report* (1912), 53; Caridad Aldecoa–Rodriguez, *History of Dumaguete City* (Dumaguete City: by the author/ Silliman University, 2001), 25.

369. Charles A. Gunn, *The Presbyterian Church and the Filipino* (New York: Board of Foreign Missions of the Presbyterian Church in the USA, 1913), microfiche, 14–15.

Silliman Institute; fourteen native ministers and eighty-five evangelists, about twenty of whom have been trained in the Union Theological Seminary in Manila.[370]

The "self-supporting Chinese congregation" that Gunn referred to was not Cebu Gospel Church but the "Chinese Presbyterian Church in Iloilo City" (detailed history in pp. 118–140), for the Chinese church in Cebu had not yet been formed in 1913. However, there is a late claim that seems to state otherwise. Emelio Pascual states that there were five church communities in 1913: "three Cebuano-speaking churches; one English church and a Chinese church plus two junior churches (young people meeting for evangelistic services)."[371] Pascual gives no reference or any other support for his statement, and mission records do not evidence support for Pascual's claim, either. On the contrary, it was stated in 1915 in the deputation report given by Robert E. Speer, Dwight H. Day and David Bovaird that there was only one Chinese congregation – the one in Iloilo. The work of the Presbyterians among the Chinese up to this stage seems to have produced only this congregation, as the following statement indicates:

> We have a small congregation among the Chinese in Iloilo where the pastor said there were about thirty Chinese Christians. The work can hardly be said to be very effective or flourishing. In Manila after an effort on the part of several of the missions to work for Chinese, their efforts were unified and the whole work placed under the care of the Episcopalians. It does not seem to have flourished any better, considering the extent of the field, than the enterprise in Iloilo. And certainly the work is no easy one.[372]

---

370. Gunn, *Presbyterian Church*, 3.

371. Pascual, "Presbyterian Protestantism," 61.

372. *Report of Deputation Sent by the Board of Foreign Missions of the Presbyterian Church in the USA in the Summer of 1915, to visit the Missions in Siam and the Philippine Islands and on the Way Home to Stop at Some of the Stations in Japan, Korea and China.* Presented by Robert E. Speer, Dwight H. Day and David Bovaird (New York: Board of Foreign Missions of the Presbyterian Church in the USA, 1916), 256.

b) Progress in Cebu Mission

Constant shuffling of missionaries may have been one reason why the missionaries did not start any work among the Chinese in Cebu before 1916, unlike the situation in Iloilo. The work among the Filipinos had better progress. According to Sitoy, the reason why the Presbyterian Church in the USA granted the Philippine Presbyterian Synod full autonomy in 1914 was because there was evidence of growing Filipino leadership in terms of numbers and capacity to take on responsible leadership positions. With the creation of this Synod, the Philippine Mission station held the last of its annual meetings in Cebu City in October 1914.[373]

The years 1916 and 1917 were a period of testing and trial for the Filipino churches. Yet at the same time the Chinese Christians were beginning to form into a congregation in Cebu City. One of the earliest evangelists and the first ordained Presbyterian minister, Rev Ricardo Alonzo, became a priest of the *Iglesia Filipina Independiente* (Philippine Independent Church/Aglipayan Church). The Aglipayans also tried to recruit Rev Jorge Patalinghug (App. DD, Fig. 1) but he rejected their offer. Around five hundred members of the Presbyterian churches in the Visayas migrated to Mindanao.[374]

In 1917 some encouraging developments began to take place, such as the Matilda Bradford Memorial Church and the Oslob Evangelical Church becoming self-supporting, and new work beginning in many places. However, due to the continuing drain in number and vitality brought about by the migration to Mindanao, the situation again became critical in 1920. The overburdened missionaries were Rev John Wallace Dunlop/ Lan Na mushi 賴約翰牧師 (1890–1937; term of service 1918–1937), who had charge of northern Cebu, and Rev Charles Edward Rath (d. 20 January 1948, term of service 1903–1934), who cared for southern Cebu and Leyte.[375] Despite these trials, these two missionaries were able to help

---

373. See App. BB for the history of the United Church of Christ in the Philippines. Cf. Sitoy, *Several Springs* 1: 187–189; Jose R. Quisumbing, *The American Occupation of Cebu: Warwick Barracks, 1899–1917* ([Dumaguete]: J. R. Quisumbing, 1983), 75.

374. Sitoy, *Several Springs* 1: 189, 213.

375. Ibid., 214. James Rodgers appraised Rev Dunlop's ministry as follows: "Mr Dunlop has been in a real sense the successor as an evangelist of Mr Jansen, the founder of the station and has scattered the seed far and wide. During the last years he has given much

the Chinese congregation after it emerged (App. CC indicates specifically the Presbyterian missionaries of the Visayan Station).

In 1921 the work in Cebu was strengthened with twelve of the eighteen congregations registering increases and six new congregations getting started. The economic conditions of the province, however, continued to fluctuate.[376] Despite these hard times, 1926 was a good year for the Cebu mission. It was in such an environment that the Chinese congregation, which the missionaries called "The Chinese Congregation in Cebu" and "The Chinese Christian Church of Cebu," (App. DD, Fig. 2 photo caption) but which later became known as Cebu Gospel Church/Suwu Jidu Jiaohui 宿務基督教會, emerged, began to take root and grow.[377] To understand the situation better, one must first gain a proper perspective of the historical context of the Chinese community of Cebu City.

c) The Chinese in Cebu City

Before going into the work of the Presbyterian missionaries among the Chinese of Cebu City, it is necessary to understand the historical background of these Chinese during the Spanish colonial period, especially at the turn of the nineteenth century and until the early decades of the twentieth century.

(1) Hispanic Period

By the middle of the sixteenth century, the port of Cebu was a prosperous entrepot having a well-established trading link with China.[378] But from

---

time to the study of the text and translation of the Cebuan [sic] version of the Bible." They never moved to another field, unlike most of the missionaries, but worked in Cebu until their retirement in 1939. See Rodgers, *Forty Years*, 97. The Chinese names given to Dunlap and Dunlop are exactly the same. This has created confusion in the memories of the CGC members, even until present times.

376. "The years 1900–1940 saw Cebu with many pressing problems such as famine, drought, pestilence, immigration, robbery, high prices of commodities, starvation and poverty." See Delilah R. Labajo, "A Historical Survey of Reformative and Dissident Religious Movement in Cebu: 1900–1990" (MA thesis, University of San Carlos, 2002), 56. See also, *Minutes of the Annual Meeting of the Presbyterian Mission in the Philippines, Cebu, October 1ˢᵗ to October 9ᵗʰ, Nineteen Twenty-six. Ninety-seventh Year*, 34.

377. See *The Philippine Presbyterian* 13, no. 4 (Oct 1922): 23, and Judson L. Underwood, "Personal Report – 1928–1929," *Annual Reports, Philippine Mission, Presbyterian Church in the USA, Dumaguete, Oriental Negros, October 5–12, 1929*, 2.

378. For details on the pre-hispanic development of trade between Cebu and China, see Bruce Leonard Fenner, *Cebu under the Spanish Flag (1521–1816): An Economic and*

pre-hispanic times, not many Chinese settled in Cebu. Due to the sporadic hostility of the native Cebuanos, the encroachment of the Portuguese and the constant threat of food shortage, Miguel Lopez de Legazpi transferred his military base from Cebu to Panay in 1569 and conquered Manila in 1570. The galleon trade was established during the 1570s. This almost entirely eliminated Cebu's traditional commercial relations with Chinese and Southeast Asian traders. Manila became the trans-shipment center of a three-cornered trade involving exchange of Chinese silk and Asian luxury goods for Mexican silver. The Spaniards disregarded native products and neglected regional development when they focused on the galleon trade centered in Manila.[379]

Following Manila's monopoly of international commerce, Cebu declined as the regional entrepot and Spanish as well as Chinese population in Cebu City decreased. In 1595, Pedro Chirino, SJ, records that approximately two hundred Chinese traders and artisans were living in the Cebu *Parian*, a segregated area located on the outskirts of the city.[380] But after the decline, many Chinese left the city, leaving only between eighteen and twenty-five residing in the *Parian* during the eighteenth century.[381] Chinese population during the seventeenth and eighteenth centuries was also adversely affected by the numerous uprisings and subsequent expulsions and massacres by the Spanish authorities. During this period, the *Parian* in Cebu became a parish of the Roman Catholic Church. It was administered by a *capitan* (captain), whose duty was to collect taxes, to ensure security, and to act as liaison between the Spaniards and Chinese.

In the early decades of the nineteenth century, the Spaniards still neglected the Visayan region. In the 1840s Cebu became one of the major

---

Social History, Humanities Series 14 (Cebu City: San Carlos Publications, 1985), 16–19. Cebu is spelled Sebú in the Spanish sources.

379. Fenner, *Cebu under the Spanish Flag*, 34–38.

380. Pedro Chirino, SJ, *Relación de las Islas Filipinas i de lo que en ellas [h]an trabajado[s] los padres de la compaña de Iesus* (The Philippines in 1600), trans. Ramon Echevarria, Historical Conservation Society 15 (Rome: *Por Estevan Paulino*, 1604; reprint, Manila: Historical Conservation Society, 1969), 306 (page citations are to the reprint edition). Also in *BRPI* 12:276. The Spanish government intentionally built *pariancillos* in Manila (see pp. 44–48), Cebu, Iloilo (see p. 92), Davao and Sulu. *Tsinoy*, 62.

381. *Cedularios 1744–52*, Philippine National Archives, 177–179; in Fenner, *Cebu under the Spanish Flag*, 41.

sugar-producing provinces in the country, and by the mid-1850s, its port once again became a regional entrepot. At the same time, the policy on immigration had also become more lenient.[382] The rapid growth of the Chinese community in Cebu actually took place after the Spanish government opened its port to international trade in 1860. By the 1880s, Cebu had become the center of distribution for the Visayas and Mindanao and the most important port for internal commerce outside Manila. It stood second to Iloilo as the next port to Manila in international commerce.[383] Thus, between the late 1840s to the mid-1890s, the number of Chinese in the province increased from eighteen to around 1,400 or 1,500.[384] Around 1886, the Chinese numbered 983, the third largest concentration of this ethnic group following Manila (51,575) and Iloilo (1,157).[385] By 1894, there were 1,416 Chinese living in the province, the majority coming from Fujian, specifically from Hosan, Xiamen 廈門禾山. Seventy-two percent of this population resided either in Cebu City or in the town of San Nicolas, an Augustinian parish located south of Cebu City.[386] Ninety percent of this number were laborers on the docks and wharves. During

382. Fenner, *Cebu under the Spanish Flag*, 85–86.

383. Peter Gordon Gowing, *Brief History of Bohol, Cebu and Negros Oriental* (Manila: Ateneo de Manila University/Institute of Philippine Culture, 1962), 5.

384. Díaz Arenas, *Memorias históricas y estadísticas de Filipinas y particularmente de la grande isla de Luzon* ([Manila]: *Imprenta del Diario de Manila*, 1850), 115; Philippine National Archives, *Padron general de los Chinos de la provincia de Cebú, 1893, 1894*, in Fenner, *Cebu under the Spanish Flag*, 84, 144.

385. Chen YanDe 陳衍德. *Xiandaizhong de Chuantong – Feilvbin Huaren Shehui Yanjiu* 現代中的傳統—菲律賓華人社會研究 (Tradition in Modern Times: A Study on Philippine Chinese Society) (Xiamen, Fujian: Xiamen University Press 廈門大學出版社, 1998), 39 [henceforth cited as *Tradition in Modern Times*]; Foreman, *Philippine Islands*, 118. Foreman gave the number for Manila as 51,539, but believed that there were around 40,000, due to differing statistics that were provided him. Foreman, *Philippine Islands*, 118.

386. Philippine National Archives, *Padron general de los Chinos de la provincia de Cebú, 1894* in Fenner, *Cebu under the Spanish Flag*, 112, 145. Fenner's work provides detailed information on the role played by immigrant Chinese and Chinese mestizos in the economic and social growth of Cebu City from 1760–1860 (chs. 3 and 4) and the ethnic diversity and social complexity of Cebuano society from 1860–1896 (ch. 5). There were four parishes in Cebu after a century of Spanish rule: The Cathedral (exclusively for Spaniards under the secular clergy), the *Parian* (exclusively for Chinese under the secular clergy), San Nicolas, and Mandaue (Jesuit parish for *indios*). The number of parishes increased in succeeding years. See Michael Cullinane and Peter Xenos, "The Growth of Population in Cebu During the Spanish Era: Constructing a Regional Demography from Local Sources," in *Population and History: The Demographic Origins of the Modern Philippines*, Center for Southeast Asian Studies Monograph 16, eds., Daniel F. Doeppers

the Philippine Revolution (1896–1898) the Spaniards massacred many Chinese. A Chinese source records that a Spanish military force was sent to quell a revolt in Cebu in 1896; almost 900 Chinese perished in the battle that ensued. In contrast, merchants of other nationalities were protected by their consuls.[387] Many of the Chinese who survived fled back to their homeland or to other countries. Thus, by mid-1899, the number of Chinese living in the Philippines had dropped to approximately 40,000, compared with more than 90,000 in the 1880s.[388] Following the Revolution, the 1899–1902 War of Independence against the Americans broke out, resulting in great loss of lives, property and normal business operations within the Chinese community.

(2) American Occupation

During the years 1899–1902, the number of Chinese all over the Philippines substantially decreased due to several factors. First and foremost was the enforcement of the Chinese Exclusion Acts (see pp. 40–41).[389] Second, the debilitating effects of revolution and war followed by a series of natural disasters combined to bring on a depressed economy. The causes include: the rinderpest of 1902 killed 90 percent of work buffalos, a severe rice shortage, locust infestation, and the cholera that killed 100,000 inhabitants in two years.[390] Third, the suspension of revenue collections from *ce-*

---

and Peter Xenos (Madison, WI: University of Wisconsin–Madison Center for Southeast Asian Studies/Ateneo de Manila University Press, 1998), 88.

387. Chen YanDe, *Tradition in Modern Times*, 39. See also Teresita Ang See/Shi Hong YuHua 施洪玉華 and Go Bon Juan/Wu WenHuan 吳文煥, *The Ethnic Chinese in the Philippine Revolution* (Manila: Kaisa Para Sa Kaunlaran, Feilübin Huayi Qingnian Lianhehui 菲律賓華裔青年聯合會, 1996), 5, for the English translation of a report in the *Star Paper* (May 1896), cited in 中國大事匯記, 卷首 《論說匯》 (Historical record of big events outside China, vol. 1, Collected Works), ed. Qi JianSheng 倚劍生.

388. Wong Kwok-chu, *The Chinese in the Philippine Economy*, 23. Another source gives an even higher number of 100,000 in 1898. See *The Encyclopedia of the Chinese Overseas*, ed. Lynn Pan (Singapore: Archipelago Press, Landmark Books, for Chinese Heritage Center, 1998), 188.

389. For a compilation in Chinese of the primary documents related to these Acts, see Go Bon Juan/Wu WenHuan 吳文煥 and Wang PeiYuan 王培元編, ed., *Jinian Paihuafa Yibai Zhounian (Fu Huagong Xielei Xiaoshuo 《 Kushehui》)* 紀念排華法一百週年 〔 附 華工血淚小說 《苦社會》 (Commemorating the centennial of the Chinese Exclusion Acts with "Bitter Society," a novel about Chinese workers in America) (Manila: Kaisa Para Sa Kaunlaran, Feilübin Huayi Qingnian Lianhehui 菲律賓華裔青年聯合會, 2002).

390. Wong Kwok-chu, *Chinese in the Philippine Economy*, 26.

dula (residence certificate), Chinese poll tax, opium contracts, and licensed gambling, adversely affected the Chinese business world and caused many Chinese to go out of business.

This deplorable state of affairs continued until 1909 when the Payne-Aldrich Act established free trade between the Islands and the United States. A sustained export-led growth of the Philippine economy ensued during the next decade (1910–1920), and the Chinese were at the forefront of this economic prosperity. As a commercial entrepot Cebu experienced the same spiraling trend in its Chinese population – from 1,662 Chinese in 1918, to 2,697 in 1933, and 6,117 in 1939. Many of the Chinese who came from what was then known as the Xiamen-Tongan district engaged in and profited from the import-export enterprise.[391] The majority of the immigrants were merchants but the number of teachers and other professionals increased as the latter group started establishing educational facilities in 1915. This was the situation of the Cebu Chinese community when a Chinese church began to take shape in 1916.

d) Presbyterian Work Among the Chinese

The English name of the Cebu Gospel Church appeared variously throughout its early history. The Presbyterian missionaries referred to it as "The Chinese Christian Church of Cebu." The earliest reference to this name, appearing as a photo caption of the small congregation, dates from 21 August 1921 (App. DD, Fig. 2). Another name found in Presbyterian publications is "The Chinese Congregation in Cebu." The UCCP, on the other hand, referred to it as either the "Cebu Chinese Church"[392] or "the UEC Chinese Congregation of Cebu."[393] The Chinese name has evolved from Suwu Zhonghua Jidu Jiaohui 宿務中華基督教會 (App. DD, Fig. 7, Cebu Chinese Church of Christ), used from 1916 to around 1934, to Suwu Jidu Jiaohui 宿務基督教會 (Cebu Christian Church or Cebu Church of Christ), used probably from 1934 onward but definitely after

---

391. See Wong Kwok-chu, *Chinese in the Philippine Economy*, 23–88 for information on the Chinese economic situation in the Philippines from 1898 to 1929.

392. *Minutes of the Executive Committee, United Church of Christ in the Philippines, Manila, December 6–11, 1954*, 35.

393. Sitoy, *Several Springs* 2: 942–943. See later section on the history of UECP.

WWII, or 1946 until the present day.[394] The church has preserved the hand-written minutes of the church council dating from 1946 until 1951, and this Chinese name appears on the cover page. There are also pictures within this time frame showing the same name. The present-day English nomenclature – Cebu Gospel Church – is not the exact translation of the Chinese name used currently.

When Sitoy discussed "UCCP Work with the Chinese Churches" in his book, he used the term "UEC Chinese Congregation of Cebu" to refer to the Cebu Chinese congregation and "Chinese United Evangelical Church of Manila" to refer to the Manila Chinese Congregation. This is actually an awkward name to use, for the term "UEC" mistakenly links the Cebu congregation to the United Evangelical Church of the Philippines (former CUEC) in Manila. These two congregations, although having the same Presbyterian heritage, are not and never have been affiliated with each other. Each developed independently and separately from the other. Sitoy's name for the Manila Chinese Congregation is in itself inaccurate, for the official name for UECP is either "Chinese United Evangelical Church" (original name used) or "United Evangelical Church of Manila" (the name used in the sixties). The fact remains that the name "UEC Chinese Congregation of Cebu" is never found in the UCCP minutes from 1950 to 1972.

(1) Emergence: People Involved

(a) The Missionaries

The CGC is now considered the second oldest Chinese church in the Philippines, although during the decade that it emerged (1916–1926), it was the third Chinese church to be formed, following the CPCI in 1900 and the SSCM in 1903. Soon after arriving in 1900, the Presbyterian missionaries started working among the Chinese of Iloilo. This is evidenced by the *Annual Reports* between the years 1901 to 1916.[395] Unlike Iloilo, however, the Mission station reports from Cebu during the same period

---

394. The Chinese names are found on photographs marked with exact dates, found in the archive of Cebu Gospel Church. The year 1934 is just an approximation, since many photographs were lost during WWII.

395. *Annual Report of the Board of Foreign Missions of the Presbyterian Church in the United States of America* (*1901*), 262; (*1909*), 374; (*1910*), 353; (*1911*), 338; (*1913*), 345–346; (*1915*), 346; (*1916*), 312.

did not mention any work being done among the Chinese. Instead, the missionaries seemed to have concentrated on evangelizing the Visayans in five circuits (Cebu City, Compostela, Dumanjug, Balamban, and Bohol) in the central region of the archipelago.[396] This lack of documentary evidence raises questions regarding the claim of Sitoy that "the Presbyterian missionaries in 1902 also started work among the local Chinese, although these early efforts were aborted either due to the lack of missionary personnel, or the departure of the most avid inquirers."[397]

The Presbyterian record likewise does not seem to support the claim of Pascual Emelio S. Pascual who wrote in his thesis that "It was Rev Charles Rath and Rev John Dunlop who started full-time mission work with the Chinese starting in the year 1918."[398] Based on CGC records and that of the Philippine Mission of the Presbyterian Church in the United States of America, the work actually started in 1916. The annual report for 1917 recorded that "a class of young Chinese of the best class has lately been formed."[399] At that time, neither Rath nor Dunlop were in Cebu City, for according to James B. Rodgers, Rath moved from Tacloban to Cebu in 1918, and the Dunlops arrived in Cebu in the same year. None of the missionaries can ever be considered as doing "full-time mission work with the Chinese" because they were all involved in doing ministry among the three people groups mentioned by George Dunlap and Charles Rath.[400] Both of them categorically stated in *The Eighty-third Annual Report* that their work was "limited to the English-speaking people, and the Visayans and the Chinese." There were around 1,000 Chinese at this time while there were only 150 English-speaking people. Their main work, however, was with the Visayan people. This is the reason why the Presbyterian Mission desired to secure a Chinese pastor for the Chinese congregation, but at that time it

---

396. Sitoy, *Several Springs* 1: 157.

397. Sitoy, *Several Springs* 2: 943. He was discussing "The UEC Chinese Congregation of Cebu" when he made this statement.

398. Pascual, "Presbyterian Protestantism," 81.

399. *The Eightieth Annual Report of the Board of Foreign Missions of the Presbyterian Church in the United States of America Presented to the General Assembly, May, 1917* (New York: Presbyterian Building, 1917), 322.

400. *The Eighty-third Annual Report of the Board of Foreign Missions of the Presbyterian Church in the United States of America Presented to the General Assembly, May, 1920* (New York: Presbyterian Building, 1920), 343.

was still too small and financially incapable of supporting a pastor. John Dunlop could not have been working full-time with the Chinese as well, for he was also well known for his indefatigable preaching tours around the whole island of Cebu, much like what his predecessor Paul Frederick Jansen had done during his term.[401]

Regarding who started the work among the Chinese in Cebu, Bishop Santiago G. Iyoy, wrote in 1961 that, "The Cebu Gospel Church . . . began its organization with a handful of Chinese communicant members in the pre-war time under the able ministration of a Presbyterian missionary – the Rev Dr George Dunlap assisted by Pastor Jorge B. Patalinghug."[402] Although Bishop Iyoy wrote this in 1961, it is the view that has been accepted throughout the decades by the Presbyterian missionaries, the Filipino Bradford United Church of Christ in the Philippines (former Matilda Bradford Memorial Church where the Chinese congregation held Sunday afternoon services), as well as the CGC, publisher of the *Gospel Quarterly*. George and Devee Dunlap were in Cebu intermittently during the years 1907, 1911 to 1918, and 1920 until they retired in 1935. Note that the Dunlaps (not the Dunlops) were in Cebu when the Chinese congregation emerged. In the October 1922 issue of *The Philippine Presbyterian* featuring the work in Cebu, George Dunlap gave a very long report on the Chinese work. Despite the fact that he does not claim to have started the work, his words show how deeply concerned and devoted he was to the work.[403] The record from CGC, on the other hand, states that it was Paul Frederick Jansen/Lan Xin mushi 蘭新牧師 who shared the gospel with the Chinese community in Cebu.[404] If so, since Jansen left Cebu in 1917, his work

---

401. In the early years (1902–1907) Jansen "traveled through the rough mountain country of Cebu following up people who had attended services in the city. On the other hand, John Dunlop went from "the extreme south to Bantayan in the north. He has sought the Visayan believers in Southern Masbate where Cebuano is the common language." See Rodgers, *Forty Years*, 91, 96–97.

402. Santiago G. Iyoy, "Cebu Gospel Church," *Wuguang* 務光 *Gospel Quarterly* 17 (Dec 1961): 47. Iyoy was bishop of the Visayas Jurisdiction of the UCCP during the sixties.

403. *The Philippine Presbyterian* 23, no. 4 (Oct, 1922): 23–24.

404. Joseph Que/Guo YuXian 郭毓賢, "Benhui Wushi Nianlai Dashiji 本會五十年來大事記 (The church's main events for the past fifty years)," 36 and Tiuⁿ Chin/Zhang ZhenZong 張振宗, "Shuwu Jidu Jiaohui Wushi Nianlai Jianshi Zheyao 宿務基督教會五十年來簡史摘要 (Summary of the history of Cebu Gospel Church for the past fifty years)," in *Cebu Gospel Church Golden Jubilee Souvenir 1916–1966 (Suwu Jidu Jiaohui Jinxi*

among the Chinese must have been done around 1916–1917, or even earlier. There is, however, no mention of this in the Presbyterian records.

(b) Rev Jorge Patalinghug

Regarding the contribution of Rev Jorge Patalinghug, Go Pang Kong/Wu BangGuang 吳邦光 supplied the following information, which he received directly from Patalinghug. During visitation rounds, the Reverend met a Chinese Christian named Tan Khim/Chen Qin 陳琴. He invited this Christian and he in turn invited the nephew of Kang Bun Pit/Jiang WenBi 江文筆 [the legal name Cang Bon Pit will henceforth be used] named Kang Tsui Leng/Jiang ShuiLong 江水龍, to attend the Filipino worship service. Cang Bon Pit was a well-respected community leader and prominent businessman in Cebu City. According to Go, however, Patalinghug was not aware of two other gentlemen – Chiu Tsong Kiau/Zhou ZongQiao 周宗橋 and Sih Eng Su/Xue YongShu 薛永黍 – who were initiating plans to hold Chinese services in the afternoon at Bradford Church. These two Chinese Christians had not talked with Patalinghug but with the American missionaries. In cooperation with the missionaries, they were instrumental in gathering communicants whom they invited to attend the worship services and Bible studies.[405]

(c) Two Chinese Christians

Chiu Tsong Kiau and Sih Eng Su can be considered as the Chinese founders of Cebu Gospel Church, alongside Patalinghug and the Presbyterian missionaries. Chiu Tsong Kiau, a graduate of the Heling Yinghua Shuyuan 鶴齡英華書院 (Anglo-Chinese College), established by the Methodists in Fuzhou, China, went to teach English at the Cebu Chinese School.[406] According to Go Pang Kong, Chiu loved the Lord dearly, was very

---

Xiantang Anmu Qingdian Tekan) 宿務基督教會金禧獻堂按牧慶典特刊 (Cebu City: Cebu Gospel Church, [1966]), 55. This source will henceforth be cited as *CGCGJS*.

405. Go Pang Kong/Wu BangGuang 吳邦光, "Shuwu Chuqi De Jidu Jiaohui 宿務初期的基督教會 (The Early Christian Church in Cebu)," in *CGCGJS*, 59.

406. The Anglo-Chinese School in Fuzhou was established in 1881 through the donation of ten thousand dollars given by the wealthy merchant and recent convert Zhang HeLing 張鶴齡 (d. 1890) and supported by the Foochow [variant spelling of Fuzhou] Annual Conference of the Methodist Episcopal Church. See Ryan Dunch, *Fuzhou Protestants and the Making of a Modern China 1857–1927* (New Haven, CT: Yale University Press, 2001), 22, 34, 38–40.

Christ-like in his relationship with people, and gave a good impression to his colleagues at school. Sih Eng Su was the chairman of the school board and was a graduate of the University of Michigan. He and his wife were likewise devoted Christians. Presbyterian records support Go's information regarding this couple's role in the Chinese church. In 1919, Olive Rohrbaugh (term of service 1917–1945), manager of the Emerson Girls' Dormitory, had a boarder by the name of a "Mrs Sy" (variant spelling for Sih). The description of her husband is the same as that given by Go, and it is further stated that she came from a Christian family in Xiamen. She had attended a mission school there and in Shanghai. Mrs Sih accompanied Olive Rohrbaugh and Theresa Margaret Kalb (term of service 1903–1934), the wife of Charles Rath, on their visits to other Chinese ladies, acting as their interpreter.[407]

It is safe to surmise that all of the above-mentioned missionaries (Jansen, Dunlap, Rath, Dunlop), Rev Patalinghug, as well as the two Chinese Christians, Chiu and Sih, were involved in starting the church. The latter, however, were most likely more effective in drawing their fellow Chinese into attending the services at Bradford Church. Their profession and social standing enabled them to reach the parents of the school children, their colleagues in school and other Chinese businessmen in society, and allowed them, gradually, to form a group that became the core members of the Chinese church.

(2) Emergence: Membership and Organization

Chiu and Sih gathered eleven people for regular Sunday worship, including Mrs Cang Bon Pit/Jiang WenBi 江文筆夫人, nee Ng Chhai Toan/Huang CaiDuan 黃彩段 (d. 1933 in China; App. DD, Fig. 3),[408] her son (Kang Sun Heng/Jiang ShunXing 江順興) and daughter-in-law (Sih Ma Bin/Xue MaMin 薛媽敏), Mrs Cang's daughter (Mrs Uy Cang Chui Siok/Huang Jiang ShuiShu 黃江水淑, 1888–1975; App. DD, Fig. 5), Mr and Mrs Ng

---

407. Theresa Kalb Rath, "Work among the Chinese in Cebu," *The Philippine Presbyterian* 10 (Jul 1919): 8–10, cited in Sitoy, *Several Springs* 2:943.

408. See App. DD, Fig. 3. Ye MingChang 葉明昌, "Daibiao Shangjia Zhici 代表喪家致詞 (Eulogy from Bereaved Family)," in *The Spring Sunshine: A Memoir of Elder Cang Chui Siok/ Chunhuiji – Huang Jian ShuiShu Zhanglao Jinian Ce*「春暉集」—黃江水淑長老紀念冊 (Caloocan City: Shangkuan Press & School Supply, n.d.), 96.

Siong Chu/Huang XiangCi 黃祥慈夫婦 and their three daughters, and Mrs Iap An Tun/Ye AnDun 葉安頓夫人 (legal name AntonYap) and her daughter. Anton Yap, like Mr Cang Bon Pit, was a prominent and wealthy businessman.[409]

Mrs Cang Bon Pit was one of the first to believe and be baptized in this emerging church. From 1918–1920, those who regularly attended the Chinese worship services were Mrs Sih Eng Su (the former Lim Pek Guat/Lin BiYue 林碧月) and the teacher Chiu Tsong Kiau. From 1921–1922, more teachers from the Tiong Hoa Hak Hao/Zhong Hua Xue Xiao 中華學校 began attending the church, namely, Go Bun Peng/Wu WenBing 吳文炳, Ng Eng Tiong/Huang YongZhang 黃永長 (legal name David Uyboco), Ng Tek Bo/Huang DeMao 黃德茂, and three gentlemen who studied at the Silliman University – Ng Teng Su/Huang DengShi 黃登仕 (legal name Uy Teng Su, also known as Tirso Uytengsu, Sr), Lim Giok Su/Lin YuSu 林玉樹 (legal name Lim Yok Su), and Lim Khai Chhun/Lin KaiChun 林開春 (legal name Lim Kay Chun).[410]

(a) Church Organization

An entry in the Presbyterians' 1922 *Annual Report* is most significant for the history of the CGC. It reads:

> [On] The first Sunday in May, 1921, the Chinese congregation was organized into a church. Two elders and a deacon were chosen from the seven young men who composed the organization. A number of months ago, at their own initiative, they decided to hold a prayer meeting each Sun [*sic*] evening in addition to the regular Sunday afternoon service. From this prayer meeting came the desire to have some special evangelistic meetings for the unconverted Chinese of the city. Three meetings were held. They were well attended, and a splendid

---

409. Go Pang Kong, "Early Christian Church," in *CGCGJS*, 59. Born in Xiamen in 1868, Yap Anton was brought over to Cebu City at age 15 to help his father's dry-goods store. Through trading in sugar, his import and export firm and other companies remained viable throughout many decades. See Wong Kwok-chu, *Chinese in the Philippine Economy 1898–1941*, 47–48.

410. Que, "The Church's Main Eevents," in *CGCGJS* 66, 36. These teachers later became the board members of the church-related Kian Kee School.

spirit was shown. The last night 38 young men signed cards expressing their desire to accept Christ as their Savior.[411]

That the Chinese congregation officially became a recognized church in 1921 is not documented in any of the five Chinese sources or in any of the interviews I conducted.[412] It seems that only the Presbyterian Mission kept this record. However, the whole congregation, together with George and Devee Dunlap and two unidentified female missionaries, are pictured in a photograph dated 21 August 1921, and this picture appeared in the *Golden Jubilee Souvenir* of the church (App. DD, Fig. 2).[413] The occasion of taking this photograph, moreover, was duly noted by Go Pang Kong in his article.[414]

411. *The Eighty–fifth Annual Report of the Board of Foreign Missions of the Presbyterian Church in the United States of America Presented to the General Assembly, May, 1922* (New York: Presbyterian Building, 1922), 388.

412. These five sources, all found in the *CGCGJS*, are: Joseph Que 郭毓賢, "Benhui Wushi Nianlai Dashiji 本會五十年來大事記 (The church's main events for the past fifty years)," 36–54; Tiuⁿ Chin Tsong/Zhang ZhenZong 張振宗, "Shuwu Jidu Jiaohui Wushi Nianlai Jianshi Zheyao 宿務基督教會五十年來建使摘要 (Summary of the history of Cebu Gospel Church for the past fifty years)," 55–58; Go Pang Kong/Wu BangGuang 吳邦光, "Shuwu Chuqi De Jidu Jiaohui 宿務初期的基督教會 (The Early Christian Church in Cebu)," 59–60; Tiuⁿ Toan Tsong/Zhang DuanZhuang 張端莊, "Zaoqi De Shuwu Jiaohui 早期的宿務教會 (The early period of the Cebu Church)," 60; and Cheng Ju/Zeng Yu 增瑜, "Cong Shuwu Jidu Jiaohui Qingzhu Jinxi Tandao Huaqiao Jidujiao Zai Nandao 從宿務基督教會慶祝金禧談到華僑基督教在南島 (Discussing the overseas Chinese Christians in Southern Philippines from the fiftieth anniversary celebration of Cebu Gospel Church)," 20–22.

413. Mrs Mercedes Cang/Jiang MianLing 江蔡綿綾, one of the great grand daughters-in-law of Mrs Cang Bon Pit, has identified some of the figures in this photograph as: Ng Siu Tin/Huang XiuZhen 黃秀珍, Kang Hu Se/Jiang FuXi 江扶西/存仁 Jose Cang, Kang Tsun Tek/Jiang ChunDe 江存德 also known as Lucas Cang, Ng Teng Su/Huang DengShi 黃登仕 also known as Uy Teng Su, 林玉樹夫人 Mrs Lim Giok Su/Lin YuShu, Mrs Kang Sun Heng/Jiang ShunXing nee Sih Ma Bin/Xue MaMin 江順興夫人薛瑪敏; Kang Tat Jin/Jiang DaRen 江達仁 Catalina Cang, Rev George Dunlap, Ng Tek Bo/Huang DeMao 黃德茂, Sih Eng Su/Xue YongCi 薛永賜 also written as Sy Eng Su, Cang Suco, Kang Sun Heng/Jiang ShunXing 江順興 also written as Cang Sun Heng, Lim Giok Su/Lin YuShu 林玉樹, Tian Su Jin/Tian ShuRen 田樹人, and Go Bun Peng/Wu WenBing 吳文炳. Mercedes Chua vda. de Cang/Jiang Cai MianLing 江蔡綿綾, interview by Jean Uayan, 25 and 29 Jun 2004, transcript, Philippine Chinese Church Archives, Biblical Seminary of the Philippines, Valenzuela City, Philippines.

414. Go Pang Kong, "Early Christian Church," in *CGCGJS*, 59.

(b) Church Activities

Thus the congregation was recognized and organized as a church in May 1921. In 1923–1924, a very substantial report was given by Rev Judson Leolin Underwood (term of service 1922–1936), who introduced himself as pastor of the Union (American) and Chinese churches in Cebu City. Underwood's description affords a glimpse of the general activities going on during this early period of the emerging church. Theresa Rath conducted a Bible class for women and the Chinese women themselves held Sunday School classes in one of their homes. The mission ladies helped in doing visitation. Four of the men took turns with the pastor in preaching during the services, after which the latter conducted a Bible class. He also conducted catechumen classes for prospective members. Most of the twenty-three new members in 1922 went through this class. This brought the membership to forty.[415]

Regular worship services were held at the Bradford Church at three o'clock in the afternoon, from 1916 to 1948, disrupted only for a few years during the Second World War (App. DD, Fig. 4). Olive Rohrbaugh briefly states that on Sundays, "There is time for dinner, and a siesta, but you will not sleep too long for at 3:00 p. m. the church bell calls the Chinese Congregation for its regular church service . . ." When I interviewed Mrs Saw Cang Iattee/Su Jiang YueZhi 蘇江悅治 (App. DD, Fig. 5), the daughter of Cang Bon Pit's "second wife," she remembers that they paid a monthly rental fee of five pesos for use of the Bradford Church.[416] As a child she was always brought to the church by Mrs Cang Ng Chhai Toan, who was the "first wife." Mrs Saw was baptized in 1923 and later became an active leader in the church.[417] There is no record that Mr Cang Bon Pit himself ever became a Christian.

---

415. *Mission Meeting Reports for 1923–1924 of the Philippine Mission, Manila, Philippine Islands, October 6–14, 1924.* See also *The Eighty-ninth Annual Report of the Board of Foreign Missions of the Presbyterian Church in the United States of America Presented to the General Assembly, May, 1926* (New York: Presbyterian Building, 1926), 234.

416. Mrs Saw Cang Iattee/Su Jiang YueZhi 蘇江悅治, audio-taped interview by Jean Uayan, 23 Jun 2004, transcript, Philippine Chinese Church Archive, Biblical Seminary of the Philippines, Valenzuela City, Philippines. At the time of the interview, Mrs Saw was 99 years old.

417. "List of Church Members and Their Dates of Baptism," in *CGCGJS*, 74.

Prayer meetings were soon added and held in the evenings.[418] It is evident from Rev Underwood's description that the missionaries were very much involved in evangelistic outreach and ecclesiastical duties among the Chinese, despite the fact that they struggled with having to rely fully on the Chinese members to act as their interpreters.[419] The Presbyterian record seems to give a more positive portrayal of the church with regard to membership – twenty-three new members in one year! Worship attendance also seemed to have been sustained. The Chinese sources, however, give the impression that attendance around the years 1923–1925 was close to the lowest possible level. The attendance seems to be only around ten, at most a few more than twenty if all the names are combined, and this is only half of the number reported by Rev Underwood. There were times when there were only six or seven, even three in attendance – one preacher (Underwood was clearly identified in Que's record), one interpreter, and one listener! Without more data from either side, however, there can be no way of reconciling these differences.[420]

Alice Fullerton started a Sunday School class with the help of a certain Mrs Lim around 1922. Fullerton stated: "I started a Sunday School in the house of one of the church members. We ver [y, *sic*] soon had twenty-five members. I hear from Mrs Lim that these numbers are keeping up."[421] Again, the Chinese record seems to give a less positive view of this ministry. What Fullerton claimed regarding her starting the Sunday School ministry in 1922 seems to be contradicted by what Tiuⁿ Chin Tsong/Zhang ZhenZong 張振宗 and Joseph Que wrote. According to them, the work began during 1923–1925 by the missionaries (when Fullerton had already

418. Charles Rath reported that "The men and women of the congregation have had prayer meetings in the home of one of the deacons and also in the home of the deaconess Mrs Cang [Bon Pit]." See "Personal Report of Charles E[dward] Rath," *Annual Reports, 1929–1930, Philippine Mission of the Presbyterian Church in the USA, Manila, October 2–9, 1930.*

419. "Personal Report of John W[allace] Dunlop," *Annual Reports for 1932–1933, Philippine Mission of the Presbyterian Church in the USA, Cebu, October 16–21, 1933.*

420. Que, "Church's Main Events," in *CGCGJS*, 36.

421. Alice Fullerton was a nurse who arrived in Cebu in 1922 but was soon after transferred to Iloilo and later served in Dumaguete City. See *Mission Meeting Reports for 1923–1924 of the Philippine Mission. Manila, Philippine Islands, October 6–14, 1924;* W. MacD[onald], "Our 'Golden Roster'" *The Philippine Presbyterian* 32, no. 4 (Dec 1940): appendix.

gone to Dumaguete City) and a lady named Ng Iap Bi Biau/Huang Ye
MeiMiao 黃葉美描, at the residence of Mrs Cang Bon Pit, but the attendance was very small. Tiu^n even wrote that this work did not continue.
However, he may not have been totally accurate on this point, based on
the testimony of Pilar Siao (Siau Pit Leng/Xiao BiLeng 蕭必冷傳道) and
her contemporaries. Pilar Siao and her two sisters were among the earliest
Sunday School children. She later became a long-term full-time worker
of CGC. Her mother was one of those who provided a vehicle to be used
for visiting the communicants and church members. She remembers that
Sunday School was held at the home of Mrs Cang Bon Pit on Sunday
mornings.[422] Despite the slight discrepancy between these two records,
which may be due to the unstable conditions at the beginning, Sunday
School work and Bible studies were undeniably key features in the survival
and continuance of this young church as the first decade progressed.

(c) Growth and Progress

By 1923–1925, the church already had two elders who took turns preaching and helping to translate Rev Underwood's messages. They were Go
Hong Tso/Wu HongZhu 吳鴻助, a teacher in the English department of
the Cebu Chinese School, and Ng Jin Seng/Huang RenSheng 黃仁聖.
Furthermore, Que mentions some new names among the regular church-
goers: Kang Tsui Leng/Jiang ShuiLong 江水龍; Tan Un Ho/Chen YunHe
陳允和; Ng Peng Hong/Huang BingHuang 黃炳煌; Ng Sih An Pa Lok/
Huang Xue AnBaLu 黃薛安巴洛; Mrs Uy Cang Chui Siok (the daughter
of Mrs Cang Bon Pit); Kang Ng Giok Pheng/Jiang Huang YuPeng 江黃
玉碰; and Kang Sih Ma Bin/Jiang Xue MaMin 江薛瑪敏 (legal name
Mameng Sy). Some of these names overlap with the list given in the article
written by Go Pang Kong.

Clearer details are given by Go Pang Kong regarding the organization,
Sunday worship service, and other activities during the earliest period
of the church. First, with regard to church organization, he wrote that
in the beginning, it was not formal because members were few. Out of

---

422. Pilar Siao/Siau Pit Leng/Xiao BiLeng 蕭必冷傳道, audio-taped interview by
Jean Uayan, 25 Jun 2004, transcript, Philippine Chinese Church Archive, Biblical Seminary
of the Philippines, Valenzuela City, Philippines.

the teachers from the Cebu Chinese School who attended, two, maybe three, were elected as elders or deacons, which agrees with Que's record. During the tenure of Rev Judson Underwood, Go, who lived in Cebu City from August 1920 to March 1925, was himself elected as an elder.[423] Second, with regard to the Sunday worship service, Go wrote that Rath and Dunlap, followed by Dunlop and Underwood, took turns preaching. The translators during this early period were Chiu Tsong Kiau and Sih Eng Su, but they later went back to China. Several others, including Go, took over the responsibility.

Go also mentions that Mr and Mrs Lim Giok Su/Lin YuShu 林玉樹 夫婦 were added to the membership roster.[424] Other truth-seekers who attended the services were Sih An Dian/Xue AnRan 薛安然 and Sih An Sim/ Xue AnXin 薛安心, Sih Bin Diong/Xue BinLiang 薛彬良 and Sih Chhai Hi/Xue CaiXi 薛彩熙, Ng Peng Hong/Huang BingHuang 黃炳煌, Ti^n Diong Kheng/Zheng LiangQing 鄭良卿, Tan Seng Cho/Chen ChengZu 陳承祖, and Kho Nga Diong/Xu YaLiang 許雅諒.

Lastly, with regard to activities, Go relates that visitation and evangelistic meetings were being done in addition to the worship service in order to draw the Chinese in the community into the faith. In 1922, such an event took place with about sixty or seventy Chinese attending, and these people had never before stepped inside a Protestant church. Dunlap would regularly invite some members to go with him to the leprosarium in the town of Consolacion or to the prison house on Martires Street, Cebu City. Every year, Christmas was something to look forward to, with all the members assisting in decorating or participating in the programs.

(d) Church Leadership

The church was not yet financially strong enough to secure a Chinese pastor, but from the start and into the early 1930s, the missionaries and the congregation continued to search for Chinese pastors in China. Charles

---

423. This statement regarding Go Pang Kong being elected as an elder does not seem to correspond to the record of Que and Tiu^n who wrote that the two elders at this time (1920–25) were Go Hong Tso and Ng Jin Seng, unless he was elected before 1923. But if this was the case, it would seem strange that the two authors did not mention it for a fact.

424. Lim Giok Su later became an elder who accomplished much for the church and the church school – Kian Kee School – in the post-war era.

Rath reported regarding this search in 1930.[425] A pastor, Rev Sih Eng Kiat/
Shi YingJi 施應吉, came from China in 1931, but he left the following
year because he could not adjust to the conditions and the church. The
leaders at this time were Go Tiong Hoa/Wu ZhongHua 吳仲華 and Mrs
Lim Hok Seng/Lin FuSheng 林福盛夫人 (nee Si Giok Pan/Shi YuPing 施
玉瓶) (App. DD, Fig. 6).

I was able to interview Mrs Lim Hok Seng in 2005. At the time she
was either 100 or 102 years old, depending on which of two dates of birth
was being used.[426] The birth date on her passport is 16 June 1903, but she
said that her real birth date is 18 December 1905. In those days it seems
there was a practice of giving false birth dates in order to make one old
enough to migrate from China. She said that she came to the Philippines
at age 24. This would mean she came in 1929, if 1905 is taken as the
year of her birth. She was from Gulangyu, Fujian, 福建鼓浪嶼, where
she had married a Christian named Lim Hok Seng, and, after converting
from her Buddhist faith, had attended the Hok Im Tong/Fuyin Tang 福
音堂 (Gospel Church) with her husband. Despite her age, she distinctly
remembers being baptized in Cebu City by Rev John Dunlop and attending services at the Bradford Church.

(e) Temporary Setback

The years 1932–1933 were the lowest point of the Chinese work, as recorded in both sources. George Dunlap painted a bleak picture in his report
when he wrote:

> We regret that this work has been most discouraging. It be-
> came necessary to ask the Chinese pastor [Rev Sih Eng Kiat]
> to return to China. For some reason or other he was not able
> to make the adjustment that was necessary to work with his
> people in another country. Then the fact that the depression
> was most noticeable among the Chinese it was necessary that

---

425. *The Eightieth Annual Report*, 322. Charles Rath first labored in Leyte from
1903 to 1908 before moving to Manila. After marrying Theresa Kalb in 1912, the couple
returned to work in Leyte in 1918 and partly got involved with the work in Cebu.

426. Si Giok Pan a.k.a Mrs Lim Hok Seng/Shi YuPing (Mrs Lin FuSheng) 施玉瓶/
林福盛夫人, audio-taped interview by Jean Uayan, 22 Apr 2005, transcript, Philippine
Chinese Church Archive, Biblical Seminary of the Philippines, Valenzuela City, Philippines.

many of them return to China. The attendance at the beginning of the year was about fourty [sic] and now about ten to fifteen.[427]

Among the "many" who returned to China were numerous teachers from the Cebu Chinese School (App. DD, Fig. 7). As the church emerged, the majority of the teachers from this school had become church members. Some of them, with names listed in the article by Tiuⁿ Chin Tsong, included: Ng Ka Lek/Huang JiaLi 黃嘉歷, Tiuⁿ Chheng Peh/Zhang QingBai 張清白, Tan Peng Jin/Chen BingRen 陳秉仁, Ng Jin Seng/Huang RenSheng 黃仁聖 (who frequently shared the word), Tan Iok Pek/Chen YueBo 陳約伯 (legal name Job Chen), who preached and translated faithfully, and Go Hong Tso.[428] This is the positive aspect of the situation, but, on the other hand, these teachers were so transient that church membership was always critically affected and constantly fluctuating. This situation was especially true during the early 1930s.

Writing for the same period, Mrs Dunlap reported that there was likewise a drop-in Sunday School attendance and that the choir had been dissolved. She lamented the death of a "Mrs Chang" who had gone back to China expecting to return shortly. Thus she lost her assistant in Sunday School work. The Dunlaps, however, remained faithful as they worked in this fledgling church and the members loved them very much. When they left Cebu in 1935, a huge crowd of sixty-five adults and twenty children came to send them off. The Chinese caption below the photograph reads "宿務中華基督教會歡送 Dr & Mrs Geo. W. Dunlap 返國紀念 (In remembrance of the Cebu Chinese Church of Christ sending off Dr and Mrs Geo. W. Dunlap as they return home)."[429]

427. George W[illiamson] Dunlap, "Personal Report," in *Annual Reports 1932–1933, Philippine Mission, Presbyterian Church in the USA, Cebu, October 16–21, 1933.*

428. Tiuⁿ Chin Tsong, "Summary of the History," in *CGCGJS*, 55. Job Chen himself testified that he was the one translating when there were only three attending the worship service. Job Chen/Chen YueBo 陳約伯, "Jiushi Chongti 舊事重提 (Re-telling past events)," in *Spring Sunshine*, 52. The mission records identify him as "Mr Chen," and Pilar Siao remembered him well during her interview.

429. Photograph, Cebu Gospel Church Archives.

(f) Period of Revival

Just before the Dunlaps left, however, Que recorded several improvements developing within the church in 1934: An evangelistic meeting was held with Simon Meek, leader of the Christian Gospel Assembly, as speaker. Thirty persons were baptized and the church was revived. A board of elders and deacons was formed, and Tiuⁿ Chin Tsong was ordained as elder. Four were elected as deacons: Tiuⁿ Phoan/Zhang Fan 張藩, Lim Jin Ki/Lin ZhenJi 林振驥, Mrs Uy Cang Chui Siok, and Siau Iuⁿ Siok Ju/Xiao Yang ShuNü 蕭楊淑女, the mother of Pilar Siao. The church invited Tiuⁿ Toan Tsong/Zhang DuanZhuang 張端莊傳道 (App. DD, Fig. 8), who became the first resident and long-term pastor of the CGC. The church also made it possible for his fiancé – O Iong So Jin/Au Yang SuRen 歐陽素仁 – to come to Cebu City. Then they arranged their wedding. The groom felt that the church was getting a daughter-in-law. Aside from rendering devoted service for seven years (from September 1934 until 1941), for which they were fondly remembered by many church members, Tiuⁿ also rendered great service to the church by introducing Rev Niu Se Ko/Liang XiGao 梁細羔牧師 (b. 15 July 1896; d. 22 November 1969; the legal name Leung Sai Ko will hereafter be used) to be its ordained minister. More of this part of the history will be taken up further on. O Iong So Jin and Pilar Siao revived the Sunday School ministry, holding classes at the residence of Mrs Uy Cang Chui Siok.[430]

Another factor that brought revival to the church was the series of revival and evangelistic meetings in Cebu, a ripple effect of the revival movement going on in China during the decade. Well-known speakers who visited Cebu City included: Betty Hu/Hu MeiLin 胡美林女士 and Alice Lan/Lan RuQi 藍如溪女士 (c. 1935–1936), Leland Wang Dai 王戴, Ong Si/John Wang Zhi 王峙, Ng Goan So/Huang YuanSu or Silas Wong 黃源素牧師, Lim Siong Hong 林翔鳳牧師, Go Jin Kiat/Wu RenJie 吳仁傑, George Sin Chiong Chua/Tsai XinZhang 蔡信彰, Tan Chhiu Kheng/Chen QiuQing 陳秋卿, Liok Tiong Sin/Lu ZhongXin 陸忠信, Chua Chi

---

430. Tiuⁿ Toan Tsong, "The Early Period of the Cebu Church," in *CGCGJS*, 60; and Que, "Church's Main Events," in *CGCGJS*, 37.

Teng/Cai ZhiCheng 蔡志澄, and Kho Chheng Thoan/Xu QingChuan 許
清傳 (c. 1938–1940).[431]

The third factor that brought steady growth until prior to the WWII
was the ministry of Rev Leung Sai Ko (App. DD, Fig. 9). Pastor Tiuⁿ Toan
Tsong was a graduate of the Wuchow Alliance Bible Seminary. Three years
after coming to Cebu, he recommended that the church should secure
his teacher and vice-president of this seminary, Leung Sai Ko, as resident
minister. The initial reaction of the church was negative, for the elders
and deacons felt that there were three impediments. First, Leung was from
Guangxi 廣西 which was so culturally distant from the predominantly
Hokkien members of the church. Second, language was seen as a vital factor. If he could not communicate directly in the *Hokkien* dialect they felt
his ministry would be hindered. Lastly, the church was financially unable
to support two pastors at the same time. Tiuⁿ Toan Tsong willingly offered
his own residence and hospitality to Leung, who finally came without his
family in October 1936. This offer essentially implied that both Leung
and Tiuⁿ had to live by faith and that whatever the latter was receiving
was shared with his colleague. Leung received no salary for twenty out of
his long term of twenty-eight years of service at Cebu Gospel Church.[432]
However, he was widely known for his simple lifestyle and the church
members treated him well. In fact, until the present he is still remembered
as a most respected and beloved pastor of Cebu Gospel Church.

(g) Ministry of Leung Sai Ko

Because of his great contribution to the church and the length of his ministry, it is fitting to include a portrait of Leung's life and ministry in China
and in Cebu. Leung was born in Guixian, Guangxi 廣西貴縣 on 15 July
1896. He was originally named Se Ko/Shi Gao 世高, literally, "higher than
earth," and he was a distinguished scholarly Christian. But he changed
his name to Se Ko/Xi Gao 細羔, literally, "little lamb." He was indeed a

---

431. Que, "Church's Main Events," in *CGCGJS*, 37–38. Simon Meek's meetings
were announced in the *Philippine Evangelist*; see "Evangelizing the Sinner," *The Philippine
Evangelist* 2, no. 8 (May 1934): 238.

432. Ng Kun Guan/Huang GenYuan 黃根源, legal name Valentin Uy, audio-tape
interview by Jean Uayan, 22 Jun 2004, transcript, Philippine Chinese Church Archive,
Biblical Seminary of the Philippines, Valenzuela City, Philippines. Valentin Uy is the second
son of Uy Cang Chui Siok and at present an elder emeritus of the Cebu Gospel Church.

gentle, dignified and devoted servant of God. In response to God's call, he studied at, then graduated from the Wuchow Alliance Bible Seminary, and was ordained in 1929. For a short period after his graduation, he pastored a church before being invited to teach in his alma mater from 1929 to 1935. Leung was later installed as the vice-president of the school. In life and in ministry, he was ably assisted by his life partner, Ge I Tek/Ni YiDe 倪懿德師母.

Poor health led Leung to change his field of service and for a short period he served at the Shenzhao ShengjJing Xueyuan 神召聖經學院 (ShenZhao Bible School). It was there, in 1935, that he received the invitation and money for his airplane ticket sent by the CGC, but he deliberated over a year before accepting the offer. When Tiuⁿ Toan Tsong wrote him a follow-up letter, he was finally moved to accept the invitation and take the journey to Manila. However, since he had bought a third-class ticket, he was quarantined for three days on board the ship that he had booked passage. All third-class passengers were quarantined for fear of carrying diseases.[433] He had left an elderly mother, his wife and children in Hong Kong but he served with fervor and devotion from 1936 to 1964, then retired and lived with his family. Except for his son, his wife and other children came only for short visits or he would spend his vacations in Hong Kong. For three years, despite his health condition, he would make the long journey to visit his beloved church in Cebu City. One notable legacy that he left behind is his method of baptism, which is still practiced today. Because of his CMA background, Leung insisted on baptism of believers by immersion, changing the practice of baptizing adults by sprinkling, a long-held practice instituted by the Presbyterian system. This was a big change and set the church apart from other churches with a similar Presbyterian heritage. In contrast, Rev Silas Wong was never able to institute the same change at CUEC, where baptism by sprinkling continues to be practiced until today.

433. Leung Sai Ko/Liang XiGao 梁細羔, "Po Ren Zhi Yan 僕人之言 (The servant's word)," in *Zhaojiu Liangyan* 造就良言 (Edifying Words), Appendix: *Liang XiGao Mushi Ganen Jinian Tekan* 梁細羔牧師感恩紀念特刊, ed. Liang ShenWei (Cebu City: Cebu Gospel Church, 1979), 26–27.

(h) Period of Building

Returning to the pre-war period, just when the church was experiencing revival and steady growth quantitatively and qualitatively, the Second World War broke out, devastating the world. The members of CGC dispersed when the Japanese burned Cebu City. The few who remained, including Mrs Saw Cang Iattee, continued to meet at the Cebu Grace Church, a Visayan-speaking church that split off from Bradford Church,[434] where Filipino and Japanese pastors took turns conducting the services. Rev Leung Sai Ko had gone to Dumaguete City for ministry and was not able to return to Cebu City. After the war, many of the members returned to the city and Leung took a long vacation to visit his family. The church was left in the care of Pastor Kepler Ting (Teng Keng Pho/Ding JingPo 丁景波), one of the founding members of the CUEC/UECP.

Before leaving in 1946 for his long-delayed vacation, Leung encouraged members of the church to embark upon a building program, indeed a giant step of faith, seeing that the economy was in shambles. Work began the next year and, in 1948, the church building as well as the school building (the Kian Kee School or Jianji Zhongxue 建基中學) were constructed at Junquera Street on property owned by the Presbyterian Church in the USA.

(3) Devolution of Cebu Gospel Church

At this point, focus must turn toward the history of the relationship of CGC and the Presbyterian Mission, followed by its relationship with the United Church of Christ in the Philippines (UCCP). Not long after the Philippine Presbyterian Synod became an independent synod, Filipino churches from the Presbyterian, Congregational, United Brethren and other denominational backgrounds united to form the United Evangelical Church of the Philippine Islands (UECPI). This union body was succeeded by the formation of the UCCP in 1948 (see full detail in App. BB). CGC had from the beginning of its existence been linked to the Presbyterian Synod, the UECPI, and the UCCP. As Bishop Santiago G. Iyoy stated in 1966: "The Cebu Gospel Church had been integrated into the United Church of Christ from the beginning of its organization, because the work among the Chinese was started by a Presbyterian missionary and a Filipino

---

434. Sitoy, *Several Springs* 2: 731.

Pastor."[435] This section will show how the Chinese church devolved into an independent body.

According to David Cheung, whose dissertation focused on how mission-established churches in South Fujian became self-supporting, self-propagating, and self-governed, devolution takes place when an organized Christian community attains structural independence and sovereign self-determination and transitions from missionary to native leadership.[436] Anne Kwantes further observes that, "the Presbyterians were impressed with the so-called Nevius method which called for self-propagation, self-government and self-support of the national church."[437] In the Philippine context, the missionaries adopted this method in theory but found it extremely difficult to apply. In the case of CGC, however, this method seemed to have been applied quite successfully and quite early in terms of self-support and self-propagation. The congregation that began in 1916 became a local church in 1921 and was soon on its way to becoming a self-supporting church. The church could have become independent at an even earlier date, according to the Presbyterian ideals, had it not been for the formation of the UCCP in 1948.

(a) Self-support

The church seemed to have started moving toward self-support less than a decade after its formation, as indicated by their ability to give regularly to the Philippine Presbyterian Mission and other immediate needs, on top of taking care of their own needs. In 1922, George Dunlap gave testimony that,

> the Chinese have never yet failed to put in their portion for our
> work when the appeal was made to them. Our little congrega-
> tion of a dozen members gave one hundred and eighty-four

---

435. Santiago G. Iyoy, *Report on the Visayan Jurisdiction to the Tenth Biennial Meeting of the General Assembly of the United Church of Christ in the Philippines, Dumaguete City, May 23–27, 1966*, 52.

436. Cheung, *Christianity in Modern China*, 3.

437. Kwantes, "Presbyterian Missionaries in the Philippines, 71. Nevius said that a missionary's "special business is to plant independent, self-supporting Christian institutions, and to raise up a native ministry." See John Livingston Nevius, *China and the Chinese* (London: Sampson Low, Son & Co., and Marston, 1869; reprint, Madras: Asian Educational Services, 1991), 352–355.

pesos. They have responded to a number of calls in the past year and a more generous spirit would be hard to find. They are always ready and willing to give no matter what the call may be. It is most interesting and encouraging to feel that the entire community has an interest in our work. And for them to have had this privilege of giving has quickened their interest in things worth while [*sic*].[438]

And yet, as a 1929 UEC conference put it, "a self-supporting church is one which pays the whole salary of its worker or pastor. The salary must be adequate for a decent livelihood. A church which has a pastor of its own who does not receive a salary from that church may be independent from the Mission but not self-supporting."[439] This ideal was expressed by Rev Leonardo Dia who was Secretary of the Bicol Conference in 1929. Based on this ideal, CGC was not yet self-supporting in the 1920s. But conditions improved in the Philippines in the next decade, as indicated by the report of the Presbyterian Mission for 1939, which stated:

> The Chinese Christians have developed a splendid program which includes zealous evangelistic work and practical assistance for their less fortunate fellow-countrymen. They have not only cared for their own expenses, but have met the needs of refugees from China. In addition to all of this they have made sacrificial gifts to aid the sufferers from war, flood, famine, and disease in the homeland.[440]

(b) Self-propagation

Ever since it emerged, the members of the CGC exhibited zeal for evangelism and mission work, as indicated by their persistence in visiting both their members and non-Christians. The Church held evangelistic meetings

---

438. George W[illiamson] Dunlap, "Dormitory Extension," *The Philippine Presbyterian* 13, no. 4 (Oct 1922): 20.

439. *Minutes of the Luzon Conference of the United Evangelical Church on Evangelism and Self-Support September 19 & 20, 1929*, 12.

440. *The One Hundred and Second Annual Report of the Board of Foreign Missions of the Presbyterian Church in the United States of America Presented to the General Assembly, May 1939* (New York: Presbyterian Building, 1939), 87.

frequently and members were also very much involved in prison and leper ministries, undertaken cooperatively with the Presbyterian missionaries. For example, between 1934 and 1940, under the aegis of the CGC the following Chinese evangelists and revivalists preached in Cebu: Simon Meek (1934), Betty Hu and Alice Lan (1935), Leland Wang Dai, John Wang Zhi, Silas Wong, Lim Siong Hong, Wu RenJie, George Sin Chiong Chua, Chen QiuQing, Lu ZhongXin, Cai ZhiCheng, and Xu QingChuan (1938–1940).[441] These meetings attracted large crowds of Chinese, so much so that, on one particular occasion, the venue had to be changed three times in order to accommodate the audience.[442]

Another way that the church aimed to sow the gospel seed was through the establishment of a Christian school, which emerged in May 1948. As mentioned above, the Kian Kee School was constructed at Junquera Street, beside the church building, on property owned by the Presbyterian Mission. The English and high school curriculum were at first offered in conjunction with the Cebu Institute (a UCCP church-related school), which was on the same property, but the Chinese institution started operating its own high school in 1955. The school started with 184 students and twenty teachers and by 1954 the student population had reached seven hundred. The two institutions later merged and became Cebu Christian School/Suwu Jianji Zhongxue 宿務建基中學. When the school began, the board members, the principal and the teachers were all Christians and members of the CGC. The stated purpose of establishing this school was to meet the physical, mental and spiritual needs of the children, to let them know Christ as the Way, the Truth and the Life. Aside from the Bible class, there were three chapel services for the different student levels. Teachers also channeled the students into the sixteen classes of the Sunday School on Sunday mornings, while the Student Fellowship was held regularly on Sunday afternoons.[443]

---

441. "The Church's Main Events," in *CGCGJS*, 37–38. Simon Meek's meetings were announced in the *Philippine Evangelist*; see "Evangelizing the Sinner," *The Philippine Evangelist* 2, no. 8 (May 1934): 238. These preachers were well-known in Southeast Asia and brought a great spiritual harvest in the region.

442. "The Church's Main Events," in *CGCGJS*, 37.

443. Go Bun Peng/Wu WenBing 吳文炳, "Xiaoshi 校史 (School History)," and Ng Hui Tsu/Huang Hui Ci 黃惠慈, "Benxiao Xuesheng Zongjiao Xiuyang Yu Jiaoyu 本校

(c) Self-government

i) Chinese Ministers

The previous sections have shown that events transpired that not only spurred the church toward financial independence but also strengthened the leadership structure of the fast-growing Chinese church. From 1916 until 1934, the Chinese congregation had had Filipino and American pastors, and Rev William Robertson Angus, Jr (1901–1984) declared that, "The CGC was from the time of its organization a member of the Cebu Presbytery and is today [1965] a member of the Cebu Annual Conference."[444] Since the congregation was part of the Matilda Bradford Memorial Church, which belonged to the Cebu Annual Conference, and Rev Jorge Patalinghug was the first Filipino pastor of this church, as well as the first pastor of the Chinese congregation, the Chinese church was also considered a part of the same Conference. A letter dated 6 June 1966, issued by the Cebu Annual Conference, states: "This is to certify that the CEBU GOSPEL CHURCH, Osmeña Boulevard, Cebu City, is a regular member of the Cebu Annual Conference, United Church of Christ in the Philippines."[445] The letter was signed by then Moderator Marcos P. Berame and Bishop Santiago G. Iyoy.

With regard to the leadership structure of the church, from the time of Tiuⁿ Toan Tsong, followed by the long service of Leung Sai Ko (1936–1964), and then his successors Rev Niu Sin Bi/Liang ShenWei 梁慎微 (Leung's son, "Liang" is the Mandarin while "Leung" is the Cantonese form), and Rev Joseph Young, the helm of leadership has been in the hands of Chinese ministers. Despite the financial challenges that Tiuⁿ and Leung faced during their terms of service, the Cebu Annual Conference did not

---

學生宗教修養與教育 (Religious education and nurture in our school children," in 菲律賓宿務建基初級中學第一、二屆畢業特刊 *Commemorating the First and Second High School Graduation of the Philippine Cebu Christian School* (Cebu City: Cebu Christian School, 1958). See also *Suwu Jianji Zhongxue Wushi Xueniandu Biye Jinian Kan* 宿務建基中學五十學年度畢業紀念刊 *Cebu Kian Kee High School Graduation Annual of 1961–1962* (Cebu City: Cebu Kian Kee High School, 1962). This source will be cited as *Kian Kee Annual 1961–1962*.

444. Berame, Marcos P. and Santiago G. Iyoy DD. Bishop of the UCCP and head of the Cebu Annual Conference, "to whom it may concern," 6 Jun 1966. Cebu Gospel Church archives, Cebu City, Philippine.

445. Ibid.

assist the church with monetary aid throughout the decades until its separation from the UCCP. Still, CGC was *nominally* attached to the Presbyterian General Assembly in the USA through the Philippine Presbyterian Synod from its beginning until 1948, and was a regular member of the UCCP from 1948 to 1966. Although the Chinese congregation provided for their pastors' salaries, yet they still met in a building erected by the Presbyterian missionaries and maintained by the Conference (the Bradford Church) until 1948, when they built their own sanctuary on Junquera Street. The attachment to the Presbyterian General Assembly in the USA was indirect because "the General Assembly at its meeting in Chicago in 8 October 1914, had ordered the establishment of the Presbyterian churches in the Islands as an independent organization."[446] But the Presbyterian Board of Foreign Mission continued to send and support the missionaries, including those involved in the Chinese work.

The sanctuary that was built at Junquera Street served its purpose until the time when the church council decided to build a bigger edifice for worship. Construction started at the end of 1964 and the new sanctuary, located on the same street (Osmeña Boulevard) as the Bradford United Church of Christ, was dedicated on 27 March 1966. Before reaching this milestone, however, a new development took place that reflected the signs of the times for the relationship between UCCP and the Chinese churches.

ii) Relationship with the UCCP

After the Communist take-over in China, missionaries belonging to the Reformed Church in America were reassigned to different Southeast Asian countries. These missionaries were under the care of the Philippine Interboard Office, and their field assignments were given by the Personnel Committee of the UCCP. They became members of the UCCP Annual Conferences in which their residences were located.[447]

---

446. *Report of Deputation*, 249. Independence of the church was the third stage in the three stages of Philippine mission work, according to James Rodgers and quoted in this *Report*. The other two stages were gospel proclamation followed by the organization of scattered congregations into churches.

447. Norwood B. Tye, *Journeying with the United Church of Christ in the Philippines: A History* (Quezon City: United Church of Christ in the Philippines, 1994), 214–215.

In 1954, the Field Committee in the Philippines of the RCA Board of Foreign Missions sent a letter to the Presbyterian General Assembly. It was evident from the letter that sending these missionaries to the Philippines was the right move, for they were from the Amoy Mission of the RCA and had worked within the Church of Christ in China, a national, united church, with a history and development similar to the UCCP churches. Having primarily worked among the *Hokkien* Chinese, they felt they were most suitable for evangelizing and shepherding this special group of people. They also observed that "Here in the Philippines most of the members of the Chinese congregations among whom we work have as a background the Church of Christ in China, either as former members, or as students in the Sunday School or in the Church or Mission schools. However, here in the Philippines their congregations and their leadership are to a large extent independent." The letter further gave the sentiments of the RCA:

> It is our hope that by our work and by our presence here we cannot only form new groups of Christian believers, but can also help these established groups to draw closer in fellowship with one another, and closer in fellowship with you, a church similar to their own in its history and government. To realize that hope, we need the benefit of your experience and of your continued full cooperation.[448]

During the early 1950s, the UCCP initiated and formed the subcommittee on Chinese work and placed it under the Philippine Board of Missions. There were three Chinese, two Filipinos and two Americans as members of the Committee, but the representation and focus were mostly in the Luzon area. This organization was reorganized in 1953 to include representation from the Visayas and Mindanao churches. But it seems that this work did not always flourish, for the Committee had to be reactivated in 1955.[449] Furthermore, the question was raised that the Chinese members of this committee were "not even from the Chinese congregations

---

448. See "Appendix IV," in *United Church of Christ in the Philippines, Minutes of the Fourth Biennial General Assembly, Los Baños, Laguna, May 17–23, 1954,* 74.

449. *United Church of Christ in the Philippines, Minutes of the Executive Committee, Manila, December 6–10, 1955, and Minutes of the Personnel Committee, December 2, 3, and 8, 1955,* 16.

organically within the structure of the United Church, and none of those
United Church Chinese congregations are represented in the Chinese Work
Committee."[450] In 1962, when the Commission on Philippine-Chinese
Mission replaced the UCCP Committee on Chinese Work, Cebu Gospel
Church, being a member of the Cebu Annual Conference, came under the
care and oversight of this Commission (see discussion in App. BB).[451]

iii) Independence from the UCCP

In 1966, however, the church council of the CGC sent a letter to the
executive committee of the Cebu Annual Conference, UCCP.[452] The decision was made in the regular monthly meeting on 6 November 1966 to the
effect that "The Cebu Gospel Church, beginning 1967, will officially withdraw her membership from the Cebu Annual Conference, United Church
of Christ in the Philippines. A special Committee will be created to discuss this matter with Bishop Santiago Iyoy, head of Visayan Jurisdiction
regarding its procedure."[453] This was truly a sudden turn of events, for on
27 March 1966 the church had just celebrated its golden anniversary and
dedicated its new sanctuary.[454] Liang ShenWei, having been approved by
the ordination committee of the Cebu Annual Conference, was ordained
by Chinese as well as UCCP ministers. Whenever major occasions took
place – be it inauguration, ordination, pastoral installation, or other events
– the bishop of the Visayan Jurisdiction of the Cebu Annual Conference

450. See "Minutes of the Joint United Church and Reformed Church Committee on
Proposed Integration of Work in the Philippines of Reformed Church with United Church,
September 12, 1962," in *United Church of Christ in the Philippines Minutes of the Executive
Committee, Quezon City, December 11–13, 1962 and January 22, 1963,* 39–43.

451. "United Church of Christ in the Philippines Organizational Set-Up, Commission
on Philippine-Chinese Mission," in *Minutes of the Ninth Biennial General Assembly, United
Church of Christ in the Philippines, Lucena City, May 31–June 5, 1964,* 164.

452. Unfortunately, I could not find any copy of this letter either in the church file
or in the UCCP office. Its existence and quotation given above are known mainly through
a follow-up letter mentioning the fact, dated 3 Feb 1967. This follow-up letter was signed
by the church secretary Que Yok Hian (Joseph Que), who in many UCCP records was at
one time a representative to the Philippine-Chinese Mission. Rev Joseph Young attested to
the content of the letter.

453. Cebu Gospel Church, Cebu, 3 Feb 1967, to the Executive Committee, Cebu
Annual Conference, United Church of Christ in the Philippines.

454. See Santiago G. Iyoy, "Report on the Visayan Jurisdiction to the Tenth Biennial
Meeting of the General Assembly of the United Church of Christ in the Philippines,
Dumaguete City, May 23–27, 1966," in *United Church of Christ in the Philippines Tenth
Post War Biennial General Assembly, May 23–May 27, 1966, Dumaguete City, Philippines,* 52.

or his representative would be part of the officiating party. In the CGC archives a letter dated 6 June 1966 attests that the church was a "regular member" of this Conference. However, by 6 November 1966, the church council had decided to withdraw from the UCCP.

Based on the Chinese source, the meeting with Iyoy took place on 22 November 1966. However, the UCCP *Minutes of the Executive Committee* records the date as 15–16 December 1966. There was a resolution "To designate the Chairman of the General Assembly and Bishop Marciano C. Evangelista, with Bishop Santiago G. Iyoy, as representatives of the United Church of Christ to confer with Cebu Gospel Church regarding reconsideration of their desire to servere [*sic*] their relationship with the United Church."[455]

Another UCCP record that confirms this development is reported by the Commission on Christian Witness and Service Division of Philippine-Chinese Mission, found in the *Minutes of the Executive Committee*, also dated 15–16 December 1966: "News has just come from Cebu that the Cebu Gospel Church has withdrawn from its organic relationship to the United Church. This [is] a development which many of us have long thought might happen, but which we hoped would not happen."[456] Angus gave this report in his capacity as Secretary of the Commission on Christian Witness and Service, Division of Philippine-Chinese Mission.

Although no other items regarding this matter appeared in succeeding minutes of the UCCP Executive Committee, a follow-up letter from Cebu Gospel Church, dated 3 February 1967, indicates a meeting did take place between the church and Bishop Iyoy. The agreement reached during this meeting was that the Church, although no longer part of the Cebu Annual Conference, would continue to have mutual fellowship and friendship with the Conference. The Church would also continue to cooperate with the UCCP in mission, Christian education (through the Cebu Christian School), and medical work (referring to the UCCP-owned

455. *Minutes of the Executive Committee, United Church of Christ in the Philippines, National Headquarters, Quezon City, December 15–16, 1966*, 51.

456. See "Appendix I: Commission on Christian Witness and Service Division of Philippine-Chinese Mission," in *United Church of Christ in the Philippines Minutes of the Executive Committee, National Headquarters, Quezon City, December 15 & 16, 1966*, 75.

Cebu Community Hospital), as well as assist the Conference financially every year.

What caused the council to arrive at this decision so suddenly? Angus, in "The United Church and the Existing Chinese Churches," indicates reasons for this sudden change of heart on the part of the Chinese church. He gave two possible reasons for this development:

> Another situation inherited by the Commission was the school situation in Cebu. To go into the details of this situation would take too much time and would perhaps do no good. I will say that many members of the congregation of the Cebu Gospel Church were displeased 1) because Mr. & Mrs. Kragt [full name Earl Nelson Kragt or 嘉立德牧師師母] were transferred from Cebu to Naga and blamed it on the United Church, and 2) because they were informed that if the church council did not wish to permit the church school to comply with the regulations for church-related schools, they would be requested to remove the school from the Presbyterian Mission property. This also is blamed on the United Church.[457]

The UCCP minutes confirm the transfer of the Kragts. The Personnel Committee had made the decision in 1965 to assign them to Naga to work among the Chinese, before they went on furlough. They were hesitant to leave Cebu, for they requested that the "assignment be left open . . . inasmuch as there are some matters related to continuing service which need more study." Apparently their desire to stay on in Cebu was not approved, for upon returning from furlough in 1966, they were assigned to Naga.[458] This incident may have been a minor cause in the souring of relationship between CGC and UCCP.

Another proposal in the same minutes, that the Cebu Christian School should be classified as Category IV, was at first rescinded but was finally carried out. The UCCP commissioned Dr Frank Wilson to conduct a survey on church-related school from 10 January to 10 March 1959. Wilson

---

457. Angus, "United Church," 28–29.

458. See "Appendix V," in *Minutes of the Tenth Post War Biennial General Assembly of the United Church of Christ in the Philippines, Dumaguete City, May 23–27, 1966*, 182.

grouped these schools into four categories, the fourth of which was one that was "strategically located with creditable programs, acceptable physical plants, competent administration and teaching personnel, with real potentialities for maximum development and useful service."[459] Maximum undergirding and expansion would be given to such an institution. According to Norwood Tye, by December 1966, category placement of the sixteen schools of the UCCP had been firmly determined, and Cebu Christian School was placed in Category IV. This reveals that UCCP recognized the potentials of this school. However, despite the aspiration of undergirding or upgrading schools with priority classification, the UCCP faced increasing limitation of financial resources to make this a reality.[460]

My review of the UCCP Executive Committee minutes from the early 1950s until 1974, showed that UCCP still considered Cebu Christian School as one of their church-related schools, even after relations had been broken off in 1966. It was the practice of the school during the 1960s and 1970s that, "in order to maintain the balance of Filipino and Chinese representation in the Board of Trustees it was an unexpressed policy to elect an American missionary for the position of director of the school, also that when the chairman of the board is of Filipino blood the vice-chairman should be of Chinese and when the chairman is Chinese the vice-chairman should be Filipino."[461] This practice of having an American missionary as Director-Principal persisted until 1970 when the last American to serve as director, Rev John Ellis Bandt/Wan YueHan 萬約翰牧師 (term of service 1964–1971), returned to the States.[462] After Bandt left, no foreign missionary has ever assumed administrative or even teaching positions in

459. See "Appendix XI," in *United Church of Christ in the Philippines, Minutes of the Executive Committee Meeting, May 11–13, 1965*, 7, 9, 71, 133, 171.

460. For a comprehensive discussion of the complex development of the UCCP ministry to church-related schools from 1948–1982, see Tye, *Journeying*, 74–80, 130–135, 186–190, 233–235, 281–285, 314–318.

461. *United Church of Christ in the Philippines, Minutes of the Executive Committee, December 7–11, 1959*, 17; Angus, "United Church," 49; and also, Pedro M. Raterta, "Report for the Visayas Jurisdiction," Appendix VII, *Proceedings of the Thirteenth Post War Biennial General Assembly of the United Church of Christ in the Philippines, Manila, May 28–June 1, 1972*, 117.

462. During school year 1961–1962, Cebu Christian School had an American missionary (Rev Robert Howard) as director of the English department, but it also had a Chinese principal (Iuⁿ Chin Seng/Yang ZhenSheng 楊振聲) for the Chinese department.

the school; all subsequent directors were Filipino Chinese Christians. The political situation (martial law period, 1972–1981) and government requirements restricting foreigners from assuming the post of directors or principals most likely led to the nationalization of this school as well as all other church-established schools.

The complete history of this school does not fall within the scope of this study, but what has been discussed sufficiently connects it to the eventual breakup of relationship between the Chinese church and the UCCP. There was increasing friction between the Chinese church and UCCP over property issues. In 1971, the United Presbyterian Church in the USA, through its executive committee, resolved to donate to Cebu Gospel Church the three pieces of land upon which the Chinese church had constructed its first sanctuary and the elementary and high school buildings.[463] Whatever may have been the circumstances surrounding this state of affairs, the fact remains that Cebu Gospel Church finally and officially broke off relations with UCCP in 1966, and the school finally broke off all connections with the UCCP when it was incorporated as the Philippine Christian Gospel School (PCGS) on 7 July 1982.[464] With this action, the Chinese church achieved full and final devolution, from being a mission-established church, to being a regular member of the UCCP, and finally, to being a totally independent Protestant Chinese church.

e) Summary

Based on the preceding narration of successive historical events, from the emergence of the Cebu Gospel Church up to developments during the 1960s and early 1970s, the history of this Chinese congregation can be divided into three segments. Although the emergence of the church resulted largely through the hard work of the earliest Chinese believers,

---

Howard was a predecessor of Rev John Bandt, during whose administration I was a student at Cebu Christian School. See *Kian Kee Annual 1961–1962*.

463. The Deed of Donation was jointly signed by Rev Byron W. Clark, duly authorized attorney of the UPCUSA and Engineer Ramon C. Lim, then chairman of the Board of Trustees on 21 Feb 1973.

464. According to Dr Wanda Po, the present director of PCGS and my former classmate, Filipinos who were members of Bradford United Church of Christ continued to serve as board members until 1982, when CCS was reorganized and became PCGS. Wanda Po Liam Giok 傅念玉博士, telephone interview by Jean Uayan, Cebu City, 15 Oct 2006.

Presentation and Evaluation of Findings

the contributions of the Presbyterian missionaries can in no way be disregarded. Consequently, the first era of the history of the CGC can be called the missionary period. This was the time when Presbyterian missionaries and Protestant Chinese made every effort, albeit not quite successfully at first, to establish a Chinese congregation (as it did in Manila and Iloilo) from 1916 to the late 1930s, just prior to WWII. The second era is the UCCP-affiliated period, roughly between 1945 to 1966, wherein the Chinese congregation was a semi-independent Chinese congregation under the oversight of the UCCP, or more specifically, the Matilda Bradford Memorial Church and the Cebu Annual Conference. The third era is the independence period, wherein the Chinese congregation, known as Cebu Gospel Church after the war, officially withdrew from the UCCP in 1966, exactly fifty years after its founding. In actuality, the church had been self-determined and self-governed ever since the time of Leung Sai Ko, and the relationship with UCCP through the Cebu Annual Conference was merely nominal. When interviewed regarding this matter, all of the elderly members and church leaders were reluctant to discuss CGC's relationship with the UCCP. Several decades after the break-off, the church continued to maintain cordial relationship with the UCCP. As a child growing up in this church during the sixties until the late seventies, I remember seeing many Filipinos, known to be members of the Bradford United Church of Christ, attending the English worship services at the Cebu Gospel Church. During the 1980s and 1990s, these people were less frequently seen during the services. Representatives from the UCCP on special occasions also diminished.

5. The Chinese United Evangelical Church

a) Chinese and English Names

The fourth Protestant Chinese congregation in Manila, established on 14 July 1929, was the Chinese United Evangelical Church/Lüfei Zhonghua Jidu Jiaohui 旅菲中華基督教會. It is presently known as the United Evangelical Church of the Philippines/Feilübin Zhonghua Jidu Jiaohui 菲律濱中華基督教會. Literally, the earliest Chinese name of this church can be translated as "Church of Christ in China Sojourning in the Philippines," and the English version of the name has been, from the official standpoint, "Chinese United Evangelical Church." However, another name – "Philippine Chinese Presbyterian Church" – appeared in a 1929 letter addressed to Rev Dr George William Wright/Liu Zhe boshi 劉哲博士 (1863–1940; term of service 1903–1938), then secretary of the United Evangelical Church.[465] It was signed by fourteen representatives of the new church. They were appealing for assistance in organizing their new congregation.[466] Suffice it to state at this point that the name was never used by the Chinese Christians in subsequent references to their new church. The Philippine Mission of the Presbyterian Church gave two other names: "Chinese Presbyterian Church–Manila" and "Chinese Presbyterian Congregation."[467] The first name appeared in a compilation of Board Letters covering the period from January 1929 to November 1931, which is around the time the church was established. The second name is found in the personal report of George Wright for the year 1929, the year it was established. Members of the congregation, however, never used these names to refer to their new church.

In its Chinese form, the term 中華基督教會 (Church of Christ in China) reflects the spiritual roots of the members of the new congregation. Since the majority of them were immigrants from southern China, they were members of either Presbyterian or Reformed churches established in South Fujian 閩南, particularly in E-Mng/Xiamen 廈門, Oaⁿ Hai/Anhai 安海, and Tsoan Chiu/Quanzhou 泉洲. In 1927 these and other churches formed a church union called the Church of Christ in China (see pp. 78–80). One of the founders of the CUEC, Keng Lin Kiat, stated that the

---

465. This name might be misconstrued as referring to a church, but it is actually referring to a union body [the United Evangelical Church of the Philippine Islands] composed of churches belonging to the Baptists, Congregationalists, Presbyterians and the United Brethren. This entity was the predecessor of the UCCP. See App. BB. See page 188 for content of the letter.

466. *Minutes of the Executive Committee of the Philippine Mission Presbyterian Church in the United States of America. Baguio, P.I. May 3–6, 1930*, 34.

467. Letter No. 513, Jul 23, 1930, in *Board Letters Nos. 488 to 527, January 1929 to November 1931, Philippine Presbyterian Mission*; Personal Report of George W. Wright, in *Annual Reports 1928–1929, Philippine Mission of the Presbyterian Church in the USA Dumaguete, Oriental Negros, October 5–12, 1929.*

sentiment of such a name indicates that "our congregation was considered an extension work of the Church of Christ in China."[468]

Another significant aspect of the Chinese name of CUEC is the term Lüfei 『旅菲』, which means "the Chinese staying overseas in the Philippines," according to Keng Lin Kiat. A better translation is "sojourning." This reflects the popular sentiment of immigrant Chinese at that time, that is, the Philippines is not a permanent place of residence, but only for sojourning. China remained the homeland to which all the Chinese residing in the Philippines at that time eventually hoped to return.

The church changed its English name to "United Evangelical Church of Manila" during the 1960s when the reality of returning to China was shattered by the Communist take-over. During the 1980s, the name was again changed to "United Evangelical Church of the Philippines." By this time, the union of Filipino evangelical churches no longer used this name, as this union body had been renamed the United Church of Christ in the Philippines (UCCP) in 1929 (see App. BB).[469]

A document entitled "Lüfei Zhonghua Jidu Jiaohui Chengli Xuanyan 旅菲中華基督教會成立宣言 (Declaration of the Founding of the Chinese Church of Christ Sojourning in the Philippines)" announced the emergence of this new Chinese church.[470] Rev Kho Seng Iam wrote this document in South Fujian on 18 August 1924. He was then a nationally known pastor of Kim Chi^n Kao Hoe/Jinjing Jiaohui 金井教會 – or as the

---

468. Keng Lin Kiat/Gong RenJie 龔人傑, "A Stormy Night," in *HDPO*, 239 (pages in Chinese style).

469. This name was first proposed on 25 Aug 1924 and became official on 15 Mar 1929. See *The Confession of Faith and Form of Government of the United Evangelical Church of the Philippine Islands Approved by the Executive Committee of the General Assembly of the United Evangelical Church, Manila, P.I.: October, 1933*, 7–8.

470. Kho Seng Iam/Xu Shengyan 許聲炎, "Lüfei Zhonghua Jidu Jiaohui Chengli Xuanyan 旅菲中華基督教會成立宣言 (Declaration of the Founding of the Chinese Church of Christ Sojourning in the Philippines)," in *Lüfei Zhonghua Jidu Jiaohui Chengli Jinian Tekan* 旅菲中華基督教會成立紀念特刊 (Special commemorative publication of the founding of the Chinese United Evangelical Church) (Manila: Chinese United Evangelical Church, n.d.). This publication, henceforth cited as the *Founding Publication*, has no consecutive paging, hence the references will be based on the title or heading of the articles. The name "Chinese Church of Christ" is used because in 1924, the Church of Christ in China had not yet been formed. When Kho used this term, he was referring to all the Protestant churches in China. Kho's work will be referred to as "Declaration" hence forward.

missionaries called it, the Church of the Golden Well – in South Fujian.[471] This indicates that as early as 1924, five years before it officially came into existence, former members of the Church of Christ in China, some of whom attended worship services at SSCM, were already aspiring to establish a church that followed the Presbyterian tradition. According to Rev Kho, there were eight reasons for this endeavor, all of them related to the greater entity known as the South Fukien (Banlam) Church of Christ in China/Minnan Zhonghua Jidu Jiaohui 閩南中華基督教會.[472] The eight reasons given by Kho are summarized in brief statements below. The whole document, with comments in footnotes, has been translated into English and condensed by the writer and can be found in Appendix EE.

b) Eight Reasons for Establishing CUEC

- First, except for a small number who were converted locally, the majority of believers in Manila come from the Banlam Chinese Church of Christ. All the churches in Banlam formerly belonged to the Presbyterian Mission and London Mission; their ecclesiastical system and liturgy differ from that of the Episcopalian system. This becomes an excuse for believers to stop attending services.

- Second, branches of the Chinese Church of Christ have already been successively established in many localities in and outside China, in order to worship and serve God.

- Third, Banlam believers who settle in the Philippines are not few, but Sunday attendance at the Episcopal Church was less than a hundred, hence, there is a need to organize a new church for those who have stopped attending services.

- Fourth, there were many Filipino churches in Manila and yet the Chinese number in the tens of thousands. If the Chinese Christians could spread the gospel widely, not only would there

---

471. Band, *Working His Purpose Out*, 429. Cf., "Xu ShengYan Mushi Xingzhuan Zhangmushi 許聲炎牧師行傳章目詩 (The Life of Rev Kho Seng Iam set as epic hymn)," in *Xu ShengIan Mushi Bainian Danchen Jiniankan* 許聲炎牧師百年誕辰紀念刊 (Commemorative publication of the centenary of the birth of Rev Kho Seng Iam), ed. John Pan 潘再恩 (Manila: n.p., 1966), 30, n. 9. This source will henceforth be cited as the *Centenary*.

472. "Declaration," in the *Founding Publication*.

be another branch of the Chinese Church of Christ, but a Cantonese congregation could possibly arise in the near future.

- Fifth, uniting churches of a different background to become a bigger Chinese Church of Christ such as in Banlam has become a trend in China. Kho felt that he could not be indifferent to such a move to establish a church [in Manila].

- Sixth, churches in China are organizing themselves into a Chinese Church of Christ, casting off their denominational ties to come under the name of Christ and becoming an indigenous Chinese church.

- Seventh, the churches in China were becoming contextualized and were also becoming self-subsisting, financially and otherwise. The aim of this new church was likewise, to attain self-reliance.

- Lastly, not only would this new church become self-reliant, it would also help the mainland churches in their development, just as other branch churches were doing. Some believers who settled outside China had ceased to attend worship and needed to be given support. With elders and deacons in the new church committed to render service, going out to reclaim believers who have ceased church attendance, the hearts of these believers would be strengthened.

Rev Kho concluded with the remark that the existence of two churches in Manila should be seen as an opportunity to work together to save the souls of the great number of Chinese settlers and to nurture the spiritual lives of the Chinese believers living overseas.

c) Other Reasons for Separating

In 1958, the late Dr Joseph Young propounded three reasons for the separation of this group of Christians from the St. Stephen's Chinese Mission.[473] Young's source for this statement was the *St. Stephen's Church Episcopal Golden Jubilee Souvenir 1903–1953 (Huaqiao Shenggonghui Wushi Zhounian Jiniankan)* 華僑聖公會五十周年紀念刊, on pages 9

---

473. Joseph Young/Yang QiYao 楊其耀, "A Survey of the Overseas Chinese in the Philippines with a Suggested Program of Evangelism for the Chinese United Evangelical Church" (Master's thesis, Columbia Bible College, 1958), 31–32. Quotations in this discussion are from this source.

and 11–13. According to his analysis, the reasons of this separation was first of all because most of the Chinese Christians came from the evangelical background, hence "they were not accustomed to the form of worship as conducted in the Episcopal Church." The so-called "evangelical background" Young is referring to is the Presbyterian background. This reason is admittedly the main reason for the separation, in my opinion.

The second reason that Young gives is that "the early Episcopalian ministers, as well as missionaries, were unable to speak the Amoy [*Hokkien*] dialect. There were no Amoy-speaking preachers to supply the needs." What has been written concerning the background of both Rev Hobart Studley and Rev Ben Ga Pay in the SSCM section clearly shows that both were fluent in the dialect. Although Pay died in 1923 and Studley left SSCM in 1931, there remained *Hokkien*-speaking preachers during the period of the separation, which was around 1928 or 1929, at least until 1933, when missionaries did begin to have this language handicap and it was difficult to find Chinese preachers from Xiamen.

The third reason given by Young is that after the arrival of "some Amoy-speaking ministers from Mainland China," the Episcopalian Church refused to open her pulpit to non-Anglican preachers. However, upon reading the *Golden Jubilee Souvenir*, I could not find anything written to this effect. Instead, from the section that follows regarding the personal background of Kho Seng Iam, it will be seen that as a Presbyterian "Amoy-speaking" minister from Fujian, he did preach in the worship service of SSCM when he visited the Philippines in 1928.[474]

d) Context of the "Declaration"

The significance of Kho Seng Iam's "Declaration" cannot be fully understood and appreciated until I introduce his own personal background and the historical backdrop of the Church of the Golden Bell, set within the ecclesiastical context of South Fujian. The history of Christianity in the Xiamen region has been covered in a previous section. Focus will now be

---

474. George Sin Chiong Chua/Tsai Xinzhang 蔡信彰, "Jiushi Chongti 舊事重提 (Recalling the past)," in *Centenary*, 72; Bill Yang, "Chinese Protestant Churches in the Philippines," 152–153.

given to the towns of Anhai and Jinjing, the origins of many founding members of the new church.

The Scottish missionary, Carstairs Douglas, visited Anhai in June 1857. The congregation in Anhai produced six pastors and a large number of non-ordained preachers. William Sutherland Swanson reported in 1868 that the Anhai congregation was growing and the gospel was spreading.[475]

Anhai was the gateway to Quanzhou 泉州, the famous ancient city of Zeitun that Marco Polo visited in 1275. Douglas entered the city in December 1859. Despite opposition from the literati, the mission rented a place in the heart of the city in 1866. The next year, the first baptism took place and fourteen Christians formed the Quanzhou Church. In 1877 the Church was able to purchase and extend their land, which led to the formation of the famous Lam Koe Ki Tok Kao Hoe/Nanjie Jidu Jiaohui 南街基督教會 (South Street Church). With this development it ceased to be a mission station and became a separate congregation no longer under the supervision of the Anhai Church. In 1895 the Se Koe Ki Tok Kao Hoe/Xijie Jidu Jiaohui 西街基督教會 (West Street Church) was opened. English Presbyterian missionaries Dr David Grant (term of service 1880–1894), Rev Colin Campbell Brown (term of service 1893–1913) and Rev A. S. Moore Anderson (term of service 1902–1949?) rendered decades of faithful service that edified the churches and schools around the Quanzhou region.[476]

On 12 January 1866, Kho Seng Iam (App. FF, Fig. 1) was born to Kho Kian Hun/Xu JianXun 許建勛 and Go Cheng Han/Wu JingXian 吳 (趙) 靜嫻, the daughter of Go Chiao Jin/Wu ZhaoRen 吳 (趙) 招認 who began attending worship service in 1869 at the Anhai Church.[477] Kho was born in Chian Pho/Qian Po village in Anhai 福建晉江安海前坡鄉. His father led a prodigal life before he was converted in Anhai at age twenty-five. On the way to sell the last piece of his family's jewelry (the wedding ring of his mother) in order to save the family from starvation, the melodious singing captivated and drew him inside a Protestant church. Soon after

475. Band, *Working His Purpose Out*, 221.

476. Ibid., 52–56, 222–223, 309–310.

477. Kho Goat Hoa/Xu YueHua 許月華, "Siyuan 思源 (Pondering on origins)," in *Centenary*, 107.

his life was totally transformed, he became an itinerant evangelist and Bible colporteur. The godly parents had many children but did their best not only to feed but also to arrange for their schooling. Kho was able to study in a primary school in Anhai, where he stayed with the family of Go Chiao Jin. Eventually, at age twenty, he married Go Cheng Han, the daughter of his benefactor, in 1886.

Kho studied at the Hui Lan College/Hui Lan Shengdao Shuyuan 迴瀾聖道書院 (1884-1886) and ministered at Koan Kio/Guanqiao 管橋 (1884), Anhai (1886), Ho Thau/Hutou 湖頭 (1887), Xiamen (1894) and finally at Jinjing (1895–1948). The Church at Kim Chi[n] was founded by Rev Kho in 1890 while he was still an itinerant preacher, and eventually this grew into five congregations, called the Five Golden Fellowship/Wujin Tuanqi 五金團契: Kim Chi[n]/ Jinjing, Kim Phoan/Jinpan 金潘, Kim Ho/Jinhu 金滬, Kim Ge/Jinya 金衙, and Kim Chhun/Jinchun 金村. He founded the Iok Eng School/Yu Ying Xuexiao 毓英學校 in 1892. Many of the alumni from this school settled in the Philippines and became well known, prosperous citizens. He founded the Ban Lam Bible School/Minnan Shengjing Xueyuan 閩南聖經學院 in 1939. According to Edward Band, Rev Kho was suspicious of the teaching of the Amoy Theological College, which had reopened in 1926 under the management of the three missions (the EPM, LMS, and RCA) and the churches in Xiamen.[478]

By 1927 the Protestant churches in China had survived a series of political upheavals that began with the Revolution of 1911 that toppled the Manchu (Qing) dynasty (AD 1644–1911/12) and turned China into a Republic, followed by years of civil war between the Communists, the Revolutionaries (Guomindang 國民黨), and the warlords. Yuan ShiKai 袁世凱 (1859–1916) temporarily dissolved the Guomindang in 1913, which led to internal disunity between the Northern and the Southern Revolutionists. When the First World War ended in 1917 the Western powers refused to admit the new Republic into the League of Nations, thus igniting a nationwide frustration over China's weakness and a gradual anti-missionary feeling,

---

478. I surmise from the general contents of the *Centenary* that the suspicion was caused by the controversy between the modernists and fundamentalists in the United States. Band, *Working His Purpose Out*, 475. Eventually, in 1946, the Ban Lam Bible School united with the Amoy Theological College.

which escalated when Sun Yat Sen/Sun ZhongShan 孫逸仙/孫中山 (born 1866) died in 1925. The alliance that had been forged between the Communists and Russian socialists, and their attacks against Christianity and Western missionaries, caused anti-Christian propaganda to rise. From 1925–1927, the Church in China suffered persecutions and attacks because of its association with foreign missionaries who were being called "capitalists" and "imperialists." Despite these upheavals, the Protestant churches in general and Presbyterian churches in particular, experienced growth and even revival in Quanzhou (1913). A program originated at a preachers' conference in July 1918. It conceived of a Five Year Evangelistic Campaign/Wu Nian Peizeng Yundong 五年倍增運動 to reach the five million inhabitants of the Banlam region.[479]

By 1927 there were signs of improvement: Fujian had come under the control of the Southern Guomindang forces, the tide had turned against Russia's influence, the extreme violence of the Communists had been checked and local bandits quelled. The Presbyterian Church of China closed its history on 29 September 1927 at Shanghai, and on 1 October, the Church of Christ in China was constituted during its first General Assembly. Representatives from seventeen provinces came and practically all the churches associated with the new entity were Calvinist in background and either Congregational or Presbyterian in polity. The Anglicans and Lutherans chose not to attend. The first moderator was Rev Seng Cheng I/Cheng JingYi (C. Y. Cheng) 誠靜怡 and Rev Kho was the vice-moderator. By now the South Fujian Church had 255 churches, 40 pastors and 150 preachers. Total membership consisted of 10,000 adults and 7,000 baptized children. Two years later, in 1929, the Five Year Evangelistic Campaign, also known as the Five Year Movement/Wu Yun 五運, was finally launched. Influenced by the Jerusalem Conference of 1928, this Movement aimed to carry out vigorous evangelistic programs in hope of doubling the number of Christians in China within five years.

Kho spearheaded the movement around the Quanzhou area. Although the goal of the Movement was not fully realized, yet there was a rich harvest

479. James Edwin Orr, *Evangelical Awakenings in Eastern Asia*. Minneapolis, MN: Bethany Fellowship, 1975), 74–80, Band, *Working His Purpose Out*, 323–325, 331–333, 394–420, 425–435.

of souls in 1935. In Shantou membership increased to about 1,000; in Fujian 1,136 new communicants were reported.[480] Chinese evangelists such as Dr John Sung/Song ShangJie boshi 宋尚節博士 (1901–1944) brought about great revival in churches within and outside of China. John Sung was the son of a Chinese Methodist pastor who became China's greatest evangelist and revivalist. He traveled through 230 cities and towns in South China and Southeast Asia and gained hundreds of thousands of converts. It is estimated that between 1933 and 1936, there were over 100,000 converts as a result of his ministry and that of the Preaching Bands that he organized.[481]

Sung and the Bethel Evangelistic Band greatly revived the Chinese churches in Southeast Asia (see pp. 202–204).[482] It should be noted that Sung had a Wesleyan rather than a Calvinist orientation, yet he was warmly accepted by the churches in the Banlam region and in the Philippines.[483] This is the backdrop of the period during which Rev Kho and his family became influential in the emergence of the CUEC in Manila.

(1) The Kho Family and CUEC

Rev Kho and his wife had twelve children: six sons and six daughters. Among these daughters, four went to live in the Philippines. Rev Kho's second daughter, Kho Goat Hoa/Xu YueHua 許月華 (a.k.a. Xu ShuZhen 許淑慎,

---

480. Band, *Working His Purpose Out*, 431–433, 469–470.

481. See Timothy Tow, *Asian Awakening* (Singapore: Christian Life Publishers, 1988), 26, and William E. Schubert, *I Remember John Sung* (Singapore: Far Eastern Bible College Press, 1976), 23.

482. Latourette, *History of Christian Missions in China*, 800–801. For details of Sung's ministry in this region, see Levi Tian-Zhen Song 利未, ed., *Lingli Jiguang – Chupu Song Shanjie De Riji Zhaichao* 靈歷集光—主僕宋尚節的日記摘抄 (The diary of the spiritual life of Dr John Song [*sic*]) (Hong Kong: Eng Yu Evangelistic Mission, 1995), 178–205; Li MingAn 李明安, "Song Shangjie Yu Malaixiya Jiaohui Zhi Shigong Yu Yingxiang 宋尚節于馬來西亞教會之事工與影響 (The ministry and influence of John Sung in Malaysia)," 79–90; and, Li JianAn 李健安, "Song Shangjie De Shuling Chuantong ji dui Huarenjiaohui De Gongxian yu Yingxiang 宋尚節的屬靈傳統及對華人教會的貢獻與影響 (The spiritual tradition of John Sung and his contribution and influence upon the Chinese churches)," in *Song ShangJie De Shenxue Yu Shuling Guan* 宋尚節的神學與屬靈觀 (The theology and spiritual view of John Sung), (Masheng) Ziyan Zhongxin ZhuantiXilie 《馬聖》資研中心專題系列〈1〉 MBS Centre for Christianity and Malaysian Studies 1 (Malaysia: Malaysia Bible Seminary, 2002), 79–90.

483. See Chin Cheak Yu, "Christian Religious Education for Awakening and Living in the Spirit: As Inspired by John Wesley and John Sung," accessed 27 Jan 2007, http://religiouseducation.net/member/ 04_papers/yu.pdf.

1894–1987) was the first to come to the Philippines (App. FF, Fig. 1). Her legal name is Phoebe Kho-Chua, also spelled as Co-Chua (variant spelling Co-Chhoa), but the name Kho Goat Hoa will be used throughout this work. She had been recommended by her father when Rev Mr Ben Ga Pay of St. Stephen's Chinese Girls' School wrote him about recruiting teachers in 1917, the year when the school was founded. Being a former student of Rev Kho, Rev Mr Pay naturally turned to him regarding the need for teachers.[484] Rev Kho himself accompanied his second daughter to the Philippines. This was his second trip. He had come in 1910 to raise funds for Iok Eng School, the school that he founded. During the 1917 visit, he went to Iloilo for a short vacation. Inside the *Commemorative publication of the centenary of the birth of Rev Kho Seng Iam* there is a picture of him reclining and reading a book during his stay in Iloilo (App. X, Fig. 2). It is significant to note that in 1917, the Iloilo Chinese congregation was already in existence. It is probable that Rev Kho, who stayed at a relative's house (as stated in the photo caption), visited the church or came into contact with the Chinese Christians there.

The third daughter to arrive in the Philippines in 1924 was Kho Ju Soat/ Xu YuXue 許逾雪 (a.k.a. Xu ShuRui 許淑瑞 1900–1981; App. FF, Fig. 1). Her legal name was Elizabeth Co, but since she is better known by her Chinese name, Kho Ju Soat will be used throughout this work. She was accompanied by her brother Rev Kho Sek Hui/Xu XiHui 許錫慧牧師 who was on a fundraising trip for his church in Eng Leng/Yong Ning 永寧. It is significant that this was the year when Rev Kho wrote the "Declaration," five years prior to the founding of CUEC. The last to emigrate in 1928 was the eldest daughter, Kho Kheng Hoa/Xu QiongHua 許瓊華 (a.k.a. Xu ShuYing 許淑英, 1891–?) – the legal form Co King Hoa will be used throughout this work. Again, her father accompanied her whole family to the Philippines. This was the last time Rev Kho visited the country, and it was a year prior to the establishment of CUEC.

---

484. Chhoa Kho Goat Hoa (a.k.a. Phoebe Kho-Chua)/Cai Xu YueHua 蔡許月華, "Shizhu Wushinian Jingguo 事主五十年經過 (Serving the Lord for fifty years)," in Chhoa Kho Goat Hoa, *Liushi Nian* (*Riji Yu Xuanwen*) 60 年 *(*日記與選文*) (*Sixty years – diary and selected articles) (Manila: by the author, 1980), 8.

Of this visit, Rev George Sin Chiong Chua (term of service 1934–1969; d. 1993) was able to recall that Kho came to raise funds for a new dormitory for his beloved school Iok Eng. At that time, Chua was a confirmed member of the St. Stephen's Chinese Mission, and Kho's two daughters, Ju Soat and Goat Hoa, were teaching in the St. Stephen's Chinese Girls' School. Rev Kho spoke one Sunday during the worship service. After the service, he conversed with some members of SSCM who were former members of the Banlam churches. Kho informed them that these churches in China were interested in establishing a Presbyterian church in Manila. The former Banlam members were of course elated by this news, but the priest-in-charge of SSCM, Rev Hobart Studley, was displeased and vehemently opposed this idea.[485] Thus it can be surmised that when Kho visited St. Stephen's Chinese Mission in 1928, he had already written the "Declaration" four years before in 1924, and in his mind, establishing a church in the Presbyterian tradition was both urgent and justifiable.

The "Declaration" written by Kho Seng Iam was printed in the Special Commemorative Publication of the Founding of the Chinese Evangelical Church of Manila (Lüfei Zhonghua Jidu Jiaohui Chengli Jinian Tekan) 旅菲中華基督教會成立紀念特刊, Founding Publication for short. Aside from this source, however, the *Historical Documentary of Protestantism in the Orient, 40th Anniversary of the United Evangelical Church of Manila (Feilübin Zhonghua Jidu Jiaohui Sishi Zhounian Lishi Wenxian Fu Yazhou Duoguo Jidu Jiaohui Lishi 1929–1969)* 菲律濱中華基督教會四十週年歷史文獻附亞洲多國基督教會歷史1929–1969 (or, *HDPO*), provides the testimonies of two of the original founding members – Keng Lin Kiat and Kho Ju Soat. Their stories need to be presented and viewed in conjunction with the events of Kho's life and involvement with the Protestant Chinese in the Philippines. Both indicate the early stage of the plan to establish a church patterned after the Presbyterian system.

---

485. No name was mentioned by Rev Chua in his article, but it can be easily surmised that Studley was the minister who opposed the suggestion. It couldn't have been Pay for he had died in 1923.

(2) First Testimony – Keng Lin Kiat

Keng Lin Kiat (App. FF, Fig. 3) was the person with whom Pastor Sia Tsu Keng had an altercation over the distribution of their church publication while he was still a member of the SSCM (see pp. 136–137). Keng Lin Kiat was born on 15 August 1901 in Anhai, Fujian 福建安海. The Presbyterians converted his wife from Buddhism, hence, they belonged to the Presbyterian church in Anhai. As a Christian, Keng would attend services in his church three times a day on Sundays. When he came to the Philippines in 1920, at the age of nineteen, he felt badly about not going to church for about three weeks. He began to inquire and found out about worship services at SSCM. Although he attended this Chinese church because the services were held in the *Hokkien* dialect, he felt that there was a need to establish a Chinese Presbyterian church.

Forty years later, Keng attested to the discussion regarding the initiatory plan in 1924.[486] He briefly wrote that "In 1924, the late Ti" Han Eng/ Zheng HanRong 鄭漢榮, Ng Ho Seng/Huang HeSheng 黃和聲, and Ti" Ka Seng/Zheng JiaSheng 鄭家聲 had already advocated the establishment of a Chinese Presbyterian church."[487] Keng himself desired as much, but because there were too many concerns, these three men lost their courage just like Peter did when he saw the waves around him (Matt 14:30). The main reason for their timidity, he went on to say, was because these people were prominent in society, and if their plan failed, they would be shamed all their lives. Hence, this plan remained idle and no progress was made toward establishing a Chinese Presbyterian church in Manila.

In the *Founding Publication* Keng wrote a four-page report entitled "Benhui Da Shiji 本會大事記 (Main Events of the Church)," detailing

---

486. Although basically the same in structure, the short articles in English and in Chinese have differences in specific details. In this study both versions have been combined to present a better picture of the event.

487. Keng Lin Kiat/Gong RenJie 龔人傑, "Chuchuang Jianshi 初創簡史 (A short history of the initial formation)," in *HDPO*, 10. The legal name of Ti" Han Eng was Ty Han Eng. He became an elder of CUEC in later years and a major supporter of the church-established school Chia-Nan School/Jianan Xuexiao 嘉南學校 (now Hope Christian High School/Jianan Zhongxue 嘉南中學) and the Evangelistic Band until he died on 23 Mar 1957. Kho Goat Hoa (a.k.a. Phoebe Kho-Chua/Cai Xu YueHua) 蔡許月華, "Retrospect at the 30th Anniversary," in *30th Anniversary Souvenir Magazine, The Evangelistic Band of the Chinese United Evangelical Church* (Manila: Chinese United Evangelical Church, 1966). This source is published bilingually; it will henceforth be cited as *Evangelistic Band.*

major events of the first year of the establishment of CUEC as follows: (1) The inaugural meeting of the church was held from eight o'clock to eleven o'clock on the evening of 14 July 1929. (2) A second meeting was held on 25 August to welcome Dr Ha Le Bun/Xia LiWen 夏禮文博士 [Dr Clarence Holleman][488] and send off two visitors from Xiamen.[489] (3) Six deacons and four elders were elected on 1 September. It was announced that if two weeks passed and no one objected to the ten being elected, then the election would become final and official on 15 September. During that event, Dr Ha Le Bun presided while Dr George William Wright gave an exhortation on the duties of church officers. (4) Dr Ha was the founder of a hospital in China that had suffered damages and needed repair. He was in the Philippines seeking financial support. While in Manila he gave much assistance to the new congregation. On 22 September, a send-off party was given in his honor. (5) The first evangelistic team, composed of eight men and women, was sent out to a place called *Sandaluo* 三答洛 [San Pablo]. There was Scripture reading, exhortation, and prayer during the meeting. Keng Lin Kiat narrated the events leading up to the formation of the new church, and six or seven persons voluntarily signed up to join the new church. (6) On 25 December, a Christmas celebration was held. The meeting place was packed. The preachers were Sia Tsu Keng and Rev Dr Wright. Rev and Mrs Charles A. Gunn (term of service 1911–1921, 1928–1939) of the Presbyterian Mission rendered a duet.[490]

(3) Second Testimony – Kho Ju Soat

The other testimony comes from Kho Ju Soat, the fourth daughter of Rev Kho Seng Iam. She related that:

---

488. By comparing the phonetic transcription and the English surname of the person concerned, and by using the background information regarding his work furnished in Keng's article in the *Founding Publication*, I have deduced that this person is Dr Clarence Holleman of the Leng Na Ai Hoa Hospital 龍巖愛華醫院 in Fujian, which was completed in early 1922. See De Jong, *Reformed Church in China*, 239–240 and Keng Lin Kiat, "Main Events of the Church," in *Founding Publication*.

489. Keng wrote that the two visitors were Madam Fu 福姑娘 and Madam Wen 文姑娘 (unidentified). Madam Fu would be Dr Tena Holkeboer/Fu YiMu guniang 福懿慕姑娘 (1895–1965). They were vacationing in Baguio around Aug 1929. Keng Lin Kiat, "Main Events of the Church," in *Founding Publication*.

490. Keng Lin Kiat/Gong RenJie 龔人傑, "Benhui Da Shiji 本會大事記 (Main Events of the Church)," in *Founding Publication*.

In 1924, . . . Mr. Tiⁿ Ka Seng came to see my brother [Rev Kho Sek Hui]. He told my brother that the Chinese Church of Christ was going to be established in Manila. Mr. Iuⁿ Khe Thai/Yang QiTai 楊啓泰 and Tiⁿ Han Eng would support the church financially. A letter had been sent to the Ban Lam Tai Hoe [Minnan Da Hui 閩南大會 or more accurately, South Fujian Synod of China/Zhonghua Jidu Jiaohui Minnan Dayihui 中華基督教會閩南大議會] pleading that they look for a Chinese pastor on their behalf. Rev Iuⁿ Hoai Tek/Yang HuaiDe 楊懷德牧師 of E-mng Kang/Xiamen Gang 廈門港 [The Church in Amoy Harbor] responded that he had recommended her brother Rev Kho Sek Hui, who would soon come to the Philippines using a business visa. Rev Yu declared that Rev Kho was young and energetic; if he were invited to minister at the church, he would accomplish much.[491]

This is another confirmation that in 1924, the Chinese Church of Christ had plans for establishing a church in Manila, and Kho Seng Iam's son was recommended as pastor. However, Kho Sek Hui could not find anyone to take his place as pastor of the two big churches in Yong Ning and Chioh Sai/Shishi 石獅, hence the plan failed to materialize. When Tiⁿ Ka Seng passed away no one else pursued a similar plan, hence, nothing happened until 1929.

Kho Ju Soat went on to reminisce about the next event leading to the formation of CUEC. Two men who had settled in the Philippines and who were both members of the Anhai Church 安海教會 in China – Keng Lin Kiat and Sio Tsong Kheng/Xiao ZongQing 蕭宗卿 (App. FF, Fig. 3), visited her elder sister Co King Hoa in May 1929. They discussed how sad they were because they could not find a suitable church to attend. They were attending the SSCM but could not get used to its rites and liturgy. How they wished that a church oriented toward the Presbyterian tradition could be formed. Co King Hoa was very sympathetic with their situation and talked to Ms Iuⁿ Bun Phek/Yang WenBi 楊文碧 about it. Those who

---

491. Kho Ju Soat/Xu YuXue 許逾雪, "Yehehua Yile – Chuqi De Jiaohui 耶和華以勒—初期的教會 (Jehovah Jireh – The early church)," in *HDPO*, 16 (English translation mine).

shared the same sentiment formed a steering committee that began to meet at the residence of U Keng Pho/Yu JingPo 于景波 (the husband of Co King Hoa). They started to invite more people to attend and to search for a place to hold worship services. The first prayer meeting was held there on 7 July 1929 with fourteen in attendance. These were: U Keng Pho, Kho Kheng Hoa, Sio Tsong Kheng, Keng Lin Kiat, Iuⁿ Bun Phek, Kho Ju Soat, Tan Tiau Lam/Chen ChaoNan (legal name I. S. Tian Nam) 陳朝南, Iuⁿ Un Tian/Yang EnDian 楊恩典, Kho Chheng Un/Xu QingEn (legal name Co Ching Hu) 許清恩, Si Sun Sam/Shi ChunSan 施純三, Kho Su Diam/ Xu ShuNian 許書念, Tiuⁿ Tsu Ai/Zhang CiAi 張慈愛, Lim Siong Hong (a.k.a. Joseph Lim Tiao Hong who became pastor of CPCI), Po Siok Bi/ Fu ShuMei 傅淑美. Some believers who were from the Kho sisters' village began to have misgivings and began to investigate these meetings. In order to prevent damaging criticisms, this group decided to publicly proclaim the birth of their church through a worship service held on 14 July 1929 (App. FF, Fig. 4).

Keng Lin Kiat related the momentous event of the birth of their new church from another angle. In 1929, he and five other people (Sio Tsong Keng, U Keng Pho, Co King Hoa, Kho Ju Soat, and Iuⁿ Bun Phek) regularly met for exercise at the Luneta Park. One day they were discussing the news of the day – the strike of some teachers of St. Stephen's Chinese Girls' School. The teachers were protesting the management style of the principal which they considered unfair.[492] As a result, the principal terminated these teachers. Another teacher who had also complained resigned. She happened to be Kho Goat Hoa, a teacher since 1917, and sister of Kho Ju Soat. As the group discussed the issue, the conversation turned toward their spiritual needs. It was Keng's opinion that the moment had come to form a new church, so he and Sio Tsong Keng decided to visit U Keng Pho and Co King Hoa. Kho Ju Soat and Iuⁿ Bun Pek were also present.

The teachers' response was enthusiastic, and they set up a prayer meeting together with the dismissed teachers. A steering committee was also formed, composed of ten people. These included Tan Tiau Lam, Teng Keng Pho/Ding JingPo 丁景波 (the legal spelling Ting Keng Po will henceforth

---

492. The principal from 1925–1931 was Dorothy Latham Mattocks, wife of then Parish Rector Rev Henry Mattocks. Botengan, "Horizon," 22.

be used; he is also known as Kepler Ting) (App. FF, Fig. 3), Iu^n Ka Bo/
Yang JiaMuo (Yuha Bo) 楊嘉謨, and Kho Chheng Un, in addition to the
six mentioned above. Keng described the meeting place as No. 602 Reina
Regente Street (App. FF, Fig. 2). He explained that the term "Lu Hui/Lü
Fei 旅菲 (sojourning in the Philippines)" indicated that this church *was*
affiliated with the Min Nan Da Hui 閩南大會 (Minnan Synod) of the
Church of Christ in China. This group of people invited Rev Ngo Keng
Seng/Wu JingXing 吳景星牧師 to come and assist the new church, but
he declined. On the evening of 14 July 1929, a Sunday, while rain poured
during a violent storm, the first worship service transpired. According to
Shih Chang Shangkuan, there were about thrity-two participants and visitors that night (Fig. 4 in App. FF).[493]

e) The Presbyterian Mission and CUEC
Among the visitors attending the historical service was Rev Dr George
William Wright, a Presbyterian missionary and then secretary of the UECPI
(now UCCP, see App. BB). He had come to the Philippines in November
1903, and had served as minister of the Ellinwood Malate Church from
1907 to1937 (hereafter Ellinwood Church). His wife, Anna Rodgers, the
sister of James Burton Rodgers, came in 1907. The reason that Wright
became involved with this new congregation was because of the action
initiated by its founders.

During their first prayer meeting they fervently prayed for a pastor. Tan
Tiau Lam suggested that they approach the Presbyterian Mission for help
regarding this matter. Kho Ju Soat explained that after they got in touch
with Wright, they found out that the Comity Agreement stipulated that
Manila was within the jurisdiction of the Episcopal Church. In reality,
the Comity Agreement stipulated that Manila was open to all Protestant
missions (see App. BB). This misunderstanding may have arisen from the
fact that the Presbyterians and Methodists had turned over their Chinese
work to SSCM in 1907. From that time until the 1920s, the idea that the
Episcopal Church had sole jurisdiction over the Chinese in Manila may
have lingered on, even though it was an incorrect inference from the 1907
incident. Wright wanted them to prepare a document listing the names

---

493. Shangkuan, "Pre-fortieth Anniversary Celebration," 143.

of the initiators and stating their intentions, so that the Episcopalians would not misunderstand and think that the Presbyterians had initiated the organization of the church. The fourteen persons who attended the prayer meeting signed their names on the document (App. GG). When the Episcopalians approached Wright about this matter, he showed them the document. Upon noticing the name of Kho Ju Soat, Rev Hobart Studley wrote to her father Rev Kho Seng Iam in Fujian and questioned him: "Why did you tell your daughter to form this church?" Her father wrote back: "I never told my daughter to form a church. I do not even know that she would form a church. If she really did form a church, you and I should be happy about it."[494] After this response, the Episcopalians never again raised the issue.

Kho's response can be perceived in one of two ways. First, he was the one who wrote the "Declaration" for founding CUEC, and he had done this in 1924. He had come in 1928 and expressed his desire for such a church to be formed. Since the plan was not carried out at that time, it is possible that at the time he received Studley's letter, he was not yet aware that it had been actualized in July 1929. This may explain why he told Studley that he did not know the church had been formed. Another way of understanding his answer is that he did not know his daughter could establish a church, that she had the capability of doing so. In light of the preceding discussion, I am more inclined to take the first perception that Kho was not aware that the event had already transpired.

The letter that was sent on 9 July 1929 to the Presbyterian Mission care of its secretary, Rev Wright, reads as follows:

> Dr. G. W. Wright,
> Secretary of the United Evangelical Church,
> Manila, P.I.
>
> Sir:
>
> In view of the necessity to have a place for common worship among the Christian Chinese, we, the undersigned who

---

494. This is my translation. In Chinese the text reads, 「我未曾叫小女設教會，我更不知道她會設教會。如果她真的設教會，你我都應該高興。」 Kho Ju Soat, "Jehovah Jireh," 16.

are initiatory to the preposition, have pledged ourselves to form what is known as the Philippine Chinese Presbyterian Church, and have hereby petitioned before you for consideration for membership in your church. Members at present rank from forty up, and we are still campaigning for the increase.

We shall deem it a great favor for any manners of courtesy extended us in helping our church formally organized.[495]

The fourteen signatories were: Co Ching Hu, I. S. Tian Nam [Tan Tiau Lam], Sio Chong Keng [Sio Tsong Keng], Yuha Bo [Yu Ka Bo], Khe Chi Liam, Keng Lin Kiat, Edward C. C. Yii, Elizabeth Co [Kho Ju Soat], Lim Ching Pung, Wen Pi Yang [Iu^n Bun Phek], Sy Sun Sam [Si Sun Sam], King Hoa Co [Kho Kheng Hoa], Ching Po Teng [Ting Keng Po], and Lee Kim Kis. Note that the group identified themselves as the "Philippine Chinese Presbyterian Church." This is probably due to the fact that the group wanted to reflect its Presbyterian affiliation. However, as far as I can determine, it is significant that this name is never found in any of the subsequent documents or literature published by or written about the church.

Among the fourteen names, Tan Tiau Lam, Sio Tsong Keng, Yu Ka Bo, Keng Lin Kiat, Kho Ju Soat, Iu^n Bun Phek, Sy Sun Sam, Kho Kheng Hoa and Ting Keng Po are clearly identifiable when compared with names found in articles of the 40th anniversary publication of the CUEC (*HDPO*). For the five names that are not identifiable, no Chinese equivalents are given. This letter serves as evidence that these people were the founding members of the Chinese United Evangelical Church. This list, however, is different from the list given by Kho Ju Soat's list of the fourteen who attended the first prayer meeting on 7 July 1929. A comparison of the two lists is given in Appendix GG.

The Foreign Board of the Presbyterian Church in the USA responded to the request positively. In a seven-page report submitted on 23 July 1930 by James Burton Rodgers, then acting executive secretary of the Philippine Mission, it was recorded: "We have been greatly interested during the year

---

495. *Minutes of the Executive Committee of the Philippine Mission Presbyterian Church in the United States of America. Baguio, P. I., May 3–6, 1930,* 34.

198
A Study on the Emergence and Early Development of
Selected Protestant Chinese Churches in the Philippines

in the development of the Chinese Presbyterian Church in Manila and we are glad to see that they plan to join with the United Evangelical Church in the Philippines [former name of UCCP]." This did not actually happen, but Wright was involved in the capacity of "advisory pastor." In his personal report in the Philippine Mission's Annual Reports for 1929–1930 and for 1932–1933, he wrote:

> Have also been privileged to serve in an advisory and pastoral way to a new <u>Chinese Presbyterian Congregation</u> organized in BINONDO and it has been an inspiration to be with them in what is a real and going work organized and managed by themselves. They come mostly from Amoy.
>
> I have also been privileged to continue as an advisory pastor to the Chinese Presbyterian Congregation in *Calle Alvarado* and have tried to help, as best as I might, with the many problems that have been before them during this past year.[496]

This advisory relationship continued until the Wright's term ended in 1937, during which occasion the Chinese church held a send-off party for the Wrights. Subsequently, he retired in 1938. Wright's portrait is printed in the *Founding Publication*, with the caption: "Zanzhu benhui Zuilizhe 贊助本會最力者 (The person who most energetically assisted our church)."

Although the advisory role did not continue for long, the friendly relationship with the Presbyterian missionaries continued over the next decade. In 1958, the Chinese United Evangelical Church applied for affiliate membership with the Philippine Federation of Christian Churches (App. BB). While acknowledging that CUEC had closely cooperated with the evangelism program of PFCC, some members of PFCC still hesitated over this application. They felt that CUEC, having split from the SSCM, was setting a "dangerous precedent" for other churches. Others, however, felt that since UCCP had in the past attempted to integrate such Chinese

---

496. Personal Report of George W. Wright, in *Annual Reports 1928–1929, Philippine Mission of the Presbyterian Church in the USA Dumaguete, Oriental Negros, October 5–12, 1929.* The letter has been quoted in whole, together with Dr Wright's emphasis by means of underscoring and capitalization. This advisory relationship lasted until the mid-sixties, for William Angus stated that Rev Dr Stephen Smith, then pastor of Ellinwood Malate Church, was given the title of "honorary pastor" of CUEC. See Angus, Jr, "United Church," 24.

churches, the PFCC should happily accept the application now that CUEC was initiating this move.[497]

No mention of the approval of the above-mentioned application is found in the Minutes of the Seventh General Assembly (1960), but it was stated that the tie between "the biggest Chinese Church located at Benavidez" [CUEC] and the Ellinwood Church, "has not been organizational but rather through choice personal links," through Rev George Wright and other pastors who succeeded him at Ellinwood Church. Rev Joseph Young had graduated from Union Theological Seminary, and CUEC was recommending that the Greater Manila Conference ordain him as a minister of the UCCP, then assign him to CUEC.[498] Perhaps if Rev Joseph Young had lived until the present or if the RCA had continued assigning missionaries to the church-related school Hope Christian High School (see discussion in App. BB), this relationship could have been sustained. During the late 1970s and 1980s, with decreasing numbers of leaders from the Ellinwood Church having any personal links with UCCP, the association dissolved on its own.

f) The Church Organized

However, the new church did not rely on non-members or any organization to administer its affairs. Just two months after its inauguration, the church had already organized itself by electing a board of elders and deacons. Four elders and six deacons were elected in September 1929. The elders were Co King Hoa, Tan Tiau Lam, Tan Beng Tek/Chen Mingde 陳明德, and Keng Lin Kiat. The deacons were Po Siok Bi, Kho Ju Soat, Iu^n Ka Bo, Ng Lip Tek/Huang Lide 黃立德, Sio Tsong Kheng, and Ting Keng Po.[499] It is significant that this plan was initiated by a group of Chinese Christians, a unique move that had not happened elsewhere in the Philippines during the 1920s. At that time the Western Protestant missions (Episcopalian and

---

497. *Minutes of the Executive Committee Meeting, Philippine Federation of Christian Churches, Union Theological Seminary Building, Manila, October 31, 1958*, Record Group A, Box 32A, Yale University Day Missions Library, Yale University, New Haven, Connecticut, 426.

498. *Minutes of the Seventh General Assembly, United Church of Christ in the Philippines, Legaspi City, May 19–24, 1960*, 110.

499. *Founding Publication*, n.p.

Presbyterian) had been the only ones forming Chinese churches in Manila and around the provinces (Cebu and Iloilo).

As this extension of the Church of Christ in China was being formed in Manila, the church members repeatedly emphasized in their writings that they were fully supported by the members themselves, that no mission organization was backing them financially or administratively, and that they were independent and self-governing. The late Rev Dr Joseph Young, writing in the fortieth anniversary publication of the church, described the church as "indigenous in that it was organized, maintained and managed by its members without foreign financial assistance."[500] In other words, they were fully self-supporting and independent right from the start.

With regard to ministerial staffing, the church immediately sought assistance from the Church of Christ in China to supply Chinese pastors from Fujian. According to Young, the first preacher to come from Xiamen in 1930 was Wu MingEn 吳明恩.[501] It is not known how long this preacher stayed, but the church soon tried to find pastors who were available locally. One of these, as recorded by Shangkuan, was Pastor Sia Tsu Keng who had by that time come into conflict with Rev Henry Mattocks and subsequently left SSCM (see pp. 136–137). CUEC invited the pastor to speak once or twice during their services in November and December.[502] The leaders of the newly organized church deliberated whether to invite him as their pastor or not. There were, moreover, dissenting voices regarding the length of his tenure should he be invited. When Sia was not invited, he affiliated with another group, the Christian Union/Feilübin Huaqiao Jidutu Lianhehui 菲島華僑基督徒聯合會, the predecessor of today's Christian Gospel Center/Jidutu Juhuisuo 基督徒聚會所 and Church Assembly Hall/Jiaohui Juhuisuo 教會聚會所,[503] the roots of which go back to the

---

500. Joseph Young, "A Brief Survey of Chinese Protestantism in the Philippines," in *HDPO*, 233 (pages in Chinese style).

501. Young, "Survey of the Overseas Chinese," 32. His source was a brief article found in the programme of the 25th anniversary of CUEC in 1954. It was entitled "Story of Our Church" and was written by Keng Lin Kiat, but unfortunately, it cannot be located in the church repository. This seemingly important information is not found in the *HDPO*, nor in all the UECP records gathered by the researcher.

502. "Schedule of Sunday Services recorded by Keng Lin Kiat," *Founding Publication*.

503. Shangkuan, "Pre-fortieth Anniversary Celebration," 143. These two groups were formed on 22 Aug 1961.

"Little Flock" or Xiaoqun 小群 movement, one of the largest indigenous churches of China famous for its leaders – Leland Wang Dai 王載 (1898–1975) and Watchman Nee/Ni TuoSheng 倪柝聲 (App. FF, Fig. 5).[504]

Nee was a third-generation Fuzhou Protestant, grandson of the first Chinese pastor in Fuzhou (affiliated with the American Board) and son of a custom official who served on the mission board of the YMCA. Nee rejected foreign mission and the YMCA style of Christianity. His group, started in the early 1920s, espoused anti-denominationalism and a non-formal church structure, and yet became an isolationist denomination operating under a complex organizational system. It is characterized by its passion for soul winning, evangelism, biblical and evangelical doctrine, a strong discipline of life in Christ, opposition to theological education and to winning souls through medical missions and Christian schools. Rejecting all former church customs, they met in rented halls and took their names from where they were located.[505]

g) *Effects of Revival in China*

(1) The Bethel Mission

The growth and expansion of CUEC was greatly spurred by the Bethel Mission 伯特利教會 of Shanghai. The evangelistic fervor of this Mission was brought about by the great revival in China that lasted from 1927 until 1939.[506] The Bethel Mission was founded by Dr Mary Stone/Shi MeiYu 石美玉醫生 (1873-1954) and Jennie V. Hughes/Hu ZunLi 胡遵理女士 (1874–1951) in September 1920. The Mission constructed the first coeducational high school and dormitory buildings in 1922. Betty Mayling Hu/

504. See Joseph Tse-Hei Lee, "Watchman Nee and the Little Flock Movement in Maoist China," *Church History* 74, no. 1 (Mar 2005): 68–96.

505. Dunch, *Fuzhou Protestants*, 195; Young, "A Brief Survey of Chinese Protestantism in the Philippines," in *HDPO*, 231–232 (pages in Chinese style); Bill Yang, "Chinese Protestant Churches in the Philippines," 157–166.

506. See Orr, *Evangelical Awakenings*, chs. 9–14, and Cao ShengJie 曹聖潔, "Zili Yundong yu Benshehua 自立運動與本色化 (The Movement of self-rule and contextualization)," in *Qianshi Buwang Houshi Zhi Shi: Diguo Zhuyi Liyong Jidujiao Qinlue Zhongguo Shishi Shuping* 前事不望後事之師：帝國主義利用基督教侵略中國史實述評 (Forget not the past, teacher of the future – a historical evaluation of the imperialist invasion of China through Christianity), ed. Luo GuanZong 羅冠宗 (Beijing: Zongjiao Wenhua Chubanshe 宗教文化出版社, 2003), 136–179. The second work clearly has a negative outlook on Christianity, but its historical information has its own value.

Hu MeiLin 胡美林 (a.k.a. Wang Mayling/Wang MeiLin 王美林) headed the high school work in 1928, and later became the superintendent of Bethel Orphanages for twenty-five years. Alice Lan (1930–1973) graduated from Asbury College and returned to Shanghai in 1928 (App. FF, Fig. 6). She volunteered as a missionary to Yunnan 雲南 for seven months, then became president of the Bethel Bible College 伯特利神學院 which was founded in 1925. Between 1934 and 1970, they made a total of eight visits to the Philippines and had the joy of watching this church grow from 30 to over 3,000 members (including all the branch churches) by 1969.[507]

One of those trained by Mary Stone was Andrew Gih/Ji ZhiWen 計志文牧師 (1901–1985) (App. FF, Fig. 5).[508] Gih was greatly challenged by the ministry of Dr Alphaeus Paget Wilkes (1871–1934) in Shanghai.[509] Wilkes, an Anglican missionary to Japan and founder of the Japanese Evangelistic Band, spoke at a conference on spiritual life in 1925 and revived the flagging spirits of the missionaries as well as energized the Chinese Christians by repeatedly insisting that the latter should be the ones to evangelize China.[510] As a result of the burden to evangelize the whole of China, the Bethel Evangelistic Band 伯特利佈道團 was formed in 1927 by Gih and other like-minded young men such as Philip Lee/Li DaoRong 李道榮, Frank Lin/ Lin JingKang 林景康牧師, Lincoln Nieh/ Nie ZiYing 聶子英, and John Shih/Shi GengMing 時賡明. This sparked the nationwide revival movement known as the Awakening of 1927–1939. The wide-reaching effects of this movement permeated all of China and extended as far as South (India) and Southeast Asia (Malaysia, Singapore,

---

507. Betty M. Hu/Hu MeiLin 胡美林, "Pioneer Days," in *HDPO*, 18–19 (pages in Chinese style); Betty M. Hu/Hu MeiLin 胡美林, "Golden Memories – A Short History of Bethel Mission of China for its Fiftieth Anniversary," in *50th Anniversary of the Bethel Mission of China, 1920–1970* (Hong Kong: Hsiang-Kang Po-Pe-Li Chiao Hui [香港伯特利教會], 1970), 1–5.

508. See Andrew Gih, *Twice Born – and Then? The Life Story and Message of Andrew Gih*, ed., Ruth J. Corbin, 2nd ed. (London: Marshall, Morgan & Scott, 1954); *Biographical Dictionary of Christian Missions*, 1998 ed., s.v. "Gih, Andrew (Ji ZhiWen)," by Donald E. MacInnis.

509. See Mary Wilkes Dunn Pattison, *Ablaze for God: The Life Story of Paget Wilkes*, 3rd ed. (London: Oliphants, 1937); I. R. Govan Stewart, *Dynamic: Paget Wilkes of Japan* (London: Marshall, Morgan & Scott, 1957).

510. Orr, *Evangelical Awakenings*, 48, 58, 61, 76–78.

Philippines). Gih invited the famous John Sung to join the band in 1931, and this association lasted for thirty fruitful months.

The Bethel Band indirectly contributed to the young church through the ministry of John Sung (App. FF, Fig. 5), who ministered independently from 1934–1944. He came to the Philippines and held evangelistic meetings on 6 June 1935, attended by thousands of people every night.[511] He passed by briefly and held another evangelistic service in 1940, at the same time organizing the City-wide Evangelistic Team 全岷佈道團, composed of members from all denominations under the leadership of Chua Heng Hok/Cai XingFu 蔡幸福.[512] However, not long after Sung left, this team quickly dissolved. Still, the fervor for evangelism remained and spurred the CUEC to organize the Evangelistic Band 播道團 on 28 October 1936, under the leadership of Kho Goat Hoa. Its members, many of whom were elderly ladies with bound feet, served as pioneers of the nationwide evangelistic campaign.[513] By the time of its 25th anniversary, the band had already established ten daughter churches.[514] Some of the pioneers in the band were Chua I Kiat/Cai WeiJie 蔡維潔 (Homer Chua), Chiu Pek Tat/Zhou BoDa 周柏達 (Peter Chiu), Lao Eng Kui/Liu RongGui 劉榮桂, Lim Eng Pang/Lin RongBang 林榮邦, Tan Chin Heng/Chen ZhenXing 陳振興, and Tan Chi Lin/Chen ZhiRen 陳志仁.[515]

---

511. Levi Song, *Lingli Jiguang* (The Diary of His Spiritual Life), 187–188.

512. Orr, *Evangelical Awakenings*, 62; George Sin Chiong Chua/Tsai XinZhang 蔡信彰, "Boteli Budaotuan Yu Lüfei Zhonghua Jidu Jiaohui 伯特利佈道團與旅菲中華基督教會 (The Bethel Worldwide Evangelistic Band and the United Evangelical Church of Manila)," in *HDPO*, 23 (pages in Chinese style).

513. See Kho Goat Hoa (a.k.a. Phoebe K. Chua)/Cai Xu YueHua 許月華, "History of the Evangelistic Band," in *Evangelistic Band.*

514. Chhoa Kho Goat Hoa, *Sixty Years*, 9, 11–25. She narrated the historical beginning of these ten churches in consecutive order, together with their exact dates of being officially recognized as daughter churches of UECP. They are: Naga (6 Jul 1939), Sta. Cruz, Laguna (24 Sep 1940), Bacolod (7 Jan 1950), Lucena (11 Jan 1953), Vigan (28 Sep 1953), Daet (12 Mar 1961), Legaspi (30 Sep 1962), Jubilee (20 Jan 1963), Pasay (28 Nov 1965), and Malabon (17 Jun 1973). These churches all have "United Evangelical Church of" as prefix in their official names, except for Bacolod Trinity Church and Jubilee Evangelical Church. See also Kho Siu Lim/Xu XiuLin 許秀琳, "Daminshi Yiwai – Lüsong Quandao Huaqiao Jiaohui Lueshi 大岷市以外—呂宋全島華僑教會略史 (Beyond Metro Manila: Historical sketch of overseas Chinese churches in Luzon Island)," in *HDPO*, 147–150 (pages in Chinese style).

515. George Chua, "Bethel Worldwide," in *Historical Documentary*, 23; Wesley Kho Shao/Shao QingZhang 邵慶彰, "Feilübin Zhonghua Jidu Jiaohui Jianshi 菲律賓中華

(2) Two Seminaries, Three Pioneers

Two institutions helped the young church through the training of the much-needed pastoral staff. One was the Wuchow Alliance Bible Seminary 梧洲宣道神學院 (now Alliance Bible Seminary in Hong Kong) in Guangxi, China 中國廣西. One of the earliest workers at CUEC was Rev George Sin Chiong Chua (App. FF, Fig. 7). He felt called to ministry in 1931 and entered this Seminary. Two years after graduation he was assigned to Anhai, Fujian, and there continued his link with the Chinese United Evangelical Church in Manila. Keng Lin Kiat invited him to become their pastor. Thus he arrived in Manila in August 1934.[516] It was Chua who urged the leaders of the church to invite evangelists from the Bethel Evangelistic Band. It was also Chua who recommended to the church council to invite the president of his seminary, Rev Ng Goan So/Huang YuanSu 黃原素 (1895–1994), popularly known as Silas Wong, to come to CUEC, where he served from 1938 to 1965.[517]

The other institution was the Bethel Bible College. Founding member of CUEC Ting Keng Po (1905–1970) (App. FF, Fig. 3) went to study at this College after he was spiritually convicted as a result of the ministry of Alice Lan and Betty Hu. In a short biographical sketch of Ting, Ong Hok Bin/Wang FuMin 王福民 wrote that Ting was born in Un Chiu, Chiat Kang/Zhejiang Wenzhou 浙江溫洲 on 20 August 1905, and was originally surnamed Lim (Lin 林). He was abducted at seven and sold to a family surnamed Ting (Ding 丁) in Jinjiang 晉江. At the age of fourteen, he came to the Philippines and worked for his uncle, but had to return because of an illness. He came back at age 18, but was sent back to manage his uncle's business enterprise in China. He married and returned to the Philippines. It was at this time that he helped form the CUEC. He is listed as one of the three founders (faqiren 發起人) in the *Founding Publication*, together

---

基督教會簡史 (A short history of the United Evangelical Church of the Philippines)," in *Arise, Shine: 70ᵗʰ Anniversary* (*Xingqi Faguang – Feilübin Zhonghua Jidu Jiaohui Qishi Zhounian Tekan 1929–1999*) 興起發光—菲律賓中華基督教會七十週年特刊*1929–1999* (Manila: United Evangelical Church of the Philippines, [1999]), 6; Joseph Young, "A Brief Survey of Chinese Protestantism in the Philippines," in *HDPO*, 232 – 233 (pages in Chinese style).

516. George Chua, "Bethel Worldwide," in *HDPO*, 23.

517. Bill Yang, "Chinese Protestant Churches," 154; "BSOP Founder Passes Away," *BSOP in Focus* (Jun 1995): 12.

with Sio Tsong Kheng and Keng Lin Kiat. He was actively involved in the Bethel evangelistic campaigns whenever their evangelists came, as well as in preaching around the provinces with Rev George Chua. While still studying in Shanghai, he was invited by the Bethel Band to travel throughout South Fujian to act as interpreter for the evangelists. After he graduated from Bethel Bible College, he returned and became a worker of CUEC. His daughter, Esther Ting Dy/Li Ding YingYing 李丁瑩瑩, remembers that they lived on the second floor of the church building. Every time a church member died, the coffin would be placed in the worship hall, hence the children of Pastor Ting would see it everyday or watch the ceremonial rites from the staircase.[518]

Another founder of the church, Sio Tsong Kheng, also studied at Bethel Bible College for a year but could not finish his studies because of his family's financial needs. He was also from Anhai and was already a believer before he came to the Philippines. He had also attended the SSCM and found the worship style discomfiting. After CUEC was established, he alternately preached with Keng Lin Kiat when there was no preacher. He also went regularly to the provinces with Yu Ka Bo to raise funds for the struggling church.[519]

Fundraising seems to have been frequently done, for the financial situation of the church was so bad in the beginning. According to Sy Chi Siong/Shi CiXiang 施慈祥 (b. 1913), who came to the Philippines in 1926, and at age 94 (when interviewed) is one of the oldest living members of CUEC/UECP, he attended the afternoon services around the time of the founding of the church, whenever he could finish buying and selling rice and returning to Manila early. He saw that when Wright was asked to officiate the Communion Service, he would regularly give five pesos (another source said ten pesos) in the offering plate. The amount of five or ten pesos

518. Esther Ting Dy/Li Ding YingYing 李丁瑩瑩, 2005. Audio-taped interview by Jean Uayan, 12 Apr 2005, 3:10–4:15 p.m., transcript, Philippine Chinese Church Archive, Biblical Seminary of the Philippines, Valenzuela City, Philippines. Wang FuMin 王福民, *Tingjingbo Xiansheng Xingshu* 丁景波先生行述 (Eulogy for Mr Ting Keng Po) (Manila, 3 Dec 1970).

519. Dy Hong Suan vda. de Siao/Xiao Li HongXuan 蕭李鳳萱, 2005. Audio-taped interview by Jean Uayan, 30 Mar 2005, 2:00–2:42 p.m. at her residence in Quezon City, transcript, Philippine Chinese Church Archive, Biblical Seminary of the Philippines, Valenzuela City, Philippines.

was considered a huge sum to give on the part of Wright, since his home allowance for 1930–1931 was only $1,925, which meant a monthly average of $160.42.[520] He was amazed because the other members could hardly give one peso each. The sum of ten or twenty centavos was already quite a sacrifice to offer, for the members received meager salaries.[521]

Sio Tsong Kheng and Ting Keng Po did not stay in the Chinese United Evangelical Church all their lives, unlike Keng Lin Kiat. Sio retired to Gulangyu, Fujian 福建鼓浪嶼 at past the age of fifty, while Ting, not long after CUEC was founded, went on to pastor many other churches, among them the United Evangelical Church of Naga and St. Stephen's Parish.[522] Kho Ju Soat established the Westminster High School in 1932 and later left CUEC when she formed the Westminster Student Church (now WSC Westminster Church, Inc.) in 1950.[523] In Chinese, the name of this church is Feilübin Zhonghua Jidujiao Xunshantang 菲律濱中華基督教 郇山堂 (literally translated, Church of Christ in China in the Philippines

---

520. This information is taken from the projected salary and allowances of missionaries of the Philippine Mission, Presbyterian Church in the USA, for the year 1930–1931. Allowances are given for those who are not on the field, and Wright's personal report just a few pages before this chart points to the fact that he and his family went on furlough in 1930–1931. For those on the field the regular salary was 2,100 pesos *per annum*. See *Annual Reports 1929–1930 Philippine Mission, Presbyterian Church in the USA, Dumaguete, Oriental Negros Oriental, October 5–12, 1929.*

521. Sy Chi Siong/Shi CiXiang 施慈祥, 2006. Audio-taped interview by Jean Uayan, 3 Jan 2006, 11:30–12:20 a.m. at his business establishment in Binondo, Manila, transcript, Philippine Chinese Church Archive, Biblical Seminary of the Philippines, Valenzuela City, Philippines. Sy Chi Siong was born in 1913 and came to the Manila at age thirteen. His brother, Peter Leoncio, who came in 1939, said that the sum was equal to a month's salary for some people. Peter Leoncio Sy/Shi LiangRui 施良瑞, 2005, 2006. Audio-taped interview by Jean Uayan, 30 Mar 2005, 8:45–11:00 a.m. at his residence in Pasay City and 3 Jan 2006, 11:30–12:20 a.m. at his office in Manila, transcript, Philippine Chinese Church Archive, Biblical Seminary of the Philippines, Valenzuela City, Philippines.

522. Siao Dy Hong Suan, 2005; Wang FuMin, Eulogy for Mr Ting Keng Po.

523. She first established the Su-Kung Elementary School in 1932 which later became the Westminster High School in 1949, giving rise to different records of the founding year. Porfirio V. Sison, "Tribute to Madam Elizabeth Kho Lu Soat," in *Xu Zhanglao YuXue Xiaozhang Jiniance Fu Zhurixue YuXuelou Fengxianli* 許長老逾雪校長紀念冊附主日學 逾雪樓奉獻禮 (Memorial book of Elder/Principal Xu YuXue with dedication ceremony of the YuXue Sunday School building) (Manila: Westminster Student Church Literature Committee, 1983), 62–65, 83 (pages in Chinese style). Cf. Amanda Shao Tan/Chen YouChun 陳友純, "Chinese Churches in the Philippines," in *United Evangelical Church of the Philippines Golden Jubilee Almanac (Feilübin Zhonghua Jidu Jiaohui Jinxi Nianjian)* 菲律 濱中華基督教會金禧年鑑 *1929–1979*, ed. S[hih] C[hang] Shangkuan (Manila: United Evangelical Church of the Philippines, [1979]), 148.

Westminster Chapel), a name that reflects the fact that this church, purposely formed to meet the spiritual needs of the students, wanted to retain its association with the Church of Christ in China. Only Keng Lin Kiat remained and served as an elder of CUEC/UECP until he passed away.

h) Summary

The Chinese United Evangelical Church was formed in Manila on 14 July 1929 through the efforts of Chinese believers who came mainly from the Presbyterian or Reformed background in South Fujian, China. These believers had come from such places as Xiamen, Anhai, Jinjing, Tongan, and Quanzhou. When they settled in Manila, they had to attend SSCM for that was the only Chinese church in existence in this city at the time. However, the desire to form a Presbyterian church kept burning deep in their hearts. After a failed attempt in 1924 to begin the process, a core group of members met on 7 July 1929 for prayer and inaugurated CUEC on 14 July 1929. This church differed greatly from the other Chinese churches in and outside Manila because they were totally independent of any Western mission influence or control, whether in terms of finance, polity or liturgy. From the very beginning, CUEC members associated and identified with the Church of Christ in China, specifically, the churches in Kim Chi[n], the Ko Long Su Hok Im Tong/Gulangyu Fuyin Tang 鼓浪嶼福音堂 (Gospel Church of Gulangyu), the AnHai Christian Church and the Quanzhou Christian Church, places where the spiritual life of the original members had taken root and had been nurtured.[524] Much like the methodology and according to the impetus of these South Fujian churches, CUEC followed the same pattern of establishing gospel stations through regular visitations and follow-up work, forming branch churches and founding church-related schools. As of 2007, CUEC/UECP had established thirty-two branch churches all over the Philippines, largely through the past efforts of the Evangelistic Band and the Church Mission Board.[525]

---

524. Because of unavailable resources, the link with these churches, except for Kim Chi[n], has not been explored, but undoubtedly, from interviews with senior members of UECP, they still have spiritual bonds with these churches. In recent decades, some even went back to help build churches and schools in their hometowns.

525. "United Evangelical Church of the Philippines: Manila's Oldest Chinese Presbyterian Church." *Philippine Panorama* (18 Jul 2004): 3; Rev Felix Ong/Wang ZhenGuo 王振國 and Rev Dr Vicente Y. Sia/Xie GuoZhi 謝國智, telephone interview by

The names of these churches are:

Bacolod Trinity Christian Church 描戈律基督教三一堂;

Diamond Jubilee Evangelical Church 鑽禧中華基督教會;

Jubilee Evangelical Church 銀禧中華基督教會, which established
  Calvary Reformed Evangelical Church 加略山歸正福音教會,
  Malabon Jubilee Christian Fellowship 瑪拉文銀禧堂佈道所,
  Marikina Jubilee Gospel Center 馬利瑾那銀禧堂佈道所 and
  Pasig Jubilee Gospel Center 巴石銀禧堂佈道所;

United Evangelical Church [UEC] of Angeles 紅奚禮示中華基督
  教會;

UEC Baguio 碧瑤中華基督教會;

UEC Balintawak 描仁斗沃中華基督教會;

Cotabato Christian Church 古島中華基督教會;

UEC Cubao 龜卯中華佈道所;

UEC Daet 迺乙中華基督教會;

UEC General Santos 南古島中華基督教會 which established
  UEC Marbel 馬伯中華基督教會;

UEC Greenhills 青山中華基督教會;

UEC La Union 拉允隆中華基督教會;

UEC Legaspi 黎牙實備中華基督教會;

UEC Lucena 羅申那中華基督教會;

UEC Malabon 嗎哪門中華基督教會;

UEC Manila (Tagalog-speaking congregation);

UEC Naga 那牙中華基督教會;

UEC Olongapo 荷浪牙波中華基督教會;

UEC Palawan 巴拉灣中華佈道所;

Jean Uayan, Manila, 3 Feb 2007. Rev Ong used to oversee twenty-four of these thirty-two
churches, while the other eight churches are considered "grand-daughter" churches under
the care of their respective mother churches.

UEC Pasay 巴西中華基督教會, which established Batangas Fellowship Evangelical Church;

UEC Pili (Tagalog-speaking congregation);

UEC San Pablo 仙答洛中華基督教會;

UEC Sta Cruz, Laguna 內湖中華基督教會;

UEC Vigan 美岸中華基督教會;

UEC Zamboanga 三寶顏中華基督教會, which established UEC Isabela 伊沙貝拉中華基督教會.

6. Davao Chinese Gospel Church

One of the leading Chinese churches in Mindanao is the Davao Evangelical Church/Namao Jidu Jiaohui 納卯基督教會 (DEC), formerly known as Davao Chinese Gospel Church/Namao Huaqiao Jidu Jiaohui 納卯華僑基督教會 (DCGC). It is located on Villamor Street corner Jacinto Extension in Davao City, a thriving metropolis on the southeastern part of Mindanao (App. A). The city of Davao was created specifically to expedite economic development in the southern Philippines.[526] Davao has the distinction of being a "melting pot" where Filipinos of various regional strains and foreigners conglomerate. Ernesto Corcino mentions "Ilocanos, Cagayanos, Novo Ecijanos, Tarlaqueños, Pampagueños, Caviteños, Batangueños, Bicolanos, Ilonggos, Capizeños, Antiqueños, Negrenses, Cebuanos, Boholanos, Leyteños, Samareños, Zamboangueños, etc."[527]

The DCGC can be considered indigenously established, since its existence came about as a result of the efforts of a few Christian individuals, such as the sisters Bona and Valeria Lim, Eng Tiong Uyboco (the legal name David Uyboco will henceforth be used), Job Chen and Mih Sek Long. On the other hand, it is also a recognized fact that the CMA was closely related to some of the pioneers of this church and was involved in its establishment. Hence, the history of the emergence of DCGC will start with the story of the CMA work in the Philippines, specifically in Mindanao.

---

526. Based on Commonwealth Act No. 51, known as the "Charter of the City of Davao," and approved on 16 Oct 1936. Galang, ed., *Filipiniana* 1: 72.

527. Ernesto I. Corcino, *Davao History* (Davao City: Philippine Centennial Movement, Davao City Chapter, 1998), 123.

a) Beginning of CMA

The CMA is an organization that emerged as a result of the merging of two bodies – the Christian Alliance and the International Missionary Alliance. Both were organized in 1887. The extremely simple organization of the former consisted of a central executive board in New York and auxiliaries and branches in other states and centers of population. The chief methods of work were through local conventions, printed publications, formation of the Highway Missions (classes at home) and rescue missions.[528] The two bodies merged on 2 April 1897.[529] The earliest mission fields of the Evangelical Missionary Alliance, another name for the International Missionary Alliance given in 1888, included countries in Africa, Asia and in South America.[530]

The founder, Albert Benjamin Simpson (1843–1919), was born in Prince Edward Island, Canada, on 15 December 1843 in the home of devout Scottish Covenanter parents. At age 21 he became pastor of Knox Presbyterian Church in Hamilton, Ontario, in 1865. Then he became pastor of Chestnut Street Presbyterian Church in Louisville, Kentucky, where, David Rambo writes, "his unusual interest in foreign missions became a passion, his antagonistic attitude toward revivalism reversed, and his narrowly denominational spirit expanded."[531]

In 1879, Simpson became pastor of the Thirteenth Street Presbyterian Church in New York City. At this time New York City was experiencing the influx (50,000 per year) of people from the hinterland and from Europe, and many of these immigrants tended to be impervious to the message

---

528. *Year Book of the Christian Alliance and the International Missionary Alliance 1893* (New York: Christian Alliance, 1893), 8, accessed 26 Aug 2005, http://apps.cmalliance.org/archives/pdfs/annual_reports/1893_yearbook.pdf.

529. George P. Pardington, *Twenty-Five Wonderful Years 1889–1914: A Popular Sketch of the Christian and Missionary Alliance* (New York: Christian Alliance, 1914), 39, accessed 29 Aug 2005, http://www.cmalliance.org/whoweare/archives/pdfs/ miscellaneous/25yrs_pardington.pdf.

530. *The Christian Alliance Yearbook 1888*, ed. A. B. Simpson (New York: Word, Work & World, [1888]), 53, accessed 26 Aug 2005, http://apps.cmalliance.org/archives/pdfs/annual_reports/1888_yearbook.pdf.

531. David Lloyd Rambo, "The Christian and Missionary Alliance in the Philippines, 1901–1970" (PhD diss., New York University, 1975; Ann Arbor, MI: University Microfilms International, 1979), 24.

and ministry of the churches. Simpson decided to leave the Presbytery.[532] Rambo attributes this to Simpson's "newly-found, non-Presbyterian belief that baptism should be administered by means of immersion."[533] Simpson's theological views had moderated from Calvinism and had leaned toward Keswick theology, which emphasized the attainability of complete sanctification.[534] He also emphasized divine healing and Holy Spirit baptism, did not share the struggles of his contemporaries over the issue of liberalism versus conservatism, was missiologically motivated by a sense of eschatological urgency, and eschewed doctrinal formulations that polarized Christians.[535] This sense of eschatological urgency was manifested in the way Simpson viewed the political turn of events in the Philippines during the late 1800s.

b) CMA in the Philippines

Even before the Spanish-American War in 1898, the CMA had already considered the Philippines an attractive mission field. In 1893, Rev D. W. Le Lacheur, the Home Superintendent of Missions of the CMA in China, went to Singapore for the purpose of establishing a mission in the Spanish colony, but the authorities refused him admission to Manila. Believing that the war would open Cuba and the Philippine Islands to the gospel, he was hoping to take a band of Christian missionaries without seeking permission

---

532. A. E. Thompson, *A. B. Simpson: His Life and Work* (Harrisburg, PA: Christian Publications, 1920), 84–85.

533. Rambo, "Christian and Missionary Alliance," 28.

534. See Paul Gibbs, "'Let Go and Let God': Keswick Movement's Lasting Impact on Fundamentalism's View of Sanctification," 1–10, accessed 30 Jan 2007, http://seminary.cbs.edu/content/events/nlc/2003/ papers/5-%20Let%20Go%20and%20Let%20God.pdf.

535. See Gerald E. McGraw, "A. B. Simpson 1943–1919: From Home Missions to a World Missionary Movement," in *Mission Legacies: Biographical Studies of Leaders of the Modern Missionary Movement*, eds. Gerald Harry Anderson, Robert T. Coote, Norman A. Horner, and James M. Phillips, American Society of Missiology Series 19 (Maryknoll, NY: Orbis, 1994), 37–47.

from Spain.[536] Providence, however, led this party to stay in China, for they felt that mission in China must be reinforced for the time being.[537]

Simpson lived at a time when the central thinking in the United States was the "manifest destiny" of advanced nations to bring the benefits of their achievements to the rest of the world. It was also a time when theology absorbed the mood of the times. Many conservatives envisioned a literal millennium of peace and prosperity prior to the visible return of Christ to earth. There was a pervasive conviction that God had guided the political destiny of America in ways that best suited Christ's Great Commission to make disciples of all the nations.[538] Thus he declared regarding the war: "It is a war in which the providence of God seems destined to have an important place in the fulfillment of prophecy, inasmuch as it is to be, we trust, God's instrumentality for striking another blow at that system of iniquity, the papacy, which looms up more and more clearly as the antichrist of the past and the future."[539] One month after the Battle of Manila, Simpson commented, "The signs are still increasing that the outcome of this war will be, not only the freedom of these oppressed lands, but the opening of their doors for the gospel of Jesus Christ."[540]

When war broke out between the Americans and the Filipinos, Simpson was already making plans to enter the Philippines. He said:

> The Philippine Islands are calling to us. The war has, of course, been a cause of delay and hindrance in the immediate starting

---

536. *Bringing in the Sheaves: Gleanings from the Mission Fields of the Christian and Missionary Alliance* (New York: Christian and Missionary Alliance, 1898), 25–26. The identity of Le Lacheur, as well as a description of the Philippines, is provided by Albert Benjamin Simpson, "Greater America and Her Missionary Opportunity," *Christian and Missionary Alliance* (Nyack and New York) 22, no. 1 (1 Dec 1898): 3–4, accessed 23 Aug 2005, http://apps.cmalliance.org/archives/alifepdf/AW–1898–12–01.pdf.

537. Albert Benjamin Simpson, "Our New Island Possessions," *Christian and Missionary Alliance* (Nyack and New York) 23, no. 15 (9 Sep 1899): 227, accessed 3 Sep 2005, http://apps.cmalliance.org/archives/alifepdf/AW–1899–09–09.pdf.

538. Rambo, "Christian and Missionary Alliance," 35–36.

539. Albert Benjamin Simpson, "The Significance of the Spanish-American War," *Christian and Missionary Alliance* 20, no. 17 (Nyack and New York, 27 Apr 1898): 396, accessed 24 Aug 2005, http://apps.cmalliance.org/archives/alifepdf/AW–1898–08–24.pdf.

540. Albert Benjamin Simpson, "The Progress of the War," *Christian and Missionary Alliance* 20, no. 22 (Nyack and New York, 1 Jun 1898): 516, accessed 24 Aug 2005, http://apps.cmalliance.org/archives/alifepdf/AW–1898–06–01.pdf.

of missions in Luzon, but it is hoped that before the close of the year the vigorous operations of the American forces, aided by the cool season will bring about a settled peace and a stable government. We already have one missionary leader appointed to this field, formerly of South America. . . . We hope other missionaries will follow ere long and we are prayerfully considering several applications. Let there be much prayer for the evangelization of the Philippine Islands."[541]

The missionary Simpson was referring to was Miss Elizabeth (also known as "Bessie" and "Ella") White, formerly connected with the Venezuelan Mission.[542] The CMA sent her to Manila in 1900.[543]

In a report White said that she traveled to the Philippines from Spain together with a Filipina named Manuela. Manuela was a native from Iloilo, hence the CMA wanted to start ministry in her hometown.[544] However, this never happened. Another interesting thing to note is that White knew Rev Eric Lund and the Filipino Braulio Manikan in Spain, before they went to Iloilo and pioneered the Baptist work.[545] Although she did not

541. Albert Benjamin Simpson, "The Islands," *Christian and Missionary Alliance* 23, no. 11 (Nyack and New York, 12 Aug 1899): 168, accessed 24 Aug 2005, http://apps.cmalliance.org/whoweare/archives/pdfs/AW–1899–08–12.pdf.

542. Bayani Y. Mendoza uses both names without explanation, but I surmise that both may have been her nicknames. See Bayani Y. Mendoza, *The Philippine Christian Alliance: First Seventy-Eight Years* (N.p.: by the author, 1985), 26–27 and compare with annual reports for 1894–1901.

543. *Annual Report of the Superintendent and Board of Managers of the Christian and Missionary Alliance 1900–1901 Presented at the Meeting of the Society, May 5, 1901* (New York: Christian and Missionary Alliance, 1901), 24–25, accessed 24 Aug 2005, http://www.cmalliance.org/whoweare/archives/pdfs/annual_reports/1900–1901_report.pdf, henceforth cited as *CMA 1900–1901*; Robert B. Ekvall et al, *After Fifty Years: A Record of God's Working through the Christian and Missionary Alliance* (Harrisburg, PA: Christian Publications, [1939]), 230. See also Rogers, *Forty Years*, 158. Cf. Ernest J. Frei, *Ventures in Cooperation* (Manila: United Church of Christ in the Philippines, 1963), 1; Enrique Sobrepeña, *That They May Be One* (Manila: United Church of Christ in the Philippines, 1964), 13–14. The last two sources trace the beginning of CMA work in the Philippines to 1905.

544. Bessie White, "God's Providences in the Entering of the Philippines," *The Christian and Missionary Alliance* 25, no. 9 (Nyack and New York, 1 Sep 1900), 118–119, accessed 29 Aug 2005, http://apps.cmalliance.org/archives/alifepdf/AW–1900–09–01.pdf.

545. For the relationship of Lund and Manikan and their ministry in Iloilo, see Nestor Distor Bunda, *A Mission History of the Philippine Baptist Churches 1898–1998 from*

mention their names in her article "The Philippines from a Missionary Standpoint," her description clearly points to their identities.[546]

Due to the "unsettled state of the country and the enormous expense of living," which was quite out of proportion to any of the other mission fields, the CMA mission board doubted whether it would be best to attempt further work at that time.[547] Rambo further notes that the "enormous amount" totaled US $700 annually.[548] Elizabeth White's association with the Presbyterians grew especially close through one of its bachelor missionaries, Paul Frederick Jansen (see pp. 88, 141–142). Within a year they were married, and the Alliance mission thereby ceased to exist. The following brief word appeared in the official organ of the CMA, *The Christian and Missionary Alliance*: "During the past year Miss E. White, of Manila, an independent missionary under the auspices of the Alliance, was married to Rev F. Jansen, a Presbyterian missionary in Manila. Her work has, therefore, been transferred from the Alliance to another society, while she is still affectionately cherished by us in Christian fellowship."[549]

The CMA did not join the Evangelical Union of the Philippines until much later when they joined the National Christian Council (formed in 1929), but they abided by the Comity Agreement on territorial assignments.[550] There were subsequent adjustments to the territorial divisions

---

a Philippine Perspective, Perspectiven der Weltmission Wissenschaftliche Beiträge Band, Vol. 30 (Aachen: Verla an der Lottbek im Besitz des Varlags Mainz, 1999), 63–66.

546. Bessie White, "The Philippines from a Missionary Standpoint," *The Christian and Missionary Alliance* 24, no. 12 (Nyack and New York, 24 Mar 1900), 177–179, accessed 27 Aug 2005, http://apps.cmalliance.org/archives/alifepdf/AW–1900–03–24.pdf.

547. *CMA 1900–1901*, 25, accessed 24 Aug 2005, http://www.cmalliance.org/whoweare/archives/pdfs/annual_reports/1900–1901_report.pdf.

548. Rambo, "Christian and Missionary Alliance," 44. In comparison, a missionary from China wrote to ask that his previous allowance of $400 be cut down to $300 because this was enough to live on in his mission field. See James C. Howe, "A Timely Missionary Testimony," *The Christian and Missionary Alliance* 23, no. 14 (Nyack and New York, 2 Sep 1899): 217, accessed 3 Sep 2005, http://apps.cmalliance.org/archives/alifepdf/AW–1899–09–02.pdf.

549. *The Fifth Annual Report of the Christian and Missionary Alliance Presented at the Meeting of the Board 1902* (New York: Christian and Missionary Alliance, 1902), 27–28, accessed 3 Sep 2005, http://www.cmalliance.org/ whoweare/archives/pdfs/annual_reports/1901–1902_report.pdf. This report was made by Dr Simpson himself, according to Mendoza. See Mendoza, *Philippine Christian Alliance*, 27. Cf. Sitoy, *Several Springs* 1: 63.

550. Rodgers, *Forty Years*, 165. This is confirmed by Rambo, "Christian and Missionary Alliance," 46.

throughout the decades until 1923 or 1925. In the final division that lasted until 1950, Mindanao was assigned to the Congregationalists, but Sulu, Basilan and the southern Zamboanga peninsula were assigned to either the CMA or the Episcopal Mission.[551]

The CMA work in Zamboanga was among "Romanists, Mohammedans, and Chinese" and other "Pagans."[552] One source states that "during that period, in the city of Zamboanga, the church labored principally among the Filipinos, but also paid attention to the needs of the large local Chinese community."[553] It is significant that in 1899 Elizabeth Jansen took an interest in the situation of the Chinese in her article, "God's Providences in the Entering of the Philippines."[554] She mentioned that the gospel was being preached to the Chinese in Iloilo as well as in Manila. She states that there were 42,000 Chinese in Manila, and "under American rule, through God's providence, the Chinese are having the gospel preached to them through their own people."[555] In 1908 she visited Zamboanga and in a letter contained in the Twelfth Annual Report of the CMA, she confirmed the work being done by the CMA among the Chinese. She commented:

> The increasingly fruitful work among the Chinese, of whom there are many in Mindanao, makes it most needful to supply your mission station with a Chinese pastor.
>
> The desire for Bible instruction among some of the Chinese enquirers is so great that Mrs [Hilda O.] Lund, shortly after her recovery from illness, took a journey of twelve miles into the country in order to help some of them. On arriving there she found that almost double the number she had expected were eager to be taught. It is hoped that nine or ten Chinese from this place alone will be baptized shortly. These with the other Chinese Christians, if given a Chinese pastor, would, after a few years at most, support their own pastor and work, as

551. Sitoy, Several Springs 1: 326.
552. Atlas Showing Mission Fields of the Christian and Missionary Alliance issued by The Foreign Department (NY: Christian and Missionary Alliance, 1922), 34.
553. Ekvall et al, *After Fifty Years*, 232.
554. Bessie White, "God's Providences in the Entering of the Philippines," 119.
555. Ibid.

well as probably assist in some measure in the missionary work among the Filipinos and Moros of the island. The persecution borne by the Chinese converts in and around Zamboanga has shown the sincere faith in their new-found Saviour.[556]

In subsequent years, specifically 1910 to 1921, I found less and less mention of the Chinese work in the annual reports. However, there is a late record where this information was given: "In Zamboanga, Jolo and other places, a Chinese evangelist who has attended the Wuchow Bible School [Wuchow Alliance Bible Seminary] is laboring among his own people, depending wholly upon the Lord for his support. Four Chinese converts have been baptized in Zamboanga during the year and there have been several definite conversions in Jolo as a result of his labors."[557] There is no specific year mentioned, but I surmise that it is not later than the year of publication – 1936. It is beyond the scope of this book to investigate the history of the Chinese church in Zamboanga, but it seems as if this work did not give rise to a formally established indigenous church during the pre-war years.

c) CMA in Davao

(1) Work among the Filipinos

The Davao Gulf region had largely been a contested area among the various tribes, and between the tribes and the Spaniards. The Spaniards had been in the region for about fifty years following the conquest of Davao by Jose Oyanguren in 1847, but their control remained unstable.[558] During this period, Davao was one of six districts in Mindanao which included Zamboanga, North Mindanao, East Mindanao, Central Mindanao and Basilan. When American occupation troops took Davao from the

---

556. "Crowned Year" 1908–1909. *The Twelfth Annual Report of the Christian and Missionary Alliance (Reorganized) Adopted at the Annual Meeting of the Society, May 25, 1909* (Nyack, NY: Christian and Missionary Alliance, 1910), 28, accessed 24 Aug 2005, http://www.cmalliance.org/whoweare/archives/pdfs/annual_reports/1908–1909.

557. "Golden Anniversary, The Christian and Missionary Alliance 1887–1937." *Fiftieth Year Annual Report to the General Council at Nyack, New York, May 19–24, 1937 for the year ended December Thirty-First, 1936* (New York: Headquarters, 1937), 111.

558. Macario D. Tiu, *Davao 1898–1910: Conquest and Resistance in the Garden of the Gods* (Quezon City: Center for Integrative and Development Studies, University of the Philippines, 2003), 1.

Spaniards in December 1899, they did in just about a decade what the Spaniards failed to do in fifty years. As the Americans consolidated their rule, they transformed the region into huge plantations. An effective colonial administrative machinery was set up, followed by educational and religious endeavors that completed the conquest of Davao.[559] Muslims provided the main bulk of plantation labor, followed by the importation of Japanese labor in 1903.[560]

Due to people movements developing around the 1930s among the various tribal peoples, some Alliance families moved to Davao.[561] Starting a church would not have been difficult except for the 1901 "territorial agreement," according to Ernest Frei.[562] However, the Congregationalists, who were assigned the area, were not adequately staffed. The ABCFM had appointed Rev Robert Franklin Black to the Philippines. He arrived in 1902 and settled in Davao in 1903, but progress was slow. It was only in 1908 when more missionaries arrived that the work grew. However, the growth of the congregation was retarded because of stiff Roman Catholic opposition and because Rev Black focused more on the work among the Bagobos. During the 1920s and 1930s, the church also lacked regular pastors.[563] Hence other mission groups who were not assigned the territory eventually started to establish their churches in Davao, and the CMA was no exception. I found this entry in the *Sixty-second Year Annual Report* for 1948: "A missionary couple were [*sic*] released for Davao City and have opened this needy city to full gospel preaching."[564]

Before this event took place, the CMA missionaries were interned during the war in Davao City. When they had no money for food, arrangements were made to borrow money through a local Chinese friend, according to Rambo.[565] Among the missionaries were Rev Ernest Francis

---

559. Tiu, *Davao 1898–1910*, 41.

560. Ibid., 65.

561. Rambo, "Christian and Missionary Alliance," 200.

562. Frei, *Ventures in Cooperation*, 1.

563. See Sitoy, *Several Springs* 1: 61–62, 64–65, 287–295.

564. *The Christian and Missionary Alliance Sixty-second Year Annual Report for 1948 and Minutes of the General Council at Rochester, New York, May 18–24, 1949* (New York: Christian and Missionary Alliance, 1949), 111.

565. Rambo, "Christian and Missionary Alliance," 158.

Gulbranson 嘉明遜牧師 (1900–1976) and W. G. Davis, both "newly-arrived missionaries among the Chinese."[566] This gives a hint that there was a ministry among the Chinese, but it is not clear whether they were assigned to Zamboanga, Davao or another field. After the War, Rev Gulbranson requested to be assigned to Davao. There he called back dispersed missionaries to Mindanao and filed war claims for them.[567]

(2) Work among the Chinese

There were only a few Chinese residing in Davao during the colonial era, although next to the Spaniards, they were the second earliest foreign settlers. As late as 1852, there were reportedly two Chinese inhabitants in the territory known as *Nueva Guipuzcoa*.[568] From 1893 to 1895 the Chinese population reached thirty-four; three years later it was thirty-seven. The first reports by American army commanders in Davao showed that until 1904 there were still only two Chinese residents in the Davao *poblacion* (town).[569] Ernesto Corcino has gathered data from three sources to show that the number increased from two in 1904 to 2,493 in 1935 and 3,595 in 1939. Around 1950, there were about 5,000 Chinese in Davao.[570] Compared to the Chinese, the Japanese, being involved in plantation work and other ventures, were more numerous before the war: 194 (1904), 13,064 (1935), and 17,888 (1939).[571] The American colonial government allowed more

566. Rev Shao gave Gulbranson this Chinese name. Uyboco writes the Chinese name as 伯蘭遜. Rev Ernest Francis Gulbranson was born in Worth Country, Iowa on 27 Feb 1900. He died in St. Petersburg, Florida, on 5 Jul 1976. McGarvey, Patty <archives@cmalliance.org>. Private email message to the writer, 29 Aug 2005. Rambo, "Christian and Missionary Alliance," 152. He says, however, that Davis was supported by the Presbyterians and not by the Alliance.

567. Rambo, "Christian and Missionary Alliance," 176.

568. *Nueva Guipozcoa* is the name given by the Spaniards to Davao. Patricio N. Abinales, *Making Mindanao: Cotabato and Davao in the Formation of the Philippine Nation-State* (Quezon City: Ateneo De Manila University Press, 2000), 73.

569. Corcino, *Davao History*, 129.

570. *Charles Eldred Notson, Davao City, to the Philippine Mission of the Southern Baptist Convention Chinese Chapel, Davao City, 6 Dec 1951*, 2. Christian and Missionary Alliance Archive.

571. See Corcino, *Davao History*, 131–132. See also Abinales, *Making Mindanao*, 80–86, which is a summary of the article "Davao-kuo: The Political Economy of a Japanese Settler Zone in Philippine Colonial Society," *Journal of American-East Asian Relations* 6, no. 1 (Spring 1997): 59–82; *Report of the War Department* (1904), *Provincial Governor's Report* (1935) and *Census of the Philippines* (1939), quoted in Corcino, *Davao History*, 130.

Japanese immigrants to enter the Philippines because they engaged in cultivation of extensive plantations, logging, fishing, and large-scale merchandising. Prior to their deportation at the end of World War II, they practically controlled every major phase of Davao's economic life, unlike other major cities in the Philippines where Chinese merchants were dominant. During the pre-war years, the Chinese were second only to the Japanese in dominating the commerce of Davao. Because of the Manchurian incident of 1931, Chinese stores refused to handle Japan-made products.

The story of the emergence of the DCGC is set in the backdrop of the post-war era. When the Japanese were deported at the end of the War, the Chinese became the dominant businessmen. Repatriation of the Japanese rendered Davao wide open for immigrants and squatters.[572] This migration made Davao increasingly a Roman Catholic zone, thus limiting Alliance ministry to the Manobo and Bagobo tribes.[573] Davao became a center of what Rambo calls "Cristiano" (converted Roman Catholic) influence. Its population had grown from 6,059 in 1903 to 95,546 in 1939, then to 225,712 in 1960.[574] Parallel to this increase the Chinese population in Davao surged from 19 in 1903 to 3,595 in 1939 (see App. K). Two prominent families of DCGC were part of this influx – the Uyboco clan and the family of Job Chen. The Uyboco family moved from Cebu City while Job Chen and his family moved from Zamboanga and he became an agent of the Caltex Company in Sta. Cruz, a town near Davao City.[575]

---

572. Rambo states that "between 1948 and 1960, nearly 380,000 new settlers came to Davao in voluntary migrations, principally from the over-crowded Visayan Islands." He is using as his source Frederick L. Wernstedt and Joseph E. Spencer, *The Philippine Island World* (Berkeley, CA: University of California Press, 1967), 530, quoted in Rambo, "Christian and Missionary Alliance," 202–203.

573. Rambo, "Christian and Missionary Alliance," 203.

574. Doeppers, "Ethnicity and Class," 93, table 2.3.

575. The patriarch of this clan, Elder and Mrs Eng Tiong (David) Uyboco 黃永長夫婦, his four sons and their families were former members of Cebu Gospel Church. In Notson's words, their move to Davao Evangelical Church "brought mature judgment as well as an exuberantly joyful enthusiasms [*sic*] on youth to this new venture of faith." See Charles Eldred Notson, "Mid-century Miracle," in *Davao Evangelical Church Fortieth Anniversary Special Publication (1951–1991) [Namao Jidu Jiaohui Sishi Zhounian Jinian Tekan (Yijiu Wuyinian-Yijiu Jiuyinian)]* 納卯基督教會四十週年紀念特刊〔一九五一年－一九九一年〕(Davao City: Davao Evangelical Church, [1991]). Henceforth, this source will be written as *DEC Fortieth*; Wesley Kho Shao/Shao QingZhang 邵慶彰, "Namao Jidu Jiaohui Chuqi Jianshi 納卯基督教會初期簡史 (Short history of the early

CMA missionaries Rev Ernest Francis Gulbranson and Rev Charles Eldred Notson (1908–2001), who was given the Chinese name Na CiEn mushi 納慈恩牧師, were instrumental in the formal establishment of DCGC around 1949, almost fifty years after mission work started in Mindanao.[576] What could have been the reasons for this long delay? For one, it may have been the small number of Chinese during this period. Second, the CMA work force in Mindanao had not always been sufficient. In 1928, there were only eleven missionaries and seven native workers. By 1938 there were twenty-two missionaries and one-hundred-thirteen native workers serving 2,780 church members.[577] This increase may have resulted from the 1925 survey done by Rev Robert A. Jaffray, then serving in South China. Shortly after his survey, an experienced missionary from South China was transferred to act as leader of the Philippine field.[578] Another reason for the delay may have been the absence of a strong language program for the China missionaries and new recruits from America, due to the belief that English would be used increasingly.[579]

---

period of Davao Evangelical Church)," in *Davao Evangelical Church Twentieth Anniversary Special Publication (Namao Jidu Jiaohui Ershi Zhounian Tekan)* 納卯基督教會二十週年特刊 (Davao City: Davao Evangelical Church, [1971]), 20. This source will be henceforth cited as *DEC Twentieth*. Job Chen, an elder of DCGC, was later assigned to Tungkalan. Two of his sons became pastors, one of whom was Rev Livingstone Chen/Chen YangSheng 陳仰聖. Rev Morino Lim/Lin HuaSheng 林華生牧師, interview by Jean Uayan, 4 Apr 2005, audio-taped transcript, Philippine Chinese Church Archive, Biblical Seminary of the Philippines, Valenzuela City, Philippines.

576. Chinese names for foreigners are transliterated phonetically, so the characters used may vary. Another form of his Chinese name is 駱德森 (*luo-de-sen*). Cf. Livingstone Chen/Chen YangSheng 陳仰聖, "Aijie 愛結 (Love bonds)," in *DEC Fortieth*, who used the characters 納德芩 (*na-de-qin*). Throughout this work, 納慈恩 (*na-ci-en*) has been used consistently. Rev Charles E. Notson was born in Heppner, Oregon, on 21 Mar 1908; he died at age 93 in Seattle, Washington, on 11 Mar 2001. He visited the Philippines frequently after transferring to another field and even after his retirement. He maintained very close contact with Davao Evangelical Church and was able to attend their fortieth anniversary in 1991.

577. *The Christian and Missionary Alliance Fifty-second Year Annual Report and Minutes of the General Council, May 18–23, 1939, for the year ended December 31, 1938* (New York: Christian and Missionary Alliance, 1939), 98.

578. Ekvall et al, *After Fifty Years*, 232–233.

579. Rambo, "Christian and Missionary Alliance," 188.

Around 1946, re-enforcements came, many of them from China, for during that time, it was getting difficult to work inside the troubled nation.[580] Rambo cites the *Annual Report* of 1949 and writes that "88 missionaries representing nearly fifteen percent of its total missionary force" had to leave China." Sixteen applied to go to the Philippines, to be added to the group of twenty-five who were already serving there. It was recorded that one of these, Ms Annetta Holsted, "on a stopover trip, went to try some Mandarin speech with the ubiquitous Chinese merchants."[581] Three of the new arrivals worked among the Chinese. However, although these missionaries had learned Mandarin while serving in China, they could not speak the *Hokkien* dialect. This was another disadvantage. Rambo also states, "the Foreign Department [of the CMA] did not view this ministry as a high-priority item."[582] In the 1948 official record this statement appears: "We regret there are no funds available for the support of Chinese work in the Philippine Islands . . ."[583] Despite this fact, however, two years later the Notsons were assigned to Davao City and given "supervision of all Chinese work of the Mission."[584]

Charles Notson himself provided two other reasons. He attributed the neglect of Alliance ministry among the Chinese to the preoccupation of the CMA missionaries with the Filipinos and the business abstraction of the Chinese. He stated: "They felt they had to make a choice and considered it best to deploy their limited resources among a people eager to hear the gospel of salvation. Because the Chinese were intent upon the development

580. See Rambo, "Christian and Missionary Alliance," 184–186. However, upon checking this source, I found that Rambo's computation is not accurate. I counted only 80 who either went to other places or returned to the United States. See *The Christian and Missionary Alliance Sixty-third Year Annual Report for 1949 and Minutes of the General Council held at Toronto, Canada May 4–9, 1950* (New York: Christian and Missionary Alliance, 1950), 50–51, 131.

581. Rambo, "Christian and Missionary Alliance," 103.

582. Ibid., 188, 229.

583. Foreign Department Minutes (New York: Christian and Missionary Alliance, 25–27 Feb 1948), quoted in Rambo, "Christian and Missionary Alliance," 229.

584. Mission Conference Minutes. Zamboanga City, Philippines (Mar 1950), quoted in Rambo, "Christian and Missionary Alliance," 229. "All" refers to the work in Zamboanga, Cotabato, Jolo, Dadiangas and Davao City, where the Chinese joined worship services with the Filipinos.

of profitable business enterprises they appeared to have no time for or interest in the gospel."[585]

However, the war made the Chinese more aware of their spiritual needs, and with the influx of CMA missionaries assigned to Chinese ministry, the stage was set for the birth of DCGC. The history of this church will be constructed mainly from the oral reports of Bona Lim/Lin LianZhu 林蓮珠傳道 (1916–2004, App. HH, Fig. 2), one of the founders and lifelong full-time worker of DCGC/DEC, and the articles of Rev Wesley Kho Shao (the first Chinese pastor of DCGC, albeit he is of Reformed persuasion), in addition to the written records found in their twentieth, fortieth and fiftieth anniversary publications.

d) Emergence of DCGC

(1) Pioneers

All the writings found in the three anniversary publications along with oral testimonies point to the Lim sisters, Bona and Valeria/Lin HeBi 林河碧 (later married to Hernando Young/Yang YongNai 楊永耐) as the ones who planted the seed from which the church grew into existence. According to Elder Prudencio S. Uyboco/Huang DengShou 黃登守長老, son of Elder David Uyboco/Huang YongChang 黃永長長老, who was among the earliest members:

> God started to prepare the ground by calling out a couple of chosen ones to fulfill His plan. Bona and Valeria Lim, two sisters who studied in a Christian girls' school in Kulangsu [Gulangyu], Amoy [Xiamen], China in the late 1930s were converted to Christianity. They returned after graduation to share their faith. As there was at that time no organized Chinese church in Davao City, they started to engage in children's work of evangelism by conducting Sunday School.[586]

Bona's own testimony confirms that their father had sent them to study at the Iok Tek All Girls' Mission School/Yude Nüzi Xuexiao 毓德女子學

---

585. Notson, "Mid-century Miracle."
586. Prudencio S. Uyboco, "The Only Foundation," in *DEC Fortieth*. This article is written in Chinese and in English but the writer is no longer living.

校 in Gulangyu, Xiamen 廈門鼓浪嶼.[587] There she was converted during a revival meeting of John Sung around 1934/1935.[588] Coming back to the Philippines in the early part of 1936, she started gathering children, around one hundred, and taught Sunday School with the help of Alliance Church member Edith Dangila.[589] Some of the early students were Tan Cheng Hi/Chen QingXi 陳清禧 (Robert Tan), Lim Siu Chin/ Lin XiuZhen 林秀真, Lim Bun Beng/Lin WenMing 林文明, Lim Hua Seng/Lin HuaSheng 林華生 (Morino Lim), Lim Kang Sui/Lin JiangShui 林江水 (Dr Antonio Lim). Bona writes that the children's ministry began as early as 1936–1940.[590] The venue was the first floor of a house where her brother lived.[591] This brother was still an unbeliever, so he used to pound upon his floor because he was irritated by the noise downstairs.[592]

Bona said that when in need of Sunday School materials, she approached the UCCP missionaries for help. Around that time she was also attending services at the UCCP church,[593] and she mentioned that "half of the members were [formerly] Alliance," probably alluding to the fact that the Congregationalists were much earlier in Davao than the Alliance. When the Alliance Church was formed, many of the UCCP members rejoined

587. Bona Lim, interview by Jean Uayan, 17 Mar 2001, at their residence in Malate, Manila, Philippines, audio-taped transcript, Philippine Chinese Church Archives, Biblical Seminary of the Philippines, Valenzuela City, Philippines.

588. In her interview she says the year was 1934, but in a written testimony in the *DEC Fortieth*, she wrote 1935. John Sung was conducting his evangelistic meetings in Gulangyu and Xiamen from October to November 1934, but he again passed through Xiamen in 1935. This confirms Bona's recollection, but her conversion most likely took place in 1934, for the meetings at Gulangyu were held on the grounds of the Anglo-Chinese School/Yinghua Shuyuan 英華書院 and she was studying at Iok Tek. See Levi Song, ed. *Diary of His Spiritual Life*, 172–182.

589. Shao, "Short History."

590. Bona Lim/Lin LianZhu 林蓮珠, "Ershi Nianlai Zhurixue Shigong De Fazhan 二十年來主日學事工的進展 (The progress of Sunday School ministry these past twenty years)," in *DEC Twentieth*, 65.

591. Bona explained that they lived in another house beside this one. These houses were near a school, which probably explains how they were able to invite many children to attend Sunday School. Bona Lim, interview.

592. Wesley K. Shao/Shao QingZhang 邵慶彰, "The Fifty Years of Davao Evangelical Church," in *Davao Evangelical Church Fifty Years 1951–2001 (Namao Jidu Jiaohui)* 納卯基督教會 (Davao City: Davao Evangelical Church, 2001), 9. This article is written in Chinese as well as in English. The publication is henceforth cited as *DEC Fifty.*

593. See Sitoy, *Several Springs* 2: 608. Although UCCP was formed in 1948, this was the term Bona used during the interview.

the Alliance Church, which in other sources is identified as the Davao Gospel Church.[594] The American Board established the Davao Evangelical Church in 1909. This name was retained until the formation of the UCCP in 1948, after which all except two churches in Mindanao retained the "Evangelical Church" appendage. Significantly, whether knowing of this church or not, DCGC changed its name to Davao Evangelical Church in 1958 (see pp. 227–228).

(2) Early Protestants and Gulbranson

This pioneer work was disrupted but not stopped when the Lim residence was burned down during WWII. According to Prudencio Uyboco, around this time, Job Chen 陳約伯 and his family came to Davao City, and he assisted in the Sunday School ministry as well as translated for guest speakers.[595] The children were gathered and meetings were held in different homes of the believers.

The second phase of the children's work started after the war, in 1947, when Bona accepted a teaching position in Davao. Together with Tan Lo Tek/Chen LuDe 陳路得 (Ruth Chen), a Christian worker from the Christian Gospel Center (Manila), Bona did personal evangelism among the children she gathered for Sunday School.[596] During these pioneer days, the Christian Gospel Center offered much help by way of sending Tan Lo Tek, Tan Bi Seh/Chen MeiXi 陳美西, Ng Zhu Ai/Huang CiAi 黃慈愛, and others. One of their key leaders, Simon Meek, often held evangelistic meetings in Davao. The following year, the believers constructed a small chapel, which facilitated the work quite well. There were two other teachers aside from Bona and Lo Tek – Ang Siu Hua/Hong XiuHua 洪秀華 and Lim Bun Beng – and the children numbered around sixty.[597] In May of 1948, Bona went to study at the Ebenezer Bible School.[598] She had wanted

---

594. Erlinda Duy Pan/Pan Rui XiuZhu 潘雷秀祝, audio-taped interview by Jean Uayan, 16 Aug 2005, Valenzuela City, audio-taped transcript, Philippine Chinese Church Archive, Biblical Seminary of the Philippines, Valenzuela City, Philippines.

595. Notson, "Mid-century Miracle."

596. A brief sketch of this group who followed Watchman Nee has been included in the history of SSCM and CUEC, see 128–129, 192–193.

597. Shao, "Short History."

598. Ibid., and Bona Lim, interview.

to study in a well-known seminary in China and was also considering the Febias Bible Institute, waiting for it to open. But she testified that the Lord himself brought her to the conviction that her roots were from Mindanao, hence, she should be trained in Ebenezer Bible School which was located in Zamboanga City. During her absence, her sister Valeria continued the children's ministry.

Right after the War, Gulbranson chose to return to Mindanao,[599] and, although the official stand was that the CMA was unable to work among the Chinese, Gulbranson was "assigned to offer part-time help and he assumed the responsibility of filling the pulpit preaching ministry with the aid of translation," according to Prudencio Uyboco.[600] Bona provides more information: When Rev and Mrs Ernest Gulbranson undertook the CMA ministry among Filipinos in Davao City, they were allowed to use the small chapel (that the Chinese believers had built) for their services. According to Bona, this was the time when Filipinos and Chinese worshiped together. The following year, the CMA bought a lot, and Filipino and Chinese Christians contributed toward the construction of the new church building, which was named Davao Gospel Church.[601] On 24 April 1949, Gulbranson baptized Ang Siu Hua, Yu Eng Nay (Valeria Lim's husband), Ng Teng Tian/Huang DengDian 黃登典 [Rolando Uyboco], Lim Bun Beng, Tan Cheng Hi, Te Pek Dian/Dai BiLian 戴碧蓮, and Kang Chui Sian/Jiang ShuiXian 江水仙.[602] Ruth Gulbranson, on the other hand, set up Sunday School teachers' training.[603] However, they left for the States, presumably around 1948/49, and when they returned in 1953, they were assigned to Manila.[604]

---

599. Patty McGarvey confirms that Gulbranson returned to the Philippines on 11 Jul 1947. McGarvey, Patty <archives@cmalliance.org>. Private email message to the writer, 29 Aug 2005.

600. Uyboco, "Only Foundation."

601. Bona Lim, "The Progress of Sunday School." Other sources give the name Davao Gospel Center. Cf. Lim Duy Un Hong/Lin Rui YunFang 林雷韻芳, "Huiyi Zhongchuqi De Namao Jidu Jiaohui 回憶中初期的納卯基督教會 (Recalling Davao Evangelical Church during the early and middle periods)," in *DEC Twentieth*, 66.

602. "Benhui Huiyou Shouxi Guizhu Nianbiao 本會會友受洗歸主年表 (List of baptized members)," in *DEC Twentieth*, 8.

603. Shao, "Short History."

604. Rambo, "Christian and Missionary Alliance," 176, 226.

The Uyboco family moved to Davao in 1948. Prudencio testifies that their family was disappointed in not finding any Chinese church, for they had been active members of Cebu Gospel Church and were longing for Christian fellowship. Although they worshiped for a while in Filipino churches, David Uyboco was delighted to make the acquaintance of the Lim sisters and some other Chinese believers. They "agreed to meet for Sunday afternoon service[s] at the ground floor of the Lim's home. Over a period, a number of evangelists and ministers from outside of Davao City were invited to come for special evangelistic meetings."[605] These meetings were held at a location opposite the public mental hospital, according to Bona Lim. Wesley Shao mentions that one of the speakers was Philip Watts; another missionary who helped was Ms Gladys Mackenzie, whom Notson identified as a nurse. This nurse was instrumental in bringing Antonio and Paz Lim to the Lord. During their illness the household was in chaos, the maids not knowing what to do. Mackenzie took charge and nursed the couple to health. This resulted in a lifelong friendship and their conversion. Thus, one by one, the Lord added to the number of the saved.[606] Bona does not mention that services were held in their home around this time, maybe because she was away at Ebenezer studying for the ministry. Another addition to the group was the family of Consul Mih Sek Long 宓錫寵領事 and his wife.[607] According to Mrs Ang Go Sun Lu/Hong Wu ChunYu 洪吳純瑜師母, the Consul was very fervent in serving the Lord.[608] He contributed much to the development of the Chinese community in Davao.[609] Wesley Shao remembers him as "the first person who suggested

---

605. See Notson, "Mid-century Miracle."

606. Uyboco, "Only Foundation."

607. The title "consul" is used to refer to diplomats sent by the government of China. In July 1898 Spain conceded the establishment of a temporary Chinese consulate. When the United States assumed control over the Islands, the consulate was confirmed as a permanent one with the first consul, Chen Gang/Tan Kong 陳綱 (a.k.a. Engracio Palanca), from China arriving in January 1899. Since that time it was an established practice to have consuls not only in Manila but also in key cities like Cebu and Davao. See Wong Kwok-chu, *Chinese in the Philippine Economy*, 233.

608. Ang Go Sun Lu/Hong Wu ChunYu 洪吳純瑜師母, also known as Rosie Go, is the wife of Rev Henry Ang/Hong KangRi 洪康日牧師, another Davaoeño interview by Jean Uayan, 18 Aug 2005, Valenzuela City, audio-taped transcript, Philippine Chinese Church Archive, Biblical Seminary of the Philippines, Valenzuela City, Philippines.

609. Bona Lim, interview.

the need for a worship service in Chinese."[610] Shao further records that during the first Chinese service, Consul Mih gave the message and his secretary translated it into the *Hokkien* dialect.[611]

(3) Formation and Organization

Aside from these key Chinese leaders, Charles and Ruth Notson, Rev and Mrs Frederick Eugene Ruhl/Lü XinMin 呂新民牧師師母,[612] and Agnes Catlin Birrel 白宣恩姑娘 (1901–1972) assisted the ministry full time during Bona's absence.[613] Ruhl and Birrel had served in China in Guizhou 桂州 and Sichuan 四川. Ruhl served in the Philippines from 1949–1964. Agnes Birrel was the daughter of veteran missionary to China, Rev and Mrs Matthew Birrel. She served in the Philippines from 1947 to 1967. The Notsons were CMA missionaries in Gansu 甘肅, China before they arrived in August 1949. Their character and performance in ministry were glowingly praised by Prudencio, who declared, "Because of their devotion to the Lord and great love for the Chinese people, they labored faithfully, untiringly and sacrificially by means of visitations, prayer meeting, Sunday School and preaching to nurture the Christian, building them up in the faith and also at winning new converts to Christ."[614] Notson became the first resident pastor of the Davao Chinese Gospel Church (DCGC) when it was formally established in June 1951.[615] This was the official name of the Chinese congregation before it was renamed Davao Evangelical Church on 28 September 1958. The reason, according to Wesley Shao, was the

---

610. Shao, "Fifty Years," 11.

611. Wesley K. Shao/Shao QingZhang 邵慶彰, *Jitanshang De Xinsheng* 祭壇上的心聲 (Witness from the Altar), Testimony and Biography Series (Hong Kong Tien Dao, 1981), 10.

612. This is the official name given in *DEC Twentieth*, 25.

613. The departure of these missionaries from China was reportedly temporary, as recorded in a news item found in *The Alliance Weekly* Vol. 84, no. 49 (3 Dec 1949): 779, accessed 31 Aug 2005, http://apps.cmalliance.org/archives/alifepdf/AW–1949–12–03.pdf. But as history later shows, they were never able to return to China.

614. Uyboco, "Only Foundation."

615. Ibid., and "Chuen Shu Bu Jin – Benhui Ershi Nianlai Dashiji 主恩數不盡 – 本會二十年來大事記 (God's infinite grace – major events for the past twenty years)," in *DEC Twentieth*, 5.

increasingly Chinese Filipino (Chinese with Filipino citizenship) composition of the church.[616]

Ruth Notson took charge of training around eight or nine Sunday School teachers, supervising a work that ministered to around ninety children, and reaching out to neighborhood children in three areas, thereby planting the seed that grew into the youth ministry. Other ministries initiated by the Notsons included the Sisters' Prayer Meeting on Tuesdays and the weekly Women's Fellowship (established in September 1950), and the Young People's Society.[617]

The Notsons nurtured the spirit of self-rule, self-support, and self-propagation. Most of the missionaries in their time felt that the Chinese were a minority group and should belong to the Filipino churches, but Notson propounded the concept that the Chinese should retain their own distinctive culture and should build up their own churches, although close relationship with the Filipino Christians should also be maintained. They recognized that the purpose of the Western missionaries in setting up churches was not to bring them under the control of the missions. When DCGC emerged, the CMA sent missionaries to assist the church, but they quickly allowed the church to manage on their own. In the beginning members of DCGC worshiped at the Filipino CMA church, but they were later able to purchase land and build their work in neighboring localities, led by the elders and deacons and involving the church members. Members were thus encouraged to give toward mission projects. They were also exhorted to build their own sanctuary. In order to do this, the Notsons taught them how to practice tithing by devising a system of using individual envelopes for the offertory.[618] From the start the Church, inspired by Notson, emphasized doing mission themselves for the ministry. With regard to church

616. "Highlights Through the Years," in *DEC Fifty*, 48–49; Shao, "Short History," 21.

617. See Bona Lim, interview; "Highlights," 49; "Jiemei Tuanqi Jianjie 姐妹團契間介 (Short introduction of the Sisters' Fellowship)," in *DEC Twentieth*, 43; and Charles Eldred Notson, *Report of the Work Among the Chinese As Given from the Viewpoint of Mr. and Mrs. C. E. Notson, December 1, 1952*, 1, from Personnel Files of Deceased Missionaries, the USA Christian and Missionary Alliance National Archives.

618. Bona Lim testifies that ever since her conversion in Xiamen until her days of worshiping with the Christian Gospel Center group, she had never heard about tithing. Bona Lim, interview; Uyboco, "Only Foundation."

administration, the Notsons clearly stipulated membership requirements and implemented careful election of church leaders.[619]

e) DCGC and CMA

Rev Wesley Shao further credits the Notsons for implementing the three-self policy that led to the quick devolution of DCGC, at the cost of their own personal disadvantage. According to Shao, Notson set down the policy of self-rule, self-support, and self-propagation as a foundation from the beginning of its existence. With regard to self-rule, the church was not under any denomination or under the Christian and Missionary Alliance Churches of the Philippines [CAMACOP]. Aside from Elder David Uyboco, the church members elected Job Chen and Antonio Lim as elders and Go He, Prudencio Uyboco, Bona Lim as deacons and deaconess. The Church was registered with the government as a local church. With regard to self-support, church members were encouraged to tithe, not to rely upon foreign sources for support, and to take care of their own needs. As to self-propagation, on the one hand the young people were encouraged to enter the seminary, while at the same time, Chinese pastors were invited to minister in the Church so that there need not be long-term reliance on the missionaries. With regard to doctrine, Notson's view that Christ is the Savior, Sanctifier, Healer, and Coming King, that inwardly, the Christian should focus on the believer's inner purity and spiritual life, and that outwardly, the emphasis should be on evangelism, whether within or without city limits, influenced the church. As a result, Sunday School was set up in four places in Toril and evangelistic teams visited Calinan and Digos. Notson even suggested that the church should build its own school, and initiated the process to buy land for this project. Initially, the Davao Christian Kindergarten/Namao Jidujiao Youzhiyuan 納卯基督教幼稚園 was established on the ground floor of the building of Lim Han Sui/Lin HanShui 林漢水 [Rafael Lim] on 14 January 1953 with fourteen students being taught by Bona Lim, Valeria Lim, and Tio So Lan/

619. Wesley Kho Shao/Shao QingZhang 邵慶彰, "Namao Jidu Jiaohui Zhi Huigu 納卯基督教會之回顧 (Remembering Davao Evangelical Church)," in *DEC Fortieth*. This translation into English is by the writer. By 2007, DEC has the distinct honor of nurturing more than 50 full-time ministers (including second-generation pastors) who are now serving all over and beyond the Philippines.

Zhao SuLan 趙素蘭. Within two years, with the sum of 30,000 pesos, a lot measuring 7,700 square meters was purchased. During the summer of 1953, the Notsons had to go on furlough. There was a faction within the Filipino CMA church that was not in agreement with Notson's view that the Chinese church should be allowed independence, hence the Notsons were reassigned to Taiwan by the Mission Board. Notson himself said, "We did not expect that our ministry in the Philippines would be terminated when we left for furlough the spring of 1953."[620]

From another angle, Notson's policy with regard to the governance of the Chinese church has been acclaimed not only by Wesley Shao but by Prudencio Uyboco as well. The church had been influenced by mainly three denominational groups – Presbyterian, CMA and Christian Gospel Center. There was bound to be some tension with regard to church polity and certain issues, such as the mode of baptism, the form of church organization, and the use of ordained clergy. From Uyboco's perspective, the following tension developed:

> For as long as the group did not favor any particular denomination, the brethren were willing to assemble and worship together, since there was no other Chinese church in the City. However, when denominational lines were drawn, the risk of a split into different factions became a strong possibility. This would mean a break-up that could be detrimental to all previous efforts to encourage cohesiveness and promote unity, not to mention a serious setback to church growth.
>
> With keen insight to the danger of disintegration, and with great spiritual vision and foresight, Rev Notson, despite his being a missionary of the Christian and Missionary Alliance, decided to obey the Lord's leading by uplifting Christ instead of emphasizing denominational tie. He, therefore, took the courageous stand of organizing an independent, local church not affiliated with any denominational [sic] not even that of his own! For this step of not integration [sic] the Chinese

---

620. Wesley Kho Shao/Shao QingZhang 邵慶彰, "Namao Jidujiao Xiaoxue Jianli Jianshi 納卯基督教小學建立簡史 (A brief history of the establishment of Davao Christian Elementary School)," in *DEC Twentieth*, 22–23; Notson, "Mid-century Miracle."

brethren into the organization [*sic*] setup of the Christian and Missionary Alliance, he was to court the criticism and misunderstanding of some members of his own Mission Board and some of his fellow missionaries. They were of the opinion the Rev Notson was being disloyal to his own organization. Later on, however, Rev Notson was able to convince his critics of the soundness and wisdom of his decision, especially by looking at it from a Scriptural standpoint and from a long-term perspective. So he fully vindicated himself of the initial misconception.[621]

It is unfortunate that a faction of the CAMACOP[622] had this negative view toward the devolution of the Chinese church when in fact, as early as 1927 the three-self policy of John Nevius (1829–1893) had already been adopted, though not immediately implemented, by the CMA.[623] Rambo points out that "the principal issue in Chinese ministry was whether to pursue a policy of integration or organizational separation."[624] This issue created a spirit of disunity among CMA missionaries during the year 1951. On 8 March, Notson's letter reported the highlights of the two-week Annual Conference at Zamboanga.[625] Before a resolution could be reached, the group spent five hours and forty-five minutes debating on a policy for Chinese work! The pro-integration side, supported by the Chairman of the Philippine Mission, held to the opinion that the Chinese believers should organize under the banner of the CMA.[626] The pro-separation side "was of the persuasion that the Chinese congregation should be allowed to arrive

---

621. Uyboco, "Only Foundation."

622. Although the CAMACOP was officially organized in 1947, their history is traced back to the pioneer days of the Christian and Missionary Alliance work in the Philippines in 1902.

623. Rambo, "Christian and Missionary Alliance," 179. See also n. 431.

624. Ibid., 230.

625. Charles Eldred Notson, En Route Cotabato on Board M/V Alex, to A. C. Snead, New York, 8 Mar 1951. From Personnel Files of Deceased Missionaries, the USA Christian and Missionary Alliance National Archives.

626. The most extreme view was expressed by this missionary's statement: "If these people are not willing to organize as an Alliance Church, let them go!" Charles Eldred Notson, Davao City, to A. C. Snead, New York, 12 Jun 1951, 2. From Personnel Files of Deceased Missionaries, the USA Christian and Missionary Alliance National Archives.

at the decision themselves."[627] Notson himself confirmed the urgency and severity of this contention in his correspondence with Dr A. C. Snead, CMA Foreign Secretary, from March to December of 1951.

Both sides had their reasons and strongly pursued their respective stands. As gleaned from the letters, the rationale of the pro-integration group included: (1) In view of what the missionaries had done, the Chinese should do so out of gratitude.[628] (2) Apparently, there was a view that if ethnic congregations were allowed, this would go against St. Paul's admonition that in Christ there is neither Jew nor Gentile (Col 3:11).[629] (3) Missionaries must insist on the Chinese congregation becoming an Alliance church in order to show loyalty to the Mission.[630]

The Conference of 1951 recommended that "the Chinese Congregations in Davao, Cotabato, and Zamboanga Cities be encouraged to organize as distinct Church bodies, and establish an affiliation with each other with a view to combined effort in reaching other places where there is not a Gospel witness especially for Chinese."[631] After voting, there were twenty-one in favor, none against, and five abstentions.[632]

The arguments given by the pro-separation side were: (1) The CMA would lose the favor of the Chinese by at least 90 percent if the attempt were made to integrate them. (2) Real CMA churches are born of a vision and not manipulated into being; they should be free to act as the Lord leads them. (3) There is a fear in the Philippine CMA church of losing the generous financial backing of some members of the Chinese congregation. Although possible, this may not necessarily happen. (4) If the Chinese Christians were divided because of this issue, they would be "torn to shreds by other groups" (most likely thinking that they would scatter and join other groups belonging to the Presbyterians, Southern Baptists, and the

---

627. Notson to Snead, 8 Mar 1951, 3.

628. Ibid.

629. Rambo, "Christian and Missionary Alliance," 230.

630. Notson to Snead, 8 Mar 1951, 3.

631. Charles Eldred Notson, Davao City, to D. I. Jeffrey, New York, 30 July 1952, 5. From Personnel Files of Deceased Missionaries, the USA Christian and Missionary Alliance National Archives.

632. Notson to Snead, 8 Mar 1951, 2.

Manila-based Christian Gospel Center).[633] (5) To top it all, Notson appealed to the words of Albert Benjamin Simpson: "Leave each Church established on the foreign field free to organize and administer its affairs as it may choose, provided that such method be scriptural in its features," and, "let us never forget the special calling of our CMA work. It is not to form a new religious denomination."[634] Interestingly, when Gulbranson and Notson were discussing this issue, they took different views. Gulbranson's opinion was "it would be better to have a handful of people left who would be loyal to the Alliance, than to hold the whole group together in an interdenominational fellowship that was not under the direct control of our Mission."[635]

This issue was finally resolved when Dr Snead delineated a policy in June 1951 that "there are satisfactory reasons from the human standpoint, for considering it proper that the Filipinos should organize their own church, and the Chinese be permitted to organize their separate church with the earnest prayer that between the two groups there will be close fellowship in Christ and true cooperation through the Spirit."[636] However, Snead did not agree that if the Chinese Christians would not completely come under CMA control, they should let go of them. Rather, they should continue to show love and fellowship in doing ministry and laboring for Christ in their midst.[637] There were some who resisted this policy, but Rambo admits that, in the end, "the allowance for separate Chinese churches certainly has contributed to the numerical growth of the Church."[638] Furthermore, he notes that when the Chinese left the CMA congregation in Davao City they were able to readily surpass them in numbers and to construct a "lovely,

---

633. Notson to Snead, 12 Jun 1951, 1–3.

634. Thompson, *A. B. Simpson*, 131; in Notson to Snead, 12 Jun 1951, 2.

635. Notson to Snead, 12 Jun 1951, 2.

636. A. C. Snead, New York to Charles Notson, Davao City, Jun 22, 1951, 1. From Personnel Files of Deceased Missionaries, the USA Christian and Missionary Alliance National Archives.

637. Snead to Notson, 22 Jun 1951, 2.

638. Rambo, "Christian and Missionary Alliance," 231.

large" church in 1956, a building that was larger than that of the Filipino congregation.[639]

It is important to note that while this issue was transpiring in 1951, RCA missionary Tena Holkeboer and three Chinese women from Manila visited Davao City, looking for a place to put missionaries who could not go back to China.[640] Encouraged by the warm response of the Chinese, she was all set, in Notson's words, to "ignore" the CMA work and take the preliminary steps toward organizing the Davao Chinese congregation as a church of the Reformed mission. Charles Notson was in Zamboanga at the time, but Ruth Notson strongly advised Holkeboer not to take such steps. She was persuaded and this incident ended only with the formation of an alumni fellowship with her former students at Iok Tek All Girls' Mission School.[641] Rev Baker James Cauthen of the Southern Baptist Convention also visited Davao City. Unlike the Reformed mission, however, a missionary couple – Rev and Mrs John Jackson – was sent to establish the Davao Chinese Baptist Church in July 1951. Notson wrote to the Philippine Mission of the Southern Baptist Convention that same year, requesting them to reconsider. Their entry into Davao presented a situation "inimical to the development of the new Church" and was putting the CMA in a dilemma, "either to surrender the field or continue to maintain its missionaries in Davao."[642]

639. The lot cost ₱ 20,000 and was about 7,500 square meters. Charles Eldred Notson, *Report of the Work among the Chinese as Given from the Viewpoint of Mr. and Mrs. C. E. Notson, December 1, 1952*, 1. From Personnel Files of Deceased Missionaries, the USA Christian and Missionary Alliance National Archives; R. M. Landis, "Philippine Islands," *The Christian and Missionary Alliance Annual Report for 1956 and Minutes of the General Council held at Charlotte, North Carolina May 15–21, 1957* (New York: Christian and Missionary Alliance, 1956), 116. See also, Rambo, "Christian and Missionary Alliance," 231.

640. Holkeboer was formerly acting principal of the Iok Tek All Girls' Mission School in Gulangyu, China; she later became a teacher and administrator at Hope Christian High School. See "Yi Ai Ren Jian 遺愛人間 (Bequeathing Love Among Men)," in *Yude Muxiao Baizhounian Jiniankan* 毓德母校百週年紀念刊 (*Commemorative publication of the centennial anniversary of alma mater Iok Tek*) (Manila: Lüfei Yude Xiaoyouhui 旅菲毓德校友會 [Philippine Iok Tek Alumni Association], [1970]), 17.

641. Notson to Snead, 22 Jun 1951, 1.

642. Charles Eldred Notson, Davao City, to The Philippine Mission of the Southern Baptist Convention Chinese Chapel, Davao City, December 6, 1951, 1–3. From Personnel Files of Deceased Missionaries, the USA Christian and Missionary Alliance National Archives.

Another group that gave Notson cause to worry was the Christian Gospel Center. On the positive side, he commented that some of the Davao Protestants were quite attached to this group because they had clearer spiritual teaching than they had previously heard and a number were saved as a result.[643] On the other hand, they were anti-denominational and the people "smelled sectarianism" (because of their seclusive tendency) in their group. Thus, in the first quarter of 1951, the CMA told their "friends in the north" (the Manila-based Christian Gospel Center) that they had the situation well in hand, and if they wished to do labor in Davao, they should consult with the CMA out of Christian courtesy. They wanted co-ordination and mutual benefits between the two groups. As a result, and at the insistence of her co-laborers in Manila, Ruth Chen returned after a few months to Manila. Notson praised her as "cooperative and helpful."[644]

Clearly then, in the short span of time when the Notsons ministered in Davao, there was tension not only within the CMA group but with other missions and Christian groups as well. Even though the Notsons were not able to return and continue their fruitful ministry, the Ruhls and Agnes Birrel continued to help the new church. Ruhl was musically gifted, hence he served as choir conductor as well as led the youth fellowship.[645]

f) The First Chinese Pastor

Before the Notsons left, they made one other lasting contribution, and that was to recommend and invite Rev Wesley Shao to be the full-time pastor. Shao had just graduated from Western Theological Seminary in Holland, Michigan in 1952, and was then on an evangelistic tour as the translator of Rev Walter De Velder and other Reformed evangelists.[646] In February 1953 they visited Davao City, where Rev De Velder had been scheduled to give the message. However, he asked Wesley Shao to speak in his place, so Shao spoke for four evenings instead of two. The following day he was informed

---

643. Notson to Snead, 12 Jun 1951, 2.

644. Charles Eldred Notson, *Report on Work Among the Chinese by Mr. and Mrs. Charles E. Notson to the Annual Conference in Zamboanga February 1951*, 1. From Personnel Files of Deceased Missionaries, the USA Christian and Missionary Alliance National Archives.

645. Ang Go Sun Lu, interview and Erlinda Duy Pan, interview.

646. Shao, *Witness*, 3. This is the autobiography of Rev Wesley Shao and gives rich details of his whole ministry experience in DCGC/DEC.

that the church board, in a meeting called by Notson, had agreed to invite him to be their pastor. After much prayer together with his wife, they accepted the invitation. They arrived on 13 June 1953 to take the helm of leadership, his service lasting until 1963/64. Shao accepted the invitation of CUEC to be their pastor, but he requested to leave on 15 November 1963 rather than on 1 July. The whole family moved to Manila in 1964, and during this year, Shao continued to go to Davao to preach occasionally, thus explaining the use of these two years as the end of his tenure.[647] From that moment on, the DCGC has consistently been a fully independent, mission-minded, healthy and growing church.

Their mission concern was not limited to local boundaries. During the 1960s, they supported Rev Augusto Chao/Zhao ShiChang 趙士昌 of Hong Kong to go to Canada to propagate the gospel among Chinese immigrants. He planted the first CMA Chinese church in North America, and this resulted in more than seventy-five CMA Chinese churches being planted all over Canada.[648] What the Notsons believed and openly advocated, at the inception of the church, was truly visionary and precedent-setting. He wrote in 1952: "A strong friendly sister Church among the Chinese, which is completely autonomous, can be a greater blessing to the Philippine Church than for it to have a few Chinese as members, or than having a Chinese congregation which is subservient to the Philippine Church."[649]

Furthermore, what Elizabeth Jansen envisioned in 1908 when she said that the "Chinese Christians, if given a Chinese pastor, would, after a few years at most, support their own pastor and work, as well as probably assist in some measure in the missionary work among the Filipinos and Moros of the island" has indeed become a reality.[650] Succeeding pastors include Rev Robin Chua/Cai ZhongYi 蔡中宜牧師 (1964–1978), Rev Sun Teck Guan/Sun DeYuan 孫德源牧師 (1973–1984), Rev Florentino Lim/ Lin JuQiang 林聚強牧師 (1984–1995), and Rev Lin Lin Chueh/Que

---

647. Shao, *Witness*, 74–75.

648. Uyboco, "Only Foundation," and Augusto Chao, "Cong Namao dao Diji 從納卯到地極 (From Davao to the Ends of the Earth)," in *DEC Fifty*, 39.

649. Charles Eldred Notson, *Report of the Work Among the Chinese As Given from the Viewpoint of Mr. and Mrs. C. E. Notson, December 1, 1952*, 2. From Personnel Files of Deceased Missionaries, the USA Christian and Missionary Alliance National Archives.

650. "Crowned Year," 29.

RenNeng 關仁能牧師 (1994–present). Noteworthy is the fact that all of these pastors served for ten years or more without leaving any leadership vacuum throughout the fifty-six-year history of the church. These pastors have also been active in getting the church involved in mission work, supporting countless Filipino pastors and missionaries throughout the years. This truly unique feature of DCGC testifies to the solid foundation set down by such founding leaders as Bona Lim, Valeria Lim Young, Job Chen and David Uyboco and the missionaries of the CMA, specifically the Rev and Mrs Charles Eldred Notson.[651]

7. Dagupan Chinese Baptist Church

The Southern Baptist Convention (SBC) had the opportunity to enter the Philippines and join the Presbyterians in doing mission work as early as 1898, but it did not do so until the 1950s. Rather, it was the Northern Baptists, under the American Baptist Missionary Union (ABMU), who were invited to a conference held on 13 July 1898, by the Executive Council of the Presbyterian Church in the United States of America.[652] The Southern Baptists were more concerned with doing mission in the Caribbean (Cuba and Puerto Rico) at that time and declined to attend the event. However, SBC missionaries were already deeply involved in doing mission in China for over sixty years before this event took place.

The SBC was organized in 1845 for the purpose of conducting mission work and benevolent enterprises in the United States and in other countries. Previously, Southern and Northern Baptists had cooperated in such enterprises under the Triennial Convention. The General Missionary Convention of the Baptist Denomination in the United States of America for Foreign Missions, also known as the Triennial Convention, was organized in 1814. The American Baptist Home Mission Society (ABHMS), founded in 1832, started foreign mission work in China in 1836.[653] This

---

651. Charles Notson died soon after sending his greetings on 27 Jan 2001 to Davao Evangelical Church on the occasion of its fiftieth anniversary. According to Bona Lim, Ruth Notson had died two or three years before him.

652. Brown, *New Era*, 176. Brown himself was the one who wrote and sent the circular letter to these mission boards.

653. *Encyclopedia of Religion in the South*, 1997 ed., s.v. "Southern Baptist Convention," by Walter B. Shurden.

was the year that Jehu Lewis Shuck (pronounced *shook*)/Shu WeiShi 叔
未士 (1812–1863) and his first wife Henrietta Hall Shuck (1817–1844)
reached Macau. In 1842 the Shucks move to Hong Kong and together with
William Dean (1807–1895) and Issachar Jacox Roberts/Luo XiaoQuan 羅
孝全 (1802–1871) formed the Hong Kong Baptist Church.[654]

However, sectional differences, most notably attitudes toward slav-
ery, caused insurmountable barriers to this cooperative mission effort.
The Southern Baptists separated from the Triennial Convention and the
ABHMS, and the SBC formed two boards, one of which, the Foreign
Mission Board, adopted China as its first mission field.[655]

a) SBC Work in China

After the SBC was organized, it was agreed that SBC and the Triennial
Convention would leave it to missionaries to decide which Convention
they would join. The Shucks are considered as pioneer SBC missionaries since they were from Virginia and they chose to join the SBC. In
1844, Issachar Roberts, who also decided to join the SBC, began work in
Guangdong, while Shuck (by this time widowed) went to Shanghai.[656]

The Southern Baptists in China employed a variety of mission strategies. Evangelism (preaching and distribution of Christian literature) and
church development formed the hub of all their ministries. They conducted Bible conferences and instituted religious and formal education.
Religious education included Sunday School, Church Training, Woman's
Missionary Union, Brotherhood, Vacation Bible School, and theological
training. Formal education covered the elementary, middle, high school

---

654. See Jonathan Spence, *God's Chinese Son: The Taiping Heavenly Kingdom of Hong
Xiuquan* (New York: W. W. Norton, 1996); Jack Gray, *Rebellions and Revolutions: China
from the 1800s to the 1980s* (Oxford: Oxford University Press, 1990), 56; and Gail Law,
ed., *Chinese Churches Handbook* (Hong Kong: Chinese Coordination Centre of World
Evangelism (CCCOWE), 1982), 53.

655. The SBC Foreign Mission Board was located in Richmond, Virginia. For the
history of SBC see, Robert Baker, ed., *A Baptist Source Book* (Nashville, TN: Broadman,
1966) and E. C. Routh, "The Foreign Mission Board – A Historical Sketch," in *Annual
of the Southern Baptist Convention, Nineteen Hundred and Forty-Six, Eighty-Ninth Session,
One Hundred and First Year, Miami, Florida, May 15 to 19, 1946* (Nashville, TN: Executive
Committee, Southern Baptist Convention, [1946]), 226–227.

656. Winston Crawley, *Partners Across the Pacific – China and Southern Baptists: Into
the Second Century* (Nashville, TN: Broadman, 1986), 38–40.

and collegiate levels (the University of Shanghai). Publication work through the China Baptist Publication Society and Bible translation comprised their literature ministry. They were also involved in women's and youth work, benevolent ministries (emergency relief, orphanages, homes for the elderly), the leper colony and medical work.[657]

In 1917, Southern Baptist missionaries recognized the importance of building up native workers and rapidly allowing them to become partners in mission work rather than subordinates under the direction of the missionaries. This mission strategy was later implemented in the Philippines during the early 1950s. One of those who went to China on 9 January 1947 was James Winston Crawley (1920–2010)[658] (App. II, Fig. 1). This is the name recorded in the SBC Roster, but he simply uses Winston Crawley. Born in Newport, Tennessee on 2 May 1920, and educated at Baylor University (BA), Vanderbilt University (MA), and Southern Baptist Theological Seminary (ThM and ThD), Crawley has been a teacher, pastor, editor, and staff member of the Southern Baptist Foreign Mission Board (now International Mission Board) for more than thirty years. He and his wife (nee Margaret Joy Lawrence) served in the Philippines after leaving China, arriving in Baguio in 30 November 1948. Their term of service ended in May or June of 1954. They helped start the Baguio Chinese Baptist Church (BCBC) in 1950 (App. II, Fig. 2, 3) and also taught at the Philippine Baptist Theological Seminary (established in 1952), which was originally set up to train Chinese workers for the new churches (see pp. 262–263). He has authored seven books and numerous articles on Christian missions. In one of these books, Crawley expressed his view that the two crises of the 1940s disrupted the Christian partnership

657. For a sample of the composite ministries of the Southern Baptist Convention and the number of their personnel in China, see "Appendix: Statistical Reports" in *Annual of the Southern Baptist Convention, Nineteen Hundred and Forty-Nine, Ninety-Second Session, One Hundred and Fourth Year, Oklahoma City, Oklahoma, May 18–22, 1949* (Nashville, TN: Executive Committee, Southern Baptist Convention, [1949]), 149–153, and Christopher Tang, *First Hundred Years*, 205–218.

658. See "Southern Baptist Convention Foreign Missionary Personnel," in *Annual of the Southern Baptist Convention, Nineteen Hundred and Forty-seven, Ninetieth Session, One Hundred and Second Year, St. Louis, Missouri, May 5–11, 1947* (Nashville, TN: Executive Committee, Southern Baptist Convention, [1947]), 126. Crawley's most recent book is World Christianity 1970–2000: Toward a New Millennium (Pasadena, CA: William Carey Library, 2001).

across the Pacific that had been so valuable in earlier years. But at the same time, it produced opportunities for "the deepening and strengthening of Christianity in China and a maturing of relationships with Christians from other lands that could become the basis for even warmer and more effective partnership."[659]

By the time the Crawleys arrived in China, the Communists were already too powerful to subdue. Warring factions and internal corruption had likewise weakened the nationalist government. Hence, after the People's Republic of China was inaugurated on 1 October 1949, the national government and its forces retreated to the island of Taiwan. Most missionaries in China withdrew ahead of the Communist advance. Rev Max Pettit/Pei MaKe 培馬可牧師, whom I interviewed personally, described the great disillusionment that he and other missionaries felt when they had to leave China:

> In September of '47 I sailed from San Francisco to Hong Kong, . . . we went to . . . Beijing and began studying the language. . . . I was in a tough time with the language but enjoyed being in Beijing and working with the language and working, . . . we began a little church there, began a little mission, and Winston Crawley was preaching there, but then the Communists got rather close, . . . and we knew that Beijing would be next. So they requested that we leave Beijing. We went to Shanghai, stayed there for three weeks, trying to decide, to determine what to do. And we decided then that we would continue our language study in Baguio. . . . We continued to try and study or get interested in studying Mandarin and as Communists were walking all over China. It was, looked rather futile to try to learn the language then . . .[660]

---

659. He is referring to the WWII and Communist overthrow of China. Crawley, *Partners across the Pacific*, 81. This view is echoed by the report of Baker James Cauthen, "The Orient in Search of Peace," in *Annual of the Southern Baptist Convention Nineteen Hundred and Forty-Six, Eighty-Ninth Session, One Hundred and First Year, Miami, Florida, May 15–19, 1946* (Nashville, TN: Executive Committee, Southern Baptist Convention, [1946]), 334.

660. Rev Max Pettit/Pei MaKe 培馬可, audio-taped interview by Jean Uayan, in Dagupan City, 16 Feb 2002, transcript, Philippine Chinese Church Archive, Biblical

By the end of 1951 all SBC missionaries had left the Chinese mainland. Between 1948 and 1951, they started new work in different fields in Asia – Macau, Hong Kong, Indonesia, Malaysia, Burma (Myanmar), Singapore, and the Philippines. They sought opportunities among the Chinese *diaspora*, aiming to continue serving in familiar Chinese settings and using the language (Mandarin) that they had already acquired. Crawley notes that in Taiwan, Hong Kong, Malaysia, and Singapore, Southern Baptists worked almost entirely with Chinese people, while in Korea, the Philippines, Thailand, and Indonesia, "their early contacts and missionary effort among Chinese minorities became a spearhead for Southern Baptist mission ministry to the majority populations of those nations."[661]

b) SBC Work in the Philippines

Between 1900 and 1946, there were only two Baptist mission groups working in the Philippines. First came Rev Eric Lund (1852–1933) of the American Baptist Missionary Union (ABMU–Northern Baptists) who arrived in Iloilo on 3 May 1900.[662] His Ilonggo teacher and coworker in translation work was Braulio Ciriaco Manikan y Miralles (b. 1870), a Filipino who had been converted and baptized by Lund in Spain.[663] The second group was the Association of Baptists for Evangelism in the Orient (ABEO), later known as Association of Baptists for World Evangelism (ABWE), which was formed by Dr Rafael Thomas when he severed ties

---

Seminary of the Philippines, Valenzuela City, Philippines. The Chinese name of Pettit was supplied by Rev Pedro Hao. Pedro Hao/Hou JunNan 侯均南, audio-taped interview by Jean Uayan, 19 Mar 2004, at his residence in Cainta, Rizal, transcript, Philippine Chinese Church Archive, Biblical Seminary of the Philippines, Valenzuela City, Philippines.

661. Crawley, *Partners across the Pacific*, 97.

662. Nestor Bunda argues that in actuality, the starting point of the Baptist work should be dated to the year 1898 when Manikan was converted and planned to return to the Philippines as a missionary to his own people. Lund, on the other hand, was reluctant to leave his work in Spain, and it was Manikan who urged him to start work in the Philippines. See Bunda, *Mission History*, 63–66. Manikan, however, dropped out of the Baptist church in 1906, when it was discovered that he was a gambler.

663. Henry Weston Munger, *Christ and the Filipino Soul* (Iloilo: Mrs Laura Lee Munger and Mrs Laura Lee Marques, 1967), 16. Cf. Henry W. Munger, "After Twenty-five Years," *Missions* 16 (Dec 1925): 34; quoted in Bunda, *Mission History*, 67. For details about the life and conversion of Manikan, see Bunda, *Mission History*, 66–74.

with the American Baptists. The work of these two groups covered mainly the Visayas and Mindanao areas.[664]

The Second World War brought the Philippines to international attention, and Western Christians saw the spiritual needs of the Filipinos. Thus, when the country was liberated, mission groups came in successive waves, including missionaries from the Southern Baptists, the Conservative Baptists, the Baptist General Conference, the Baptist Bible Fellowship, and the General Baptists.[665]

The SBC missionaries originally came to the Philippines to study Mandarin at the Chinese language school in Baguio, not to start a mission program. There was a lingering hope that the political situation in China would change and that they would be able to return.[666] When this hope dimmed, it was only normal that they turned their attention toward the Chinese people and began witnessing to them. Thus, Crawley stated that,

> The Southern Baptist mission program in the Philippines began as witness to the Chinese minority population. That was natural enough, since its pioneers were displaced China missionaries. In fact, that same general pattern was followed in all of our new Southeast Asian fields. Relocated China missionaries began a ministry to Chinese minority groups, which served as a spearhead for the opening of work also with the majority population in each country.[667]

Indeed, the Chinese population in the Philippines at this time was still considered a minority when compared with other nations in Southeast Asia. Around 1949 there were probably six million Chinese in Taiwan, two million in Hong Kong, a quarter of a million in Macau, three million in

664. See Catalino P. Pamplona, *Baptist History for Church Leaders* (Makati City: Church Strengthening Ministry, 1992), 303–319.

665. Elaine J. Kennedy, *Baptist Centennial History of the Philippines (1900–1999)* (Makati City: Church Strengthening Ministry, 1999), 162.

666. Winston Crawley, "From China to the Philippines: A Turn in the Road," in *Let the Philippine Islands Be Glad. Stories of the Development and Growth of God's Kingdom in the Philippines through the Philippine Baptist Mission 1948–1998*, comp. Jan Hill ([Baguio City]: Bundok Press, 1999), 12.

667. Winston Crawley, *Into a New World* (Nashville, TN: Convention Press, 1958), 38–39.

Singapore and Malaya, another three million in Thailand, and more than two million in Indonesia. In contrast, the number of Chinese people in the Philippines was estimated to range from 150,000 to 300,000.[668] About half of this number was concentrated in Manila, with the rest scattered throughout the provinces. In Baguio there were only about twelve- to fifteen-hundred Chinese immigrants.

The 1949 report on the "Orient," submitted by then SBC Secretary for the Orient Baker James Cauthen, simply stated, "Facilities for Chinese language study were organized in Baguio in the Philippine Islands and a group of new missionaries, many of them with little children, were placed there so their study could be continued."[669] This implies that the SBC expected to redeploy their missionaries; it also showed the Mission's respect for the Northern Baptists who were already doing mission work in the Islands.

The missionary sent to organize the language school in Baguio was Fern Harrington/Han MuLan jiaoshi 韓慕蘭教士 (1915–2006, term of service 1948–1962)[670] (App. II, Fig. 1). She had been called to China in December 1937, arriving there in 1940. Because of the Sino-Japanese War, the Beijing Chinese Language School, with four Chinese language teachers accompanying the missionaries, was relocated to Baguio, Philippines in March

---

668. Crawley, *Partners across the Pacific*, 95 and Crawley, *Into a New World*, 39.

669. Baker James Cauthen, "The Orient," in *Annual of the Southern Baptist Convention Nineteen Hundred and Forty-Nine, Ninety-Second Session, One Hundred and Fourth Year, Oklahoma City, Oklahoma, May 18–22, 1949* (Nashville, TN: Executive Committee, Southern Baptist Convention, [1949]), 126.

670. According Winston Crawley and the editors of the 50th anniversary publication of the Dagupan Chinese Baptist Church, published in 2002, Fern Harrington married Herbert J. Miles when she was about 65 years old and already retired from missionary service in Taiwan. See Dagupan Chinese Baptist Church/Laguban Huaqiao Jinxinhui 拉古扳華僑浸信會, *Christ Preeminent 50th Anniversary* (*Zhu Ju Shouwei*) 主居首為 (Dagupan City: Dagupan Chinese Baptist Church, 2002), inside back cover. This source is henceforth cited as *Christ Preeminent*. See also Winston Crawley, <winstoncrawley@yahoo.com>. Private email message to the writer, 25 Jul 2005. She passed away on 31 Mar 2006 and bequeathed a collection of her letters (written while serving as a Philippine missionary) to BSOP. Throughout this study the name Fern Harrington or Harrington will be used to refer to this pioneer missionary during the time of her service in the Philippines. However, in more recent works her married name – Fern Harrington Miles – is used. She should not be confused with Julia Virginia Miles, another SBC missionary who served in the Philippines from 1949–1959.

1941.[671] But the Japanese army occupied that city on 27 December 1941. Together with eight other Southern Baptist missionaries, Fern Harrington was among the five hundred Americans interned in the Japanese camp.[672] The first concentration camp was set up inside Washington Hotel at the top of Session Road, then moved to Camp John Hay, and finally to Camp Holmes, now Camp Dangwa. When the country was liberated, Harrington returned to the United States hoping never to return to the Philippines. She went back to China in 1947, but again, in 1948, circumstances forced her to re-enter the country that held painful memories of captivity. Her first reaction was to decline Cauthen's invitation to help the language school in Baguio. But while praying for God's guidance, she recalled an incident that happened during her captivity. She witnessed the burial of a Chinese prisoner living in the barrack beside the American barrack, and she found herself saying, "Lord, if I ever have a chance again to give the gospel to the Chinese in Baguio, I will do it."[673]

Fern Harrington gave the reason in her report that the pre-war language school in Baguio was open to missionaries of all denominations, whereas the post-war school was financed by the Baptist mission board exclusively for their missionaries.[674] She said that there were eighty-five language students in the first school, of whom eight were missionaries, when the Japanese occupied Baguio. When the Japanese imprisoned the Chinese and Americans, this must have disbanded the school. In 1949 four language teachers fled from Beijing; three of these had taught in the pre-war school.[675]

---

671. See W. Carl Hunker, "Waiting and Watching," in *Let the Philippine Islands Be Glad*, 6.

672. See Cheng and Bersamira, *Ethnic Chinese in Baguio*, 223.

673. Fern Harrington Miles, "God's Call to the Philippines," in *Let the Philippine Islands Be Glad*, 3–4. She has written a book on this episode of her life entitled *Captive Community: Life in a Japanese Internment Camp, 1941–1945* (San Angelo, TX: Mossy Creek Place, 1987).

674. Fern Harrington Miles, "The Opening of Southern Baptist Work in the Philippines," in *Let the Philippine Islands Be Glad*, 1–3. See also Fern Harrington Miles, *Account of Opening Baptist Work in the Philippines*, TMs (photocopy), 197, Special Collections, Philippine Chinese Church Archives, Biblical Seminary of the Philippines Library, Valenzuela City. In succeeding pages, the exact dates of events related to the establishment of BCBC and DCBC are provided by Miles' notes in this collection.

675. See Winston Crawley, <winstoncrawley@yahoo.com>. Private email message to the writer, 25 Jul 2005.

But why was Baguio chosen as the center for language learning? Harrington stated that Cauthen decided to set up the language school there because "housing was available."[676] But Crawley indicated that the Philippines was actually a third choice for Cauthen. The first choice was Canton, but he was warned by the American Consulate that Americans ought to leave China. The second was Hong Kong, but at that time the British government did not want to receive any more Americans into their colony.[677]

Fern Harrington listed the names of those who arrived in Baguio during 1948–1949. There were eleven couples (Winston and Margaret Crawley, Max and Ann Pettit, Henry and Helen Turlington, Charles and Donal Culpepper, Clyde and Alcie May Jowers, Wesley and Geraldine Lawton, W. Carl and Jeanette Hunker, James and Zelma Foster, Willie Alsberry [Bill] and Ella Ruth Solesbee, Clifton and Ann Harris, Bettie and Bob Ricketson), four single ladies (Margaret Collins, Mrs Buford Nichols, Theresa Anderson, and Fern Harrington), four Chinese teachers (Mr and Mrs H. T. Yeh/Ye XinYu 葉信余, Bai Tse-fang [characters for Chinese name not known], and his daughter Bai QiWen 白琦文), and Yeh's teenage daughter Ling Kang [characters for Chinese name not known]. Most of the missionaries came for language study, which began on 17 January 1949 at #4 Carino Street in Baguio.

Before undertaking mission work in the Philippines, the Foreign Mission Board of SBC had asked Harrington to survey three potential mission fields. She recounted that she sent out questionnaires and interviewed missionaries and Filipino leaders in Baguio, Manila, and Iloilo (the Northern Baptist headquarter). Her report included three maps and indicated: "(1) areas assigned to various mission groups according to the Comity Agreement; (2) distribution of population, typography, and principal cities with more than 20,000 population; and (3) distribution of people according to religious background – pagan, Muslim, and Roman Catholic." The conclusion of the survey was that the Southern Baptists should focus on evangelizing the Chinese in the Philippines, since the missionaries all spoke

---

676. Miles, "God's Call," 3.
677. Crawley, "From China," 12.

Chinese. They failed to realize that the *lingua franca* of the Chinese in the Philippines was either the *Hokkien* or Cantonese dialect, not Mandarin, despite the fact that the latter was the national language. Also, in view of the Comity Agreement, it was felt that the newcomers had no opening to work among the Filipinos.[678]

The Chinese work eventually served as a springboard to a much greater ministry among the Filipinos, and in spite of the Comity Agreement, Filipino congregations were established within stipulated areas designated for other mission groups by this agreement. The SBC justified this by the following reasons: First, WWII had shifted the population, leading to problems of maintaining the original comity divisions. Second, the evangelical witness of the original mission boards agreeing to the Comity Agreement was inadequate, and the Filipinos themselves had sought out the Southern Baptist missionaries to work among them.[679] On 30 August 1950, the establishment of the SBC Philippine Mission, composed of twenty-three missionaries, inaugurated the official launching of permanent mission work in the Philippines.[680]

(1) SBC Work in Baguio

In 1899, Benguet province was organized by the government of the newly formed Republic of the Philippines. In November 1899, however, the Americans arrived and set up a military government at La Trinidad and in February 1900, made Baguio the capital of Benguet. From that year until the Jones Act of 29 August 1916, when the government personnel were Filipinized, Benguet Province was staffed by American governors and officers. Baguio became a chartered city on 1 September 1909. The Tydings-McDuffie Law (adopted in the Philippines on 1 May 1934) created the

---

678. Miles, "Opening of Southern Baptist Work," 1–2.

679. Ibid., 2.

680. Crawley, "Into a New World," 42. See also Jesse Earl Posey, Jr, "A Historical Study of Baptist Missions in the Philippines 1900–1967" (ThD dissertation, New Orleans Baptist Theological Seminary, 1968), 143. The Southern Baptist mission work in the Philippines was formally reported for the first time in the *Annual of the Southern Baptist Convention Nineteen Hundred and Fifty, Ninety-Third Session, One Hundred and Fifth Year, Chicago, Illinois, May 9–12, 1950* (Nashville, TN: Executive Committee, Southern Baptist Convention, [1950]), accessed 15 Sep 2005, https://solomon.imb.org/public/ws/oldmin/www2/minutesp/Record.

Commonwealth of the Philippines on 15 November 1935, ushering in a ten-year transition period preparatory to the granting of independence on 4 July 1946. Before this could happen, the Second World War devastated the Philippines. Baguio was the first place in the Philippines to be struck when the Japanese bombed Camp John Hay on 8 December 1941. It was declared an open city on 27 December and Japanese rule was in force until the Americans liberated Baguio on 26 April 1945.[681]

The Protestant Episcopal Church was the first to enter the Mountain Province as a mission field when Bishop Charles Henry Brent and Rev Walter Clapp made an initial survey in 1903.[682] Rev John Armitage Staunton, Jr founded the Sagada mission with a dispensary and vocational school in 1904. Rev S. S. Drury opened the Easter School in Baguio in 1905, and Bishop Charles Henry Brent and the Rev Remsen B. Ogilby established the Baguio School for Boys (now Brent School) in 1909. Bishop Brent built the Church of the Resurrection, which was inaugurated on 24 April 1904, on top of the Constabulary Hill.[683] When the Evangelical Union of Protestant Churches was formed in Manila on 26 April 1901, the provinces of La Union, Ilocos Norte, and Ilocos Sur were assigned to the United Brethren Church (UBC). Much later, Bontoc, Abra and Lepanto were added to their jurisdiction, and a UBC church was built on 19 February 1904 in Baguio.[684] Other mission groups came later and gradually the number of Protestants increased. By 1950 there were around 25,654 Protestants in the Mountain Province, according to the Roman Catholic Church religious census taken on 30 June 1950.[685]

---

681. Established by General Order No. 43 of Gen. Otis, this was the first provincial civil government under American auspices. See *Report of the Philippine* Commission, 1901, Vol. 1, 69; quoted in Robert R. Reed, *City of Pines: The Origins of Baguio as a Colonial Hill Station and Regional Capital* (Baguio City: A-Seven, 1976), 67; Laurence L. Wilson, *The Skyland of the Philippines* (Baguio: L. L. Wilson/Bookman, 1965), 74–80, 87– 90, 107; Charles L. Cheng and Katherine Bersamira, *The Ethnic Chinese in Baguio and in the Cordillera Philippines: The Untold Stories of Pioneers* (Baguio City: Unique Printing, 1997), 109, 216, 223.

682. Myrick, "Episcopal Church in the Philippines," 5. See p. 118 and Brown, *New Era*, 185, 187.

683. Myrick, "Episcopal Church in the Philippines," 5–7.

684. Brown, *New Era*, 190–191.

685. Wilson, *Skyland of the Philippines*, 97.

When the SBC missionaries arrived in Baguio in 1948, they settled down for language study with the four Chinese language teachers. Classes were held in a rented building near the Burnham Park. The missionaries, according to W. Carl Hunker, "worshiped with Filipinos in the basement of a bombed-out church building of the United Church of Christ."[686]

The opening for work among the Chinese came when the principal of the Chinese Patriotic School, Mr S. C. Lee, visited Fern Harrington on 2 April 1949. Mr Lee knew her from having taught in the interdenominational language school in Baguio prior to WWII. The principal requested for missionaries to teach English remedial classes during the summer vacation. At first hesitant because all of the missionaries were occupied with language study, she testified that, "God's small voice spoke, 'I sent these men. They are handing you the key to the door you have been trying to open.'"[687] Through these English classes they became acquainted with the Chinese children and began to dream of a Sunday School for them. The best venue for this would be the Chinese school. After much prayer she approached Mr Lee and told him the teachers refused to accept any pay for teaching English classes, but asked for the favor of being allowed to use the school building for a Chinese Sunday School. The principal responded positively, "I've heard a lot about the Bible but have never had a chance to study it. This would be a wonderful opportunity for our children."[688] He cooperated by sending addresses of parents so they could send out publicity. Harrington described the Sunday School classes, the first one held on 29 May 1949, conducted by missionaries, who had neither funds, teaching curriculum, nor sufficient language skills, in the following way:

> First we worked out a curriculum with stories on the life of Christ, to be followed by stories from Genesis after the first of the next year. Since no one could speak Chinese fluently, we took turns leading the songs and telling the Bible story for the week to the entire group in the opening assembly. Then we divided the children into four classes, from preschoolers to

686. Hunker, "Waiting," 7.
687. Miles, "Opening," 2, 8–9.
688. Ibid., 9.

teenagers, where we would teach them a memory verse and review the lesson with suitable activities.

To finance the project, we set up a Storehouse Fund to which most of us gave our tithes . . . On Sunday afternoons we met as a group for prayer and worship, and took up offerings for the Storehouse Fund.[689]

About forty children came to that first Sunday School, gradually increasing over the year. It was reorganized in 1951 into the Primary, Junior and Intermediate Departments and taught by the missionaries and Chinese Christians.[690] Bible classes for young people and adults began three weeks later, on 19 June 1949, and were held on Sunday afternoons because the Chinese kept their stores open in the mornings. They borrowed a place in the United Church to hold these classes. Also on this date, regular worship services in Chinese in conjunction with these Sunday afternoon Bible classes began, with male missionaries taking turns to preach. By 29 May 1950 the Baguio Chinese Baptist Church/Biyao Huaqiao Jinxinhui 碧瑤華僑浸信會 was organized with twelve Chinese charter members and with Crawley as the first pastor.[691] In the *Hokkien* vernacular, they called him Keh Bun Seng Bok Su (Reverend) or in Mandarin, Guo WenSheng mushi 郭文生牧師.[692] By the middle of September they were averaging a combined attendance of over one hundred in the morning and afternoon services.[693]

---

689. Ibid., 9.

690. James A. Foster, "Report of the Baguio Station," in *Minutes of the Philippine Mission of the Southern Baptist Convention 1950–51, Annual Session – Aug 27–31, Baguio City, Minutes of the 1950–51 Executive Committee Constitution, Theme: By My Spirit* (Baguio: Baguio Printing & Publishing, [1951]), 18. Hereafter, *Minutes 1950–51*. Some of the teachers were Elaine Crotwell, Mrs Hou, Wu Yu Ying, Mrs Hung and Miles (primary department); Mrs Peng, Mr Hung (Junior); Victoria Parsons and Mrs Zelma Rosa Foster.

691. Winston Crawley, "In the Philippines with God," in *Let the Philippine Islands Be Glad*, 19. For the names and background information on these twelve members, see Cheng and Bersamira, *Ethnic Chinese in Baguio*, 254–256 and "Baptist Work in the Philippines," in Baguio Chinese Baptist Church/Biyao Huaren Jinxinhui 碧瑤華人浸信會. *Blueprints BCBC 1950–2000* (Baguio City: Baguio Chinese Baptist Church, 2000), n.p.

692. Pedro Hao, interview and Crawley, *Partners*, 11.

693. Fern Harrington Miles, "The Breakthrough," in *Let the Philippine Islands Be Glad*, 10. See also Winston Crawley, "Report of the Baguio Station," in *Minutes of the First Annual Session of the Philippine Mission of the Southern Baptist Convention 1950, Aug 29–Sep*

Crawley was in charge of the baptismal class; of this group eleven were baptized on 28 May 1950. One of the first Christians in Baguio was Pedro Hao/Hou JunNan 侯均南 (1924–2004); his conversion took place on 4 December 1949. He and his wife, Rosa Chua/Lin JiaBao 林佳寶, were among the twelve charter members. Hao was born in Manila on 26 November 1924. His Buddhist parents left Lam Oaⁿ/Nan-An, Fujian 福建南安, to come to work in the Philippines during the Spanish regime. When he was 22 years old, he went to Baguio to work in a hardware store as a clerk. It was there that the missionaries visited and invited him to join their meetings. He did not do so at once, because there was no one to go with him, but he was already very curious about these Americans who could speak Mandarin so well. Then he met a Mr Ang who had also been invited and who felt the same curiosity as Hao. They attended the worship service for an hour, then the Bible study afterward. The biggest attraction for them was the fact that these missionaries, especially Winston Crawley, could speak and read the Bible in fluent Mandarin, so they started attending the meetings every week, and were among those baptized in 1950.[694]

In an unsigned report that was probably written in 1954, a glowing appraisal was given regarding Pedro Hao:

> One of these young men, Pedro Hao, was anxious to study the Scriptures and learn more about the God and the faith he had accepted. From the beginning of his Christian life, he was always willing and eager to serve in any way. Because he was very capable, opportunities came not only for him to interpret for the missionaries but also for personal witnessing and, later, even to preach himself. He refused his father's offer of a much better business opportunity in another city because he preferred to stay in Baguio, where he could study, worship, and serve his God as a growing Christian should. Now he is a ministerial student in our seminary in Baguio and is a challenge even to the older Christians there.[695]

1, *Theme: Advance with Christ* (Baguio: Baguio Printing & Publishing, [1950]), 16–18. Hereafter cited as *Minutes 1950*.

694. Hao interview.
695. Crawley, "In the Philippines with God," 19.

According to Crawley, having no building of its own, the BCBC met in three different places: the children's Sunday School was held in the Chinese school, the adult Bible classes and Sunday worship in the United Church of Christ, and the weekly prayer meetings in the building used for language classes. By the end of 1951, the mission was looking forward to some church members assuming the teaching responsibilities and eventually taking over the entire church program. They foresaw little problem in the church becoming self-supporting financially. But they admitted that the deficiency of the missionaries in using *Hokkien*, the Roman Catholic influence, and the materialism and indifference of a large part of the Chinese community were seen as problems facing the mission.[696]

Writing around 1957, Crawley noted that progress of missions among overseas Chinese business communities in Southeast Asia was slow but steady. Converts from the Chinese community were usually "very capable and dependable."[697] The BCBC already had its own building in the downtown area, an ideal location to attract the Chinese who lived in the business district. The church was under the leadership of missionary-pastor James A. Foster and was giving half of its offering to support two missions, one at San Fernando and the other at Tarlac. Mission work in San Fernando began in March 1951 in a soap factory under the general headship of the BCBC.[698] This was the situation of the Baguio Chinese Baptist Church seven years after it was established. Not only was the first Chinese church established by the SBC able to become entirely self-supporting, it also started to support two mission stations.

(2) SBC Work in Dagupan

Geographically, Dagupan City is located in the mid-north section of the province of Pangasinan, at the foot of the Lingayen Gulf and lying in the southwestern part of Region I (see App. A). The city was originally named Bacnotan (sometimes spelled Bagnotan) and was renamed Dagupan

---

696. Crawley, "Report of the Baguio Station," *Minutes 1950*, 17–18.

697. Crawley, *Into a New World*, 42.

698. Foster, "Report of the Baguio Station," *Minutes 1950–51*, 18, and Crawley, "Into a New World," 42.

(meaning "a meeting place") in 1720.[699] Although initially overshadowed by Lingayen (with its Chinese-*mestizo pariancillo*) and Calasiao, but because it was located along the coast and the sandbars found at the mouth of the Agno River which formed excellent anchorage for boats engaged in the coastwise trade, it became a growing commercial center.[700] On 23 November 1892, the railroad traversing Manila to Dagupan was opened and run by an English company.[701] This was the only railroad in the country when the Americans occupied the Philippines, but it facilitated the growth of commerce in the province of Pangasinan. Civil government was established on 16 February 1901.[702]

(a) Christianity in Dagupan City

When the Spaniards conquered and set up the *alcaldia* (province) of Pangasinan in 1572, a significant number of the people were converted to Roman Catholicism. In 1614 the Augustinians turned Dagupan over to the charge of the Dominican Order.[703] Under a policy of centralization the different regions were slowly, if unevenly, integrated over a period of 300 years.[704] Under the Spanish insular government, the province was ruled first by *encomenderos* (land-owning colonizers), then by the *alcaldes* (mayors), and finally by civil governors. The people were subjected to heavy taxes and endured a defective fiscal system.[705] Despite having to acculturate themselves to Spanish social, cultural and political developments for three centuries, the people of Pangasinan, however, did not lose their identity and dignity. This found final expression in the revolution of 1896, when the yoke of Spanish sovereignty was overthrown. The province was freed on 22 July 1898 when Spanish officials surrendered at Dagupan.

---

699. Doeppers, "Ethnicity and Class," 72–73; Rosario Mendoza Cortes, *Pangasinan, 1572–1800* (Quezon City: New Day, 1974), 100.

700. Doeppers, "Ethnicity and Class," 73; Cortes, *Pangasinan, 1572–1800*, 134.

701. Devins, *Observer in the Philippines*, 77–78; Foreman, *Philippine Islands, Vol 2*, 265–267.

702. "Welcome to Dagupan City – City Profile – History," accessed 17 Mar 2004, http://cityhall.dagupan.com/aboutus.htm.

703. Cortes, *Pangasinan, 1572–1800*, 100; Doeppers, "Ethnicity and Class," 72.

704. Rosario Mendoza Cortes, *Pangasinan, 1901–1986: A Political, Socioeconomic and Cultural History* (Quezon City: New Day, 1990), 5.

705. For further discussion see Foreman, *Philippine Islands*, 211–242.

Soon after the American military entered the Philippines, missionaries of several Protestant groups followed.[706] Following the Comity Agreement, the Methodist Episcopal Church was assigned an area that included Dagupan. In 1906, through the efforts of Rev Ernest S. Lyons and accompanied by traveling evangelist Felipe Marquez who was also a ranking Katipunan officer, the Methodists were able to make the first converts among the ranks of the Katipuneros in Dagupan.[707] According to Homer Stuntz, eight churches with a total membership of eight hundred were set up after only seven months![708] The *Iglesia Evangelica Metodista en las Islas Filipinas* (IEMELIF), led by Rev Nicolas V. Zamora, broke away from the Methodist Episcopal Church on 28 February 1909.[709] Soon after, Pastor Hipolito Guirnalda succeeded in planting an IEMELIF church in Dagupan in 1911.

After WWII many more denominations established mission work in the province, such as the Wesleyan Methodists under Romeo Boronia in 1949. Joseph Pitts and John Pattee of the Church of the Nazarene, through their evangelistic work, likewise planted churches in Pangasinan.[710] From Baguio City, the Southern Baptist missionaries spread the gospel to Dagupan City in February 1950. Before this part of history is discussed, however, it is important to first understand the background of the Chinese living in Dagupan City.

---

706. The first Protestant missionaries to visit Manila and conduct evangelistic meetings were Rev and Mrs Charles Owens, who were Methodists. This was in November 1898. James Thoburn followed afterwards, in March 1899, and established the first Methodist church. Pamplona, *Baptist History*, 297. See also Floyd T. Cunningham, "Diversities within Post-war Philippine Protestantism," *The Mediator* 5 (Oct 2003): 42–143.

707. Cortes, *Pangasinan, 1572–1800*, 100. See also Trinidad, *Monument*, 86.

708. Stuntz is not always a reliable source, but this is what he recorded in his book, *Philippines and the Far East*, 451.

709. Trinidad, *Monument*, x. Trinidad writes from a very nationalistic view of the IEMELIF when he narrates the founding of this breakaway group of Filipino Methodists led by Nicolas Zamora, see pp. 99–135 of his book.

710. Cunningham, "Diversities," 112–114.

(b) Chinese in Dagupan City

In 1903, there were 413 Chinese merchants and tradesmen in Dagupan.[711] In contrast, according to Benito Lim in an article written in 1997, there were 7,000 ethnic Chinese in Dagupan City, and over 70 percent of them had parents, grandparents, or great-grandparents who had lived in or were still living in this city.[712] During the mid-nineteenth century, Chinese traders crossed the South China Sea or Nan Yang 南洋, sailing in Chinese junks from Fujian province (primarily Quanzhou and Xiamen) and landing in ports on the western coast of Luzon. Sta. Cruz, Bolinao, Anda, Lingayen, Sual, Vigan served as entry points. Historians Yang Li 楊力 and Ye XiaoDun 葉小敦 also state that during the 1890s, there were about 6,000–7,000 *Hokkien* Chinese families in Luzon.[713] When surveyed by Benito Lim in 1997, most immigrants claimed that they learned about Dagupan from relatives who immigrated there around 1850–1900.[714] A few attested that their ancestors came during the Spanish colonization period; others even said that they were descendants of the sailors left behind by the retreating forces of the pirate Lin Feng.[715] He had set up a fortified settlement near the Pangasinan River and resisted Spanish forces for three months in 1575 before escaping by building small boats out of burnt ships. Those who descended from Lin Feng's crew opened many kinds of shops (saw mills, rice mills, copra mills, and others), settling first in Binmaley and doing business as far as Dagupan, Lingayen, Urdaneta, Manaoag and Tarlac (see map in App. A).[716]

---

711. Doeppers, "Ethnicity and Class," 75. Comparatively, there was a total population of 7,140 in the nuclear settlement around Dagupan in the same year.

712. Benito Lim, "The Dagupan Chinese," in *The Ethnic Chinese as Filipinos (Part 2) Proceedings of the National Conference on "The Ethnic Chinese as Filipinos" held in Quezon City 10–11 Nov 1995*, by the Philippine Association for Chinese Studies, ed. Teresita Ang See/Shi Hong YuHua 施洪玉, *Chinese Studies Journal* 7 (Quezon City: Philippine Association for Chinese Studies (PACS), 1997), 16.

713. Yang Li 楊力 and Ye XiaoDun 葉小敦, *Dongnanya de Fujianren* 東南亞的福建人 (The Fujianese of Southeast Asia), Huaqiao Huaren Yanjiu Congshu 華僑華人研究叢書 (Series on Overseas Chinese Studies) (Fujian: Fujian Renmin Chubanshe 福建人民出版社, 1993), 25–26.

714. Lim, "Dagupan Chinese," 17.

715. *BRPI* 6: 92–125. See pp. 33–34, and p. 44 note 41.

716. Lim, "Dagupan Chinese," 18.

At the turn of the nineteenth century most of the Chinese were traders and since they came mostly from South Fujian, they spoke *Hokkien*. Doeppers' research shows that these traders were mainly from the Jinjiang county 晉江縣, specifically Quanzhou city.[717] A figure given in a Chinese source states the number of Chinese in the Philippines during 1898 was 100,000.[718] According to an account of the business sector in Dagupan in 1910, the Chinese who lived in this area opened general stores, bakeries, and other shops near the river along *Avenida Torres Bugallon* (now Angel B. Fernandez, the main street). Daniel Doeppers remarked that retail trade was dominated by the Chinese.[719] Their goals during the 1920s and 1930s were to accumulate enough wealth to bring home to their family in China, to own and manage their own businesses in the Philippines, and to raise their social stature within the Dagupan Chinese community and in China.[720]

After the WWII, external circumstances hastened the acculturation of the Dagupan Chinese into the Filipino society. According to school authorities interviewed by Benito Lim in 1997, about 95 percent of the third and fourth generation Dagupan Chinese can still speak their mother tongue (*Hokkien*), but only 30 percent speak and read Mandarin. Most of these Chinese are fluent in the Pangasinan dialect and English, and can speak a little Ilocano and Tagalog.[721]

c) *Emergence of DCBC*

(1) The Initial Contact

After this brief introduction to the Chinese community in Dagupan, the history of the emergence of the Dagupan Chinese Baptist Church/ Laguban Huaqiao Jinxinhui 拉古板華僑浸信會 can be gathered from the personal testimonies of the missionaries and early converts, specifically those of Rev Max Pettit, Fern Harrington Miles, and Rev Pedro Hao, as

---

717. See Doeppers, "Ethnicity and Class," 108, for the distribution of the *Hokkien* in the cities of Dumaguete, Dagupan and Davao by county of origin. Compare App. D and E for the different categories in the division of Fujian province.

718. See Yang and Ye, *Fujianese of Southeast Asia*, 310.

719. See Doeppers, "Ethnicity and Class," 72–80.

720. Lim, "Dagupan Chinese," 19.

721. Ibid., 30.

well as from the minutes of the Philippine Mission of the SBC. Crawley writes that during the 1950s, "the business life of the city [Dagupan] was carried on largely by the two thousand Chinese who lived there."[722] On 20 February 1950, four SBC missionaries – Fern Harrington (1914–2006), Theresa K. Anderson/Yin MuJie 因慕潔教士 (1917–2010), Max Pettit (1922–2012), Bill Solesbee/Sha WeiRen 沙衛仁牧師 (1919–2006) – and one Protestant Chinese, Pedro Hao, paid a visit to one of the Chinese groceries in Dagupan.[723] Jesse Earl Posey states that weekend trips from Baguio to Dagupan began in July 1950.[724] The February date, however, is recorded in mission records and confirmed by Pedro Hao in *Christ Preeminent*, the fiftieth anniversary publication of DCBC, as marking the beginning of SBC mission work in Dagupan.[725]

Fern Harrington further recorded that it was only on 2 June that they were able to contact Mr Chua Ke Kan/Cai JiGan 蔡繼干 (App. II, Fig. 4), the grocery store owner.[726] Whereas Catalino Pamplona states in his book, *Baptist History for Church Leaders*, that the missionaries "found a group of Chinese believers meeting in their own homes and studying the Bible," the method actually used by the missionaries during the initial trip was not to go to the residence but to the stores in search of Chinese businessmen, and they started from the main street of Dagupan where the stores were concentrated.[727] They distributed flyers announcing their meetings and initially did not meet good response. On their second trip, Harrington and Collins met Christians from Manila who were attending a funeral service. The deceased was the brother of a Mr Chua, later identified by Hao as Chua Ke Kan.[728] Except for Mr Chua and his family, all of the ten earliest members

---

722. Crawley, *Into a New World*, 38.

723. Pedro Hao/Hou JunNan 侯均南, "Laguban Huaqiao Jinxinhui Huishi 拉古扳華僑浸信會史 (History of the Dagupan Chinese Baptist Church)," in *Christ Preeminent*, n.p.

724. Cf. Posey, "Historical Study of Baptist Missions," 143 and Pamplona, *Baptist History*, 344. Kennedy's work, *Baptist Centennial History of the Philippines*, is too concise to offer specific details concerning the history of DCBC.

725. Hao wrote that it was in the "spring/chuntian 春天" of 1950. See Hao, "History," in *Christ Preeminent*, n.p.

726. Harrington, "Report of the Dagupan Work," in *Minutes 1950*, 19.

727. Pamplona, *Baptist History*, 344.

728. Hao interview.

were converted in Dagupan, according to Hao. Furthermore, the division of work among the missionaries was not that clearly assigned. Hao said that they took turns leading the different meetings, because some of them, such as Max Pettit and Margaret Collins (who had to teach Sunday School using English), were not as fluent in Mandarin as Crawley and Harrington.

(2) Testimony of Fern Harrington

The beginnings of DCBC are carefully recorded in the *Minutes of the First Annual Session of the Philippine Mission of the Southern Baptist Convention* (1950). This report by Fern Harrington is quoted in Appendix JJ to give full detail regarding the process that SBC missionaries used to start work in Dagupan. The report can be summarized thus: Dr Baker Cauthen suggested that SBC missionaries explore the vicinity of Baguio where large numbers of Chinese lived. The first exploration took place in February 1950. They discovered around 2,000 Chinese in Dagupan City who were mostly *Hokkien* Chinese. Mandarin was usable with everyone they met except the very young and the very old. After Dr Cauthen approved the work, Fern Harrington and Margaret Collins went to Dagupan City on 2 June 1950. At first the missionaries could not locate any Protestant Chinese, but due to a funeral event they became acquainted with a new contact – Chua Ke Kan. The first service was held in the Chua residence on 9 July 1950. During the following weeks they started to hold services at the Filipino First Methodist Church, for their request to use the Chinese school in Dagupan had been turned down. Aside from the two female missionaries, others involved in this work were Oswald "Oz" Quick, Bill Solesbee, Max Pettit and Clyde Jowers. Collins and Harrington moved to Dagupan City on 15 September 1950.[729]

(3) Testimony of Pedro Hao

Pedro Hao was another eyewitness of the establishment of DCBC (App. II, Fig. 4).[730] He reports that while conversing with Mrs Ngo Niu Siao Kia^n/Wu Liang ShaoJing 伍梁少京太太 [of the Baguio Chinese Baptist Church] about the Mission's desire to bring the gospel to places with a large

---

729. Harrington, "Dagupan Work," *First Annual Session 1950*, 19–21.

730. The sources for Hao's testimony include my interview with him and his own written article, "History," in *Christ Preeminent*, n.p.

population of Chinese, she suggested that they visit Dagupan. Upon her recommendation, they did just that.

At first, while surveying for Chinese Christians among the storefronts on *Avenida Torres Bugallon*, they met much resistance and could find no Christians. Finally, they met Chua Ke Kan, who owned the grocery store. Rev Pettit called him "Mr Tsai," using the Mandarin form instead of "Chua," which is the *Hokkien* form. He was a Protestant Chinese connected with CUEC; he had gone to Dagupan from Manila because his brother had died and he had to take over his business. His wife and son, Samuel Chua or Chua Khe Beng/Cai QiMing 蔡啟明, were also Christians.

When Chua Ke Kan transferred to Dagupan, he was disappointed to find no Protestant Chinese church, so he asked the help of the CUEC Evangelistic Band to start such a church. Mrs Wu, who suggested that the missionaries visit Dagupan, was a friend of Mrs Peng Sia Kiat Ying/Peng Xie JieYing 彭謝潔瑩太太, another translator for the missionaries. Mrs Peng was in the hotel and restaurant business. She was asked to be a full-time worker of the Baguio congregation by the CUEC Evangelistic Band, but because of her business she only served part-time as a female preacher. When Crawley went on a mission trip, she would preach in Baguio.[731] Upon learning about the plan of the Evangelistic Band, the missionaries and Pedro Hao were dismayed, for they did not want to compete and thought it better to do mission work elsewhere. They asked Mr Chua to give them the name and address of the chairman of the Evangelistic Band, and met with this person the following Saturday. This chairman could not confirm that CUEC had concrete plans to do mission work in Dagupan and told them that they would be informed if no work could be carried out. After three weeks, the call finally came and the CUEC representative asked the Baptists to initiate the work.

Another problem was the place of meeting. The group gathered by the missionaries started holding evangelistic meetings during Saturday evenings at the First Methodist Church, when the place was not being used.

731. Crawley notes that the Chinese had no problem with a "woman preacher" and she did an "excellent job." When the Philippine Baptist Theological Seminary was formed, she represented the Chinese on the board of trustees, being "one of the most grounded biblically." Crawley, "From China to the Philippines," 13.

Sunday School was temporarily held at the Chua residence. Harrington says that they "had 25 children for Sunday School, then an Adult Bible class followed by a worship service."[732] This situation continued until September 1950, when they rented a big room on the second floor of the Galvan Building, a place they used until 1964.

The Saturday night meetings usually started with a film, then the gospel message, handled by Max Pettit and Oswald Quick.[733] Harrington took charge of the Sunday School and Samuel Chua helped translate the Mandarin lessons into *Hokkien*. Pedro Hao handled the Adult Class, which was regularly attended by Mr and Mrs Chua Ke Kan, his younger brother Chua Tek Chuan/Cai DeQuan 蔡德泉 and his wife, a Mrs Wang 王太太, and an elderly man surnamed Wu 吳老先生. By September the Sunday School class had increased to 40–50 children. Harrington and Collins moved to Dagupan and hired a Chinese helper to prepare invitations and translate from Mandarin to *Hokkien* during the services. Harrington said in her letter that she was "often discouraged because of the lack of interest among adults who would say 'I'm too busy'" whereas "many children were enthusiastic about activities for them."[734] She assisted this work until May 1951 when she went to Manila to help Theresa Anderson. Rev and Mrs Solesbee moved to Dagupan after she left. When they went on furlough, the Mission invited Pedro Hao, then a student at the Philippine Baptist Theological Seminary and Bible School (PBTSBS)/Meinan Jinxinhui Shengjing Xuexiao 美南浸信會聖經學校, to assist the ministry (see pp. 262–264).

d) The Church Organized

On 19 February 1952 the Dagupan Chinese Baptist Church formally came into existence with ten charter members. These ten charter members included the first seven who were baptized: Chua Keng Hu/Cai JingXu 蔡經許, Di Kok Chim/Li GuoZhen 李國箴, Ong Si Pek Tin/Wang Shi BiZhen 王施碧珍, Dy Tan Siu Theng/Li Chen XiuTing 李陳秀婷, Chua

732. Fern Harrington Miles, "Down Memory's Lane in Dagupan, Philippines," in *Christ Preeminent*, n.p.

733. Oswald Quick died on 13 Jan 1997.

734. Harrington, "Down Memory's Lane."

260
A Study on the Emergence and Early Development of
Selected Protestant Chinese Churches in the Philippines

Dy Siu Kin/Cai Li XiuJin 蔡李秀瑾, Chua Khe Beng/Cai QiMing 蔡啟明, and Kua Kim Hui/Ke JinHui 柯金輝. Aside from these seven who were baptized in January and February of 1952, three other members were Rev Bill Solesbee, female preacher Peh Ki Bun/Bai QiWen 白琦文傳道, and Ngo Bun Be/Wu WenMai 吳文麥 (already baptized).[735]

After Bill Solesbee, the next pastors at DCBC were Rev Dr Winston Crawley (1953), Rev Wesley Lawton/Lu WeiLi 陸衛理牧師 (1954), Rev James Foster/Fu YaGe 富雅各牧師, and Rev R. Edward Gordon/Gao ErDeng 高爾登牧師 (1955). In 1956, Pedro Hao became the first ordained Chinese minister of DCBC and served until 1968. The location of the church moved from the Galvan Building to a rented house on Rivera Street in 1964, then a church edifice was finally built in 1965, with inauguration on 16 April 1965.

Leonard Tuggy and Ralph Toliver, who planted Conservative Baptist churches in the Philippines, observed that the Southern Baptists entered the country with determination to evangelize, plant churches, and carry forward a denominational program. The two authors postulate that this system works and offers the following advantages: (1) emotionally, the missionaries feel at home in this system because they have been in it all their lives; (2) socially, the interpersonal relationships of the missionaries function better if they all think in the same patterns; (3) practically, the systems provides 10,000 pieces of ready-made materials to cover every religious need from the cradle to the grave. The missionary only has to get a piece translated into a local dialect.[736]

Southern Baptist missionaries also arrived just when their home denomination was expanding across America from the south to the west and north. The same expansion seems to have taken place here but in reverse direction: from the north to the south. They gave special attention to cities, although their churches can now be found in many Philippine barrios

---

735. "History of Dagupan Chinese Baptist Church," in *Christ Preeminent*, n.p.; Hao, "History," in *Christ Preeminent*, n.p. In the first source Cai JingXu 蔡經許 is written as Cai JingPing 蔡經評. It also distinguished the male from the female members by using "brother" and "sister" after each name, which is actually redundant since an additional surname indicates the bearer as a married woman.

736. See A. Leonard Tuggy and Ralph Toliver, *Seeing the Church in the Philippines* (Manila: OMF, 1972), 60–62.

and towns. Some of these cities are Baguio, Dagupan, Cabanatuan, Cavite, Cebu, Cagayan de Oro, Iligan, Pagadian, Cotabato, General Santos, and Davao.[737]

The same mission strategy seems to have been uniformly applied to both Filipino and Chinese churches. Although the Philippine Baptist Mission first initiated church planting among the Chinese communities in northern Luzon, Filipino churches very quickly became established. In Baguio, for example, work among Filipinos started in 1953 in the Aurora Hill district, growing out of Bible studies conducted in the homes of the missionaries.[738] In Dagupan, a few weeks after the Chinese church was established, there were six Filipinos who were converted and the church that subsequently formed was the Dagupan Baptist Church. This was the first Filipino Southern Baptist church organized in the Philippines.[739] However, work among Filipinos grew more rapidly and extensively than among the Chinese. In 1953, Rev and Mrs Edward Gordon (who later helped DCBC in 1955–1956) were the first missionaries assigned to work among Filipinos. They would continue their ministry until 1982, and as a result of their efforts many Filipino daughter churches were planted in the surrounding countryside.

e) Devolution of DCBC

The early development of DCBC and other Chinese Baptist churches established by the Philippine Mission of SBC shows that the devolution of these churches, especially in terms of self-support and self-government, took place within a decade or two of their founding.

(1) Financial Stability

In terms of financial stability, the Chinese Baptist churches became self-supporting earlier than the Filipino Baptist churches. When asked what the biggest difference was between Filipino and Chinese Baptist churches, Hao answered that it was financial stability – the Chinese Baptist churches were more financially stable than their Filipino counterparts. This is evident

---

737. See Pamplona, *Baptist History*, 341–365.

738. Mary Lucile Saunders, "Church in the Making," *The Commission: A Baptist World Journal* 17, no. 7 (Jul 1954), 208–209.

739. Pamplona, *Baptist History*, 345.

from the fact that in 1965, when DCBC dedicated its church building, it was the fourth Chinese Baptist church to have its own building.[740] (App. II, Fig. 5)

(2) The First Chinese Pastor

The missionaries were not in the forefront of shepherding the Chinese Baptist churches for long periods of time. Most of them stayed less than five years, and quickly turned the leadership mantle over to locally trained Chinese pastors such as Rev Pedro Hao. In the case of DCBC, the turnover was even much earlier, considering that they invited a Chinese brother of the Christian Gospel Center as early as 1950, two years before it was formally organized. Lim Tek Beng/Lin DeMing 林德明 was invited to help the ministry, but, according to Hao, he was from the Christian Gospel Center and his belief system was incompatible with that of the Baptists. Until today, the Christian Gospel Center trains their own workers but do not ordain them as pastors. Therefore, he did not stay long. It was in 1956 that Hao formally took the helm of leadership. However, prior to being ordained as their minister, he had already been helping the church while still undergoing training at PBTSBS.

(3) Locally Trained Pastors

That Hao could be trained at the same time as SBC missionaries were planting Chinese churches in Baguio and Dagupan was made possible because the SBC purposely established the Philippine Baptist Theological Seminary and Bible School, now called Philippine Baptist Theological Seminary (PBTS), in order to train Chinese pastors. In the 1951 session of the Philippine Mission, a Bible school committee was formed to plan for the opening of the seminary in the summer of 1952. The Committee met in Manila on 11 December 1951 and immediately took steps to have the seminary incorporated with the Philippine government. Dr Francis Pugh Lide (term of service 1951–1963) was elected as president. Crawley went to the USA to secure books and returned just a few days before school opened on 15 July 1952 (App. II, Fig. 6). Aside from Lide and Crawley, the

---

740. "History of Dagupan Chinese Baptist Church," in *Christ Preeminent*, n.p. Hao, interview.

other faculty members for the first year were the Mandarin instructor Yeh XinYu (assigned to teach Chinese Composition) and Dr Robert Fleming Ricketson. Eight students registered for classes, which were held at the facilities of the BCBC. There were only two books on the Old Testament before Crawley returned with more resources.[741] At the end of the first year the plan had shifted in focus. There were now two divisions, the Chinese and the English, and eight Filipinos were admitted, while the number of six Chinese students remained unchanged.[742]

Such seminary training gave momentum to the rapid turnover of leadership in the Chinese Baptist churches. Since their initial intention was to train Chinese pastors, the first group of six graduates were Chinese. Out of these six graduates, three became ministers of Chinese Baptist churches: Rev Pedro Hao served at DCBC from 1956 to 1968; Rev Samuel Chua became the fourth pastor (from 1960–1966) of the Manila Chinese Baptist Church 馬尼拉華僑浸信會 (MCBC), after American pastors Rev Clyde Jowers 趙凱雲牧師 (1952), Rev Ivan Larson 孫約翰牧師 (1952–1953),[743] and Rev Wesley Lawton (1953–1955); and Dim Lam Thian/Ren NanTian 任南添傳道, who served in MCBC from 1955–1957. After serving at DCBC, Hao became the fourth ordained minister of MCBC, serving from 1968 until his retirement in 1989, with an interim of three years serving at BCBC (1982–1985).[744] MCBC has presently become the central

741. *Minutes of the Philippine Mission of the Southern Baptist Convention 1951–52. Annual Session—Aug. 11–14, 1952 Manila. 1951–52 Executive Committee Minutes Constitution. Theme: Be Filled with the Spirit* ([Baguio City:] Baguio Printing & Publishing, [1952]), 23–28.

742. *Minutes of the Philippine Mission of the Southern Baptist Convention 1952–53. Annual Session – Aug 17–21, 1953 Baguio City. 1952–53 Executive Committee Minutes Constitution. Theme: Able through Christ* ([Baguio City:] Baguio Printing & Publishing, [1953]), 40. Hereafter, *Minutes 1952–53*.

743. The mission report of 1952 lists the arrival of Mr and Mrs Ivan Larson, while the 1952–1953 report states that the Lawtons arrived in August 1953. The Larsons left on emergency sick leave in March 1953, leaving the church without a pastor for five months. See Mary Lucile Saunders, "Mission to the Filipino People," in *Annual of the Southern Baptist Convention Nineteen Hundred and Fifty-three, Ninety-sixth Session One Hundred and Eighth Year, Houston, Texas May 6–10, 1953* (Nashville, TN: Executive Committee, Southern Baptist Convention, [1953]), 173–174 and Mary Lucile Saunders, "Report of the Manila Station," in *Minutes 1952–53*, 25–28.

744. "The History of Manila Chinese Baptist Church," TMs (photocopy) (Manila: Manila Chinese Baptist Church, n.d.), 1, 2.

headquarter overseeing pastoral placements and coordinating annual conferences attended by all the Chinese Baptist churches.

During the 1970s and 1980s many of the pastors serving in the Chinese Baptist churches were trained at the Biblical Seminary of the Philippines (BSOP)/Feilübin Shengjing Shenxueyuan 菲律濱聖經神學院, although a few still continue to be trained at PBTS. Some of the BSOP-trained workers include the current (fifth) pastor of MCBC, Rev Romeo Yu/Yang JianMing 楊建明 and his wife, Phebe Lim/Lin RenZhe 林仁哲 (started in 1990), Rosa Cong/Kang JianLi 康健麗 (Caloocan Christian Baptist Church), and Christine Ngo/Wu ShuangYue 伍霜月.[745] The reason why these Chinese Baptists chose BSOP as a training ground maybe due to the fact that soon after the first six Chinese graduated from PBTS, the seminary began focusing on training Filipino students. Today the PBTS student body is dominantly Filipino; the rest include Koreans, a few Chinese, and other nationalities.

The above events show that the SBC missionaries originally did not intend to stay long in the Philippines, using Baguio only as a transitory language training center. Upon seeing the needs of the Chinese in Baguio, they began their ministry among them and focused on establishing Chinese churches (see App. II, Fig. 7), unlike the Presbyterian Mission which considered Chinese work subsidiary. For several decades, these churches remained under the overall supervision of the Philippine Mission of the Foreign Mission Board of the SBC, which was responsible for assigning missionaries and funding their support. During the 1960s, mission records continued to report on each of these churches. At present, a cordial relationship with these churches still exists but these churches have devolved and are completely independent in terms of finance, governance by native leadership and propagation.

---

745. Now deceased, Christine was first trained in BSOP, then in PBTS and was a full-time worker of DCBC from 1985–1988. Biblical Seminary of the Philippines Academic Office records.

CHAPTER 4

Summary, Conclusion and Recommendations

A. Introduction

Six Chinese churches have been studied in the preceding chapter with special focus on their emergence and early history. These six churches, arranged chronologically according to their dates of founding, are the "Chinese Presbyterian Church in Iloilo/CPCI" (established in 1900), the St. Stephen's Chinese Mission/SSCM (1903), the Cebu Gospel Church/CGC (1916), the Chinese United Evangelical Church/CUEC (1929), the Davao Chinese Gospel Church/DCGC (1951), and the Dagupan Chinese Baptist Church/DCBC (1952). An assessment of each of the histories of these churches as they unfolded individually reveals common and converging as well as distinctive and diverging patterns. The first procedure in this analysis will discuss and compare the common and distinct patterns. Next, the unique features of each of these six churches, where discernable, will be examined. Finally, personal observations, recommendations, applicable correlations to present-day situation and a conclusion bringing together everything that has been studied will be made.

B. Emergence of the Six Chinese Churches

Before making any assessment of these six Protestant Chinese churches, a summary of the historical emergence of each of these churches, presented in detail in the previous section, will first be given.

1. "Chinese Presbyterian Church in Iloilo"

The first Sunday Service in Iloilo for English-speaking people, held on 8 April 1900, was attended by the Chinese, Malay, Spanish, *mestizo* Filipinos, English and American. The Presbyterian missionaries who were serving at that time were Dr and Mrs David Sutherland Hibbard, and Dr and Mrs Joseph Andrew Hall, all of whom arrived in Iloilo on 13 February 1900. The ministry among the Chinese began in the same month when Hall and Hibbard assisted a Chinese suffering from serious mental illness. Soon after, services were held in a shop on *Calle Real* where the medical assistance took place. Two Protestant Chinese who had been connected with the London Missionary Society in Xiamen assisted the missionaries as translators. Soon a group of eleven members, all of them from Xiamen, formed a Chinese congregation which the missionaries considered as "an important branch" of their work. However, mission records failed to indicate the name of this church. They do reveal that it was disbanded around 1928, shortly after the Presbyterians turned over their field in Panay to the Northern Baptists in 1925. The only recorded Chinese workers of this church were Tan Su Wong and Yung Kuanty (variant spelling Wung Kuanty).

2. St. Stephen's Chinese Mission

Formally initiated by Bishop Charles Henry Brent with Rev Hobart Earl Studley as full-time priest-in-charge, the congregation of SSCM first met on 4 October 1903 in a rented room on *Calle San Fernando* in San Nicholas, although the church now celebrates its anniversary on 8 November. Among those who attended the inaugural meeting were members of the Anglican, Congregationalist, Methodist, Presbyterian and English Wesleyan Communions. Studley conducted the meeting in *Hokkien*, as he had formerly been a missionary in Xiamen and spoke the dialect fluently. By 1905, SSCM was able to pay for the salary and rent of its priest. The Chinese communicants of the Methodist and Presbyterian Filipino churches were turned over to SSCM in 1907. Less than a decade after its founding, a two-story building was completed in 1912 for use as worship venue and pastoral residence. The St. Stephen's Chinese Girls' School was established in 1917 and maintained on the same grounds as the church without financial assistance from the Episcopalian mission.

Although self-sufficient a decade after its founding, it took several decades more before it could have a strong native leadership. Before WWII, pastoral staffing was provided by the PEC. Western missionaries were assigned to pulpit and supervisory duties whenever the Studleys went on furlough. The period from 1923–1933 was the most critical in terms of pastoral understaffing, and it was in 1929 when a majority of its members left to form two other Chinese congregations. It was only on 23 February 1941, that SSCM was formally inaugurated as a self-supporting parish with the first Chinese rector who served for twenty-five years. Since the PEC was overseeing the Chinese work, it was also its mission board that formed the Cantonese congregation – St. Peter's Chinese Mission – in 1932. Hence, SSCM was neither self-propagating nor self-governed (by Chinese pastors) for three decades after it emerged.

3. Cebu Gospel Church

A handful of Chinese communicant members in Cebu City, through the initiative of two Protestant Chinese, namely Chiu Tsong Kiau and Sih Eng Su, together with Presbyterian missionary Rev Dr George Williamson Dunlap and Rev Jorge Patalinghug, the Filipino pastor of the Matilda Bradford Memorial Church (Presbyterian), formed the CGC in 1916. Initially, CGC was a Chinese congregation of Bradford Church, and both the Chinese and the Filipino congregations recognized Patalinghug as their first pastor. Together with the American congregation, all three groups used the church building located at Jones Avenue, but worshiped at different hours. These three congregations were the fruits of the hard work done by missionaries Paul Frederick and Elizabeth Jansen who prepared the seedbed in Cebu City from 1902 to 1917. The founding of CGC in 1916 is comparatively late, considering that the Presbyterian mission work had begun in Cebu City more than a decade before.

However, less than a decade after its formation, the church was sustaining its own needs as well as assisting the Presbyterian Mission financially. Soon after it emerged, the church leaders and members began to evangelize their fellow Chinese in Cebu. This was done through regular visitation and special meetings where famous evangelists from Manila and China shared the gospel. They also got involved with the Presbyterian mission work among prisoners and lepers. Although its first pastor was a Filipino and the pulpit and Sunday School ministries were initially under the charge of this pastor and other Western missionaries, there were already elected elders and deacons within the first decade of its history. During the second decade, pastors from China were invited and by 1934, Chinese pastoral leadership was already stable. From that time onward, the oversight of the whole church was in the hands of the Chinese. However, nominal ties with the Presbyterian Mission and UCCP continued until 1966 when CGC formally withdrew from "organic relationship" with the UCCP.

4. Chinese United Evangelical Church

CUEC was formed in Manila on 14 July 1929 through the efforts of Chinese believers who mainly came from a Presbyterian background but were previously worshiping in SSCM. This church differed greatly from the other Chinese churches in and outside Manila because from its very beginning it was totally independent from any foreign mission influence on making decisions or control, whether in terms of finance, polity or liturgy. Furthermore, there was a special connection between CUEC and the Church of Christ in China, specifically the Jinjing Christian Church, the Anhai Christian Church and the Quanzhou Christian Church in South Fujian, because its founding members came from these churches. The pastor who ministered to all these churches, Rev Kho Seng Iam, was also directly connected with the founding of CUEC. Three of his daughters were among those who initiated the separation from SSCM and formation of CUEC. Soon after it emerged, elders and deacons were elected and a Chinese pastor from Xiamen was invited. It was also self-propagating in that, following the same pattern as the CCC, evangelistic meetings were conducted in cooperation with the Bethel Mission. Through the efforts of its Mission Board and the Evangelistic Band, CUEC established another congregation seven years after its emergence and many more in succeeding decades.

5. Davao Chinese Gospel Church

Two sisters – Bona and Valeria Lim – who were converted while studying in Gulangyu, Xiamen, began holding Sunday School classes in their home in Davao around 1936–1940. WWII did not disrupt this work, and classes were held in various homes of the believers. When Bona went to

Zamboanga in 1948 to study for the ministry, her sister remained to oversee the work. During this time, Rev Ernest Francis Gulbranson, a Christian and Missionary Alliance missionary, had returned to Davao, after being confined in a Japanese concentration camp in Manila. He began to assist by preaching to the Chinese and Filipinos who worshiped in a small chapel built by the Protestant Chinese. The number of Chinese believers increased when Job Chen, David Uyboco and his family and Consul and Mrs Mih Sek Long joined the small group. Soon they decided to hold their own worship service, with Consul Mih as preacher. In 1949, CMA missionaries Rev and Mrs Charles Notson, Rev and Mrs Frederick Ruhl and Ms Agnes Birrel assisted the Chinese congregation. Notson became the first resident pastor of the DCGC when it was formally established in June 1951. Two years later, Rev Wesley K. Shao became the first Chinese pastor and the church became self-governing. Five years later, DCGC was able to purchase land and construct not only a church building but a school as well. The church also engaged in missionary endeavors locally as well as supported a Chinese missionary in Canada.

6. Dagupan Chinese Baptist Church

Missionaries from the Southern Baptist Convention, displaced by the Communist take-over of China, went to Baguio to undergo Chinese language training, hoping to return to China when its doors reopened. During this time, they began work among the Chinese in Baguio and its vicinity. As a result the Baguio Chinese Baptist Church was formed in 1950, while at the same time the groundwork was being done in Dagupan City. A convert and BCBC-charter-member, Pedro Hao, and Chua Ke Kan, a Protestant Chinese who transferred to Dagupan from CUEC, assisted the missionaries and formed DCBC, which was formally organized on 19 February 1952. The early members of DCBC first met at the residence of Chua Ke Khan, then moved to a rented house on Rivera Street in 1964. Using their own resources, the members of DCBC built a church edifice in 1965, just over a decade after its emergence. In the beginning, the SBC missionaries – Bill Solesbee (1952), Winston Crawley (1953), Wesley Lawton (1954), James Foster, and Edward Gordon (1955) – acted as interim pastors of DCBC. In 1956, Pedro Hao became the first ordained Chinese minister of this church.

Table 2 gives an overview of what has been discussed regarding these six
Protestant Chinese churches. The mission agencies closely connected with
the emergence and early development of these six churches, as well as during the period of UCCP relationship with CGC and CUEC, are listed in
alphabetical order. The names of the missionaries who worked with or were
related to these Chinese churches are given in the last column.

**Table 2: Agencies and Missionaries Engaged in Chinese Mission Work in the
Philippines (1900–1960s)**

Church and Mission Agency	Chinese Church	Missionaries Involved with the Chinese Churches
Board of Foreign Missions of the Presbyterian Church in the United States of America (BFM-PCUSA)	Cebu Gospel Church	Paul Frederick and Elizabeth White Jansen; George Williamson and Devee Taylor Dunlap 蘭納牧師, John Wallace and Antonia Forni Dunlop, Olive Rohrbaugh, Charles Edward and Theresa Kalb Rath, Judson Leolin and Minnie Kemp Underwood
	"Chinese Presbyterian Church in Iloilo"	Joseph Andrew Hall 浩醫生, David Sutherland Hibbard
	Chinese United Evangelical Church	George William Wright 劉哲博士
Christian and Missionary Alliance Foreign Mission Board (CMAFMB)	Davao Chinese Gospel Church	Ernest Francis Gulbranson 嘉明遜牧師, Charles Eldred Notson 納慈恩牧師 and his wife Ruth
Protestant Episcopal Church Board of Foreign and Domestic Missions (PrECBFDM)	St. Stephen's Chinese Mission	Hobart Earl and Edith Holbrow Studley 施和力牧師師母, supervised by Charles Henry Brent

Reformed Church in America Board of World Mission (RCABWM)	Cebu Gospel Church	John Ellis Bandt 萬約翰牧師 (1960s)
	CUEC/United Evangelical Church of the Philippines	Joseph R. and Marion Boot Esther 伊樹德牧師師母, Tena Holkeboer 福懿慕姑娘 (1950s)
Southern Baptist Convention Foreign Mission Board (SBCFMB)	Dagupan Chinese Baptist Church	James Winston Crawley 郭文生 牧師, Margaret Collins 柯慕德教 士, Fern Harrington Miles 韓慕蘭 教士, Max and Ann Pettit 培馬可 牧師, Clyde and Alcie May Jowers 趙凱雲牧師, Willie Alsberry (Bill) and Ella Ruth Solesbee 沙衛仁牧 師

Note: The RCA missionaries became associated with CGC and CUEC during the 1950s to the 1960s and were not technically involved in the emerging years, but since the ministries of the Bandts, the Esthers and Holkeboer were discussed in the preceding chapter, their names are included in this table. The Chinese names and titles are written as found in the Chinese sources. English titles are omitted for reason of space.

C. Discerning the Patterns of Emergence

The summary statements in the preceding section regarding the emergence and early development of each of the six Protestant Chinese churches will now facilitate the assessment of both discernable common and distinct patterns. There are at least eight common patterns that can be discerned when one observes the histories of these six churches. These patterns neither apply to *all* of the churches at *all* points nor strictly within the emerging period, but can be discerned as generally true to majority of the churches being studied. The first pattern is that majority of the four mission organizations did not originally intend to work among the Chinese. Second, all six churches were related to Protestant missions in one way or another. A third pattern that can be discerned is the method used by the early founders or workers to draw unbelievers into the church. Another common thread is that there already were Protestant Chinese in these five cities, that they came in contact with the missionaries, and that they later became core members or leaders of these churches. The fifth pattern is the generally long service of missionaries who were involved in Chinese work. The sixth pattern is the lack of skill, on the part of the missionaries, to speak the *Hokkien* dialect. The seventh pattern that one notices is the presence of willing and capable Chinese leaders and pastors from the inception and during the early years of these churches. Lastly, most of these churches devolved rapidly, that is, they became self-perpetuating, self-governing, and self-supporting churches within or slightly over a decade after they emerged.

1. Original Intention

Except for the Episcopalian mission, the rest of the mission organizations did not actually have any plan or intention of initiating work among the Chinese before or right at the moment of contact. In the case of the Presbyterians, there was explicit awareness and concern for the salvation of the Chinese, but the history of the emergence of CPCI, CGC and CUEC gives the following impressions about their intention. For CPCI, the Presbyterian mission's first concern, explicitly recorded in their reports, was really directed toward the Filipinos. Their involvement with the Chinese resulted more from happenstance than from intentional search. Being unprepared linguistically in the *Hokkien* dialect, the missionaries had to rely heavily on Chinese translators or on pastors from China, and yet during the nineteenth century, language study was the standard and priority procedure to take before or right after entering a mission field.

When CGC emerged sixteen years after CPCI, there is little evidence that the Presbyterians were working among the Chinese in Cebu during this same amount of time, but there is ample evidence that they were concentrating on evangelizing the Filipinos of the Visayan region. It was only in 1920 that the missionaries categorically expressed that the Chinese were among the three groups that were part of their mission work.

Lastly, when CUEC approached the United Evangelical Church of the Philippine Islands (UECPI, later United Church of Christ in the Philippines), specifically Presbyterian missionary Rev Dr George Wright, to consider accepting the new congregation as a member of the union body of Protestant Filipino churches, Wright was very cautious in handling the matter. Hence, no formal relationship developed between the UECPI and CUEC, but Wright frequently preached at CUEC.

In the case of the Christian and Missionary Alliance, work among the Chinese started fifty years after CMA missionaries entered the Mindanao field. Despite the initial interest in the Chinese at the beginning of the ministry of Elizabeth White (who later became a Presbyterian missionary as wife of Paul Frederick Jansen) around 1900, by 1948, the Foreign Department of CMA still did not consider this ministry a high priority and no funds were available to support this work. Rev Ernest Francis Gulbranson was assigned to assist part-time as preacher. Rev Charles Eldred Notson himself wrote that the CMA missionaries were preoccupied with the Filipino work. Eventually in 1950, he and his wife were assigned to Davao City and given supervision over the Chinese work. However, their relocation to the Philippines from Gansu, China, was due to its mission doors closing in 1949. Were it not for the availability of Gulbranson and Notson, it is quite possible that the CMA would not have gotten involved with the ministry to the Chinese.

Another group affected by China's regime change was the Southern Baptist Convention. It has been clearly shown that initially they considered language training in Baguio as a temporary situation and the missionaries fully intended to return to China. This group, however, adjusted very quickly to the reality of their circumstances and took up the responsibility of evangelizing the Chinese, starting from the north of Luzon and eventually reaching Mindanao. Nevertheless, based on their reports for the 1950s, it didn't take many years before majority of their missionaries (including Max Pettit and Fern Harrington) transferred to Taiwan, leaving only a small work force in the Philippines.

2. Mission-Established or Mission-Assisted?

By mission-established I mean that mission agencies through their missionaries were instrumental in laying the groundwork and/or in the formation of the Chinese congregations. This covers the emerging stage of a church but can overlap with the stage when a church becomes formally organized. Mission-assisted, on the other hand, signifies that missionaries had nothing to do with the emergence or formal organization of the church. All of these six churches were either established or assisted by missionaries belonging to the following mission boards, using their more established names: Christian and Missionary Alliance Foreign Mission Board

(CMAFMB), Board of Foreign Missions of the Presbyterian Church in the United States of America (BFM-PCUSA), Protestant Episcopal Church Board of Foreign and Domestic Missions (PrECBFDM), Reformed Church in America Board of World Mission (RCABWM), and Southern Baptist Convention Foreign Mission Board (SBCFMB).

These mission organizations were involved with the six churches as follows: CPCI, CGC and CUEC were related to the BFM-PCUSA and during the 1950s and 1960s, to the RCABWM. The first two churches were established by the BFM-PCUSA, with Presbyterian missionaries closely overseeing the work. Both CPCI and CGC were initially part of a much larger mission circuit in and near the cities of Iloilo and Cebu. Missionaries conducted and preached during the worship services, despite their handicap in Mandarin or *Hokkien*. In the beginning, when neither Chinese nor Filipinos were able to understand the English language, the *lingua franca* was Spanish and messages had to be translated. The Chinese work was part of the reports submitted to the annual mission meetings. In addition to Presbyterian missionaries, RCA missionaries working in tandem with the UCCP assisted CGC from the 1950s to the 1970s. When Protestant Chinese who had separated from the SSCM established CUEC, Rev George Wright of the BFM-PCUSA assisted through preaching and in an advisory role.

The PrECBFDM established the St. Stephen's Chinese Mission. Its mission targets were not Roman Catholic Filipinos, but non-Christian Chinese, tribal peoples, and Muslims. The full-time overseer of the SSCM was Hobart Studley who faithfully did his task until he retired and returned to the United States. He and his wife Edith were directly and deeply involved with the Chinese work – Hobart in a pastoral capacity as well as an administrator of the church school, and Edith as principal and teacher in this school throughout her tenure of service.

Similarly, SBC missionaries established the Dagupan Chinese Baptist Church. Since they were able to preach in Mandarin, the missionaries attracted many Chinese hearers and soon began to form Chinese congregations in Baguio and in Dagupan. Eventually, they gave full attention to building up these congregations into full-fledged Chinese churches;

at the same time, they began to establish Filipino churches. Missionaries were assigned responsibilities for preaching and teaching Sunday School. However, unlike the Presbyterians, the SBC quickly established a seminary to train Chinese pastors. One of the earliest to be trained was Pedro Hao; he became an invaluable helper to the missionaries as well as to all the Chinese Baptist churches in Luzon (Baguio, Dagupan, and Manila). Four churches – CPCI, SSCM, CGC, and DCBC – can be considered mission-established.

The case of Davao Chinese Gospel Church is special because it can be considered a mission-assisted church, and the groundwork was laid by Protestant Chinese before two CMA missionaries (Gulbranson and Notson) arrived in Davao. Bona and Valeria Lim initiated the work by conducting Sunday School classes. During this period the adult believers worshiped with the Filipinos and Gulbranson assisted by preaching. Eventually, when the Notsons came, CMA involvement entered a deeper level and the Notsons became fully occupied with the various activities of DCGC. It can be considered as mission-assisted only in the sense that the missionaries helped to organize the church and its ministries.

Of these six churches only one can be said to be truly indigenous, that is, it was an exception to the general trend. CUEC was formed in 1929 solely through the efforts of Protestant Chinese from China who were then living in the Philippines. Although the founding members approached Rev George Wright when the church was being formed, he declined to become involved administratively, for fear of causing any misunderstanding with SSCM. The minister who was closely connected with the failed move in 1924 to form a Presbyterian-oriented Chinese church was Rev Kho Seng Iam of the Church of the Golden Well in Quanzhou. He was the one who wrote the "Declaration of the Founding of the Chinese Church of Christ Sojourning in the Philippines," giving eight reasons for its coming into existence. Recognizably, the Church of Christ in China (CCC), specifically in the Quanzhou district, did not give rise to the new church in Manila, yet Kho Seng Iam, his daughters, and members of his church or sister churches (such as the church in Anhai), were part of CUEC's pre-emergence and emergence stages. Not only was this church identified with the Church of

Christ in China through its name, the polity, liturgy and doctrinal beliefs of CUEC were clearly patterned after the South Fujian churches of CCC.

3. Common Methodology

The missionaries employed similar methods in reaching and evangelizing the Chinese in these urban communities. The first thing they did was to visit the Chinese, whether unbelievers or Protestant Chinese, who had come to the cities to set up their businesses or who were employees of Chinese business owners. Mostly, these Chinese were found in their shops or workplaces, as in the case of Pedro Hao and the Iloilo Protestants.

Whenever missionaries approached and made personal contacts with the Chinese immigrants or when the early Protestant Chinese visited their fellow countrymen, the process of evangelism was initiated. After frequent visits the missionaries became more acquainted with these contacts, and friendly relations were established. The contacts of the Protestant Chinese, on the other hand, included total strangers as well as their friends and colleagues. In the first case, if the Protestant Chinese were renowned men or women, as in the case of CGC members, the friendship process and the building of trust were much easier. Many of the early members of CGC were teachers of a well-known Chinese school. Hence, their reputation had preceded and even influenced their evangelistic outreach. One of the founding leaders of CGC was the wife of a prominent businessman in Cebu City. It was through her efforts and personal impact that numerous non-believers were drawn into the church.

When worship services or other meetings began, these contacts were invited to attend. As Pedro Hao testified, he and his friend were invited by the visiting missionaries, and they decided to attend because they were drawn to these foreigners who could speak Mandarin so fluently. In such areas as Manila and Davao, there were already Protestant Chinese wishing and waiting for the opportunity to gather together as a Chinese congregation, hence all the missionaries had to do was to arrange the venue and schedule, and to provide the speaker and form of worship. No doubt their denominational background was another factor that attracted these early contacts to attend the services. In Iloilo, for example, the background of the Protestant Chinese was either Presbyterian or Congregational; therefore, the Presbyterian worship style was very suitable to their needs.

There were also cases when the early contacts came from one denominational background but ended up becoming members of a church belonging to a different denomination. The formation of the SSCM is a case in point. The early contacts had been Presbyterians, Congregationalists, Methodists, and even a few Roman Catholics, but eventually they all became part of the Episcopalian church. In Dagupan, one of the early contacts was originally from CUEC, a Presbyterian church. But when he had to remain in Dagupan after burying his brother and taking over his business, he became a key person in the SBC Chinese ministry. Eventually, he and his family became the core members of DCBC.

The only exception to this common pattern is again the case of CUEC. The method, since there was indication of intention in the 1924 "Declaration," was one of church division and not of conversion or transplantation. The core members of this church, as it emerged in 1929, had already belonged to the Episcopalian Chinese church – SSCM. Therefore, as a splinter church, the members were already pre-existent. It can be said that the emergence of CUEC was initiated by a group of Christians rather than by either missionaries or pastors. The members were there, but a full-time minister was lacking, which is why, in the early years, the founding leaders were preoccupied with the search for a pastor from China. The circumstances surrounding the formation of this church manifestly was not very pleasant, since it involved church division and brought with it unfortunate consequences, including ill-feelings with the rest of the SSCM members and with the priest-in-charge, Hobart Studley. After the early members of CUEC had formed into a new congregation, they employed the usual manner of visitation-invitation-following up.

4. From Contacts to Core Members

After befriending their Chinese contacts, the missionaries or Protestant Chinese invited them to attend either Sunday worship services or other meetings. Once a group became regular in attending the worship services, it formed a congregation or a church. After some time had passed, these early contacts became the core members of the churches. Although there was always the possibility that, as sojourners, the church members had to go back to China (as in the Iloilo case) or move to another place (as in the case of the CGC teachers), nevertheless, a core group remained and church membership steadily increased over the years. There were also instances when some communicants lapsed into Roman Catholicism or married Roman Catholics and altogether stopped attending services in the Protestant churches. Such cases, however, were rare and did not constitute a significant loss to the latter churches. Once a core group was formed, they then tried to secure pastors for these local congregations while, during the interim, missionaries served as pastors, advisory pastors or regular preachers. Key leaders soon emerged from among these core members. This phenomenon has been repeated throughout the history of the universal church, and these six Chinese churches were no exceptions.

5. Long Terms of Service

Another phenomenon is that the missionaries who worked among the Chinese, with only a few exceptions, rendered long years of service to the Chinese congregations that they established. The missionaries who served the longest among the Chinese congregations were: Hobart and Edith Studley 施和力牧師師母 (SSCM, 1903–1931), George Dunlap 蘭納牧師 (CGC, 1916–1935), John Dunlop [賴約翰牧師] (CGC, 1918–1939). Another missionary couple, Judson and Minnie Underwood, served only seven years in Cebu, from 1922–1929, but compared to Presbyterian missionaries in other fields, this is considered a long tenure.[1] Fern Harrington 韓慕蘭教士 was in the Philippines from 1941–1962, while her connection with DCBC lasted twelve years (1950–1962). Margaret Collins 柯慕德教士 became involved with DCBC a year after she arrived in the Philippines in 1949, her service lasting from 1950 to 1963.[2]

---

1. Cf. the tenures of Rev and Mrs William J. Smith (Cebu, 1911–1913), Rev and Mrs J. Leon Hooper (Dumaguete, 1927–1931). See Rodgers, *Forty Years*, 201–204.

2. See Baker James Cauthen, *Foreign Missionaries: Southern Baptist Convention, 1845–1969 – A Supplement to Advance: A History of Southern Baptist Foreign Missions* (N.p.: n.p., 1970).

The notable exceptions are: Gulbranson and Notson in DCGC (although Notson's re-assignment was not of his choice) and the SBC missionaries (Max Pettit, Bill Solesbee, Winston Crawley, Wesley Lawton, James Foster and Edward Gordon) in DCBC, who served less than five years. Another missionary who might fit into this category was Paul Frederick Jansen. Although he worked in Cebu for fifteen years (1902–1917), the Chinese congregation was formed only during the last few years of his service in Cebu City. Even if clear records are lacking, it would seem that the Presbyterian missionaries who served in Iloilo were also not involved with the Chinese congregation for long periods of time. Hall may have been a key person who initiated the Chinese work, but being a full-time physician and hospital administrator during his stay in Iloilo, it is doubtful that he devoted a major portion of his time to this ministry.

In contrast, there were many Chinese ministers with decades of service: Ben Ga Pay/Bai MingYa 白萌芽牧師 of SSCM (1907-1923), Tiuⁿ Toan Tsong/Zhang DuanZhuang 張端莊傳道 of CGC (1934–1941), Niu Se Ko/Leung Sai Ko 梁細羔牧師 of CGC (1936–1964), George S. C. Chua/Tsai XinZhang 蔡信彰牧師 of CUEC (1934–1962), Silas Wong/ Huang YuanSu 黃源素牧師 of CUEC (1938–1962), Pedro Hao/Hou JunNan 侯均南牧師 of DCBC (1956–1968), and Wesley Kho Shao/Shao QingZhang 邵慶彰牧師 of DCGC (1953–1963/64). The devotion and faithful labor of these pioneer pastors were extremely influential in building up the churches. In the case of Pay, Zhang, Leung, Hao, and Shao, their long term of service was also a fitting complement to the contribution of the Western missionaries who were their contemporary coworkers.

6. Lack of Language Training
In South Fujian, China, the pioneer mission groups that planted the seed of the gospel were the RCA, the EPM and the LMS. Upon reaching Xiamen, the missionaries who served long terms proficiently learned the *Hokkien* dialect and were very successful in their evangelistic, educational, and medical endeavors. Not long after, churches were established which mostly devolved rapidly into independent units. These became financially stable, native clergymen were trained, and the churches multiplied, resulting in

quantitative growth.[3] Undoubtedly, one of the primary factors spurring this growth was the ability of the missionaries to speak the local dialect.

In the Philippines, however, all of the missionaries listed in table 2, except for Hobart Studley and Joseph Esther who had come from South China and had already learned the *Hokkien* dialect there, did not have any training in speaking the dialect. Some missionaries could speak Spanish, so it became the medium of communication in preaching and in conversation during the initial years of Chinese mission work. English, of course, later became the popular medium. The native Chinese needed to translate either languages during worship and other services. Educated Protestant Chinese who were present in Cebu, Iloilo, Manila, Davao and Dagupan translated the sermons of the missionaries from Spanish or English to *Hokkien*, or, as in the case of the Baptists, from English to Mandarin. It is no surprise then that, under the leadership of Studley for more than thirty years, SSCM grew steadily during the first decades of its establishment, because he was fluent in *Hokkien*. There were, however, other factors of church growth beside language proficiency. During the 1950s, missionaries who were forced to leave China were reassigned to the Philippines. Such workers, among them the SBC and the RCA missionaries, were able to speak either Mandarin or *Hokkien*. This greatly facilitated their work among the Chinese.

The question, however, is this: why did the Presbyterian missionaries, especially the long-staying ones, not take time to learn the *Hokkien* dialect as their colleagues did in China? Again, the answer reverts to the issue of who were the main targets for mission. Except for Studley, Notson, Harrington, and Collins, these missionaries were not working full time among the Chinese. Their duties required them to minister foremost to the Filipinos, as Filipino churches were sprouting up in Luzon, the Visayas, and Mindanao. This circumstance leads to another reason: because of the need to oversee so many churches, they did not have time to learn the dialect. A third reason would be, as James Rodgers expressly stated, it was ideal and seemingly easy to look for pastors serving in

---

3. See De Jong, *Reformed Church in China*, 91–117.

Fujian and invite them to come to the Philippines. This proved too idealistic and quite unattainable, however, as the cases of CGC and CUEC show. Although a pastor from Xiamen went to CGC, he stayed only one year. CUEC did not have a Chinese pastor for over five years after its emergence.

And yet, it is also a fact that the minister who stayed the longest (Leung Sai Ko) never preached in *Hokkien*. Does this mean that it was not necessary for a Chinese pastor to be able to speak the *Hokkien* dialect? Language may not necessarily be the key factor. Leung loved CGC, and many of the older generation of CGC members admired and loved him as well. He was able to converse with his church members in Mandarin and in broken *Hokkien*. For these members, Mandarin was a "second" language compared to English, which would have been a "foreign" language. Hence, it did not matter whether the medium of communication was Mandarin or *Hokkien*. As long as the missionaries knew one or the other, he or she was at a vantage point. But if they could only speak in English, there would be a certain level of distance with church members who could not speak English well.

7. Chinese Leadership

All of the six churches had capable, dedicated and consecrated leaders rendering invaluable service during the time of the emergence and early development period. Table 3 lists the early leaders and pastors of the six churches under study. The Chinese leaders served as preachers, translators, elders, deacons, and Sunday School teachers, some before the churches emerged and others not long afterward. Many of them served for several decades. Aside from these leaders, most of the churches were able to secure pastors who were either trained in the Philippines (Pr. Bona Lim, Rev Pedro Hao), in China (the reverends Sih Eng Kiat, Tiu^n Toan Tsong, Leung Sai Ko, George S. C. Chua, Silas Wong, Tan Su Wong, Wung or Yung Kuanty) or in the United States (Rev Wesley Kho Shao). Most of these pastors rendered long years of service and led the churches toward steady growth and stability.

Table 3: Leaders and Workers of the Six Protestant Chinese Churches

Chinese Churches	Pioneer Leaders	Early/Long-Term Chinese Workers
"Chinese Presbyterian Church in Iloilo"	Unknown	Tan Su Wong, Wung or Yung Kuanty (Chinese names unknown)
St. Stephen's Chinese Mission 菲律賓華僑聖公會司提芬堂	Yang NaiFu 楊迺甫牧師, Wang YiMa 王翼麻, Luo HuoQing 羅火慶, Hong DunYou 洪敦友, Li YongAn 李永安[a]	Rev Mr Ben Ga Pay 白明芽牧師
Cebu Gospel Church 宿務基督教會	Chiu Tsong Kiau 周宗橋, David Eng Tiong Uyboco 黃永長, Go Pang Kong 吳邦光, Mrs Cang Ng Chhai Toan 江黃彩段夫人, Sih Eng Su 薛永黍, Go Hong Tso 吳鴻助, Ng Jin Seng 黃仁聖, Mrs Uy Cang Chui Siok 黃江水淑	Rev Sih Eng Kiat 施應吉牧師, Pastor Tiuⁿ Toan Tsong 張端莊傳道, Rev Leung Sai Ko 梁細羔牧師, Rev Liang ShenWei 梁慎微
Chinese United Evangelical Church 旅菲中華基督教會	Keng Jin Kiat 龔人傑, Sio Tsong Kheng 蕭宗卿, Ting Keng Pho 丁景波, Kho Goat Hoa 許月華, Kho Ju Soat 許逾雪	Rev George S. C. Chua 蔡信彰牧師, Rev Silas Wong 黃源素牧師
Davao Chinese Gospel Church 納卯華僑基督教會	Valeria Lim Young 楊林冽碧, David Eng Tiong Uyboco 黃永長, Job Chen 陳約伯, Consul Mih Sek Long 宓錫寵領事	Pastor Bona Lim 林蓮珠傳道, Rev Wesley Kho Shao 邵慶彰牧師
Dagupan Chinese Baptist Church 拉古扳華僑浸信會	Chua Ke Khan 蔡繼干, Samuel Chua 蔡啟明	Rev Pedro Hao 侯均南牧師

Sources: MacGillivray, ed., *The China Mission Year Book*, 579–580; Rodgers, *Twenty Years of Presbyterian Work*, 55; St. Stephen's Golden Jubilee, 29–30; *Cebu Gospel Church Golden Jubilee Souvenir*; DCBC's *Christ Preeminent 50th Anniversary* 主居首位; *DEC's Fifty Years 1951–2001 Anniversary Souvenir; and the Special Commemorative Issue of the Founding of the Chinese Evangelical Church of Manila*.

a. These five names were listed as departed pioneer leaders of SSP in the St. Stephen's Golden Jubilee. Yang NaiFu was an ordained minister from Pechuia Chapel in South Fujian, but in Manila, he served as the fourth principal of the Anglo-Chinese School 中西學校. He was also well known for operating the Yang Juan Drugstore 楊眷西藥房.

8. Rapid Devolution

Jonathan Chao pointed out in his book that in China, the chronological pattern for the missionary-established churches was self-support (S), self-government (G), and then, self-propagation (P) (i.e. S → G → P), while the pattern for the churches established by the Protestant Chinese was self-propagation by the leaders and church members, then self-government, and then self-support, with the calling of a pastor (i.e. P → G → S).[4] Missionaries began their work with the purchase of buildings as bases for educational work and medical work as means to evangelism, using funds that came from their mission boards or the churches from which they originated. In the Philippines, the same pattern was evident in Cebu City when the Presbyterians purchased a piece of land, after which they built mission residences and the Bradford Church, where CGC emerged. Self-support became the goal as congregations began to form.

It seems that the second pattern (P → G → S) that was evident within the Chinese churches in China was replicated to a certain extent in the Philippines. SSCM, CUEC, and DCBC used rented halls as venues for worship, and it took many years, even decades, before these churches built edifices on lots that they owned. These churches attained self-propagation before reaching a sustainable level of self-rule, then they grew financially strong enough to purchase land and build church buildings.

All of the six churches experienced devolution in one way or another, some sooner and others at a later time. With regard to self-propagation, there is enough evidence to show that the pioneer members of these churches (with the exception again of CPCI) were fervent in evangelism and in outreach work. Today, the United Evangelical Church of the Philippines is most widely known for its Evangelistic Band that propagated many satellite churches all over the Philippine archipelago.

When it comes to self-government, three of these churches (DCGC, SSCM and CUEC) reached enough competency to administer their own affairs within a decade of their emergence. The five pioneer leaders of SSCM listed in table 3 became board members of the vestry, but it reached the status of a parish church only in 1941. CUEC elected six deacons and four elders on 1 September 1929, barely two months after its emergence.

---

4. Jonathan Chao, "Chinese Indigenous Church," 65–89, n. 21, 22.

284
A Study on the Emergence and Early Development of
Selected Protestant Chinese Churches in the Philippines

DCGC elected three elders and three deacons soon after being established. Although DCBC did not practice a system of rule by elders and deacons, Pedro Hao was ordained and installed just four years after the church was officially organized.

The devolution of CGC seems relatively slower. CGC was still under the oversight of the Presbyterian missionaries and did not have a structured council of elders and deacons in place until 1934 (almost twenty years after it emerged). However, the CGC *Golden Jubilee Souvenir* records that there were some deacons and elders, whose main duties were to translate during worship services and to visit members and non-Christians, during the time of Judson Underwood (1923–1925), only two years after the church was formally organized in 1921.

In terms of self-support, five of the six churches quickly reached the financial capability to support their own needs. The "Chinese Presbyterian Church in Iloilo" may have been an exception, since the Presbyterian mission records continually stated that CPCI was in need of financial assistance from the Mission. The Chinese church could hardly pay for the theological training and salary of their pastor, and in 1915 the members were finding it hard to meet expenses.[5] This is not to say that the rest of the churches quickly became wealthy. Reading the testimonies or anniversary souvenirs of these five churches, one easily notes that they were struggling financially in the first decade of their history. But Chinese believers were very frugal with their own needs and generous when it came to church needs. In fact, when the CCC and China as a whole was facing economic crisis during the Sino-Japanese War, Protestant Chinese in the Philippines kept sending monetary contributions into China.[6] Hence, until this day, they are still known for giving more than enough to meet the financial needs of their churches, as well as being generous donors to Christian causes worldwide.

---

5. See MacGillivray, ed., *China Mission Year Book*, 579–580.

6. "The Chinese Christians have developed a splendid program which includes zealous evangelistic work and practical assistance for their less fortunate fellow-countrymen. They have not only cared for their own expenses, but have met the needs of refugees from China. In addition to all of this they have made sacrificial gifts to aid the sufferers from war, flood, famine, and disease in the homeland." These words of praise were recorded in *The One Hundred and Second Annual Report of the Board of Foreign Missions of the Presbyterian Church in the United States of America Presented to the General Assembly, May, 1939* (New Y:ork Presbyterian Building, 1939), 87.

D. Unique Features

In surveying the emergence and early development of the six Chinese churches, three unique features stand out. The first has to do with the growth of CUEC as an indigenous church that bears the stamp of influence from the CCC, and, in particular, from the satellite churches that Kho Seng Iam was overseeing. It is also related to the fervor created by the John Sung evangelistic meetings and the spirit of revival pervading during the 1930s. The second feature concerns the overseas mission effort of DCGC. The third feature looks at an aspect of devolution within the SBC-established Chinese churches that concerns the issue of leadership training.

1. Growth of an Indigenous Church

As previously discussed, CUEC was the only true indigenous church established by a group of Protestant Chinese in Manila. Among the six churches, and even when compared to later churches that emerged, CUEC is uniquely unsurpassed in that it is the only church to have produced thirty-two satellite churches in the Philippines as of 2007. This number refers only to the existing satellite churches, for there were other gospel stations, such as the Laoag Gospel Station, which did not develop into churches or were later discontinued.[7] No other Protestant Chinese church in the Philippines comes close to this record.[8] In relation to self-propagation, the creation of the Evangelistic Band greatly enhanced the outreach program of CUEC. Significantly, it was Kho Goat Hua, daughter of Kho Seng Iam, who headed the band for many decades. Since its inception in 1936, teams sent by this band had gone as far north as Tuguegarao and as far south as Jolo, Sulu.[9] The energetic fervor that resulted from John Sung's campaigns

---

7. For a detailed history of the ministry of the Evangelistic Band, see Phoebe K. Chua, "History of the Evangelistic Band," in *Evangelistic Band*, written in English (n.p.) and Chinese (4–10). For an analysis of its methods, see Joseph Too Shao, "A Channel of Blessings in God's Hands: Chinese Protestant Churches in the Philippines," in *Chapters in Philippine Church History*, ed. Anne Catherine Laninga Kwantes (Mandaluyong City: OMF, 2001), 413–428.

8. The Local Church or Little Flock groups have many branches nationwide but there is no official record available, hence this statement pertains only to the rest of the Philippine Protestant Chinese churches.

9. See further, Joseph Young, "Brief Survey," 232–233 (pages in Chinese style).

and the revival ministry of Betty Hu and Alice Lan propelled the growth of CUEC satellite churches for several decades.

In contrast, mission-established churches such as SSCM, DCBC, and CGC have barely produced any satellite churches. Today, SSP has a mission outreach in Marikina City, but its growth has been stagnant. Although CGC assisted many churches in the Visayas and Mindanao throughout the decades, it has produced only one branch church in Surigao City. The Surigao Gospel Church/Shuliyao Jidu Jiaohui 樹里爻基督教會 was established in 1968, more than fifty years after the emergence of CGC, and its membership remains small.[10]

Can an implication be drawn that being an indigenous church and having the *Minnan* sector of the Church of Christ in China as model, as well as a close relationship with the Bethel Mission in Shanghai, CUEC/UECP was in a better position to conduct a systematic and productive outreach program than the mission-established churches? Such churches would logically be in a better position to multiply since there were missionaries around to lead and stimulate the work, but it turned out differently. It is also significant that from the 1950s until the 1970s, the CUEC Evangelistic Band was capably assisted by Rev Joseph Esther and Ms Tena Holkeboer, former RCA missionaries in China who were fluent in *Hokkien*, but the mission impetus came mainly from the Protestant Chinese themselves.

2. DCGC and Mission Work

DCGC has gained the reputation of being the first Protestant Chinese church in the Philippines to engage in pioneering overseas missions. Rev Augusto Chao was sent from Hong Kong to be the pastor of an Alliance church in Canada. A group of Protestant Chinese had already formed a fellowship in this place in 1955, but this small congregation was unable to support a pastor who had six dependents. DCGC set aside the whole year collection of its Mission Fund and used it to support Chao and his family for a year. He arrived in Regina on 2 June 1960 and became the first

---

10. Siao Muy Tie/Siao MeiZhi 蕭梅治, "Suwu Jidu Jiaohui Bashi Nianlai Huihu 宿務基督教會八十年來回溯 (Reminiscing the past eighty years of Cebu Gospel Church)," in *Cebu Gospel Church Eightieth Anniversary Special Edition (Suwu Jidu Jiaohui Bashi Zhounian Zuanxi Qingdian Tekan)* 宿務基督教會八十週年鑽禧慶典特刊 (Cebu City: Cebu Gospel Church, 1996), 7.

Chinese pastor of the Regina Chinese Alliance Church, the first one to be formally organized on 29 January 1961 in North America. As a result of such a vision for mission, seventy-five Chinese Alliance churches have since been planted in Canada.[11]

When DCGC started to support overseas mission, the church had not yet even reached its tenth anniversary. It had just constructed a new building in 1956 without financial assistance from the CMA, yet, just four years later it was able to support Chao. Over the decades since then, DCGC has supported many overseas missionaries, Filipino pastors and cross-cultural missionaries, as well as mission agencies, one of which is the Overseas Missionary Fellowship.[12]

3. SBC and Leadership Training

A positive indication of ecclesiastical devolution is how soon an institution is created in order to provide leadership training. The Philippine Mission of SBC acted with bold foresight when it established the PBTS in 1952, the year when DCBC emerged. PBTS was the first Chinese Bible school in the Philippines, since the faculty all spoke Mandarin and the students were Chinese.

Despite its shaky beginning, the establishment of a seminary to train Chinese and Filipino pastors displayed wisdom and clarity of purpose on the part of the Southern Baptists. With China closing its doors to the world and to Christianity, and with the church in China facing an unknown future, Chinese churches in the Philippines, as well as in other Asian countries, were suddenly left on their own to supply pastoral staff for their constituents.

Although other missions had established training schools in the Philippines, the Presbyterians in particular started several training

---

11. Leung Ka-lun/Liang JiaLin 梁家麟, *Huaren Xuandaohui Bainianshi* 華人宣導會百年史, A Centenary History of the Chinese C&MA (Hong Kong: Alliance Bible Seminary Christianity and Chinese Culture Research Centre, 1998), 144, 146; Augusto Chao/Zhao ShiChang 趙士昌, "Shusuan Shenen 數算神恩 (Count God's Blessings)," in *DEC Fortieth*, n.p.; Augusto Chao/Zhao ShiChang 趙士昌, "Cong Namao Dao Diji 從納卯到地極 (From Davao to the Ends of the Earth)," in *DEC Fiftieth*, 38–39.

12. He/Wu ChangXi 吳長熙. "Benhui Xuandao Ji Zhaojiu Rencai de Yixiang 本會宣道及造就人才的異象 (Our church's vision for mission and pastoral training)," in *DEC Fortieth*, n.p.

institutions in the provinces and in Manila, one of which – the Union Theological Seminary (UTS) – was formed in 1907.[13] However, the difference between Presbyterians and the Baptists was that the SBC embarked on the endeavor with a focus on training *Chinese* pastoral candidates in the Philippines and in less than a year had put their plan in motion. In contrast, Rev William Robertson Angus reported to the General Assembly of the UCCP in 1954, stating:

> We need your help and guidance in . . . leadership train-ing. We have new [Chinese] Christian groups forming in various parts of the Philippines, and the opportunities are many, but we have not as yet the leaders for these groups. I am happy to say that there are a few Chinese students in Union Theological Seminary and in the School of Theology at Silliman [University]. I am particularly happy, because it is near to me, that last year a first Chinese student entered the Albay Bible School in Legaspi. I hope that many more will enter all of these institutions, and that our Field Committee and the Chinese congregations may be guided into full coop-eration with you in meeting in the fullest possible manner this very important need.[14]

Evidently, Angus also perceived the great need for training Chinese pastors, but even as he was bringing this need to the attention of the General Assembly, the Southern Baptists were already *meeting* this need through their Seminary in Baguio. Angus would later head the Philippine-Chinese Commission of the UCCP, and he could have been in the posi-tion to attempt to unite the Chinese churches into attaining his desired "full cooperation" had he stayed longer in the Philippines and had a group of Protestant Chinese from several Chinese churches not formed the Bible Institute of the Philippines (BIOP), now Biblical Seminary of the Philippines (BSOP) in 1957.

---

13. The UTS was a union of two Bible schools operated by the Presbyterian and the Methodist Episcopal churches. See Sitoy, *Several Springs* 1: 162–164.

14. *United Church of Christ in the Philippines Minutes of the Fourth Biennial General Assembly, Los Banos, Laguna, May 17–23, 1954*, 9–10.

In recounting the history of BSOP, one of its founders, Henry Co See Cho/Xu ShuChu 許書楚, mentions that in 1952, the administrators of UTS requested Joseph Esther to set up a meeting with key leaders of the Chinese churches. UTS was planning to invite all the Chinese churches to work together to establish a Chinese seminary, and all the funds that the Presbyterians used to finance seminaries in China was ready to be transferred to the Philippines.[15] UTS would finance all the needs: faculty, library and facilities. Those who attended the meeting would become board members of the seminary. But, according to Henry Co, who was among those invited, the Chinese leaders were like "'blocks of wood' that night, unmoved by the Spirit and unwilling to do anything except to say a polite 'Thank you.'"[16] Needless to say, they made no move to get involved and turned down the offer. Instead, two pastors, Rev Silas Wong and Rev Raymond William Frame/Fei ShuKai 費述凱牧師 of the Overseas Missionary Fellowship who served in BIOP/BSOP from 1950 to 1977, together with seven Protestant Chinese from different churches started to pray at Rev Frame's residence regarding the need to train pastors in a Chinese Bible school. After one year of prayer, with seven men in the Board of Trustees, BIOP was established on 15 June 1957 and classes started on 15 July 1957.[17]

E. Observations and Recommendations

My analyses bring out the need for further studies to be made. Four aspects specially call for broader investigations: inter-faith and inter-cultural, ecclesiological, missiological and theological.

---

15. See Homer Chua/Cai WeiJie 蔡維潔, "上帝給我們看到的異象 (The vision that God gave us)," in 菲律濱聖經神學院三十週年特刊 BSOP 30th Foundation Anniversary (Valenzuela City: Biblical Seminary of the Philippines, [1987]), 8.

16. Henry Co See Cho/Xu ShuChu 許書楚, "菲聖首二十年史略 (The First Twenty Years of BSOP)," in 菲律濱聖經神學院45週年院慶特刊 Biblical Seminary of the Philippines 45th Anniversary Special Edition, trans. Jean Uayan (Valenzuela City: Biblical Seminary of the Philippines, 2004), 34.

17. Henry Co See Cho/Xu ShuChu 許書楚, "菲律濱聖經神學院 簡史 (Brief history of the Biblical Seminary of the Philippines)," in BSOP 30th Foundation Anniversary, 10.

1. Inter-faith and Inter-cultural Studies

As far as I am aware, this work is but one of a handful of attempts to study the history of Protestant Chinese in the Philippines. This field of interest definitely needs more research since the scope of this work has been purely historical. It has not investigated, for example, how the Protestant Chinese handled the tension of living out their faith among their Roman Catholic or Buddhist compatriots during the same time frame of this study. A virtually unexplored field of study concerns the beliefs and practices of the Protestant in comparison to the Roman Catholic Chinese in the Philippines. This study has brought out the fact that there were Roman Catholics who converted to Protestantism or joined SSCM during the beginning of the twentieth century, but what was the relationship between Protestant Chinese and Roman Catholic Chinese at that time and how is it applicable to the present situation?

How about Chinese Filipinos who adhered to traditional Chinese belief systems such as Buddhism, Confucianism, Daoism and animism? When the pre-WWII Protestant Chinese pursued the goal of self-propagation, how did they attempt to evangelize their compatriots who belonged to these traditional religions? If answers to these questions can be found through historical research, they might be useful to the programs of evangelism and mission that Philippine Protestant Chinese churches are carrying out today.

This research has been more qualitative than quantitative. Much work can be done in terms of statistical studies on membership growth or male-female ratio changes in these churches throughout the past hundred years. The growth of the Protestant and the Roman Catholic Chinese churches during certain periods can also be compared. Still another investigation that can be attempted is to find out how high a percentage of Chinese *mestizos* became members of the pre-WWII Protestant Chinese churches. If the findings turn up very minimal, then the question is why? What was the view of the missionaries regarding this matter? Was there cultural or racial marginalization taking shape within the Protestant Chinese churches at this early stage?

2. Ecclesiological Investigations

As I am trained neither in missiology nor ecclesiology, many aspects of the early history of these Chinese churches worth examining at a deeper level must be undertaken by experts in these disciplines. One such aspect is this: what, missiologically speaking, are the long-term effects of being a mission-established or a mission-assisted church? Today there are many organizational and ecclesiological aspects in the church system set in place by the PrEC within SSP that are worth exploring. Studies comparing SSCM and Filipino parishes with regard to devolution and examinations analyzing the Episcopalian in relation to other forms of church polity (Presbyterian, Baptist, Congregational) in particular historical contexts can also be made.

Can the patterns of emergence presented in this study provide relevant strategies for forming churches today? Which patterns have direct impact on church growth? Regarding the medium of communication, if missionaries were able to conduct services and preach even with deficient language skills, does it mean that present-day pastors can minister effectively without the same skill? The Chinese churches in the Philippines are struggling at present with the problem of language. The younger generation can hardly speak fluent *Hokkien* or Mandarin; neither can they read the Chinese Bible. Increasingly, pastors-in-training at BSOP are struggling with these challenges. Yet there are still thousands of Chinese in the Chinatown (Binondo) district, not to mention the incoming "*xin qiao* 新僑" or new immigrants, who are proficient in many Chinese dialects and/or Mandarin. The language factor also poses another problem for evangelism, as these *xin qiao* are no longer predominantly from South Fujian, and even those from this region now feel more at ease using Mandarin than their hometown dialects.

Is it more difficult today for the contact-turned-core members paradigm to take shape? Is the solid ground of having core members who are dedicated and zealous in proclaiming the gospel and building up the church being eroded by the phenomenon of modern-day "church hopping" or "sermon shopping" Protestant Chinese? Was there such a phenomenon during the emerging and early development stage of the Protestant Chinese churches? Many Chinese pastors are realizing that not a few in their congregations follow after "good" preachers or inspiring worship styles, so that their members attend other Chinese or Filipino churches, and cause numbers in their congregation to become fluid and fluctuating.[18]

Another area worth studying is the length of time that pastors stay in one field of ministry and how this impacts church growth. How long do pastors, especially young ministers, stay in one location and why? What are the factors causing ministers to transfer from one church to another? Does the problem lie in the pastor or the church or both? Or is the length of a pastor's service in one location even a factor for church growth at all? A study could be made comparing the length and quality of service of pastors in different eras – the emerging and early period with the modern period.

One last area to investigate is the devolution of the smaller satellite churches that were established by UECP and by other Protestant Chinese churches such as Bacolod Trinity Christian Church (Iloilo Trinity Christian Church), Grace Gospel Church (Grace Gospel Church – North), Jubilee Evangelical Church (four daughter churches).[19] How fast are these satellite churches approaching independence in terms of self-governance, self-support and self-perpetuation? Is their devolution more or less rapid than the devolution of such churches as CGC or DCBC? What similarities or dissimilarities can be observed regarding devolution in these different historical eras?

3. Missiological Concerns

An interesting aspect worth investigating is the relationship between Protestant missions working among the Chinese. As observed in the cases of DCBC and CUEC, whenever there was a possibility that misunderstanding might occur between two mission agencies interested in the same people as mission targets, the best way to handle the situation was to avoid conflict by opening communication lines with the party involved. The initial contact of the SBC missionaries was Chua Ke Khan, a member of CUEC. He requested the CUEC Evangelistic Band to help set up a daughter church in Dagupan City. The CUEC did take measures to invite a woman to act as pastor of the newly formed Baguio Chinese Baptist

---

18. There is no hard data nor has any formal study been conducted regarding this issue, but I have constantly heard these observations being discussed by senior pastors of Protestant Chinese churches in Manila.

19. See complete list in pp. 208–209.

Church. The next step would have been for this lady to oversee the work in Dagupan, but she declined the invitation. Seeing that CUEC was making these moves, the SBC missionaries took measures to avoid inter-mission conflict. Presbyterian missionary Dr George Wright, as previously noted, also took steps to avoid giving the impression that his mission was some-how involved in the breaking away of CUEC from SSCM. Such incidents can be compared with similar events that transpired within the Filipino churches during the era of the Comity Agreement.

With regard to the methods used by both missionaries and pioneer Chinese church leaders, is the visitation-invitation-follow-up cycle still workable today? True, all Chinese church workers today engage in the task of visiting non-believing Chinese, but will those visited come to church services when the invitation is extended? The attraction of a fair-skinned foreigners speaking fluent Mandarin may no longer be a reality. What sub-stitutes can be found that will create an impact at the moment of contact?

A study can be made detailing how the various mission agencies con-ducted mission among the Chinese, then a comparison can be made with how they established Filipino churches. A macro-study of the devolutionary process experienced by Chinese churches can be made and compared with the experience of Filipino mission-established churches. A wider field of study is a comparison between the devolutionary experiences of Philippine Protestant churches and other *Minnan*-related churches in Southeast Asia, such as Singapore and Malaysia, for example.

The Chinese churches of the Philippines must pay close attention to the urgent needs created by the *xin qiao* phenomenon and the fast church growth in China. The government of China has lifted the Communist-era policy of restricting its subjects from traveling or migrating to other countries. The Philippines and the People's Republic of China (PRC) pres-ently enjoy very close economic and cultural ties, especially now that pro-fessionals and businessmen from both countries can come and go much more freely. Citizens from both nations are cross-living in urban centers for extended periods of time due to the demands of their work. Many Chinese churches in Manila are facing this reality by forming "Mandarin Fellowships" for truth-seekers or by conducting separate worship servic-es for Mandarin-speaking believers. Will this situation eventually lead to new Chinese congregations emerging on Philippine soil? At this stage, the Christian church in China is facing its need for trained workers and pastors by setting up "training centers" inside multi-story buildings where systematic programs of instruction are conducted on a daily basis and over long periods of time, or by sending its people to undergo training outside China. This is far from meeting the needs of evangelizing China's billions of lost souls or staffing churches that are emerging at astonishing speed. And yet, even as more Chinese schools in the Philippines are hiring teachers from PRC, will the time soon arrive when China will again supply evangelists and pastors to minister to Chinese believers and non-believers who are scattered throughout Asia, the Americas and Europe? On a global scale, how can Chinese churches in the Philippines cooperate with the church in China in the task of sending cross-cultural Chinese missionaries to the unreached peoples of Central Asia, Eastern Europe and the Middle East? The findings of my study could be used as a jumping board to launch into these macro-studies.

4. Theological Reflection

Very little has been done to study the historical development of the theological framework of the Protestant Chinese churches in the Philippines. Considering that these churches have come into contact with the theological viewpoints of the CMA, Episcopal, Little Flock, Presbyterian, Reformed, UCCP and other mission or church-related entities, there is a vast area to be explored with regard to how these varied viewpoints have affected the theological outlook of these churches. The question concerning how the theological standpoints of pioneers Studley (Reformed turned Episcopal), Silas Wong or Leung Sai Ko (Alliance), Crawley or Harrington (Baptist), affected the thinking and belief system of the members of CGC, CUEC, DCGC, DCBC and SSCM during the emerging period and the theological heritage that has been passed on, needs to be answered. The past connection between CUEC and the Church of Christ in China, especially with regard to the issues of nationalism, liberal theology and ecumenism, and how these issues affected the Philippine Chinese churches, need to be analyzed in depth.[20] John Sung's Keswick heritage and its influence on the Chinese founders or leaders of these and other Philippine Protestant churches is also worth exploring, since more studies on his theology have come out.[21] It will be a great contribution to investigate just how much Sung's thought-life and his ministry have affected the Chinese churches in the Philippines.[22]

F. Conclusion

Most of the recorded history of the Philippine Protestant Chinese churches point to Protestant Chinese as their founders, while a minority recognize that missionaries from the Christian and Missionary Alliance, Episcopalian, Presbyterian and Southern Baptist mission organizations assisted in the establishment of such Chinese churches, without giving extensive details of their ministry.[23] This book has shown that there were Protestant Chinese in the Philippines during the Spanish regime, but no church was formed until the coming of the Protestant missionaries during the American occupation. This study of six representative Protestant Chinese churches in the Philippines has further shown that CPCI, CGC, DCBC, and SSCM emerged as a result of the labor of Western Protestant missionaries and

---

20. Wing-hung Lam, *Chinese Theology in Construction* (Pasadena, CA: William Carey Library, 1983) explores the different ways Christians responded to the intellectual ferment of the 1920s in China.

21. John Sung's thoughts and beliefs can be gleaned from his diary, see Levi Tian-Zhen Song, 靈歷集光 (The Diary of His Spiritual Life). His sermons and Bible study notes have also been transcribed.

22. See sample study of Li MingAn 李明安, "Song Shangjie yu Malaixiya Jiaohui Zhi Shigong Yu Yingxiang 宋尚節于馬來西亞教會之事工與影響 (The ministry and influence of John Sung in Malaysia)," in 宋尚節的神學與屬靈觀 (The Theology and Spiritual View of John Sung), 《馬聖》資研中心專題系列〈1〉 MBS Centre for Christianity and Malaysian Studies 1, 79–90. Malaysia: Malaysia Bible Seminary, 2002.

23. CGC celebrated its 90th anniversary on 16–20 March 2006 and consequently published *Proclaim God's Enduring Faithfulness:90th Anniversary/Xinshichang, Wuenyang* 信實長、務恩揚 *1916–2006* (Cebu City: Cebu Gospel Church, 2006). On page 16, Valentin Uy simply wrote: "Cebu Gospel Church was founded in 1916. In the beginning American missionary Rev and Mrs Jansen shared the gospel with the Chinese. Mrs Cang Bon Pit nee Ng Chhai Toan accepted the Lord and became the first Chinese believer in Cebu City. Several years later, local businessmen and teachers became believers, were baptized into the church. . . ." It is a good thing that the *CGCGJS* preserved more details in Chinese in previous anniversary publications, but the younger generation is beginning to lose their church's rich heritage.

Protestant Chinese and Filipinos. The ground was prepared for the founding of DCGC by two sisters who were later joined by other Protestant Chinese, but the formal organization of the church was assisted by CMA missionaries. Only CUEC can be considered as a fruit of the labor of a group of Protestant Chinese as a result of being closely connected to the Church of Christ in China and without the official involvement of any mission agency.

In the course of doing this research, many discoveries have been made and many uncertainties clarified. First, the earliest Protestant Chinese church to be established in the Philippines is *not* St. Stephen's Parish (former SSCM), as generally acknowledged by the Philippine Chinese community. It is rather the congregation that this study has named the "Chinese Presbyterian Church in Iloilo." No clear record of this church can be found in the historical publications of the Philippine Protestant Chinese community. Now detailed knowledge can be made public. Second, a long lost or neglected declaration of the need to establish CUEC written by a key figure of the Church of Christ in China, five years before the church emerged, has been rediscovered and its implications re-visited. Third, the circumstances surrounding the separation of CUEC from SSCM have been scrutinized from both perspectives. Fourth, the complex relationship between CGC and UCCP, which has been clouded with uncertainties, has been disentangled and can finally be laid bare. Lastly, the contributions rendered by the Western missionaries, the Chinese workers and a Filipino pastor to the six Protestant Chinese churches can now be fully appreciated, but all glory belongs to the Chief Cornerstone and Foundation of the Protestant Chinese churches of the Philippines.

Appendices

Appendices

Location of Six Philippine Protestant Chinese Churches

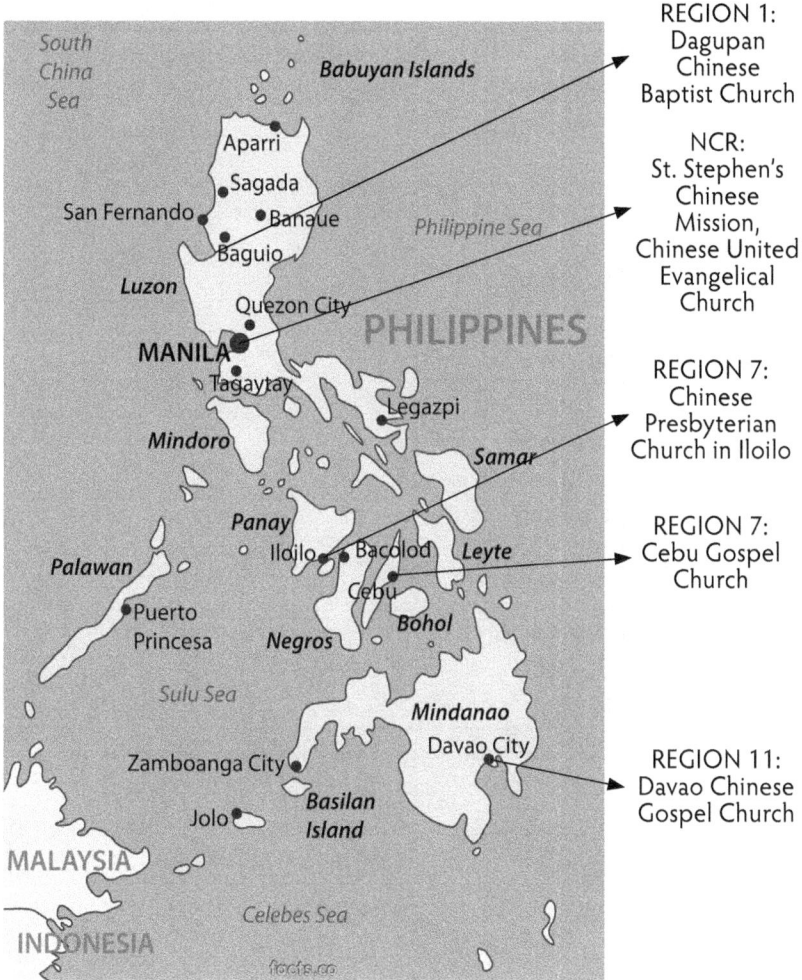

REGION 1:
Dagupan Chinese Baptist Church

NCR:
St. Stephen's Chinese Mission, Chinese United Evangelical Church

REGION 7:
Chinese Presbyterian Church in Iloilo

REGION 7:
Cebu Gospel Church

REGION 11:
Davao Chinese Gospel Church

List and Profiles of Interviewees

Date and Place of Interview	Interviewee	Affiliation	Family Origin in/Connection to China
17 Mar 2001 Malate, Manila	Pr Bona Lim 林蓮珠傳道 (1916–2004)	Davao Evangelical Church	Studied at Iok Tek Girls' School, Xiamen 廈門毓德女學校
19 Dec 2001 Dumaguete City	Elder Agapito Cang 江維勝長老 b. 17 Sep 1922; d. 11 Mar 2005	Dumaguete Evangelical Church	
	Caridad Cang vda. de Sun (sister of Elder Agapito Cang) 孫江心意 b. 1919	Dumaguete Evangelical Church	
	Peter Chuang 莊嘉聲 b. 1938	Dumaguete Evangelical Church	
16 Feb 2002 Dagupan City	Rev Max Pettit 培馬可牧師 b. 28 Sep 1922; d. 26 Mar 2012	Former missionary to Dagupan Chinese Baptist Church	Missionary to China (prior to 1949)

Date and Place of Interview	Interviewee	Affiliation	Family Origin in/Connection to China
16 Dec 2003 Sta. Cruz, Manila	Rev Wesley Shao 邵慶彰牧師 b. 17 June 1917; d. 4 Jan 2012	United Evangelical Church of the Philippines, former pastor of Davao Evangelical Church	Tongan, Fujian 福建同安
19 Mar 2004 Cainta, Rizal	Rev Pedro Hao 侯均楠牧師 b. 26 Nov 1924; d. 2004	Manila Chinese Baptist Church, former pastor of Dagupan Chinese Baptist Church	
22 Jun 2004 Country Club Village, Cebu City	Elder Valentin Uy 黃根源長老 b. 24 Feb 1924	Cebu Gospel Church	Siming, Xiamen, Fujian 福建廈門思明
23 Jun 2004 Maria Luisa Estate Park, Cebu City	Cang Saw Iattee 江蘇悅治 b. 1905	Cebu Gospel Church	Heshan, Xiamen, Fujian 福建廈門禾山
25 Jun 2004 Ramos St., Cebu City	Pr Pilar Siao 蕭必冷傳道 b. 10 Oct 1924	Retired church worker, Cebu Gospel Church	Siming, Xiamen, Fujian 福建廈門思明
25 and 29 Jun 2004 Cebu City	Mercedes Cang 江蔡綿綾 b. 15 Sep 1918	Cebu Gospel Church	Shishi, Jinjiang, Fujian 福建晉江石獅
26 Feb 2005 Caloocan City	Elder Elena Co Sy (Mrs Sy Seng Cho) 許秀琳長老 (施承祖夫人) b. 17 Jun 1928	United Evangelical Church of the Philippines	Fulin, Jinjiang, Fujian 福建晉江福林

Date and Place of Interview	Interviewee	Affiliation	Family Origin in/Connection to China
12 Mar 2005 Caloocan City	Elder Sy Seng Cho 施承祖長老 b. 18 Apr 1927	United Evangelical Church of the Philippines	Fulin, Jinjiang, Fujian 福建晉江福林
30 Mar 2005 Pasay City	Mr & Mrs Peter Leoncio Sy (nee Kwok Mei Mei) 施良瑞, 許白菊 b. 18 Aug 1922; 9 Mar 1926	United Evangelical Church of the Philippines	Qiangang, Jinjiang, Fujian 福建晉江前港
30 Mar 2005 New Manila, Quezon City	Pr Helen Kho Sia 謝許玉英傳道 b. 3 Apr 1950	Jubilee Evangelical Church	Jinmen, Fujian 福建金門
30 Mar 2005 Quezon City	Mrs Siao Dy Hong Suan 蕭李鳳萱		
4 Apr 2005 Davao City	Rev Morino Lim 林華生牧師 b. December 26, 1936 Mrs Josephine Hu 羅碧娟	Davao Evangelical Church Davao Chinese Baptist Church	
4 Apr 2005 BSOP, Valenzuela City	Rev Wilson Go Kiao 吳家順牧師 b. 11 Sep 1948	Diamond Jubilee Evangelical Church	Nan-an, Fujian 福建南安
7 Apr 2005 Quezon City	Rev Chua Ong Kim Ja 蔡王錦霞牧師 b. 6 Jan 1927	Westminster Student Church	Jinjiang, Fujian 福建晉江

Date and Place of Interview	Interviewee	Affiliation	Family Origin in/Connection to China
7 Apr 2005 City of Manila	Dr Lim Diong Su 林忠恕醫生 (b. 1922)	St. Stephen's Parish	Heshan, Xiamen, Fujian 福建廈門禾山
10 Apr 2005 Vigan City	Elder Franco Chua 蔡世芳長老	United Evangelical Church of Vigan	
12 Apr 2005 Sta. Cruz, Manila	Elder Esther Ting Dy 李丁瑩瑩長老 b. 27 Jun 1933	United Evangelical Church of the Philippines	Chendai, Jinjiang, Fujian 福建晉江陳埭
12 Apr 2005 Sta. Cruz, Manila	Elder Shao Hui Cheng vda. de Tan 陳邵惠卿長老 (b. 1918)	United Evangelical Church of the Philippines	Tongan, Fujian 福建同安
19 Apr 2005 Cebu City	Mercedes Chua vda. de Cang 江蔡綿綾 b. 15 Sep 1918 Rev Agustin Bacon (b. 1910) Jonathan L. Bacon	Cebu Gospel Church

Bradford UCCP Church | |
| 20 Apr 2005 Cebu City | Pablo Moreno | Bradford UCCP Church | |
| 20 Apr 2005 Cebu City | Si Giok Pan/Shi YuPing (Mrs Lim Hok Seng) 施玉瓶 (林福盛夫人) b. 16 Jun 1905 | Cebu Gospel Church | Tongan, Fujian 福建同安 |

Date and Place of Interview	Interviewee	Affiliation	Family Origin in/Connection to China
22 Apr 2005 Sto. Niño Village, Cebu City	Si Giok Pan/Shi YuPing (Mrs Lim Hok Seng) 施玉瓶 (林福盛夫人) b. 16 Jun 1905	Cebu Gospel Church	Tongan, Fujian 福建同安
28 Apr 2005 Dumaguete City	Rev Jesus GoChioco 吳光迪牧師 Mrs Filomena Tan vda. de Cang 江陳秀敏	Dumaguete Evangelical Church Dumaguete Evangelical Church	
29 Apr 2005 Dumaguete City	Dr T. Valentino Sitoy, Jr	Silliman University	
4 May 2005 Iloilo City	Go To Kang 吳道巷	Iloilo Christian Gospel Assembly Center, Inc.	
4 May 2005 Iloilo City	Tan Tay San 鄭泰山	Iloilo Trinity Christian Church	
23 Jun 2005 Sta. Cruz, Manila	Lim Giok Khun 林玉崑 b. 6 Jul 1918; d. 31 Oct 2014	St. Stephen's Parish	Xiamen, Fujian 福建廈門
9 Jul 2005 Malabon City	Lim King Hua vda. de Lim Siong Hong (1905–1990) 林璟華 (林翔鳳師母) b. 18 Dec 1928	United Evangelical Church of Malabon	Quanzhou, Fujian 福建泉州

Date and Place of Interview	Interviewee	Affiliation	Family Origin in/Connection to China
16 Aug 2005 BSOP, Valenzuela City	Pr Erlinda Duy Pan 潘雷秀祝傳道 b. 22 Dec 1933; d. 26 Nov 2013	United Evangelical Church of the Philippines	Nan-an, Fujian 福建南安
18 Aug 2005 BSOP, Valenzuela City	Pr Rosie Ang (nee Go Sun Lu) 洪吳純瑜傳道 b. 19 Nov 1939	United Evangelical Church of the Philippines	Xiwu, Jinjiang, Fujian 福建晉江棲梧
6 Oct 2005 Sampaloc, Manila	Kua Bee Tin 柯美珍 Kua Ka Tin 柯佳珍		
3 Jan 2006 Binondo, Manila	Peter Leoncio Sy & Sy Chi Siong 施良瑞, 施慈祥 (b. 1913)	United Evangelical Church of the Philippines	Qiangang, Jinjiang, Fujian 福建晉江前港
12 Apr 2006 Cebu City	Phoned Li Tiong Chi, talked to Mrs Li Tiong Chi 陳長志夫婦	Cebu Gospel Church	
12 Apr 2006 Cebu City	Elder Adon Ong 王亞倫長老	Cebu Gospel Church	
12 Apr 2006 City of Manila	Pr Ho Wei Tuan 何慰端傳道	United Evangelical Church of the Philippines	
15 Oct 2006 Cebu City	Dr Wanda Po Liam Giok 傅念玉博士 b. 22 Oct 1954	Cebu Gospel Church; Philippine Christian Gospel School	

Date and Place of Interview	Interviewee	Affiliation	Family Origin in/Connection to China
8 Mar 2007 City of Manila	Rev Romeo Yu 楊建明牧師	Manila Chinese Baptist Church	
9 Apr 2007 Cebu City Quezon City	Pr Pilar Siao 蕭必泠傳道	Cebu Gospel Church	Siming, Xiamen, Fujian 福建廈門思明
	Mercedes Cang 江蔡綿綾	Cebu Gospel Church	Shishi, Jinjiang, Fujian 福建晉江石獅
	Rev Chua Ong Kim Ja 蔡王錦霞牧師	Westminster Student Church	Jinjiang, Fujian 福建晉江

Significant Events Affecting Chinese Immigration During the Spanish Regime (1561–1899)

Year	Number of Chinese	Uprisings/ Incidents	Restrictions/ Massacres	Result
1561	150[a]			
1574		Lin Feng's attack		
1582			*Parian* segregation (destroyed in 1860)	
1585/ 88	10,000[b]			Chinese entrusted to Dominicans
1593		P'an Ho Wu's mutiny[c]		
1594-1596	24,000		Royal decree – first expulsion (12,000)[b]	
1603	30,000	Uprising in Manila	25,000 + killed	Letter of apology to China
1606, 1616, 1622	Restricted to 6,000		Travel restricted	
1635	30,000[d]			
1639	40,000	Uprising in Calamba, Laguna[e]	22,000–24,000 Chinese, 300 Filipinos and 45 Spaniards killed	

Year	Number of Chinese	Uprisings/ Incidents	Restrictions/ Massacres	Result
1662		Koxinga letter[f] *Parian* revolt	Filipinos from Pampanga sent to quell revolt, hundreds killed	
1686		Tingco and eleven men looted houses of mayors[a]	Expulsion decree of Charles II	Many embraced Christianity, some for convenience
1702	40,000+			
1709		Accused of rebellion	Many expelled	
1744			Expulsion decree of Philip V	Many embraced Christianity
1755	1,515		All non-Christian Chinese expelled	1,000 added to 515 Chinese Christians
1766		Some Catholic Chinese assisted British during brief occupation (1762–1764)	Anda's decree - thousands expelled, 6,000 killed	Workmen allowed to enter two years later
1789			Expelled except for artisans	
1804			Only agriculturists and artisans allowed	
1810	7,000[g]			
1820		Wrongly accused after cholera epidemic	Europeans, Americans and Chinese killed	

Year	Number of Chinese	Uprisings/ Incidents	Restrictions/ Massacres	Result
1828			New system of taxation called *Captacion de Chinos*	
1840-46	Only 5,000		Categorized into "transients" and "residents"	
1864	8,000			Treaty of Tientsin recognized China as most favored nation in the Philippines
1876	30,000			
1886	100,000		Chinese forbidden to live permanently in the provinces or to trade with Muslims	
1888			Chinese forbidden to reside in Mindanao	
1896			900 Chinese in Cebu massacred[a]	
1898			Chinese Exclusion Acts enforced in the Philippines by American government	
1899	40,000			

Sources: The data in this table is drawn from the following works: Khin Khin Myint Jensen, "The Chinese in the Philippines During the American Regime: 1898–1946" (PhD diss., University of Wisconsin, 1956), 6–45; *Census of the*

310
A Study on the Emergence and Early Development of
Selected Protestant Chinese Churches in the Philippines

Philippine Islands Taken under the Direction of the Philippine Commission in the Year 1903. Volume II: Population. Director J. P. Sanger (Washington, DC: United States Bureau of the Census, 1905), 39, 319, 489; Tomás S. Fonacier, "The Chinese in the Philippines During the American Administration" (PhD diss., Stanford University, 1932), xii; *Tsinoy: The Story of the Chinese in Philippine Life*, ed. Teresita Ang See, Go Bon Juan, Doreen Go Yu, Yvonne Chua (Manila: Kaisa Para Sa Kaunlaran *Feilübin Huayi Qingnian Lianhehui* 菲律賓華裔青年聯合會, 2005), 54, 58–62; Tomas de Comyn, *Estado de las islas Filipinas en 1810* (State of the Philippines in 1810: Being an Historical, Statistical, and Descriptive Account of the Interesting Portion of the Indian Archipelago), trans. William Walton. Filipiniana Book Guild, 15 (Madrid: *Imprenta de Repulles*, 1820; reprint, Manila: Filipiniana Book Guild, 1969), 146. This work is henceforth cited as *State of the Philippines in 1810*.

---

[a] *Tsinoy*, 54, 58-62.

[b] Fonacier, "The Chinese in the Philippines During the American Administration," xii.

[c] P'an Ho Wu/Pan HeWu 潘和五 led 250 conscripted Chinese galley rowers to mutiny against Governor General Gomez Perez Dasmariñas on 25 Oct 1593, whose son, Luis Perez Dasmariñas, governor from 1593–1596, led the massacre of 25,000 Chinese in 1603.

[d] Figure given by Grau Monfalcón, according to Fonacier, see note b.

[e] See *BRPI* 29:208–258.

[f] Called "Cotsen" by the Spaniards, Koxinga 國姓爺, or Zheng Chenggong 鄭成功 (1624–1662) was a merchant turned rebel, of Chinese and Japanese parentage, who grew up in Quanzhou. Failing to defeat the Qing government forces, he moved on to conquer Taiwan, defeating the Dutch on 1 Feb 1662. On 10 May 1662, Koxinga sent Fray Victorio Riccio/Vittorio Ricci (1621–1685), a relative of the famous Matteo Ricci, with a letter to the Spanish governor accusing the Spaniards of oppressing the Chinese and demanding that the Philippines submit to him as King of Taiwan. Ricci had been a missionary to the Chinese in the *Parian* for seven years (1648–1655), and later served in Xiamen and Fuzhou. He spent his last days as Vicar of Cavite and the *Parian*, where he died on 17 Feb 1685. Koxinga died soon after this incident, but the Chinese had revolted on 25 May 1662 in fear of what the enraged Spanish authorities would do. There were attempts on both sides to pacify, but in the end, Filipino troops were sent to the *Parian* where scores were killed. Those who fled to the provinces were hunted and killed as well. Thousands fled to China or Taiwan in trading junks. See *BRPI*, 36:218–260.

[g] Comyn, *State of the Philippines in 1810*, 146.

Source Areas of *Hokkien* Migration to the Philippines

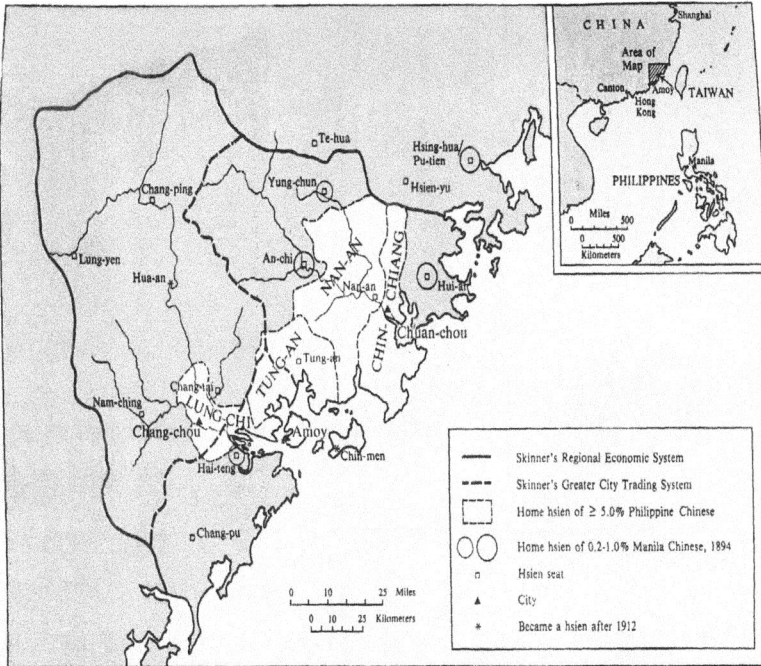

Wade-Giles, Hanyu Pinyin and Chinese place names:

Tung-an = Tongan 同安

Nan-an = Nanan 南安

Chin-chiang = Jinjiang 晉江

Hsing-hua/Pu-tien = Xinghua/Putian 興化/莆田

Chuan-chou = Quanzhou 泉州

Amoy = Xiamen 廈門

Chin-men = Jinmen 金門

Chang-pu = Zhangpu 漳浦

Lung-chi = Longxi 龍溪

An-chi = Anxi 安溪

Yung-chun = Yongchun 永春

Hai-teng = Haideng 海澄

Hsien-yu = Xianyou 仙游

Hui-an = Huian 惠安

Te-hua = Dehua 德化

Nan-ching = Nanjing 南靖

Hua-an = Huaan 華安

Lung-yen = Longyan 龍岩

Chang-tai = Changtai 長泰

Chang-chou = Zhangzhou 漳州

Chang-ping = Zhangping 漳平

Source: The map is from Daniel Frederick Doeppers, "Destination, Selection and Turnover Among Chinese Migrants to Philippine Cities in the Nineteenth Century," *Journal of Historical Geography* 12, 4 (1986): 386. Reprinted with the permission of the author.

Note: *Hanyu Pinyin* and Chinese place names are added to the Wade-Giles notation for the convenience of modern readers.

The Origin of the Chinese Population of Manila and the Philippines 1822 and 1890s

(As percentage by year)

Native place	Manila		51 Provincial Centers[a]
	1822	1894	1890s
Quanzhou 泉州 greater-city trading system	46.9	59.6	52.5
Jinjiang 晉江 (Chincan)[b]	6.5	10.5	9.3
Nanan 南安 (Lamua)	0	0.9	0
Huian 惠安 (Juyua)	0.8	0.6	0.2
Anxi 安溪 (Anque)	1·2	0.3	0.3
Yongchun 永春 (Yengchun/Ingchun)	1.2	0.3	0.3
(Subtotal)	(55.4)	(71.9)	(62.3)
Xiamen 廈門 and Zhangzhou 漳州 greater-city trading system			
Tongan 同安 (Tangua-Emuy)[c]	17.5	9.9	27.0
Haideng 海澄 (Jaytin)	3.7	0.2	0.1
Longxi 龍溪 (Leonque)	22.1	7.5	7.1
Nanqing 南靖 and Changtai 長泰 (Lamching and Tintiu)	0.9	0	0
(Subtotal)	(44.2)	(17.6)	(34.2)
Xinghua/Putian 興化/浦田 (Joingua)[d]	0	1.0	0.1
Cantonese (Canton, Macao)	n/g[e]	9.5	3·3
Others and unlocated[f]	0.4	0	0.1
Total percentage	100.0	100.0	100.0
N	*1,200[g]*	*2,056[g]*	*13,261*

Source: Calculated from the listings of individuals in the *Padrones de Chinos* for Manila 1822 and 1894, and the provinces for various years between 1891 and 1896, all in the Philippine National Archives (PNA). The 1822 *padron* omits Christian Chinese. Locations confirmed with the aid of Rev L. W. Kip's Vicinity Map of the *Hokkien* region (E-mng Si-ui E Te-to/Xiamen Siwei de Ditu 廈門 四圍的地圖), London: Unwin Brothers, Lithographers, *c.* 1890 from a copy held by the American Geographical Society, and by the kind assistance of Edgar Wickberg and Chester Wang. Doeppers, "Destination, Selection and Turnover," 388. Reprinted with the permission of the author.

Note: Doeppers originally used the Wade-Giles Mandarin romanization. I have added the *Hanyu pinyin* system for the place names as well as supplied the Chinese characters, in order to be complete. Except for this alteration and addition, the whole chart has been reproduced verbatim with permission from the author. The terms that were altered from Wade-Giles romanization to *Hanyu pinyin* include: Ch'uan-chou = Quanzhou, Chin-chiang = Jinjiang, Nan-an = Nanan, Hui-an = Huian, An-chi = Anxi, Yung-ch'un = Yongchun, Amoy = Xiamen, Chang-chou = Zhangzhou, Tung-an/Amoy = Tongan/Xiamen, Hai-teng = Haideng, Lung-chi = Longxi, Nam-ching = Nanqing, Chang-tai = Changtai, and Hsing-hua/Pu-tien = Xinghua/Putian. See *Doeppers, "Destination, Selection and Turnover,"* 388.

---

[a] Not including Manila. For list, see App. F.

[b] Wade-Giles Mandarin romanization as provided by Edgar Wickberg and, in parentheses, the Spanish rendering of local *Hokkien* pronunciation. Jinjiang here includes a small number of persons giving Quanzhou city [76]/prefecture [16] as their native place. The numbers in brackets refer to the 51 provincial cities. None of these entries are for Zhangzhou city/prefecture, here represented by Longxi *xian*.

[c] The island and port of Xiamen remained part of the Tongan *xian* through the entire Qing period, but the increased role of Xiamen as a center of both commerce and population led to its outstripping the rest of the *xian* in importance, and, eventually, to being declared a special district. A number of Philippine Chinese came from the rural portion of Xiamen Island, later known as the special district of Heshan 禾山. In the nineteenth century these persons tended to give Tongan as their native place – at least this is what several immigrants from Heshan said when interviewed in 1969 and 1973 in Dumaguete and Cebu cities. Likewise the few persons arriving from Jinmen 金門 (Quemoy, Kim-mng) may have listed either Tongan or Xiamen.

[d] The name Xinghua 興化 is associated with the locality of Putian 浦田 *xian*, but in its use by immigrants it may have been meant to refer to the prefecture of Xinghua which included Dehua 德化, Xianyou 仙游, and other *xians* in addition to Putian. Tombstone censuses in various cities reveal that all three of these places sent a few men to the Philippines in the twentieth century.

[e] It is likely that a few hundred Cantonese lived in the city in 1822 and were enrolled in a separate and unlocated register of *Macanistas*. In the 1890s, a few immigrants gave Hong Kong as their native place. These have been included here.

[f] Persons for whom no data were given are omitted.

[g] The 1822 data are based on a 50% stratified random sample of the surviving half of the register. The 1894 data represent a 10% stratified random sample.

APPENDIX F

Chinese in Philippine Cities and Towns by *Xian* of Origin

Predominant *xian* [縣]	Jinjiang 晉江	Jinjiang 晉江	Tongan/ Xiamen 同安/廈門	Nanan 南安(N) Longxi 龍溪(L)
Percentage of Chinese[a]	75–100	40–74	75–100 40–74	40–50 Mixed (M) No group ≥ 40
	Daet	Balayan	*Jolo	
	Jaro, L	Cavite[b]	Cotabato	Paranas (N)
	Alongalong, L	Tambobong	*Zamboanga	
	Abuyog, L	Tabaco, A	Dumaguete	Ilagan (L)
	Palo, L	MANILA		
	Dagami, L	Lipa	--	Capiz/Roxas (M)
	Vigan	Malolos		
	Baruga, L	Catbalogan	Silay	
	Burauen, L	Baliuag	La Carlota	
	Dulag, L	San Isidro	CEBU	
	*Carigara, L	*Aparri	Bacolod	
	Laoag	Navotas	*Guinobatan, A	
	*Naga	*DAGUPAN	San Fernando, P	
	*Tacloban, L	*Tuguegarao	Legaspi, A[b]	
	Surigao	*Calbayog	Angeles, P	
	Guivan	Guagua, P		
	Batangas	ILOILO		
	Santa Cruz	Sorsogon		
	Ligao, A			

Source: Calculated from the *Padrones de Chinos* for various years between 1891 and 1896. See *Doeppers*, "Destination, Selection and Turnover," 389. Reprinted with the permission of the author.

* Centers with 300–450 Chinese residents. L=Leyte, A=Albay, P=Pampanga.

---

[a] Listed in descending order.

[b] Cavite includes San Roque; Iloilo includes Jaro, Molo, and La Paz; Cebu includes San Nicolas, and Legaspi includes Albay.

Political Divisions of Fujian Province circa 1912

Quanzhoufu 泉州府 3,000,000	Zhangzhoufu 漳州府 2,500,000	Dingzhoufu 汀洲府 3,500,000	Yongchunfu 永春府 500,000	Longyanfu 寵巖府 500,000
Jinjiang *xian* 晉江縣	Longxi *xian* 龍溪縣	Shanghang *xian* 上杭縣	Dehua *xian* 德化縣	Zhangping *xian* 漳平縣
Nan-an *xian* 南安縣	Zhangpu *xian* 漳浦縣	Changding *xian* 長汀縣	Datian *xian* 大田縣	Ningyang *xian* 甯洋縣
Huian *xian* 惠安縣	Nanjing *xian* 南靖縣	Ninghua *xian* 甯化縣		
Anxi *xian* 安溪縣	Changtai *xian* 長泰縣	Wuping *xian* 武平縣		
Tongan *xian* 同安縣	Pinghe *xian* 平和縣	Liancheng *xian* 連城縣		
	Zhaoan *xian* 詔安縣	Qingliu *xian* 清流縣		
		Yongding *xian* 永定縣		
		Guihua *xian* 歸化縣		

Source: Philip Wilson Pitcher, *In and About Amoy*, 10–12. The Wade-Giles place names have been changed to present day *Hanyu pinyin*.

Note: This is a chart showing the political divisions by *fu* 府 (prefecture or administrative jurisdiction) and *xian* 縣 (county) with estimated population per prefecture given as follows:

Fu 府 cities: Quanzhou 泉州 (est. 150,000); Zhangzhou 漳州 (est. 200,000); Dingzhou 汀洲 (est. 100,000)

Xian 縣 cities: Tongan 同安 (est. 40,000); Pinghe 平和 (est. 10,000); Nanan 南安 (est. 5,000); Anxi 安溪 (est. 3,000); Huian 惠安 (est. 20,000); Nanjing 南靖 (est. 10,000)

Zhou 洲 cities: Yongchun 永春 (est. 30,000); Longyan 龍巖 (est. 20,000)

Other towns: Chiohbe/Shimei 石美 (est. 60,000); Pechuia/Baishuiying 白水營 (est. 5,000); Wahai/Anhai 安海 (est. 20,000)

Migration from Xiamen, circa 1912

NATIVE SAILING VESSEL (JUNK)

EMIGRANTS LEAVING AMOY.

Chinese junk (top) and emigrants leaving Xiamen

Source: Pitcher, *In and About Amoy*, facing 130, 244.

Emigration Statistics for 1904, 1905, 1906, 1909

Destination	1904	1905	1906	1909
To Formosa	5,415	4,897	5,126	4,155
To Hong Kong	5,643	6,337	6,738	10,260
To Coast Ports	16,261	5,917	7,528	11,080
To Straits	70,000	53,729	67,612	41,963
To Manila	5,080	5,392	4,628	3,855
To Others	457	57	30	518
Totals	102,856	76,329	91,667	71,771
*Inland Waters			335,126	249,785

Destination	1904	1905	1906	1909
From Formosa	6,549	5,557	5,471	7,027
From Hong Kong	19,871	16,887	16,490	15,092
From Coast Ports	14,594	6,898	7,699	13,998
From Straits	28,000	18,920	14,447	21,486
From Manila	1,059	1,185	2,348	4,137
From Others	294	138	15	90
Totals	70,767	49,085	46,500	61,330
*Inland Waters			243,566	245,179

Source: Pitcher, *In and About Amoy*, 160.

* These figures on inland waters have nothing to do with emigration. They merely show the immense passenger traffic between Xiamen and places like Chiohbe [Shima], Chiang Chiu [Zhangzhou], Tsoanchiu [Quanzhou], Oa^n Hai [Anhai] and Tang Oa^n [Tongan] using the waterways. [The names in this note by Pitcher have been rendered into the Romanization style used consistently in this study, and provided with the *Hanyu pinyin* equivalents.]

APPENDIX J

Number of Chinese in Manila and Provinces, 1899–1909

Year	Basis of Estimate	No. in Provinces	No. in Manila	Total Population
1899	Estimate of the Schurman Commission	17,000	23,000	40,000
1903	Census of 1903[a]	19,952	21,083	41,035
1904	Registered Chinese under the act of 1903	22,189	27,474	49,663
1908	Estimate of the Bureau of Customs	36,000	20,000	56,000
1909	Estimate of the Bureau of Customs	36,500	20,500	57,000

Source: Annual Report of the Acting Insular Collector of Customs for the Fiscal year ended June 30, 1909, 125; Annual Report of the Philippine Commission, IX:2:734; in Graciano Cabusora Abulog, "The Chinese Immigration Question in the Philippines" (MA thesis, University of California, 1940), 89.

---

[a]There seems to be a slight difference in the figures given by Abulog with regard to the Census of 1903. In the Census, the number of Chinese in Manila was recorded as 21,500, while those in the provinces numbered 19,535. The total of 41,035, however, is the same for both records.

Chinese Population in the Philippines, Manila and More Heavily Populated Provinces, 1903, 1918, 1939

City/Province	Chinese Population			Times Increase 1939/1903
	1903	1918	1939	
Manila	21,083	17,760	46,233	2.19
Cebu	1,164	1,662	6,117	5.26
Rizal	524	645	5,431	10.36
Zamboanga	618	1,340	4,167	6.74
Tayabas	479	1,274	4,069	8.49
Davao	19	762	3,595	189.21
Iloilo	1,587	1,693	3,511	2.21
Leyte	1,787	2,246	3,076	1.72
Philippines	41,035	43,082	117,487	2.86

Sources: Census 1903, II:262; *Census 1918*, II:354–353; *Census 1939*, II:428; cited in Wong Kwok-chu. *The Chinese in the Philippine Economy 1898–1941*, 17. Reprinted with permission of The Ateneo de Manila University Press.

Note: There seems to be a discrepancy between these two appendices on the total number of Chinese in the country for the years 1918 and 1939. The numbers 43,802 and 43,082 may be different due to typographical errors. Unfortunately, Wong does not give his source(s).

Manila in the Late Eighteenth Century

Source: Reprinted from *The Chinese in Philippine Life 1850–1898*, 27 by Edgar Wickberg by permission of The Ateneo de Manila University Press.

Map of the City of Manila, Philippine Islands 1913

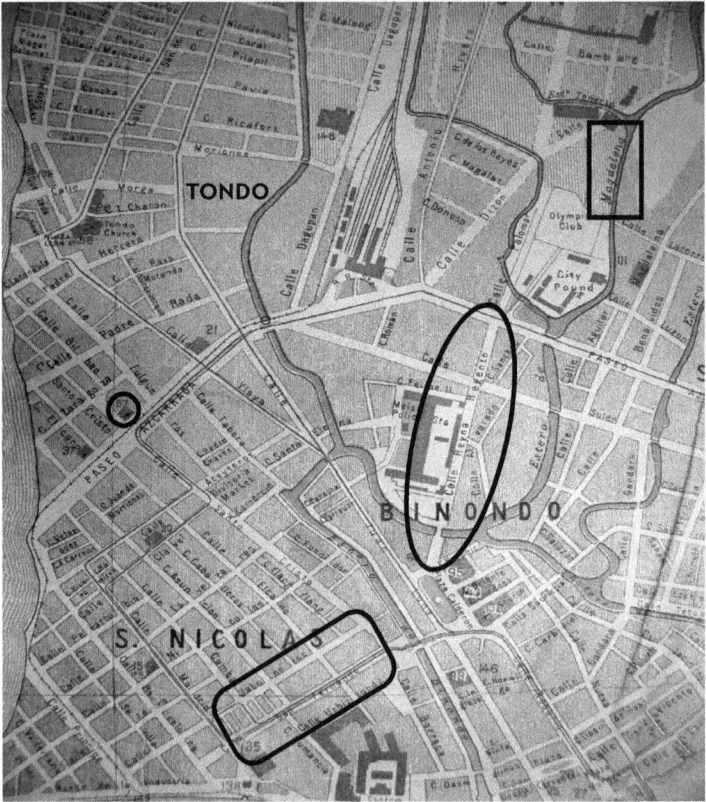

This map, showing the location of the Tondo Presbyterian Church (small circle on the left), the Trozo Presbyterian Church (bold rectangle on the upper right), *Calle Reyna Regente* (elongated circle, center), and *Calle San Fernando* (rectangle on the lower center) is part of a bigger map labeled "City of Manila, Philippine Islands," published by John Bach and F. H. Jaeger of the Bureau of Lands, U.S. Army, on December 1913.

Source: Digital image taken with permission of Filipiniana Section, University of the Philippines, July 6, 2005.

Map of Manila (2006)

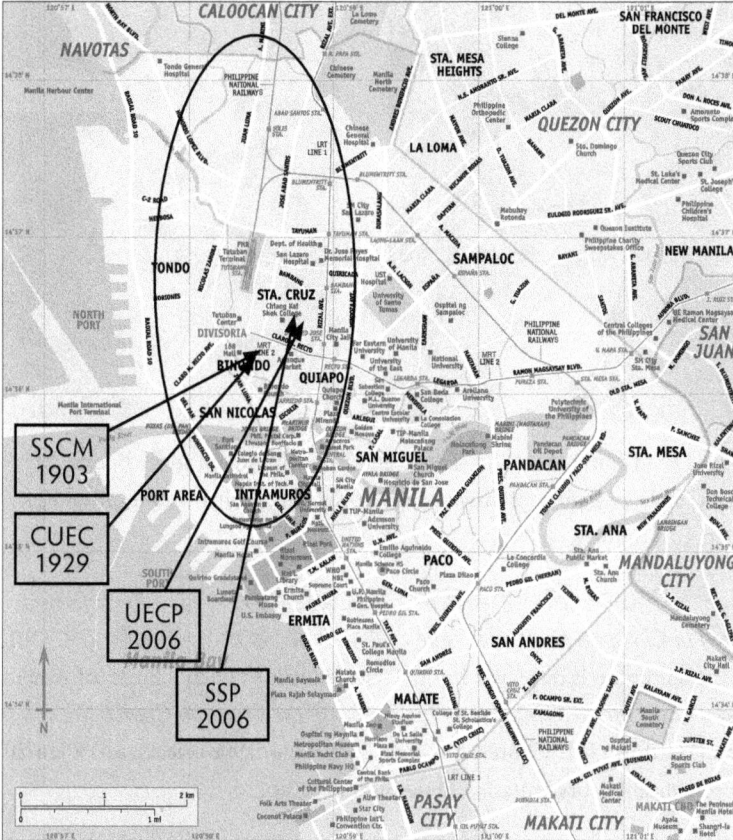

This map is contemporary, with additional markers provided by the writer. The encircled area is where the Chinese population has been concentrated since the days of the Spanish regime. The former and present sites of the SSCM/SSP and the CUEC/UECP are also indicated on the map.

Source: Accessed 7 March 2017, https://en.wikipedia.org/wiki/File:Ph_map_manila.svg

Two Pioneer Missionaries in Xiamen

Rev Dr David Abeel III (1804–1846) and Bishop William Jones Boone, Sr (1811–1864), two pioneer missionaries in Xiamen, China who inspired Rev Hobart Earl Studley.

Source: 杰拉德·F.德庸著，美國歸正教在廈門 *1842–1951 (The Reformed Church in China 1842–1951).* 楊麗、葉克豪譯 (臺北市: 龍圖騰文化, 2013), 25. The left photo is displayed in the First Reformed Dutch Church of Athens in New York. *Project Canterbury: The Bishops of the American Church Mission in China* (Hartford, CT: Church Missions Publishing, 1906), accessed 15 Jan 2016, http://anglicanhistory.org/asia/china/ bishops1908/.

Mission Work in China before and after 1842

Year	Mission	Missionary	Base/Field
1807	London Missionary Society (LMS, 1795) 英國倫敦會	Robert Morrison 馬禮遜 (1782–1834)	Malacca
1827, 1831–33	Netherlands Missionary Society (NMS, 1797) 荷蘭傳教會	Karl Friedrich August Gutzlaff 郭實獵 (1803–1851)	Java, Bangkok China coast
1830	American Board of Commissioners for Foreign Missions (ABCFM, 1810) 美國公理會	Elijah Coleman Bridgman 裨治文 (1801–1861) David Abeel III 雅裨理 (1804–1846)	Guangdong Singapore
1833–1834, 1836	American Baptist Missionary Union/ American Baptist Foreign Mission Society (ABF, 1814) 大美國浸禮會差會 Board of Foreign Missions of the Northern Baptist Convention 美北浸禮會	John Taylor Jones 祝恩賜 (1802–1851) Jehu Lewis Shuck 叔未士 (1812–1863) William Dean 鄰為仁 (1807–1843)	Bangkok Macau, Hong Kong, Shanghai; Bangkok, Hong Kong
1835, 1837	Board of Foreign Missions of the Protestant Episcopal Church in the United States/Episcopal China Mission/American Church Mission (ACM, 1821) 美國聖公會中國差會	Henry Lockwood 駱武 and Francis R. Hanson 韓森 (1807–1873) William Jones Boone 文惠廉 (1811–1864)	Java Java, Xiamen, Shanghai

Year	Mission	Missionary	Base/Field
1837, 1844	Church of England Missionary Society/Church Missionary Society (CMS, 1812) 英行教會	Edward B. Squire 施愛華 George Smith 四美 (d. 1887); Thomas McClatchie 麥麗芝	Singapore, Macau Visited 5 ports, Hong Kong; Ningpo, Shanghai
1838	Board of Foreign Missions of the American Presbyterian Church (APM/PN, 1822) 美國長老總差會	Robert W. Orr 何牧師 (1837–1841); John A. Mitchell 密牧師 (d. 1838, 1837–1838)	Singapore
1842	Dutch Reformed Church in America [under ABCFM (1826–1857)] (RCA, 1857) 大美國歸正教會	David Abeel III William Jones Boone, Sr	Guangdong, Southeast Asia, Xiamen
1842 1844	Board of Foreign Missions of the American Presbyterian Church/ American Presbyterian Mission (APM/PN) 美國長老總差會	Walter Macon Lowrie 婁理華(1819–1847, 1842–1847) Andrew Patton Happer 哈巴安德 (d. 1894, 1844–1894)	Macau, Shanghai, Ningpo Guangdong
1845	General Baptist Missionary Society (UK, BMS) 英國普通浸禮會	Thomas Hall Hudson 胡德邁; William Jarrom 耶翁	Ningbo
1846	Board of Foreign Missions of the Southern Baptist Convention in the United States (BFMSBC, 1845) 美國南浸信傳道會	Samuel Cornelius Clopton 咖笋頓 (1816–1847); George Pearcy 嗶士; Issachar Jacox Roberts 羅孝全 (1802–1871)	Macau, Hong Kong, Guangdong Nanjing, Shanghai
1846	Board of Foreign Missions of the Southern Presbyterian Church (PS) 美國南長老會	Elias B. Inslee 應思理 (1822–1871, 1856–1871)	Ningpo, Shanghai, Zhejiang, Hangzhou

Year	Mission	Missionary	Base/Field
1846, 1847	Evangelical Missionary Society at Basel (1815) 巴色會/崇真會	Gutzlaff; Theodore Hamberg 韓山文; Rudolp Lechler 黎力基	Hong Kong, Guangdong
1847	Rhenish Missionary Society (RM, 1828) 禮賢會/巴勉會	Ferdinand Genahr 葉納清; Heinrich Küster 柯士德	Hong Kong, Guangdong
1847	Seventh Day Baptist Missionary Society (SDB) 安息日浸禮會	Solomon Carpenter 賈本德; Nathan Wardner 華納單	Shanghai
1847	American Methodist Episcopal Missionary Society (MEFB, 1844) 美國衛理宗美以美會	Judson Dwight Collins 柯林 (1822–1852); Moses Clark White 懷德 (1819–1900)	Fuzhou
1847, 1852	Foreign Mission Board of the Presbyterian Church of England (EPM, 1844) 英國長老會	William Chalmers Burns 賓維廉 (1815–1868)	Hong Kong, Guangdong, Xiamen
1848, 1849	American Southern Methodist Episcopal Mission, (MES, 1846) 美南監理會	Charles Taylor 戴醫生; Benjamin Jenkins 秦右	Shanghai
1850	Berlin Missionary Society for China (BN, 1850) 巴陸會/柏林會	Robert Neumann 萬羅伯; August Hanspach 韓士伯	Hong Kong, Guangdong
1852	English Wesleyan Missionary Society (WMMS) 英國循道會	George Piercy 俾士	Guangzhou
1854	Chinese Evangelization Society (CES, 1854) 中華傳道會	James Hudson Taylor 戴德生 (1832–1905)	Shanghai, Jiangsu, Zhejiang, Guangdong

Year	Mission	Missionary	Base/Field
1860	New Connection Methodist Missionary Society in England 聖道公會	William Nelthorpe Hall 郝為廉 (d. 1878); John Innocent 殷約翰	Shanghai, Tianjin
1862	Chinese Inland Evangelization Society/ United Presbyterian Church of Scotland (UPCS) 蘇格蘭長老會	William Parker 巴格爾 (1824–1863)	Ningpo
1865	China Inland Mission (CIM, 1865) 內地會	James Hudson Taylor	Eleven provinces

Sources: Kenneth Scott Latourette, *History of Christian Missions*; Christopher Tang, *The First Hundred Years*; Alexander Wylie, *Memorials of Protestant Missionaries to the Chinese*; Wang ZhiXin's *History of Christianity in China*; and encyclopedic works on mission and church history.

Note: Dates in italics refer to term of service in China. Christopher Tang's book is by far the most comprehensive work on this subject, giving specific details on foreign and Chinese missionaries and systematic geographical treatment of mission throughout the empire. However, it covers only 100 years, until 1907. For a geographical treatment of mission agencies working in China from 1807 to 1917, see Zha ShiJie, *Anthology on the History of Christianity*, 13–20. The life and writings of the missionaries are found in Wylie, *Memorials of Protestant Missionaries to the Chinese*, 1967. Wang's book lists in chart form the mission agencies, representative missionary, mission base and districts from 1807 to 1921.

Map of Fujian (2003)

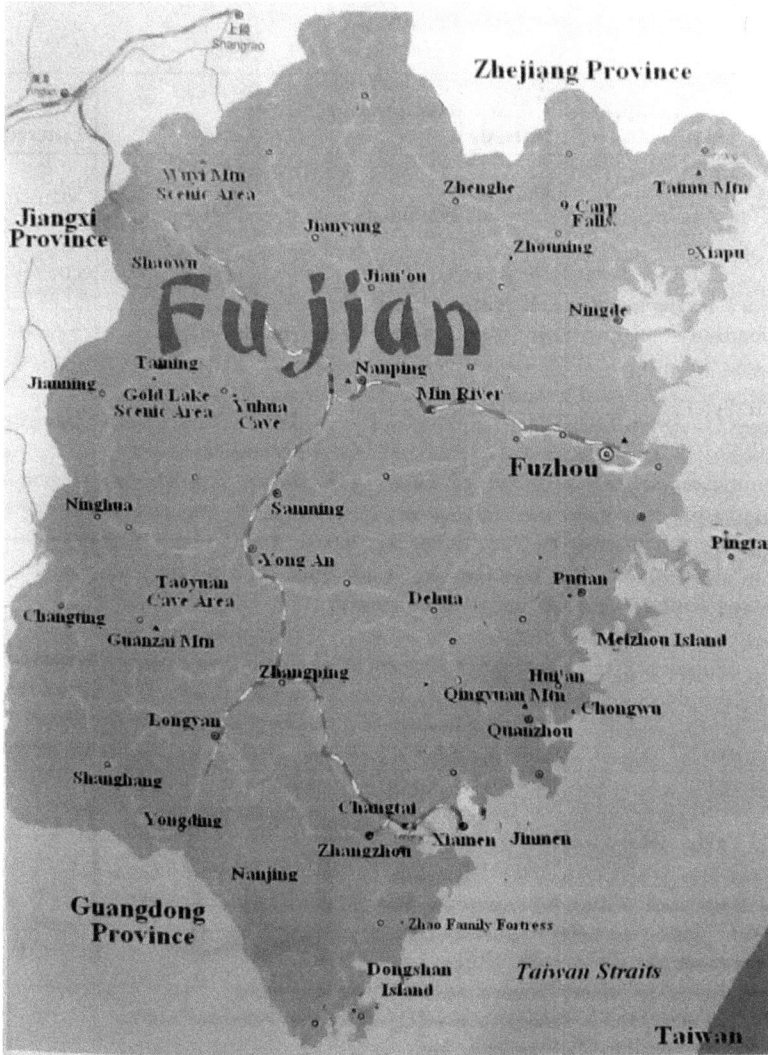

Source: William N. Brown, *Meili Fujian* 魅力福建 *Fujian Adventure* (Xiamen: Lu Jiang Chu Ban She 鷺江出版社, 2003), facing 16. Reproduced with the permission of Dr William N. Brown.

APPENDIX R

Initial Phase of Mission Work in Fujian Province

Mission Agency	Year Started	Missionaries	Field Entered
American Board of Commissioners for Foreign Mission (ABCFM)	1842–1857 1847	David Abeel III 雅裨理 (1804–1846); Stephen Johnson; Rev & Mrs Lyman Birt Peet 弼 (1809–; *1846–1847*)	Xiamen Fuzhou
Board of Foreign Missions of the Presbyterian Church of the United States (APM/PN)	1842	Thomas L. MacBryde (*1842–1843*); James C. Hepburn (*1843–1845*), Walter Macon Lowrie (*1843*), John Lloyd 盧壹 (1813–1848, *1844–1848*), Hugh A. Brown (*1845–1847*)	Xiamen
Board of Foreign Missions of the Protestant Episcopal Church in the United States (ACM)	1842–1845	William Jones Boone, Sr 文惠廉 (1811–1864, *1842*)	Xiamen
Board of Foreign Missions of the Reformed Protestant Dutch Church (now BFMRCA)	1842 1844 1847	David Abeel III; Elihu and Eleanor Ackley Doty 羅啻 (1809–1864, *1844–1865, 1844–1845*); William John and Theodosia Scudder Pohlman 波羅滿 (1812–1849, *1844–1849, 1844–1845*); John Van Nest and Abby Woodruff Talmage 打馬字 (1819–1892, *1847–1892, 1850–1862*)	Xiamen

London Missionary Society (LMS)	1844, 1846	Alexander Stronach 施敦力亞力山大 (1800–1879; *1846–1870*); John Stronach 施敦力約翰 (1810–1888, *1844–1845, 1853–1876*); William Young 楊威廉 (*1848–1854*)	Xiamen
Methodist Episcopal Missionary Society (MEMS)	1848	Robert Samuel Maclay 賣利和 (1824–1907, *1848–1871*)	Fuzhou
Church Missionary Society (CMS)	1850	William Welton 溫敦醫生 (d. 1858)	Fuzhou
Mission of the Presbyterian Church of England (EPM)	1850 1852 1853 1855	James Hume Young 養醫生 (d. 1854, *1850–1854*); William Chalmers Burns 賓維廉 (1815–1868, *1847–1868*); James Johnston 認信 (*1853–1855*); Carstairs Douglas 杜嘉德 (1829–1877, *1855–1877*)	Xiamen

Sources: Latourette, *History of Christian Missions*; Tang, *The First Hundred Years*; Wylie, *Memorials of Protestant Missionaries to the Chinese*; De Jong, *The Reformed Church in China*; Band, *Working His Purpose Out*; various encyclopedic works on mission and church history.

Note: Dates in italics refer to term of service in China.

APPENDIX S

International Settlement in Gulangyu

Gulangyu showing large houses with European designs (1912)

Source: Pitcher, *In and About Amoy,* facing 208.

334

William Burns, Iap Han Chiong and Carstairs Douglas

William Chalmers Burns/Bin WeiLian 賓維廉 (1815–1868), left photo, and Iap Han Chiong/Ye HanZhang 葉漢章 (1832–1914), on the right.

Source: William Brown, *Amoy Magic*, 99, and *The 150ᵗʰ Founding Anniversary of the Xinjie Christian Chapel of Xiamen City*, 16. Reproduced with the permission of Dr William N. Brown (left photo).

還在許牧師在安海童年時代，時
一八七五年清光緒元年，該西人
係首先來安海傳道之杜嘉德牧師
Rev. Cosataid Douglas, L.L.D.
和一位老姊妹學習廈語。

Carstairs Douglas/Du JiaDe 杜嘉德
(b. 1839; d. July 26, 1877)

This photo is taken from the *Commemorative publication of the centenary of the birth of Rev Kho Seng Iam*, 133. The Chinese caption reads "During the childhood days of Reverend Kho [Seng Iam] in Anhai, in 1875, this Westerner, Rev Cosataid ["Carstairs" wrongly spelled] Douglas, L.L.D., was the first man to preach the Gospel in Anhai, here seen taking *Hokkien* lessons with an elderly lady."

Xiamen Churches Past and Present

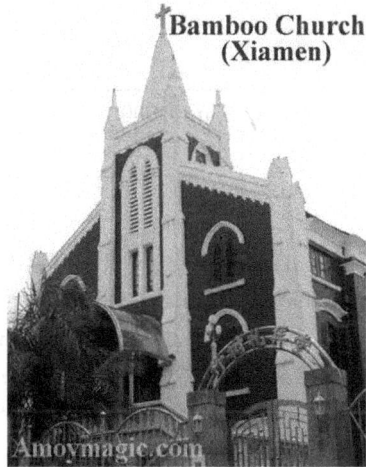

Upper photos (L-R): Sinkoe "New Street" Chapel 新街堂會 (built 1848) and Tekchhiukha "Bamboo Tree Foot" Chapel 竹樹腳堂會 (built 1859), and as the two churches appear today (lower photos, L-R).

Source: Pitcher, *In and About Amoy,* facing 198 (upper left photo); William *Brown, Amoy Magic,* 33, 95. Reproduced with the permission of Dr William Brown.

Protestant Expansion, 1842–1905

Year	Communicants/ Church Members
1842	6
1853	350
1857	400
1863	1,974
1865	3,132
1869	5,753
1873	9,715
1876	13,035
1883	21,560
1889	37,287
1893	55,093
1898	80,682
Early 1900	112,808[a]
Late 1900	95,943[b]
1905	178,251[c]

Source: David Cheung, "The Growth of Protestantism in China: The Role of the Chinese Christians, 1860–1900" (MA thesis, University of London, 1997), 9–10. Cheung's sources include: Donald MacGillivray, ed. *The China Mission Year Book Being "The Christian Movement in China" 1910* (Shanghai: Christian Literature Society for China, 1910), 91–92; Charles Luther Boynton and Charles Dozier Boynton, *1936 Handbook of the Christian Movement in China under Protestant Auspices* (Shanghai: Kwang Hsueh Publishing, 1936), viii–ix; *Records of the General Conference of the Protestant Missionaries of China held at Shanghai, May 10–24, 1877* (Shanghai: Presbyterian Mission Press, 1878; rep. Taiwan: Ch'eng Wen Publishing, 1973), 486, cf. 480–485; *Records 1890*, 732, as cited in J. W. Davies, "Protestant Missionary Work in China," *Chinese Recorder* 23 (1892): 512 (cf. also MacGillivray who gave 37,287 "church members" for 1890 in *China Mission Year Book 1915*, 91–92); *China Mission Handbook* (1896), 325; "Dawn on the Hills of T'ang" (Student Volunteer Movement 1898) as cited in Arthur Henderson Smith, *Rex Christus. An Outline Study of China* (NY: Macmillan, 1903), 250–251; cf. also Harlan P. Beach, "Recent Statistics of Missions in China," *China's Millions*, New Series 13 (1905):145–148; and Warneck's higher figure of 99, 281 (see MacGillivray, *China Mission Year Book 1915*, 91–92).

---

[a] Harlan P. Beach, "Recent Statistics of Missions in China," *China's Millions*, New Series 13 (1905):145–158.

[b] The figure 95,943 which excluded Formosa was reported by Hartmann according to Beach, *China's Millions* (1905):147. "Hartman's" [*sic*] "Survey of Protestant Missions in China" is reproduced in Marshall Broomhall, ed., *Martyred Missionaries of the China Inland Mission, with a Record of the Perils & Sufferings of Some Who Escaped* (London: Morgan & Scott, 1901), 316–323 (originally from Prof Warneck's *Allgemeine Missions Zeitschrift* [May 1900]). Cf. MacGillivray (*China Mission Year Book 1915*, 91–92) who mistakenly reckoned the *Martyred Missionaries* as reporting a pre-1900 figure (i. e. 95, 943); the figure of 85,000 as in Milton Theobald Stauffer, Tsinforn C. Wong and Malcolm Gardner Tewksbury, *The Christian Occupation of China: A General Survey of the Numerical Strength and Geographical Distributon [sic] of the Christian Forces in China, Made by the Special Committee on Survey and Occupation, China Continuation Committee, 1918–1921* (Shanghai: China Continuation Committee, 1922), 38.

[c] Adding together the 178,251 baptized members and 78,528 catechumens yields a combined number of 256,779 for 1905. See W. Nelson Bitton, "Statistics of the Work of Protestant Missions in China for the Year Ending 1905. Prepared for this volume by W. Nelson Bitton" in Donald MacGillivray, ed., *A Century of Protestant Missions in China (1807–1907), Being the Centenary Conference Historical Volume*, CMC Reprint Series 72 (San Francisco: CMC, 1977; reprint, Shanghai: American Presbyterian Mission Press, 1907), 671; also reproduced in *China Centenary Missionary Conference Records. Report of the Great Conference Held at Shanghai, April 25 to May 8 1907* (New York: American Tract Society, 1907), 767. Cf. 178,251 "church members" in MacGillivray, *China Mission Year Book 1915*, 91–92.

Map of Iloilo and Guimaras, circa 1899

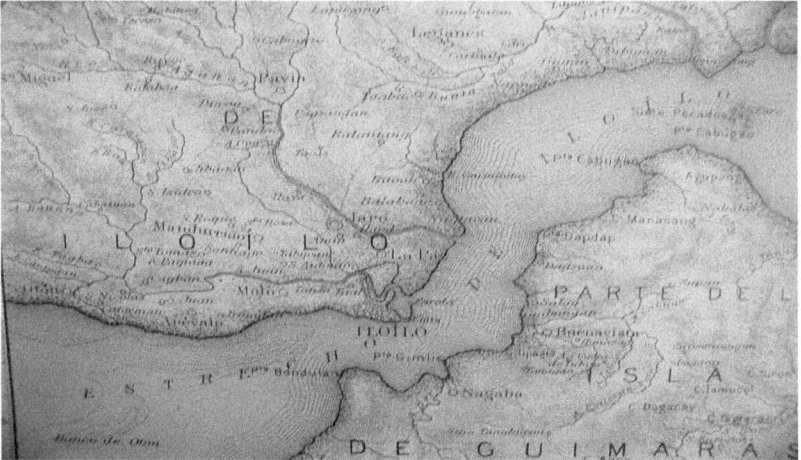

Source: P. José Algué, S.J., *Atlas de Filipinas: Collecion de 30 Mapas. Trabajados por delineantes Filipinos bajo la direccion del P. José* Algué, *S. J. Director del Observatorio de Manila, 1899* (Washington, DC: Government Printing Office, 1900). Reproduced with permission of the University of the Philippines Archives.

APPENDIX X
Archival Photographs of Iloilo Mission

Fig. 1 Photo at left shows Rev D. Donald Sutherland Hibbard and Laura Crooks Hibbard at the time of their missionary appointment. The right photo shows the Executive Committee of the Presbyterian Mission, circa 1923, with Dr Andrew Hall (center), Rev Dr George William Wright (second from right) and Rev Paul Frederick Jansen (far right).

Source: Arthur Leroy Carson, *Silliman University 1901–1959* (New York: United Board for Christian [Higher] Education in Asia, 1965), 63; *Philippine Presbyterian* 14, no. 1 and 2 (Jan–Apr 1923): 3. Reproduced with permission from Silliman University and Union Theological Seminary Archives.

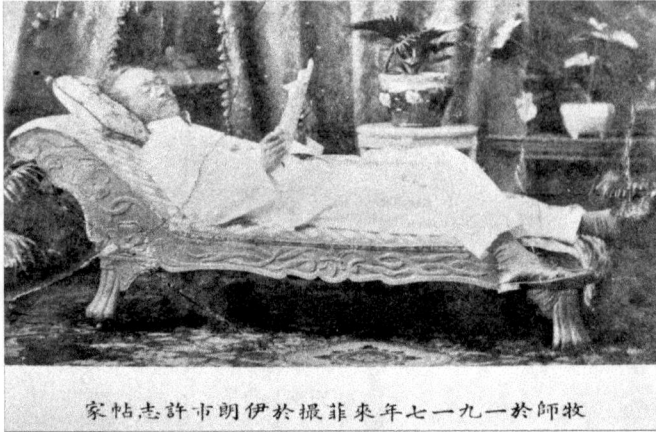

Fig. 2 Rev Kho Seng Iam in Iloilo circa 1917

Source: Commemorative publication of the centenary of the birth of Rev Kho Seng Iam, 118. The Chinese caption reads: "The Reverend [Kho Seng Iam] came to the home of Kho Chi Thiap in Iloilo City, Philippines in 1917."

Fig. 3 Rev Lim Siong Hong (a.k.a. Joseph Lim Tiao Hong) 林翔鳳牧師 (L) and Mr Ong Siong Kim 王尚琴先生 (R)

Reproduced with permission from Lim and Ong families.

APPENDIX Y

Archival Photographs of St. Stephen's Chinese Mission

Fig. 1 Bishop Charles Henry Brent and Rev Hobart Earl Studley

Source: Vincent Herbert Gowen, *Philippine Kaleidoscope: An Illustrated Story of the Church's Mission* (New York: The National Council, Protestant Episcopal Church, n.d.), 6, and *Historical Documentary of Protestantism in the Orient*, 142.

Fig. 2 View of St. Stephen's Chinese Mission, circa 1924. This photo, when compared with Fig. 3, shows the church building from another angle.

Source: Studley, "Chinese Experiment," 578, and Gowen, *Philippine Kaleidoscope*, 21.

ST. STEPHEN'S MISSION FOR CHINESE, MANILA
The small building at the left is the church. It is now quite inadequate to accommodate the constantly growing congregation

Fig. 3 Photo above shows the church (left) and school building (right) of St. Stephen's Chinese Mission, circa 1924. The street in front is *Calle Reina Regente*.

Source: Studley, "Chinese Experiment," 578, and Gowen, *Philippine Kaleidoscope*, 21.

Fig. 4 Rev Mr Ben Ga Pay 白萌芽牧師

Source: Handbooks on the Mission of the Episcopal Church No. III: Philippine Islands (New York: The National Council of the Protestant Episcopalian Church Deparment of Missions, 1923), 24.

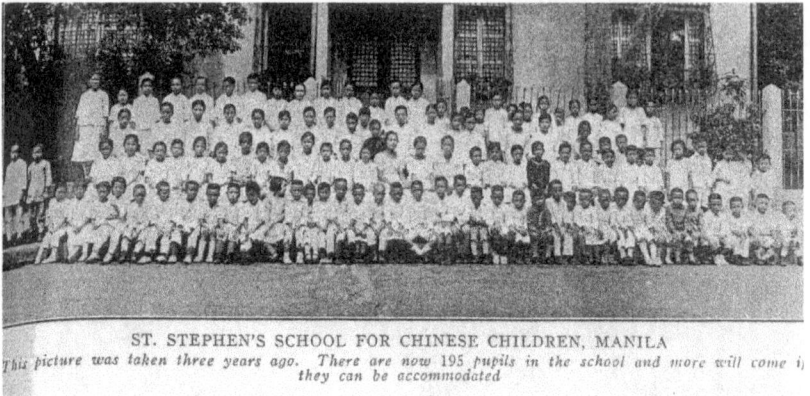

ST. STEPHEN'S SCHOOL FOR CHINESE CHILDREN, MANILA
This picture was taken three years ago. There are now 195 pupils in the school and more will come if they can be accommodated

Fig. 5 St. Stephen's School for Chinese Children, Manila, circa 1921

Source: Studley, "Chinese Experiment," 579.

THE RECTOR, PRINCIPAL AND CHINESE STAFF OF ST. STEPHEN'S SCHOOL
The Rev. Hobart E. Studley, the founder of St. Stephen's Mission, stands in the center of the rear; in front of him sits Miss Georgie M. Brown, the American principal of the school

Fig. 6 Rev Hobart Studley, Ms Georgie Brown and Chinese Staff

Source: Studley, "Chinese Experiment," 577.

Fig. 7 St. Stephen's Parish, c. 1950s (top photo) and at present

Source: Historical Documentary of Protestantism in the Orient, 234 and 142.
Reproduced with the permission of the United Evangelical Church of the
Philippines.

Growth of the Philippine Methodist Church, 1904–1907

Categories/Year	1904	1905	1906	1907
Foreign missionaries – Men		1	1	1
Foreign missionaries – Women		1	1	1
National unordained preachers	2	6	1	
Native preachers				2
Other helpers			7	
Members	10	25	11	16
Probationers	65	51	46	47
Total members and probationers	[75]	[76]	57	63
Other adherents			25	25
Adults baptized		2	1	8
Children baptized		4	1	1
Number of other elementary or day schools		1	1	
Number of high schools, boarding schools, and seminaries			1	
Number of teachers in same			4	
Number of day pupils		18	20	
Number of other elementary or day schools			1	
Number of other day pupils			70	
Number of Sabbath schools			1	1
Number of Sabbath scholars			30	60
Number of halls and other rented places of worship			3	
Number of church and chapel				1
Estimated value of churches and chapels				40,000
Debt on rental estate				10,000

Categories/Year	1904	1905	1906	1907
Collected for self-support				4,000
Total under instruction		18		
Collection for church building and repairing		300		20,000
Collection for other local purposes		380	3,245	
Total contributions on the field		740	3,245	24,000

Source: This is a compilation of data from the following reports: *Eighty-sixth Annual Report of the Missionary Society of the Methodist Episcopal Church for the year 1904* (New York: Missionary Society of the Methodist Episcopal Church, 1905), 274; *Eighty-seventh Annual Report of the Missionary Society of the Methodist Episcopal Church for the Year 1905* (New York: Missionary Society of the Methodist Episcopal Church, 1906), 284; *Eighty-eighth Annual Report of the Missionary Society of the Methodist Episcopal Church for the Year 1906* (New York: Missionary Society of the Methodist Episcopal Church, 1907), 299; *Annual Report of the Board of Foreign Missions of the Methodist Episcopal Church for the Year 1907* (New York: Board of Foreign Missions of the Methodist Episcopal Church, 1908), 376–377.

Progress of St. Stephen's Chinese Mission, 1923–1929

	1923	1926	1927	1929
Infants baptized	18	19	24	18
Adults baptized	9	30	10	6
Total baptized	27	49	34	24
Confirmation	18	36	17	0
Marriages	14	30	45	8
Burials	4	0	2	5
Communicants	228	174	190	195
Baptized Persons	580	650	682	500
Schools: Day	1	1	1	–
Teachers	12	16	17	–
Pupils	98	273	295	–
School: Sunday	1	1	1	–
Teachers	7	8	9	–
Pupils	95	133	110	–
Services	150	220	200	–
Total receipts	₱19,638.61	₱16,296.82	₱17,155.73	–
Total expenses	₱18,861.23	₱12,089.40	₱11,542.54	–

Source: The Eighteenth Annual Report of the Missionary District of the Philippine Islands for the Year Ending December 31, 1923 (Manila, published by the secretary, 1924), 34; *The Nineteenth Annual Report of the Missionary District of the Philippine Islands for the Year Ending December 31, 1926* (Manila, published by the secretary, 1927), 12; *The Twentieth Annual Report of the Missionary District of the Philippine Islands for the Year Ending December 31, 1927* (Manila, published by the secretary, 1928), 24; *The Twentieth-second Annual Report of the Missionary District of the Philippine Islands for the Year Ending December 31, 1929* (Manila: by the secretary, 1930), appendix.

The United Church of Christ in the Philippines and the Protestant Chinese Churches

The United Church of Christ in the Philippines (UCCP, or Feilübin Lianhe Jiaohui 菲律賓聯合教會 as it was known to the Chinese churches) was formed in 1948.[1] The UCCP monitored and coordinated the multi-faceted ministries of autonomous church units. The work of former Presbyterian missionaries among the Chinese and Filipinos in the Philippines came under the evangelistic and ecclesiastical supervision of the UCCP. After the Second World War, the Filipino Protestant churches had reached a new level of independence from foreign missions, despite being closely linked to the various home bases of their various denominational roots.

A. The Evangelical Union

Not long after the American occupation of the Philippines, seven Protestant missions, arriving between 1899 and 1902, began doing mission work in the Islands. These denominations and their mission organizations were: the American Baptists (American Baptist Board – ABB), the Congregationalists

1. The earliest source describing the plan and execution of the union movement up to the year 1929 is found in *The Confession of Faith and Form of Government of the United Evangelical Church of the Philippine Islands approved by the Executive Committee of the General Assembly of the United Evangelical Church, Manila, P. I.: October, 1933.* For a detailed and more up-to-date description of the precedings and succeeding events regarding the formation of the Evangelical Union and the UCCP, see Sitoy, *Several Springs,* 1:321–427. However, only two volumes of the projected five-volume work have been published. Hence, the history of UCCP covers only up to the year 1958. Other useful sources include Sobrepeña, *That They May Be One,* 28–98; and Rodgers, *Forty Years,* 162–175. More recent studies deal with this issue from a skewed perspective, in my view, focusing on the context of the struggle for national identity and integrity of the UCCP. Two examples are Hilario M. Gomez, Jr and Leomyr L. de Jesus, eds., *Commitment and Struggle: The Life and Ministry of the United Church of Christ in the Philippines: A Festschrift for Bishop Erme R. Camba* (Quezon City: United Church of Christ in the Philippines, 1998), and Mariano C. Apilado, *Revolutionary Spirituality: A Study of the Protestant Role in the American Colonial Rule of the Philippines, 1898–1928* (Quezon City: New Day Publishers, 1999).

(American Board of Commissioners for Foreign Missions – ABCFM), the Disciples of Christ also known as The Christian Church, the Episcopalians (Protestant Episcopal Church), the Methodists (Missionary Society of the Methodist Episcopal Church – MSMEC), the Presbyterians (Board of Foreign Missions of the Presbyterian Church in the United States of America – BFMPCUSA), and the United Brethren in Christ. The Christian and Missionary Alliance came in 1905, followed by the Seventh-Day Adventists in 1906.[2] Concern over the potential problem of territorial overlaps as well as the desire to attain smooth relations and better cooperation in the mission field led to the formation of the "Evangelical Union in the Philippine Islands" (also known as the Federation of the Evangelical Missions) in April 1901, with the Christian and Missionary Alliance, the Seventh-Day Adventists and the Episcopalians declining to join.[3]

The move toward cooperation was preceded by the "Ministerial Alliance" formed by the Presbyterian and Methodist missionaries on 11 Jun 1900.[4] The Union formed an Executive Committee consisting of two representatives from each of the member missions. Its objective was "to unite all the evangelical forces in the Philippine Islands for the purpose of securing comity and effectiveness in their missionary operations."[5] Its ultimate goal, however, was the union of all churches into one Evangelical or Protestant Church. In order to achieve the first objective, a Committee on Division of Territory was also formed which divided the Philippines into areas of responsibility according to geographical and ethno-linguistic lines.

1. The Comity Agreement

In the final division that would last until 1950, Manila from the very beginning was considered a common area for all mission groups. The Methodists

---

2. For the early mission attempts of the Christian and Missionary Alliance prior to 1905, see section on Davao Evangelical Church. Seventh-Day Adventists such as Elder G. A. Irwin, R. Caldwell, and E. H. Gates had briefly visited the Philippines in 1905 but only to explore possibilities, hence their mission work actually began with the coming of Elder and Mrs J. Lamar McElhany on 13 Apr 1906. See Sitoy, *Several Springs*, 1: 66.

3. *A Unified Program for the Philippines. Findings of the Conference held in Manila, March 19–21, 1929.* Manila: National Christian Council of the P.I. May, 1929, 19–20.

4. "The Evangelical Union," *The Philippine Presbyterian* 12 (April 1921): 3, quoted in Sitoy, *Several Springs*, 1: 321.

5. James B. Rodgers in *The Evangelist* (20 Jun 1901), quoted in Dean, *Cross of Christ*, 228.

had Luzon north of Manila except for La Union (under the United Brethren), and the two Ilocos provinces, and Abra (under the Disciples). The Presbyterians held Luzon south of Manila, as well as the Palawan group and the eastern Visayas. The Baptist were assigned the Ilonggo-speaking western Visayas, Negros Occidental, Romblon and nearby islands. The Presbyterians withdrew from southern Iloilo and Antique in 1925. Mindoro was under the aegis of the Presbyterians and Methodists, while the Congregationalists pioneered in Mindanao, except for Sulu, Basilan, the southern Zamboanga peninsula, and certain pockets in Cotabato, which were entrusted to the Christian and Missionary Alliance and, for the non-Christian peoples, who were entrusted to the Episcopalians.

2. The Evangelical Church

In order to achieve the ultimate goal, it was agreed that all Protestant churches in the Philippines would adopt a common name – *La Iglesia Evangelica* ("The Evangelical Church") – followed by the geographical location and the denominational title (in parentheses). In 1914, the Committee on Union Church was formed in answer to the pleading of Filipino ministers and the growing occurrences of schisms within different denominations.[6] The committee met to formulate a plan for a federation of churches, for conventions in districts and island capitals. But many still held back from supporting the union plan.[7] This was also the year when the General Assembly in session in Chicago Synod established the Philippine Presbyterian Synod as an independent Synod. This meant that the Presbyterian churches in the Philippines no longer had any ecclesiastical relation with the church in the United States.[8] Soon after, the church union plan of 1915 was drawn up, but encountered a snag when the Baptists and the Disciples became concerned over the clause regarding the General Advisory Council and the power it would hold. The rest of the churches

6. The Methodist Episcopal Church experienced schisms in 1905, 1909, and later in 1933 and in 1913, the Presbyterian Church was divided resulting in the formation of another body, the *Iglesia de los Cristianos Filipinos*. See Gerald Harry Anderson and Peter G. Gowing, *Four Centuries of Christianity in the Philippines: An Interpretation*. Reprint from *Encounter* 25, 3, n.d. (Indianapolis, IN: Christian Theological Seminary, n.d.), 363.

7. See Sitoy, *Several Springs*, 1: 323–330; Rodgers, *Forty Years*, 162–169.

8. See *The Philippine Presbyterian*, 15, 4 (Oct 1924): 32–34, for a detailed explanation of "The Movement for Church Union in the Philippines."

hesitated from implementing the plan since there were dissenting groups. The 1920s was also the time when churches in the United States were racked by the "liberal-fundamentalist" controversy, and the ripples of this controversy spilled into the Philippines. The Disciples and the Baptists, in particular, were buffeted by inner tensions and conflicts.[9]

3. The Evangelical Church of the Philippines

In 1920 the Evangelical Union amended its constitution to admit Filipino members. Among those who agreed to the plan there developed a stand to enter into union without those who disagreed. In 1921, the Presbyterians and Congregationalists took a definite step during their meeting and united into one church, taking the name "The Churches of Christ in the Philippines."[10] They proposed that the form of government would be worked out after the union was effected, and that the doctrinal standards accepted by the union theological seminaries in Manila and Nanking and other federations elsewhere be adopted. This proposed scheme of union was adopted with slight modifications by the Philippine Presbyterian Synod meeting in Cebu in 1922. The name was modified to "The Evangelical Church of the Philippines (Presbyterian-Congregational)" until such time as others joining the union would propose another name. After 1922, the call for union fell into the hands of the churches entirely and the Filipino leaders almost wholly conducted union negotiations.

4. The United Evangelical Church of the Philippine Islands

In 1924, church units from the United Brethren, Baptists, Congregationalists and Presbyterians formed "The United Church of Manila," a name that was chosen over "The United Church of the Philippines" as originally proposed. This was different from the Evangelical Union which was made up of individual members rather than church units. It was also different from the Union Church of Manila, the inter-denominational American

---

9. For a clearer picture of the controversy that rocked these two groups, see Mark Maxey, *History of the Philippine Mission of the Churches of Christ* (San Clemente, CA: Go Ye Books, n.d.).

10. See Sitoy, *Several Springs*, 1: 336–340; *The Confession of Faith and Form of Government of the United Evangelical Church of the Philippine Islands approved by the Executive Committee of the General Assembly of the United Evangelical Church, Manila, October, 1933*, 4–6. This source will henceforth cited as *Confession of Faith* (1933).

congregation in Ermita. This organization paved the way for final approval for forming the union that would be called "The United Evangelical Church of the Philippine Islands." The original name proposed was "The United Church of Christ in the Philippines," but it would take twenty more years before this name would be used for the much bigger union that exists until the present day.

The Evangelical Church of the Philippines (Independent Presbyterian), the Presbytery of Cagayan (Congregationalist), the Philippine Conference of the Church of the United Brethren in Christ, and the independent congregation of the United Church of Manila signified their intention to join the proposed united Church. Three representatives from each of these groups met in Manila in August 1924, where the General Committee on Church Union adopted the Nanking Agreement as doctrine and chose the name "The United Church of Christ in the Philippines," similar to the names of other federations in Canada, China and other countries.[11] However, when the Philippine Synod met in Cebu in 1926, the delegates formulated a fuller confession of faith and adopted the name "United Evangelical Church of the Philippine Islands" in their desire to retain the term "evangelical." This was later modified as "The United Evangelical Church of the Philippines." When the Basis of Union was drawn up in 1928, the final name that appeared was "the United Evangelical Church in the Philippine Islands" (UECPI).

The historic union assembly was held in Manila on 14–19 March 1929, with the first session held at the United Church of Manila on *Calle Azcarraga* and the rest of the meetings at the Union Theological Seminary on Taft Avenue. On 15 March, the participants accepted the Basis of Union, the Confession of Faith, and the Form of Government as they were submitted.[12] The governing bodies of this new entity were: the local

---

11. The principal reference document was the union plan of the United Church of Christ in Canada. Other names include the Church of Christ in China and the United Church of South India.

12. The National Christian Council would later describe this form of government as an amalgamation of "the democracy of the Baptists and Disciples [as well as Congregationalists], the efficiency and connectionalism of the Methodists, and the representative authority of the Presbyterians." See *Minutes and Reports of the Enlarged Meeting of the Executive Committee of the National Christian Council of the Philippines, Manila, April 2–7, 1932*, 83; quoted in Sitoy, *Several Springs*, 1: 374 and *Confession of Faith* (1933).

Church Council, the District Conference, and the General Assembly.[13] At the time of this merger, there were five district conferences, namely: the Northern Luzon District Conference, the Manila District Conference, the Cebu District Conference, the Dumaguete District Conference, and the Mindanao District Conference, the last replacing the Presbytery of Cagayan. The UECPI drew up a Constitution setting down its life and mission. More significantly, with regard to the relationship of the united church and the cooperating mission bodies, the Second General Assembly of 1931 declared that "The missions should continue to exist, but should work through the native church, transferring to the church the responsibilities belonging to it" and that "the term and extent of the interdenominational cooperation should be determined by the native church.[14]

That the missionaries should become members of the Conference was an adoption of the action taken by the Church of Christ in China (CCC), whereby missionaries were permitted by the Presbyterian Church in the United States of America to "continue in the Church of Christ in China in any and all relationships which the Church of Christ in China pleases to grant while at the same time conserving all the implications of membership as an ordained minister in full standing in the Presbyterian Church in the United States of America."[15] The UECPI simply replaced the name "Church of Christ in China" with its name and with such a declaration, the Filipino Christian churches became an independent entity.

5. The National Christian Council of the Philippines

In the same month as the formation of the United Evangelical Church, the National Christian Council of the Philippines was also organized, superseding the old Evangelical Union. The leadership was almost completely Filipino, and the voice of the churches carried more weight than that of the missions. However, it continued to uphold the comity and unity originally

---

13. See *Constitution of the United Evangelical Church* for the full description of the composition and organizational functions of these three bodies. Cf. Sitoy, *Several Springs*, 1: 374–377.

14. *Minutes of the Meeting of the Second General Assembly of the United Evangelical Church of the Philippines April 16th–20th, 1931*, 45–46.

15. *Minutes of the Third General Assembly of the United Evangelical Church of the Philippines Held in Cebu, April 19th–22nd, 1933*, 13.

articulated by the Evangelical Union of 1901. To promote the common interests of its member churches, it also created various standing committees on church relations, social and moral welfare, stewardship, Bible circulation, evangelism, educational institutions, publications, and religious education. In 1938, the United Evangelical Church, the Methodist Episcopal Church, the Church of Christ (Disciples), and the Philippine Baptist Church were organized as the Philippine Federation of Evangelical Churches.

6. The War Time Union

From 1929-1941, there was great gain in the areas of education, leadership training, medical missions in addition to that of evangelism and conversion. When war broke out, the Japanese occupation forces reorganized the Philippine Federation of Evangelical Churches (PFEC) in 1942. Unity within this Federation was almost shattered by accusations against Enrique C. Sobrepeña, then presiding bishop of the Evangelical Church and president of the Federation. Some groups within these two bodies charged him with being a Japanese collaborator, but the court verdict found him not guilty. This issue was peacefully resolved eventually.[16] This time, in addition to the United Church of Christ in the Philippines, the United Methodist Church and its splinter groups (the *Iglesia Evangelica Metodista En Las Islas Filipinas*/IEMELIF and *Iglesia Evangelica Unida de Cristo*/UNIDA),[17] the Convention of Philippine Baptist Churches, the *Iglesia Filipina Independiente* (Philippine Independent Church) and the Philippine Episcopal Church participated in the Council.[18]

---

16. See Norwood B. Tye, *Journeying with the United Church of Christ in the Philippines: A History* (Quezon City: United Church of Christ in the Philippines, 1994), 12–16, for a concise discussion on the matter.

17. The *Iglesia Evangelica Unida de Filipinas* was founded on 3 Jan 1932, but because the English translation turned out to be similar to the United Evangelical Church of the Philippines, it was amended to *La Iglesia Evangelica Unida de Cristo* ("The United Evangelical Church of Christ"). The shortened form UNIDA became more popularly used. The *Iglesia Evangelica Metodista en las Islas Filipinas*/IEMELIF ("The Evangelical Methodist Church in the Philippine Islands"), led by Rev Nicolas V. Zamora, separated from the Methodist Church in 1909.

18. Arthur Leonard Tuggy and Ralph E. Toliver, *Seeing the Church in the Philippines* (Manila: OMF Publishers, 1972), 42–43; Estanislao Q. Abainza, et. al., *Enrique C. Sobrepeña: His Life and Work,* eds., Fern Babcock Grant, Domini Torrevillas-Suarez, and Leon O. Ty (Quezon City: The Sponsorship Committee, 1975), 98–188. Cf. Douglas J.

All Protestant church groups, including some that did not participate in the pre-war federation, had to join the PFEC. They also encouraged the continuation of the united church, known then as the Evangelical Church in the Philippines. However, there was great resistance against this new version of the United Church, which eventually led to a division of allegiance between the Evangelical Church in the Philippines and the reconstituted United Evangelical Church in the Philippines.[19] By the time of liberation, the union disintegrated and a new organization, the National Council of Churches in the Philippines (NCCP), formed on November 7, 1963 and officially related to the World Council of Churches (WCC), succeeded the Philippine Federation of Evangelical Churches.

7. Church-Missions Relation

The first post-war General Assembly of the revived United Evangelical Church (the eighth since 1929) was held at Dumaguete on May 14–19, 1946. The Assembly made a landmark decision that the General Moderator and District Conference involved should be consulted in matters of appointing missionaries to the field. This would have far reaching consequences on the relationship of both the churches in the Philippines and the mission boards.

On 16–17 September 1946, the historic Special Church-Mission Meeting was held at Silliman University, attended by the Executive Committee of the United Evangelical Church, eight representatives of the deputation from the American mission boards, and a few local representatives from the American Board and the Presbyterian Mission. An excerpt of the declaration stated:

> Believing that the time has come for the complete unification of the program of the United Evangelical Church and Mission Boards related to the Church which in the past has

---

Elwood, "Varieties of Christianity in the Philippines," in *Studies in Philippine Church History*, ed. Gerald H. Anderson (Ithaca and London: Cornell University Press, 1969), 366–386.

19. The Evangelical Church in the Philippines was composed of the Ilocano Convention of the Disciples, the Philippine Methodist Church, congregations of the UNIDA and IEMELIF, and the Ilocano and Tagalog segments. The reconstituted United Evangelical Church in the Philippines was composed mostly of conferences in the Visayas and Mindanao and half of the Tagalog and Bicol conferences

been carried on under parallel lines of activities, and assuming that the right to the management of its own internal affairs inheres in the Church. We propose the transfer to the Church of all ecclesiastical functions, the philanthropic service, and the missionary expansion previously carried on by the Missions.[20]

The transfer was to take effect on 1 October 1947. In the same year, the Committee on Church Union of the Philippine Federation of Evangelical Churches appointed a sub-committee to draft an enlarged Basis of Union, which dealt with the categories of faith, order and practical measures in five articles. The name of the organization was the United Church of Christ in the Philippines.

8. The United Church of Christ in the Philippines

On 25 May 1948 delegates from the Evangelical Church, the Philippine Methodist Church, and the United Evangelical Church met at the Ellinwood Malate Church in Manila. They agreed upon the Basis of Union and submitted a Declaration of Union signed by the 173 delegates and visitors. The whole text of the Declaration, the election of officers, the government and heritage of faith of the UCCP can be found in the works of Enrique C. Sobrepeña and T. Valentino Sitoy, Jr[21] The four bishops who had joint oversight over the entire UCCP, and their respective jurisdictions, were Enrique C. Sobrepeña (Northern Luzon), Cipriano Navarro (Southern Luzon), Leonardo G. Dia (Visayas), and Proculo A. Rodriguez (Mindanao). Rev Stephen L. Smith, pastor of Ellinwood Malate Church served as General Secretary, with Mr Jose L. Navarro as General Treasurer and Rev Hugh N. Bousman as General Evangelist.

There were ten standing commissions for the ministry, evangelism and missions, Christian religious education, audio-visual education, education, finance, Christian literature and publication, women's work, rural life, polity, and church and missions board relations. At the time of the union,

---

20. *Minutes of the Planning Conference (September 16–17, 1946)*, 15; quoted in Sitoy, *Several Springs*, 1: 478. The above summary of the war-time union and postwar rehabilitation of the United Evangelical Church of the Philippines is based on Sitoy, *Several Springs*, 1: 429–483.

21. Sobrepeña, *That They May Be One*, 72–98 and Sitoy, *Several Springs*, 1: 494–501.

the UCCP had a communicant membership of about 130,000 and a constituency of over 330,000 gathered in 1,000 organized local churches and hundreds of unorganized congregations.

B. The UCCP and Chinese Churches

After the UCCP was organized, a new situation within the Chinese community began to take shape. Beginning in 1949, the Communist regime forced Chinese Christians and foreign missionaries to withdraw from China, thus creating successive waves of immigrants entering countries surrounding China. The Philippines was a prime destination for the exodus of missionaries, but the emigration policy set by the government limited the entry of Chinese Christians. The UCCP was quick to respond to the situation. It formed a sub-committee on Chinese work that was placed under the Philippine Board of Missions, composed of three Chinese, two Filipinos and two Americans. Rev George Sin Chiong Chua of the Chinese United Evangelical Church headed the Chinese representatives.[22]

1. Relocated Missionaries

Not long after, the Reformed Church in America missionaries reassigned to the Philippines reinforced the UCCP personnel. Two resolutions appeared in the 1950 minutes of the Second General Assembly of the UCCP:

> VOTED: That we extend a cordial invitation to missionaries in China who are ecumenically-minded and who use the Amoy dialect, to come to the Philippines to work among the Chinese along educational and evangelistic lines in conjunction with the UCCP and that this invitation be sent to the National Christian Council of China.

> VOTED: That we express an active interest in the temporary assignment for service with the UCCP of missionaries of the American and Presbyterian Boards whose services in China

---

22. *Minutes of the Second General Assembly, United Church of Christ in the Philippines, April 25–30, 1950*, 20. See pp. 190 and 204 for more information on Rev Chua.

are at present temporarily restricted and whose experiences and interests would fit them for service in the Philippines.[23]

This overture signaled the beginning of the cooperative mission enterprise between the RCA and the UCCP.[24] The RCA affiliated itself with the UCCP because, according to Rev William Robertson Angus, Jr/Hong WeiLin 洪為霖牧師 (1901–1984), "this followed the settled policy of its Board [of World Missions of the Reformed Church in America] and its denomination not to perpetuate its own name and its own denomination on the mission field, but to cooperate in the organization, establishments, and fostering of indigenous evangelical churches in each of the countries where its missionaries are at work."[25] Nevertheless, although its missionaries were under the direction of and were appointed by the Personnel Committee of the UCCP, they had their own Field Committee, and more than half of their work force ministered to the Chinese congregations that were not formally affiliated with the UCCP.

The first Reformed Church missionaries, who came in 1950, were Rev Joseph R. Esther/Yi ShuDe 伊樹德 and his wife Marion Boot Esther. They had served in China from 1946–1949.[26] All in all fifteen RCA missionaries who had served in the Amoy Mission (Xiamen), and who spoke *Hokkien*, came to the Islands.[27] In 1952, William Angus and his wife Agnes Joyce Buikema Angus, who had served in China since 1925, had to leave their ministry in Xiamen, and were reassigned to the Philippines. They were first assigned to Legaspi to work among the Chinese, then to Cagayan de Oro

---

23. *Minutes of the Second General Assembly*, 15.

24. A detailed report of the deliberations concerning this venture can be found in the "Discussion of Proposed Integration of Work in the Philippines of Reformed Church in America with the United Church of Christ in the Philippines," in *Minutes of the Joint United Church and Reformed Church Committee on Proposed Integration of Work in the Philippines of Reformed Church with United Church, September 12, 1962*, 39–43.

25. Angus, "The United Church and the Existing Chinese Churches," 26.

26. The Esthers served in the United Evangelical Church of Manila (former CUEC) from 1951–1961. For their autobiography, see Joseph R. Esther, *"This Is the Way, Walk Ye in It" Isaiah 30:21* (Redlands, CA: by the author, 1977).

27. In 1954, there were three missionaries in Manila, six in Cebu, and two each in Dumaguete, Lucena, and Legaspi. See "Appendix VI," *United Church of Christ in the Philippines, Minutes of the Fourth Biennial General Assembly, Los Baños, Laguna, May 17–23, 1954*, 74.

(ministering at Cagayan Gospel Church, a Chinese congregation), and finally, to Manila, where they served until their retirement in 1967.

Fig. 1. Joseph R. Esther and Marion Boot Esther (L) and William Robertson Angus, Jr with his wife, Agnes Joyce Buikema Angus (R)

Source: Esther, *"This Is the Way, Walk Ye in It"* and Angus Papers, reprinted with permission from Joint Archives of Holland, Hope College.

2. Relating to the Philippine Chinese Churches

Angus aptly summarized the hard lessons the RCA missionaries had to learn on what could be accomplished in their Chinese work. They started out assuming that the Chinese churches would cooperate willingly in evangelism and other types of ministry, eventually uniting with the UCCP, but this did not become a reality. Next, they hoped that they could form a Chinese annual conference, either independently but still cooperating with the UCCP or better still, under the UCCP. This, too did not happen as they desired. Finally, they hoped that "the United Evangelical Church of Manila [as CUEC had become known by the mid-1960s] might form such an annual conference."[28] This also did not come to pass. The minutes of the Executive Committee Meeting of the Philippine Federation of Christian Churches (PFCC) indicated that the CUEC did apply for affiliate membership with the PFCC in 1958. The minutes of the Seventh

---

28. William Robertson Angus, Jr, "The Commission on Philippine-Chinese Mission – Talk to Moderator's Seminar, 1963," in *United Church of Christ in the Philippines: Commission on Philippine-Chinese Mission – Communications, Reports, Minutes, Talks 196–65.* H00=1381 Box 1. Angus Papers. Joint Archives of Holland, Hope College, Holland, Michigan, 3.

General Assembly held in 1960, however, showed no record that this application ever became a reality, and part of the text of the PFCC meeting manifests the reason why. It states,

> But like any other Chinese organizations, the Chinese church has had a minority group who are fearful of being absorbed into a non-Chinese entity, like the UCC[P]. This is the main reason why the Chinese church may perhaps always remain an independent church organization. To disturb that status would result to a division of the congregation which the chinese [*sic*] church leaders would not want to happen. The independent-mindedness of the Chinese churches throughout the country inhibits them to integrate [*sic*] with our national churches.[29]

This assessment points to the cultural factor that hindered the Chinese churches from fully identifying or integrating with the UCCP, which, to these churches, was considered a Filipino entity. However, as will be seen in the next section, there was another reason for this hindrance.

Despite this bleak state of affairs, the Reformed Board continued throughout the 1950s and the better part of the 1960s to work closely with the Chinese. They did this mostly by placing personnel in two Chinese churches and their church-related schools: the United Evangelical Church of Manila (former CUEC) and Hope Christian High School/Jianan Zhongxue 嘉南中學,[30] and the Cebu Gospel Church and Cebu Christian School/Shuwu Jianji Zhongxue 宿務建基中學, which was a union of the Kian Kee High School/Shuwu Jianji Zhongxue 宿務建基中學 and Cebu Institute (UCCP church-related school).[31]

---

29. *Minutes of the Executive Committee Meeting, Philippine Federation of Christian Churches, Union Theological Seminary Building, Manila, October 31, 1958*, Record Group A, Box 32A, Yale University Day Missions Library, Yale University, New Haven, CT, 426; *Minutes of the Seventh General Assembly, United Church of Christ in the Philippines, Legaspi City, May 19–24, 1960*, 110.

30. For a short history of this school, see Board of Trustees, "A Quarter-Century of Progress," in *Jianan Zhongxue Yinxi Tekan* 嘉南中學銀禧特刊 (Twenty-fifth anniversary special publication of Hope Christian High School) (Manila: Hope Christian High School, 1972), 18–19.

31. Some of the RCA missionaries involved in education, in or before the year 1964, included: the Esthers; Tena Holkeboer, who served in China from 1920–1948, then in

3. The Commission on Philippine Chinese Mission

The integration of the RCA and the UCCP was formally recorded in the 1962 report of the Department of Evangelism, as follows:

> 62–25 VOTED: That the General Assembly receive with appreciation the announcement of the contemplated plan of the Reformed Church in America to integrate its work in the Philippines with that of the United Church of Christ, and that it designate the Chairman, the General Secretary, and the General Treasurer of the United Church to constitute a committee of three to meet with a committee of similar number representing the Reformed Church in America to work out the plans for integration.[32]

In the 1960s, the UCCP entity that had direct relationship with the Chinese churches, particularly in Cebu and Manila, was the Department on Evangelism. During the Executive Committee meeting held on December 11–13, 1962, this Department reported that as a result of the integration of the work of the RCA and the UCCP, a new program for the Chinese was being given new attention in line with their commitment to "join in an active participation in provincial evangelistic rallies and preaching missions with Chinese evangelists and missionaries.[33] This joint effort created a committee composed of representatives from both bodies and these recommended a plan to establish the Commission on Philippine-Chinese Mission (henceforth written as CPCM). The purpose of the CPCM would be

> to win Chinese for Christ and to create a climate in which these new Christians can experience unity with their Filipino

---

Manila at the Hope Christian High School from 1951–1961; Rev Earl Nelson Kragt and his wife Hazel Vander Woude in Cebu Gospel Church; and Mr and Mrs Robert B. Howard in Cebu Christian School. See *United Church of Christ in the Philippines, Minutes of the Executive Committee, December 10 & 11, 1964*, 126, 128. The school was originally called Cebu Gospel School, then Cebu Christian School. Today it is known as Philippine Christian Gospel School. See further pp. 175–178.

32. See "Appendix VIII: Report of the Sub-Committee submitted by Enrique Sobrepeña," *United Church of Christ in the Philippines, Minutes of the Executive Committee, Quezon City, December 11–13, 1962 and January 22, 1963*, 97. Note that the number 62-25 refers to the record number in the minutes.

33. Ibid., 68–69.

brethren. In pursuing this purpose, the Commission will foster cooperation between the UCCP and the Chinese congregations that are not members of it. The Commission will foster fraternal relations and develop a working partnership with
these associated Chinese congregations. The Commission
looks upon the whole Chinese community as an area for fostering unity between Chinese and Filipinos, bringing to bear
upon the relation of these two peoples the witness and resources of the Gospel of Christ.[34]

In its administrative structure, the CPCM was designed to be directly under the Executive Committee of the UCCP, consisting of from 10 to 12
persons: five representatives from the Chinese churches organically related
to the United Church of Christ, the pastor and a layman whenever possible
(two from the Cebu Gospel Church; two from the Westminster Student
Church; and one from the United Evangelical Church of Sta. Cruz); three
from among the Reformed Church missionaries; and three members from
the UCCP. Co-opted members may be invited from the Chinese churches
not yet related to the UCCP, if the CPCM agreed to do so.[35]

The CPCM replaced the Field Committee of the Reformed Board.
For the CPCM to work well, a "capable Chinese or a missionary of the
Reformed Church" was recommended, although this person need not work
full-time. Ever since the 1950s, Rev Wesley Shao, who was still the minister
of DCGC/DEC at the time, had been recommended by the CPCM either
as representative for the Mindanao area or as the director of the Chinese
work in the Department of Evangelism.[36] He, however, did not seem to be
the suitable person for this task.

34. *Minutes of the Ninth Biennial General Assembly, United Church of Christ in the Philippines, Lucena City, May 31–June 5, 1964*, 164.

35. See Angus, "The United Church," 26.

36. See *United Church of Christ in the Philippines, Minutes of the Mid-Year Meeting, Executive Committee, Manila, November 25–27, 1953*, 13; *United Church of Christ in the Philippines, Minutes of the Executive Committee, Quezon City, December 11–13, 1962 and January 22, 1963*, 22. Rev Wesley Shao's surname was wrongly spelled as "Shiao" in the second source.

After the UCCP approved the recommendation, the Board of World Missions of the RCA also consented to full relationship with the UCCP. The Executive Committee Minutes for May 22-24, 1963 recorded that,

> The Board of World Missions of the Reformed Church in America has voted, at its meeting May 7-19, 1963, to enter into full relationship with the United Church of Christ in the Philippines beginning January 1, 1964, by having its missionaries working with and under the direction of the United Church of Christ in the Philippines, without prejudice to present assignments.[37]

When the CPCM was finally formed, William Angus was elected as its first secretary. In 1963, he reported that there were three Chinese congregations in the UCCP: the Westminster Student Church/Feilübin Zhonghua Jidu Jiaohui Xunshantang 菲律賓中華基督教會郇山堂 (a member of the Greater Manila Annual Conference), the United Evangelical Church of Santa Cruz, Laguna/Neihu Zhonghua Jidu Jiaohui 內湖中華基督教會 (a member of the Southern Tagalog Annual Conference), and the Cebu Gospel Church/Shuwu Jidu Jiaohui 宿務基督教會 (a member of the Cebu Annual Conference).[38] There were also missionaries who worked with Chinese congregations that did not have organic relationship with the UCCP.

Part of the process of integration was the full membership of the Board of World Mission of the Reformed Church in America into the Philippines Interboard Committee in New York and into the Philippines Interboard Office.[39] The Interboard Office was the liaison not only between the UCCP and the American churches that had sent missionaries to the Philippines, it

37. "Full Relationship of RCA Board with United Church of Christ," in *United Church of Christ in the Philippines, Minutes of the Executive Committee, Quezon City, May 22–24, 1963*, 17.

38. Angus, "The Commission on Philippine-Chinese Mission," 3. He noted that the Westminster Student Church, although cordial toward the RCA missionaries, never attended meetings of the Commission. On the other hand, the United Evangelical Church of Sta. Cruz, Laguna is a branch church of the United Evangelical Church of Manila (former CUEC), as well as a member of the Southern Tagalog Annual Conference, a unique dual relationship.

39. Tye, *Journeying*, 105–106.

was also a liaison between each of the missionaries and his or her supporting agency, and between them as a group and their several boards. Hence,
most foreign personnel received salaries, allowances, and various benefits
through this office. This relationship took effect on 1 January 1964. On
8 April 1964, the CPCM called its first meeting and formed the Luzon
Area Work Committee and the Visayas-Mindanao Area Work Committee.
With this integration in motion, the UCCP became fully concerned with
and responsible for the work among the Chinese in the Philippines, but the
relationship was tenuous and ultimately unsustainable.[40]

Angus assessed the situation of the Chinese Christians quite well as he
took the mantle of heading the CPCM. Aside from the three Chinese congregations in the UCCP, there were Chinese members and church-goers
in other congregations. Then there were the associated Chinese churches
that had a different relationship with the UCCP. Their ties with the UCCP
were informal, with the latter offering facilities for worship, assisting in
the securing and ordaining of their pastors, helping to solve their property
and other legal problems, or rendering assistance whenever needed. Both
the Cebu Gospel Church and the United Evangelical Church of Manila
experienced such a relationship with the UCCP. A discussion of the relationship between the Cebu Gospel Church and the UCCP is found on
pages 171–179.

4. The Widening Gap
The CPCM did not last long. In 1966 the church council of the Cebu
Gospel Church sent a letter to the Executive Committee of UCCP care
of the Cebu Annual Conference and in January 1967, the church officially withdrew from the Conference. The natural reaction of the UCCP
was of course to persuade the church to reconsider, but to no avail. The
UCCP had become increasingly identified not only with liberal theology but also with the ecumenical movement. This perceived openness to

40. Santiago G. Iyoy, *Report on the Visayan Jurisdiction to the Tenth Biennial Meeting of the General Assembly of the United Church of Christ in the Philippines, Dumaguete City, May 23–27, 1966,* 68. See "Appendix VI," in *Minutes of the Ninth Biennial General Assembly of the United Church of Christ in the Philippines, Lucena City, May 31–June 5, 1964,* 49.

ecumenism is not without factual basis.[41] In 1967, the Division of Mission
and Ecumenical Relations of the UCCP presented an article on "Fostering
the Growth of the Ecumenical Movement." A statement in this article declared: "By General Assembly action, the United Church of Christ in the
Philippines warmly encourages the holding of interchurch conferences,
dialogues and seminars, including those which involve Roman Catholic as
well as Protestant people."[42]

Arthur Leonard Tuggy and Ralph E. Toliver commented in their book
Seeing the Church in the Philippines that "although the ecumenical current
has carried the U.C.C.P. a remarkable distance," in terms of membership
and institutional commitment to the nation's welfare, yet at the same time,
they wondered, "How far will the ecumenical spirit take the U.C.C.P.?"
The cause for tension and apprehension stems from the ecumenical activities that the UCCP engaged in jointly with the Roman Catholic Church in
their pursuit of "Christian unity." On 26 January 1968, the *Weekly Calendar*
of Silliman University carried the news item entitled "Ecumenism" which
described an ecumenical prayer service held inside the university attended
by 2,000 Catholics and Protestants. Then on 31 December 1968, another
"Ecumenical Rally for Peace" was held in Cebu City that ended with a
Roman Catholic mass.[43]

This shift from a joint prayer rally to a Roman Catholic mass, participated in by ministers of the UCCP, greatly alarmed the more evangelical-
leaning members in the UCCP and the non-UCCP Protestant congregations in the Philippines. It particularly disturbed the conservative Chinese
congregations, even those that had had a long history of cordial relationship with the UCCP, such as the Cebu Gospel Church. From this period
onward, a majority of these congregations either distanced themselves or
completely severed their ties with the UCCP. For some, such as the United

---

41. The UCCP published a book in 1998 entitled *Commitment and Struggle* wherein
two articles on theology clearly lean toward praxis theology and radical socialism which
conservative evangelicals find difficult to accept. See Gomez and de Jesus, eds. *Commitment
and Struggle*, 95–130.

42. See "Appendix II, Division of Philippine-Chinese Mission, 1967," in *United
Church of Christ in the Philippines, Minutes of the Executive Committee, National Headquarters,
Quezon City, December 8–9, 1967*, 97.

43. See Tuggy and Toliver, *Seeing the Church*, 26–33.

Evangelical Church of the Philippines (former CUEC/UECM), there was always a tension between the desire to be related functionally to the union bodies and Filipino churches, and the fear of what full integration entailed. An event in the late 1960s clearly displays this tension.

Adding to these factors that gradually widened the gap between the Chinese churches and the UCCP was the withdrawal of the RCA cooperation from the UCCP. A consultation with Dr James J. Thomas, area secretary of the RCA Board of World Missions, in 1967, acknowledged the concern that the RCA was losing its qualification of doing specialized work among the Chinese. The Anguses and Muilenburgs[44] were leaving for good. Rev and Mrs John P. Muilenburg had been serving in the Philippines among the Chinese (partly in Hope Christian High School) since 1952. He was designated to succeed Rev William Angus as Director of the CPCM, but Muilenburg served only until the end of 1967, upon his withdrawal from the UCCP. This left only one Chinese-speaking couple, the Esthers. The RCA would continue working with the UCCP Interboard Committee, but felt it best that leadership should be in the hands of this Committee, that is, in the hands of the Chinese and Filipinos. The RCA Board would also no longer send any career missionaries to the Philippines after the Esthers retired. Dr Thomas even expressed the feeling that the Division "should not anymore waste time with the Chinese established congregations." Dr Enrique Sobrepeña, however, remarked that "the UCCP will continue its fraternal relations with these congregations but that the thrust of its missionary program will be towards the un-churched Chinese and will not force any unnecessary pressure for their integration."[45] Therefore, in later decades, the relationship between the UCCP and the Chinese churches remained "fraternal" and they continued to cooperate in evangelistic endeavors, such as the Billy Graham Crusades, but the Chinese churches refrained from integrating into the UCCP.

---

44. See "Appendix XI," *United Church of Christ in the Philippines, Minutes of the Executive Committee Meeting, May 11–13, 1965*, 128. *United Church of Christ in the Philippines, Tenth Post War Biennial General Assembly, Dumaguete City, Philippines, May 23–27, 1966*, 179–180.

45. "Appendix II, Division of Philippine-Chinese Mission, 1967," 89–90.

5. Abolishing the CPCM

With such sentiments circulating at the end of the 1960s, the Division on Philippine-Chinese Mission, as it had become known in 1970, was asking: "Must the Division be abolished or can the Church take full responsibility of supporting and continuing [the ministry to the Chinese]." This was brought about by the impending withdrawal, no matter partial or total, of the RCA from the program of the UCCP, as well as from the plan of restructuring the latter body. The Division itself gave a bleak report:

> The last two years were difficult and trying ones in the life and work of the Division of Philippine Chinese Mission. Plagued by the sudden departure of Chinese speaking missionaries and the absence of a full-time director and needed personnel that can speak Chinese, we nevertheless tried the best we can to carry on the objective for which the Division was established.
>
> However, we have to honestly admit that we can point to no visible accomplishments in so far as our main objectives are concerned; namely, that of attracting and winning Chinese churches into the United Church of Christ and the evangelization of the many still unchurched Chinese.[46]

The end finally came in 1972, for this last item appeared in the minutes of the Thirteenth Biennial General Assembly, under the heading "Appointment of Directors for the Divisions of Mission and Ecumenical Relations, Philippine-Chinese Mission, and Evangelism and Stewardship." The General Assembly did not act on the recommendation of the Committee on Executive Committee Minutes to appoint nominees for the directorship of these Divisions, "because of the impending recommendation of the Committee on General Affairs declaring the offices of the division directors and staff vacant by the end of November 1972, in line with the restructuring of the Church."[47]

---

46. See "Appendix VI, Report of the Commission on Christian Witness and Service," *Proceedings of the Twelfth Post War Biennial General Assembly of the United Church of Christ in the Philippines, Baguio City, May 24–28, 1970,* 107–108.

47. *Proceedings of the Thirteenth Post War Biennial General Assembly of the United Church of Christ in the Philippines, Manila, May 28–June 1, 1972,* 38.

Succeeding meetings of the General Assembly no longer recorded anything on the Division of Philippine-Chinese Mission. Despite the lack of any direct statement regarding its official dissolution, it can be safely assumed that after the re-structuring of the UCCP, around 1972–1974, the Division no longer existed. Following this, the relationship between the Chinese churches and UCCP deteriorated as well, with the negative perception of the UCCP, because of its ecumenical stance, lasting in the minds of the Protestant Chinese until the present time.

Presbyterian Missionaries in the Philippines, circa 1925

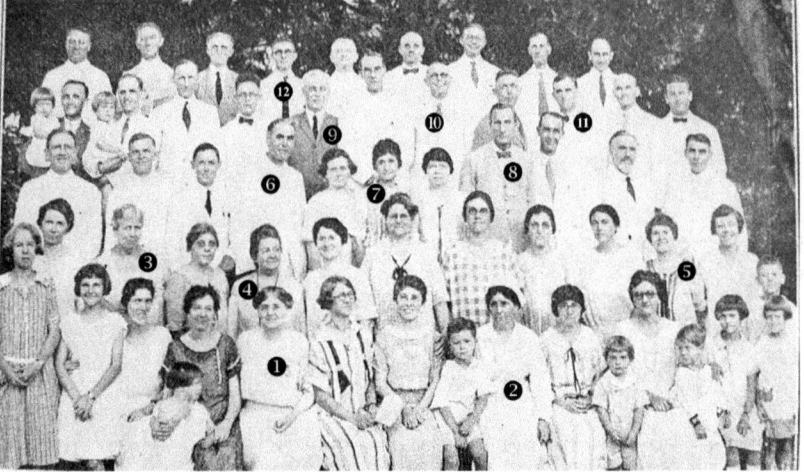

First row: 1 – Dyvee Taylor Dunlap; 2 – Alice Fullerton. Second row: 3 – Jean Russell Hall; 4 – Olive Rohrbaugh; 5 – Laura Crooks Hibbard. Third Row: 6 – Rev Dr George Dunlap; 7 – Minnie Kemp Underwood; 8 – Dr Joseph Andrew Hall. Fourth row: 9 – Rev Dr James Burton Rodgers; 10 – Rev John Wallace Dunlop; 11 – Rev Charles Edward Rath. Fifth row: 12 – Rev Judson Leolin Underwood. Reproduced with permission from Union Theological Seminary Archive.

Source: Station Report of Philippine Presbyterian Mission 1920–1925, 15.

Archival Photographs of Cebu Gospel Church

Fig. 1 Rev Dr George Williamson Dunlap (L), Rev Jorge Patalinghug (M) and Rev Paul Frederick Jansen (R)

Source: Cebu Gospel Church Golden Jubilee Souvenir, 37; *Philippine Presbyterian* 14, no.1, 2 (Jan–Apr 1923): 3. Reproduced with the permission of Cebu Gospel Church and the Union Theological Seminary Archives.

Fig. 2 The Chinese Christian Church of Cebu (1921) with Rev George Williamson Dunlap (seated 6th from the right on the second row); to his right with head turned is Mrs Devee Dunlap.

Source: Reproduced with permission of the Cebu Gospel Church.

Fig. 3 The above photo was taken in 1932 in front of the Bradford Church. The elderly lady seated fourth from right is Mrs Cang Bon Pit.

Source: Reproduced with permission of the Cebu Gospel Church.

Fig. 4 Left photo shows a view of Jones Avenue in the 1920s with the Matilde Bradford Memorial Church on the left. The right photo shows the Bradford United Church of Christ in the Philippines as it appears today. It is now a historical landmark in Cebu City.

Source: Left photo – *Cebu City: The Early Years Celebrating the Silver Jubilee of the Cebuano Studies Center 2000* (Cebu City: University of San Carlos, 2001), 8. Reprinted with the permission of the University of San Carlos Cebuano Studies Center. The right photo was taken with a digital camera by the author on 7 January 2002.

Fig. 5 Left photo: Mrs Uy Cang Chui Siok 黃江水淑 (1888–1975), daughter of Mrs Cang Bon Pit 江文筆夫人. At right is Mrs Saw Cang Iattee 蘇江悅治 at the age of 99 when she was interviewed.

Source: The left photo is reproduced with the permission of Elder Valentin Uy 黃根源長老 of Cebu Gospel Church, son of the late Uy Cang Chui Siok. The right photo was taken by the author in Cebu City on 23 June 2004.

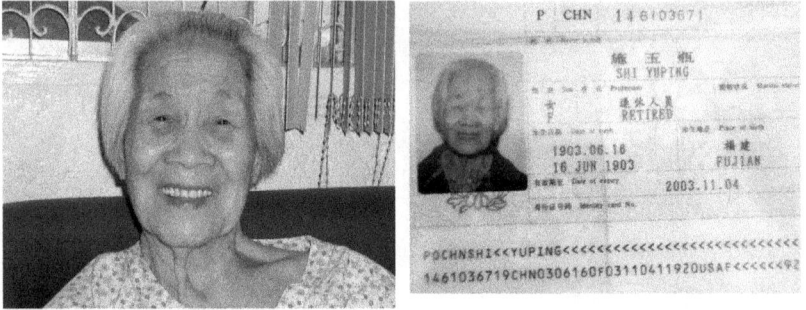

Fig. 6 Mrs Lim Hok Seng 林福盛夫人 (nee Si Giok Pan/Shi Yu Ping 施玉瓶), oldest living member of Cebu Gospel Church. Her passport on the right indicates her birth date as 16 June 1903.

Source: These photographs were taken by the author at the interviewee's residence in Cebu City on 22 April 2005.

Fig. 7 An early photo indicating the "Members of Cebu Chinese Church of Christ" in Chinese text, taken on 8 October 1926. On the first row from left are: Rev George Dunlap (3rd), Rev John Dunlop (4th) and Rev Jorge Patalinghug (5th). Many of the Chinese men in this photo were teachers of Zhong Hua Xue Xiao.

Source: Reproduced with permission of the Cebu Gospel Church.

Fig. 8 First resident pastor of Cebu Gospel Church – Pr Tiu^n Toan Tsong 張端莊 傳道. At right is Rev John Wallace Dunlop.

Source: 30th Anniversary Souvenir Magazine, Pearl 1939–1969 Jubilee 哪呀中華 基督教會成立三十週年紀念特刊 (Naga City: United Evangelical Church of Naga, 1969), 11; *Cebu Gospel Church Golden Jubilee Souvenir*, 38.

Fig. 9 Rev Niu Se Ko/Leung Sai Ko 梁細羔牧師 and his son and successor at CGC Rev Niu Sin Bi/Liang ShenWei 梁慎微牧師.

Source: Reproduced with permission of the Cebu Gospel Church.

Fig. 10 Cebu Gospel Church at Junquera Street, dedicated in 1948, and at its present location at Osmeña Boulevard (former Jones Avenue), dedicated in 1966.

Source: Reproduced with permission of the Cebu Gospel Church.

"Declaration of the Founding of the Chinese Church of Christ Sojourning in the Philippines"

By Rev Kho Seng Iam

Christ is not the sole property of any individual denomination or nation. Christianity came to China from the European and American countries, and the churches that were established became the Church of Christ in China/ Zhonghua Jidu Jiaohui 中華基督教會. The establishment in Manila of a Chinese Church of Christ is not a matter of division or rivalry but of the expansion of Christianity.[1] Only a small portion of the believers in Manila are converted locally; the rest come from "Banlam/Min Nan 閩南" [South Fujian]. All the churches in Banlam formerly belonged to the Presbyterian Mission and London Mission. Their ecclesiastical system and liturgy are different from that of the Episcopalian system. Because there were no other Chinese churches, those who came to Manila had to worship at the existing St. Stephen's Chinese Mission (SSCM). Many soon grew cold and quit attending services, making the excuse that they were not accustomed to the different liturgy.[2] This is the first reason for organizing this church.

Chinese churches, whether in or outside China, were established according to the size of the local Chinese population because of the need to have a place to worship and serve God. Branches of the Chinese Church

---

1. I have translated 中華基督教會 as "Chinese Church of Christ" in order to differentiate it from the Church of Christ in China which was nationally constituted in October 1927. This Declaration was written on August 18, 1924, but the South Fukien Church of Christ 閩南中華基督教會 was established on January 6, 1920, hence, this is what Rev Kho Seng Iam was referring to by this name.

2. In the 1909, 1910 and 1912 reports of Hobart Studley regarding the SSCM, he mentioned that many of his communicants were from "various Protestant denominations in Southern Fukien, China" and that they "had been full members of Protestant churches in or near Amoy." See *JAC* (1909): 40; *JAC* (1910): 19; (1912): 34.

of Christ have already been successively established in many localities in China and wherever the Chinese have settled in other Asian countries. This is the second reason.

Christians from Banlam who settled in the Philippines were numerous, although there are no exact figures. And yet the attendance in SSCM number less than a hundred.[3] Many Chinese believers were not attending because of the difference in ecclesiastical background. Believers who make such excuses need to be led back into the sheepfold, hence, there is a need to organize this new church. This is the third reason.

There are already many Filipino churches in Manila and yet the Chinese are also quite numerous, numbering in the tens of thousands. If the Chinese Christians could spread the Gospel widely, not only would there be another branch of the Chinese Church of Christ, but a Cantonese congregation could possibly arise in the near future. All these churches can unite and fulfill the Lord's commission. By so doing, these churches outside China would follow in the spirit of the great Five Year Movement of the mainland churches.[4] This is the fourth reason for organizing this church.

Uniting churches of a different background to become a bigger Chinese Church of Christ, as it was being done in Banlam, has become a trend in China. How can I, being a part of this Church, be indifferent to such a move to establish a church? This is the fifth reason for organizing this church.

The churches in China belong to more than a hundred denominations of diverse foreign backgrounds. Now these churches in China are organizing themselves into the Chinese Church of Christ, and are casting off their denominational ties to come under the name of Christ and become an indigenous Chinese church. This is the sixth reason for organizing this church.

Those who brought the Gospel to China not only desired to save souls, but to serve sacrificially. Initially the churches were financially reliant, thus

---

3. The statistical report of the SSCM for the year ending 1923 gave the number of communicants as 228. Kho wrote this in 1924 and he is talking about worship attendance. Either he had another source that is not given in the official report or he may have made the remark without this knowledge. See *The Eighteenth Annual Report of the Missionary District of the Philippine Islands for the Year ending December 31, 1923* (Manila: published by the secretary, 1924), 34.

4. The plan for the Five Year Evangelistic Campaign to reach the people in the Banlam region was conceived in 1918 (see pp. 187–188).

giving the impression that the believers were after material gains. Now that the churches were becoming contextualized, they were also becoming self-subsisting. Just like children who have become mature no longer need to rely upon their parents, but becomes independent, financially and otherwise. The aim of this new church was likewise, to attain self-reliance. This is the seventh reason.

Lastly, not only would this new church become self-reliant, but it would also help the mainland churches in their development. Many of the churches in China were already self-governing, self-supporting, and self-propagating, despite being greatly affected by the political and economic turmoil in past years. Many believers who left for overseas to seek livelihood in other lands were elites, causing a drain to the mother church. These, nevertheless, were also stouthearted, able to survive and even give assistance to the church in China. However, there were some who settled outside China who had ceased to attend worship services, becoming weak in their faith and drifting away from their churches. These people needed to be given support. Thus with the new church organized, with elders and deacons committed to render service, going out to reclaim these believers and strengthen their faith, the hearts of these believers would be strengthened. If a minister were enlisted to teach and to administer, this new church would eventually become capable of extending assistance to the mother church in China, similar to what the Cantonese believers residing in America were able to accomplish. They not only established their own churches in many American cities, they also sent financial support to the Cantonese churches in China. In order to supplement the mother church, this is the eighth reason.

Note: This condensed English translation of Rev Kho Seng Iam's "Lüfei Zhonghua Jidu Jiaohui Chengli Xuanyan 旅菲中華基督教會成立宣言 (Declaration of the Founding of the Chinese Church of Christ Sojourning in the Philippines)" was reviewed by Dr Jonathan Lu, former president of Holy Light Theological Seminary who was born in Quanzhou, China, residing there until 1947. He is very familiar with the style of Kho's writing. The church whose founding was declared by Kho is translated literally as "Chinese Church of Christ Sojourning in the Philippines" because in 1924, the Chinese United Evangelical Church or CUEC was not yet inaugurated.

Archival Photographs of Chinese United Evangelical Church

Fig. 1 Rev Kho Seng Iam 許聲炎牧師 and his daughters Kho Goat Hoa/Xu YueHua 許月華/許淑慎 (M) and Kho Ju Soat/Xu YuXie 許逾雪/許淑瑞 (R).

Source: Historical Documentary of Protestantism in the Orient, 17 and the descendants of Kho Seng Iam. Reproduced with the permission of the United Evangelical Church of the Philippines and Mrs Edith Beltran 蔡許韻琛, daughter of Kho Goat Hoa.

Fig. 2 The second meeting place of CUEC, circa 1929, was in the *accessoria* located on *Calle Reina Regente*. Arrow points to the unit where CUEC meetings took place. A Chinese flag hangs outside the window.

Source: Historical Documentary of Protestantism in the Orient, 11. Reproduced with the permission of the United Evangelical Church of the Philippines.

Front row, L-R: Tan Beng Tek 陳明德, Po Siok Bi 傅淑美, Kho Ju Soat 傅淑美, Tan Tiau Lam 陳朝南.
Second row, L-R: Ting Keng Po 丁景波, Keng Lin Kiat 龔人,傑, Sio Tsong Kheng 蕭宗卿, Ng Lip Tek 黃立德, Iuⁿ Ka Bo 楊嘉謨

Fig. 3 Three of the founders of CUEC (L-R): Keng Lin Kiat 龔人傑, Ting Keng Po 丁景波, and Sio Tsong Kheng 蕭宗卿. Right photo: First group of elders and deacons.

Source: These photos are found in the *Special Commemorative Issue of the Founding of the Chinese Evangelical Church of Manila* 旅菲中華基督教會成立紀念特刊. The original of the left photo is still with the daughter-in-law of Sio Tsong Kheng. Reproduced with the permission of Mrs Siao Dy Hong Suan 蕭李鳳萱, wife of Siao Hok Bin 蕭福民 (deceased), son of Sio Tsong Kheng, and the United Evangelical Church of the Philippines.

Fig. 4 Inaugural worship service of the Chinese United Evangelical Church on 14 July 1929. Rev Dr George Wright is seated on the front row with a child on his lap.

Source: Historical Documentary of Protestantism in the Orient, 12. Reproduced with the permission of the United Evangelical Church of the Philippines.

Fig. 5 Chinese preachers of the 1930s: left photo (L-R) Dr John Sung 宋尚節博士, Dr Leland Wang 王載博士, Watchman Nee 倪柝聲. Right photo: Rev Andrew Gih 計志文牧師.

Source: Historical Documentary of Protestantism in the Orient, 17, 78. Reproduced with the permission of the United Evangelical Church of the Philippines Collections.

Fig. 6 Betty Hu 胡美林女士 (L) and Alice Lan 藍如溪女士 (R) circa 1970s
and 1930s.

Source: Betty Hu, *50th Anniversary of the Bethel Mission of China 1920–1970*
(Hong Kong : Hsiang-Kang Po-Pe-Li Chiao Hui, 1970), 60. Reproduced with
the permission of Yale University archivist Martha Smalley.

Fig. 7 Rev George Sin Chiong Chua 蔡信彰牧師 (L) and Rev Silas Wong/Ng
Goan So 黃源素牧師 (R) circa 1970s.

Source: Arise, Shine: United Evangelical Church of the Philippines 70th Anniversary
興起發光— 菲律濱中華基督教會七十週年特刊 *1929–1999* (Manila:
United Evangelical Church of the Philippines, [1999]), 124. Reproduced with
the permission of the United Evangelical Church of the Philippines Collections.

Founding Members of The Chinese United Evangelical Church

List of Chinese Names by Kho Ju Soat	List of English Names in Letter to Wright
U KENG PHO 于景波	EDWARD C. C. YII
Kho Kheng Hoa 許瓊華	*King Hoa Co* [legal name of Kho Kheng Hoa]
Sio Tsong Kheng 蕭宗卿	Sio Chong Keng
Keng Lin Kiat 龔人傑	Keng Lin Kiat
Iuⁿ Bun Phek/Yang WenBi 楊文碧	*Wen Pi Yang*
Kho Ju Soat/Xu YuXue 許逾雪	*Elizabeth Co* [legal name of Kho Ju Soat]
Tan Tiau Lam/Chen ChaoNan 陳朝南	I. S. Tian Nam
Iuⁿ Un Tian/Yang EnDian 楊恩典	Yuha Bo [Yu Ka Bo 楊嘉謨]
Kho Chheng Un/Xu QingEn 許清恩	Co Ching Hu
Si Sun Sam/Shi ChunSan 施純三	Sy Sun Sam
KHO SU DIAM/XU SHUNIAN 許書念	LEE KIM KIS
TIUⁿ TSU AI/ZHANG CIAI 張慈愛	LIM CHING PUNG
LIM SIONG HONG/LIN XIANGFENG (A.K.A. JOSEPH LIM TIAO HONG) 林翔鳳牧師	CHING PO TENG [legal name of TING KENG PO 丁景波]
PO SIOK BI/FU SHUMEI 傅淑美	KHECHI LIAM

Note: The list on the left column refers to those who attended the CUEC prayer meeting on 7 July 1929, while the list on the right is found in the 9 July 1929 letter submitted to the Presbyterian Mission care of Rev George Wright. Italicized names are female. Note that the names that match (shown in lower case) have slightly different spelling. This can be attributed to the form of their legal names being different from the names that have been phonetically transcribed from Chinese characters. The five names that are in upper case in both columns do not match. Since the prayer meeting was held on 7 July 1929 and the letter was written two days after, it is logical to assume that the fourteen who attended the prayer meeting would have been the ones signing the letter. However, no other document has been found to explain why the names in the two lists are not completely identical. There are only two possible explanations for this. First, the names, especially of the men (not italicized), may have been in legal form. Second, since the letter was written two days after the prayer meeting, six other persons who were not present during this meeting may have been asked to or may have volunteered to sign the letter. I am inclined toward the second explanation as more logical.

Archival Photographs of Davao Chinese Gospel Church

Fig. 1 Charles Eldred and Ruth Notson 納慈恩牧師師母 during the fifties (L) and the nineties.

Source: Davao Evangelical Church Fifty Years 1951-2001 Anniversary Souvenir (*Namao Jidu Jiaohui*) 納卯基督教會 (Davao City: Davao Evangelical Church, [2001]), 6. Reproduced with the permission of the Davao Evangelical Church.

390
A Study on the Emergence and Early Development of
Selected Protestant Chinese Churches in the Philippines

Fig. 2 Pr Bona Lim 林蓮珠傳道 (L) and a very early photo (circa 1946) of the Sunday School being held at her residence in Davao City.

Source: Davao Christian High School Golden Jubilee 1953-2003 (Davao City: Davao Christian High School, [2003]); Bona Lim personal collection. Reproduced with permission from Bona Lim before her death.

Fig. 3 Rev and Mrs Frederick Eugene Ruhl 呂新民牧師 and their children (L). At right is Ms Agnes Catlin Birrel.

Source: Davao Evangelical Church Fifty Years 1951–2001 Anniversary Souvenir, 72. Reproduced with permission of the Davao Evangelical Church.

Fig. 4 The first resident Chinese pastor of DCGC/DEC – Rev Wesley Kho Shao 邵慶彰牧師, his wife Too Siu Pao/Du XioBao 杜秀寶 (1924–1988) and five children.

Source: Personal collection of Rev Wesley Shao. Reproduced with the permission of the Shao family.

Archival Photos of Dagupan Chinese Baptist Church

Fig. 1 A recent photograph of Rev Dr James Winston Crawley (L) and one of Fern Harrington (R) taken during the fifties and in recent times.

Source: Personal photograph (Crawley) and *BCBC 1950–2000* (Harrington). Reproduced with the permission of Dr Winston Crawley and the Baguio Chinese Baptist Church.

The TWELVE CHARTERED MEMBERS OF THE BAGUIO CHI-
NESE BAPTIST CHURCH. Seated L-R: Mrs. Pansy Sam,Mrs. Celine
Ng, Ms.Yook Ying Chao,Ms. Josephine Lo, Mrs. Rosa Hao.
  Standing L-R: Ms. Ling Kang, Mr Edward Pang, Mr. Ang Cho
Sam, Mr. H.Y.Yeh, Mr. Pedro Hao, Mr. George Co, Mrs.- Kit Ying
Pand.

Fig. 2 First Charter Members of the Baguio Chinese Baptist Church

Source: BCBC 1950–2000. Reproduced with the permission of the Baguio
Chinese Baptist Church.

Fig. 3 Baguio Chinese Baptist Church (organized on 29 May 1950)

Source: BCBC 1950–2000. Reproduced with permission of the Dagupan Chinese
Baptist Church.

394
A Study on the Emergence and Early Development of
Selected Protestant Chinese Churches in the Philippines

Fig. 4 (Left) Rev Pedro Hao 侯均南 and (right) Chua Ke Kan 蔡繼干 standing second from right with his family in front of their grocery store.

Source: BCBC 1950–2000 and *DCBC 50th Anniversary*. Reproduced with permission of the Baguio Chinese Baptist Church and Dagupan Chinese Baptist Church.

Dr. Frank Lide, Dr. Winston Crawley, First Seminarians & church members

Fig. 5 Philippine Baptist Theological Seminary Faculty and Seminarians circa 1952. The four Chinese students are shown seated on the front row, Pedro Hao is on the left and Bai QiWen on the right. Guests from Baguio Chinese Baptist Church are shown standing at the back.

Source: BCBC 1950–2000. Reproduced with the permission of the Baguio Chinese Baptist Church.

Fig. 6 Dagupan Chinese Baptist Church (organized 19 February 1952). This building was erected in April 1965, but the 1990 earthquake caused it to tilt and sink into the ground.

Source: DCBC 50th Anniversary. Reproduced with the permission of the Dagupan Chinese Baptist Church.

SOUTHERN BAPTIST MISSION WORK IN THE PHILIPPINES
— 1 9 5 3 —

— FILIPINO WORK, LUZON —

BAGUIO . . .
Filipino Department, Seminary
and Bible School (1952)
Filipino Work Opened (1953)
3 Missionaries:
Dr. and Mrs. R. F. Ricketson
Miss Virginia Miles

DAGUPAN . . .
Dagupan Baptist Church (1955)
Bonuan Baptist Center (1953)
San Carlos, Out-Station
Barrio Work
3 Missionaries:
Rev. and Mrs. R. E. Gordon
Miss Margaret Collins

MANILA . . . ALL P. I.
Literature and Promotion
2 Missionaries:
Miss Virginia Mathis
Miss Mary Lucile Saunders

— FILIPINO WORK, MINDANAO —

Cotabato Baptist Church, affiliated in 1952.

DAVAO . . .
Immanuel Baptist Church (1952)
Other Week-Day Groups (5)
Bunawan Baptist Church (1951),
Out-Station
Bahac, Samal; Calinan; Talicud:
Out-Stations
3 Missionaries:
Rev. and Mrs. W. A. Solesbee
Miss Elaine Crotwell

MATI . . .
Medical Clinic (1952)
1 Missionary: Miss Vicky
Parsons

— ON FURLOUGH —
Dr. Frank Lide
Rev. and Mrs. J. E.
Jackson

— CHINESE WORK, LUZON —

BAGUIO . . .
Chinese Baptist Church (1950)
Chinese Department, Seminary
and Bible School (1952)
4 Missionaries:
Dr. and Mrs. Winston Crawley
Rev. and Mrs. J. A. Foster

DAGUPAN . . .
Chinese Baptist Church (1952)
1 Missionary:
Miss Fern Harrington

MANILA . . .
Chinese Baptist Church (1952)
3 Missionaries:
Rev. and Mrs. W. W. Lawton
Miss Theresa Anderson

— CHINESE WORK, MINDANAO —

DAVAO . . .
Chinese Baptist Church (1952)
2 Missionaries:
Rev. and Mrs. Clyde Jewers
(Mrs. Elaine Crotwell)

Fig. 7 Southern Baptist mission work in the Philippines, circa 1953. This map
shows five mission stations of the SBC in 1953. Note Fern Harrington's name
under DCBC.

*Source: Minutes of the Philippine Mission of the Southern Baptist Convention
1952–53. Annual Session – August 17–21, 1953 Baguio City. 1952–53 Executive
Committee Minutes Constitution. Theme: Able through Christ* ([Baguio City]:
Baguio Printing & Publishing, [1953]). Reproduced with permission from
Philippine Baptist Theological Seminary Archives.

APPENDIX JJ

Fern Harrington's Report

As I look back over the beginnings of the work in Baguio and Dagupan, the progress in Baguio seems to have made in a series of plateaus whereas the Dagupan work has been a series of mountain peaks and dark valleys.

In discussing plans for the future in the Philippines early this year [1950], Dr. [Baker James] Cauthen suggested that investigations be made of places near Baguio having large Chinese populations where work might be started in order to give the group still studying more opportunity for practical experience in using the language. Thus in February, a group went down to Dagupan to look over the situation there. We found a typical dusty lowland town with a thriving business district run almost entirely by Chinese – the estimated Chinese population of Dagupan being well over two thousand. We learned that the Chinese elementary school uses Mandarin as the medium of instruction although actually most explanations are made in Fukienese [*Hokkien*], since the pupils are almost entirely Fukienese. We found Mandarin usable with all except the very young and the very old. The Chinese whom we contacted that day did not know of any Christians among the Chinese and could not tell us where any of the Filipino churches were. Later we found three churches very near the business district—Methodist, Aglipayan (Filipino Catholic), and Roman Catholic. All these buildings are huge stone, rather dilapidated looking buildings, indicating a lack of religious emphasis in the life of the Filipinos as well as the Chinese. We came back to Baguio thrilled with the possibilities of preaching the Gospel there.

By the time we received Dr. Cauthen's approval for opening the work in Dagupan, we were involved in Vacation Bible School in Baguio, so that it was June before we were able to make further investigations as to the best avenue of approach in opening the work. At that time the most logical approach seemed to be through the Chinese school. Some weeks previously I had had the opportunity to be of some assistance to the principal of the Dagupan Chinese school when he brought a group of Boy Scouts and Girl

Scouts to Baguio for a weekend. At that time I had made colored slides of the group, the showing of which I felt might be the means of putting us before the Chinese community in one of their programs.

On June 2, Margaret Collins and I went to Dagupan to make arrangements for such an entree. The principal of the school was out of town, which, at first, made our trip seem fruitless. The keenness of our disappointment was softened only by the thought that perhaps God had a better plan. We went to call on all the Chinese we had met on the trip before, and at the very last place someone remembered that there was a group of Chinese up from a church in Manila, and perhaps we would like to meet them. From these people we learned that a man from Dagupan had died of cancer in a Manila hospital. Shortly before his death he had accepted Christ and died a glorious death of testimony of Christ's love. These had come to Dagupan for the funeral to bear a Christian witness for him. Through them we found there were a few Christians in Dagupan, among them a brother of the man who died. We talked to him about the possibility of opening work, and he was most enthusiastic.

Upon returning to Baguio, the group felt that no time should be wasted in taking advantage of this interest aroused in Christianity. The following Sunday [June 4] Oz [Oswald] Quick, Bill Solesbee and I returned to Dagupan. We learned then that the Chinese church in Manila [Evangelistic Band of the Chinese United Evangelical Church] had promised to send someone to hold services regularly for the people in Dagupan and were going to discuss the details in Manila the following evening. I was invited to go to Manila to take part in this planning meeting and see if they would be willing for us to take up the work in Dagupan.

The conference in Manila [June 5] was very difficult, but I left it with peace in my heart that I had done all I could and that the matter was in the Lord's hands. After three busy weeks, with the matter completely surrendered to the Lord, a letter came stating that Manila had no one to send to Dagupan and they would be most happy for us to go ahead with our plans for beginning work there. The following Sunday, July 2, several of us went to Dagupan and discussed our plans with the Christians there, who were most enthusiastic.

The program outlined to them was a Saturday evening service featuring group singing and some type of visual aid program such as religious slides or movies, to be under the supervision of Max Pettit; a Sunday School to be conducted by Margaret Collins, and a worship service under the leadership of Clyde Jowers. We held our first services [July 9] in a home the following weekend and were surprised and thrilled to see the initiative the people took for getting the work started. One man was selected as interpreter, plans were worked out for taking care of our meals and lodging with Christians, and a request had been sent to the Chinese school asking permission to hold our services there. During the next few weeks, while awaiting the answer on this, we started holding our services in the Filipino Methodist Church in order to accomodate [sic] the number attending.

We found these weekend trips most strenuous, but the response and the warm interest shown made it seem most worthwhile. We returned to Baguio each week walking on clouds. We stayed on this mountain top all of July, and then finally received a formal refusal to our request to use the school. As the weeks passed, need for a suitable meeting place became more urgent while the interest of the people in getting such a place seemed to be declining. Thus at the present time we feel that our work has reached a point beyond which it cannot progress until we have a meeting place adequate for our needs. At this moment we are standing in a dark valley, but we are heartened at the thought of the widow's acceptance of Christ as Saviour, by a young man's statement that he is seeking God's will as to whether he should be a missionary, by the new radio program started August 27 under the direction of Bill Solesbee. This program gives promise of a wide ministry not only to English speaking Chinese but to Filipinos as well.

God has provided in a wonderful way for missionary personnel willing to help project the work. Oz Quick and Bill Solesbee are taking over the work of Max Pettit and Clyde Jowers. Margaret Collins and I plan to move within the next two weeks to Dagupan [they did on September 15]. Continue to pray with us for our efforts there and bear in mind that life moves at ox cart pace in the lowlands and not always as fast as we would like.

Source: Fern Harrington, "Report of the Dagupan Work," *Minutes of the First Annual Session of the Philippine Mission of the Southern Baptist Convention 1950, August 29–September 1*, 19–21.

Note: The dates and names in bracket are supplied in other documents belonging to Fern Harrington.

Bibliography

English Sources

I. Archival Materials

A. Personal Papers

Abeel, David. *Journal of a Residence in China and the Neighboring Countries from 1829 to 1833*. New York: Leavitt, Lord & Co., 1834.

Angus, William Robertson, Jr "The Commission on Philippine-Chinese Mission – Talk to Moderator's Seminar, 1963." In *United Church of Christ in the Philippines: Commission on Philippine-Chinese Mission – Communications, Reports, Minutes, Talks 1964–65*. TMs (photocopy), H00=1381 Box 1, Angus Papers, Joint Archives of Holland, Hope College, Hope, MI.

———. "The United Church and the Existing Chinese Churches." In *United Church of Christ in the Philippines: Commission on Philippine-Chinese Mission – Communications, Reports, Minutes, Talks 1964–65*. TMs (photocopy), 24, H00=1381 Box 1, Angus Papers, Joint Archives of Holland, Hope College, Hope, MI.

Archives of the Presbyterian Church in the U.S.A. Board of Foreign Missions, 1833–1964. Special Collections. Text-fiche. Yale Divinity School. New Haven, CT.

Berame, Marcos P. and Santiago G. Iyoy D. D., Bishop of the UCCP and head of the Cebu Annual Conference, "to whom it may concern." 6 June 1966. Cebu Gospel Church Archives, Cebu City, Philippines.

Brent, The Rt Rev Charles Henry D. D., Bishop of the Philippine Islands. Correspondence. Archives of the Protestant Episcopal Church, Austin, Texas. Record Group 76, Boxes 9–18. Quoted in Norbeck, Mark Douglas. "The Protestant Episcopal Church in the City of Manila, Philippine Islands from 1898–1918: An Institutional History." MA thesis, The University of Texas at El Paso, 1992.

Brent, The Rt. Rev Charles Henry D. D., First Missionary Bishop of the
    Philippines, Protestant Episcopal Church in the USA (PECUSA), Box 2,
    1901–1906. St. Andrew's Seminary Archives, Quezon City, Philippines.
———, First Missionary Bishop of the Philippines, Protestant Episcopal
    Church in the USA (PECUSA), Box 3, 1907–1908. St. Andrew's Seminary
    Archives, Quezon City, Philippines.
———, First Missionary Bishop of the Philippines, Protestant Episcopal
    Church in the USA (PECUSA), Box 4, 1909–1910. St. Andrew's Seminary
    Archives, Quezon City, Philippines.
———, First Missionary Bishop of the Philippines, Protestant Episcopal
    Church in the USA (PECUSA), Box 6, 1914–1918. St. Andrew's Seminary
    Archives, Quezon City, Philippines.
———, S. S. Zieten (ship), Gulf of Suez, to Dr Lloyd, New York, 15 July 1904.
    St. Andrew's Seminary Archives, Quezon City, Philippines.
———, Manila, to Dr John W. Wood, New York, 15 February 1906, 2, 8. St.
    Andrew's Seminary Archives, Quezon City, Philippines.
———, Manila, to Dr. John W. Wood, New York, 18 July 1906. St. Andrew's
    Seminary Archives, Quezon City, Philippines.
———, Manila, to Dr. John W. Wood, New York, 31 July 1906. St. Andrew's
    Seminary Archives, Quezon City, Philippines.
———, Zamboanga, to Dr John W. Wood, New York, 10 August 1906. St.
    Andrew's Seminary Archives, Quezon City, Philippines.
———, Manila, to Dr John W. Wood, New York, 16 November 1906. St.
    Andrew's Seminary Archives, Quezon City, Philippines.
———, Manila to Dr John W. Wood, New York, 20 May 1907, RG76-13. St.
    Andrew's Seminary Archives, Quezon City, Philippines.
———, Manila to Dr John W. Wood, New York, 27 May 1907. St. Andrew's
    Seminary Archives, Quezon City, Philippines.
———, Manila, to Dr John W. Wood, New York, 27 December 1909, 3. St.
    Andrew's Seminary Archives, Quezon City, Philippines.
———, France, to Dr John W. Wood, New York, 2 February 1918. St. Andrew's
    Seminary Archives, Quezon City, Philippines.
———, Paris, France, to Dr John W. Wood, New York, 4 April 1918. St.
    Andrew's Seminary Archives, Quezon City, Philippines.
Cebu Gospel Church, Cebu, 3 February 1967, to the Executive Committee,
    Cebu Annual Conference, United Church of Christ in the Philippines.
Hall, Joseph Andrew, Iloilo, P[hilippine] I[slands], to Dr Ellinwood, New York
    City, 1 May 1900. Yale Divinity School Library Special Collection, text-
    fiche, 1–2, Sp. Col. Film, MS 11 Reel 287. Yale University, New Haven, CT.

———, Iloilo, to Dr Ellinwood, New York City, 15 June 1903. Yale Divinity School Library Special Collection, text-fiche, 2, Sp. Col. Film, Ms 11 Reel 288. Yale University, New Haven, CT.

Hibbard, David Sutherland, Manila, to Dr Francis F. Ellinwood, New York City, 28 November 1899, 1–2. Archives of the Presbyterian Church in the USA Board of Foreign Missions, 1833–1964, MS 11, Reel 287. Special collection, Day Missions Library, Yale Divinity School, New Haven, CT.

Hills, Leander (a.k.a. Leon) C. (1874–1950), Iloilo, to Dr Ellinwood, New York City, 29 October 1901. Yale Divinity School Library Special Collection, text-fiche, 1–2, Sp. Col. Film, MS 11 Reel 288. Yale University, New Haven, CT.

Leger, Samuel Howard. "The Successes and Failures of the Devolution Process in the Mid-Fukien and North Fukien Synods 1927–1944" (1917–1932, 1944). *American Board of Commissioners for Foreign Missions Foochow, Peking Fukien Christian University (1917–1944),* 4p. report. Yale Divinity Archives Record Group No. 8, Box 114. Guide to the China Records Project Miscellaneous Personal Papers Collection. Yale Divinity Library, Yale University, New Haven, CT.

Letter No. 513, 23 July 1930. In Board Letters Nos. 488 to 527, January 1929 to November 1931, Philippine Presbyterian Mission, 33–34. New York: The Board of Foreign Missions of the Presbyterian Church in the U.S.A., n.d.

Lingle, William H. Manila, Philippine Islands and the United States of America, to Rev Frank Field Ellinwood, New York, 17 January 1899. Yale Divinity School Library Special Collection, Sp. Col. MS 11 287. Yale Divinity Library, Yale University, New Haven, CT.

Mosher, Rt. Rev Governeur Frank, Box 18, 1927–1930. St. Andrew's Seminary Archives, Quezon City, Philippines.

———, Manila, to Dr John W. Wood, New York, 30 August 1920. St. Andrew's Seminary Archives, Quezon City, Philippines.

———, Manila, to Dr John W. Wood, New York, 23 March 1926. St. Andrew's Seminary Archives, Quezon City, Philippines.

———, Manila, to Dr John W. Wood, New York, 30 November 1926. St. Andrew's Seminary Archives, Quezon City, Philippines.

———, Manila, to Dr John W. Wood, New York, 22 April 1927. St. Andrew's Seminary Archives, Quezon City, Philippines.

———, Manila, to Dr John W. Wood, New York, 2 July 1927. St. Andrew's Seminary Archives, Quezon City, Philippines.

———, Manila, to Dr John W. Wood, New York, 26 July 1927. St. Andrew's Seminary Archives, Quezon City, Philippines.

———, Manila, to Dr John W. Wood, New York, 11 June 1930. St. Andrew's Seminary Archives, Quezon City, Philippines.

————, Manila, to Dr John W. Wood, New York, 22 July 1930. St. Andrew's Seminary Archives, Quezon City, Philippines.

————, Manila, to Dr John W. Wood, New York, 28 July 1930. St. Andrew's Seminary Archives, Quezon City, Philippines.

Notson, Charles Eldred, Davao City, to A. C. Snead, New York, 8 March 1951. From Personnel Files of Deceased Missionaries, the USA Christian and Missionary Alliance National Archives.

Notson, Charles Eldred, Davao City, to A. C. Snead, New York, 12 June 1951. From Personnel Files of Deceased Missionaries, the USA Christian and Missionary Alliance National Archives.

————, Davao City, to A. C. Snead, New York, 22 June 1951. From Personnel Files of Deceased Missionaries, the USA Christian and Missionary Alliance National Archives.

————, Davao City, to D. I. Jeffrey, New York, 30 July 1952. From Personnel Files of Deceased Missionaries, the USA Christian and Missionary Alliance National Archives.

————, Davao City, to The Philippine Mission of the Southern Baptist Convention Chinese Chapel, Davao City, 6 December 1951. From Personnel Files of Deceased Missionaries, the USA Christian and Missionary Alliance National Archives.

————, En Route Cotabato on Board M/V Alex, to A. C. Snead, New York, 8 March 1951. From Personnel Files of Deceased Missionaries, the USA Christian and Missionary Alliance National Archives.

————, Report of the Work among the Chinese as Given from the Viewpoint of Mr and Mrs C. E. Notson, 1 December 1952. From Personnel Files of Deceased Missionaries, the USA Christian and Missionary Alliance National Archives.

————, Report on Work among the Chinese by Mr and Mrs Charles E. Notson to the Annual Conference in Zamboanga February 1951. From Personnel Files of Deceased Missionaries, the USA Christian and Missionary Alliance National Archives.

Papers of the American Board of Commissioners for Foreign Missions, ABC 16: Missions to Asia, 1827–1919. Vol. 1, Amoy Mission, Borneo, Canton, Siam, 1827–1846. Unit 3, Reel 231, 16.3.3: Amoy Mission, vol. 1.

Purcell, Francis J. Presbyterian Mission, Cebu, to Dr Arthur J. Brown, New York City, 9 September 1903. MS 11, Reel 287. Special collection, Day Missions Library, Yale Divinity School, New Haven, CT.

Report of the Bishop of the Missionary District of the Philippine Islands, 1913. Manila: by the Secretary, 1914. Box 1, RG76-13. St. Andrew's Seminary Archives, Quezon City, Philippines.

Rodgers, James Burton. Presbyterian Mission, Manila, to Dr Francis F. Ellinwood, New York City, 5 March 1903. MS 11, Reel 287. Yale Divinity Library, Yale University, New Haven, CT.

Snead, A. C., New York to Charles Notson, Davao City, 22 June 1951. From Personnel Files of Deceased Missionaries, the USA Christian and Missionary Alliance National Archives.

Studley, Hobart Earl, Manila, to [first name not recorded] Kimber, 23 March 1904, RG76-73. St. Andrew's Seminary Archives, Quezon City, Philippines.

———, to Kimber, 29 June 1907, RG76-13. St. Andrew's Seminary Archives, Quezon City, Philippines.

Underwood, Judson Leolin. Personal Report. In *Annual Reports 1928-1929, Philippine Mission of the Presbyterian Church in the U.S.A. Dumaguete, Oriental Negros, October 5–12, 1929.*

———. Personal Report. 1923–1924. In *Mission Meeting Reports for 1923–1924 of the Philippine Mission, Manila, Philippine Islands, October 6–14, 1924.*

United Church of Christ in the Philippines: Commission on Philippine-Chinese Mission—Communications, Reports, Minutes, Talks 1964-65. H00 1381 Box 1. Angus Papers. Joint Archives of Holland, Hope College, Holland, MI.

Williams, Samuel Wells to Rev Elijah Coleman Bridgman, D. D. Macao 8 July 1844, "Family Papers" (1774–1938). Sterling Library. Yale University. New Haven, CT.

Wood, Dr John W., New York, to The Rt Rev Charles Henry Brent, Paris, France, 8 February 1918. St. Andrew's Seminary Archives, Quezon City, Philippines.

———, New York, to The Rt Rev Charles Henry Brent, Paris, France, 5 March 1918. St. Andrew's Seminary Archives, Quezon City, Philippines.

———, New York, to Rt Rev Governeur Frank Mosher, Manila, 27 February 1926. St. Andrew's Seminary Archives, Quezon City, Philippines.

———, New York, to Rt. Rev Gouvernor Frank Mosher, Manila, 2 November 1929. St. Andrew's Seminary Archives, Quezon City, Philippines.

B. China Missions Reports

Bell, Henry Thurburn Montague, and Henry George Wandesforde Woodhead, eds. *The China Year Book, 1912.* Nendeln, Liechtenstein: Kraus-Thomson; Reprint, Germany: Lessingdruckerei Wiesbaden, 1969.

Chiang Ting-fu. "China's Foreign Relations in 1939." In *The China Mission Year Book, 1924 (Twelfth Issue),* ed. Frank Rawlinson. Shanghai: Christian Literature Society, 1924.

China and the Gospel: An Illustrated Report of the China Inland Mission 1907. London: China Inland Mission, 1907.

China Christian Church Year Book. 1914–1925.

Fisher, A. J. "South China." In *The China Mission Year Book, 1924 (Twelfth Issue)*. Edited by Frank Rawlinson. Shanghai: Christian Literature Society, 1924.

Hodous, Lewis. "Fukien." In *The China Mission Year Book, 1917 (Eighth Issue)*. Edited by E. C. Lobenstine, The China Continuation Committee. Shanghai: Christian Literature Society for China, 1917.

MacGillivray, Donald. *A Century of Protestant Missions in China (1807–1907), Being the Centenary Conference Historical Volume*. CMC Reprint Series 72. Reprint, Shanghai: American Presbyterian Mission Press, 1907. San Francisco: CMC, 1977.

> A compendious volume providing historical sketches of the work of various Protestant missions in China in the period 1807–1907. The materials in this volume were gathered from sources in both China and the West, covering missions from Britain, the United States, Germany, Norway, Canada, New Zealand, and other Western countries. Each mission is given a concise but comprehensive summary of its origin, organization, and its work. The appendices include a brief chronology, a list of martyrs, a list of books, and index of persons. There is also an index of missions at the beginning.

———, ed. *The China Mission Year Book Being "The Christian Movement in China" 1910*. Shanghai: Christian Literature Society for China, 1910.

———. *The China Mission Year Book Being "The Christian Movement in China" 1913*. Shanghai: Christian Literature Society for China, 1913.

———. *The China Mission Year Book Being "The Christian Movement in China"1915*. Shanghai: Christian Literature Society for China, 1913.

Records of the General Conference of the Protestant Missionaries of China, Held at Shanghai, May 10–24, 1877. Shanghai: Presbyterian Mission Press, 1878. Reprint, Taipei: Ch'eng Wen Publishing, 1973.

C. Mission Reports

1. American Board of Commissioners for Foreign Missions

Anderson, Rufus. *History of the Missions of the American Board of Commissioners for Foreign Missions to the Oriental Churches, Republication of the Gospel in Bible Lands*, Vol. 1 and 2. Boston: Congregational Publishing Society, 1872.

Year Book of Missions, The American Board, the Woman's Board, 1917. Continuing the Almanac of Missions of the American Board and the Calendar of Prayer of the American Board and Woman's Board. Bethlehem, PA: Preservation Resources, 1917–1937. Microfilm.

2. Christian and Missionary Alliance

Annual Report of the Superintendent and Board of Managers of the Christian and Missionary Alliance 1900-1901 Presented at the Meeting of the Society, May 5,

1901. New York: Christian and Missionary Alliance, 1901, 24. Accessed 24
   August 2005, http://www. cmalliance.org/whoweare/ archives/pdfs/annual_
   reports/1900-1901_report.pdf.
Annual Survey and Report of the Christian and Missionary Alliance 1903-1904.
   Accessed 26 August 2005, http://www.cmalliance.org/whoweare/archives/
   pdfs/annual_reports/1904_survey.pdf.
The Christian Alliance Yearbook 1888. New York: Word, Work & World
   Publishing, (1888), 53. Accessed 26 August 2005, http://apps.cmalliance.
   org/archives/pdfs/annual_reports/1888_yearbook.pdf.
*The Christian and Missionary Alliance Fifty-second Year Annual Report and Minutes
   of the General Council, May 18–23, 1939, for the year ended December 31,
   1938*. New York: The Christian and Missionary Alliance, 1939.
*The Christian and Missionary Alliance Sixty-second Year Annual Report for 1948
   and Minutes of the General Council at Rochester, New York, May 18–24, 1949*.
   New York: The Christian and Missionary Alliance, 1949.
*The Christian and Missionary Alliance Sixty-third Year Annual Report for 1949 and
   Minutes of the General Council held at Toronto, Canada May 4–9, 1950*. New
   York: The Christian and Missionary Alliance, 1950.
*"Crowned Years." The Twelfth Annual Report of the Christian and Missionary
   Alliance (Reorganized)*. Adopted at the Annual Meeting of the Society, 25
   May 1909. Nyack, NY: The Christian and Missionary Alliance, 1910, 29.
   Accessed 24 August 2005, http://www.cmalliance.org/whoweare/archives/
   pdfs/annual_reports/1908-1909.
"The Fields." In *Year Book of the Christian Alliance and the International
   Missionary Alliance 1893*. New York: The Christian Alliance Publishing,
   1893), 14–22. Accessed 26 August 2005, http://apps.cmalliance.org/
   archives/pdfs/annual_reports/1893_yearbook.pdf.
"The Fields." In *Report of the Sixth Year of the International Missionary Alliance
   Presented at the Annual Meeting, October 13, 1894. An Annual Report of the
   International Missionary Alliance Presented at the Annual Meeting, October
   19, 1894*. New York: The International Missionary Alliance, 1894, 31, 46.
   Accessed 26 August 2005, http://apps.cmalliance.org/whoweare/archives/
   pdfs/annual_reports/ 1894_report.pdf.
*The Fifth Annual Report of the Christian and Missionary Alliance Presented at
   the Meeting of the Board 1902 Annual Report of the President and Board of
   Managers*. New York: The Christian and Missionary Alliance, 1903, 28.
   Accessed 24 August 2005, http://apps.cmalliance.org/whoweare/archives/
   pdfs/annual_reports/1902_report.pdf.
*Golden Anniversary, The Christian and Missionary Alliance 1887–1937. Fiftieth
   Year Annual Report to the General Council at Nyack, New York, May*

19–24, 1937 for the Year Ended December Thirty-First, 1936. New York: Headquarters, 1937.

Howe, James C. "A Timely Missionary Testimony." *The Christian and Missionary Alliance* 23 (2 Sep 1899): 217. Accessed 3 September 2005, http://apps. cmalliance.org/archives/alifepdf/AW-1899-09-02.pdf.

Landis, R. M. "Philippine Islands." In *The Christian and Missionary Alliance Annual Report for 1956 and Minutes of the General Council held at Charlotte, North Carolina May 15–21, 1957.* New York: The Christian and Missionary Alliance, 1956.

Report in Part. The Eighth Year. The International Missionary Alliance 1895–1896. New York: The International Missionary Alliance, 1896, 19, 31. Accessed 26 August 2005, http://apps.cmalliance.org/whoweare/archives/pdfs/annual_ reports/1895_report.pdf.

The Sixth Annual Report of the Christian and Missionary Alliance 1903. Presented at the Sixth Annual Meeting of the Board Officers, June 5, 1903. Accessed 26 August 2005, http://apps.cmalliance.org/whoweare/archives/pdfs/annual_ reports/1903_survey.pdf.

Souvenir and Survey of the Work of the Christian and Missionary Alliance, 1899. Accessed 26 August 2005, http://www.cmalliance.org/whoweare/archives/ pdfs/annual_reports/1899_survey.pdf.

A Week of Years. The Annual Report of the International Missionary Alliance 1894–1895. New York: The International Missionary Alliance, 1895, 10, 69. Accessed 26 August 2005, http://apps.cmalliance.org/whoweare/archives/ pdfs/annual_reports/1895_report.pdf.

Year Book of the Christian Alliance and the International Missionary Alliance 1893. New York: The Christian Alliance Publishing, 1893, 5. Accessed 26 August 2005, http://apps.cmalliance.org/archives/pdfs/annual_reports/1893_ yearbook.pdf.

3. Methodist Episcopal Church

Annual Report of the Missionary Society of the Methodist Episcopal Church for the Year 1907. New York: Missionary Society of the Methodist Episcopal Church, 1908.

Annual Report of the Board of Foreign Missions of the Methodist Episcopal Church for the Year 1908. New York: Board of Foreign Missions of the Methodist Episcopal Church, 1909.

Annual Report of the Board of Foreign Missions of the Methodist Episcopal Church for the Year 1909. New York: Board of Foreign Missions of the Methodist Episcopal Church, 1910.

Eighty-fourth Annual Report of the Missionary Society of the Methodist Episcopal Church for the Year 1902. New York: Missionary Society of the Methodist Episcopal Church, 1903.

Eighty-fifth Annual Report of the Missionary Society of the Methodist Episcopal Church for the Year 1903. New York: Missionary Society of the Methodist Episcopal Church, 1904.

Eighty-sixth Annual Report of the Missionary Society of the Methodist Episcopal Church for the Year 1904. New York: Missionary Society of the Methodist Episcopal Church, 1905.

Eighty-seventh Annual Report of the Missionary Society of the Methodist Episcopal Church for the Year 1905. New York: Missionary Society of the Methodist Episcopal Church, 1906.

Eighty-eighth Annual Report of the Missionary Society of the Methodist Episcopal Church for the Year 1906. New York: Missionary Society of the Methodist Episcopal Church, 1907.

4. Philippine Episcopal Church

Annual Report of the Missionary District of the Philippine Islands for the Year Ending December 31, 1907. Manila: Published by the Printing Committee, 1908.

Annual Report of the Missionary District of the Philippine Islands for the Year Ending May 31, 1917. Manila: Published by the Printing Committee, 1918.

Brent, Charles Henry. "The Church in the Philippines: A Review of Events Since 1898." In *First Annual Report of the Bishop*.

———. *Report of the Bishop of the Missionary District of the Philippine Islands, 1906–1907*.

———. *Report of the Bishop of the Missionary District of the Philippine Islands, 1911–12. The Church in the Philippines: A Review of Events since 1898, with Bishop Brent's First Annual Report*, 2nd ed. Photocopy. New York: Protestant Episcopal Church of the USA, 1904.

Handbooks on the Missions of the Episcopal Church, Number 3: Philippine Islands. New York: The National Council of the Protestant Episcopal Church Department of Missions, 1923.

The Journal of the Bishops Clergy and Laity assembled in General Convention in the City of San Francisco on the First Wednesday in October A.D. 1901 with Appendices. Boston: Alfred Mudge & Son, 1902.

The Journal of the Fourth Annual Convocation of the Missionary District of the Philippine Islands held in the Cathedral Church of S. Mary and S. John, Manila, January 23–25, 1907. Manila: by the Secretary, 1907.

The Journal of the Sixth Annual Convocation of the Missionary District of the Philippine Islands Held in the Cathedral Church of S. Mary and S. John, Manila, August 10–11, 1909. Manila: by the Printing Committee, 1909.

The Journal of the Seventh Annual Convocation of the Missionary District of the Philippine Islands held in the Cathedral Church of S. Mary and S. John, Manila, August 3, 1910. Manila: by the Printing Committee, 1910.

The Journal of the Ninth Annual Convocation of the Missionary District of the Philippine Islands held in the Cathedral Church of S. Mary and S. John, Manila, August 3, 1912. Manila: by the Printing Committee, 1912.

The Journal of the Tenth Annual Convocation of the Missionary District of the Philippine Islands held in the Cathedral Church of S. Mary and S. John, Manila August 4, 1913. Manila: by the Printing Committee, 1913.

The Journal of the Eleventh Annual Convocation of the Missionary District of the Philippine Islands Held in the Cathedral Church of S. Mary and S. John, Manila September 30, 1914. Manila: by the Printing Committee, 1914.

The Journal of the General Convention of the Protestant Episcopal Church in the United States of America Held in the City of Boston from October 5th to October 25th, Inclusive in the Year of Our Lord 1904 with Appendices. New York City: Winthrop Press, 1905.

The Journal of the General Convention of the Protestant Episcopal Church in the United States of America Held in the City of Richmond from October Second to October Nineteenth, Inclusive in the Year of Our Lord 1907 with Appendices. New York: Winthrop Press, 1907.

The Journal of the Proceedings of the Bishops Clergy and Laity of the Protestant Episcopal Church in the United States of America Assembled in a General Convention Held in the City of Washington from October 5 to October 25 Inclusive in the Year of Our Lord 1898 with Appendices. Boston: Alfred Mudge & Son, 1899.

"Philippine Islands – 1923, Supplement No. 1 to the Philippine Handbook." In *Handbooks on the Missions of the Episcopal Church, Number 3: Philippine Islands.* New York: The National Council of the Protestant Episcopal Church Department of Missions, 1923, n.p.

Studley, Hobart Earl. "Report of the Cathedral Mission of St. Stephen." In *Journal of the Annual Convention,* 1913, 12.

———. "Report of the Cathedral Mission of St. Stephen, Manila." In *Journal of the Annual Convention,* 1908, 14. In *Journal of the Annual Convention,* 1911, 21.

———. "Report to the Cathedral Mission St. Stephen's for Chinese for the Year Ending December 1905." In *Journal of the Annual Convention,* 1905, 30.

The Twentieth Annual Report of the Missionary District of the Philippine Islands for the Year Ending December 31, 1927. Manila: by the Secretary, 1928.

The Twenty-first Annual Report of the Missionary District of the Philippine Islands for the Year Ending December 31, 1928. Manila, by the Secretary, 1929.

The Twentieth-second Annual Report of the Missionary District of the Philippine Islands for the Year Ending December 31, 1929. Manila: by the Secretary, 1930.

The Twentieth-third Annual Report of the Missionary District of the Philippine Islands for the Year Ending December 31, 1930. Manila: by the Secretary, 1931.

The Twenty-fourth Annual Report of the Missionary District of the Philippine Islands for the Year Ending December 31, 1931. Manila, by the Secretary, 1932.

The Twenty-fifth Annual Report of the Missionary District of the Philippine Islands for the Year Ending December 31, 1932. Manila, by the Secretary, 1933.

The Twenty-sixth Annual Report of the Missionary District of the Philippine Islands for the Year Ending December 31, 1933. Manila, by the Secretary, 1934.

5. Philippine Mission/Presbyterian Mission/UCCP

Annual Reports 1929-1930 Philippine Mission, Presbyterian Church in the USA, Dumaguete, Oriental Negros Oriental, October 5–12, 1929.

"Appendix I: Commission on Christian Witness and Service Division of Philippine-Chinese Mission." In *United Church of Christ in the Philippines, Minutes of the Executive Committee, National Headquarters, Quezon City, December 15 & 16, 1966*.

"Appendix II, Division of Philippine-Chinese Mission, 1967." In *United Church of Christ in the Philippines, Minutes of the Executive Committee, National Headquarters, Quezon City, December 8–9, 1967*.

"Appendix VIII: Report of the Sub-Committee submitted by Enrique Sobrepeña." In *United Church of Christ in the Philippines, Minutes of the Executive Committee, Quezon City, December 11–13, 1962 and January 22, 1963*.

"Appendix XI." In *United Church of Christ in the Philippines, Minutes of the Executive Committee Meeting, May 11–13, 1965*.

"Appendix IV." In *United Church of Christ in the Philippines, Minutes of the Fourth Biennial General Assembly, Los Baños, Laguna, May 17–23, 1954*.

"Appendix VI." In *United Church of Christ in the Philippines, Minutes of the Fourth Biennial General Assembly, Los Baños, Laguna, May 17–23, 1954*.

"Appendix VI." In *Minutes of the Ninth Biennial General Assembly of the United Church of Christ in the Philippines, Lucena City, May 31–June 5, 1964*.

"Appendix V." In *Minutes of the Tenth Post War Biennial General Assembly of the United Church of Christ in the Philippines, Dumaguete City, May 23–27, 1966*.

"Appendix VI, Report of the Commission on Christian Witness and Service." In
    *Proceedings of the Twelfth Post War Biennial General Assembly of the United
    Church of Christ in the Philippines, Baguio City, May 24–28, 1970.*

*The Confession of Faith and Form of Government of the United Evangelical Church
    of the Philippine Islands approved by the Executive Committee of the General
    Assembly of the United Evangelical Church, Manila, P. I.: October, 1933.*

"Discussion of Proposed Integration of Work in the Philippines of Reformed
    Church in America with the United Church of Christ in the Philippines."
    In *Minutes of the Joint United Church and Reformed Church Committee
    on Proposed Integration of Work in the Philippines of Reformed Church with
    United Church, September 12, 1962.*

Dunlap, George Williamson. Personal Report. In *Annual Reports 1932–1933,
    Philippine Mission of the Presbyterian Church in the USA, Cebu, October
    16–21, 1933.*

Dunlop, John Wallace. Personal Report. In *Annual Reports 1928-1929, Philippine
    Mission of the Presbyterian Church in the USA, Dumaguete, Oriental Negros,
    October 5–12, 1929.*

———. Personal Report. In *Annual Reports 1932–1933, Philippine Mission of the
    Presbyterian Church in the USA, Manila, October 2–9, 1930.*

———. Personal Report. In *Annual Reports 1932–1933, Philippine Mission of the
    Presbyterian Church in the USA, Cebu, October 16–21, 1933.*

*The Eightieth Annual Report of the Board of Foreign Missions of the Presbyterian
    Church in the United States of America Presented to the General Assembly, May,
    1917.* New York: Presbyterian Building, 1917.

*The Eighty-first Annual Report of the Board of Foreign Missions of the Presbyterian
    Church in the United States of America Presented to the General Assembly, May,
    1918.* New York: Presbyterian Building, 1918.

*The Eighty-third Annual Report of the Board of Foreign Missions of the Presbyterian
    Church in the United States of America Presented to the General Assembly, May,
    1920.* New York: Presbyterian Building, 1920.

*The Eighty-fourth Annual Report of the Board of Foreign Missions of the Presbyterian
    Church in the United States of America Presented to the General Assembly, May,
    1921.* New York: Presbyterian Building, 1921.

*The Eighty-fifth Annual Report of the Board of Foreign Missions of the Presbyterian
    Church in the United States of America Presented to the General Assembly, May,
    1922.* New York: Presbyterian Building, 1922.

*The Eighty-ninth Annual Report of the Board of Foreign Missions of the Presbyterian
    Church in the United States of America Presented to the General Assembly, May,
    1926.* New York: Presbyterian Building, 1926.

"Full Relationship of RCA Board with United Church of Christ." In *United Church of Christ in the Philippines, Minutes of the Executive Committee, Quezon City, May 22–24, 1963.*

Iyoy, Santiago G. "Report on the Visayan Jurisdiction to the Tenth Biennial Meeting of the General Assembly of the United Church of Christ in the Philippines, Dumaguete City, May 23–27, 1966." In *United Church of Christ in the Philippines Tenth Post War Biennial General Assembly, May 23–May 27, 1966, Dumaguete City, Philippines.*

Jansen, Paul Frederick. Personal Report. In *Annual Reports 1928–1929, Philippine Mission of the Presbyterian Church in the USA, Dumaguete, Oriental Negros, October 5–12, 1929.*

Minutes and Reports of the Enlarged Meeting of the Executive Committee of the National Christian Council of the Philippines, Manila, April 2–7, 1932.

Minutes of Annual Meeting, Philippine Mission, Held in Manila December 18th to the 19th, 1900. Yale Divinity School Library Special Collection, text-fiche, Sp. Col. Film, MS 11 Reel 289. Yale University, New Haven, CT.

Minutes of the Annual Meeting of the Presbyterian Mission in the Philippines, Manila Oct. 6th–14th Nineteen Twenty-four.

Minutes of the Annual Meeting of the Presbyterian Mission in the Philippines, Cebu, October 1st to October 9th, Nineteen Twenty-six. Ninety-seventh Year.

Minutes of the Executive Committee of the Presbyterian Mission in the Philippines, Manila, October Ninth through the Twenty First Nineteen Twenty-Two.

Minutes of the Executive Committee of the Presbyterian Mission in the Philippine Islands, Iloilo, March Sixteenth through the Twentieth Nineteen Twenty-Five.

Minutes of the Executive Committee of the Philippine Mission of the Presbyterian Church in the United States of America, Baguio, P.I., May 3–6, 1930.

Minutes of the Executive Committee Meeting, Philippine Federation of Christian Churches, Union Theological Seminary Building, Manila, October 31, 1958. Record Group A, Box 32A, Yale University Day Missions Library, Yale University, New Haven, CT.

"Minutes of the Joint United Church and Reformed Church Committee on Proposed Integration of Work in the Philippines of Reformed Church with United Church, September 12, 1962." In *United Church of Christ in the Philippines Minutes of the Executive Committee, Quezon City, December 11–13, 1962 and January 22, 1963.*

Minutes of the Luzon Conference of the United Evangelical Church on Evangelism and Self-Support September 19 & 20, 1929.

Minutes of the Meeting of the Executive Committee – United Evangelical Church of the Philippines Manila, October 2, 1933.

Minutes of the Meeting of the United Evangelical Church of the Philippines March 14th–19th, 1929.

Minutes of the Meeting of the Second General Assembly of the United Evangelical Church of the Philippines April 16th–20th, 1931.

Minutes of the Second General Assembly, United Church of Christ in the Philippines, April 25–30, 1950.

Minutes of the Ninth Biennial General Assembly, United Church of Christ in the Philippines, Lucena City, May 31–June 5, 1964.

Minutes of the Seventh General Assembly, United Church of Christ in the Philippines, Legaspi City, May 19–24, 1960.

Minutes of the Third Annual Meeting of the Philippine Mission, Iloilo, P[hilippine] I[slands], December 8-15, 1902. Yale Divinity School Library Special Collection, text-fiche, Sp. Col. Film, Ms 11 Reel 289. Yale University, New Haven, CT.

Minutes of the Third General Assembly of the United Evangelical Church of the Philippines Held in Cebu, April 19th–22nd, 1933.

Mission Meeting Reports for 1923–1924 of the Philippine Mission, Manila, Philippine Islands, October 6–14, 1924.

The One Hundred and Second Annual Report of the Board of Foreign Missions of the Presbyterian Church in the United States of America Presented to the General Assembly, May, 1939. NY: Presbyterian Building. 1939.

Proceedings of the Thirteenth Post War Biennial General Assembly of the United Church of Christ in the Philippines, Manila, May 28–June 1, 1972.

Raterta, Pedro M. "Report for the Visayas Jurisdiction," Appendix VII. *Proceedings of the Thirteenth Post War Biennial General Assembly of the United Church of Christ in the Philippines, Manila, May 28–June 1, 1972.*

Rath, Charles Edward. Personal Report. *Annual Reports, 1929–1930, Philippine Mission of the Presbyterian Church in the USA, Manila, October 2–9, 1930.*

Report of Deputation Sent by the Board of Foreign Missions of the Presbyterian Church in the U.S.A. in the Summer of 1915, to visit the Missions in Siam and the Philippine Islands and on the Way Home to Stop at Some of the Stations in Japan, Korea and China. Presented by Robert E. Speer, Dwight H. Day and David Bovaird. New York City: The Board of Foreign Missions of the Presbyterian Church in the USA, 1916.

The Sixty-second Annual Report of the Board of Foreign Missions of the Presbyterian Church in the United States of America, presented to the General Assembly, May, 1899. New York: Presbyterian Building, 1899. Microfilm SD1620. Yale Divinity Library, Yale University, New Haven, CT.

The Sixty-third Annual Report of the Board of Foreign Missions of the Presbyterian Church in the United States of America, presented to the General Assembly, May, 1900. New York: Presbyterian Building, 1900.

The Sixty-fourth Annual Report of the Board of Foreign Missions of the Presbyterian Church in the United States of America, presented to the General Assembly, May, 1901. New York: Presbyterian Building, 1901.

The Sixty-seventh Annual Report of the Board of Foreign Missions of the Presbyterian Church in the United States of America, presented to the General Assembly, May, 1904. New York: Presbyterian Building, 1904.

The Seventy-first Annual Report of the Board of Foreign Missions of the Presbyterian Church in the United States of America Presented to the General Assembly, May, 1908. New York: Presbyterian Building, 1908.

The Seventy-second Annual Report of the Board of Foreign Missions of the Presbyterian Church in the United States of America Presented to the General Assembly, May, 1909. New York: Presbyterian Building, 1909.

The Seventy-third Annual Report of the Board of Foreign Missions of the Presbyterian Church in the United States of America Presented to the General Assembly, May, 1910. New York: Presbyterian Building, 1910.

The Seventy-fourth Annual Report of the Board of Foreign Missions of the Presbyterian Church in the United States of America Presented to the General Assembly, May, 1911. New York: Presbyterian Building, 1911.

Station Reports of Philippine Presbyterian Mission 1920–1925, Marking Completion of Quarter Century of Service Force List for Entire Period/Statistics for year 1924–1925.

A Unified Program for the Philippines. Findings of the Conference held in Manila, March 19–21, 1929. Manila: National Christian Council of the P.I. May, 1929.

United Church of Christ in the Philippines, Minutes of the Executive Committee, December 7–11, 1959.

United Church of Christ in the Philippines, Minutes of the Executive Committee, December 10 & 11, 1964.

United Church of Christ in the Philippines Minutes of the Fourth Biennial General Assembly, Los Banos, Laguna, May 17–23, 1954, 9–10.

United Church of Christ in the Philippines, Minutes of the Mid-Year Meeting, Executive Committee, Manila, November 25–27, 1953.

United Church of Christ in the Philippines, Tenth Post War Biennial General Assembly, Dumaguete City, Philippines, May 23–27, 1966.

"United Church of Christ in the Philippines Organizational Set-Up, Commission on Philippine-Chinese Mission." In *Minutes of the Ninth Biennial General Assembly, United Church of Christ in the Philippines, Lucena City, May 31–June 5, 1964.*

Wright, George William. Personal Report. In *Annual Reports 1928–1929, Philippine Mission of the Presbyterian Church in the USA, Dumaguete, Oriental Negros, October 5–12, 1929.*

———. Personal Report. In *Annual Reports 1932–1933, Philippine Mission of the Presbyterian Church in the USA, Cebu, October 16–21, 1933.*

6. Reformed Church in America

Thirty-second Annual Report of the Board of Foreign Missions of the Reformed Church in America . . . for the Year Ending April 30th, 1864. New York: Board of Publication of the Reformed Protestant Dutch Church, 1864, 14. Accessed 24 September 2015, http://digitalcommons.hope.edu/cgi/viewcontent.cgi?article=1006&context=world_annual_report.

The Fortieth Annual Report of the Board of Foreign Missions of the Reformed Church in America . . . for the Year Ending April 30, 1872. New York: Board of Publications of the Reformed Church in America, 1872, 11. Accessed 24 September 2015, http://digitalcommons.hope.edu/cgi/viewcontent.cgi?article=1014&context=world_annual_report.

7. Southern Baptist Convention

Annual of the Southern Baptist Convention Nineteen Hundred and Forty-six. Eighty-ninth Session One Hundred and First Year. Miami, Florida, May 15–19, 1946. Nashville, TN: Executive Committee, Southern Baptist Convention, [1946].

Annual of the Southern Baptist Convention Nineteen Hundred and Forty-seven. Ninetieth Session One Hundred and Second Year. St. Louis, Missiouri, May 7–11, 1947. Nashville, TN: Executive Committee, Southern Baptist Convention, [1947].

Annual of the Southern Baptist Convention Nineteen Hundred and Forty-Nine. Ninety-Second Session, One Hundred and Fourth Year. Oklahoma City, Oklahoma, May 18–22, 1949. Nashville, TN: Executive Committee, Southern Baptist Convention, [1949].

Annual of the Southern Baptist Convention Nineteen Hundred and Fifty, Ninety-Third Session, One Hundred and Fifth Year, Chicago, Illinois, May 9–12, 1950. Nashville, TN: Executive Committee, Southern Baptist Convention, 1950. Accessed 15 September 2005, https://solomon.imb.org/public/ws/oldmin/www2/minutesp/Record.

Annual of the Southern Baptist Convention Nineteen Hundred and Fifty-first. Ninety-fourth Session One Hundred and Sixth Year. San Francisco, California, June 20–24, 1951. Nashville, TN: Executive Committee, Southern Baptist Convention, 1951.

Annual of the Southern Baptist Convention Nineteen Hundred and Fifty-two. Ninety-fifth Session One Hundred and Seventh Year. Miami, Florida, May 14–18, 1952. Nashville, TN: Executive Committee, Southern Baptist Convention, 1952.

Annual of the Southern Baptist Convention Nineteen Hundred and Fifty-three. Ninety-sixth Session One Hundred and Eighth Year. Houston, Texas, May 6–10, 1953. Nashville, TN: Executive Committee, Southern Baptist Convention, 1953.

Annual of the Southern Baptist Convention Nineteen Hundred and Fifty-fourth. Ninety-seventh Session One Hundred and Ninth Year. St. Louis, Missiouri, June 2–5, 1954. Nashville, TN: Executive Committee, Southern Baptist Convention, 1954.

Annual of the Southern Baptist Convention Nineteen Hundred and Fifty-fifth. Ninety-eighth Session One Hundred and Tenth Year. Miami, Florida, May 18–21, 1955. Nashville, TN: Executive Committee, Southern Baptist Convention, 1955.

Annual of the Southern Baptist Convention Nineteen Hundred and Fifty-sixth. Ninety-ninth Session One Hundred and Eleventh Year. Kansas City, Missiouri, May 30–June 2, 1956. Nashville, TN: Executive Committee, Southern Baptist Convention, 1956.

"Appendix: Statistical Reports." In *Annual of the Southern Baptist Convention, Nineteen Hundred and Forty-Nine, Ninety-Second Session, One Hundred and Fourth Year, Oklahoma City, Oklahoma, May 18–22, 1949*, 149–153. Nashville, TN: Executive Committee, Southern Baptist Convention, 1949.

Cauthen, Baker James. "The Orient." In *Annual of the Southern Baptist Convention Nineteen Hundred and Forty-Nine. Ninety-Second Session One Hundred and Fourth Year. Oklahoma City, Oklahoma, May 18–22, 1949*, 125–126. Nashville, TN: Executive Committee, Southern Baptist Convention, 1949.

———. "The Orient in Search of Peace." In *Annual of the Southern Baptist Convention Nineteen Hundred and Forty-Six. Eighty-Ninth Session One Hundred and First Year. Miami, Florida, May 15–19, 1946*, 233–238. Nashville, TN: Executive Committee, Southern Baptist Convention, 1946.

Crawley, Winston. "Report of the Baguio Station." In *Minutes of the First Annual Session of the Philippine Mission of the Southern Baptist Convention 1950, August 29–September 1, Theme: Advance with Christ.* Baguio: Baguio Printing & Publishing, 1950.

Foster, James A. "Report of the Baguio Station." In *Minutes of the Philippine Mission of the Southern Baptist Convention 1950–51, Annual Session – August 27–31, Baguio City, Minutes of the 1950–51 Executive Committee Constitution, Theme: By My Spirit*, 18–19. Baguio: Baguio Printing & Publishing, 1951.

Foster, Zelma Van Osdol. "Amazing Growth in Philippine Missions." In *Annual of the Southern Baptist Convention 1954. 97th Session 109th Year. St. Louis,*

Missiouri, June 2–5, 1954, 173–175. Nashville, TN: Executive Committee, Southern Baptist Convention, 1954.

Harrington, Fern. "Report of the Dagupan Work." In *Minutes of the First Annual Session of the Philippine Mission of the Southern Baptist Convention 1950, August 29–September 1, Theme: Advance with Christ*, 19–21. Baguio: Baguio Printing & Publishing, 1950.

Minutes of the First Annual Session of the Philippine Mission of the Southern Baptist Convention 1950 August 28–September 1. Theme: Advance with Christ. Baguio City: Baguio Printing & Publishing, 1950.

Minutes of the Philippine Mission of the Foreign Mission Board Southern Baptist Convention 1961–62. Baguio City, Philippines – May 26–June 6, 1962. Baguio City: Baguio Printing & Publishing, 1962.

Minutes of the Philippine Mission of the Foreign Mission Board Southern Baptist Convention 1962–63. Baguio City, Philippines. Baguio City: Baguio Printing & Publishing, 1963.

Minutes of the Philippine Mission of the Southern Baptist Convention 1950–51. Annual Session – Aug 27–31, 1951 Baguio City. Minutes of the 1950–51 Executive Committee Constitution. Theme: By My Spirit. Baguio City: Baguio Printing & Publishing, 1951.

Minutes of the Philippine Mission of the Southern Baptist Convention 1951–52. Annual Session – Aug. 11–14, 1952 Manila. 1951–52 Executive Committee Minutes Constitution. Theme: Be Filled with the Spirit. Baguio City: Baguio Printing & Publishing, 1952.

Minutes of the Philippine Mission of the Southern Baptist Convention 1952–53. Annual Session – August 17–21, 1953 Baguio City. 1952–53 Executive Committee Minutes Constitution. Theme: Able through Christ. Baguio City: Baguio Printing & Publishing, 1953.

Minutes of the Philippine Mission of the Southern Baptist Convention 1953–54. Annual Session – June 21–25, 1954 Manila. 1953–54 Executive Committee Minutes Constitution. Theme: The Love of Christ Constraineth Us. Baguio City: Baguio Printing & Publishing, 1954.

Minutes of the Philippine Mission of the Southern Baptist Convention 1954–55. Annual Session – June 21–28, 1955 Manila. 1954–55 Executive Committee Minutes. Baguio City: Baguio Printing & Publishing, 1955.

Minutes of the Philippine Mission of the Southern Baptist Convention 1955–56. Annual Session – June 21–28, 1956 Manila. 1955–56 Executive Committee Minutes. Baguio City: Baguio Printing & Publishing, 1956.

Minutes of the Philippine Mission of the Southern Baptist Convention 1956–57. Annual Session – June 6–13, 1957 Manila. 1956–57 Executive Committee Minutes. Baguio City: Baguio Printing & Publishing, 1957.

Minutes of the Philippine Mission of the Southern Baptist Convention 1957–58. Annual Session – May 29–June 6, 1958 Baguio City. Baguio City: Baguio Printing & Publishing, 1958.

Minutes of the Philippine Mission of the Southern Baptist Convention 1958–59. Annual Session – May 29–June 3, 1959 PBTS, Baguio City. Baguio City: Baguio Printing & Publishing, 1959.

Minutes of the Philippine Mission of the Southern Baptist Convention 1959–60. Annual Session – May 25–June 1, 1960 PBTS, Baguio City. Baguio City: Baguio Printing & Publishing, 1960.

Minutes of the Philippine Mission of the Southern Baptist Convention 1960–61. Annual Session – May 31–June 8, 1961 Baguio City. Theme: God's Word . . . His Accomplishment . . . Our Joy. Baguio City: Baguio Printing & Publishing, 1961.

Nichols, B. I. "Gleanings from Letters: A Unique Missionary Ministry." In *Annual of the Southern Baptist Convention 1946. 89th Session 101st Year. Miami, Florida, May 15–19, 1946*, 238–240. Nashville, TN: Executive Committee, Southern Baptist Convention, 1946.

"Philippine Islands." In *Annual of the Southern Baptist Convention 1952. 95th Session 107th Year. Miami, Florida, May 14–18, 1952*, 174–176. Nashville, TN: Executive Committee, Southern Baptist Convention, 1952.

Rankin, M. Theron. "One Hundred and First Annual Report Foreign Mission Board." In *Annual of the Southern Baptist Convention 1946. 89th Session 101st Year. Miami, Florida, May 15–19, 1946*, 225–226. Nashville, TN: Executive Committee, Southern Baptist Convention, 1946.

Routh, E. C. "The Foreign Mission Board – A Historical Sketch." In *Annual of the Southern Baptist Convention 1946. 89th Session 101st Year. Miami, Florida, May 15–19, 1946*, 226–227. Nashville, TN: Executive Committee, Southern Baptist Convention, 1946.

Saunders, Mary Lucile. "Mission to the Filipino People." In *Annual of the Southern Baptist Convention 1953. 96th Session 108th Year. Houston, Texas, May 6–10, 1953*, 173–174. Nashville, TN: Executive Committee, Southern Baptist Convention, 1953.

———. "Report of the Manila Station." In *Minutes of the Philippine Mission of the Southern Baptist Convention 1952–53, Annual Session–August 17–21, 1953 Baguio City, 1952–53 Executive Committee Minutes Constitution, Theme: Able Through Christ*, 25–28. Baguio: Baguio Printing & Publishing, 1953.

"Southern Baptist Convention Foreign Missionary Personnel." In *Annual of the Southern Baptist Convention, Nineteen Hundred and Forty-seven, Ninetieth Session, One Hundred and Second Year, St. Louis, Missouri, May 5–11,*

1947, 125–126. Nashville, TN: Executive Committee, Southern Baptist
Convention, 1947.

II. Official Documents and Anniversary Publications

Anglo Chinese School Golden Jubilee Book: 1899–1949. Manila: n.p., 1949.

Annual Report of Major General Arthur MacArthur, US Army, Commanding, Division of the Philippines. Military Governor in the Philippine Islands, Reports of the Military Governor, Vol. 2. Manila: n.p., 1901.

Annual Report of the Military Governor in the Philippine Islands, 1899–1903, 6 vols. Manila: n.p., 1899–1903.

Apilado, Mariano Casuga. "The United Church of Christ in the Philippines: A Historical Essay." In *The Church for the Life of the World. The 40th Anniversary Souvenir Magazine of the United Church Letter, May 22, 1988*. N.p.: n.p., n.d.

The Association for Promotion of Chinese Theological Education, Editorial Committee. *A Report on the Consultation of Chinese Theological Educators and Church Leaders. 10th–13th Jan 1972*. Kowloon, Hong Kong: Christian Witness Press for the Association for Promotion of Chinese Theological Education, 1973.

Banzuelo, Edilberto V. "Entrance of Evangelical Christianity." In *Golden Jubilee Almanac 1929–1979 (Feilübin Zhonghua Jidu Jiaohui Jinxi Nianjian)* 菲律濱中華基督教會金禧年鑑, ed. S[hih] C[hang] Shangkuan, 132–139 (pages in Chinese style). Manila: United Evangelical Church of the Philippines, 1979.

"Baptist Work in the Philippines." In Baguio Chinese Baptist Church/Biyao Huaren Jinxinhui 碧瑤華人浸信會. *Blueprints BCBC 1950–2000*. Baguio City: Baguio Chinese Baptist Church, 2000.

Beard, Willard L. "Recent Developments in Chinese Church Life." In *The China Mission Year Book, 1924 (Twelfth Issue)*, ed. Frank Rawlinson. Shanghai: Christian Literature Society, 1924.

Board of Trustees, "A Quarter-Century of Progress." In *Jianan Zhongxue Yinxi Tekan* 嘉南中學銀禧特刊 (Twenty-fifth anniversary special publication of Hope Christian High School), 18–19. Manila: Hope Christian High School, 1972.

Botengan, Kate Chollipas. "The Horizon of the Past." In *Pearl for the Episcopal Diocese of Central Philippines – Recapturing the Zeal for Mission*, 1–23. Quezon City: The Episcopal Diocese of Central Philippines, 2002.

————. *Transformed by the Word; Transforming the World: One Hundred Years of Episcopal Church in the Philippines.* Quezon City: The Episcopal Church in the Philippines (ECP), 2001.

Canlas, Querubin D. "A Brief History of Philippine Christianity." In *Golden Jubilee Almanac 1929-1979 (Feilübin Zhonghua Jidu Jiaohui Jinxi Nianjian)* 菲律濱中華基督教會金禧年鑑, ed. S[hih] C[hang] Shangkuan, 122–131 (pages in Chinese style). Manila: United Evangelical Church of the Philippines, 1979(?).

The Confession of Faith and Form of Government of the United Evangelical Church of the Philippine Islands Approved by the Executive Committee of the General Assembly of the United Evangelical Church, Manila, P.I.: October, 1933.

"Document 539 Agreement between the Sulu Sultan and Datus and General John C. Bates (Jolo, August 20, 1899)." In *Documentary Sources of Philippine History*, compiled by Gregorio F. Zaide, additional notes by Sonia M. Zaide, 10: 143–147. Metro Manila: National Book Store, 1990.

"Document 544, Spread of the Gospel through the Bible." In *Documentary Sources of Philippine History*, compiled by Gregorio F. Zaide, additional notes by Sonia M. Zaide, 10: 210–215. Metro Manila: National Book Store, 1990.

"Evangelistic Work: A Chinese Woman Preaches." *The Philippine Presbyterian* 13, no. 1 (Jan 1922): 9.

"Factsheet 1 by the Kaisa Para Sa Kaunlaran/Feilübin Huayi Qingnian Lianhehui 菲律濱華裔青年聯合會." Accessed 3 November 2006, http://www.philonline.com.ph/~kaisa/kaisa_fact.html).

First General Assembly United Church of Christ in the Philippines Ellinwood-Malate Church, May 25–27, 1948 – Proceedings. Quezon City: n.p., 1992.

For All the Peoples of Asia: Federation of Asian Bishops' Conferences Documents from 1970 to 1991, Vol. 1, eds. Gaudencio B. Rosales, D. D. and C. G. Arevalo, S.J. Quezon City: Claretian Publications, 1997.

For All the Peoples of Asia: Federation of Asian Bishops' Conferences Documents from 1991 to 1996, Vol. 2, ed. Franz-Josef Eilers, SVD. Quezon City: Claretian Publications, 1997.

Gamboa, Jose, Jr, Gamaliel T. de Armas, Jr, Roela Victoria Rivera, Sharon Paz C. Hechanova. *Methodism in the Philippines: A Century of Faith and Vision.* Manila: Philippine Central Conference, The United Methodist Church, 2003.

"The History of Manila Chinese Baptist Church." TMs (photocopy). Manila: Manila Chinese Baptist Church, n.d.

Hu, Betty Mayling /Hu MeiLin 胡美林. "Pioneer Days." In *Historical Documentary of Protestantism in the Orient. 40th Anniversary of the United Evangelical Church of Manila (Feilübin Zhonghua Jidu Jiaohui Sishi Zhounian*

Lishi Wenxian Fu Yazhou Duoguo Jidu Jiaohui Lishi 1929–1969) 菲律賓中華基督教會四十週年歷史文獻附亞洲多國基督教會歷史*1929-1969*, 18–19 (pages in Chinese style). Manila: United Evangelical Church of Manila, 1969.

Kho Goat Hoa (a.k.a. Phoebe Kho-Chua)/Cai Xu YueHua 許月華. "Retrospect at the 30th Anniversary." In *30th Anniversary Souvenir Magazine, The Evangelistic Band of the Chinese United Evangelical Church*. Manila: Chinese United Evangelical Church, 1966.

———. "History of the Evangelistic Band." In *30th Anniversary Souvenir Magazine, The Evangelistic Band of the Chinese United Evangelical Church*. Manila: Chinese United Evangelical Church, 1966.

Manual of the Board of Foreign Missions of the Reformed Church in America: For the Use of Missions and Missionaries. New York: The Board of Foreign Missions, 1948.

Miles, Fern Harrington. "Down Memory's Lane in Dagupan, Philippines." In Dagupan Chinese Baptist Church/Laguban Huaqiao Jinxinhui 拉古板華僑浸信會. *Christ Preeminent 50th Anniversary (Zhu Ju Shouwei)* 主居首位. Dagupan City: Dagupan Chinese Baptist Church, 2002.

Notson, Charles Eldred. "A Mid-century Miracle." In *Davao Evangelical Church Fortieth Anniversary Special Publication (1951-1991) [Namao Jidu Jiaohui Sishi Zhounian Jinian Tekan (Yijiu Wuyinian-Yijiu Jiuyinian)]* 納卯基督教會四十週年紀念特刊〔一九五一年～一九九一年〕. Davao City: Davao Evangelical Church, 1991.

Palugod, Sylvia. *The Chinese in the Philippines: A Demographic and Socio-Cultural Profile*. Manila: CCOWE Fellowship Philippines, 1993.

Report of the Philippine Commission to the President. Vol. 1, *January 31, 1900*. Washington, DC: Government Printing Office, 1900.

Scott, Roderick. "The Christian Movement in China in a Period of National Transition." In T.C. Chao and Roderick Scott, ed. *The Christian Movement in China in a Period of National Transition*. Three papers prepared at the request of the Department of Social and Industrial Research for the Tambaram Meeting of the International Missionary Council. Mysore: Wesley Press & Publishing, 1938.

Shao, Wesley Kho/Shao QingZhang 邵慶彰. "The Fifty Years of Davao Evangelical Church." In *Davao Evangelical Church Fifty Years 1951–2001 (Namao Jidu Jiaohui)* 納卯基督教會, 9–17. Davao City: Davao Evangelical Church, 2001.

Tan, Amanda Shao/Chen YouChun 陳友純. "Chinese Churches in the Philippines." In *United Evangelical Church of the Philippines Golden Jubilee Almanac (Feilübin Zhonghua Jidu Jiaohui Jinxi Nianjian)* 菲律賓中華基督教會金禧年鑑*1929–1979*, ed. S[hih] C[hang] Shangkuan, 147–154 (pages in Chinese style). Manila: United Evangelical Church of the Philippines, 1979.

Traffic in Opium and Other Dangerous Drugs: Report by the Government of the United States of America. Washington DC: US Government Printing Office, 1931.

US Bureau of the Census. *Census of the Philippine Islands Taken Under the Direction of the Philippine Commission in the Year 1903.* Vol. 1: *Geography, History, and Population.* Washington, D.C.: United States Bureau of the Census, 1905.

US Congress, Senate. The Library of Congress. The Bureau of Insular Affairs, War Department. *Bibliography of the Philippine Islands.* 57th Cong., 2nd sess., 1903. S. Doc. 74. Washington, DC: Government Printing Office, 1903. Reprint, Manila: National Historical Institute, 1994.

Uyboco, Prudencio S. "The Only Foundation." In *Davao Evangelical Church Fortieth Anniversary Special Publication (1951–1991) [(Namao Jidu Jiaohui Sishi Zhounian Jinian Tekan (Yijiu Wuyinian—Yijiu Jiuyinian)]* 納卯基督教會四十週年紀念特刊 *(一九五一年～一九九一年).* Davao City: Davao Evangelical Church, 1991.

Young, Joseph/Yang Qiyao 楊其耀. "A Brief Survey of Chinese Protestantism in the Philippines." In *Historical Documentary of Protestantism in the Orient. 40th Anniversary of the United Evangelical Church of Manila (Feilübin Zhonghua Jidu Jiaohui Sishi Zhounian Lishi Wenxian Fu Yazhou Duoguo Jidu Jiaohui Lishi)* 『菲律賓中華基督教會四十週年歷史文獻附亞洲多國基督教會歷史』 *1929–1969,* 226–235 (pages in Chinese style). Manila: United Evangelical Church of Manila, 1969.

III. Interviews and Other Materials

Ang, Rosie Sun Lu Go/Hong Wu ChunYu 洪吳純瑜 (b. 1939; former member and Christian worker, Davao Evangelical Church). Audio-taped interview by Jean Uayan, 18 August 2005, at Biblical Seminary of the Philippines, Valenzuela City, Philippines. Transcript. Philippine Chinese Church Archives, Biblical Seminary of the Philippines, Valenzuela City, Philippines.

Bacon, Agustin and Jonathan L. Bacon (former minister, Bradford UCCP and his son). Telehone interview by Jean Uayan, 19 April 2005, in Cebu City, Philippines. Transcript. Philippine Chinese Church Archives, Biblical Seminary of the Philippines, Valenzuela City, Philippines.

Cang, Agapito/Jiang WeiSheng 江維勝 (1922–2005; elder, Dumaguete Christian Church). Audio-taped interview by Jean Uayan, 19 December 2001, at his residence in Dumaguete City, Philippines. Transcript. Philippine Chinese Church Archives, Biblical Seminary of the Philippines, Valenzuela City, Philippines.

Cang, Caridad vda. de Sun/Sun Jiang XinYi 孫江心意 (b. 1919; sister of
    Agapito Cang). Audio-taped interview by Jean Uayan, 19 December 2001,
    in Dumaguete City, Philippines. Transcript. Philippine Chinese Church
    Archives, Biblical Seminary of the Philippines, Valenzuela City, Philippines.

Chua, Mercedes vda. de Cang/Jiang Cai MianLing 江蔡綿綾 (b. 1918; member,
    Cebu Gospel Church). Audio-taped interview by Jean Uayan, 25 and 29
    June 2004, at Cebu Gospel Church, Cebu City, Philippines. Transcript.
    Philippine Chinese Church Archives, Biblical Seminary of the Philippines,
    Valenzuela City, Philippines.

———. Audio-taped interview by Jean Uayan, 19 April 2005, at Cebu Gospel
    Church, Cebu City, Philippines. Transcript. Philippine Chinese Church
    Archives, Biblical Seminary of the Philippines, Valenzuela City, Philippines.

Crawley, Winston <winstoncrawley@yahoo.com>. Private email message to the
    writer, 25 July 2005.

Divinagracia, Rocky (chairman, Tondo Evangelical church). Telehone interview
    by Jean Uayan, 27 June 2005, in Manila, Philippines. Transcript. Philippine
    Chinese Church Archives, Biblical Seminary of the Philippines, Valenzuela
    City, Philippines.

Dy, Esther Ting/Li Ding YingYing 李丁瑩瑩 (b. 1933; elder, United Evangelical
    Church of the Philippines). Audio-taped interview by Jean Uayan, 12
    April 2005, at her residence in Sta. Cruz, Manila, Philippines. Transcript.
    Philippine Chinese Church Archives, Biblical Seminary of the Philippines,
    Valenzuela City, Philippines.

Dy Hong Suan vda. de Siao/Xiao Li HongXuan 蕭李鳳萱 (b. 1931; daughter-
    in-law of Sio Tsong Kheng). Audio-taped interview by Jean Uayan, 30
    March 2005, at her residence in Quezon City, Philippines. Transcript.
    Philippine Chinese Church Archives, Biblical Seminary of the Philippines,
    Valenzuela City, Philippines.

Go Bon Juan/Wu WenHuan 吳文煥 (board member, KAISA Foundation).
    Telephone interview by Jean Uayan, Manila, 19 December 2006.

Go To Kang/Wu DaoHang 吳道巷 (member, Iloilo Christian Gospel Assembly,
    Center, Inc.). Audio-taped interview by Jean Uayan, 4 May 2005, at his
    residence, Iloilo City, Philippines. Transcript. Philippine Chinese Church
    Archives, Biblical Seminary of the Philippines, Valenzuela City, Philippines.

GoChioco, Jesus/Wu GuangTi 吳光迪 (minister-at-large, Dumaguete City).
    Personal interview by Jean Uayan, 28 April 2005, in Dumaguete City,
    Philippines. Transcript. Philippine Chinese Church Archives, Biblical
    Seminary of the Philippines, Valenzuela City, Philippines.

Hao, Pedro/Hou JunNan 侯均南 (1924–2004; former minister, Dagupan
    Chinese Baptist Church). Audio-taped interview by Jean Uayan, 19 March
    2004, at his residence in Cainta, Rizal, Philippines. Transcript. Philippine

Chinese Church Archives, Biblical Seminary of the Philippines, Valenzuela City, Philippines.

Hu, Josephine/Luo BiJuan 羅碧娟 (b. 1930; former member, Baguio Chinese Baptist Church). Audio-taped telephone interview by Jean Uayan, 4 April 2005, at his residence in Cainta, Rizal, Philippines. Transcript. Philippine Chinese Church Archives, Biblical Seminary of the Philippines, Valenzuela City, Philippines.

Kua Bee Tin/Ke MeiZhen 柯美珍 and Kua Ka Tin/Ke JiaZhen 柯佳珍 (daughters of Kua Eng Chiong/Ke RongZhang 柯榮章). Telephone interview by Jean Uayan, Manila, 6 October 2005. Audio-tape transcript. Philippine Chinese Church Archives, Biblical Seminary of the Philippines, Valenzuela City, Philippines.

Lim, Bona/Lin LianZhu 林蓮珠 (1916–2004; former church worker, Davao Evangelical Church) and Valeria Lim/Yang Lin HeBi 楊林何碧. Audio-taped interview by Jean Uayan, 17 March 2001, at their residence in Malate, Manila, Philippines. Transcript. Philippine Chinese Church Archives, Biblical Seminary of the Philippines, Valenzuela City, Philippines.

Lim Diong Su/Lin ZhongShu 林忠恕 (b. 1922; former Senior Warden, St. Stephen's Parish). Audio-taped telephone interview by Jean Uayan, 17 April 2005, at his residence in Sta. Cruz, Manila, Philippines. Transcript. Philippine Chinese Church Archives, Biblical Seminary of the Philippines, Valenzuela City, Philippines.

Lim Giok Khun/Lin YuKun 林玉崑 (b. 1918; former Senior Warden, St. Stephen's Parish). Audio-taped interview by Jean Uayan, 23 June 2005, at his residence in Sta. Cruz, Manila, Philippines. Transcript. Philippine Chinese Church Archives, Biblical Seminary of the Philippines, Valenzuela City, Philippines.

Lim King Hua vda. de Ong/Wang Lin JingHua 王林璟華 (b. 1928; daughter of Lim Siong Hong). Personal interview by Jean Uayan, Malabon City, 9 July 2005. Transcript. Philippine Chinese Church Archives, Biblical Seminary of the Philippines, Valenzuela City, Philippines.

Lim, Morino/Lin HuaSheng 林華生 (b. 1936; minister, Davao Evangelical Church). Audio-taped telephone interview by Jean Uayan, 4 April 2005, at his residence in Davao City, Philippines. Transcript. Philippine Chinese Church Archives, Biblical Seminary of the Philippines, Valenzuela City, Philippines.

McGarvey, Patty <archives@cmalliance.org>. Private email message to the writer, 29 August 2005.

Moreno, Pablo (member, Bradford UCCP). Audio-taped telephone interview by Jean Uayan, 20 April 2005, in Cebu City, Philippines. Transcript. Philippine

Chinese Church Archives, Biblical Seminary of the Philippines, Valenzuela
City, Philippines.

Ong, Felix/Wang ZhenGuo 王振國. Telephone interview by Jean Uayan,
Manila, 3 February 2007.

Ong Kim Ja vda. de Chua/Cai Wang JinXia 蔡王錦霞 (b. 1927; minister,
Westminster Student Church). Telephone interview by Jean Uayan,
Quezon City, 9 November 2004 and 7 April 2005. Transcript. Philippine
Chinese Church Archives, Biblical Seminary of the Philippines, Valenzuela
City, Philippines.

Pan, Erlinda Duy/Pan Rui XiuZhu 潘雷秀祝 (b. 1933; member, United
Evangelical Church of the Philippines). Audio-taped interview by Jean
Uayan, 16 August 2005, at Biblical Seminary of the Philippines, Valenzuela
City, Philippines. Transcript. Philippine Chinese Church Archives, Biblical
Seminary of the Philippines, Valenzuela City, Philippines.

Pettit, Max/Pei MaKe 培馬可 (b. 1922; retired missionary, Southern Baptist
Convention). Audio-taped interview by Jean Uayan, 16 February 2002, in
Dagupan City, Philippines. Transcript. Philippine Chinese Church Archives,
Biblical Seminary of the Philippines, Valenzuela City, Philippines.

Po, Wanda Liam Giok 傅念玉博士 (b. 1954; Director, Philippine Christian
Gospel School). Telephone interview by Jean Uayan, 15 October 2006, in
Cebu City, Philippines. Transcript. Philippine Chinese Church Archives,
Biblical Seminary of the Philippines, Valenzuela City, Philippines.

Saw Cang Iattee/Su Jiang YueZhi 蘇江悅治 (b. 1905; member, Cebu Gospel
Church). Audio-taped interview by Jean Uayan, 23 June 2004, at her
residence in Cebu City, Philippines. Transcript. Philippine Chinese Church
Archives, Biblical Seminary of the Philippines, Valenzuela City, Philippines.

Shao Hui Cheng vda. de Tan/Chen Shao HuiQing 陳邵惠卿 (b. 1918; elder,
United Evangelical Church of the Philippines). Audio-taped interview
by Jean Uayan, 12 April 2005, at her residence in Sta. Cruz, Manila,
Philippines. Transcript. Philippine Chinese Church Archives, Biblical
Seminary of the Philippines, Valenzuela City, Philippines.

Shao, Wesley/Shao QingZhang 邵慶彰 (b. 1917; retired minister, United
Evangelical Church of the Philippines). Audio-taped interview by
Jean Uayan, 16 December 2003, at his residence in Sta. Cruz, Manila,
Philippines. Transcript. Philippine Chinese Church Archives, Biblical
Seminary of the Philippines, Valenzuela City, Philippines.

Si Giok Pan/Shi YuPing 施玉瓶 a.k.a Mrs Lim Hok Seng (Mrs Lin FuSheng)
林福盛夫人 (b. 1905; member, Cebu Gospel Church). Audio-taped
telephone interview by Jean Uayan, 20 April 2005, at her residence in Cebu
City, Philippines. Transcript. Philippine Chinese Church Archives, Biblical
Seminary of the Philippines, Valenzuela City, Philippines.

————. Audio-taped interview by Jean Uayan, 22 April 2005 at her residence in Cebu City, Philippines. Transcript. Philippine Chinese Church Archives, Biblical Seminary of the Philippines, Valenzuela City, Philippines.

Sia, Vicente Y./Xie GuoZhi 謝國智. Telephone interview by Jean Uayan, Manila, 3 February 2007.

Siao, Pilar/Siau Pit Leng/Xiao BiLeng 蕭必冷 (b. 1924; retired Christian worker, Cebu Gospel Church). Audio-taped interview by Jean Uayan, 25 June 2004, at her residence in Cebu City, Philippines. Transcript. Philippine Chinese Church Archives, Biblical Seminary of the Philippines, Valenzuela City, Philippines.

Sitoy, T. Valentino, Jr (Professor, Silliman University). Audio-taped interview by Jean Uayan, 29 April 2005, at Cang's Store, Dumaguete City, Philippines. Transcript. Philippine Chinese Church Archives, Biblical Seminary of the Philippines, Valenzuela City, Philippines.

Sy Chi Siong/Shi CiXiang 施慈祥 (b. 1913; member of United Evangelical Church of the Philippines). Audio-taped interview by Jean Uayan, 3 January 2006, at his business establishment in Binondo, Manila, Philippines. Transcript. Philippine Chinese Church Archives, Biblical Seminary of the Philippines, Valenzuela City, Philippines.

Sy, Elena Co/Shi Xu XiuLin 施許秀琳 (b. 1928; elder, United Evangelical Church of the Philippines). Audio-taped interview by Jean Uayan, 26 February 2005 at her residence in Caloocan City, Philippines. Transcript. Philippine Chinese Church Archives, Biblical Seminary of the Philippines, Valenzuela City, Philippines.

Sy, Peter Leoncio/Shi LiangRui 施良瑞 (b. 1922) and Kwok Mei Mei Sy/Shi Xu BaiLi 施許白莉 (b. 1926; members, United Evangelical Church of the Philippines). Audio-taped interview by Jean Uayan, 30 March 2005, at his residence in Pasay City, Philippines. Transcript. Philippine Chinese Church Archives, Biblical Seminary of the Philippines, Valenzuela City, Philippines.

Sy Seng Cho/Shi ChengZu 施承祖 (b. 1927; elder, United Evangelical Church of the Philippines). Audio-taped interview by Jean Uayan, 12 March 2005, at his residence in Caloocan City, Philippines. Transcript. Philippine Chinese Church Archives, Biblical Seminary of the Philippines, Valenzuela City, Philippines.

Tan, Filomena vda. de Cang/Jiang Chen XiuMin 江陳秀敏 (b. 1929, wife of Agapito Cang). Audio-taped interview by Jean Uayan, 28 April 2005, Dumaguete City, 28 April 2005. Transcript. Philippine Chinese Church Archives, Biblical Seminary of the Philippines, Valenzuela City, Philippines.

Tan Tay San/Zheng TaiShan 鄭泰山 (member, Iloilo Trinity Christian Church). Telephone interview by Jean Uayan, 4 May 2005, at his residence, Iloilo

City, Philippines. Transcript. Philippine Chinese Church Archives, Biblical Seminary of the Philippines, Valenzuela City, Philippines.

Tanhuanco, Patrick/Chen LiangShou 陳良壽 (Canon, St. Stephen's Parish). Telephone interview by Jean Uayan, Manila, 7 November 2005.

Uy, Valentin/Huang GenYuan 黃根源 (b. 1924; elder, Cebu Gospel Church). Audio-taped interview by Jean Uayan, 22 June 2004, at his residence in Cebu City, Philippines. Transcript. Philippine Chinese Church Archives, Biblical Seminary of the Philippines, Valenzuela City, Philippines.

IV. Books

Abainza, Estanislao, Q., et. al. *Enrique C. Sobrepeña: His Life and Work*. Edited by Fern Babcock Grant, Domini Torrevillas-Suarez, and Leon O. Ty. Quezon City: The Sponsorship Committee, 1975.

Abel, Clarke. *Narrative of a Journey in the Interior of China, and a Voyage to and from That Country, in the Years 1816 and 1817; Containing an Account of the Most Interesting Transaction of Lord Amherst's Embassy to the Court of Pekin, and Observations of the Countries Which It Visited*. London: Longman, Hurst, Rees, Orme, & Brown, 1818.

Abinales, Patricio N. *Making Mindanao: Cotabato and Davao in the Formation of the Philippine Nation-State*. Quezon City: Ateneo de Manila University, 2000.

Aldecoa-Rodriguez, Caridad. *History of Dumaguete City*. Dumaguete City: by the author/Silliman University, 2001.

Alejandrino, Clark L. *A History of the 1902 Chinese Exclusion Act: American Colonial Transmission and Deterioration of Filipino-Chinese Relations*. Manila: Kaisa Para Sa Kaunlaran, Feilübin Huayi Qingnian Lianhehui 菲律濱華裔青年聯合會, 2003.

Alip, Eufronio Melo. *The Chinese in Manila*. Manila: National Historical Commission, 1974.

———. *Political and Cultural History of the Philippines*. Vol. 1: *Since Time Began to British Occupation*. Manila: Alip & Sons, 1967.

———. *Ten Centuries of Philippine-Chinese Relations (Historical, Political, Social, Economic)*. Manila: Alip & Sons, 1959.

Amyot, Jacques, S. J. *The Chinese Community of Manila: A Study of Adaptation of Chinese Familism to the Philippine Environment*. Research Series, no. 2. Chicago, IL: Philippine Studies Program, Department of Anthropology, University of Chicago, 1960.

———. *The Manila Chinese: Familism in the Philippine Environment*. Institute of Philippine Culture Monographs, no. 2. Quezon City: Ateneo De Manila University Press, Institute of Philippine Culture, 1973.

Anderson, Gerald Harry, ed. *Studies in Philippine Church History.* Ithaca and London: Cornell University Press, 1969.

Anderson, Gerald Harry, and Peter G. Gowing. *Four Centuries of Christianity in the Philippines: An Interpretation.* Reprint from *Encounter* 25, 3, n.d. Indianapolis, IN: Christian Theological Seminary, n.d.

Anderson, Gerald Harry, Robert T. Coote, Norman A. Horner, James M. Phillips, eds. *Mission Legacies: Biographical Studies of Leaders of the Modern Missionary Movement.* American Society of Missiology Series, no. 19. Maryknoll, NY: Orbis, 1994.

Anderson, William Hart. *The Philippine Problem.* New York: G. P. Putnam's Sons, 1939.

Andrade, Pio, Jr "The Ethnic Chinese in Paracale 1571–1995." In *The Ethnic Chinese as Filipinos* (Part 2) *Proceedings of the National Conference on "The Ethnic Chinese as Filipinos."* Conference Held in Quezon City 10–11 November 1995, ed. Teresita Ang See 施洪玉華. *Chinese Studies Journal* 7 (1997): 16–36.

Ang See, Teresita/Shi Hong YuHua 施洪玉華. "The Chinese and the *Parian.*" In Jose S. Arcilla. *Kasaysayan: The Story of the Filipino People.* Vol. 3, *The Spanish Conquest,* ed. Gina Apostol, 136–137. Hong Kong: Asia Publishing, 1998.

———. "The Chinese Filipinos as Manilans." In *The Ethnic Chinese as Filipinos* (Part 2) *Proceedings of the National Conference on "The Ethnic Chinese as Filipinos."* Conference Held in Quezon City 10–11 November 1995, ed. Teresita Ang See 施洪玉華. *Chinese Studies Journal* 7 (1997): 16–36.

———. *The Chinese in the Philippines: Problems and Perspectives.* Vol. 1. Manila: Kaisa Para Sa Kaunlaran, Feilübin Huayi Qingnian Lianhehui 菲律濱華裔青年聯合會, 1997.

———. *The Chinese in the Philippines: Problems and Perspectives.* Vol. 2. Manila: Kaisa Para Sa Kaunlaran, Feilübin Huayi Qingnian Lianhehui 菲律濱華裔青年聯合會, 1997.

———, ed. *The Chinese Immigrants: Selected Writings of Professor Chinben See (Huaren Yimin: Shi ChenMin Jiaoshou Jinian Wenji)* 華人移民: 施振民教授紀念文集. Manila: Kaisa Para Sa Kaunlaran, Feilübin Huayi Qingnian Lianhehui 菲律濱華裔青年聯合會 and Chinese Studies Program, De La Salle University, 1992.

Ang See, Teresita/Shi Hong YuHua 施洪玉華 and Lily T. Chua 蔡麗麗, ed. *Crossroads: Short Essays on the Chinese Filipinos (Feihua Shehui Wenji)* 菲華社會文集. Manila: Kaisa Para Sa Kaunlaran, Feilübin Huayi Qingnian Lianhehui) 菲律濱華裔青年聯合會, 1988.

Ang See, Teresita/Shi Hong YuHua 施洪玉華 and Go Bon Juan/Wu WenHuan 吳文煥. *The Ethnic Chinese in the Philippine Revolution.* Manila: Kaisa Para

Sa Kaunlaran, Feilübin Huayi Qingnian Lianhehui 菲律濱華裔青年聯合會, 1996.

Apilado, Mariano Casuga. *Revolutionary Spirituality: A Study of the Protestant Role in the American Colonial Rule of the Philippines, 1898–1928*. Quezon City: New Day Publishers, 1999.

Arcilla, Jose S., S. J. *Recent Philippine History 1898–1960*. 2nd ed. Quezon City: Ateneo de Manila University Press, 1990.

Atlas Showing Mission Fields of the Christian and Missionary Alliance Issued by the Foreign Department. New York: Christian & Missionary Alliance, 1922.

Bagamaspad, Anavic. "History of the Baguio Chinese: Integration into the Baguio Community." In *The Ethnic Chinese as Filipinos* (Part 2) *Proceedings of the National Conference on "The Ethnic Chinese as Filipinos."* Conference Held in Quezon City 10–11 November 1995, ed. Teresita Ang See 施洪玉華. *Chinese Studies Journal* 7 (1997): 6–15.

Baker, Robert ed. *A Baptist Source Book*. Nashville, TN: Broadman Press, 1966.

Band, Edward. *Working His Purpose Out: The History of the English Presbyterian Mission 1847–1947*. London: Presbyterian Church of England, 1947. Reprint, Taipei: Ch'eng Wen Publishing, 1972.

Bankoff, Greg, and Kathleen Weekley. *Celebrating the Centennial of Independence: Postcolonial National Identity in the Philippines*. Aldershot, Hampshire: Ashgate Publishing, 2002. Reprint, Manila: De La Salle University Press, 2004.

Banzuelo, Edilberto V. *The Beginnings of Evangelical Christianity in the Philippines*. Valenzuela City: Febias College of Bible, 1998.

Barnes, Lemuel Call. *Two Thousand Years of Missions before Carey*. The Advanced Christian Culture Courses, Vol. 2. Chicago: Christian Culture Press, 1900.

Barranco, Vicente. "The Chinese among Us." In *Chinese Participation in Philippine Culture and Economy*, ed. Shubert S. C. Liao, 191–194. Manila: by the editor, 1964.

Barrows, David P. *A Decade of American Government in the Philippines*. Yonkers-on-Hudson, NY: World Book, 1914.

Baviera, Aileen S[an] P[ablo] and Teresita Ang See/Shi Hong YuHua 施洪玉華, ed. *China, across the Seas/The Chinese As Filipinos*. Quezon City: Philippine Association for Chinese Studies, 1992.

Bays, Daniel H. "The Growth of Independent Christianity in China, 1900–1937." In *Christianity in China: From the Eighteenth Century to the Present*, ed. Daniel H. Bays, 307–316. Stanford, CA: Stanford University Press, 1996.

Beyer, H. Otley. "Philippine Prehistoric Contacts with Foreigners." In *Chinese Participation in Philippine Culture and Economy*, ed. Shubert S. C. Liao, 2–18. Manila: by the editor, 1964.

Beets, Henry. *The Christian Reformed Church: Its Roots, History, Schools and Mission Work, AD 1857 to 1946*. Grand Rapids, MI: Baker, 1946.

Benitez, Conrado. *History of the Philippines: Economic, Social, Political*. Boston: Ginn & Co., 1940.

———. *Philippine Progress Prior to 1898: The Old Philippines' Industrial Development. Chapters of an Economic History*. Publications of the Filipiniana Book Guild, 15. Manila: Filipiniana Book Guild, 1969.

Bernad, Miguel A., S. J. *The Christianization of the Philippines: Problems and Perspectives*. Manila: Filipiniana Book Guild, 1972.

Bernstein, David. *The Philippine Story*. New York: Farrar, Straus & Co., 1947.

Boone, Muriel. *The Seed of the Church in China*. Philadelphia: United Church Press, 1973.

Botengan, Kate Chollipas, "The Rt. Rev Frederick Rogers Graves, D.D." In *Transformed by the Word; Transforming the World: One Hundred Years of Episcopal Church in the Philippines*, 113. Quezon City: The Episcopal Church in the Philippines (ECP), 2001.

Bourne, Edward Gaylord. *Discovery, Conquest, and Early History of the Philippine Islands*. Cleveland, OH: Arthur H. Clark, 1907.

Bowring, John. *A Visit to the Philippine Islands (In 1858)*. London: Smith, Elder & Co., 1859. Reprint, Manila: Filipiniana Book Guild, 1963.

Boxer, Charles Ralph. *South China in the Sixteenth Century: Being the Narratives of Galeote Periera, Fr. Gaspar Da Cruz, O.P., and Fr. Martin De Rada, O.E.S.A*. London: Hakluyt Society, 1953.

Briggs, Charles Whitman. *The Progressing Philippines*. Philadelphia: Griffith Rowland Press, [1913].

Bringing in the Sheaves: Gleanings from the Mission Fields of the Christian and Missionary Alliance. New York: Christian & Missionary Alliance, 1898.

Brown, Arthur Judson. *The Foreign Missionary Yesterday and Today*. New York: Revell, 1907.

———. *The New Era in the Philippines*. New York: Revell, 1903.

———. *Report of a Visitation of the Philippine Islands*. New York: The Board of Foreign Missions of the Presbyterian Church in the United States of America, 1902.

Brown, G. Thompson. *Earthen Vessels and Transcendent Power: American Presbyterians in China, 1837–1952*. Maryknoll, NY: Orbis, 1997.

Brown, William N. *Amoy Magic: Guide to Xiamen (Meili Xiamen: Xiamen Zhinan)* 魅力廈門: 廈門指南. Xiamen: Xiamen University Press, 2003.

———. *Fujian Adventure (Meili Fujian)* 魅力福建. Xiamen: Lu Jiang Chu Ban She 鷺江出版社, 2003.

Bunda, Nestor Distor. *A Mission History of the Philippine Baptist Churches 18981998 from a Philippine Perspective*. Perspektiven der Weltmission, Bd. 30. Aachen: Verlag an der Lootbek im Besitz des Verlags Mainz, 1999.

The Cambridge History of China Vol. 12: *Republican China 1912–1949, Part 1*, ed. John K. Fairbank. Cambridge: Cambridge University Press, 1983.

The Cambridge History of China Vol. 13: *Republican China 1912–1949, Part 2*, ed. John K. Fairbank. Cambridge: Cambridge University Press, 1983.

Campbell, William. *A Dictionary of the Amoy Vernacular Spoken throughout the Prefectures of Chin-Chiu, Chiang-Chiu and Formosa (Taiwan) (Xiamenyin Xinzidian)* 廈門音新字典, 19th ed. Tainan: Ren Guang Chubanshe 人光出版社, 1997.

Caoili, Manuel A. *The Origins of Metropolitan Manila: A Social and Political Analysis*. Quezon City: University of the Philippines Press, 1999.

Cariño, Theresa Chong. *China and the Overseas Chinese in Southeast Asia*. Quezon City: New Day Publishers, 1985.

———, ed. *Chinese in the Philippines*. Manila: De La Salle University Press, China Studies Program, 1985.

Carlson, Ellsworth C. *The Foochow Missionaries 1847–1880*. Cambridge, MA: East Asian Research Center, Harvard University Press, 1974.

Carpenter, Joel A., and Wilbert R. Shenk, eds. *Earthen Vessels: American Evangelicals and Foreign Missions, 1880–1980*. Grand Rapids, MI: Eerdmans, 1990.

Cary-Elwes, Columba. *China and the Cross: Studies in Missionary History*. London: Longmans, Green & Co., 1957.

Cauthen, Baker James, et. al. *Foreign Missionaries: SBC, 1845–1969 – A Supplement to "Advance: A History of Southern Baptist Foreign Missions."* N.p.: by the author, 1970.

Chang, Lit-sen 章力生. *Strategy of Missions in the Orient: A Christian Impact on the Pagan World*. Hong Kong: World Outreach, 1968.

Chau Ju-Kua/Zhao RuGua 趙汝适. *His Work on the Chinese and Arab Trade in the Twelfth and Thirteenth Centuries, Entitled Chu-fan-chi* 諸蕃志 (now written as *Zhu Fan Zhi*, literally, All barbarians of Southseas – record, viz., Reports on the South Seas barbarians, or An Account of Various Barbarians). Translated and annotated by Friedrich Hirth and W. W. Rockhill. Originally published as *Chu-fan-chi (*諸蕃志*)* in 1225. St. Petersburg: Imperial Academy of Sciences, 1911.

Chen, Ta. *Emigrant Communities in South China: A Study of Overseas Migration and Its Influence on Standards of Living and Social Change*, ed. Bruno Lasker. New York: Secretariat, Institute of Pacific Relations, 1940.

Cheng, Charles L. and Katherine Bersamira. *The Ethnic Chinese in Baguio City and in the Cordillera: The Untold Story of Pioneers*. Baguio City: Unique Printing Press, 1997.

Cheong, Caroline Mar Wai Jong. *The Chinese-Cantonese Family in Manila: A Study in Culture and Education*, eds. Paz Policarpio Mendez and F. Landa Jocano. Manila: Centro Escolar University Research & Development Center, 1983.

Cheung, David (Chen Yiqiang 陳貽強). *Christianity in Modern China: The Making of the First Native Protestant Church*. Studies in Christian Mission, ed. Marc R. Spindler, 28. Leiden: Brill, 2004.

The China Mission Handbook. First Issue. Shanghai: American Presbyterian Mission Press, 1896. Reprint, Taipei: Ch'eng Wen Publishing, 1973.

Chinese around the World 2003 Pu Shi Hua Ren 普世華人. Edited by Elson Chow and Dora Sze. Hong Kong: Chinese Coordination Centre of World Evangelism, 2003.

Chinese-Filipinos (Huafei) 華菲. Edited by Jonathan Chua. Quezon City: Ateneo de Manila University Chinese Studies Program, Xavier School, Jesuit Communications Foundation, 2003.

The Christianization of the Philippines. Translated by Rafael Lopez, O.S.A. and Alfonso Felix, Jr Manila: Historical Conservation Society, University of San Agustin, 1965.

Christlier, Theodore. *Protestant Foreign Missions: Their Present State. A Universal Survey*. Translated by David Allen Reed. Boston: Congregational Publishing Society, 1880.

Cleope, Earl Jude Paul L. *Bandit Zone: A History of the Free Areas of Negros Island during the Japanese Occupation (1942-1945)*. Manila: by the author and University of Santo Tomas Publishing House, 2002.

Clymer, Kenton J. *Protestant Missionaries in the Philippines, 1898–1916: An Inquiry into the American Colonial Mentality*. Urbana: University of Illinois Press, 1986.

Cohen, Paul A. *Discovering History in China: American Historical Writing on the Recent Chinese Past*. New York: Columbia University Press, 1984.

Conger, Emily Bronson. *An Ohio Woman in the Philippines Giving Personal Experiences and Descriptions Including Incidents of Honolulu, Ports in Japan and China*. Akron, OH: Richard H. Leighton, 1904.

Constantino, Renato. *Neocolonial Identity and Counter-Consciousness: Essays on Cultural Decolonization*. London: Merlin Press, 1978.

Corcino, Ernesto I. *Davao History*. Davao City: Philippine Centennial Movement Davao City Chapter, 1998.

Coronel, Hernando M., Msgr. *The Early Filipino Priests: Boatmen for Christ*. Manila: Reyes Publishing, for Catholic Book Center, 1998.

Cortes, Rosario Mendoza. *Pangasinan 1572–1800*. Quezon City: New
Day, 1975.

———. *Pangasinan 1801–1900: The Beginning of Modernization*. Quezon City:
New Day, 1990.

———. *Pangasinan 1901–1986: A Political, Socioeconomic and Cultural History*.
Quezon City: New Day, 1990.

Craig, Austin, and Conrado Benitez, *Philippine Progress Prior to 1898: A Source
Book of Philippine History to Supply a Fairer View of Filipino Participation
and Supplement the Defective Spanish Accounts*. Manila: Philippine Education
Co., 1916.

Crawley, James Winston. "From China to the Philippines: A Turn in the Road."
In *Let the Philippine Islands Be Glad. Stories of the Development and Growth
of God's Kingdom in the Philippines through the Philippine Baptist Mission
1948–1998*, comp. Jan Hill, 12–15. [Baguio City]: Bundok Press, 1999.

———. "In the Philippines with God." In *Let the Philippine Islands Be Glad.
Stories of the Development and Growth of God's Kingdom in the Philippines
through the Philippine Baptist Mission 1948–1998*, comp. Jan Hill, 18–22.
[Baguio City]: Bundok Press, 1999.

———. *Into a New World*. Nashville, TN: Convention Press, 1958.

———. *Partners across the Pacific – China and Southern Baptists: Into the Second
Century*. Nashville, TN: Broadman Press, 1986.

———. *World Christianity, 1970–2000: Toward a New Millennium*. Pasadena,
CA: William Carey Library, 2001.

Crow, Carl. *America and the Philippines*. Garden City, NY: Doubleday, 1914.

Cuesta, Angel Martinez. *History of Negros*. Translated by Alfonso Felix, Jr and Sor
Caritas Sevilla. Historical Conservation Society and The Recollect Fathers
32. Manila: The Historical Conservation Society, 1980.

Cullinane, Michael and Peter Xenos. "The Growth of Population in Cebu
During the Spanish Era: Constructing a Regional Demography from
Local Sources." In *Population and History: The Demographic Origins of the
Modern Philippines*. Center for Southeast Asian Studies Monograph 16, eds.
Daniel F. Doeppers and Peter Xenos, 71–137. Madison, WI: University of
Wisconsin-Madison Center for Southeast Asian Studies/Ateneo de Manila
University Press, 1998.

Cushner, Nicholas P. *The Isles of the West: Early Spanish Voyages to the Philippines,
1521–1564*. Quezon City: Ateneo de Manila University Press, 1966.

De Jong, Gerald Francis. *The Reformed Church in China 1842–1951*. The
Historical Series of the Reformed Church in America, no. 22. Grand
Rapids, MI: Eerdmans, 1992.

de La Costa, Horacio, S. J., ed. *Readings in Philippine History: Selected Historical
Texts Presented with a Commentary*. Manila: Bookmark, 1965.

Deats, Richard L. *The Story of Methodism in the Philippines*. Manila:
National Council of Churches in the Philippines, for Union Theological
Seminary, 1964.

Dean, John Marvin. *The Cross of Christ in Bolo-land*. Chicago: Revell, 1902.

Dean, William. *The China Mission: Embracing a History of the Various Missions of
All Denominations among the Chinese with Biographical Sketches of Deceased
Missionaries*. New York: Sheldon & Co., 1859.

Devins, John Bancroft. *An Observer in the Philippines or Life in Our New
Possessions*. Boston, MA: American Tract Society, 1905.

Diokno, Maria Serena I. "The Rise of the Chinese Trader." In *Kasaysayan: The
Story of the Filipino People*. Vol. 4, *Life in the Colony*, by Maria Serena I.
Diokno and Ramon N. Villegas, ed. Ricardo de Ungria, 46–69. Hong
Kong: Asia Publishing Co., 1998.

Dunaway, David K., and Willa K. Baum, ed. *Oral History: An Interdisciplinary
Anthology*. 2nd ed. Walnut Creek, CA: AltaMira Press/Sage, 1996.

———. "Introduction: The Interdisciplinarity of Oral History." In *Oral History:
An Interdisciplinary Anthology*. 2nd ed., eds. David K. Dunaway and Willa
K. Baum, 7–22. Walnut Creek, CA: AltaMira Press/Sage, 1996.

Dunch, Ryan. *Fuzhou Protestants and the Making of a Modern China 1857–1927*.
New Haven: Yale University Press, 2001.

Duus, Peter. "Science and Salvation in China: The Life and Work of W. A.
P. Martin (1827–1916)." In *American Missionaries in China: Papers from
Harvard Seminars*, ed. Kwang-Ching Liu, 11–41. Cambridge, MA: East Asia
Research Center, Harvard University Press, 1966.

Eberhard, Wolfram. *Moral and Social Values of the Chinese Collected Essays*.
Chinese Materials and Research Aids Service Center Occasional Series, ed.
Robert L. Irick, no. 6. Taipei: Ch'eng Wen Publishing Co., 1971.

Ekvall, Robert B., Harry M. Shuman, John H. Cable, William Christie, Alfred
C. Snead, Howard Van Dyck, and David J. Fant. *After Fifty Years: A Record
of God's Working through the Christian and Missionary Alliance*. Harrisburg,
PA: Christian Publications, [1939].

Elwood, Douglas J. "Varieties of Christianity in the Philippines." In *Studies in
Philippine Church History*, ed. Gerald H. Anderson, 366–386. Ithaca and
London: Cornell University Press, 1969.

The Encyclopedia of the Chinese Overseas, ed. Lynn Pan. Singapore: Archipelago
Press, Landmark Books, for Chinese Heritage Center, 1998.

Entenmann, Robert E. "Catholics and Society in Eighteenth-Century Sichuan."
In *Christianity in China*, ed. Daniel H. Bays, 8–23. Stanford, CA: Stanford
University Press, 1996.

The Episcopal Church in the Philippines Celebrating One Hundred Years of Ministry.
Accessed 14 June 2005, http://episcopalphilippines.net/History1.htm.

Escoda, Jose Ma. Bonifacio M. *Warsaw of Asia: The Rape of Manila*. Quezon
City: Giraffe Books, 2000.

Esther, Joseph R. *"This Is the Way, Walk Ye In It" Isaiah 30:21*. Redlands, CA: by
the author, 1977.

Fagg, John Gerardus. *Forty Years in South China: The Life of Rev John Van Nest
Talmage, D.D.* New York: A. D. F. Randolph & Co., 1894. Reprint,
Whitefish, MT: Kessinger Publishing, 2004.

Fairbank, John K., ed. *The Missionary Enterprise in China and America*.
Cambridge, MA: Harvard University Press, 1974.

Faust, Karl Irving. *Campaigning in the Philippines*. San Francisco: Hicks-Judd
Co., 1899.

Fee, Mary Helen. *A Woman's Impressions of the Philippines*. Chicago, IL: A. C.
McClurg & Co., 1910.

Felix, Alfonso, Jr, ed. *The Chinese in the Philippines: 1570–1770*. Vol. 1. Manila:
Solidaridad Publishing, 1966.

———. *The Chinese in the Philippines 1770–1898*. Vol. 2. Manila: Solidaridad
Publishing, 1969.

Fenner, Bruce Leonard. *Cebu under the Spanish Flag (1521–1896): An
Economic and Social History*. Humanities Series 14. Cebu City: San Carlos
Publications, 1985.

Fernandez, Doreen, ed. *Kasaysayan: The Story of the Filipino People*. Vol. 10. *A
Timeline of Philippine History*, ed. Henry S. Totanes. Hong Kong: Asia
Publishing Co., 1998.

*For Christ in Fuh-kien: Being a New Edition (the Fourth) of the Story of the Fuh-
kien Mission of the Church Missionary Society*. London: Church Missionary
Society, 1904.

Forbes-Lindsay, C. H. *The Philippines under Spanish and American Rules*.
Philadelphia: John C. Winston Co., 1906.

Foreman, John. *The Philippine Islands: A Political, Geographical, Ethnographical,
Social and Commercial History of the Philippine Archipelago Embracing the
Whole Period of Spanish Rule with an Account of the Succeeding American
Insular Government*. 3rd ed. Filipiniana Book Guild, 2nd series, Vol. 2. New
York: Charles Scribner's Sons, 1906. Reprint, Manila: Filipiniana Book
Guild, 1980.

Forman, Charles W., ed. *Christianity in the Non-Western World*. Freeport, NY:
Books for Libraries Press, 1967. Reprint, n.p.: n.p., 1970.

Foronda, Marcelino A. *Kasaysayan: Studies on Local and Oral History*. Manila: De
La Salle University Press, 1991.

Frei, Ernest J. *Ventures in Cooperation*. Manila: United Church of Christ in the
Philippines, 1963.

Furth, Charlotte. "Intellectual Change: From the Reform Movement to the May Fourth Movement, 1895–1920." In *The Cambridge History of China Vol. 12: Republican China 1912–1949*. Part 1. Edited by John K. Fairbank, 322–405. Cambridge: Cambridge University Press, 1983.

Galang, Zoilo M., ed. *Filipiniana* Vol. I: *Land and People*. Manila: Philippine Education Co., 1937.

Gibson, John Campbell. *Mission Problems and Mission Methods in South China: Lectures on Evangelistic Theology*. Edinburgh: Oliphant, Anderson & Ferrier, 1901. Reprint, Boston, MA: Elibron Classics, 2003.

Gih, Andrew. *Twice Born – and Then? The Life Story and Message of Andrew Gih*. Edited by Ruth J. Corbin. 2nd ed. London: Marshall, Morgan & Scott, 1954.

Giles, Herbert Allen. *China and the Chinese*. New York: Columbia University Press, MacMillan, 1902.

Giordano, Pasquale T. S. J. *Awakening to Mission: The Philippine Catholic Church 1965–1981*. Quezon City: New Day, 1988.

Glasser, Arthur F. "China (The People's Republic of China)." In *The Church in Asia*, ed. Donald E. Hoke, 130–179. Chicago, IL: Moody Press, 1975.

Gleeck, Lewis E., Jr *Americans on the Philippine Frontiers*. Manila: Carmelo & Bauerman, 1974.

———. *Dissolving the Colonial Bond: American Ambassadors to the Philippines, 1946–1984*. Quezon City: New Day, 1988.

———. "Iloilo: Missionaries, Merchants and the Colonial Establishment I–IV." In *Iloilo in American Times: Excerpts from Bulletin of the American Historical Collection* 23, 7–104. Manila: American Historical Collection Foundation, 1995.

———. *The Manila Americans (1901–1964)*. Manila: Carmelo & Bauermann, 1977.

Go Bon Juan/Wu WenHuan 吳文煥 and Teresita Ang See/Shi Hong YuHua 施洪玉華, ed. *Heritage: A Pictorial History of the Chinese in the Philippines (Wenhua Chuantong – Feihua Lishi Tupian)* 文化傳統 – 菲華歷史圖片. Manila: Kaisa Para Sa Kaunlaran, Feilübin Huayi Qingnian Lianhehui 菲律濱華裔青年聯合會 and Professor Chinben See Memorial Trust Fund/ Jinian Shi Chenmin Jiaoshou Jiangxuejin Jijinhui 紀念施振民教授獎學金基金會, 1987.

Goddard, Burton L., ed. *The Encyclopedia of Modern Christian Missions*. Camden, NJ: Thomas Nelson, 1967.

Golvers, Noël, ed. *The Christian Mision in China in the Verbiest Era: Some Aspects of the Missionary Approach*. Louvain Chinese Studies 6. Leuven: Leuven University Press/Ferdinand Verbiest Foundation, 1999.

Gomez, Hilario M., Jr, and Leomyr L. De Jesus, ed. *Commitment and Struggle: The Life and Ministry of the United Church of Christ in the Philippines: A Festschrift for Bishop Erme R. Camba.* Quezon City: United Church of Christ in the Philippines, 1998.

Vincent, Herbert. *Philippine Kaleidoscope: An Illustrated Story of the Church's Mission.* New York: The National Council, Protestant Episcopal Church, n.d.

Gowing, Peter Gordon. *Brief History of Bohol, Cebu and Negros Oriental.* Manila: Ateneo de Manila University/Institute of Philippine Culture, 1962.

————. "Christianity in the Philippines: Yesterday and Today." In *Historical Documentary of Protestantism in the Orient. 40th Anniversary of the United Evangelical Church of Manila (Feilübin Zhonghua Jidu Jiaohui Sishi Zhounian Lishi Wenxian Fu Yazhou Duoguo Jidu Jiaohui Lishi)* 『菲律賓中華基督教會四十週年歷史文獻附亞洲多國基督教會歷史』 *1929–1969*, 200–225 (pages in Chinese style). Manila: United Evangelical Church of Manila, 1969.

————. *Islands under the Cross.* Manila: National Council of Churches in the Philippines, 1967.

————. *Mandate in Moroland: The American Government of Muslim Filipinos 1899–1920.* Quezon City: New Day, 1983.

Gray, Jack. *Rebellions and Revolutions: China from the 1800s to the 1980s.* Oxford: Oxford University Press, 1990.

Guillermo, Merlyn L. and L. P. Verora. *Handbook on Protestant Churches and Missions in the Philippines* Vol. 1. *National Council of Churches in the Philippines.* Valenzuela: World Vision Philippines, 1982.

Gunn, Charles A. *The Presbyterian Church and the Filipino.* New York: Board of Foreign Missions of the Presbyterian Church in the USA, 1913, 14–15, microfiche.

Gutierrez, Lucio, O.P. *The Archdiocese of Manila: A Pilgrimage in Time (1565–1999).* Vol. 1. Edited by Crisostomo A. Yalung. Manila: Roman Catholic Archbishop of Manila, 1999.

Haines, J. Harry. *Chinese of the Diaspora.* World Council of Churches Commission on World Mission and Evangelism Research Pamphlet, no. 14. London: Edinburgh House Press, 1965.

Hall, Joseph Andrew. "Conference on the Philippines." In *Men and Modern Missionary Enterprise: History, Call, Addresses, Deliverances, Conferences and Deliberations of the First Inter-Synodical Foreign Missionary Convention for Men, Held at Omaha; Nebraska, February 19–21, 1907*, ed. Charles Edwin Bradt, 145–149. Chicago: Winona Publishing, 1907.

Halsema, James J. *Bishop Brent's Baguio School: The First 75 Years.* Baguio: Brent School, 1988.

Halsey, Abram Woodruff. *Presbyterian Medical Missions: A Sketch of the Medical and Philanthropic Work of the Board of Foreign Missions of the Presbyterian Church in the USA.* New York: Board of Foreign Missions of the Presbyterian Church in the USA, 1914.

Harper, Anna Maria L. *Santa Cruz Church: A Living Heritage.* Manila: Sta. Cruz Parish Pastoral Council, 2004.

Hartendorp, A. V. H. *History of Industry and Trade of the Philippines.* Manila: American Chamber of Commerce of the Philippines, 1958.

Higdon, E. K. *Why Protestantism in the Philippines.* San Fernando, La Union: Ilocano Printing, 1937.

Hill, Jan, comp. *Let the Philippine Islands Be Glad. Stories of the Development and Growth of God's Kingdom in the Philippines through the Philippine Baptist Mission 1948–1998.* [Baguio]: Bundok Press, 1999.

Holkeboer, Tena. *God's Bridge or the Story of Jin-Gi.* W88-0055 Holkeboer Papers, 1920–1963. Grand Rapids, MI: Eerdmans, 1944.

Horne, C. Silvester. *The Story of the L.M.S. 1795–1895.* London: London Missionary Society, 1894.

Hsü, Immanuel C. Y. *The Rise of Modern China.* 3rd ed. New York: Oxford University Press, 1983.

Hu, Betty Mayling/Hu MeiLin 胡美林. "Golden Memories – A Short History of Bethel Mission of China for Its Fiftieth Anniversary." In *50th Anniversary of the Bethel Mission of China, 1920–1970.* Hong Kong: Hsiang-Kang Po-Pe-Li Chiao Hui [香港伯特利教會], 1970.

———. *Precious Jewels.* Pasadena, CA: Bethel Mission of China, 1952.

Hu, Betty Mayling/Hu MeiLin 胡美林 and Alice Y. Lan 藍如溪. *We Flee from Hong Kong (Ritai Xia Shanggang De Yiyu)* 日台下香港的一隅. Hong Kong: Bethel Mission of China, 1944, rep. 2000.

Hunker, W. Carl. "Waiting and Watching." In *Let the Philippine Islands Be Glad. Stories of the Development and Growth of God's Kingdom in the Philippines through the Philippine Baptist Mission 1948–1998*, comp. Jan Hill, 18–22. [Baguio City]: Bundok Press, 1999.

Hunt, Everett N., Jr "John Livingston Nevius 1829–1893: Pioneer of Three-self Principles in Asia." In *Mission Legacies: Biographical Studies of Leaders of the Modern Missionary Movement*, eds. Gerald Harry Anderson, Robert T. Coote, Norman A. Horner, and James M. Phillips, American Society of Missiology Series, 19, 190–196. Maryknoll, NY: Orbis, 1994.

Institute of Religion and Culture Research Committee, ed. *Profiles in Protestant Witness: The First Fifty years of Evangelical Christianity in the Philippines (1898-1948).* Muntilupa City: Institute of Religion and Culture, 1999.

Intal, Ponciano S., Jr *Essays on Philippine Colonial Economy: Balance of Payments and Trade, 1870s to 1930s.* Manila, De La Salle University Press, 2003.

Jesuit Missionary Letters from Mindanao Volume Three: The Davao Mission.
Translated and edited by Jose S. Arcilla. Quezon City: University of the
Philippines – Center for Integrative and Development Studies, National
Historical Institute, the UP Press and the Archives of the Philippine
Province of the Society of Jesus, 1998.

Kennedy, Elaine J. *Baptist Centennial History of the Philippines (1900–1999).*
Makati City: Church Strengthening Ministry, 1999.

Kitagawa, Joseph Mitsuo. *The Christian Tradition: Beyond Its European Captivity.*
Philadelphia: Trinity Press International, 1992.

Kroeger, James H. *Asia-Church in Mission: Exploring* Ad Gentes *Mission
Initiatives of the Local Churches in Asia in the Vatican II Era.* Quezon City:
Claretian Communications, 1999.

Kwantes, Anne Catherine Laninga. *Presbyterian Missionaries in the Philippines:
Conduits of Social Change (1899–1910).* Quezon City: New Day, 1989.

———, ed. *Chapters in Philippine Church History.* Mandaluyong City: OMF
Literature, 2001.

———, ed. *Supplement to Chapters in Philippine Church History.* Mandaluyong
City: OMF Literature, 2002.

Lam, Wing-hung. *Chinese Theology in Construction.* Pasadena, CA: William
Carey Library, 1983.

Latourette, Kenneth Scott. *The Chinese: Their History and Culture.* 3rd ed. New
York: Macmillan, 1949.

———. *A History of Christian Missions in China.* New York: MacMillan, 1929.

———. *A History of the Expansion of Christianity.* Vol. 7. *Advance through the
Storm AD 1914 and after, with Concluding Generalizations*, 1945. Reprint,
Grand Rapids, MI: Zondervan, 1971.

Lau Yee-cheung and Lee Kam-keung, "An Economic and Political History." In
Fujian: A Coastal Province in Transition and Transformation, eds. Yue-man
Yeung and David K. Y. Chu, 25–55. Hong Kong: Chinese University
Press, 2000.

Laufer, Berthold. *The Relations of the Chinese to the Philippines.* Smithsonian
Miscellaneous Collections Vol. 50. Washington, DC: Smithsonian
Institution, 1907. Reprint, Manila: Philippine Historical Association, 1967.

Laubach, Frank Charles. *The People of the Philippines: Their Religious Progress and
Preparation for Spiritual Leadership in the Far East.* New York: George H.
Doran Co., 1925.

———. *Seven Thousand Emeralds.* New York: Friendship Press, 1929.

Law, Gail, ed. *Chinese Churches Handbook.* Hong Kong: Chinese Coordination
Centre of World Evangelism (CCCOWE), 1982.

Le Roy, James Alfred. *The Philippines Circa 1900: Book One. Philippine Life
in Town and Country.* Reprint, Manila: Filipiniana Book Guild, 1968.

Filipiniana Book Guild, 13. Originally published as *Philippine Life in Town and* Country. New York: G. P. Putnam's Sons, 1907.

Lee, Joseph Tse-Hei. *The Bible and the Gun: Christianity in South China, 1860–1900*. East Asia: History, Politics, Sociology, Culture. Edited by Edward Beauchamp. New York: Routledge, 2003.

Lee, Witness 李常受. *The History of the Church and the Local Churches*. Anaheim, CA: Living Stream Ministry, 1991.

Legarda, Benito J., Jr *After the Galleons: Foreign Trade, Economic Change & Entrepreneurship in the Nineteenth-Century Philippines*. Quezon City: Ateneo de Manila University Press, 1999.

———. *Occupation '42*. Manila: De La Salle University Press, 2003.

Leslie, Lyall T. *John Sung*. London: China Inland Mission, 1954.

Liao, Shubert S.C. "How the Chinese Lived in the Philippines from 1570 to 1898." In *Chinese Participation in Philippine Culture and Economy*. Edited by Shubert S. C. Liao, 19–33. Manila: by the editor, 1964.

———, ed. *Chinese Participation in Philippine Culture and Economy*. Manila: by the editor, 1964.

Licuanan, Virginia Benitez, and Jose Llavador Mira, ed. *The Philippines Under Spain*. Book 1, *(1518–1565) Voyages of Discovery*. Manila: The National Trust for Historical and Cultural Preservation of the Philippines/The International Fund for the Promotion of Culture, n.d.

———. *The Philippines under Spain*. Book 2, *(1564–1573) The Legazpi Expedition Conquest and Civilization*. Manila: The National Trust for Historical and Cultural Preservation of the Philippines/The International Fund for the Promotion of Culture, 1990.

[Lieutenant] X [Aime Ernest Motsch]. *The Diary of a French Officer on the War in the Philippines 1898*. Translated by Marietta Enriquez-de La Haye Jousselin. Manila: National Historical Institute, 1994.

Lim, Benito. "The Dagupan Chinese." In *The Ethnic Chinese as Filipinos (Part 2) Proceedings of the National Conference on "The Ethnic Chinese as Filipinos" Conference Held in Quezon City 10–11 November 1995*, by the Philippine Association for Chinese Studies, ed. Teresita Ang See/Shi Hong YuHua 施洪玉華, *Chinese Studies Journal* 7, 16–36. Quezon City: Philippine Association for Chinese Studies (PACS), 1997.

Lipphard, William B. *Out of the Storm in China: A Review of Recent Developments in Baptist Mission Fields*. Philadelphia: Judson Press, 1932.

Lippiello, Tiziana and Roman Malek, ed. *"Scholar from the West" Giulio Aleni S.J. (1582–1649) and the Dialogue between Christianity and China*. Annali/Fondazione Civilta Bresciana, 9; Monumenta Serica Monograph Series, no. 42. Brescia: Fondazione Civilta Bresciana; Sankt Augustin: Monumenta Serica Institute, 1997.

The Living Church Annual and Whittaker's Churchman's Almanac: A Church Cyclopedia and Almanac 1910, 333. Milwaukee: Young Churchman Co., 1910.

Lutz, Jessie Gregory. *Chinese Politics and Christian Missions: The Anti-Christian Movements of 1920–1928*. The Church and the World. Vol. 3. Edited by Cyriac C. Pullapilly. Notre Dame, IN: Cross Cultural Publications, Cross Cultural Books, 1988.

———. "A Profile of Chinese Protestant Evangelists in the Mid-Nineteenth Century." In *Authentic Chinese Christianity: Preludes to Its Development (Nineteenth and Twentieth Centuries)*, eds. Ku Wei-ying and Koen De Ridder, 67–85. Leuven: Leuven University Press Ferdinand Verbiest Foundation, 2001.

Ma, Wonsuk, and Julie C. *Asian Church and God's Mission: Studies Presented in the International Symposium on Asian Mission in Manila, January 2002*. Mandaluyong City: OMF Literature, 2003.

Manuel, E. Arsenio. *Documenting Philippineasian*. Quezon City: The Philippineasian Society, 1994.

Martin, William Alexander Parsons. *The Awakening of China*. London: Hodder & Stoughton, 1907.

Maxey, Mark. *History of the Philippine Mission of the Churches of Christ*. San Clemente, CA: Go Ye Books, n.d.

Mayo, Katherine. *The Isles of Fear: The Truth about the Philippines*. New York: Harcourt Brace, 1925.

McBeath, Gerald A. *Political Integration of the Philippine Chinese*, Research Monograph no. 8. Berkeley, CA: Research Monograph Series, Center for South and Southeast Asia Studies, University of California, 1973.

McGraw, Gerald E. "A. B. Simpson 1943–1919: From Home Missions to a World Missionary Movement." In *Mission Legacies: Biographical Studies of Leaders of the Modern Missionary Movement*, eds. Gerald Harry Anderson, Robert T. Coote, Norman A. Horner, and James M. Phillips, American Society of Missiology Series, 19. Maryknoll, NY: Orbis, 1994.

McLeish, Alexander. *A Christian Archipelago: A Review of Religion in the Philippines*. Rev. ed. War-Time Survey Series, no. 2. London: World Dominion Press, 1941.

Mendoza, Bayani Y. *The Philippine Christian Alliance First Seventy-Eight Years*. N.p.: by the author, 1985.

Mercader, Cesar, and Felix Noel Mercader. *The Evangelization of Cebu (Cradle of Christianity in the Philippines)*. Dumanjug, Cebu: by the authors, 1970.

Mercado, Cesar M. *A New Approach to Social Research/Thesis Writing*. Quezon City: Development Consultants for Asia Africa Pacific, 2004.

Michael, Franz H. with Chung-li Chan. *The Taiping Rebellion: History and Documents*. 3 vols. Seattle and London: University of Washington Press, 1966–1971.

Miles, Fern Harrington. *Account of Opening Baptist Work in the Philippines*, TMs (photocopy), Special Collections, Philippine Chinese Church Archives, Biblical Seminary of the Philippines Library, Valenzuela City.

———. "The Breakthrough." In *Let the Philippine Islands Be Glad. Stories of the Development and Growth of God's Kingdom in the Philippines through the Philippine Baptist Mission 1948–1998*, comp. Jan Hill, 8–10. [Baguio City]: Bundok Press, 1999.

———. *Captive Community: Life in a Japanese Internment Camp, 1941–1945*. San Angelo, TX: Mossy Creek Place, 1987.

———. "God's Call to the Philippines." In *Let the Philippine Islands Be Glad. Stories of the Development and Growth of God's Kingdom in the Philippines through the Philippine Baptist Mission 1948–1998*, comp. Jan Hill, 3–4. [Baguio City]: Bundok Press, 1999.

———. "The Opening of Southern Baptist Work in the Philippines." In *Let the Philippine Islands Be Glad. Stories of the Development and Growth of God's Kingdom in the Philippines through the Philippine Baptist Mission 1948–1998*, comp. Jan Hill, 1–3. [Baguio City]: Bundok Press, 1999.

Miller, Stuart Creighton. *"Benevolent Assimilation" The American Conquest of the Philippines, 1899–1903*. New Haven: Yale University Press, 1982.

"Miscellanies." In *The Chinese Repository*, Vol. 2, *from May, 1833, to April, 1934*, 2nd ed., 350–355. Canton: Printed for the Proprietors, 1834.

Miyahara, Gyo. "The Status of the Chinese Filipinos in the 1950s, Cebu: An Analysis of Articles in Two Local Newspapers." In *The Ethnic Chinese as Filipinos* (Part 2) *Proceedings of the National Conference on "The Ethnic Chinese as Filipinos" Conference Held in Quezon City 10–11 November 1995*, by the Philippine Association for Chinese Studies, ed. Teresita Ang See 施洪玉華, *Chinese Studies Journal* 7, 73–90, 1997.

Moffett, Samuel Hugh. *A History of Christianity in Asia*. Vol. 1: *Beginnings to 1500*. Rev. ed. Maryknoll, NY: Orbis, 1998.

———. *A History of Christianity in Asia*. Vol. 2: *1500–1900*. Maryknoll, NY: Orbis Books, 2005.

Mojares, Resil B. *The War against the Americans: Resistance and Collaboration in Cebu: 1899–1906*. Quezon City: Ateneo de Manila University Press, 1999.

Morrison, Eliza. *Memoirs of the Life and Labors of Robert Morrison*. London: Longmans, Orme, Green & Longmans, 1839.

Morse, Hosea Ballou. *The International Relations of the Chinese Empire*. Vol. 1. *The Period of Conflict 1834–1860*. New York: Paragon Book Gallery, 1910.

———. *The International Relations of the Chinese Empire*. Vol. 2. *The Period of Submission 1861–1893*. New York: Paragon Book Gallery, 1910.

———. *The International Relations of the Chinese Empire*. Vol. 3. *The Period of Subjection 1894–1911*. New York: Paragon Book Gallery, 1918.

Mullen, Shirley A. "Between 'Romance' and 'True History': Historical Narrative and Truth Telling in a Postmodern Age." In *History and the Christian Historian*, ed. Ronald A. Wells, 23–40. Grand Rapids, MI: Eerdmans, 1998.

"A Multicultural Connection." In *Kasaysayan: The Story of the Filipino People*. Vol. 3, *The Spanish Conquest*, by Jose S. Arcilla. Edited by Gina Apostol, 112–137. Hong Kong: Asia Publishing Co., 1998.

Munger, Henry Weston. *Christ and the Filipino Soul*. Iloilo: Mrs Laura Lee Munger and Mrs Laura Lee Marques, 1967.

Myrick, Conrad "The Episcopal Church in the Philippines." In Joseph Graessle Moore, *A Study of the Episcopal Church in the Missionary District of the Philippines*. Quezon City: n.p., 1962.

Nakpil, Carmen Guerrero. *The Philippines and the Filipinos*. Vol. 1. Quezon City: Vibal Publishing, 1977.

Naraval, Thelma F. *The Southern Cross: A History of the Christian and Missionary Alliance Churches of the Philippines and the Ebenezer Bible College*. Vol. 1. Cagayan de Oro City: Bustamante Press & Publishing, 1977.

Nariko Sugaya. "Chinese Immigrant Society in the Latter Half of the 18th-Century Philippines." In *Intercultural Relations, Cultural Transformation, and Identity – The Ethnic Chinese: Selected Papers Presented at the 1998 International Society for the Study of Chinese Overseas (ISSCO) Conference*. Conference Held in Manila 26–28 November 1998, ed. Teresita Ang See 施洪玉華, 553–570. Manila: Kaisa Para Sa Kaunlaran, Feilübin Huayi Qingnian Lianhehui 菲律濱華裔青年聯合會, 2000.

Nash, Ronald H. *Christian Faith and Historical Understanding*. Grand Rapids, MI: Zondervan/Probe Ministries International, 1984.

Nee, Watchman 倪柝聲. *The Normal Christian Church Life*. Anaheim, CA: Living Stream Ministry, 1980.

Nevius, John Livingston. *China and the Chinese*. London: Sampson Low, Son and Marston, 1869. Reprint, Madras: Asian Educational Services, 1991.

Newspaper Syndicate Color Photos of America's New Possessions. Chicago: The Press Association, 1900.

Noll, Mark A. "The Potential of Missiology for the Crises of History." In *History and the Christian Historian,* ed. Ronald A. Wells, 106–123. Grand Rapids, MI: Eerdmans, 1998.

Noyes, Harriet Newell. *History of the South China Mission of the American Presbyterian Church 1845–1920*. Shanghai: Presbyterian Mission Press, 1927.

Okihiro, Gary Y. "Oral History and the Writing of Ethnic History." In *Oral History: An Interdisciplinary Anthology*. 2nd ed., eds. David K. Dunaway and Willa K. Baum, 199–214. Walnut Creek, CA: AltaMira Press/Sage, 1996.

Omohundro, John Thomas. *Chinese Merchant Families in Iloilo: Commerce and Kin in a Central Philippine City*. Quezon City: Ateneo de Manila University Press, 1981.

―――. "A Fukienese Immigrant Adaptation to a Central Philippines Social Environment." In *Cultural-ecological Perspectives on Southeast Asia: A Symposium*. Edited by William Wood. Athens: n.p., 1977.

The Order of Confirmation. Accessed 12 November 2006, http://prayerbook.ca/bcp/confirmation. html.

Orr, James Edwin. *Evangelical Awakenings in Eastern Asia*. Minneapolis, MN: Bethany Fellowship, 1975.

Osias, Camilo, and Avelina Lorenzana. *Evangelical Christianity in the Philippine*. Dayton, OH: United Brethren Publishing, 1931.

Our Islands and Their People as Seen with Camera and Pencil. Introduction by Major General Joseph Wheeler, United States Army. With Special Descriptive Matter and Narrations by José De Olivares. Vol. 2. St. Louis: N.D. Thompson Publishing, 1899.

Pamplona, Catalino P. *Baptist History for Church Leaders*. Makati City: Church Strengthening Ministry, 1992.

Pardington, George P. *Twenty-Five Wonderful Years 1889–1914: A Popular Sketch of the Christian and Missionary Alliance*. New York City: Christian Alliance Publishing, 1914. Accessed 29 August 2005, http://www.cmalliance.org/whoweare/archives/pdfs/miscellaneous/25yrs_pardington.pdf.

Parker, Edward Harper. *China and Religion*. New York: E. P. Dutton & Co., 1905.

Pattison, Mary Wilkes Dunn. *Ablaze for God: The Life Story of Paget Wilkes*, 3rd ed. London: Oliphants, 1937.

Pelmoka, Juana Jimenez. *Pre-Spanish Philippines*. Caloocan City: by the author and Elenita Pelmoka Ujano, 1996.

Peralta, Jesus T., and Lucila A. Salazar. *Pre-Spanish Manila: A Reconstruction of the Pre-History of Manila*. Manila: National Historical Society, 1993.

The Philippine Islands, 1493–1898 (electronic resource). Edited and translated by Emma Helen Blair and James Alexander Robertson. CD-ROM design and programming, Antonio E. A. Defensor. Cleveland, OH: Arthur H. Clark Co., 1903–1909; Quezon City: Bank of the Philippine Islands, 2000.

Pier, Arthur Stanwood. *American Apostles to the Philippines*. Biography Index Reprint Series. Freeport, NY: Books for Libraries Press, 1950, reprint, 1971.

Pitcher, Philip Wilson. *Fifty Years in Amoy or, a History of the Amoy Mission, China, Founded February 24, 1842.* New York: Reformed Church in America, 1893.

———. *In and About Amoy: Some Historical and Other Facts Connected with One of the First Open Ports in China.* 2nd ed. Shanghai and Foochow: Methodist Publishing House in China, 1912.

Poethig, Richard P. *60 Years Mission in Manila.* Manila, Ellinwood Malate Church, 1967.

Polo, Marco. *The Travels of Marco Polo: The Complete Yule-Cordier Edition, Including the Unabridged Third Edition (1903) of Henry Yule's Annotated Translation, as Revised by Henri Cordier; Together with Cordier's Later Volume of Notes and Addenda (1920).* Vol. 2. New York: Dover Publications, 1993.

Porter, Lucius Chapin. *China's Challenge to Christianity.* New York: Missionary Education Movement of the United States and Canada, 1924.

"Pro-Catheral." *An Episcopal Dictionary of the Church.* Edited by Don S. Armentrout and Robert Boak Slocum, 417. New York: Church Publishing, 2000.

Quisumbing, Jose R. *The American Occupation of Cebu: Warwick Barracks, 1899–1917.* [Dumaguete]: J. R. Quisumbing, 1983.

Racelis, Mary, and Judy Celine Ick, eds. *Bearers of Benevolence: The Thomasites and Public Education in the Philippines.* Pasig City: Anvil Publishing, 2001.

Reed, Robert R. *City of Pines: The Origins of Baguio as a Colonial Hill Station and Regional Capital.* Baguio City: A-Seven Publishing, 1976.

Regalado, Felix B. and Quintin B. Franco. *History of Panay.* Edited by Eliza U. Griño. Jaro, Iloilo City: Central Philippine University Press, 1973.

Regan, Joseph W. *The Philippines: Christian Bulwark in Asia.* Maryknoll, NY: World Horizon Reports, 1957.

Reilly, Thomas H. *The Taiping Heavenly Kingdom: Rebellion and the Blasphemy of Empire.* Seattle: University of Washington Press, 2004.

Renbord, Bertil Arne. *International Drug Control: A Study of International Administration.* Washington, DC: League of Nations, [1944].

Reynolds, I. Hubert, and Harriet R. Reynolds. *Chinese in Ilocos: 1950s–1960s.* Part 1 & 2. Edited by Teresita Ang See 施洪玉華. Manila: Kaisa Para Sa Kaunlaran, Feilübin Huayi Qingnian Lianhehui 菲律濱華裔青年聯合會, 1998.

[Louis] *Richard's Comprehensive Geography of the Chinese Empire and Dependencies.* Translated, revised and enlarged by M. Kennelly, S.J. Shanghai: T'usewei Press, 1908. Reprint, Washington, DC: Ross & Perry, 2001. Originally published as *Géographie de l'Empire de Chine.* Shanghai: T'usewei Press, 1905.

Robequain, Charles. *Malaya, Indonesia, Borneo, and the Philippines* (Le monde malais). Translated by E. D. Laborde. London: Longmans, Green & Co. and the Institute of Pacific Relations, 1954.

Robert, Dana L. "'The Crisis of Missions': Premillennial Mission Theory and the Origins of Independent Evangelical Missions." In *Earthen Vessels: American Evangelicals and Foreign Missions, 1880-1980*, eds. Joel A. Carpenter and Wilbert R. Shenk, 33–39. Grand Rapids, MI: Eerdmans, 1990.

Robinson, Albert B. *Historical Sketch of the Missions in China, under the Care of the Board of Foreign Missions of the Presbyterian Church*. Philadelphia: Woman's Foreign Missionary Society of the Presbyterian Church, 1881.

Robles, Eliodoro G. *The Philippines in the Nineteenth Century*. Quezon City: Malaya Books, 1969

Rodgers, James Burton. *Forty Years in the Philippines: A History of the Philippine Mission of the Presbyterian Church in the United States of America 1899–1939*. New York: The Board of Foreign Missions of the Presbyterian Church in the United States of America, 1940.

———. *Twenty Years of Presbyterian Work in the Philippines Supplement to the Philippine Presbyterian, Being a Summary of Preceding Years and the History of the Year Nineteen-ninteen [sic] as Shown by Station Reports*. Manila: n.p., 1920.

Rodrigo, Raul. *Phoenix: The Saga of the Lopez Family* Vol. 1: *1800–1972*. Manila: Eugenio López Foundation, 2000.

Rogers, Jack. *Presbyterian Creeds: A Guide to the Book of Confessions*. Louisville, KY: Westminster John Knox Press, 1985.

Rommerskirchen, Johannes, founder. *Bibliographia Missionaria LX=1996*. Pontifical Missionary Library. Vatican City: Pontifical Urban University, 1997.

Ronan, Charles E., S.J. and Bonnie B. C. Oh, ed. *East Meets West: The Jesuits in China, 1582–1773*. Chicago: Loyola University Press, 1988.

Rosa, Rolando V. de la, O.P. *Beginnings of the Filipino Dominicans: A Critical Inquiry into the Late Emergence of Native Dominicans in the Philippines and Their Attempt at Self-government*. Quezon City: Dominican Province of the Philippines, 1990.

Rubinstein, Murray A. *The Origins of the Anglo-American Missionary Enterprise in China, 1807–1840*. ATLA Monograph Series no. 33, ed. Kenneth E. Rowe. Lanham, MD: Scarecrow Press, 1996.

Saito, Shiro. *Philippine Ethnography: A Critically Annotated and Selected Bibliography*. Honolulu, HI: University Press of Hawaii, 1972.

Salamanca, Bonifacio S. *The Filipino Reaction to American Rule 1901–1913*. Quezon City: New Day, 1984.

Sancianco y Goson, Gregorio. *The Progress of the Philippines: Economic,*
Administrative and Political Studies. Translated by Encarnacion Alzona.
Madrid: Imprenta de la viuda de J. M. Perez, 1881. Reprint, Manila:
National Historical Institute, 1975.

Santamaria, Alberto, O.P., "The Chinese *Parian* (El Parian de los Sangleyes)." In
The Chinese in the Philippines: 1570–1770. Edited by Alfonso Felix, Jr, 1:
67–72. Manila: Solidaridad Publishing, 1966.

Santos, Ruperto C., STL. *Anales Ecclesiasticos de Philipinas 1574–1682,* Vol.
1 and 2. *Philippine Church History: A Summary Translation.* Manila:
The Roman Catholic Archbishop of Manila and Rev Fr Ruperto C.
Santos, 1994.

Sa-onoy, Modesto P. *A Brief History of the Church in Negros Occidental.* Bacolod
City: Bacolod Publishing, 1976.

Schafer, Edward H. *The Empire of Min.* Rutland, VT: Charles E. Tuttle
Co., 1954.

Schirokauer, Conrad. *A Brief History of Chinese and Japanese Civilization.* New
York: Harcourt Brace Jovanovich, 1978.

Schmidlin, Joseph. *Catholic Mission History.* Techny, IL: Mission Press, 1933.

Schreurs, Peter, MSC. *Caraga Antigua 1521–1910: The Hispanization and
Christianization of Agusan, Surigao and East Davao.* 2nd ed. Manila:
National Historical Institute, 2000.

Schubert, William E. *I Remember John Sung.* Singapore: Far Eastern Bible
College Press, 1976.

Schumacher, John N. S.J. *Readings in Philippine Church History.* 2nd ed. Quezon
City: Loyola School of Theology/Ateneo de Manila University, 1987.

———. *Revolutionary Clergy: The Filipino Clergy and the National Movement,
1850–1903.* Quezon City: Ateneo de Manila University Press, 1981.

Scott, William Henry. *Barangay: Sixteenth-Century Philippine Culture and Society.*
Quezon City: Ateneo de Manila University Press, 1994.

See, Chinben/Shi ZhenMin 施振民 and Teresita Ang See/Shi Hong YuHua 施
洪玉華. *Chinese in the Philippines: A Bibliography.* Manila: De La Salle
University Press, China Studies Program, 1990.

Shalom, Stephen Rosskamm. *The United States and the Philippines.* Quezon City:
New Day, 1986.

Shao, Joseph Too. "A Channel of Blessings in God's Hands: Chinese Protestant
Churches in the Philippines." In *Chapters in Philippine Church History*, ed.
Anne Catherine Laninga Kwantes, 413–428. Mandaluyong City: OMF
Literature, 2001.

Sison, Porfirio V. "Tribute to Madam Elizabeth Kho Lu Soat." In *Xu Zhanglao
YuXue Xiaozhang Jiniance Fu Zhurixue YuXuelou Fengxianli* 許長老逾雪校
長紀念冊附主日學逾雪樓奉獻禮 (Memorial book of Elder/Principal Xu

YuXue with dedication ceremony of the Ju Soat Sunday School building), 82–83 (pages in Chinese style). Manila: Westminster Student Church Literature Committee, 1983.

Sitoy, T. Valentino, Jr *A History of Christianity in the Philippines*. Vol. 1: *The Initial Encounter*. Quezon City: New Day, 1985.

———. "The Making of Negros: A Brief History." In *Kabilin: Legacies of a Hundred Years of Negros Oriental*, eds. Merlie M. Alunan and Bobby Flores Villasis, 1–28. Negros Oriental: Negros Oriental Foundation, 1993.

———. *Several Springs, One Stream: The United Church of Christ in the Philippines*. Vol. 1: *Heritage and Origins (1898–1948)*. Quezon City: United Church of Christ in the Philippines, 1992.

———. *Several Springs, One Stream: The United Church of Christ in the Philippines*. Vol. 2: *The Formative Decade (1948–1958)*. Quezon City: United Church of Christ in the Philippines, 1997.

"Sketch Reports." *The China Mission Handbook* (1896), 4–7.

Skivington, S. Robert. *Mission to Mindanao: A Study in the Principle of Church Planting Strategy for the Philippines*. Quezon City: Conservative Baptist Publications, 1977.

Sly, Virgil A. *The Philippines: A Christian Opportunity (Philippines Mission of Disciples of Christ)*. N.p.: Department of the Orient, The United Christian Missionary Society, n.d.

Smith, Arthur H. *The Uplift of China*. Rev. ed. New York: Eaton & Mains, 1907. Reprint, Cincinnati, OH: Jennings & Graham, 1912.

Smith, Eugene R., ed. *The Gospel in All Lands. Illustrated*. New York: Eaton & Mains, 1898.

Sobrepeña, Enrique C. *That They May Be One*. Manila: United Church of Christ in the Philippines, 1954.

Spence, Jonathan D. *God's Chinese Son: The Taiping Heavenly Kingdom of Hong Xiuquan*. New York: W. W. Norton, 1996.

Spence, Jonathan D., and Annping Chin. *The Chinese Century: A Photographic History of the Last Hundred Years*. New York: Random House, 1996.

The Spring Sunshine: A Memoir of Elder Cang Chui Siok (Chunhuiji – Huangjiang Shuishu Zhanglao Jiniance) 「春暉集」—黃江水淑長老紀念冊. Caloocan City: Shangkuan Press and School Supply, n.d.

Standaert, Nicolas, ed. *Handbook of Christianity in China*. Volume One: *635–1800*. Handbook of Oriental Studies Section 4, eds. Erik Zürcher, S. F. Teiser, M. Kern, vol. 15/1. Leiden: Brill, 2001.

Stanley, Peter W. *A Nation in the Making: The Philippines and the United States, 1899–1921*. Harvard Studies in American-East Asian Relations, no. 4. Cambridge, MA: Harvard University Press, 1974.

————, ed. *Reappraising an Empire: New Perspectives on Philippine-American History*. Harvard Studies in American-East Asian Relations, no. 10. Cambridge, MA: Harvard University Press and the Committee on American-East Asian Relations, 1984.

Starr, Louis. "Oral History." In *Oral History: An Interdisciplinary Anthology*. 2nd ed., eds. David K. Dunaway and Willa K. Baum, 39–61. Walnut Creek, CA: AltaMira Press/Sage, 1996.

Staunton, John A., Jr *An Open Letter to the Rt. Rev F. R. Graves, D.D., Bishop of Shanghai; and Bishop in Charge of the Missionary District of the Philippine Islands: From the Rev John A. Staunton, Jr, Priest-in-Charge of the Mission of St. Mary the Virgin, Sagada, Philippine Islands*. Sagada: Igorot Press, 1919.

Stevens, Joseph Earle. *The Philippines Circa 1900: Book Two. Yesterdays in the Philippines*. Publications of the Filipiniana Book Guild, 13. Manila: Filipiniana Book Guild, 1968. Originally published as *Yesterdays in the Philippines*. New York: Scribner, 1898.

Stewart, I. R. Govan. *Dynamic: Paget Wilkes of Japan*. London: Marshall, Morgan & Scott, 1957.

Stewart, James Alexander. *William Chalmers Burns: A Man with a Passion for Souls*. Philadelphia, PA: Revival Literature, 1964.

Stock, Eugene. *The Story of the Fu-kien Mission of the Church Missionary Society*. London: Seeley, Jackson, & Halliday, Church Missionary Society, 1877.

Storey, Moorfield, and Marcial P. Lichauco. *The Conquest of the Philippines by the United States 1898–1925*. New York: G. P. Putnam's Sons, 1926. Reprint, Mandaluyong, Metro Manila: Cacho Hermanos, 1985.

The Story of the Christian and Missionary Alliance. Nyack, NY: Christian & Missionary Alliance, 1900, 95. Accessed 29 August 2005, http://www.cmalliance.org/whoweare/archives/ pdfs/miscellaneous/story_cma.pdf.

Stuntz, Homer Clyde. *The Philippines and the Far East*. Cincinnati, OH: Jennings & Pye, 1904.

Suarez, Oscar S. *Protestantism and Authoritarian Politics: The Politics of Repression and the Future of Ecumenical Witness in the Philippines*. Quezon City: New Day, 1999.

Swanson, William Sutherland. "In Memoriam: Dr. Talmage – the Man and the Missionary." In John Gerardus Fagg, *Forty Years in South China*, 108–116. New York: A. D. F. Randolph & Company, [1894]. Reprint, Whitefish, MT: Kessinger Publishing, 2004.

————. "His Missionary Career." In John Monteath Douglas, Memorials of Rev Carstairs Douglas, MA, LL.D., Missionary of the Presbyterian Church of England at Amoy, China. London: Waterlow & Sons, 1878.

Sy, Dionisio A. *A Short History of Cebu, 1500–1890's and the Anti-Spanish Revolution in Cebu*. Cebu: Bathalad, 1996.

Tan, Antonio/Chen ShouGuo 陳守國. *The Chinese Mestizos and the Formation of the Filipino Nationality*. Quezon City: University of the Philippines Asian Center, n.d. Reprint, Manila: Kaisa Para Sa Kaunlaran, Feilübin Huayi Qingnian Lianhehui 菲律濱華裔青年聯合會, 1987.

Tan, Chee-Beng. "Culture, Ethnicity and Economic Activities: The Case of the People of Chinese Descent with Special References to Southeast Asia." In *The Ethnic Chinese (Hua Ren)* 華人. *Proceedings of the International Conference on Changing Identities and Relations in Southeast Asia*. Conference Held in Manila 8–10 November 1991, eds. Teresita Ang See 施洪玉華 and Go Bon Juan 吳文煥, 27–59. Manila: Kaisa Para Sa Kaunlaran, Feilübin Huayi Qingnian Lianhehui 菲律濱華裔青年聯合會; Chinben See Memorial Trust Fund (Jinian Shi Chenmin Jiaoshou Jiangxuejin Jijinhui) 紀念施振民教授獎學金基金會; Chinese Studies Program, De La Salle University, 1994.

Tan, Samuel K. *The Filipino-American War 1899–1913*. Quezon City: University of the Philippines Press, 2002.

———. *A History of the Philippines*. Manila: Manila Studies Association, Philippine National Historical Society, 1997.

Tang Tack. "The Chinese in the Philippines – A Synthesis." In *Chinese Participation in Philippine Culture and Economy*, ed. Shubert S. C. Liao, 393–397. Manila: by the editor, 1964.

Thompson, A. E., *A. B. Simpson: His Life and Work*. Harrisburg, PA: Christian Publications, 1920.

Tiu, Macario D. *Davao 1898–1910: Conquest and Resistance in the Garden of the Gods*. Quezon City: Center for Integrative and Development Studies, University of the Philippines, 2003.

Tolliver, Ralph E. "The Philippines." In *The Church in Asia*, ed. Donald E. Hoke, 524–552. Chicago: Moody Press, 1975.

———. *The Philippines: Pear of the Orient*. Fields for Reaping, 8. London: China Inland Mission/Overseas Missionary Fellowship, 1955.

Tow, Timothy. *The Asian Awakening*. Singapore: Christian Life Publishers, 1988.

Trinidad, Ruben F. *A Monument to Religious Nationalism: History and Polity of the IEMELIF Church*. Quezon City: Evangelical Methodist Church in the Philippines, 1999.

Tsinoy: The Story of the Chinese in Philippine Life. Edited by Teresita Ang See, Go Bon Juan, Doreen Go Yu, and Yvonne Chua. Manila: Kaisa Para Sa Kaunlaran, Feilübin Huayi Qingnian Lianhehui 菲律濱華裔青年聯合會, 2005.

Tucker, Ruth A. "Women in Missions: Reaching Sisters in 'Heathen Darkness.'" In *Earthen Vessels: American Evangelicals and Foreign Missions, 1880–1980*, eds. Joel A. Carpenter and Wilbert R. Shenk, 253–256. Grand Rapids, MI: Eerdmans, 1990.

Tuggy, Arthur Leonard. *The Philippine Church: Growth in a Changing Society*. Grand Rapids, MI: Eerdmans, 1971.

Tuggy, Arthur Leonard and Ralph E. Toliver. *Seeing the Church in the Philippines*. Manila: OMF Publishers, 1972.

Tye, Norwood B. *Journeying with the United Church of Christ in the Philippines: A History*. Quezon City: United Church of Christ in the Philippines, 1994.

Van Sickle, Emily. *The Iron Gates of Santo Tomas: The Firsthand Account of an American Couple Interned by the Japanese in Manila, 1942–45*. Chicago: Academy Chicago Publishers, 1992.

Villarroel, Fidel, O.P., ed. *The Dominicans and the Philippine Revolution (1896–1903)*. Documents on the Church and the Philippine Revolution. Translated by Luis Antonio Mañeru and Fidel Villarroel. Manila: UST Publishing House, 1999.

Von Brevern, Marilies. *"Once a Chinese, Always a Chinese?" The Chinese of Manila – Tradition and Change*. Manila: Marilies von Brevern, 1988.

Waley-Cohen, Joanna. *The Sextants of Beijing: Global Currents in Chinese History*. New York: W. W. Norton & Co., 1999.

Wang GungWu. *China and the Chinese Overseas*. Ethnic Studies Series. Singapore: Times Media Private Limited, Eastern Universities Press by Marshall Cavendish, 1991.

———. "Ethnic Chinese: The Past in Their Future." In *Intercultural Relations, Cultural Transformation, and Identity – The Ethnic Chinese – Selected Papers Presented at the 1998 International Society for the Study of Chinese Overseas (ISSCO) Conference*. Conference Held in Manila 26–28 November 1998, ed. Teresita Ang See 施洪玉華, 1–20. Manila: Kaisa Para Sa Kaunlaran, Feilübin Huayi Qingnian Lianhehui 菲律濱華裔青年聯合會, 2000.

———. *The Nanhai Trade: Early Chinese Trade in the South China Sea*. Singapore: Eastern Universities Press, 2003.

Wang, Peter Chen-Main. "Contextualizing Protestant Publishing in China: The Wenshe, 1924–1928." In *Christianity in China: From the Eighteenth Century to the Present*, ed. Daniel H. Bays, 292–306. Stanford, CA: Stanford University Press, 1996.

Wang Teh-Ming. *Sino-Filipino Historico-Cultural Relations*. Quezon City: University of the Philippines Press, 1967.

Watterson, Henry. *History of the Spanish-American War Embracing a Complete Review of Our Relations with Spain*. New York: Werner Co., 1898.

Wei AnGuo 魏安國. *The Chinese Mestizo in Philippine History (Feilübin Lishishang de Huaren Hunxieer)* 菲律濱歷史上的華人混血兒. Translated by Go Bon Juan 吳文煥譯. Manila: Kaisa Para Sa Kaunlaran, Feilübin Huayi Qingnian Lianhehui 菲律濱華裔青年聯合會, 2001.

Wentzel, Constance White. *A Half Century in the Philippines.* New York, NY: The National Council, 1952.

Wickberg, Edgar. *The Chinese in Philippine Life 1850–1898.* New Haven and London: Yale University Press, 1965. Reprint, Quezon City: Ateneo De Manila University Press, 2000.

Williams, Samuel Wells. *The Middle Kingdom: A Survey of the Geography, Government, Literature, Social Life, Arts and History of the Chinese Empire and its Inhabitants*, 2 vols. (*Zhongguo Zonglun*) 中國總論. Rev. ed. New York: Charles Scribners Sons, 1883. Reprint, Taipei: Ch'eng Wen Publishing, 1965.

Willis, Henry Parker. *Our Philippine Problem: A Study of American Colonial Policy.* New York: Henry Holt & Co., 1905.

Wilson, Andrew. "Compradors or Cabecillas? Colonial Manila as 'Treaty Port'." In *Intercultural Relations, Cultural Transformation, and Identity – The Ethnic Chinese – Selected Papers Presented at the 1998 International Society for the Study of Chinese Overseas (ISSCO) Conference.* Conference Held in Manila 26–28 November 1998, ed. Teresita Ang See 施洪玉華, 571–586. Manila: Kaisa Para Sa Kaunlaran, Feilübin Huayi Qingnian Lianhehui 菲律濱華裔青年聯合會, 2000.

Wilson, Laurence L. *The Skyland of the Philippines.* Baguio: L. L. Wilson/ Bookman, 1965.

Wionzek, Karl-Heinz, ed. *Germany, the Philippines, and the Spanish-American War: Four Accounts by Officers of the Imperial German Navy.* Translated by Thomas Clark. Manila: National Historical Institute, 2000.

Wong Kwok-chu. *The Chinese in the Philippine Economy 1898–1941.* Quezon City: Ateneo de Manila University Press, 1999.

Woods, L. Shelton. *A Broken Mirror: Protestant Fundamentalism in the Philippines.* Quezon City: New Day, 2002.

Worcester, Dean Conant. *The Philippine Islands and Their People: A Record of Personal Observation and Experience with a Short Summary of the More Important Facts in the History of the Archipelago.* New York: Macmillan, 1898.

Wu Ching-hong 吳景宏. "Discussion on a New Outline of the History of the Chinese in the Philippines during the Spanish Period." In *Proceedings of the First International Conference of Historians of Asia. Philippine Historical Association. Held in Manila November 25–30, 1960*, 67–72. Manila: Philippine Historical Association, 1962.

Wylie, Alexander. *Memorials of Protestant Missionaries to the Chinese: Giving a List of their Publications, and Obituary Notices of the Deceased. With Copius*

Indexes. Shanghai: American Presbyterian Mission Press, 1867. Reprint, Taipei: Ch'eng Wen Publishing, 1967.

Yamamoto Sumiko. *History of Protestantism in China: The Indigenization of Christianity.* Tokyo: The Tōhō Gakkai (The Institute of Eastern Culture), 2000.

Yeung, Yue-man, and David K. Y. Chu, ed. *Fujian: A Coastal Province in Transition and Transformation.* Hong Kong: Chinese University Press, 2000.

Yin BinYong 尹斌庸, and Mary Felley. *Chinese Romanization, Pronunciation and Orthography* (Hanyu pinyin he zhengcifa 漢語拼音和正詞法). Beijing: Sinolingua, 1990.

Yue-man Yeung, "Introduction." In *Fujian: A Coastal Province in Transition and Transformation,* eds. Yue-man Yeung and David K. Y. Chu, 1–24. Hong Kong: Chinese University Press, 2000.

Yung Li Yuk-wai. *The Huaqiao Warriors: Chinese Resistance Movement in the Philippines 1942–1945.* Quezon City: Ateneo de Manila University Press, 1996.

Zabriskie, Alexander C. *Bishop Brent: Crusader for Christian Unity.* Philadephia: Westminster Press, 1948.

Zarco, Ricardo M. "The Philippine Chinese and Opium Addiction." In *The Chinese in the Philippines 1770–1898,* 96–109, ed. Alfonso Felix, Jr, Vol. 2. Manila: Solidaridad Publishing, 1969.

Zürcher, Erik. "Aleni in Fujian, 1630–1640: The Medium and the Message." In *"Scholar from the West" Giulio Aleni S.J. (1582–1649) and the Dialogue between Christianity and China.* Edited by Tiziana Lippiello and Roman Malek. Annali/ Fondazione Civilta Bresciana 9. Monumenta Serica Monograph Series 42. Brescia: Fondazione Civilta Bresciana; Nettetal: Sankt Augustin Steyler Verlag, Monumenta Serica Institute, 1997.

V. Articles and Addresses

Abad, Ricardo G. "Religion in the Philippines." *Philippine Studies* 49 (Third Quarter 2001): 337–367.

Adams, George Burton. "History and the Philosophy of History." *American Historical Review* 14 (1909): 223, 226.

Andrews, David. "Pastor and Poet." *The Joint Archives Quarterly* (Spring 2001): 1–4.

Angus, William Robertson, Jr "Chinese Church Life in the Philippines." *Church and Community* 7 (May–June 1967): 19–24.

"Announcements Concerning Missionaries." *The Spirit of Missions* 70 (January 1905): 52.

The American Chamber of Commerce Journal 10, 1 (January 1930): 10.

Andrews, David. "Pastor and Poet." *The Joint Archives Quarterly* (Spring 2001): 1–2.

Arcilla, Jose S., S.J. "The Christianization of Davao Oriental: Excerpt from Jesuit Missionary Letters." *Philippine Studies* 19 (October 1971): 639–724.

Barrett, John. "The New Treaties: The Future of the Philippines; Siam; and the Open Door." Address given before the Imperial Educational Society, Tokyo, 25 December 1898. Hongkong: Kelly & Walsh, 1899.

———. "The Philippine Islands and America's Interests in the Far East." Address given before the Shanghai General Chamber of Commerce, Shanghai, 12 January 1899, together with extracts from addresses delivered before the Oriental Society of Tokio and the Odd Volumes Society of Hongkong. Hong Kong: Kelly & Walsh, 1899.

———. "The Situation in the Far East, as Affected by the Results of the Late War." Address given before the Old Volumes Society in Hongkong, 2 February 1899. Hong Kong: Kelly & Walsh, 1899.

Bohr, P. Richard. "The Legacy of William Milne." *International Bulletin of Missionary Research* 25, 1 (October 2001): 173–178.

Brent, Charles Henry. "'My Little Book of Praise' A Miscellany of Meditations and Views on Church Unity from the Unpublished Personal Papers of Bishop Charles Henry Brent (1862–1929)." Edited by Frederick Ward Kates. *Historical Magazine of the Protestant Episcopal Church* 27 (June 1958): 89–111.

———. "Religious Conditions in the Philippine Islands." *Missionary Review of the World* 28 (January 1905): 49–56.

———. "Sixteen Years in the Philippines." *The Spirit of Missions* 82 (March 1918): 163–185.

———. "Various Notes on Philippine Matters." *The Spirit of Missions* 71 (May 1906): 372–377.

Briggs, Charles W. "Christian Missions in Our New Possessions." *Missionary Review of the World* 23 (March 1900): 205–208.

"BSOP Founder Passes Away." *BSOP in Focus* (June 1995): 12.

Chan, Alberto. "Chinese-Philippine Relations in the Late Sixteenth Century and to 1603." *Philippine Studies* 26 (1978): 51–82.

Chin Cheak Yu. "Christian Religious Education for Awakening and Living in the Spirit: As Inspired by John Wesley and John Sung." Accessed 27 January 2007, http://religiouseducation.net/ member/04_papers/yu.pdf.

Chu, Richard T. "The 'Chinese' and the 'Mestizos' of the Philippines: Towards a New Interpretation." *Philippine Studies* 50 (2002): 327–370.

Chua, S. C. (a.k.a. George Sin Chiong)/Tsai XinZhang 蔡信彰. "The Chinese United Evangelical Church." In *Fifty Years of Protestantism in the Philippines:*

The Manila Time (Morning Daily) and the Daily Mirror, 63–65. Manila:
Manila Times Publishing, 1949.

Clapp, Walter C. "Some Note of Matters Philippine." *The Spirit of Missions* 68
(May 1903): 329–330.

Cooke, William. "Domestic Manila." *The Philippine Presbyterian* 2 (March
1911): 5–8.

Cunningham, Floyd T. "Diversities within Post-war Philippine Protestantism."
The Mediator 5 (October 2003): 42–143.

"Davao-kuo: The Political Economy of a Japanese Settler Zone in Philippine
Colonial Society." *Journal of American-East Asian Relation* 6 (Spring
1997): 59–82.

Doeppers, Daniel Frederick. "Destination, Selection and Turnover among
Chinese Migrants to Philippine Cities in the Nineteenth Century." *Journal
of Historical Geography* 12, no. 4 (1986): 381–401.

Dunlap, George Williamson. "The Chinese Work." *The Philippine Presbyterian*
13, no. 4 (October 1922): 23–24.

———. "Dormitory Extension." *The Philippine Presbyterian* 13, no. 4 (October
1922): 20–21.

———. "A Forward Look; Cebu and Her Needs." *The Philippine Presbyterian* 13,
no. 4 (October 1922): 21–22.

———. "History of Cebu Station." *The Philippine Presbyterian* 13, no. 4
(October 1922): 10–11.

Edmonds, H. Wesley. "Among the Ataos in the Philippines." *The Alliance Weekly*
71 (1 August 1936). Accessed 30 August 2005, http://apps.cmalliance.org/
whoweare/archives/alifepdfs/ AW_1936/07.pdf.

"Evangelizing the Sinner." *The Philippine Evangelist* 2, no. 8 (May 1934): 238.

"The Foochow Conference." *The Gospel in All Lands* (July 1898): 304–311.

Foster, Zelma. "Dedicated to Training." *The Commission: A Baptist World Journal*
19 (January 1956): 10–13.

Gibbs, Paul. "'Let Go and Let God': Keswick Movement's Lasting Impact on
Fundamentalism's View of Sanctification," 1–10. Accessed 30 January 2007,
http://seminary.cbs.edu/content/ events/nlc/2003/papers/5-%20Let%20
Go%20and%20Let% 20God.pdf.

Go Bon Juan/Wu WenHuan 吳文煥. "Gems of History: Earliest Chinese
Drawings." *Tulay Fortnightly* (23 May 2006): 5–6.

———. "Ma'I in Chinese Records – Mindoro or Bai? An Examination of a
Historical Puzzle." *Philippine Studies* 53 (2005): 119–138.

Graham, Lilian Holmes. "Cebu Special." *The Philippine Presbyterian* 13, no. 4
(October 1922): 10.

Hamilton, Charles R. "The Movement for Church Union in the Philippines."
The Philippine Presbyterian 15 (October 1924): 32–36.

Harrington, Fern. "Prayer, Our Most Effective Weapon." *The Commission: A Baptist World Journal* 17 (November 1954): 316–317.

"The Historical Background of the Present Union of the United Church of Christ in the Philippines." In *Fifty Years of Protestantism in the Philippines: The Manila Time (Morning Daily) and the Daily Mirror*, 38–40. Manila: Manila Times Publishing, 1949.

Hykes, John R. "Missionary Opportunity in the Philippines." *Missionary Review* 22 (May 1899): 359–362.

"Iloilo Mission Hospital at the Forefront of Caring: A Hundred Years and Beyond." *News Today* (12–18 February 2001): 14.

"Iloilo Station." *The Philippine Presbyterian* 13 (January 1922): 8–9.

Iyoy, Santiago G. "Cebu Gospel Church." *Wuguang* 務光 *Gospel Quarterly* 17 (December 1961): 47.

Johnson, Todd. "The Crisis of Mission: The Historical Development of the Idea of the Evangelization of the World by the Year 1900." *Mission Frontier Supplement* 10, no. 8 (August 1988): 2–32. Accessed 11 October 2006, http://www.missionfrontiers.org/1988/08/a8812.htm.

Le Roy, James A. "Chinese Exclusion in the Philippines." *Independent* 55 (15 January 1903): 140–143.

Lee, Joseph Tse-Hei. "Watchman Nee and the Little Flock Movement in Maoist China." *Church History* 74, no. 1 (March 2005): 68–96.

Lerrico, P. H. J. "The Prime Need of the Filipinos: The Place of Religion in the Educational System in the Philippines." *Missionary Review of the World* 37 (July 1914): 525–530.

Liu Chi-tien. "Centuries of Sino-Philippine Relations." Edited by Philip H. and Liu Chi-tien. *Sino-Philippine Research Journal* 1 (September 1940): 20–28.

MacD[onald], W. "Our 'Golden Roster'" *The Philippine Presbyterian* 32, no. 4 (December 1940): appendix.

McKee, J. A. "Alliance Mission." *The Christian and Missionary Alliance* 31 (31 October 1903): 303. Accessed 3 September 2005, http://apps.cmalliance.org/archives/alifepdf/AW-1903-10-31.pdf.

———. "Shall the Moros Be Evangelized; or Shall an Unwise American Treaty Succeed in Shutting Out the Gospel?" *The Christian and Missionary Alliance* 29 (2 August 1902): 57–58. Accessed 2 September 2005, http://apps.cmalliance.org/archives/alifepdf/AW-1902-08-02.pdf.

"The Meeting of the Board of Missions December 13, 1904." *The Spirit of Missions* 70 (January 1905): 50–51.

Mencarini, Juan. "The Philippine Chinese Labour Question." *Journal of the China Branch of the Royal Asiatic Society for the Year 1900–1901*. Vol. 33. Reprint, Nendeln, Liechtenstein: Kraus Reprint Ltd., 1967, 158–185.

Meyer, Milton Walter. "The Course of Early Baptist Mission in the Philippines
   (1) – The First Decade: 1900–1910." *The American Era in the Philippines.*
   Bulletin of the American Historical Collection 15, no. 59 (April–June
   1987): 7–23.
———. "The Course of Early Baptist Mission in the Philippines (2)." *The
   American Era in the Philippines. Bulletin of the American Historical Collection*
   15, no. 60 (July–September 1987): 38–57.
"Mid Shrine and Crescent in the Southern Philippines." *The Alliance Weekly* 71
   (7 November 1936). Accessed 30 August 2005, http://apps.cmalliance.org/
   whoweare/archives/alifepdfs /AW_1936/07.pdf.
"Missionaries for the Philippines." *Independent* 52 (March 1, 1900): 566–567.
Mosher, Governeur Frank. "The Conference of the Anglican Communion in
   China, March 27th to April 4th, 1909." *The Spirit of Missions: An Illustrated
   Monthly Review of Christian Missions* (May 1909): 466.
"The Movement for Church Union in the Philippines." *The Philippine
   Presbyterian* 15, no. 4 (October 1924): 32–34.
Munson, E. H. "The Study of Methods and Results of the Fukien Provincial
   Evangelistic Campaign, 1914." *The Chinese Recorder and Missionary Journal*
   47 (1916): 616–626.
Norbeck, Mark Douglas. "False Start: The First Three Years of Episcopal
   Missionary Endeavor in the Philippine Islands, 1898–1901." *Anglican and
   Episcopal History* 62 (June 1993): 215–236.
———. "The Legacy of Charles Henry Brent." *International Bulletin of
   Missionary Research* 20 (October 1996): 163–168.
"Outline History of the Missionary Society of the Methodist Episcopal Church,
   1894–1897." *The Gospel in All Lands* (March 1898): 121–129.
The Outlook 63 (11 November 1899): 611–612. Accessed 31 December
   2015, https://www.unz.org/Pub/Outlook-1899nov11-00611.
The Outlook 63 (9 December 1899): 611–612. Quoted in Donald Dean Parker,
   "Church and State in the Philippines 1896–1906." PhD diss., University of
   Chicago, 1936, 178.
Pakenham-Walsh, W. S. "Methods of Administration and Church Organization
   in the Diocese of Fuhkien." *The Chinese Recorder and Missionary Journal* 46
   (1915): 293–296.
Palanca, Ellen H. "The Economic Position of the Chinese in the Philippines."
   Philippine Studies 25 (1977): 80–94.
Pierce, Charles C. "Philippine Beginnings and Philippine Possibilities." *The Spirit
   of Missions* 65 (1900): 378–381.
Potter, Henry C. "Bishop Potter: On the Church Question in the Philippines."
   The Churchman (24 March 1900): 354. Quoted in Mark Douglas Norbeck,
   "The Protestant Episcopal Church in the City of Manila, Philippine Islands

from 1898–1918: An Institutional History." MA thesis, The University of Texas at El Paso, 1992, 193–194.

Rath, Theresa Kalb. "Work among the Chinese in Cebu." *The Philippine Presbyterian* 10 (July 1919): 8–10.

Reilly, Michael C. "Charles Henry Brent: Philippine Missionary and Ecumenist." *Philippine Studies* 24 (1976): 303–325.

Robinson, Albert Gardner. "The Religious Question in the Philippines." *Independent* 52 (22 February 1900): 476–478.

Rodgers, James Burton. "Religious Conditions in the Philippines." *Missionary Review of the World* 24 (July 1901): 510–516.

Rohrbaugh, Olive. "A Sunday in Cebu." *The Philippine Presbyterian* 13, no. 4 (October 1922): 13.

Saunders, Mary Lucile. "Church in the Making." *The Commission: A Baptist World Journal* 17 (July 1954): 208–209.

Schumacher, John N., S.J. "The Early Filipino Clergy: 1698–1762." *Philippine Studies* 51 (2003): 7–62.

Shao, Joseph Too. "Heritage of the Chinese-Filipino Protestant Churches." *Journal of Asian Mission* 1 (1999): 93–99.

Shenk, Wilbert R. "Toward a Global Church History." *International Bulletin of Missionary Research* 20, no. 2 (April 1996): 50–57.

Simpson, Albert Benjamin. "Greater America and Her Missionary Opportunity." *Christian and Missionary Alliance* 22 (1 December 1898): 3–4. Accessed 23 August 2005, http://apps.cmalliance.org/archives/alifepdf/AW-1898-12-01.pdf.

———. "The Islands." *Christian and Missionary Alliance* 23 (12 August 1899): 168. Accessed 24 August 2005, http://apps.cmalliance.org/whoweare/archives/pdfs/AW-1899-08-12.pdf.

———. "Our New Island Possessions." *Christian and Missionary Alliance* 23 (9 September 1899): 227. Accessed 3 September 2005, http://apps.cmalliance.org/archives/alifepdf/AW-1899-09-09.pdf.

———. "The Progress of the War." *Christian and Missionary Alliance* 20 (1 June 1898): 516. Accessed 24 August 2005, http://apps.cmalliance.org/archives/alifepdf/AW-1898-06-01.pdf

———. "The Significance of the Spanish-American War." *Christian and Missionary Alliance* 20 (27 April 1898): 396. Accessed 24 August 2005, http://apps.cmalliance.org/archives/alifepdf/AW-1898-08-24.pdf.

Smith, W. T. "My Impression of Cebu." *The Philippine Presbyterian* 3 (May 1912): 5–6.

The Spirit of Missions 63 (1898): 26.

"Statistics Showing Work of the Protestant Church in the Philippines." *The Philippine Presbyterian* 5 (August 1914): 2–3.

Studley, Hobart Earl. "A Chinese Experiment in Christian Union: The Fruits of Twenty Years' Effort Are Worthy of the Effort Made." *The Spirit of Missions* 89 (September 1924): 576–579.

———. "Report of St. Stephen's Mission for Chinese." In *Journal of the Annual Convocation of the Missionary District of the Philippine Islands* (3 August 1912). Accessed 31 December 2015, https://imageserver.library.yale.edu/digcoll:239983/500.pdf.

Stuntz, Homer C. "Protestant Missions and Reform Movements in the Philippine Islands." *Missionary Review of the World* 33 (July 1910): 522–528.

Thoburn, James Mills et al. "The Philippines as a Mission Field." *The Gospel in All Lands* (October 1898): 467–468.

Thompson, Lanny. "Representation and Rule in the Imperial Archipelago: Cuba, Puerto Rico, Hawai'i and the Philippines Under US Dominion After 1898." *American Studies Asia* 1 (2002): 3–39.

Uayan, Jean. "The Manila Connection: The Philippines as a Land-bridge for Roman Catholic Mission to China during the 16th and 17th Centuries." Lecture, Asia Graduate School of Theology, Taytay, Philippines, 26 February 2004.

Underwood, Judson Leolin. "Cebu Special." *The Philippine Presbyterian* 16 (January 1925): 17–18.

"United Evangelical Church of the Philippines: Manila's Oldest Chinese Presbyterian Church." *Philippine Panorama* (18 July 2004): 3.

Walton, Jean R. "Elihu Doty's Garden – New Brunswick, Borneo and China." *Journal of the New Jersey Postal History Society* 32, no. 4 (November 2004): 127–142. Accessed 5 October 2007, http://www.bernehistory.org/local/ELIH_DOTY_NJPH_article.pdf.

Warren, James F. "Sino-Sulu Trade in the Late Eighteenth and Nineteenth Centuries." *Philippine Studies* 25 (1977): 50–79.

Wei, J. B. (a.k.a. HsiJin)/Wei XiRen 魏希仁. "A Brief Note on St. Stephen's Parish." In *Fifty Years of Protestantism in the Philippines: The Manila Time (Morning Daily) and the Daily Mirror*, 66–67. Manila: Manila Times Publishing, 1949.

"Welcome to Dagupan City – City Profile – History." Accessed 17 March 2004, http://cityhall.dagupan.com/aboutus.htm; Internet.

White, Bessie [Elizabeth]. "God's Providences in the Entering of the Philippines." *The Christian and Missionary Alliance* 25 (1 September 1900), 118–119. Accessed 29 August 2005, http://apps.cmalliance.org/archives/alifepdf/AW-1900-09-01.pdf.

———. "The Philippines from a Missionary Standpoint." *The Christian and Missionary Alliance* 24 (24 March 1900), 177–179. Accessed 27 August 2005, http://apps.cmalliance.org/archives/alifepdf/ AW-1900-03-24.pdf.

Winthrop, W. "The Problem of the Philippines: Racial, Commercial, Religious, Political and Social Conditions." *Outlook* 59 (11 June 1898): 377–383.

Wright, Gregory, FSC. "United States '*Foreign Entanglements*,' 1775–1941." *American Studies Asia* 1 (2003): 3–21.

Wu JingHong 吳景宏. "References to the Chinese in the Philippines during the Spanish Period Found in the Philippine Islands by Blair and Robertson." *The Bulletin of the Institute of Southeast Asia* 1. Singapore: Nanyang University, 1959, F1-90.

———. "A Study of References to the Philippines in Chinese Sources from Earliest Times to the Ming Dynasty." *Philippine Social Science and Humanities Review* 24 (1959): 1–181.

———. "Supplements to a Study of References to the Philippines in Chinese Sources from Earliest Times to the Ming Dynasty (?–1644)." *University of Manila Journal of East Asiatic Studies* 7 (1958): 307–393.

VI. Dissertations and Theses

Abulog, Graciano Cabusora. "The Chinese Immigration Question in the Philippines." MA Thesis, University of California, 1940.

Alfabeto, Edgardo A. *Polarization in the Local Chinese Community: Its Implications on National Security*. Social Science 288. Metro Manila: National Defense College of the Philippines, 1977.

Baldemor, Oscar C. "The Spread of Fire: A Study of Ten Growing Churches in Metro Manila." ThM thesis, Fuller Theological Seminary, 1990.

Blaker, James Ronald. "The Chinese in the Philippines: A Study of Power and Change." PhD diss., Ohio State University, 1970.

Cartmel, Daryl Westwood. "Mission Policy and Program of A. B. Simpson." MA thesis, Kennedy School of Missions of the Hartford Seminary Foundation, 1963.

Chao, Jonathan T'ien-en 趙天恩. "The Chinese Indigenous Church Movement, 1919–1927: A Protestant Response to the Anti-Christian Movements in Modern China." PhD diss., University of Pennsylvania, 1986.

Cheung, David. "Ecclesiastical Devolution and Union in China: The Emergence of the First Native Protestant Church in South Fujian, 1842–1863." PhD diss., University of London, 2002.

———. "The Growth of Protestantism in China: The Role of the Chinese Christians, 1860–1900." MA thesis, University of London, 1997.

Doeppers, Daniel Frederick. "Ethnicity and Class in the Structure of Philippine Cities." PhD diss., Syracuse University, 1971.

Fonacier, Tomás S. "The Chinese in the Philippines during the American Administration." PhD diss., Stanford University, 1932.

Go, Shirley. "A Short Historical and Cultural Study of Chinese in the
Philippines." MA thesis, Biblical Seminary of the Philippines, 1982.

Hess, Robert Reuel. "Mid Crucifix, Crescent and Shrine: Alliance Mission in
Southern Mindanao and Sulu." BD thesis, National Bible School, 1941.

Jensen, Khin Khin Myint. "The Chinese in the Philippines during the American
Regime: 1898–1946." PhD diss., University of Wisconsin, 1956.
This work has been translated into Chinese as *(Meitong Shiji De Feilübin
Huaren)* 美統世紀的菲律濱華人 (1898–1946). Translated by Go Bon
Juan 吳文煥. Manila: Kaisa Para Sa Kaunlaran, Feilübin Huayi Qingnian
Lianhehui 菲律濱華裔青年聯合會; United Daily News (Lianhe Ribao) 聯
合日報, 1991.

Kwantes, Anne Catherine Laninga. "Presbyterian Missionaries in the Philippines:
A Historical Analysis of Their Contributions to Social Change (1899–
1910)." PhD diss., University of the Philippines, 1988.

Labajo, Delilah R. "A Historical Survey of Reformative and Dissident
Religious Movement in Cebu: 1900–1990." MA thesis, University of San
Carlos, 2002.

Norbeck, Mark Douglas. "The Protestant Episcopal Church in the City of
Manila, Philippine Islands from 1898–1918: An Institutional History." MA
thesis, The University of Texas at El Paso, 1992.

Pascual, Pascual Emelio S. "Presbyterian Protestantism in Cebu: A Historical
Study, 1902–1938." MA thesis, University of San Carlos, 1988.

Pe, Susan L. "The Dominican Ministry among the Chinese in the *Parian*, Baybay
and Binondo: 1587–1637." MA thesis, Ateneo de Manila University, 1983.

Pinto, Sonia L. "The *Parian*, 1581–1762." MA thesis, Ateneo de Manila
University, 1964.

Po, Wanda Liam Giok. "A Philosophical Analysis of Filial Piety: An Integrated
Approach." EdD diss., Asia Graduate School of Theology, 1997.

Posey, Jesse Earl, Jr "A Historical Study of Baptist Missions in the Philippines
1900–1967." ThD dissertation, New Orleans Baptist Theological
Seminary, 1968.

Pradhan, Himlal. "The Protestant Churches and Their Contribution to the
Socio-Economic and Cultural Development of Cebu City, 1916–1988."
MA thesis, University of San Carlos, 1995.

Rambo, David Lloyd. "The Christian and Missionary Alliance in the Philippines,
1901–1970." PhD diss., New York University, 1975. Reprint, Ann Arbor,
MI: University Microfilms International, 1979.

Reynolds, Harriet R. "Continuity and Change in the Chinese Family in
the Ilocos Provinces, Philippines." PhD Diss., The Hartford Seminary
Foundation, 1964.

Sia, Vicente Y./Xie GuoZhi 謝國智. "Factors Affecting Church Growth in Selected Filipino-Chinese Churches." DMin diss., Dallas Theological Seminary, 2001.

Skivington, S. Robert. "Baptist Methods of Church Growth in the Philippines." MA thesis, Fuller Theological Seminary, 1970.

Weightman, George Henry. "The Philippine Chinese: A Cultural History of a Marginal Trading Community." PhD diss., Cornell University, 1960.

Uy, Bi Chin Y./Huang Yao MeiZhen 黃姚美真. "Chinese Education in Philippine Society: An Analysis of Its Structure and Implications." EdD diss., Philippine Women's University, 1969.

Yang, Bill T. C./Yang DongChuan 楊東川 (a.k.a. William Young). "The Chinese Protestant Churches in the Philippines." PhD diss., University of Santo Tomas, 1980.

Young, Joseph/Yang QiYao 楊其耀. "A Survey of the Overseas Chinese in the Philippines with a Suggested Program of Evangelism for the Chinese United Evangelical Church." MA thesis, Columbia Bible College, 1958.

French and Spanish Sources

Alcantara y Antonio, Teresita. *Views on Philippine Revolution*. Vol. 1 and 2. Edited by Lydia Arcella. Quezon City: Teresita Antonio Alcantara Pub., 2002.

A collection of seven works translated from Spanish by a team of UP professors led by Teresita Alcantara y Antonio: *Decrees by the General Government of the Philippines* (1896), translated by Felina G. Mapa; *Philippine Campaign: General Blanco and the Insurrection* (1897) by Filipe Trigo, translated by Edgardo M. Tiamson; *The Philippine Insurrection: The Four Truths by Javier Borres y Romero* ((1897), translated by Rosa Maria M. Icagsi; *The Origins and Causes of the Philippine Revolution* (1899) by Juan Alvarez Guerra, translated by Teresita Alcantara y Antonio; *The Religion of the Katipunan or The Old Beliefs of the Filipinos* (1901) by Isabelo de los Reyes, translated by Joseph Martin Yap; *The Capture of Manila* (1928) by Lt. Col. I.E.F. y S., translated by Pacita G. Fernandez; and *The Trial of the Thirteen Martyrs of Cavite* (1936) by Jose Nava, translated by Thaddeus L. Bautista.

Alencon, Ferdinand Philippe Marie d'Orleans, duc d' (Duke of Alencon). *Luçon et Mindanao. Extraits d'un journal de voyage dans l'Extrême Orient* (Luzon and Mindanao. Translated by E. Aguilar Cruz. Paris: *Michel Lévy frères*, 1870. Reprint, Manila: National Historical Institute, 1986.

Algué, P. José, S. J., *Atlas de Filipinas: Collecion de 30 Mapas. Trabajados por delineantes Filipinos bajo la direccion del P. José Algué, S. J. Director del Observatorio de Manila, 1899.* Washington DC: Government Printing Office, 1900.

Alvarez y Tejero, Don Luis Prudencio. *De las Islas Filipinas. Memoria* (Memoirs of the Philippine Islands). Translated by Lourdes R. Arespacochaga. Valencia: *Imprenta de Carerizo*, 1842. Reprint, Manila: National Historical Institute, 1998.

Chirino, Pedro, S.J. *Relacion de las Islas Filipinas i de lo que en ellas [h]an trabajado[s] los padres de la compaña de Iesus* (The Philippines in 1600). Translated by Ramon Echevarria. Historical Conservation Society 15. Roma: *Por Estevan Paulino*, 1604. Reprint, Manila: Historical Conservation Society, 1969.

Cobo, Juan, O. P. *Pien Cheng-chiao Chen-ch'uan Shih-Lu. Apologia de la Verdadera Religion. Testimony of the True Religion.* Edited by Fidel Villarroel. Manila: n.p., 1593. Reprint, Manila: UST Press, 1986.

Comenge y Dalmau, Rafael. *Cuestiones Filipinas 1a Parte Los Chinos (Estudio Social Y Politico)* [Philippine questions: Part 1, the Chinese (social and political studies)]. Manila: Tipo-litografia de Chofre y Comp., 1894.

de Comyn, Tomas. *Estado de las islas Filipinas en 1810* (State of the Philippines in 1810: Being an Historical, Statistical, and Descriptive Account of the Interesting Portion of the Indian Archipelago). Translated by William Walton. Filipiniana Book Guild, 15. Madrid: *Imprenta de Repulles*, 1820. Reprint, Manila: Filipiniana Book Guild, 1969.

de Morga, Antonio. *Sucesos De Las Islas Filipinas* (Events in the Philippine Islands). Translated by J. S. Cummins. Mexico: Shop of Geronymo Balli, 1609. Reprint, Cambridge: Cambridge University Press for the Hakluyt Society, 1972.

de San Agustin, Fray Gaspar. *Conquista de las islas Filipinas.* Madrid: Imprenta de Manuel Ruiz de Murga, 1698.

de Togores y Saravia, Jose Roca. *Bloquco y sitio de Manila en 1898* (Blockade and Siege of Manila in 1898). Huesa: L. Perez Printing Press, 1908. Reprint, Manila: National Historical Institute, 2002.

Díaz Arenas, Rafael. *Memoria sobre el comercio y navegacion de las islas Filipinas* (Report on the Commerce and Shipping of the Philippine Islands). Translated by Encarnacion Alzona. Cadiz: *Imprenta de Domingo Féros*, 1838. Reprint, Manila: National Historical Institute, 1979.

———. *Memorias históricas y estadísticas de Filipinas y particularmente de la grande isla de Luzon.* [Manila]: *Imprenta del Diario de Manila*, 1850.

Lannoy, Pierre Joseph. *Les îles Philippines. De leur situation ancienne et actuelle. Population, mœurs, administration, législation, commerce, industrie, agriculture, finances, force militaire, marine coloniale, clergé, etc.* (The Philippine Islands: Of Their Condition in Ancient Times and at Present). Brussels: *Impr. de Delevingne et Callewaert*, 1849. Reprint, Manila: National Historical Institute, 2003.

Los Chinos en Filipinas (The Chinese in the Philippines). *Males que se experimentan actualmente y peligros de esa creciente inmigracion. Observaciones, hechos y cifras que se encuentran en articulos que* "La Oceanía Española," *periodico de Manila, ha dedicado al estudio de este problema social.* Manila, Establecimiento tipografico de La Oceanía Española, 1886.

Mallat, Jean. *Les Philippines: histoire, géographie, mœurs, agriculture, industrie, et commerce des colonies espagnoles dans l'Océanie* (The Philippines: History, Geography, Customs, Agriculture, Industry and Commerce of the Spanish Colonies to Oceania). Translated by Pura Santillan-Castrence and Lina S. Castrence. Edited by Arthus Bertrand. Paris: *Librarie de la Societe de Geographie*, 1846. Reprint, Manila: National Historical Institute, 1983.

Martinez de Zuñiga, Joaquin, O. S. A. *Estadismo de las Islas Filipinas ó Mis Viajes por Este País. Publica esta obra por primera vez extensamente anotada W. E. Retana* (Status of the Philippines in 1800). Translated by Vicente del Carmen. Filipiniana Book Guild, 21. Madrid: *Imprenta de la viuda de M. Minuesa de lor Ríos*, 1893. Reprint, Manila: Filipiniana Book Guild, 1973.

Domingo Fernandez Navarrete. *Tratados historicos, politicos, ethicos, y religiosos de la monarchia de China* (An Account of the Empire of China, also Many Remarkable Messages and Things Worth Observing in Other Coasts in several Voyages. Madrid: Imprenta Real, 1676, quoted in *Census of the Philippine Islands Taken Under the Direction of the Philippine Commission in the Year 1903, Vol. 1: Geography, History, and Population*. Washington, DC: United States Bureau of the Census, 1905.

Pastells, Pablo, S. J. *Misión de la Compañía de Jesus de Filipinas en el Siglo XIX*. (Vol. 1, Mission to Mindanao 1859–1900). Translated by Peter Schreurs, MSC. Barcelona: Tipo-litografia Y Lib. Editorial Barcelonesa, 1916. Reprint, Cebu City: San Carlos Publications, 1994.

———. *Mission to Mindanao 1859–1900*. Vol. 2. Translated by Peter Schreurs, MSC. Quezon City: Claretian Publications, 1998.

———. *Mission to Mindanao 1859–1900*. Vol. 3. Translated by Peter Schreurs, MSC. Quezon City: Claretian Publications, 1998.

Chinese Sources

I. Anniversary Publications

Arise, Shine: United Evangelical Church of the Philippines 70th Anniversary (Xingqi Faguang—Feilübin Zhonghua Jidu Jiaohui Qishi Zhounian Tekan 1929–1999) 興起發光— 菲律賓中華基督教會七十週年特刊 *1929-1999*. Manila: United Evangelical Church of the Philippines, [1999].

Baguio Chinese Baptist Church/Biyao Huaren Jinxinhui 碧瑤華人浸信會. *Blueprints BCBC 1950–2000*. Baguio City: Baguio Chinese Baptist Church, 2000.

"Benhui Huiyou Shouxi Guizhu Nianbiao 本會會友受洗歸主年表 (List of baptized members)." In *Davao Evangelical Church Twentieth Anniversary Special Publication (Namao Jidu Jiaohui Ershi Zhounian Tekan)* 納卯基督教會二十週年特刊, 8. Davao City: Davao Evangelical Church, [1971].

Cai ZhiXin 蔡志信. "Shu Wu Hua Qiao Kai Shu 宿務華僑概述." In *Feilübin Shuwu Dongfang Zhongxue Jinqing Tekan* 菲律濱宿務東方中學金慶特刊 (Golden anniversary commemorative publication of the Cebu Eastern High School of the Philippines). Manila: Grace Trading, [1954].

Cebu Gospel Church Golden Jubilee Souvenir 1916–1966 (Suwu Jidu Jiaohui Jinxi Xiantang Anmu Qingdian Tekan) 宿務基督教會金禧獻堂按牧慶典特刊. Cebu City: Cebu Gospel Church, [1966].

Cebu Gospel Church Eightieth Anniversary Special Edition (Suwu Jidu Jiaohui Bashi Zhounian Xuanzuanxi Qingdian Tekan) 宿務基督教會八十週年選鑽禧慶典特刊. Cebu City: Cebu Gospel Church, 1996.

Chao, Augusto/Zhao ShiChang 趙士昌. "Shushuan Shen En 數算神恩 (Count God's blessings)." In *Davao Evangelical Church Fortieth Anniversary Special Publication (1951–1991) [Namao Jidu Jiaohui Sishi Zhounian Jinian Tekan (Yijiu Wuyinian—Yijiu Jiuyinian)]* 納卯基督教會四十週年紀念特刊〔一九五一年~一九九一年〕. Davao City: Davao Evangelical Church, [1991].

———. "Cong Namao dao Diji 從納卯到地極 (From Davao to the ends of the earth)." In *Davao Evangelical Church Fifty Years 1951–2001 (Namao Jidu Jiaohui)* 納卯基督教會, 38–39. Davao City: Davao Evangelical Church, [2001].

Chen, Job/Chen YueBo 陳約伯. "Jiushi Chongti 舊事重提 (Re-telling past events)." In *The Spring Sunshine: A Memoir of Elder Cang Chui Siok/ Chunhuiji – Huang Jian ShuiShu Zhanglao Jinian Ce*「春暉集」—黃江水淑長老紀念冊, 52. Caloocan City: Shangkuan Press and School Supply, n.d.

Chen, Livingstone/Chen YangSheng 陳仰聖. "Aijie 愛結 (Love bonds)." In *Davao Evangelical Church Fortieth Anniversary Special Publication (1951–1991) [Namao Jidu Jiaohui Sishi Zhounian Jinian Tekan (Yijiu Wuyinian – Yijiu Jiuyinian)]* 納卯基督教會四十週年紀念特刊〔一九五一年－一九九一年〕. Davao City: Davao Evangelical Church, [1991].

Cheng Ju/Zeng Yu 增瑜, "Cong Shuwu Jidu Jiaohui Qingzhu Jinxi Tandao Huaqiao Jidujiao Zai Nandao 從宿務基督教會慶祝金禧談到華僑基督教在南島 (Discussing the overseas Chinese Christians in Southern Philippines from the fiftieth anniversary celebration of Cebu Gospel Church)." In *Cebu Gospel Church Golden Jubilee Souvenir 1916–1966 (Suwu Jidu Jiaohui Jinxi Xiantang Anmu Qingdian Tekan)* 宿務基督教會金禧獻堂按牧慶典特刊, 20–22. Cebu City: Cebu Gospel Church, [1966].

———. "Jiushi Chongti 舊事重提 (Recalling the past)." In *Xushengyan Mushi Bainian Danchen Jiniankan* 許聲炎牧師百年誕辰紀念刊 (Commemorative publication of the centenary of the birth of Rev Kho Seng Iam), ed. John Pan 潘再恩, 72. N.p.: n.p., 1966.

Chhoa Kho Goat Hoa (a.k.a. Phoebe Kho-Chua)/Cai Xu YueHua 蔡許月華. "Shizhu Wushinian Jingguo 事主五十年經過 (Serving the Lord for fifty years)." In Chhoa Kho Goat Hoa, *Liushi Nian (Riji Yu Xuanwen)* 60 年 *(*日記與選文*) (*Sixty years – diary and selected articles), 8–9. Manila: by the author, 1980.

Chua, George Sin Chiong/Tsai Xinzhang 蔡信彰. "Boteli Budaotuan Yu Lüfei Zhonghua Jidu Jiaohui 伯特利佈道團與旅菲中華基督教會 (The Bethel Worldwide Evangelistic Band and the United Evangelical Church of Manila)." In *Historical Documentary of Protestantism in the Orient. 40th Anniversary of the United Evangelical Church of Manila (Feilübin Zhonghua Jidu Jiaohui Sishi Zhounian Lishi Wenxian Fu Yazhou Duoguo Jidu Jiaohui Lishi)* 菲律賓中華基督教會四十週年歷史文獻附亞洲多國基督教會歷史 *1929–1969*, 23 (pages in Chinese style). Manila: United Evangelical Church of Manila, 1969.

Chua, Homer/Cai WeiJie 蔡維潔. "Shangdi Gei Women Kandao de Yixiang 上帝給我們看到的異象 (The vision that God gave us)." In *BSOP 30th Foundation Anniversary (Feilübin Shengjing Shenxueyuan Shanshi Zhounian Tekan)* 菲律濱聖經神學院三十週年特刊, 8. Valenzuela City: Biblical Seminary of the Philippines, [1987].

"Chuen Shu Bu Jin – Benhui Ershi Nianlai Dashiji 主恩數不盡—本會二十年來大事記 (God's infinite grace – major events for the past twenty years)." In *Davao Evangelical Church Twentieth Anniversary Special Publication (Namao Jidu Jiaohui Ershi Zhounian Tekan)* 納卯基督教會二十週年特刊, 5–19. Davao City: Davao Evangelical Church, [1971].

Co, Henry See Cho/Xu ShuChu 許書楚. "Feilübin Shengjing Shenxueyuan Jianshi 菲律濱聖經神學院 簡史 (Brief history of the Biblical Seminary of the Philippines)." In *BSOP 30th Foundation Anniversary (Feilübin Shengjing Shenxueyuan Shanshi Zhounian Tekan)* 菲律濱聖經神學院三十週年特刊, 10–11. Valenzuela City: Biblical Seminary of the Philippines, [1987].

———. "Feishengshou Ershinian Shilue 菲聖首二十年史略 (The first twenty years of BSOP)." In *Biblical Seminary of the Philippines 45th Anniversary Special Edition (Feilübin Shengjing Shenxueyuan 45 Zhounian Yuanqing Tekan)* 菲律濱聖經神學院45週年院慶特刊, 14–21. Translated by Jean Uayan. Valenzuela City: Biblical Seminary of the Philippines, 2004.

Dagupan Chinese Baptist Church/Laguban Huaqiao Jinxinhui 拉古板華僑浸信會. *Christ Preeminent 50th Anniversary (Zhu Ju Shouwei)* 主居首位. Dagupan City: Dagupan Chinese Baptist Church, 2002.

Davao Evangelical Church Twentieth Anniversary Special Publication (Namao Jidu Jiaohui Ershi Zhounian Tekan) 納卯基督教會二十週年特刊. Davao City: Davao Evangelical Church, [1971].

Davao Evangelical Church Fortieth Anniversary Special Publication (1951–1991) [Namao Jidu Jiaohui Sishi Zhounian Jinian Tekan (Yijiu Wuyinian – Yijiu Jiuyinian)] 納卯基督教會四十週年紀念特刊〔一九五一年 - 一九九一年〕. Davao City: Davao Evangelical Church, [1991].

Davao Evangelical Church Fifty Years 1951–2001 (Namao Jidu Jiaohui) 納卯基督教會. Davao City: Davao Evangelical Church, [2001].

Diamond Jubilee: Sixtieth Anniversary Souvenir of the St. Stephen's Parish (Feilübin Huaqiao Shenggonghui Liushi Zhounian Jinian Tekan) 菲律賓華僑聖公會六十周年紀念特刊. Manila: St. Stephen's Parish, [1963].

Go, He/Wu ChangXi 吳長熙. "Benhui Xuandao ji Zaojiu Rencai de Yixiang 本會選道及造就人才的異象 (Our church's vision for mission and pastoral training)." In *Davao Evangelical Church Fortieth Anniversary Special Publication (1951–1991) [Namao Jidu Jiaohui Sishi Zhounian Jinian Tekan (Yijiu Wuyinian – Yijiu Jiuyinian)]* 納卯基督教會四十週年紀念特刊〔一九五一年 - 一九九一年〕. Davao City: Davao Evangelical Church, [1991].

Go Bun Peng/Wu WenBing 吳文炳. "Xiaoshi 校史 (School history)." In *Feilübin Suwu Jianji Chuji Zhongxue Diyi, Erjie Biye Tekan* 菲律賓宿務建基初級中學第一、二屆畢業特刊 (Commemorating the First and Second High School Graduation of the Philippine Cebu Kian Kee High School). Cebu City: Cebu Kian Kee High School, 1958.

Go Pang Kong/Wu BangGuang 吳邦光. "Shuwu Chuqi De Jidu Jiaohui 宿務初期的基督教會 (The early Christian Church in Cebu)." In *Cebu Gospel Church Golden Jubilee Souvenir 1916–1966 (Suwu Jidu Jiaohui Jinxi*

Xiantang Anmu Qingdian Tekan) 宿務基督教會金禧獻堂按牧慶典特刊, 59–60. Cebu City: Cebu Gospel Church, [1966].

Golden Jubilee Almanac 1929–1979 (Feilübin Zhonghua Jidu Jiaohui Jinxi Nianjian) 菲律賓中華基督教會金禧年鑑, ed. by S[hih] C[hang] Shangkuan. Manila: United Evangelical Church of the Philippines, [1979].

Hao, Pedro/Hou JunNan 侯均南, "Laguban Huaqiao Jinxinhui Huishi 拉古扳華僑浸信會會史 (History of the Dagupan Chinese Baptist Church)." In Dagupan Chinese Baptist Church/Laguban Huaqiao Jinxinhui 拉古板華僑浸信會. *Christ Preeminent 50th Anniversary (Zhu Ju Shouwei)* 主居首位. Dagupan City: Dagupan Chinese Baptist Church, 2002.

Historical Documentary of Protestantism in the Orient. 40th Anniversary of the United Evangelical Church of Manila (Feilübin Zhonghua Jidu Jiaohui Sishi Zhounian Lishi Wenxian Fu Yazhou Duoguo Jidu Jiaohui Lishi 1929–1969) 菲律賓中華基督教會四十週年歷史文獻附亞洲多國基督教會歷史 *1929–1969*. Manila: United Evangelical Church of Manila, 1969.

"Jiemei Tuanqi Jianjie 姐妹團契間介 (Short introduction of the Sisters' Fellowship)." In *Davao Evangelical Church Twentieth Anniversary Special Publication (Namao Jidu Jiaohui Ershi Zhounian Tekan)* 納卯基督教會二十週年特刊, 43–44. Davao City: Davao Evangelical Church, [1971].

Keng Lin Kiat/Gong RenJie 龔人傑. "Chuchuang Jianshi 初創簡史 (A short history of the initial formation)." In *Historical Documentary of Protestantism in the Orient. 40th Anniversary of the United Evangelical Church of Manila (Feilübin Zhonghua Jidu Jiaohui Sishi Zhounian Lishi Wenxian Fu Yazhou Duoguo Jidu Jiaohui Lishi)* 菲律賓中華基督教會四十週年歷史文獻附亞洲多國基督教會歷史 *1929–1969*, 1 (pages in Chinese style). Manila: United Evangelical Church of Manila, 1969.

———. "Benhui Da Shiji 本會大事記 (Main events of the Church)." In *Lüfei Zhonghua Jidu Jiaohui Chengli Jinian Tekan* 旅菲中華基督教會成立紀念特刊 (Special commemorative publication of the founding of the Chinese United Evangelical Church). Manila: Chinese United Evangelical Church, n.d.

———. "A Stormy Night." In *Historical Documentary of Protestantism in the Orient. 40th Anniversary of the United Evangelical Church of Manila (Feilübin Zhonghua Jidu Jiaohui Sishi Zhounian Lishi Wenxian Fu Yazhou Duoguo Jidu Jiaohui Lishi)* 菲律賓中華基督教會四十週年歷史文獻附亞洲多國基督教會歷史 *1929–1969*, 239 (pages in Chinese style). Manila: United Evangelical Church of Manila, 1969.

Kho Goat Hoa (a.k.a. Phoebe Kho-Chua)/Xu YueHua 許月華. "Siyuan 思源 (Pondering on origins)." In *Xushengyan Mushi Bainian Danchen Jiniankan* 許聲炎牧師百年誕辰紀念刊 (Commemorative publication of the centenary of the birth of Rev Kho Seng Iam), ed. John Pan 潘再恩, 107–108. N.p.: n.p., 1966.

Kho Ju Soat/Xu YuXue 許逾雪. "Yehehua Yile – Chuqi De Jiaohui 耶和華以勒—初期的教會 (Jehovah Jireh – The Early Church)." In *Historical Documentary of Protestantism in the Orient. 40th Anniversary of the United Evangelical Church of Manila (Feilübin Zhonghua Jidu Jiaohui Sishi Zhounian Lishi Wenxian Fu Yazhou Duoguo Jidu Jiaohui Lishi)* 菲律賓中華基督教會四十週年歷史文獻附亞洲多國基督教會歷史 *1929–1969*, 16 (pages in Chinese style). Manila: United Evangelical Church of Manila, 1969.

Kho Seng Iam/Xu ShengYan 許聲炎. "Lüfei Zhonghua Jidu Jiaohui Chengli Xuanyan 旅菲中華基督教會成立宣言 (Declaration of the Founding of the Chinese Church of Christ Sojourning in the Philippines)." In *Lüfei Zhonghua Jidu Jiaohui Chengli Jinian Tekan* 旅菲中華基督教會成立紀念特刊 (Special commemorative publication of the founding of the Chinese United Evangelical Church). Manila: Chinese United Evangelical Church, n.d.

Kho Siu Lim/Xu XiuLin 許秀琳. "Daminshi Yiwai – Lüsong Quandao Huaqiao Jiaohui Lueshi 大岷市以外—呂宋全島華僑教會略史 (Beyond Metro Manila: historical sketch of overseas Chinese churches in Luzon Island)." In *Historical Documentary of Protestantism in the Orient. 40th Anniversary of the United Evangelical Church of Manila (Feilübin Zhonghua Jidu Jiaohui Sishi Zhounian Lishi Wenxian Fu Yazhou Duoguo Jidu Jiaohui Lishi 1929–1969)* 菲律賓中華基督教會四十週年歷史文獻附亞洲多國基督教會歷史 *1929–1969*, 147–150 (pages in Chinese style). Manila: United Evangelical Church of Manila, 1969.

Leung Sai Ko 梁細羔. "Puren Zhiyan 『僕人之言』." In (*Zaojiu Liangyan*) 造就良言 (Edifying words), Appendix: *Liang XiGao Mushi Ganen Jinian Tekan* 梁細羔牧師感恩紀念特刊, ed. Liang ShenWei 梁慎微, 22–27. Cebu City: Cebu Gospel Church, 1979.

Lim, Bona/Lin LianZhu 林蓮珠, "Ershi Nianlai Zhurixue Shigong De Fazhan 二十年來主日學事工的進展 (The progress of Sunday School ministry these past twenty years)." In *Davao Evangelical Church Twentieth Anniversary Special Publication (Namao Jidu Jiaohui Ershi Zhounian Tekan)* 納卯基督教會二十週年特刊. Davao City: Davao Evangelical Church, [1971].

Lim Duy Un Hong/Lin Rui YunFang 林雷韻芳, "Huiyi Zhongchuqi De Namao Jidu Jiaohui 回憶中初期的納卯基督教會 (Recalling Davao Evangelical Church during the early and middle periods)." In *Davao Evangelical Church Twentieth Anniversary Special Publication (Namao Jidu Jiaohui Ershi Zhounian Tekan)* 納卯基督教會二十週年特刊, 66. Davao City: Davao Evangelical Church, [1971].

"List of Church Members and Their Dates of Baptism." In *Cebu Gospel Church Golden Jubilee Souvenir 1916–1966 (Suwu Jidu Jiaohui Jinxi Xiantang Anmu Qingdian Tekan)* 宿務基督教會金禧獻堂按牧慶典特刊, 74–75. Cebu City: Cebu Gospel Church, [1966].

Lüfei Zhonghua Jidu Jiaohui Chengli Jinian Tekan 旅菲中華基督教會成立 紀念特刊 (Special commemorative publication of the founding of the Chinese United Evangelical Church). Manila: Chinese United Evangelical Church, n.d.

Ng Hui Tsu/Huang HuiCi 黃惠慈. "Benxiao Xuesheng Zongjiao Xiuyang Yu Jiaoyu 本校學生宗教修養與教育 (Religious Education and Nurture in Our School Children)." In *Feilübin Suwu Jianji Chuji Zhongxue Diyi, Erjie Biye Tekan* 菲律賓宿務建基初級中學第一、二屆畢業特刊 (Commemorating the First and Second High School Graduation of the Philippine Cebu Christian School). Cebu City: Cebu Kian Kee High School, 1958.

Pan, John C.H./Pan ZhenHan 潘振漢. "Yijiulingshannian Souci Juhui – Feilübin Jidu Jiaohui Fayuan Shihua 一九〇三年首次聚會—菲律賓基督 教會發源史話 (First meeting in 1903: Historical beginnings of the Chinese Filipino Protestant churches)." In *Historical Documentary of Protestantism in the Orient. 40th Anniversary of the United Evangelical Church of Manila (Feilübin Zhonghua Jidu Jiaohui Sishi Zhounian Lishi Wenxian Fu Yazhou Duoguo Jidu Jiaohui Lishi 1929–1969)* 菲律賓中華基督教會四十週年 歷史文獻附亞洲多國基督教會歷史 *1929–1969*, 139 (pages in Chinese style). Manila: United Evangelical Church of Manila, 1969.

Pan, John C. H./Pan ZhenHan 潘振漢, ed. *The 70th Anniversary of the St. Stephen's Parish (Feilübin Huaqiao Shenggonghui Qishi Zhounian Jiniance)* 菲 律賓華僑聖公會七十週年紀念冊. Manila: St. Stephen's Parish Philippine Episcopal Church, [1973].

Proclaim God's Enduring Faithfulness 90th Anniversary (Xinshichang, Wuenyang) 信實長, 務恩揚. Cebu City: Cebu Gospel Church, 2006.

Que, Joseph/Guo YuXian 郭毓賢. "Benhui Wushi Nianlai Dashiji 本會五十 年來大事記 (The church's main events for the past fifty years)." In *Cebu Gospel Church Golden Jubilee Souvenir 1916–1966 (Suwu Jidu Jiaohui Jinxi Xiantang Anmu Qingdian Tekan)* 宿務基督教會金禧獻堂按牧慶典特刊, 39–54. Cebu City: Cebu Gospel Church, [1966].

Rong En 榮恩. "Feilübin Huaqiao Shenggonghui Biannian Jianshi 菲律賓華 僑聖公會編年簡史 (Short history of the Philippine Episcopal Church)." In *The 70th Anniversary of the St. Stephen's Parish (Feilübin Huaqiao Shenggonghui Qishi Zhounian Jiniance)* 菲律賓華僑聖公會七十週年紀念 冊. Edited by John C. H. Pan 潘振漢, 12–13. Manila: St. Stephen's Parish Philippine Episcopal Church, [1973].

Shangkuan, Shih Chang 上官世璋. "Benhui Sishi Zhounian Qingdianjian
Manila Huaqiao Jidu Jiaohui Jianshi 本會四十周年慶典前馬尼拉市華
僑基督教會簡史 (Pre-fortieth anniversary celebration: short history of
overseas Chinese Christian churches in Manila)." In *Historical Documentary
of Protestantism in the Orient. 40th Anniversary of the United Evangelical
Church of Manila (Feilübin Zhonghua Jidu Jiaohui Sishi Zhounian Lishi
Wenxian Fu Yazhou Duoguo Jidu Jiaohui Lishi 1929–1969)* 菲律賓中華
基督教會四十週年歷史文獻附亞洲多國基督教會歷史 *1929–1969*,
141–146 (pages in Chinese style). Manila: United Evangelical Church of
Manila, 1969.

———. "Xinyang Chunzheng Baochi Wei Difang Benshe Jiaohui – Feilübin
Nandao Huaqiao Jidu Jiaohui Shilue 信仰純正保持為地方本色教會—
菲律賓南島華僑基督教會史略 (Pure faith preserved in contextualized
local churches: History of overseas Chinese Christianity in the Southern
Philippines)." In *Feilübin Zhonghua Jidu Jiaohui Sishi Zhounian Lishi
Wenxian Fu Yazhou Duoguo Jidu Jiaohui Lishi* 菲律賓中華基督教會四
十週年歷史文獻附亞洲多國基督教會歷史 *Historical Documentary of
Protestantism in the Orient. 40th Anniversary of the United Evangelical Church
of Manila 1929–1969*, 151–154 (pages in Chinese style). Manila: United
Evangelical Church of Manila, 1969.

Shao, Wesley Kho/Shao QingZhang 邵慶彰. "Feilübin Zhonghua Jidu
Jiaohui Jianshi 菲律賓中華基督教會簡史 (A short history of the United
Evangelical Church of the Philippines)." In *Arise, Shine: 70th Anniversary
(Xingqi Faguang – Feilübin Zhonghua Jidu Jiaohui Qishi Zhounian Tekan
1929–1999)* 興起發光 – 菲律賓中華基督教會七十週年特刊 *1929–
1999*, 3–10. Manila: United Evangelical Church of the Philippines, [1999].

———. "Namao Jidu Jiaohui Chuqi Jianshi 納卯基督教會初期簡史 (Short
history of the early period of Davao Evangelical Church)." In *Davao
Evangelical Church Twentieth Anniversary Special Publication (Namao Jidu
Jiaohui Ershi Zhounian Tekan)* 納卯基督教會二十週年特刊, 20–21.
Davao City: Davao Evangelical Church, [1971].

———. "Namao Jidu Jiaohui Zhi Huigu 納卯基督教會之回顧 (Remembering
Davao Evangelical Church)." In *Davao Evangelical Church Fortieth
Anniversary Special Publication (1951–1991) [Namao Jidu Jiaohui Sishi
Zhounian Jinian Tekan (Yijiu Wuyinian—Yijiu Jiuyinian)]* 納卯基督教會
四十週年紀念特刊〔一九五一年~一九九一年〕. Davao City: Davao
Evangelical Church, [1991].

———. "Namao Jidujiao Xiaoxue Jianli Jianshi 納卯基督教小學建立簡史 (A
brief history of the establishment of Davao Christian Elementary School)."
In *Davao Evangelical Church Twentieth Anniversary Special Publication*

(*Namao Jidu Jiaohui Ershi Zhounian Tekan*) 納卯基督教會二十週年特刊,
22–23. Davao City: Davao Evangelical Church, [1971].

Shi Feng. "Feiguo Dier Da Doushi – Su Wu 菲國第二大都市—宿務." In
Feilübin Suwu Dongfang Zhongxue Jinqing Tekan 菲律濱宿務東方中學
金慶特刊 (Golden anniversary commemorative publication of the Cebu
Eastern High School of the Philippines). Manila: Grace Trading, [1954].

Siao Muy Tie/Siao MeiZhi 蕭梅治. "Suwu Jidu Jiaohui Bashi Nianlai Huihu
宿務基督教會八十年來回溯 (Reminiscing the past eighty years of Cebu
Gospel Church." In *Cebu Gospel Church Eightieth Anniversary Special Edition*
(*Suwu Jidu Jiaohui Bashi Zhounian Zuanxi Qingdian Tekan*) 宿務基督教會
八十週年鑽禧慶典特刊, 6–8. Cebu City: Cebu Gospel Church, 1996.

St. Stephen's Church Episcopal Golden Jubilee Souvenir 1903–1953 (*Huaqiao
Shenggonghui Wushi Zhounian Jiniankan*) 華僑聖公會五十周年紀念刊.
Manila: St. Stephen's Parish, [1953].

"*Suwu Dongfang Xueyuan Xiaoshi* 宿務東方學院校史 (History of Cebu Eastern
College)." In *Feilübin Su Wu Dongfang Xueyuan Chuangli Qishiwu Zhounian
Jinian Tekan 1915–1990* 菲律濱宿務東方學院創立七十五週年紀念特
刊 *1915–1990* (Cebu Eastern College diamond anniversary commemorative
publication 1915–1990). Cebu City: Cebu Eastern College, [1990].

Suwu Jianji Zhongxue Wushi Xueniandu Biye Jinian Kan 宿務建基中學五十
學年度畢業紀念刊 *Cebu Kian Kee High School Graduation Annual of
1961–1962*. Cebu City: Cebu Kian Kee High School, 1962.

*30th Anniversary Souvenir Magazine, Pearl 1939–1969 Jubilee (Naya Zhonghua
Jidu Jiaohui Chengli Sanshi Zhounian Jinian Tekan)* 哪呀中華基督教
會成立三十週年紀念特刊. Naga City: United Evangelical Church of
Naga, 1969.

Tiu[n] Chin Tsong/Zhang ZhenZong 張振宗. "Shuwu Jidu Jiaohui Wushi
Nianlai Jianshi Zheyao 宿務基督教會五十年來簡史摘要 (Summary
of the history of Cebu Gospel Church for the past fifty years)." In *Cebu
Gospel Church Golden Jubilee Souvenir 1916–1966* (*Suwu Jidu Jiaohui Jinxi
Xiantang Anmu Qingdian Tekan*) 宿務基督教會金禧獻堂按牧慶典特刊,
55–58. Cebu City: Cebu Gospel Church, [1966].

Tiu[n] Toan Tsong/Zhang DuanZhuang 張端莊, "Zaoqi De Shuwu Jiaohui 早
期的宿務教會 (The early period of the Cebu Church)." In *Cebu Gospel
Church Golden Jubilee Souvenir 1916–1966* (*Suwu Jidu Jiaohui Jinxi
Xiantang Anmu Qingdian Tekan*) 宿務基督教會金禧獻堂按牧慶典特刊,
60. Cebu City: Cebu Gospel Church, [1966].

Uy, Valentin 黃根源. "Meng Zhuen Shenhou De Suwu Jidu Jiaohui 蒙主恩
深厚的宿務基督教會 (Cebu Gospel Church: richly blessed by God)."
In *Proclaim God's Enduring Faithfulness 90th Anniversary (Xinshichang,
Wuenyang)* 信實長, 務恩揚, 16. Cebu City: Cebu Gospel Church, 2006.

Uyboco, Prudencio S. "The Only Foundation." In *Davao Evangelical Church Fortieth Anniversary Special Publication (1951–1991) [Namao Jidu Jiaohui Sishi Zhounian Jinian Tekan (Yijiu Wuyinian – Yijiu Jiuyinian)]* 納卯基督教會四十週年紀念特刊〔一九五一年--一九九一年〕. Davao City: Davao Evangelical Church, [1991].

Wang FuMin 王福民. *Tingjingbo Xiansheng Xingshu* 丁景波先生行述 (Eulogy for Mr Ting Keng Po). Manila, 3 December 1970.

Wong, Silas/Huang YuanSu 黃原素. "Wo Zai Feidao De Gongzuo yu Shenghuo 我在菲島的工作與生活 (My life and ministry in the Philippines)." In *Golden Jubilee Almanac (Feilübin Zhonghua Jidu Jiaohui Jinxi Nianjian 1929–1979)* 菲律賓中華基督教會金禧年鑑 *1929–1979*. Edited by S[hih] C[hang] Shangkuan, 17–19 (pages in Chinese style). Manila: United Evangelical Church of the Philippines, [1979].

Wu WenBing 吳文炳. "Sishi Nianqian Su Wu Qiaojiao De Qingkuang 四十年前宿務僑教的情況 (Educational conditions in Cebu forty years ago)." In *Feilübin Su Wu Dongfang Zhongxue Jinqing Tekan* 菲律濱宿務東方中學金禧大慶特刊. Manila: Grace Trading, [1954].

"Xiaoshi 校史 (1915-1975) (School History, 1915–1975)." In *Feilübin Suwu Dongfang Xueyuan Chuangxiao Liushi Zhounian Jinian Tekan* 菲律濱宿務東方學院創校六十週年紀念特刊 (Cebu Eastern College sixtieth anniversary commemorative publication) *1915–1975*. Cebu City: Cebu Eastern College, n.d.

Xin Jie Chapel Elders and Deacons Committee 新街堂長執會編, ed. *Xiamenshi Jidujiao Xinjietang Jiantang 150 Zhounian (1848–1998) Jinian Tekan* 廈門市基督教新街堂建堂*150*週年〔*1848–1998*〕紀念特刊 (The 150th founding anniversary of the Xinjie Christian Chapel of Xiamen City). Xiamen: Xiamenshi Jidujiao Xinjietang 廈門市基督教新街堂 (Xiamen City Xinjie Christian Chapel), 1998.

Xu ShengYan Mushi Bainian Danchen Jiniankan 許聲炎牧師百年誕辰紀念刊 (Commemorative publication of the centenary of the birth of Rev Kho Seng Iam), ed. John Pan 潘再恩. Manila: n.p., 1966.

"Xu ShengYan Mushi Xingzhuan Zhangmushi 許聲炎牧師行傳章目詩 (The Life of Rev Kho Seng Iam set as epic hymn)." In *Xu ShengYan Mushi Bainian Danchen Jiniankan* 許聲炎牧師百年誕辰紀念刊 (Commemorative publication of the centenary of the birth of Rev Kho Seng Iam), ed. John Pan 潘再恩, 28–30. Manila: n.p., 1966.

Xu Zhanglao YuXue Xiaozhang Jiniance Fu Zhurixue Yuxuelou Fengxianli 許長老逾雪校長紀念冊副主日學逾雪樓奉獻禮 (Memorial book of Elder/Principal Xu YuXue with dedication ceremony of the Ju Soat Sunday School building). Manila: Westminster Student Church Literature Committee, 1983.

Ye MingChang 葉明昌. "Daibiao Shangjia Zhici 代表喪家致詞 (Eulogy from
    Bereaved Family)." In *The Spring Sunshine: A Memoir of Elder Cang Chui
    Siok/Chunhuiji – Huang Jian ShuiShu Zhanglao Jinian Ce*「春暉集」– 黃
    江水淑長老紀念冊, 94–97. Caloocan City: Shangkuan Press and School
    Supply, n.d.

"Yi Ai Ren Jian 遺愛人間 (Bequeathing Love among Men)." In *Yude Muxiao
    Baizhounian Jiniankan* 毓德母校百週年紀念刊 (*Commemorative
    publication of the centennial anniversary of alma mater Iok Tek*), 16–17.
    Manila: Lüfei Yude Xiaoyouhui 旅菲毓德校友會 (Philippine Iok Tek
    Alumni Association), [1970].

"Yude Muxiao Chuangli Bainian De Huigu 毓德母校創立百年的回顧
    (Reminiscing during the centennial of alma mater Iok Tek)." In *Yude
    Muxiao Baizhounian Jiniankan* 毓德母校百週年紀念刊 (*Commemorative
    publication of the centennial anniversary of alma mater Iok Tek*), 1–2. Manila:
    Philippine Iok Tek Alumnae, 1970.

Zhu Shu Chapel Elders and Deacons Committee 竹樹堂會長執會編, ed.
    *Xiamenshi Jidujiao Zhushutanghui Jiantang Lihui 150 Zhounian (1850–
    2000) Jinianche* 廈門市基督教竹樹堂會建堂立會150週年〔1850–2000
    〕紀念冊 (The 150th founding anniversary of the Zhushu Christian Chapel
    of Xiamen City). Xiamen: Xiamenshi Jidujiao Zhushutang 廈門市基督教
    竹樹堂 (Xiamen Zhushu Christian Chapel), 2000.

II. Books

Cao ShengJie 曹聖潔, "Zili Yundong yu Benshehua 自立運動與本色化 (The
    movement of self-rule and contextualization)." In *Qianshi Buwang Houshi
    Zhi Shi: Diguo Zhuyi Liyong Jidujiao Qinlue Zhongguo Shishi Shuping* 前事
    不望後事之師: 帝國主義利用基督教侵略中國史實述評 (Forget not
    the past, teacher of the future – a historical evaluation of the imperialist
    invasion of China through Christianity), ed. Luo GuanZong 羅冠宗, 136–
    179. Beijing 北京: Zongjiao Wenhua Chubanshe 宗教文化出版社, 2003.

Chao, Jonathan/Zhao TianEn 趙天恩 and Rosanna Chong/Zhuang WanFang
    莊婉芳. *Dangdai Zhongguo Jiddujiao Fazhanshi* 當代中國基督教發展史
    (A History of Christianity in Socialist China) 1949–1997. Edited by Amos
    Wang/Wang RuiZhen 王瑞珍 and Susanna Chen/Chen Yu 陳漁. Taipei:
    CMI Publishing, 1997.

Chen JingHe 陳荊和. *Shiliu Shiji Zhi Feilübin Huaqiao* 十六世紀之菲律濱
    華僑 / Chen Ching-ho. *The Overseas Chinese in the Philippines during the
    Sixteenth Century.* Monograph Series 2. Hong Kong: Southeast Asia Studies
    Section, New Asia Research Institute, 1963.

Chen LieFu 陳烈甫. *Dongnan Yazhou de Huaqiao, Huaren yu Huayi* 東南亞洲的華僑, 華人與華裔 (Huaqiao, huaren and huayi of Southeast Asia). Taipei: Zhengzhong Shuju 正中書局, 1979.

———. *Feilübin yu Zhonghua Guanxi* 菲律濱與中華關係 (Relationship between the Philippines and China). Hong Kong: Nanyang Yanjiu Chubanshe 南洋研就出版社, 1955.

Chen TaiMin 陳台民. *Zhongfei Guanxi yu Feilübin Huaqiao* 中菲關係與菲律濱華僑 (Sino-Philippine relations and the Philippine Chinese). Hong Kong: Chao Yang Chubanshe 朝陽出版社, 1985. Originally published as two volumes in 1961.

Chen YanDe 陳衍德. *Xiandaizhong de Chuantong – Feilübin Huaren Shehui Yanjiu* 現代中的傳統—菲律濱華人社會研究 (Tradition in modern times: a study on Philippine Chinese society). Xiamen, Fujian 福建廈門: Xiamen Daxue Chubanshe 廈門大學出版社 (Xiamen University Press), 1998.

Chen ZhiPing 陳支平, ed. *Fujian Zongjiao Shi* 福建宗教史 (Religious history of Fujian). Fuzhou, Fujian 福建福州: Fujian Jiaoyu Chubanshe 福建教育出版社 (Fujian Educational Publishing), 1996.

Chen ZhiPing 陳支平 and Li ShaoMing 李少明. *Jidujiao yu Fujian Minjian Shehui* 基督教與福建民間社會 (Christianity and the folk community of Fujian). Xiamen, Fujian 福建廈門: Xiamen Daxue Chubanshe 廈門大學出版社 (Xiamen University Press), 1992.

Chow, YiFu 周億孚. *Jidujiao yu Zhongguo* 基督教與中國 (Christianity and China). Hong Kong: The Council on Christian Literature for overseas Chinese (Jidujiao Fuqiao Chubanshe) 基督教輔僑出版社, 1965.

Fan FengJuan 潘鳳娟. *Xi Lai Kong Zi Ai Ru Lue—Geng Xin Bian Hua De Zhong Jiao Hui Yu* 西來孔子艾儒略—更新變化的宗教會遇 (Confucius from the west: Giulio Aleni (1582-1649) and the religious encounter between the Jesuits and the Chinese). Taipei: Christian Olive Foundation, Scripture Resource Center, 2002.

Fujian Archival Committee 福建省黨案舘編, ed. *Fujian Huaqiao Dangan Shiliao* (*Shang*) 福建華僑黨案史料 （上） (Historical archives of overseas Chinese from Fujian, Part 1). Fujian 福建: Dangan Chubanshe 黨案出版社, 1990.

Gao Zhuru 高祖儒. *Huashang Tuozhi Feidao Shilue* 華商拓殖菲島史略 (History of Chinese business ventures in the Philippine Islands). Manila: by the author, 1969.

Go Bon Juan/Wu WenHuan 吳文煥. *Guanyi Huaren Jingji Qiyi de Shenhua* 關於華人經濟奇跡的神話 (Myths about the ethnic Chinese "Economic Miracle"). Translated by Joaquin Sy 施華謹譯. Manila: Kaisa Para Sa

Kaunlaran, Feilübin Huayi Qingnian Lianhehui 菲律濱華裔青年聯合會, 1996.

———. *Suwu Huaren de Jingji – Shehui Shi (Fu: Cong Tangye Kan Feilübin Huaren)* 宿務華人的經濟—社會史〔附：從糖業看菲律濱華人〕(A social history of the economy of the Chinese in Cebu/Chinese in the Philippines from the perspective of the sugar industry). Manila: Kaisa Para Sa Kaunlaran, Feilübin Huayi Qingnian Lianhehui 菲律賓華裔青年聯合會, 2004.

———, ed. *Huafei Ziku Shi Yijia: Feiren Yu Huananren Yuanyuan Zhiliao Huibian* 華菲自古是一家：菲人與華南人淵源質料匯編 (One family since ancient times). Manila: Kaisa Para Sa Kaunlaran, Feilübin Huayi Qingnian Lianhehui 菲律賓華裔青年聯合會, 2002.

Go Bon Juan/Wu WenHuan 吳文煥 and Teresita Ang See/Shi Hong YuHua 施洪玉華, eds. *Heritage: A Pictorial History of the Chinese in the Philippines (Wenhua Chuantong – Feihua Lishi Tupian)* 文化傳統—菲華歷史圖片. Manila: Kaisa Para Sa Kaunlaran 菲律賓華裔青年聯合會 and Professor Chinben See Memorial Trust Fund 紀念施振民教授獎學金基金會, 1987.

Go Bon Juan/Wu WenHuan 吳文煥 and Wang PeiYuan 王培元編, eds. *Jinian Paihuafa Yibai Zhounian (Fu Huagong Xielei Xiaoshuo《Kushehui》)* 紀念排華法一百週年〔附華工血淚小說《苦社會》(Commemorating the centennial of the Chinese Exclusion Acts with "Bitter Society," a novel about Chinese workers in America). Manila: Kaisa Para Sa Kaunlaran, Feilübin Huayi Qingnian Lianhehui 菲律濱華裔青年聯合會, 2002.

Haiwai Huaren Yanjiu de Dashiye Yu Xinfangxiang: Wang GengWu Jiaoshou Lunwenxuan 海外華人研究的大視野與新方向—王賡武教授論文選 (Bigger vision and new direction in studying overseas Chinese – the Collected works of Professor Wang GengWu). Edited by Liu Hong 劉宏 and Huang JianLi 黃堅立. River Edge, NJ: Bafang Wenhua Qiye Gongsi 八方文化企業公司 (Global Publishing), 2002.

Han ZhenHua 韓振華. *Zhufanzhi Zhubu* 諸蕃志注補 (Supplement to *Zhufanzhi*). Hong Kong: Center of Asian Studies, The University of Hong Kong, 2000.

Hsiao Shi-Ching 蕭曦清. *Zhongfei Waijiao Guanxi Shi* 中菲外交關係史 *Chinese-Philippine Diplomatic Relations 1946–1975*. Quezon City: Bookman Printing, 1975.

———. *Zhongfei Huaqiao Guanxi Shi* 中菲華僑關係史 *History of Chinese-Philippine Relations*. 2nd ed. Quezon City: Bookman Printing, 1998.

Hsu, Princeton S. 徐松石, ed. *Huaren Jinxinhui Shilu* 華人浸信會史錄 (A history of Chinese Baptist churches). (Xianxian Chuanlue Diwuji) 先賢傳略第五輯. Biographies of Former Leaders 5. Hong Kong: Baptist Press, 1972.

Huang WenJiang 黃文江. *Kuawenhua Shiyexia de Jindai Zhongguo Jidujiaoshi Lunji* 跨文化視野下的近代中國基督教史論集 (Collected works on the trans-cultural vision of the modern history of Christianity in China). Taipei: Cosmic Light Holistic Care Organization, 2006.

Huang ZhiSheng 黃滋生. *Feihua Wenti Lunbian - Huang ZhiSheng Jiaoshou Lunwen Xuanpian* 菲華問題論辯—黃滋生教授論文選篇 (Essays on the Philippine-Chinese problem: Collected works of Professor Huang ZhiSheng). Translated by Go Bon Juan 吳文煥. Manila: Kaisa Para Sa Kaunlaran, Feilübin Huayi Qingnian Lianhehui 菲律賓華裔青年聯合會, 1999.

Huaqiao Huaren Baike Quanshu 華僑華人百科全書 Encyclopedia of Chinese Overseas. Twelve volumes. Beijing 北京: Zhongguo Huaqiao Chubanshe 中國華僑出版社 (Chinese Overseas Publishing), 1999.

Lee, Christopher Chun Kwan 李振群. *Toushi Liangqiannian. Juansi: Shenxue Shixiangshi, Zhongguo Jiaohuishi* 透視二千年. 券四: 神學思想史、中國教會史 (In these two thousand years. Volume 4: The history of Christian thought and the Chinese church). Malaysia: Partners Training Centre, 1999.

Leung Ka-lun/Liang JiaLin 梁家麟. *Huaren Xuandaohui Bainianshi* 華人宣導會百年史 (A centenary history of the Chinese C&MA). Hong Kong: Alliance Bible Seminary Christianity and Chinese Culture Research Centre, 1998.

Li JianAn 李健安. "Song Shangjie De Shuling Chuantong ji dui Huarenjiaohui De Gongxian yu Yingxiang 宋尚節的屬靈傳統及對華人教會的貢獻與影響 (The spiritual tradition of John Sung and his contribution and influence upon the Chinese churches)." In *Song ShangJie De Shenxue yu Shuling Guan* 宋尚節的神學與屬靈觀 (The theology and spiritual view of John Sung), (Masheng) Ziyan Zhongxin ZhuantiXilie 《馬聖》資研中心專題系列〈1〉 MBS Centre for Christianity and Malaysian Studies 1, 67–78. Malaysia: Malaysia Bible Seminary, 2002.

Li JinMing 李金明. *Xiamen Haiwai Jiaotong* 廈門海外交通 (Foreign relations of Xiamen). Xiamen Wenhua Congshu 廈門文化叢書 (The culture of Xiamen series). Xiamen 廈門: Lujiang Chubanshe 鷺江出版社, 1996.

Li MingAn 李明安. "Song Shangjie Yu Malaixiya Jiaohui Zhi Shigong Yu Yingxiang 宋尚節於馬來西亞教會之事工與影響 (The ministry and influence of John Sung in Malaysia)." In *Song ShangJie De Shenxue yu Shuling Guan* 宋尚節的神學與屬靈觀 (The theology and spiritual view of John Sung), (Masheng) Ziyan Zhongxin ZhuantiXilie 《馬聖》資研中心專題系列〈1〉 MBS Centre for Christianity and Malaysian Studies 1, 79–90. Malaysia: Malaysia Bible Seminary, 2002.

Li RongMei 李榮美. *Rongru Zhuliu Shehui: Feilübin Huayi Zuqun de Weiyi Xuanze* 溶入主流社會：菲律濱華裔族群的唯一選擇 (Integrating into the mainstream society: the only alternative for the Chinese descendants in the Philippines). Feihua Congshu 菲華叢書 (Philippine-Chinese Series), no. 11. Manila: Yuyitong Jijinhui 于以同基金會 (Yuyitong Foundation), 2001.

Li TianXi 李天錫. *Quanzhou Huaqiao Huaren Yanjiu* 泉州華僑華人研究 (A study of overseas Chinese from Quanzhou). Beijing 北京: Zhongyang Wenxian Chubanshe 中央文獻出版社, 2006.

Li WeiKan 李維幹. *Fujian Shigao* 福建史稿（上，下冊）(History of Xiamen, Vol. 1 and 2). Fujian 福建: Fujian Jiaoyu Chubanshe 福建教育出版社, 1985, 1986.

Liang YuanSheng 梁元生. "Panluanzhe: Jidujiao yu Taiping Tianguo 叛亂者：基督教與太平天國 (The rebel: Christianity and the Taiping heavenly kingdom)." In *Jidujiao yu Zhongguo* 基督教與中國 (Christianity and China). Malisun Ruhua Xuanjiao Erbainian Jinian Wenji – Lunwen 馬禮遜順入華宣教200年紀念文集—論文 (Collected essays in commemoration of the 200th year of Morrison's entry into China), 87–106. Taipei: 基督教宇宙光全人關懷機構 Cosmic Light Holistic Care Organization, 2006.

Lin ChaoCe 林朝策. "Tongan Tanghui Shilue 同安堂會史略 (Short history of Tongan Chapel)." In *Minnan Zhonghua Jidu Jiaohui Jianshi* 閩南中華基督教會簡史 (Short history of Minnan Christian Church of China), vol. 4, *Xiamenqi Jiuguizheng Gonghui Getanghui Jianshi* 廈門區舊歸正公會各堂會簡史, ed. Xu ShengYan 許聲炎, 7–10. N.p.: Zhonghua Jidu Jiaohui Chubanshe 中華基督教會出版社, 1934.

Liao DaKe 廖大珂. *Fujian Haiwai Jiaotongshi* 福建海外交通史 (An overseas maritime history of Fujian). Fujian 福建: Fujian Renmin Chubanshe 福建人民出版社, 2002.

Lin JinShui 林金水. *Fujian Jidujiaoshi Chutan* 福建基督教使初探 (Initial studies on Christianity in Fujian). Malisun Ruhua Xuanjiao Erbainian Jinian Wenji – Lunwen 馬禮遜入華宣教200年紀念文集—論文 (Collected essays in commemoration of the 200th year of Morrison's entry into China) 12. Taipei: Caituan Faren Jidujiao Yuzhou Quanren Guanhuai Jigou/Shijie Huaren Fuyin Shigong Lianluo Zhongxin 財團法人基督教宇宙光全人關懷機構; 世界華人福音事工聯絡中心 Cosmic Light Holistic Care Organization/Chinese Coordination Center for World Evangelism, 2006.

Lin MeiMei Rose 林美玫. "Zhongguo Kaimen: Wen Huilian Zhujiao yu Shijiu Shiji Zhongye Meiguo Shenggonghui zaihua Caichuan Shiye de Kaichuang 中國開門：文惠廉主教與十九世紀中葉美國聖公會在華差傳事業的開創 (China's door opens: Bishop Boone and 19th century mission enterprise of the American Episcopal Church in China)." In *Zuixun Caichuan Zuji – Meiguo Shenggonghui Zaihua Caichuan Tanxi (1835-1920)* 追尋差傳足跡—美國聖公會在華差傳探析 *(1835-1920)* (In search of missionary footsteps: the study of Protestant Episcopal Mission and its

A Study on the Emergence and Early Development of
480
Selected Protestant Chinese Churches in the Philippines

development in China from 1835 to 1920), 85–140. Taipei: Cosmic Light
Holistic Care Organization, 2006.

———. *Zhuxun Caichuan Zhuji: Meiguo Shenggonghui Zaihua Caichuan Tanxi*
追尋差傳足跡：美國聖公會在華差傳探析 (1835–1920) (In search
of missionary footsteps: the study of Protestant Episcopal Mission and its
development in China from 1835 to 1920). Taipei: Cosmic Light Holistic
Care Organization, 2006.

Lin WenRen 林溫人, "Zhushu Tanghui Jianshiy 竹樹堂會簡史 (Short history
of Tekchhiu Chapel). In *Minnan Zhonghua Jidu Jiaohui Jianshi* 閩南中華基
督教會簡史 (Short history of Minnan Christian Church of China), vol. 4,
Xiamenqu Jiuguizheng Gonghui Getanghui Jianshi 廈門區舊歸正公會各堂
會簡史 (Short history of Reformed chapels in the Xiamen district), ed. Xu
ShengYan 許聲炎, 4–5. N.p.: Zhonghua Jidu Jiaohui Chubanshe 中華基
督教會出版社, 1934.

Lin ZhiPing 林治平. *Jidujiao yu Zhongguo Lishi Tupian Lunwenji* 基督教與中
國歷史圖片論文集 (Pictorial anthology of the history of Christianity and
China). Taipei: Cosmic Light, 1979.

Liu ZhiTian 劉芝田. "Jiushi Nianlai Feilübin yu Huaqiao 九十年來菲律濱與
華僑 (The Philippines and the overseas Chinese these past ninety years)."
In *Feilübin Huaqiao Shanju Gongsuo Jiushi Zhounian Jinian* 菲律濱華僑善
舉公所九十週年紀念 *90th Anniversary Yearbook of the Philippine-Chinese
Charitable Association 1877–1967*. Manila: Philippine-Chinese Charitable
Association, 1968.

———, ed. *Zhongfei Guanxi Shi* 中菲關係史 (History of Chinese-Philippine
relations). Taipei: Zhengzhong Shuju 正中書局, 1964.

Loh, Philip 羅腓力. *Xuanjiao Yu Zhongguo – Xuandaohui Zhaoqi Zaihua
Xuanjiao Shilue* 宣道與中國 —宣道會早期在華宣教史略 (Send the
doves to the dragon: Footprints of Christian Alliance Missionaries in the
early 20th century China) Hong Kong, China Alliance Press, 1997.

Luo GuanZong 羅冠宗主編, ed. *Qianshi Buwang Houshi Zhishi – Diguo Zhuyi
Liyong Jidujiao Qinlue Zhongguo Shishi Shuping* 前事不忘後事之師—帝國
主義利用基督教侵略中國史實述評 (Forget not the past, teacher of the
future—a historical evaluation of the imperialist invasion of China through
Christianity). Beijing 北京: Zongjiao Wenhua Chubanshe 宗教文化出版
社, 2003.

Ng, Kinia C./Huang CaiLian 黃彩蓮. *Xianggang Minnan Jiaohui Yanjiu* 香港
閩南教會研究 (Research on Hong Kong Min-Nam Church). (Fangyan
Jiaohui Yanjiu Xilie Zhiyi) 方言教會研究系列之一 Chinese Study Series
6. Hong Kong: Alliance Biblical Seminary, 2005.

Peng JiaLi 彭家禮. "Shijiu Shiji Xifang Qinluezhe dui Zhongguo Laogong de
Lulue 十九世紀西方侵略者對中國勞工的擄掠 (Abduction of Chinese

labourers by western invaders in the nineteenth century)." In *Huagong Chuguo Shiliao Huibian* 華工出國史料匯編 (Collection of historical materials on the export of Chinese labourers). Edited by Chen HanSheng 陳翰笙. Beijing 北京: Zhonghua Shuju 中華書局, 1981.

Poppen Alvin John 卜沃文. *Ya Bi Li De Shengping* 雅裨理的生平 (The Life of David Abeel), trans. Li HuaDe 李華德譯. Hong Kong: Jidujiao Fuqiao Chubanshe 基督教輔僑出版社, 1963.

Ren Na 任娜. *Feilübin Shehui Shenghuozhong de Huaren 1935–1965* 菲律濱社會生活中的華人 1935–1965 (The Chinese in Philippine Social Life, 1935–1965). Guiyang 貴陽: Guizhou Renmin Chubanshe 貴州人民出版社, 2004.

Shao, Wesley/Shao QingZhang 邵慶彰. *Jitanshang De Xinsheng* 祭壇上的心聲 (Witness from the Altar), Testimony and Biography Series. Hong Kong: Tien Dao Publishing, 1981.

———. *Ta Chuangshi Ta Chengzhong – Shao Qingzhang Mushi De Shengming Pianzhang* 祂創始祂成終—邵慶彰牧師的生命篇章 (God, the author and perfecter – the life of Rev Wesley Shao). Taipei: Cosmic Light Holistic Care Organization, 2006.

Shen YiMin 沈益民 and Tong ChengZhu 童乘珠. *Zhongguo Renkou Qianyi* 中國人口遷移 (The population migration in China: Historical and contemporary perspectives). Beijing 北京: Zhongguo Tongji Chubanshe 中國統計出版社, 1992.

Shi Fang 石方. *Zhongguo Renkou Qianyi ShiGao* 中國人口遷移史稿. Harbin 哈爾濱: Heilongjiang Renmin Chubanshe 黑龍江人民出版社, 1990.

Song, Levi Tian-Zhen 利未, ed. *Lingli Jiguang – Chupu Song Shanjie De Riji Zhaichao* 靈歷集光—主僕宋尚節的日記摘抄 (The diary of the spiritual life of Dr John Song). Hong Kong: Eng Yu Evangelistic Mission, 1995.

Tan, Antonio/Chen ShouGuo 陳守國. *Feilübin Wubainian De Fanhua Qishi* 菲律濱五百年的反華歧視 (Five hundred years of anti-Chinese prejudice). Translated by Joaquin Sy 施華謹. Manila: Kaisa Para Sa Kaunlaran, Feilübin Huayi Qingnian Lianhehui 菲律濱華裔青年聯合會, 1989.

Tan Chee-Beng/Chen ZhiMing 陳志明 and Zhang XiaoJun 張小軍, ed. *Fujian ji Minnan Xinyang Yanjiu Wenxian Xuanji* 福建暨閩南信仰研究文獻選輯 (Bibliography of studies on Fujian with special reference to Minnan). Hong Kong: Xiang Gang Zhongwen Daxue, Xiang Gang Yatai Yanjiusuo 香港中文大學, 香港亞太研究所, 1999.

Tang, Christopher/Tang Qing 湯清. *Zhongguo Jidujiao Bainianshi* 中國基督教百年史 (The first hundred years of Protestant mission in China). Edited by John Fan 范約翰. Hong Kong: Tao Sheng Publishing, 1987.

Wang ZhiXin 王治心. *Zhongguo Jidujiao Shigang* 中國基督教史綱 (Outline history of Christianity in China). Shanghai 上海: Shanghai Guji Chubanshe 上海古籍出版社, 2004.

Wong Man-Kong Timothy 黃文江. *Kua Wenhua Shiyexia De Jindai Zhongguo Jidujiaoshi Lunji* 跨文化視野下的近代中國基督教史論集 (Collected works on the trans-cultural vision of the modern history of Christianity in China). Taipei: Cosmic Light Holistic Care Organization, 2006.

Wu YiXiong 吳義雄. *Kaiduan yu Fazhan – Huanan Jindai Jidujiaoshi Lunji* 開端與發展—華南近代基督教史論集 (Beginning and progress: collected works on the modern history of Christianity in South China). Taipei: Cosmic Light Holistic Care Organization, 2006.

Wu YouXiong 吳幼雄. *Quanzhou Zongjiao Wenhua* 泉州宗教文化 (Religion and culture of Quanzhou). (Quanzhou Xue Yan Jiu Xiao Congshu) 泉州學研究小叢書 (Mini-series on studies on Quanzhou). Edited by Lin HuaDong 林華東. Fuzhou 福州: Fujian Renmin Chubanshe 福建人民出版社, 1998.

(Xiamen Huaqiao Zhi) Bianweihui 〈廈門華僑志〉編委會, ed. *Xiamen Huaqiao Zhi* 廈門華僑志 (Xiamen overseas Chinese gazetteer). Xiamen 廈門: Lu Jiang Chubanshe 鷺江出版社, 1991.

Xu ShengYan 許聲炎. "Anhai Tanghui Shilue 安海堂會史略 (Short history of Anhai chapel)." In *Minnan Zhonghua Jidu Jiaohui Jianshi* 閩南中華基督教會簡史 (Short history of Minnan Christian Church of China), vol. 3, *Beifang Jiaohui Shilue* 北方教會史略 (Short history of northern churches), 1–8. Edited by Xu ShengYan 許聲炎. N.p.: Zhonghua Jidu Jiaohui Chubanshe 中華基督教會出版社, 1934.

———. "Shima Tanghui Shilue 石碼堂會史略 (Short history of Shima Chapel)." In *Short history of Minnan CCC*, vol. 5, *Guizheng Zhanglaohui Shilue* 歸正長老會史略 (Short history of the Reformed Presbyterian Church), 1–4. Edited by Xu ShengYan 許聲炎. N.p.: Zhonghua Jidu Jiaohui Chubanshe 中華基督教會出版社, 1934.

Yang Li 楊力 and Yeh XiaoDun 葉小敦. *Dongnanya De Fujianren* 東南亞的福建人 (The Fujianese of Southeast Asia). Huaqiao Huaren Yanjiu Congshu 華僑華人研究叢書 (Series on the Study of Overseas Chinese). Fujian 福建: Fujian Renmin Chubanshe 福建人民出版社, 1993.

Yao MinQuan 姚民權 and Luo ChuanHong 羅傳紅. *Zhongguo Jidujiao Jianshi* 中國基督教簡史 (Short history of Christianity in China). (Zongjiao Zhishi Congshu) 宗教知識叢書 Religious Knowledge Series. Beijing 北京: Zongjiao Wenhua Chubanshe 宗教文化出版社, 2000.

Zha ShiJie 查時傑. *Minguo Jidujiaoshi Lunwenji* 民國基督教史論文集 (Anthology on the history of Christianity in the Republic of China). Taipei: Christian Cosmic Light Communication Center, 1993.

Zhang Xie 張燮. *Dongxi Yangkao* 東西洋考. *Juan Wu Lüsong Tiao* 卷五呂宋 (Studies on the ocean east and west: volume five, Luzon). N.p.: n.p., 1618; reprint Beijing: (Zhonghua Shuju) 中華書局, 1981. In Chen TaiMin 陳台民. *Zhongfei Guanxi yu Feilübin Huaqiao* 中菲關係與菲律濱華僑 (Sino-Philippine relations and the Philippine Chinese). Hong Kong: Chao Yang Chubanshe 朝陽出版社, 1985.

Zhang ZhongXin 張鍾鑫. "Bentuhua yu Xinyi Congjian – Jindai Quanzhou Jidujiao De Bentuhua Licheng 本土化與信譽重建—近代泉州基督教的本土化歷程 (Reconstructing localization and prestige: the journey of localizing Christianity in Modern Quanzhou)." In Lin JinShui 林金水. *Fujian Jidujiaoshi Chutan* 福建基督教史初探 (Initial studies on Christianity in Fujian). Malisun Ruhua Xuanjiao Erbainian Jinian Wenji—Lunwen 馬禮遜入華宣教200年紀念文集—論文 (Collected essays in commemoration of the 200th year of Morrison's entry into China) 12, 179–227. Taipei: Cosmic Light Holistic Care Organization/Chinese Coordination Centre for World Evangelism, 2006.

Zhou NanJing 周南京. *Feilübin yu Huaren* 菲律濱與華人 (The Philippines and the Chinese). Edited by Go Bon Juan 吳文煥編. Manila: Kaisa Para Sa Kaunlaran, Feilübin Huayi Qingnian Lianhehui 菲律濱華裔青年聯合會, 1993.

III. Articles and Addresses

Chao, Jonathan T'ien-en 趙天恩. "*MinNan Ziyang Jiaohui De Dianfan* 閩南自養教會的典範 (The model of the self-supporting MinNan Church)." In *Shijie Huaren Jiaohui Zengzhang Yantao Huibao* 世界華人教會增長研討會報, 237-247. Taipei: Chinese Coordinating Council on World Evangelism, Shijie Huaren Fuyin Shigong Lianluo Zhongxin 世界華人福音事工聯絡中心, 1981.

Chen QiuQing 陳秋卿. "Minnan Gulangyu Zhonghua Jidu Jiaohui 閩南鼓浪嶼中華基督教會 (The Minnan Gulangyu Church of Christ in China)." *Zhonghua Jidu Jiaohui Nianjian* 中華基督教會年鑑 *Chinese Christian Church Yearbook* 7 (1921): 100–101.

———. "Minnan Jiaohui Heyi De Jingguo 閩南教會合一的經過 (The process of the union of the Minnan Churches)." *Zhonghua Jidu Jiaohui Nianjian* 中華基督教會年鑑 *Chinese Christian Church Yearbook* 6 (1921):184–188.

———. "Minnan Zhanglao Lundun Lianghui Heyi Zhi Jinbu 閩南長老倫敦兩會合一之進步 (The progress of the union of the Presbyterian and London Missions in Minnan)." *Zhonghua Jidu Jiaohui Nianjian* 中華基督教會年鑑 *Chinese Christian Church Yearbook* 1 (1914): 25–26.

———. "Minnan Zhonghua Jidu Jiaohui 閩南中華基督教會 (The Minnan Church of Christ in China)." *Zhonghua Jidu Jiaohui Nianjian* 中華基督教會年鑑 *Chinese Christian Church Yearbook* 8 (1925): 71–72.

Jiang JiaRong/Keung Ka Wing 姜嘉榮. "Jindai Zhongguo Zili yu Heyi Yundong Zhishiyuan: Minnan Jiaohui 近代中國自立與合一運動指始源: 閩南教會 (The origins of the independent and ecumenical movement in China: the church in Southern Fujian)." *Jindai Zhongguo Jidujiaoshi Yanjiu Jikan* 近代中國基督教史研究集刊 *Journal of the History of Christianity in Modern China* 5 (2002/2003): 5–20.

Leung Sai Ko/Liang XiGao 梁細羔, "Po Ren Zhi Yan 僕人之言 (The servant's word)." In *Zhaojiu Liangyan* 造就良言 (Edifying Words), ed. Liang ShenWei, 22–27. Cebu City: Cebu Gospel Church.

Li ChaoRan 李超然. "Kanna! Shende Puren – Cong (Shigao) dao (Xigao)] 看哪! 神的僕人 — 從『世高』到『細羔』 (Behold! The servant of God – from 'Shi Gao' to 'Xi Gao')." *Wuguang* 務光 *Gospel Quarterly* 17 (December 1961): 6.

Lu Yangge 魯陽戈. "Minnanhua zai Feilübin 閩南話在菲律濱 (The Minnan Dialect in the Philippines." *Huaqiaoshi* 華僑史 5 (December, 1992): 135–137.

Que, Joseph/Guo YuXian 郭毓賢. "Benhui Xintang Libai Anli Zhanglao Ji Muzheng Jiuzhi Shengdian 本會新堂開堂禮拜按立長老暨牧正就職盛典 (New sanctuary dedication service, elders' ordination and installation of the minister)." *Wuguang* 務光 *Gospel Quarterly* 10 (March 1966): 7–9.

Wu BingYao 吳炳耀. "Bainianlai De Minnan Jidu Jiaohui 百年來的閩南基督教會 (Minnan Christian Church after a Hundred Years)." 廈門文史資料, 第13輯 *Literary and Historical Sources from Xiamen* 13 (1998): 78.

Xu ShengYan 許聲炎. "Minnan Zhonghua Jidu Jiaohui Tuijin Ziliziyang De Kaikuang 閩南中華基督教會推進自立自養的概況 (An overview of the Minnan Church of Christ in China pursuing self-support and self-governance)." In *Zhonghua Jidu Jiaohui Nianjian* 中華基督教會年鑑 *Chinese Christian Church Yearbook* 12 (1933): 79–83.

Person Index

Place Index

Subject Index

Langham
PARTNERSHIP

Langham Literature and its imprints are a ministry of Langham Partnership.

Langham Partnership is a global fellowship working in pursuit of the vision God entrusted to its founder John Stott –

> *to facilitate the growth of the church in maturity and Christ-likeness through raising the standards of biblical preaching and teaching.*

Our vision is to see churches in the majority world equipped for mission and growing to maturity in Christ through the ministry of pastors and leaders who believe, teach and live by the Word of God.

Our mission is to strengthen the ministry of the Word of God through:
- nurturing national movements for biblical preaching
- fostering the creation and distribution of evangelical literature
- enhancing evangelical theological education

especially in countries where churches are under-resourced.

Our ministry

Langham Preaching partners with national leaders to nurture indigenous biblical preaching movements for pastors and lay preachers all around the world. With the support of a team of trainers from many countries, a multi-level programme of seminars provides practical training, and is followed by a programme for training local facilitators. Local preachers' groups and national and regional networks ensure continuity and ongoing development, seeking to build vigorous movements committed to Bible exposition.

Langham Literature provides majority world preachers, scholars and seminary libraries with evangelical books and electronic resources through publishing and distribution, grants and discounts. The programme also fosters the creation of indigenous evangelical books in many languages, through writer's grants, strengthening local evangelical publishing houses, and investment in major regional literature projects, such as one volume Bible commentaries like *The Africa Bible Commentary* and *The South Asia Bible Commentary*.

Langham Scholars provides financial support for evangelical doctoral students from the majority world so that, when they return home, they may train pastors and other Christian leaders with sound, biblical and theological teaching. This programme equips those who equip others. Langham Scholars also works in partnership with majority world seminaries in strengthening evangelical theological education. A growing number of Langham Scholars study in high quality doctoral programmes in the majority world itself. As well as teaching the next generation of pastors, graduated Langham Scholars exercise significant influence through their writing and leadership.

To learn more about Langham Partnership and the work we do visit **langham.org**